Library of America, a nonprofit organization, champions our nation's cultural heritage by publishing America's greatest writing in authoritative new editions and providing resources for readers to explore this rich, living legacy.

AFRICAN AMERICAN POETRY

African American Poetry

250 YEARS OF STRUGGLE & SONG

Kevin Young, *editor*

THE LIBRARY OF AMERICA

Published in the United States by Library of America.
Visit our website at www.loa.org.

Some of the material in this volume is reprinted with the
permission of holders of copyright and publishing rights.
Acknowledgments begin on page 1021.

This paper exceeds the requirements of
ANSI/NISO z39.48–1992 (Permanence of Paper).

Distributed to the trade in the United States
by Penguin Random House Inc.
and in Canada by Penguin Random House Canada Ltd.

Library of Congress Control Number: 2019954344
ISBN 978–1–59853–666–9

First Printing
The Library of America—333

Manufactured in the United States of America

African American Poetry: 250 Years of Struggle & Song
is the centerpiece of

Lift Every Voice:
Why African American Poetry Matters

a national public humanities initiative
made possible with support from
The National Endowment for the Humanities,
the Andrew W. Mellon Foundation,
and Emerson Collective.

CONTENTS

FIVE: IDEAS OF ANCESTRY 1959–1975

SIX: BLUE LIGHT SUTRAS 1976–1989

FRED MOTEN

JOHN MURILLO

GREGORY PARDLO

WILLIE PERDOMO

CARL PHILLIPS

KHADIJAH QUEEN

CLAUDIA RANKINE

REGINALD SHEPHERD

EVIE SHOCKLEY

TRACY K. SMITH

EIGHT: AFTER THE HURRICANE 2009–2020

JAMILA WOODS

INTRODUCTION

The Difficult Miracle

BY KEVIN YOUNG

This is the difficult miracle of Black poetry in America:
that we persist, published or not, and loved or unloved: we persist.

—June Jordan

For more than 250 years, African Americans have written and recited and published poetry about beauty and injustice, music and muses, Africa and America, freedoms and foodways, Harlem and history, funk and opera, boredom and longing, jazz and joy. They wrote about what they saw around them and also what they dreamt up—even if it was a dream deferred, derailed, or flat-out denied. In sonnets and anthems, odes and epics, Black poets in the Americas confronted violence and indifference, legal barriers to reading and writing, illegal suppression of voting rights, and outright threats to their personhood, livelihood, and neighborhoods. They wrote from a world they made and a world that, at times, seemed designed to distract at best, to dis or destroy at worst. For African Americans, the very act of composing poetry proves a form of protest.

In this profound work they were participating in a long line of creation, spanning back to the enslaved "Black and Unknown Bards" of the Negro spirituals, who transformed traditions and invented language to describe and change their conditions—and to take pleasure and power in their own inventiveness. *African American Poetry: 250 Years of Struggle & Song* captures a quarter-millennium of Black poetry in the Americas, from Phillis Wheatley to the present day. Whether we consider that time span to consist of what June Jordan calls "the difficult miracle of Black poetry in America," what Amiri Baraka names "the changing same," or the pleasure that Toi Derricotte invokes when she says "joy is an act of resistance," this anthology provides a comprehensive look at the centuries of song and struggle that make up African American verse, a legacy that is fruitful and large enough to barely be represented by one volume.

Black poetry has always lived beyond books. Although Wheatley was the first to publish a volume, in 1773—one she had to go to England to find support for—the first poem of record by a person of African descent in North America is Lucy Terry's untitled poem known as "Bars Fight." Composed orally in 1746, the poem was passed around for generations till first mentioned in print in 1819 and first published in 1855, the same year as Walt Whitman's *Leaves of Grass*. Poet Jupiter Hammon published several of his works, often pious, in newspapers and other outlets, starting in 1760; he is the first African American to publish poetry in a magazine. But it wasn't till Wheatley that an entire tradition began to emerge in her poems addressed to British royalty, General Washington, and Greek myth, contemplating creativity and creation and a freedom she ultimately would write herself into.

This book is organized in eight linked sections. **Section One: Bury Me in a Free Land (1770–1899)** features a rich array of poets, from Wheatley to Frances Ellen Watkins Harper, all of whom encountered (and wrote against) bondage in some way. **Section Two: Lift Every Voice (1900–1918)** considers poets from Paul Laurence Dunbar on, and those who signal the advent of the New Negro, including W.E.B. Du Bois; novelist, poet, and anthologist James Weldon Johnson; poet and playwright Angelina Weld Grimké; and publisher and poet Fenton Johnson, whose prose poems inaugurate a modernist moment. **Section Three: The Dark Tower (1919–1936)** focuses on the Harlem Renaissance and beyond, especially what James Weldon Johnson in his introduction to Sterling Brown's *Southern Road* in 1932 called the "Younger Group" of Claude McKay, Countee Cullen, Langston Hughes, Jean Toomer, and Brown himself—a list notably missing any of the women writers of the time, such as Gwendolyn B. Bennett, Georgia Douglas Johnson, Anne Spencer, and the neglected by nearly all quarters Mae V. Cowdery, all robustly represented here. Indeed, this Dark Tower argues in its selections for women writers and LGBTQ voices sometimes ignored, and for a Renaissance that stretches from Paris to Philadelphia, from D.C. to the American South and the Caribbean.

Section Four: Ballads of Remembrance (1936–1959) takes us through the Chicago Renaissance of Gwendolyn Brooks and other poets of the wartime and postwar periods, considering the era between the end of the Harlem Renaissance and the emergence of the Black Arts Movement. The poems often consider place, and range across the land—from Alabama to Cleveland to New Orleans to San Francisco. The work of these poets has too often fallen by the wayside. This grouping includes everyone from Beat poet Bob Kaufman to Margaret Walker, the first Black person to win the Yale Younger Poets Prize (and the only one for nearly seventy years afterwards).

The book's second half charts the ongoing boom in Black poetry, starting with the Black Arts Movement featured in **Section Five: Ideas of Ancestry (1959–1975)**. This intense artistic and political outburst could fill, and has filled, many anthologies, but stands out for its foment in a short, intense period— from figures such as Amiri Baraka and Sonia Sanchez—much like the Harlem Renaissance before it. By expanding the period beyond the revolutions and unrest of the 1960s, we discover other poets who wrote alongside the movement, including Michael S. Harper and Audre Lorde, who continued the work (and outlook) in the decades after, often shaped by Black Arts freedoms but also embracing a multitude of influences. **Section Six: Blue Light Sutras (1976–1989)** presents poets such as Ai, who almost exclusively wrote persona poems, as well as iconoclasts like Sherley Anne Williams and Christopher Gilbert—not to mention Pulitzer Prize winners Rita Dove and Yusef Komunyakaa—all of whom wrote in personal ways about history and its many musics. This array of voices embodies the artistic freedoms all generations seek.

The book ends with what is arguably another, more current renaissance, an explosion of talent and culmination of tradition dating from the early 1990s. **Sections Seven: Praise Songs for the Day (1990–2008)** and **Eight: After the Hurricane (2009–2020)** consider what appears now as two generations of "furious flowering"—borrowing a phrase from Gwendolyn Brooks that became the name of the important festivals and poetry center formed by scholar JoAnne Gabbin in 1994. One is tempted to say that over these last two decades we are newly in a time of writing collectives, but this would be ignoring the presence, going back through time, of June Jordan's Poetry for the People in the 1990s, the Umbra group in the 1960s, the Black Opals or Saturday Evening Quills of the 1920s, or even groups like the French-language Les Cenelles in the nineteenth century. Yet, this tradition found recent form in the Dark Room Collective, whose emergence in the late 1980s after the funeral of James Baldwin helped galvanize the current that eventually included Natasha Trethewey and Tracy K. Smith, two Pulitzer Prize–winning poets who have also served as U.S. Poets Laureate. (I was also a member.) That Trethewey and Smith have since been joined, in the Pulitzer alone, by Tyehimba Jess, Gregory Pardlo, and now Jericho Brown is representative of increased and overdue recognition of African American excellence. That both Trethewey and Smith first also won the Cave Canem Poetry Prize, founded by and named for an institution that has now nurtured two generations of Black poets, should also be noted. Of course, there are many other recent collectives, collaborations, reading and writing groups, workshops, slams, and cohorts—from the Black Took Collective to the Affrilachian Poets—who take up experimentation, place, and poetry as their basis of community.

As a whole these pages reflect the poets we read and study and sometimes aspire to be and contain poems we memorize, pass around, carry in our memory, and literally inscribe in stone. While limited by paper and permissions, the inclusive scope of the anthology embraces significant longer poems that define the tradition, from Robert Hayden's "Middle Passage" to Robin Coste Lewis's "Voyage of the Sable Venus," as well as rarely considered works like Fenton Johnson's prose poems or Russell Atkins's experimental concrete verse. Due to space constraints, I have reluctantly excluded the rich Black tradition of verse for young people, as well as the folk songs and ballads that have substantially inspired and influenced the formal poetic tradition, including some of the spirituals and blues and hip-hop that the writers themselves reference. While this anthology can only touch on such Black vernacular traditions that are surveyed in depth elsewhere, the sense of the spoken and sung and seen tradition is ever present in the poets here, from James Weldon Johnson's "O Black and Unknown Bards" to Danez Smith's "dinosaurs in the hood." I have also included jump rope rhymes gathered by Lucille Clifton that have never before been published, and the poetry of poet-songwriters like Andy Razaf and Gil Scott-Heron. Readers are encouraged to consult other volumes that account for this vernacular "orature," including my own *Blues Poems* and *Jazz Poems* anthologies.

As with Clifton's efforts to capture what are usually Black and female folk rhymes, archival work is essential to this project, and indeed to the literature. Archives created by African Americans, and archives about African Americans, help us understand American history; poetry archives provide an important lens on Black lives, often giving us a private view of public works. Such is the case with Wheatley's pointed letter to Reverend Samson Occom, a member of the Mohegan peoples, when she wrote him that "in every human Breast, God has implanted a Principle, which we call Love of Freedom; it is impatient of Oppression, and pants for Deliverance; and by the Leave of our modern Egyptians I will assert, that the same Principle lives in us." This now-famous letter was itself published in the March 11, 1774, edition of the *Connecticut Gazette*, announcing early the connection of biblical belief and the doctrine of freedom, all from the archive. Examining archives for this book has already yielded a number of discoveries of lesser-known poets from the nineteenth century to the twentieth, reminding us of the ways poetry itself, especially African American poetry, still awaits discovery. Poet Robert Hayden would conjure this in his letter-poem from Wheatley to Obour Tanner, also enslaved and of African descent, found here.

In this way, *African American Poetry: 250 Years of Struggle & Song* seeks to amend and expand the record. Following in the tradition of previous Black anthologists dating back to James Weldon Johnson's *Book of American Negro Poetry* (1922), this anthology includes Caribbean poets such as Claude McKay and Derek Walcott who have spent significant time in the United

States, and others such as Cuban poet Nicolás Guillén and Puerto Rico–born Julia de Burgos, who wrote of their Black heritage and proved an undeniable influence on mainland-U.S. poets (and vice versa). In something of a break from tradition, the anthology also includes poems in translation by American poets of African descent writing in languages other than English, among them free Creoles of color from Louisiana who published *Les Cenelles: Choix de Poésies Indigènes* in 1845—marking the first anthology of African American poetry published in the United States. That these poets, as well as several modern Caribbean poets, were often translated by such culturally central figures as Langston Hughes indicates their significance to and influence on the African American poetic tradition.

Except in the first section, which is of necessity roughly chronological, individual poets appear alphabetically within sections, meant to give a sense of the poetry's movements and generations. No sense of generations can prove exact, but it is hoped that the poets are less divided by era than joined—rather than an arrangement purely by poets' dates of birth, here the successive eras can give a sense of the steady march and percussive drum circle of poetry. This fruitful connectivity becomes more pointed the further we go in the anthology, as poets we think of as peers turn out to have begun publishing decades apart whether choosing or being unable to publish till they were older. Angelina Weld Grimké, for instance, is often classified as a Harlem Renaissance writer—a framing that assesses her work in the various publications of the 1920s but doesn't convey her groundbreaking anti-lynching play *Rachel* from 1916, not to mention her early writing of the private love poems that give context and even redefinition to her better-known work. She never did publish a book of poetry. To include the recently discovered, early unpublished love poems of Grimké written to a woman in the 1890s connects us to generations of writers forgotten, overlooked, left out, suppressed as being gay or women or as not having a book, not to mention connecting her and us to poets writing through the AIDS crisis and in our current fraught moment of another pandemic. What does it mean to read her radical renderings alongside her turn-of-the century peers, rather than the next generation who embraced her, at least in part? How to situate her last years of seeming silence?

Whatever the answers, we must read past any divisions to the poetry itself, which aims for immortality.

SECTION ONE: BURY ME IN A FREE LAND (1770–1899)

The African American poetic tradition begins with Phillis Wheatley, the first Black woman to publish a book while in the Americas. Seized from what is now Senegal or Gambia around the age of seven, surviving the Middle Passage, she was sold in 1761 to the Wheatley family of Boston, who enslaved her and renamed her Phillis after the ship that stole her. Soon after, she learned English and published her first poem in 1770. That her *Poems on Various Subjects, Religious and Moral* (1773) is older than the United States yet was printed in England speaks to the politics of enslavement and freedom—as well as its author's savvy. In an age when books required advanced subscribers, Wheatley's poems achieved popularity in newspapers and among a burgeoning readership—ensuring not only her book's publication but, ultimately, her freedom. The task required her to negotiate the literal rough waters between her newfound home and its colonizer in the midst of war, an achievement we should celebrate as much as the requirement by the prominent white dignitaries and slaveholders of the time that she prove to them she wrote her own book.

I wish to highlight Wheatley's mobility, her literal crossing of the Black Atlantic—first as part of the transatlantic slave trade on the ship *Phillis* she was, cruelly, named for; and later, rather triumphantly, back across the ocean to England where her *Poems on Various Subjects* was being prepared and where, simply touching its soil, she was legally free. Captivity and freedom, exile and migration, transport both literal and metaphoric: these are themes Wheatley offers us. "Inspire, ye sacred nine, / Your vent'rous *Afric* in her great design": she ventures and versifies freedom, starting with the imagination.

Wheatley and her fellow early African American poets underscore several other themes that will dominate centuries of Black poetry: "Bars Fight," the lone surviving poem by oral poet Lucy Terry, is often spoken of as the first (or first known) work of African American literature, composed in 1746. Besides its siding with the settlers against Natives in a battle for the land that would be America, it is a poem that, while regularly recited, would not see print until over a century later. The poem reminds us of the conflicts in the Colonies— and that the American Revolution's seeking to throw off the chains of tyranny doesn't mean the colonists ultimately didn't impose chains and "bars" of their own. But its import speaks to the ways Black poetry would remain consumed with history—as seen in Robin Coste Lewis's twenty-first-century take on Terry, crafting a poetics not only from her public poem but from her private preparations for her marriage. These women poets have inspired us to speak on all frequencies, lower and higher.

Lucy Terry may reveal another theme: one of an oral poetry, a verse of speech and even of song. Such speech as verse ultimately returns in the modern era, finding its way into Paul Laurence Dunbar's dialect and Alice Dunbar-Nelson's oratory, Langston Hughes and Zora Neale Hurston, Fenton Johnson and James Weldon Johnson, and the contemporary performance poetry and slam poetry scenes. As with Claude McKay and his protest sonnets, many poets avail themselves of both oral and more formal traditions, seeing no reason to choose.

Jupiter Hammon's poem written to Wheatley displays a final important theme found throughout Black poetry: that of community, broadly defined. Hammon reminds us that he knew Wheatley, as did Scipio Moorehead, the Black artist who likely crafted the frontispiece profile portrait of the author found in her *Poems on Various Subjects.* In return, she wrote "To S.M., A Young African Painter, on Seeing His Works," honoring him. Wheatley's poems and her visible relationships with peers highlight that she was in touch with and writing to fellow Black artists. Together with her friend, correspondent, and confidant, Obour Tanner, Wheatley was sustained by Black connections and art. This upends easy notions of Wheatley merrily (or morbidly) isolated. While we can neither ignore nor underestimate the power and pain of her conscripted existence under white would-be slave owners, we needn't have her affected in her imagination, that liberating force she wrote of beautifully. She would go on to sign now-treasured copies of her famed poems, as any other author might.

Even as we consider the steady march to freedom, we see the connection of Black creators to each other, and to a Black literary tradition they forged, embraced, and extended. This making was often physical, as in the poet-potter David Drake—once known as Dave the Potter (or even Dave the Slave)—enslaved and yet crafting unparalleled pots inscribed with his own verse. Or George Moses Horton, whose poems were composed orally and written down and offered for sale in order to purchase the poet's freedom. All these poets were seeking freedom in some form, as realized in the poetry of Frances Ellen Watkins Harper, who closes (and titles) the first section. Her poems like "Bury Me in a Free Land" echo the Negro spirituals and their persistent pursuit of liberty, whether achieved in this life or in the hereafter.

SECTION TWO: LIFT EVERY VOICE (1900–1918)

For the poets writing toward freedom at the start of the African American tradition, found at the beginning of this book, enslavement was a reality, or a constant threat, or an immediate memory. For those poets in this second section, while in touch with the trauma of slavery as all subsequent generations have been, they often had enslaved parents yet were not necessarily enslaved themselves.

The era starts with Paul Laurence Dunbar, whose work creates and constitutes the first modern Black poetry. His work, too, takes up the themes of written qualities versus spokenness—a Black dialect that Dunbar perfected and made newly popular. He also gave voice to life "behind the veil"—or within "the mask," as he called it—Black life beyond whiteness, but also facing it. The verse that followed Dunbar's 1893 debut *Oak and Ivy* and the widespread, popular reprints of his work at the turn of the twentieth century explored formality, but also freedom—much of it, from Fenton Johnson and Angelina Weld Grimké, in verse that called itself free.

Women writers here made their mark in ways not always recognized and sometimes hard to track, despite the broad

Black print culture that sprang up in the late nineteenth and early twentieth centuries. Besides the religious verse often found in the self-published or church-sponsored publications of this era, the writers at the time explored forms that remain popular in Black poetics, from odes to the ordinary wherein the extraordinary lies (see Olivia Ward Bush's "Driftwood" or Eloise Bibb Thompson's "Ode to the Sun") to tribute verses to Frederick Douglass, poet Charlotte Forten Grimké, and Dunbar himself. Robert Kerlin in his 1923 anthology *Negro Poets and Their Poems* describes how "The mention of Attucks, Black Sampson, Sojourner Truth, Harriet Tubman, and others like these, all practically unknown to white readers, is frequent, and reverential odes and sonnets to Douglass, Toussaint L'Ouverture, Washington, Dunbar, are many and enthusiastic." These tributes to the world and to the word help create and celebrate "The New Negro" of the time, not to mention carrying over into current Black poetics.

James Weldon Johnson, whose career would span decades yet be cut short by a fatal automobile accident in 1938, literally looked ahead with his *Anthology of Negro Poetry* in 1922, a groundbreaking effort that laid the foundation for poetics to come. In his selections and introduction Johnson inaugurates, after the Dunbar Readers and emphasis on Black oratory at the turn of the century, the use of Black anthologies to preserve and promote Black poetry—indeed Johnson felt art could also ratify Black humanity. "A people may become great by many means, but there is only one measure by which its greatness is recognized and acknowledged," he wrote. "The final measure of the greatness of all peoples is the amount and standard of the literature and art they have produced." Whether such a task can be achieved by poetry, or whether convincing anyone of one's humanity is a thankless task, Johnson sought to set the bar in his own crucial work: composing what soon became known as the Negro National Anthem, "Lift Every Voice and Sing," with music by his brother Rosamund, at the turn of the twentieth century; writing his own dialect poetry, as in "Sence You Went Away"; crafting the Black epic of "Fifty Years" after Emancipation (too long, unfortunately, to feature here); and then finding his looser, influential vernacular sermons in *God's Trombones* (1927). This period reaches its height with the prescient and powerful work of Chicagoan Fenton Johnson, whose free verse—whether read as prose poems or Whitman-esque long lines—offers a powerful protest that mirrors the blues in both tone and topic. He is the forerunner to much of what makes Black poetry modern.

Fenton and James Weldon Johnson, Alice Dunbar-Nelson and Paul Laurence Dunbar, James Cotter both Sr. and Jr., Carrie Williams Clifford and the remarkable Angelina Weld Grimké, all reveal just how the modern moment would embrace both sides of speech and formality—that false divide—in ways the Harlem Renaissance, with its protest sonnets, jazz epics, and vernacular verses, would fully realize in the era to come.

SECTION THREE: THE DARK TOWER (1919–1936)

We could date the start of that phenomenon most popularly known as the Harlem Renaissance from any number of events: the return of the Black soldiers from the front of World War I and the backlash of the "Red Summer" of 1919; Langston Hughes's writing the Whitmanesque "The Negro Speaks of Rivers" or Claude McKay's publishing "If We Must Die," both in 1919; or the appearance of McKay's *Harlem Shadows* and Georgia Douglas Johnson's *Bronze* in 1922; or Jean Toomer's genre-bending *Cane* from the following year. We certainly should consider as germinal the publications of the magazines *The Crisis*, the *Messenger*, and *Opportunity*, or their related poetry prizes and banquets from that time, starting with the first in 1924. Out of this very dinner came the special issue of *Survey Graphic* that soon became *The New Negro* anthology edited by Alain Locke in 1925, which cemented the movement. We could tell the story of not just the Harlem Renaissance but of African American thought through anthologies such as Locke's and Johnson's, and down to the present day.

However we date it, the Renaissance coalescing in Harlem contended with the legacy of Africa, following in Wheatley's footsteps. Poems like Countee Cullen's "Heritage" asked *What is Africa to me?* while poets like Hughes, starting with his book *The Weary Blues* in 1926, celebrated the continent, as well as their dark selves, journeying toward both. Often Africa meant yearning, as in Gwendolyn B. Bennett's own "Heritage":

> I want to see the slim palm-trees,
> Pulling at the clouds
> With little pointed fingers . . .
>
> I want to see lithe Negro girls,
> Etched dark against the sky
> While sunset lingers.

Bennett's ellipses, found in the original, are a poignant elision of the Middle Passage that both linked and divided African Americans from their forebears. But in work like Hughes's "The Negro Speaks of Rivers," the "I" is triumphant in its relationship to the Nile and the Congo, *ancient as the world and older than the flow of human blood in human veins,* unerringly Black and human.

In the relationship with Africa there would appear another seeming divide between the classical and the vernacular. Cullen and Hughes both engage form in ways that are organic and received, inherited and their own. Cullen wrote epigrams with a recognition of race, and work that, differently from McKay's militant sonnets, still sonneted their own kind of politics in "Yet Do I Marvel" and "From the Dark Tower." Hughes created the blues poem and refined the jazz poem, recognizing that innovation and rhyme, rhythm and tradition, however new, could coexist. Other poets of the time, such as Georgia Douglas Johnson, often made it so, using traditional English verse and rhyme to contain modern thoughts that now strike us as racial, gendered, womanist, radical.

The women's poetry of this time has thankfully been greatly recovered, though there's still work to be done identifying and promoting the work of those who didn't always reap the benefits of the publication surge the Renaissance undoubtedly offered. Georgia Douglas Johnson was one of the few women to publish a book of poems, whereas Jessie Redman Fauset, Gwendolyn B. Bennett, Clarissa Scott Delaney, Helene Johnson, and Anne Spencer—and the earlier generation represented by Angelina Weld Grimké—would appear in the magazines of the time, but never issue a volume. The work of scholars Gloria T. Hull, Maureen Honey, and the late Cheryl Wall reminds us that the Harlem Renaissance is always an act of recovery—both then and now.

The Black women writers of the time speak eloquently of their situation. Anita Scott Coleman's poem "Denial" ends with a declaration that combats any notion of her obscurity: *My silence wears the ecstasy of song.* The ecstasy of song is felt in the verses of these key voices in the long Black tradition, when song became poem, poem became song, and all were underscored by the language of longing—the very kind found in the blues.

SECTION FOUR: BALLADS OF REMEMBRANCE (1936–1959)

Less well-known than the Harlem Renaissance but just as influential, the so-called Chicago Renaissance takes place in the late 1930s and early 1940s, expressing something particular and necessary about poetic craft and continuity. Poets such as Gwendolyn Brooks, the first African American to win a Pulitzer Prize, Frank Marshall Davis, Margaret Walker, Richard Wright, and others gathered in the Windy City, capitalizing on Chicago's earlier cultural foment as represented by Fenton Johnson two decades before. The result was work of humane sophistication that looked at city life as well as politics after the Depression was well under way.

Expanding our view out from Chicago, we see in this era before and after World War II a real sense of craft and the tradition's span, from Robert Hayden's Detroit and Russell Atkins's Cleveland to Margaret Walker's Alabama and Bob Kaufman's invented "Oregon" providing a growing sense of locality and place quite different from the Harlem Renaissance's internationalism. We also encounter here not just the Caribbean diasporic tradition, but also the Afro-Latino and Nuyorican one, in one of its pioneers: Julia de Burgos. To many, Burgos is emblematic, writing out of her experience in Puerto Rico but also in Manhattan in what used to be called Spanish Harlem; often considered the first Nuyorican poet, Burgos made her way to New York where she wrote a very few poems in English before dying at thirty-nine after collapsing on the street in El Barrio. Her being buried in a potter's field before being reclaimed and properly honored, speaks to her necessary legacy, in writing about her Black heritage in a postcolonial or territorial context throughout her too short life.

History becomes a focus for these poets, finding its way into long poems, whether in Hayden's "Middle Passage", Pauli Murray's "Dark Testament", Melvin B. Tolson's "Dark Symphony", Owen Dodson's mythic song cycles, or Walker's prophetic verse, all featured here in whole or in part. The postwar poets continue to explore and explode diverse poetic forms, including ballads, blues, and haiku. We must remember that during this period Langston Hughes was also publishing his mid-career masterpiece, the urban, bebop epic *Montage of a Dream Deferred* (1951), with its "disc-storted" lines and fragmented yet fertile sense of community. The long poetic line of Fenton Johnson and Hughes would become Walker's, then Kaufman's and Ted Joans's—a line inherited from Whitman that would prove flexible and fantastical, jazzlike and germane.

This engagement with form also proved a politics—one where freedom found in form, often organic, stood in for other freedoms, argued over and soon assumed. The poets here are engaged with change, and soon, revolution.

SECTION FIVE: IDEAS OF ANCESTRY (1959–1975)

The revolution may not have been televised, but for a time in the 1960s, it appeared it might be poeticized. The Black Arts Movement, growing out of the Black Power movement and, in the end, shaping it—so much so that Black Power is sometimes said to be the political wing of what was really an artistic movement—proved crucial in providing a language, forms, and forums for new Black voices. These voices were often collective, as in the Umbra group founded in 1962, which led to a magazine by that name, and included Lorenzo Thomas, Ishmael Reed, and musicians such as Archie Shepp and Cecil Taylor (who also wrote poetry); such voices were deeply unique, as in the work of concrete poet N. H. Pritchard (himself part of Umbra). Groups and key individuals founded Black-based organizations, magazines, and presses like Broadside Press and Third World, which is still operating; they agitated for transformation and revolution and changed their names; they read in bars to workers and worked at universities to change the culture and the canon. Popular anthologies like *Black Fire, Black Voices, Soulscript, The Black Woman, Jump Bad, The Black Poets, Black Spirits,* and *Giant Talk* appeared from editors who were often writers themselves. Langston Hughes also put his stamp on the movement, editing *New Negro Poets: U.S.A.* and revising, with Arna Bontemps, the colossal *Poetry of the Negro* collection first published in 1949. This was a publishing revolution as much as a political one.

Building on the writings of the Harlem Renaissance, Black thinkers and poets theorized the tradition and sought to forge a new one. This manifesto quality of the era is as important as the poetry, though it is the poetry that executed the ideas—and sometimes outlasted them. Their work was radical in all senses—politically, but also experimentally. *The master's tools will never dismantle the master's house,* Audre Lorde wrote, an idea that might help us interrogate whether the forms African American poets had inherited could be made to critique the very system that still dogged them.

"Black, lesbian, mother, warrior, poet," as she put it, Lorde also reveals the limits of the Black Arts Movement, and the ways that aesthetic strictures and often strict gender alignments often failed to reconcile with the freedoms that philosophy already insisted on. Poets like Lorde, Michael S. Harper, and Lucille Clifton all found their way in Black Arts, emerging with ideas of identity, music, and spirituality in ways not always anticipated. Another way to put this is that, looking back, Black Arts was broader than it seems, and indeed was often broader than its tenets.

Black Arts was not always interested in history as much as it was in charting a new future. The poems that stay with us consider, celebrate, and embody music—not only free jazz or the "new thing" as it was known, but the music of the page that Black Arts poets embraced.

> A political art, let it be
> tenderness, low strings the fingers
> touch
>   (Amiri Baraka)

ain't no tellen
    where the jazz of yo/songs.
    wud have led us.
                (Sonia Sanchez)

I must become
I must become a menace to my enemies
                (June Jordan)

Lord she's gone done left me done packed / up and split
and i with no way to make her
come back and everywhere the world is bare
                (Etheridge Knight)

June Jordan called this "vertical rhythm," describing how the Black Arts–era poem not only trips down the page, but springs across it, often suggesting Billie Holiday, John Coltrane, Eric Dolphy, and other musicians who made an impression on the culture, and whose early deaths seemed both tragic and symbolic.

The influence of this new sound, a reimagining of ancestry, has been widespread. We cannot imagine the likes of performance poetry, contemporary sound poetry, or the slam poetry scene without the work of Sonia Sanchez or the late Amiri Baraka, Haki Madhubuti or dearly departed Jayne Cortez, to say nothing of those found here who recorded influential poetic albums, including Gil Scott-Heron and Sarah Webster Fabio. The vernacular made its mark. Poets were looking not just for new Black forms but also for new ways of communicating with the audience they sought and, in the end, created.

In battling history, the Black Arts era was deeply concerned with legacy. Jordan would put it this way in an urgent manifesto that considers Phillis Wheatley, but that applies to the tradition entire. "This is the difficult miracle of Black poetry in America: that we persist, published or not, and loved or unloved: we persist."

SECTION SIX: BLUE LIGHT SUTRAS (1971–1989)

The poets who began publishing in earnest after the mid-1970s mark a return to history. This is not just a public history, or a

sense of the ever-present found in the blues and Black Arts, but
a personal history meant to reflect a broader one. Following
the focus on the future and protest of the present, the poets of
this era sought connections between both public and personal
histories in order to say something about the course of Black
life in America.

Though deeply personal, Black Arts wasn't exactly autobio-
graphical. (Of course, since the spirituals at least, Black culture
had in its music and meanings focused more on an "I" that
was often a "we.") Even if there's no such thing in poetry
as "strictly" autobiographical, the poets who followed Black
Arts and often published alongside it relied on telling their
own family's stories. Rita Dove and Yusef Komunyakaa, the
first poets to win the Pulitzer Prize after Gwendolyn Brooks
in 1950, did so by mythologizing and personalizing stories of
their grandparents (Dove's *Thomas and Beulah*) or making sur-
real and rather capturing the surreality of serving in the Viet-
nam War and growing up in Louisiana (Komunyakaa's *Neon
Vernacular*). Even poets, as in the case of a persona poet like
Ai who wrote in the voice of everyone from John F. Kennedy
to an abused child or wife—or, hauntingly, an abuser—used
personal voices to tell the private, imagined side of public sto-
ries. The sense of history for these poets was lived and living—a
long tradition African American poetry would continue.

These poets would write with an assuredness that spoke of
Black poetry's place in the conversation. Yet publishing oppor-
tunities dried up for all but a few, with the 1980s seeing a severe
contraction of publishing for Black poets. This was true, too, of
the Black Arts poets who were still very much writing but saw
less work appear between the covers of a book. The 1980s, like
the 1910s and 1930s before them, became a time when Black
poetry didn't have the numbers or kind of support that made
for the booms that surrounded them. It was a lean time.

Yet out of the leanness came the kinds of innovation that
emerged out of earlier, far more limited times a century
before—and a century after Dunbar's debut, poetry would
encounter the start of another new era. This newer genera-
tion would eventually found the institutions that would spread
Black poetry beyond its imposed limits or past shores, and into
the future and foundation of the African American Renais-
sance found today.

SECTION SEVEN: PRAISE SONGS FOR THE DAY
(1990–2008)

The poets whose work first took flight in the 1990s found themselves part of history but also furthering it as a topic for poetry. Foremost among these was the Dark Room Collective, the Boston-based group that sprang from wanting to honor the ancestors, while also taking up themes like "Total Life Is What We Want" from Black Arts–era poet and editor Clarence Major. Many such forerunners appeared in the Dark Room Reading Series, which paired established with emerging writers to affirm continuity, going beyond Black Arts but emerging out of it. Collectives would lead to poetry collections, anthologies, and ultimately, to a change in the American poetic landscape. The Dark Room also appeared in *The New Yorker* in a photo feature with words by Cornelius Eady, who went on to found Cave Canem—Latin for "beware the dog," taken from a tile at Pompeii—with fellow poet Toi Derricotte. Throughout the last three sections of this book, the generations are not only interrelated but often inseparable.

That both Dark Room members and future Poets Laureate Natasha Trethewey and Tracy K. Smith were selected for the Cave Canem Poetry Prize also shines light on the linked inheritance of the two Black organizations, as well as cohorts, and speaks to the literary landscape that both groups have helped to change. Prizes never tell the whole story, but to take just the Pulitzer, before this era there were only three Pulitzer Prizes awarded to Black poets, with a large gap between Gwendolyn Brooks in 1950 and Rita Dove and Yusef Komunyakaa (1987 and 1994, respectively). Yet with Trethewey's winning the Pulitzer in 2007, there have been five Black winners in the years since, with many more recognized by other prizes and institutions. At Cave Canem, the full flourishing of new poets would take place alongside the honoring of ancestors—much as in the slam and performance poetry scene as manifested on HBO's Def Poetry Jam, which ended each episode with an elder reading to the eager, typically younger, audience. That audience grew, met the poetry where it lived, and helped make its urgency known. Often, the audience members would, in turn, become poets themselves.

Some of this generation was captured in *Giant Steps* (2000), an anthology that I edited at the turn of the millennium, setting out to capture the new energy afoot. This was the first of a flurry of other anthologies like *Step into a World* (2000) and *Bum Rush the Page* (2001), collections that were often multigenre, as was *Giant Steps*, self-consciously evoking *The New Negro* anthology. As I said there, this generation of writers curated and included pop culture the way poets of the Harlem Renaissance had folk culture. They also employed what may still best be called the hip-hop aesthetic—an ability to draw from any source, white or Black or beyond, from outerspace to innervisions, from television shows to Black psychics and the blues. There is here a vernacular in search of new forms, and new forms that took up the vernacular in order to harness the energy that the poets observed and sought.

Around this time, Black poets began to get national recognition in ways that earlier generations had foreseen and made possible, starting with Brooks's Pulitzer Prize, her stint as the Poetry Consultant to the Library of Congress (now known as Poet Laureate) in the 1970s, and Maya Angelou's inaugural poem at President Clinton's ceremony in 1993. In the coming years, Black poets would win the National Book Award and MacArthur Fellowships, earn more Pulitzer Prizes, be named Poets Laureate, and become best sellers. Such influence is symbolized by Elizabeth Alexander, one of the first poets to publish in the era with her *Venus Hottentot* (1990), who then read the title poem for the first inauguration of President Barack Obama in 2009, found here in full. It is this election of the first Black president of the United States that helps bring the book full circle, calling back to Phillis Wheatley writing to General George Washington, who would become the first president of the land.

Language was a big part of the innovation here, one that engaged with the American avant-garde, but also recognized its shared Black origins. Poets like Claudia Rankine with her best-selling and influential *Citizen* managed to innovate in topic and form, as much an evolution in language as experimentation. The old artificial divide between vernacular and formal nearly disappeared; poetry's experimentation and play also often meant popularity, and the stage and the page met in the middle. For his part, whether he's writing "American sonnets" in the tradition of Wanda Coleman or creating a form based on Gwendolyn Brooks's "We Real Cool" now known as the golden shovel, poet Terrance Hayes embodies this characteristic searching, hip-hop and Generation X to the core. *What we / break is what we hold.* Not just content to reinhabit older forms, poets invented new ones in the 1990s and early 2000s, from Afaa Michael Weaver's "bop" to Natasha Trethewey's mirrored stanzas to Jericho Brown's "duplex," part sonnet and all blues. (And just as we were going to press, Brown's latest book was awarded the Pulitzer Prize.) This versatile verse means that the poets writing at the millennium's turn conjure a shifting perspective, a tone of one's own.

SECTION EIGHT: AFTER THE HURRICANE (2009–2020)

In this last section, we encounter the latest group of Black poets. Many of them not only grew up attending Cave Canem, but presumed Black poets' presences in the academy, at awards ceremonies, and in the news of the day. This coming to the craft already believing there was a Black and distinguished canon—and seeking no one's acknowledgment of their humanity—has, in this youngest generation, made a poetry by turns wise and innocent, a verse well aware of tradition but at times blissfully beyond it.

Their work proves eclectic and energetic, which is to say, Black to the bone. A poem like "dinosaurs in the hood" by Danez Smith imagines a movie that no Quentin Tarantino could make—or should be allowed to—one in which the Black protagonist not only lives but thrives: *This movie can't be about race. / This movie can't be about black pain or cause black people pain. / This movie can't be about a long history of having a long history with hurt.* Poets conjure up Emmett Till and the President's wife, nature and its clichés, civilization and its survivors, police violence and protest—or powerfully refusing to be *about a long history of having a long history with hurt.* This thriving is found in the questions of the day, ones that are political and aesthetic, contemplating gender and race, history and freedom, enlightenment and inclusion—or perhaps these are the same questions that faced, say, the poets of enslavement or the Harlem Renaissance, only with different answers.

As a kind of coda, this book's final section can only hope to provide an overview of our current moment and mood, whose vibrancy and varied voices follow in the footsteps of the hundreds of years (and pages) before. One selection per poet can merely hint at the new songs being written, the struggles always under way, and those yet to come. I eagerly await the anthologies and gatherings this younger generation will surely undertake.

All have learned from the tradition and are continuing it as they examine an America whose imagination, from Wheatley's "On Imagination" down to the present day, hasn't always included Black people. Throughout history poets have continued to write tribute poems in memory—and protest—of their fallen brothers and sisters, especially as victims of police or mob violence at the hands of whites. You could say that this too stems from Wheatley: her poem "On the Affray in King Street" describes the Boston Massacre in 1770, praising Crispus Attucks, the former enslaved runaway who was first among the dead. In full it reads:

> With Fire enwrapt, surcharg'd with sudden Death,
> Lo, the pois'd Tube convolves its fatal breath!
> The flying Ball with heaven-directed Force,
> Rids the Spirit of the fallen corse.
> Well sated Shades! let no unwomanly Tear
> From Pity's Eye, disdain in your honour'd Bier;
> Lost to their View, surviving Friends may mourn,
> Yet on thy Pile shall Flames celestial burn;
> Long as in *Freedom's* Cause the wise contend,
> Dear to your unity shall Fame extend;
> While to the World, the letter'd *Stone* shall tell,
> How *Caldwell*, *Attucks*, *Gray*, and *Mav'rick* fell.

With his lynching in 1955 spurring along the modern Civil Rights Movement, Emmett Till's may be the most mentioned name in the modern era; poems about him by Gwendolyn Brooks, Eve L. Ewing, and myself are just some of the testimony offered here, with many more that could be included and those yet to be written.

As the poets here well know, Till's mournful memory evokes a centuries-old Freedom Struggle still underway, attested by *African American Poetry*'s roll call of ongoing victims of racist violence—whether Trayvon Martin or Michael Brown, Eric Garner or Sandra Bland (evoked in work here by Claudia Rankine, Khadijah Queen, Major Jackson, Ross Gay, Jericho Brown, and Aja Monet), unidentified women (as in Toi Derricotte) or anonymous men (as in Anthony Walton)—and even the imagined Black phantoms that racism brings to life, conjured by Cornelius Eady, Alison C. Rollins, and numerous others. African American poetry has long borne witness to and sustained social change; our time, with growing protests over the pandemic of racist violence against the unarmed, the young, the trans, the sleeping, the walking, the jogging—all those who have the audacity to breathe while Black—has only given Black poetry, intimate with struggle, more urgency to sing of. The African American experience, these poets know, is a central part of the nation's chorus, with Black poetry offering up a daily epic of struggle and song.

Juneteenth 2020

ONE
BURY ME IN A FREE LAND
(1770–1899)

PHILLIS WHEATLEY

On Imagination

Thy various works, imperial queen, we see,
How bright their forms! how deck'd with pomp by thee!
Thy wond'rous acts in beauteous order stand,
And all attest how potent is thine hand.

From *Helicon's* refulgent heights attend,
Ye sacred choir, and my attempts befriend:
To tell her glories with a faithful tongue,
Ye blooming graces, triumph in my song.

Now here, now there, the roving *Fancy* flies,
Till some lov'd object strikes her wand'ring eyes,
Whose silken fetters all the senses bind,
And soft captivity involves the mind.

Imagination! who can sing thy force?
Or who describe the swiftness of thy course?
Soaring through air to find the bright abode,
Th' empyreal palace of the thund'ring God,
We on thy pinions can surpass the wind,
And leave the rolling universe behind:
From star to star the mental optics rove,
Measure the skies, and range the realms above.
There in one view we grasp the mighty whole,
Or with new worlds amaze th' unbounded soul.

Though *Winter* frowns to *Fancy's* raptur'd eyes
The fields may flourish, and gay scenes arise;
The frozen deeps may break their iron bands,
And bid their waters murmur o'er the sands.
Fair *Flora* may resume her fragrant reign,
And with her flow'ry riches deck the plain;
Sylvanus may diffuse his honours round,
And all the forest may with leaves be crown'd:

Show'rs may descend, and dews their gems disclose,
And nectar sparkle on the blooming rose.

Such is thy pow'r, nor are thine orders vain,
O thou the leader of the mental train:
In full perfection all thy works are wrought,
And thine the sceptre o'er the realms of thought.
Before thy throne the subject-passions bow,
Of subject-passions sov'reign ruler Thou,
At thy command joy rushes on the heart,
And through the glowing veins the spirits dart.

Fancy might now her silken pinions try
To rise from earth, and sweep th' expanse on high;
From *Tithon's* bed now might *Aurora* rise,
Her cheeks all glowing with celestial dies,
While a pure stream of light o'erflows the skies.
The monarch of the day I might behold,
And all the mountains tipt with radiant gold,
But I reluctant leave the pleasing views,
Which *Fancy* dresses to delight the *Muse*;
Winter austere forbids me to aspire,
And northern tempests damp the rising fire;
They chill the tides of *Fancy's* flowing sea,
Cease then, my song, cease the unequal lay.

On Recollection

Mneme begin. Inspire, ye sacred nine,
Your vent'rous *Afric* in her great design.
Mneme, immortal pow'r, I trace thy spring:
Assist my strains, while I thy glories sing:
The acts of long departed years, by thee
Recover'd, in due order rang'd we see:
Thy pow'r the long-forgotten calls from night,
That sweetly plays before the *fancy's* sight.

    Mneme in our nocturnal visions pours
The ample treasure of her secret stores;
Swift from above she wings her silent flight
Through *Phoebe's* realms, fair regent of the night;
And, in her pomp of images display'd,
To the high-raptur'd poet gives her aid,
Through the unbounded regions of the mind,
Diffusing light celestial and refin'd.
The heav'nly *phantom* paints the actions done
By ev'ry tribe beneath the rolling sun.

    Mneme, enthron'd within the human breast,
Has vice condemn'd, and ev'ry virtue blest.
How sweet the sound when we her plaudit hear?
Sweeter than music to the ravish'd ear,
Sweeter than *Maro's* entertaining strains
Resounding through the groves, and hills, and plains.
But how is *Mneme* dreaded by the race,
Who scorn her warnings and despise her grace?
By her unveil'd each horrid crime appears,
Her awful hand a cup of wormwood bears.
Days, years mispent, O what a hell of woe!
Hers the worst tortures that our souls can know.

    Now eighteen years their destin'd course have run,
In fast succession round the central sun.
How did the follies of that period pass
Unnotic'd, but behold them writ in brass!
In Recollection see them fresh return,
And sure 'tis mine to be asham'd, and mourn.

    O *Virtue*, smiling in immortal green,
Do thou exert thy pow'r, and change the scene;
Be thine employ to guide my future days,
And mine to pay the tribute of my praise.

    Of *Recollection* such the pow'r enthron'd
In ev'ry breast, and thus her pow'r is own'd.
The wretch, who dar'd the vengeance of the skies,
At last awakes in horror and surprize,

By her alarm'd, he sees impending fate,
He howls in anguish, and repents too late.
But O! what peace, what joys are hers t'impart
To ev'ry holy, ev'ry upright heart!
Thrice blest the man, who, in her sacred shrine,
Feels himself shelter'd from the wrath divine!

On the Death of the
Rev. Mr. George Whitefield. *1770*

HAIL, happy saint, on thine immortal throne,
Possest of glory, life, and bliss unknown;
We hear no more the music of thy tongue,
Thy wonted auditories cease to throng.
Thy sermons in unequall'd accents flow'd,
And ev'ry bosom with devotion glow'd;
Thou didst in strains of eloquence refin'd
Inflame the heart, and captivate the mind.
Unhappy we the setting sun deplore,
So glorious once, but ah! it shines no more.

Behold the prophet in his tow'ring flight!
He leaves the earth for heav'n's unmeasur'd height,
And worlds unknown receive him from our sight.
There *Whitefield* wings with rapid course his way,
And sails to *Zion* through vast seas of day.
Thy pray'rs, great saint, and thine incessant cries
Have pierc'd the bosom of thy native skies.
Thou moon hast seen, and all the stars of light,
How he has wrestled with his God by night.
He pray'd that grace in ev'ry heart might dwell,
He long'd to see *America* excel;
He charg'd its youth that ev'ry grace divine
Should with full lustre in their conduct shine;
That Saviour, which his soul did first receive,
The greatest gift that ev'n a God can give,

He freely offer'd to the num'rous throng,
That on his lips with list'ning pleasure hung.

"Take him, ye wretched, for your only good,
Take him ye starving sinners, for your food;
Ye thirsty, come to this life-giving stream,
Ye preachers, take him for your joyful theme;
Take him my dear *Americans*, he said,
Be your complaints on his kind bosom laid:
Take him, ye *Africans*, he longs for you,
Impartial Saviour is his title due:
Wash'd in the fountain of redeeming blood,
You shall be sons, and kings, and priests to God."

Great *Countess*,* we *Americans* revere
Thy name, and mingle in thy grief sincere;
New England deeply feels, the *Orphans* mourn,
Their more than father will no more return.

But, though arrested by the hand of death,
Whitefield no more exerts his lab'ring breath,
Yet let us view him in th' eternal skies,
Let ev'ry heart to this bright vision rise;
While the tomb safe retains its sacred trust,
Till life divine re-animates his dust.

To S. M. a young African Painter, on seeing his Works

TO show the lab'ring bosom's deep intent,
And thought in living characters to paint,
When first thy pencil did those beauties give,
And breathing figures learnt from thee to live,
How did those prospects give my soul delight,
A new creation rushing on my sight?

* The Countess of *Huntingdon*, to whom Mr. *Whitefield* was Chaplain.

Still, wond'rous youth! each noble path pursue,
On deathless glories fix thine ardent view:
Still may the painter's and the poet's fire
To aid thy pencil, and thy verse conspire!
And may the charms of each seraphic theme
Conduct thy footsteps to immortal fame!
High to the blissful wonders of the skies
Elate thy soul, and raise thy wishful eyes.
Thrice happy, when exalted to survey
That splendid city, crown'd with endless day,
Whose twice six gates on radiant hinges ring:
Celestial *Salem* blooms in endless spring.

Calm and serene thy moments glide along,
And may the muse inspire each future song!
Still, with the sweets of contemplation bless'd,
May peace with balmy wings your soul invest!
But when these shades of time are chas'd away,
And darkness ends in everlasting day,
On what seraphic pinions shall we move,
And view the landscapes in the realms above?
There shall thy tongue in heav'nly murmurs flow,
And there my muse with heav'nly transport glow:
No more to tell of *Damon's* tender sighs,
Or rising radiance of *Aurora's* eyes,
For nobler themes demand a nobler strain,
And purer language on th' ethereal plain.
Cease, gentle muse! the solemn gloom of night
Now seals the fair creation from my sight.

To His Excellency General Washington

SIR,
I Have taken the freedom to address your Excellency in the
enclosed poem, and entreat your acceptance, though I am
not insensible of its inaccuracies. Your being appointed by
the Grand Continental Congress to be Generalissimo of the

armies of North America, together with the fame of your vir-
tues, excite sensations not easy to suppress. Your generosity,
therefore, I presume, will pardon the attempt. Wishing your
Excellency all possible success in the great cause you are so
generously engaged in. I am,

Your Excellency's most obedient humble servant, PHILLIS
WHEATLEY. *Providence, Oct. 26, 1775. His Excellency Gen.
Washington.*

Celestial choir! enthron'd in realms of light
Columbia's scenes of glorious toils I write.
While freedom's cause her anxious breast alarms,
She flashes dreadful in refulgent arms.
See mother earth her offspring's fate bemoan,
And nations gaze at scenes before unknown!
See the bright beams of heaven's revolving light
Involved in sorrows and the veil of night!

The goddess comes, she moves divinely fair,
Olive and laurel binds her golden hair:
Wherever shines this native of the skies,
Unnumber'd charms and recent graces rise.

Muse! bow propitious while my pen relates
How pour her armies through a thousand gates:
As when Eolus heaven's fair face deforms,
Enwrapp'd in tempest and a night of storms;
Astonish'd ocean feels the wild uproar,
The refluent surges beat the sounding shore;
Or thick as leaves in Autumn's golden reign,
Such, and so many, moves the warrior's train.
In bright array they seek the work of war,
Where high unfurl'd the ensign waves in air.
Shall I to Washington their praise recite?
Enough thou know'st them in the fields of fight.
Thee, first in place and honours,—we demand
The grace and glory of thy martial band.
Fam'd for thy valour, for thy virtues more,
Hear every tongue thy guardian aid implore!

One century scarce perform'd its destin'd round,
When Gallic powers Columbia's fury found;
And so may you, whoever dares disgrace
The land of freedom's heaven-defended race!
Fix'd are the eyes of nations on the scales,
For in their hopes Columbia's arm prevails.
Anon Britannia droops the pensive head,
While round increase the rising hills of dead.
Ah! cruel blindness to Columbia's state!
Lament thy thirst of boundless power too late.

Proceed, great chief, with virtue on thy side,
Thy ev'ry action let the goddess guide.
A crown, a mansion, and a throne that shine,
With gold unfading, WASHINGTON! be thine.

JUPITER HAMMON

An Address to Miss Phillis Wheatly, Ethiopian Poetess, in Boston

who came from Africa at eight years of age, and soon became acquainted with the gospel of Jesus Christ

Miss Wheatly, pray give me leave to express as follows:

1.

O Come you pious youth! adore
   The wisdom of thy God,   Eccles. xii. 1.
In bringing thee from distant shore,
   To learn his holy word.

2.

Thou mightst been left behind,
   Amidst a dark abode;   Psal. cxxxvi. 1, 2, 3.
God's tender mercy still combin'd,
   Thou hast the holy word.

3.

Fair wisdom's ways are paths of peace,   Psal. i. 1, 2, 3.
   And they that walk therein,   Prov. iii. 7.
Shall reap the joys that never cease,
   And Christ shall be their king.

4.

God's tender mercy brought thee here,
   Tost o'er the raging main;   Psal. ciii. 1, 2, 3, 4.
In Christian faith thou hast a share,
   Worth all the gold of Spain.

5.

While thousands tossed by the sea,
  And others settled down,   Death.
God's tender mercy set thee free,
  From dangers still unknown.

6.

That thou a pattern still might be,
  To youth of Boston town,   2 Cor. v. 10.
The blessed Jesus set thee free,
  From every sinful wound.

7.

The blessed Jesus, who came down,
  Unvail'd his sacred face,   Rom. v. 21.
To cleanse the soul of every wound,
  And give repenting grace.

8.

That we poor sinners may obtain
  The pardon of our sin;   Psal. xxxiv. 6, 7, 8.
Dear blessed Jesus now constrain,
  And bring us flocking in.

9.

Come you, Phillis, now aspire,
  And seek the living God,   Matth. vii. 7, 8.
So step by step thou mayst go higher,
  Till perfect in the word.

10.

While thousands mov'd to distant shore,
  And others left behind,   Psal. lxxxix. 1.
The blessed Jesus still adore,
  Implant this in thy mind.

11.

Thou hast left the heathen shore,
   Thro' mercy of the Lord;   Psal. xxxiv. 1, 2, 3.
Among the heathen live no more,
   Come magnify thy God.

12.

I pray the living God may be,
   The shepherd of thy soul;   Psal. lxxx. 1, 2, 3.
His tender mercies still are free,
   His mysteries to unfold.

13.

Thou, Phillis, when thou hunger hast,
   Or pantest for thy God;   Psal. xlii. 1, 2, 3.
Jesus Christ is thy relief,
   Thou hast the holy word.

14.

The bounteous mercies of the Lord
   Are hid beyond the sky,   Psal. xvi. 10, 11.
And holy souls that love his word,
   Shall taste them when they die.

15.

These bounteous mercies are from God,
   The merits of his Son;   Psal. xxxiv. 15.
The humble soul that loves his word;
   He chooses for his own.

16.

Come, dear Phillis, be advis'd,
   To drink Samaria's flood;   John iv. 13, 14.
There nothing is that shall suffice,
   But Christ's redeming blood.

17.

While thousands muse with earthly toys,
   And range about the street,   Matth. vi. 33.
Dear Phillis, seek for heaven's joys,
   Where we do hope to meet.

18.

When God shall send his summons down,
   And number saints together,   Psal. cxvi. 15.
Blest angels chant, (triumphant sound)
   Come live with me for ever.

19.

The humble soul shall fly to God,
   And leave the things of time,   Mar. v. 3, 8.
Start forth as 'twere at the first word,
   To taste things more divine.

20.

Behold! the soul shall wast away,
   Whene'er we come to die,   Cor. xv. 51, 52, 53.
And leave its cottage made of clay,
   In twinkling of an eye.

21.

Now glory be to the Most High,
   United praises given,   Psal. cl. 6.
By all on earth, incessantly,
   And all the host of heav'n.

LUCY TERRY

[*Bars Fight*]

August 'twas the twenty-fifth,
Seventeen hundred forty-six;
The Indians did in ambush lay,
Some very valient men to slay,
The names of whom I'll not leave out.
Samuel Allen like a hero fout,
And though he was so brave and bold,
His face no more shall we behold.
Eleazer Hawks was killed outright,
Before he had time to fight,—
Before he did the Indians see,
Was shot and killed immediately.
Oliver Amsden he was slain,
Which caused his friends much grief and pain.
Simeon Amsden they found dead,
Not many rods distant from his head.
Adonijah Gillett we do hear
Did lose his life which was so dear.
John Sadler fled across the water,
And thus escaped the dreadful slaughter.
Eunice Allen see the Indians coming,
And hopes to save herself by running,
And had not her petticoats stopped her,
The awful creatures had not catched her,
Nor tommy hawked her on her head,
And left her on the ground for dead.
Young Samuel Allen, Oh lack-a-day!
Was taken and carried to Canada.

BENJAMIN BANNEKER

A Mathematical Problem in Verse

A Cooper and Vintner sat down for a talk,
Both being so groggy, that neither could walk.
Says Cooper to Vintner, 'I'm the first of my trade,
There's no kind of vessel, but what I have made,
And of any shape, Sir,—just what you will,—
And of any size, Sir,—from a ton to a gill!'
'Then,' says the Vintner, 'you're the man for me,—
Make me a vessel, if we can agree.
The top and the bottom diameter define,
To bear that proportion as fifteen to nine;
Thirty-five inches are just what I crave,
No more and no less, in the depth, will I have;
Just thirty-nine gallons this vessel must hold,—
Then I will reward you with silver or gold,—
Give me your promise, my honest old friend?'
'I'll make it to-morrow, that you may depend!'
So the next day the Cooper his work to discharge,
Soon made the new vessel, but made it too large;—
He took out some staves, which made it too small,
And then cursed the vessel, the Vintner and all.
He beat on his breast, 'By the Powers!'—he swore,
He never would work at his trade any more!
Now my worthy friend, find out, if you can,
The vessel's dimensions and comfort the man!

GEORGE MOSES HORTON

To Eliza

Eliza, tell thy lover why
Or what induced thee to deceive me?
Fare thee well—away I fly—
I shun the lass who thus will grieve me.

Eliza, still thou art my song,
Although by force I may forsake thee;
Fare thee well, for I was wrong
To woo thee while another take thee.

Eliza, pause and think a while—
Sweet lass! I shall forget thee never;
Fare thee well! although I smile,
I grieve to give thee up forever.

Eliza, I shall think of thee—
My heart shall ever twine about thee;
Fare thee well—but think of me,
Compell'd to live and die without thee.
"Fare thee well!—and if forever,
Still forever fare thee well!"

The Slave's Complaint

Am I sadly cast aside,
On misfortune's rugged tide?
Will the world my pains deride
Forever?

Must I dwell in Slavery's night,
And all pleasure take its flight,

Far beyond my feeble sight,
Forever?

Worst of all, must Hope grow dim,
And withhold her cheering beam?
Rather let me sleep and dream
Forever?

Something still my heart surveys,
Groping through this dreary maze;
Is it Hope?—then burn and blaze
Forever?

Leave me not a wretch confined,
Altogether lame and blind—
Unto gross despair consigned,
Forever!

Heaven! in whom can I confide?
Canst thou not for all provide?
Condescend to be my guide
Forever.

And when this transient life shall end,
Oh, may some kind eternal friend
Bid me from servitude ascend,
Forever!

On hearing of the intention of a gentleman to purchase the Poet's freedom

When on life's ocean first I spread my sail,
I then implored a mild auspicious gale;
And from the slippery strand I took my flight,
And sought the peaceful haven of delight.

Tyrannic storms arose upon my soul,
And dreadful did their mad'ning thunders roll;
The pensive muse was shaken from her sphere,
And hope, it vanish'd in the clouds of fear.

At length a golden sun broke thro' the gloom,
And from his smiles arose a sweet perfume—
A calm ensued, and birds began to sing,
And lo! the sacred muse resumed her wing.

With frantic joy she chaunted as she flew,
And kiss'd the clement hand that bore her thro'
Her envious foes did from her sight retreat,
Or prostrate fall beneath her burning feet.

'Twas like a proselyte, allied to Heaven—
Or rising spirits' boast of sins forgiven,
Whose shout dissolves the adamant away
Whose melting voice the stubborn rocks obey.

'Twas like the salutation of the dove,
Borne on the zephyr thro' some lonesome grove,
When Spring returns, and Winter's chill is past,
And vegetation smiles above the blast.

'Twas like the evening of a nuptial pair,
When love pervades the hour of sad despair—
'Twas like fair Helen's sweet return to Troy,
When every Grecian bosom swell'd with joy.

The silent harp which on the osiers hung,
Was then attuned, and manumission sung;
Away by hope the clouds of fear were driven,
And music breathed my gratitude to heaven.

Hard was the race to reach the distant goal,
The needle oft was shaken from the pole;
In such distress, who could forbear to weep?
Toss'd by the headlong billows of the deep!

The tantalizing beams which shone so plain,
Which turn'd my former pleasures into pain—
Which falsely promised all the joys of fame,
Gave way, and to a more substantial flame.

Some philanthropic souls as from afar,
With pity strove to break the slavish bar;
To whom my floods of gratitude shall roll,
And yield with pleasure to their soft control.

And sure of Providence this work begun—
He shod my feet this rugged race to run;
And in despite of all the swelling tide,
Along the dismal path will prove my guide.

Thus on the dusky verge of deep despair,
Eternal Providence was with me there;
When pleasure seemed to fade on life's gay dawn,
And the last beam of hope was almost gone.

Division of an Estate

It well bespeaks a man beheaded, quite
Divested of the laurel robe of life,
When every member struggles for its base,
The head; the power of order now recedes,
Unheeded efforts rise on every side,
With dull emotion rolling through the brain
Of apprehending slaves. The flocks and herds,
In sad confusion, now run to and fro,
And seem to ask, distressed, the reason why
That they are thus prostrated. Howl, ye dogs!
Ye cattle, low! ye sheep, astonish'd, bleat!
Ye bristling swine, trudge squealing through the glades,
Void of an owner to impart your food!
Sad horses, lift your heads and neigh aloud,
And caper frantic from the dismal scene;
Mow the last food upon your grass-clad lea,

And leave a solitary home behind,
In hopeless widowhood no longer gay!
The trav'ling sun of gain his journey ends
In unavailing pain; he sets with tears;
A king sequester'd sinking from his throne,
Succeeded by a train of busy friends,
Like stars which rise with smiles, to mark the flight
Of awful Phoebus to another world;
Stars after stars in fleet succession rise
Into the wide empire of fortune clear,
Regardless of the donor of their lamps,
Like heirs forgetful of parental care,
Without a grateful smile or filial tear,
Redound in rev'rence to expiring age,
But soon parental benediction flies
Like vivid meteors; in a moment gone,
As though they ne'er had been. But O! the state,
The dark suspense in which poor vassals stand,
Each mind upon the spire of chance hangs fluctuant;
The day of separation is at hand;
Imagination lifts her gloomy curtains,
Like ev'ning's mantle at the flight of day,
Thro' which the trembling pinnacle we spy,
On which we soon must stand with hopeful smiles,
Or apprehending frowns; to tumble on
The right or left forever.

The Art of a Poet

True nature first inspires the man,
But he must after learn to scan,
    And mark well every rule;
Gradual the climax then ascend,
And prove the contrast in the end,
    Between the wit and fool.

A fool tho' blind, may write a verse,
And seem from folly to emerge,

And ryme well every line;
One lucky, void of light, may guess,
And safely to the point may press,
   But this does not refine.

Polish mirror, clear to shine,
And streams must run if they refine,
   And widen as they flow;
The diamonds water lies concealed,
Till polished it is ne'er revealed,
   Its glory bright to show.

A bard must traverse o'er the world,
Where things concealed must rise unfurled,
   And tread the foot of yore;
Tho' he may sweetly harp and sing,
But strictly prune the mental wing,
   Before the mind can soar.

George Moses Horton, Myself

I feel myself in need
   Of the inspiring strains of ancient lore,
My heart to lift, my empty mind to feed,
   And all the world explore.

I know that I am old
   And never can recover what is past,
But for the future may some light unfold
   And soar from ages blast.

I feel resolved to try,
   My wish to prove, my calling to pursue,
Or mount up from the earth into the sky,
   To show what Heaven can do.

My genius from a boy,
   Has fluttered like a bird within my heart;

But could not thus confined her powers employ,
   Impatient to depart.

She like a restless bird,
   Would spread her wing, her power to be unfurl'd,
And let her songs be loudly heard,
   And dart from world to world.

SARAH LOUISA FORTEN

An Appeal to Woman

Oh, woman, woman, in thy brightest hour
Of conscious worth, of pride, of conscious power,
Oh, nobly dare to act a Christian's part,
That well befits a lovely woman's heart!
Dare to be good, as thou canst dare be great;
Despise the taunts of envy, scorn and hate;
Our 'skins may differ,' but from thee we claim
A sister's privilege, in a sister's name.

We are thy sisters,—God has truly said,
That of one hand, the nations he has made.
Oh, christian woman, in a christian land,
Canst thou unblushing read this great command?
Suffer the wrongs which wring our inmost heart
To draw one throb of pity on thy part;
Our 'skins may differ,' but from thee we claim
A sister's privilege, in a sister's name.

Oh, woman!—though upon thy fairer brow
The hues of roses and of lilies glow—
These soon must wither in their kindred earth,
From whence the fair and dark have equal birth.
Let a bright halo o'er thy virtues shed
A lustre, that shall live when thou art dead;
Let coming ages learn to bless thy name
Upon the altar of immortal fame.

The Grave of the Slave

The cold storms of winter shall chill him no more,
His woes and his sorrows, his pains are all o'er,—

The sod of the valley now covers his form,
He is safe in his last home, and fears not the storm.

The poor slave is laid all unheeded and lone,
Where the rich and the poor find a permanent home;
No master can raise him, with voice of command,
He knows not, he hears not, his cruel demand.

Not a tear, not a sigh, to embalm his cold tomb,
No friend to lament him, no child to bemoan;
Not a stone marks the place, where he peacefully lies,
The earth for his pillow, his curtain the skies.

Poor slave! shall we sorrow that death was thy friend?
The last, and the kindest, that Heaven could send:—
The grave to the weary is welcomed and blest;
And death, to the captive, is freedom and rest.

DAVID DRAKE

Concatination
[Selected Pottery Verses, 1834–1862]

Concatination

––––

horses mules and hogs—
all our cows is in the bogs—
there they shall ever stay
till the buzzards take them away =

––––

a better thing, I never saw
when I shot off, the lions Jaw

––––

whats better than Kissing—
while we both are at fishing

––––

Give me silver or; either Gold =
Though they are dangerous; to our Soul =

––––

Dave belongs to Mr. Miles /
wher the oven bakes & the pot biles ///

––––

another trick is worst than this +
Dearest miss: spare me a Kiss +

––––

not counted

––––

cash wanted

––––

I wonder where is all my relations
Friendship to all—and every nation

———

I made this Jar = for cash,
though it is called lucre trash

———

A noble jar
For lard or tar

———

when you fill this Jar with pork or beef
Scot will be there; to Get a peace,—

———

the sun moon and—stars =
In the west are a plenty of—bears

———

I saw a leppard, & a lions face,
Then I felt the need of—Grace.

———

nineteen days before Christmas—Eve—
Lots of people after its over, how they will greave,

———

Mark and
—Dave—

———

made at stoney bluff,
for making or adgin enuff

———

the fouth of July—is Surely come
to blow the fife = and beat the drum //

———

I Saw a leopard, & a lions face =
Then I felt, the need of Grace =

———

I, made this Jar, all of a cross
If, you dont repent, you will be, lost =

ANN PLATO

The Natives of America

Tell me a story, father please,
And then I sat upon his knees.
Then answer'd he,—"what speech make known,
Or tell the words of native tone,
Of how my Indian fathers dwelt,
And, of sore oppression felt;
And how they mourned a land serene,
It was an ever mournful theme."
Yes, I replied,—I like to hear,
And bring my father's spirit near;
Of every pain they did forego,
Oh, please to tell me all you know.
In history often I do read,
Of pain which none but they did heed.

He thus began. "We were a happy race,
When we no tongue but ours did trace,
We were in ever peace,
We sold, we did release—
Our brethren, far remote, and far unknown,
And spake to them in silent, tender tone.
We all were then as in one band,
We join'd and took each others hand;
Our dress was suited to the clime,
Our food was such as roam'd that time,
Our houses were of sticks compos'd;
No matter,—for they us enclos'd.

But then discover'd was this land indeed
By European men; who then had need
Of this far country. Columbus came afar,
And thus before we could say Ah!
What meaneth this?—we fell in cruel hands.
Though some were kind, yet others then held bands

28

Of cruel oppression. Then too, foretold our chief,—
Beggars you will become—is my belief.
We sold, then some bought lands,
We altogether moved in foreign hands.

Wars ensued. They knew the handling of firearms.
Mothers spoke,—no fear this breast alarms,
They will not cruelly us oppress,
Or thus our lands possess.
Alas! it was a cruel day; we were crush'd;
Into the dark, dark woods we rush'd
To seek a refuge.

My daughter, we are now diminish'd, unknown,
Unfelt! Alas! no tender tone
To cheer us when the hunt is done;
Fathers sleep,—we're silent every one.

Oh! silent the horror, and fierce the fight,
When my brothers were shrouded in night;
Strangers did us invade—strangers destroy'd
The fields, which were by us enjoy'd.

Our country is cultur'd, and looks all sublime,
Our fathers are sleeping who lived in the time
That I tell. Oh! could I tell them my grief
In its flow, that in roaming, we find no relief.

I love my country; and shall, until death
Shall cease my breath.

Now daughter dear I've done,
Seal this upon thy memory; until the morrow's sun
Shall sink, to rise no more;
And if my years should score,
Remember this, though I tell no more."

Reflections

Written on Visiting the Grave of a Venerated Friend

Deep in this grave her bones remain,
She's sleeping on, bereft of pain,
Her tongue in silence now does sleep,
And she no more time's call can greet.

She liv'd as all God's saints should do,
Resign'd to death and suffering too;
She feels not pain or sin oppress,
Nor does of worldly cares possess.

White were the locks that thinly shed
Their snows around her honor'd head,
And furrows not to be effac'd
Had age amid her features trac'd.

I said, my sister, Do tread light,
Faint as the stars that gleam at night,
Nor pluck the tender leaves that wave
In sweetness over this sainted grave.

The rose I've planted by her side,
It tells me of that fate decri'd;
And bids us all prepare to die,
For that our doom is hast'ning nigh.

Oh! that the gale that sweeps the heath,
Too roughly o'er your leaves should breathe,
Then sigh for her—and when you bloom
Scatter your fragrance o'er her tomb.

Alone I've wander'd through the gloom,
To pour my lays upon her tomb;
And I have mourn'd to see her bed
With brambles and with thorns o'erspread.

O, surely, round her place of rest
I will not let the weed be blest,
It is not meet that she should be
Forgotten or unblest by me.

My sister said, "tell of this grave!"
Go ask, said I, the thoughtless wave;
And spend one hour in anxious care—
In duty, penitence, and prayer.

Farewell! let memory bestow,
That all may soon be laid as low,
For out of dust, God did compose,
We turn to dust, to sleep, repose.

LES CENELLES

Armand Lanusse

"Do you not wish to renounce the Devil?"
Asked a good priest of a woman of evil
Who had so many sins that every year
They cost her endless remorse and fear.
"I wish to renounce him forever," she said,
"But that I may lose every urge to be bad,
Before pure grace takes me in hand,
Shouldn't I show my daughter how to get a man?"

Translated by Langston Hughes

Camille Thierry

IDEAS

To my friend P. Dalcour

Poor Child! Had I had, to make myself shine forth
    A brilliant, striking garment,
Across the mist and haze, I would perhaps have seen
    A glowing ray of sunshine!

What if I went to her and begged her thus: "Madame,
    My love will surely kill me
But one consoling word from there within your soul,
    Will revive my hope again";

What if I went, as free as during festivals,
    To say to her: "My love,

Your voice will be mine too, and never will the storm
  Cast shadows o'er our days."

What if I went, casting off the chains of the elite,
  Like the mocking child
To say to her: "Woman! my profound woes must have
  The sighs of your heart";

What if I went, a frail craft battered by the storm,
  Tormented by the swells,
To say to her: "Be for me the light on the shores,
  The hope of the sailor";

What if I went to her and cried: "What good is chastity!
  Adultery is a word
Which in our pampered hearts, our hearts devoid of faith
  No longer finds an echo!"

But no, I will not go!—for I have picked, as guide
  And for support, pride.
But no, for my despair dwells upon suicide—
  The dark and final reef!

Another would not have feared to show his misery,
  To suffer an affront!
But no, I will not risk a stinging injury
  To cause me to blush.

I wished, by way of vengeance on my too wanton heart,
  To pierce it with a knife.
Instead a secret voice whispered to my pain
  "Damned are self murderers!"

I must then, without fear, prepare to spread your sails
  In the tempest of the night!
To pierce your delicate skin, the swells recite without cease:
  Sailor, hope is no more!

    Translated by Régine Latorture and Gleason R. W. Adams

Pierre Dalcour

VERSE WRITTEN IN THE ALBUM OF
MADEMOISELLE————

The evening star that in the vaulted skies
Sweetly sparkles, gently flashes,
To me is less lovely than a glance of your eyes
    Beneath their brown lashes.

Translated by Langston Hughes

———————

Victor-Ernest Rillieux

LOVE AND DEVOTION

For Miss Ida B. Wells

Selfless to serve God and the human race:
Such, faith's devotion that naught can efface!
    To calm wounds' agony,
Dry tears, suppress injustices, protect
The orphan, hold the vile assassin checked,
    The soul must stalwart be!

For what fine cause, O harmony divine,
I temper in your fires this talent mine!
    A heavenly angel fair
Stood tall against the sky; and her reviled
Race asks that my poor pen, for this pure child,
    Compose a paean's air.

In days of old, a maid—guileless, like you—
To save her people in Bethulia, grew
    Dauntless and bold. Her name?
Judith, who Holofernes slew, beside

The city wall: forever glorified.
    Writ in the stars, her fame!

Centuries pass, and in France—beauteous nation—
Bereaved, the people seek God's liberation.
    Lo! Joan of Arc appears!
Virgin invincible, she routs the foe,
And, from the stake, her halo's flame, aglow,
    Eternal, lights the years!

But you, O virgin brown of skin, and who
Dwell in the Brute's wild land, with words you do
    Your deeds, for freedom's sake.
Your vanguard heart holds high the burning brand,
And your soft angel tread, over the land,
    Leaves no blood in its wake.

No! Never! For your race all crime abhors,
And would elect the victim's role as yours,
    And not the villain's, whose
Lynchings, guns, gallows, stakes make manifest
That arrogance throughout the Southland blessed,
    And sins of gloomiest hue!

Speak then! Let your oppressed soul shriek, cry out,
And let Europe, distressed, have little doubt
    About the fate abject
Of those a young America, each day—
Expert at torture!—immolates to pay
    A heathen god respect!

May Joan of Arc and Judith light your path!
The White Hoods cower, fearing that your wrath
    Your victory foretells;
And folk courageous, loving, bowed in woe,
Entreat eternal God, that He bestow
    His gifts on Ida Wells!

Translated by Norman R. Shapiro

JAMES M. WHITFIELD

America

America, it is to thee,
Thou boasted land of liberty,—
It is to thee I raise my song,
Thou land of blood, and crime, and wrong.
It is to thee, my native land,
From whence has issued many a band
To tear the black man from his soil,
And force him here to delve and toil;
Chained on your blood-bemoistened sod,
Cringing beneath a tyrant's rod,
Stripped of those rights which Nature's God
    Bequeathed to all the human race,
Bound to a petty tyrant's nod,
    Because he wears a paler face.
Was it for this, that freedom's fires
Were kindled by your patriot sires?
Was it for this, they shed their blood,
On hill and plain, on field and flood?
Was it for this, that wealth and life
Were staked upon that desperate strife,
Which drenched this land for seven long years
With blood of men, and women's tears?
When black and white fought side by side,
    Upon the well-contested field,—
Turned back the fierce opposing tide,
    And made the proud invader yield—
When, wounded, side by side they lay,
    And heard with joy the proud hurrah
From their victorious comrades say
    That they had waged successful war,
The thought ne'er entered in their brains
That they endured those toils and pains,
To forge fresh fetters, heavier chains
For their own children, in whose veins

36

Should flow that patriotic blood,
So freely shed on field and flood.
Oh no; they fought, as they believed,
    For the inherent rights of man;
But mark, how they have been deceived
    By slavery's accursed plan.
They never thought, when thus they shed
    Their heart's best blood, in freedom's cause
That their own sons would live in dread,
    Under unjust, oppressive laws:
That those who quietly enjoyed
    The rights for which they fought and fell,
Could be the framers of a code,
    That would disgrace the fiends of hell!
Could they have looked, with prophet's ken,
    Down to the present evil time,
    Seen free-born men, uncharged with crime,
Consigned unto a slaver's pen,—
Or thrust into a prison cell,
With thieves and murderers to dwell—
While that same flag whose stripes and stars
Had been their guide through freedom's wars
As proudly waved above the pen
Of dealers in the souls of men!
Or could the shades of all the dead,
    Who fell beneath that starry flag,
Visit the scenes where they once bled,
    On hill and plain, on vale and crag,
By peaceful brook, or ocean's strand,
    By inland lake, or dark green wood,
Where'er the soil of this wide land
    Was moistened by their patriot blood,—
And then survey the country o'er,
    From north to south, from east to west,
And hear the agonizing cry
Ascending up to God on high,
From western wilds to ocean's shore,
    The fervent prayer of the oppressed;
The cry of helpless infancy
    Torn from the parent's fond caress

By some base tool of tyranny,
   And doomed to woe and wretchedness;
The indignant wail of fiery youth,
   Its noble aspirations crushed,
Its generous zeal, its love of truth,
   Trampled by tyrants in the dust;
The aerial piles which fancy reared,
   And hopes too bright to be enjoyed,
Have passed and left his young heart seared,
   And all its dreams of bliss destroyed.
The shriek of virgin purity,
   Doomed to some libertine's embrace,
Should rouse the strongest sympathy
   Of each one of the human race;
And weak old age, oppressed with care,
   As he reviews the scene of strife,
Puts up to God a fervent prayer,
   To close his dark and troubled life.
The cry of fathers, mothers, wives,
   Severed from all their hearts hold dear,
And doomed to spend their wretched lives
   In gloom, and doubt, and hate, and fear;
And manhood, too, with soul of fire,
And arm of strength, and smothered ire,
Stands pondering with brow of gloom,
Upon his dark unhappy doom,
Whether to plunge in battle's strife,
And buy his freedom with his life,
And with stout heart and weapon strong,
Pay back the tyrant wrong for wrong,
Or wait the promised time of God,
   When his Almighty ire shall wake,
And smite the oppressor in his wrath,
And hurl red ruin in his path,
And with the terrors of his rod,
   Cause adamantine hearts to quake.
Here Christian writhes in bondage still,
   Beneath his brother Christian's rod,
And pastors trample down at will,
   The image of the living God.

While prayers go up in lofty strains,
   And pealing hymns ascend to heaven,
The captive, toiling in his chains,
   With tortured limbs and bosom riven,
Raises his fettered hand on high,
   And in the accents of despair,
To him who rules both earth and sky,
   Puts up a sad, a fervent prayer,
To free him from the awful blast
   Of slavery's bitter galling shame—
Although his portion should be cast
   With demons in eternal flame!
Almighty God! 't is this they call
   The land of liberty and law;
Part of its sons in baser thrall
   Than Babylon or Egypt saw—
Worse scenes of rapine, lust and shame,
   Than Babylonian ever knew,
Are perpetrated in the name
   Of God, the holy, just, and true;
And darker doom than Egypt felt,
May yet repay this nation's guilt.
Almighty God! thy aid impart,
And fire anew each faltering heart,
And strengthen every patriot's hand,
Who aims to save our native land.
We do not come before thy throne,
   With carnal weapons drenched in gore,
Although our blood has freely flown,
   In adding to the tyrant's store.
Father! before thy throne we come,
   Not in the panoply of war,
With pealing trump, and rolling drum,
   And cannon booming loud and far;
Striving in blood to wash out blood,
   Through wrong to seek redress for wrong;
For while thou 'rt holy, just and good,
   The battle is not to the strong;
But in the sacred name of peace,
   Of justice, virtue, love and truth,

We pray, and never mean to cease,
    Till weak old age and fiery youth
In freedom's cause their voices raise,
And burst the bonds of every slave;
Till, north and south, and east and west,
The wrongs we bear shall be redressed.

To Cinque

All hail! thou truly noble chief,
    Who scorned to live a cowering slave;
Thy name shall stand on history's leaf,
    Amid the mighty and the brave:
Thy name shall shine, a glorious light
    To other brave and fearless men,
Who, like thyself, in freedom's might,
    Shall beard the robber in his den.
Thy name shall stand on history's page,
    And brighter, brighter, brighter glow,
Throughout all time, through every age,
    Till bosoms cease to feel or know
    "Created worth, or human woe."
Thy name shall nerve the patriot's hand
    When, 'mid the battle's deadly strife,
The glittering bayonet and brand
    Are crimsoned with the stream of life:
When the dark clouds of battle roll,
And slaughter reigns without control,
Thy name shall then fresh life impart,
And fire anew each freeman's heart.
Though wealth and power their force combine
    To crush thy noble spirit down,
There is above a power divine
    Shall bear thee up against their frown.

CHARLES L. REASON

Hope and Confidence

! What a strange thing is the human heart!
   With its youth, and its joy and fear!
It doats upon creatures that day-dreams impart,—
Full sorely it grieves when their beauties depart,
   And weeps bitter tears over their bier.

The veriest gloamings that dart into birth,
   Reveal to its being of light:
The dimliest shadows that flit upon earth,
Allure it, with promise of pleasure and mirth
   In a country, where never is night.

It leaves the sure things of its own real home,
   To pursue the mere phantoms of thought!
Well knowing, that certain, there soon must come,
An end to the visions, that so gladsome,
   It bewilder'd, has eagerly sought.

It fleeth the wholesome prose of life,
   With its riches all sure and told:
And scorning the beauties, that calmly in strife
Truth fashions, it longs for the things all rife
   With glitter, and color, and gold.

It buildeth its home 'neath an ever calm sky,
   Near streams wherein crown-jewels sleep,—
And there it reposeth: while soothingly nigh,
Some loved one, perchance, doth most wooingly sigh,
   As the zephyrs all full-laden creep.

Thus it musingly wasteth its strength, in dreams
   Of bliss, that can never prove true:
And ever it revels amid what seems,

A paradise smiling with Hope's warm beams,
   And flowers all spangled with dew.

But, even as flowers are broken and fade,
   And yield up their perfumes—their souls,—
So vanish the colors of which dreams are made,—
So perish the structures on which Hope is staid,
   And the treasures to which the heart holds.

In vain does it follow the wandering forms
   That promise, yet always recede:—
Too briefly the sunshine is darken'd by storms:
Hope minstrels it onward, yet never informs
   Of the dangers unseen, that impede.

The Heart trusts the outward: "Of man 'tis the whole."
   Thus Confidence clings to decay!
It feels the sweet homage that riches control,—
And laughs in contempt at the wealth of the soul:
   And behold! now, friends wait for their prey.

It trusteth in glory, and beauty, and youth,—
   In love-vows that ne'er are to die:
But soon the Death-king, in whose heart is no ruth,
Enfolds it,—and mounting aloft, of Truth
   Thus sings, as turns glassy the eye.

"There's nothing so lovely and bright below,
   As the shapes of the purified mind!
Nought surer to which the weak heart can grow,
On which it can rest, as it onward doth go,
   Than that Truth which its own tendrils bind.

"Yes! Truth opes within a pure sun-tide of bliss,
   And shows in its ever calm flood,
A transcript of regions, where no darkness is,
Where HOPE its conceptions may realize,
   And CONFIDENCE sleep in 'The Good.'"

GEORGE B. VASHON

A Life-Day

(The following poem, written in 1864, is founded upon inci-
dents which took place in one of our Southern states. The
judge referred to, has recently figured as a provisional governor
in President Johnson's plan of reconstruction.

Pittsburgh, March 5th, 1866.   G. B. V.)

MORNING

The breeze awakes with morn's first ray,
Like childhood roused from sleep to play;
The sunshine, like a fairy sprite,
Comes to undo the wrong of night,
And earth is jocund with the glee
That swells from hill and vale and tree.
It echoes music fitly set
For mocking-bird and paroquet;
And, joyous as a ransomed soul,
It hears the notes of the oriole.
The murmur of the wide swept cane
Hymneth the rapture of the plain,
And mingles with the brooklet's song.
    A mirthful brook with fitful gleam,
    Hasting to Mississippi's stream,
And glad'ning both its banks along,
Surely, to be mid scenes like this
Doth render life a dream of bliss—
A treasure-house without alloy;—
Here's Joy's alive, and Life is joy.
Oh! what a joy it is to him
    Who for this scene has left the room
Where sickness, hollow-eyed and grim,
    Hath held, for years, its court of gloom,—
Whose shrunken limbs too clearly own

43

That there the monster had his throne!
They tell not all his tale of woe,—
    How friends and brothers from him fled,
And left him to the fever's glow,
    The ulcered frame, the throbbing head,
With no defense against the grave
Save this—the care of one poor slave.
That faithful one is by his side;—
What more of bliss can now betide?
What matter that the earth is fair?
    What matter that the glad birds sing?
His pleasure is that she doth share
    The balmy breeze's welcoming.
Her sweet smile is the sunshine bright
That floods the landscape wide with light;
Her gladsome youth the genial morn
That doth his happy day adorn,
And her soft voice the music sweet
With which no warbler can compete.
And now that Life and Hope again
Ope to him paths long closed by pain,—
Now, while her tawny cheek, her eye,
Are bright with modest ecstasy,
The hushed shades of the orange grove
Smilingly hear his tale of love.

NOON

How swiftly glide our mortal years,
    When Love doth wing each blissful hour,—
When all our hopes, and all our fears,
    Are minions of his magic power!
Twelve years! Twelve moments in her life,
Since she became a happy wife!
All chains are riven save the tie
Which links her to his destiny.
What cares he for the glance of scorn
    That mocks him in his daily walk?
What, that each coming night and morn
    Echoes his neighbors' gibing talk?

She, once his slave and now his bride,
Outvalues all the earth beside.
And 'neath the orange-trees he strays
With her, as in their younger days;
But not with her alone; for now
His hand doth press a maiden's brow
Whose flaxen curls and eyes of blue
From her fond sires have caught their hue.
Beside them stands a dark-eyed boy,
Whose laugh rings out his infant joy,
As, now and then, comes flashing by
The many-colored butterfly.
Oh! with such pledges of fond love
    As thou dost mark in either boon,
Say, mother, hath not He above
    Granted thy morn a fitting noon?

NIGHT

Alas! that noon should yield to night
Its treasured joys of life and light!
Alas! that sun-bright happiness
Should be o'clouded by distress!
The noble soul who gladly gave
A wife's name to his faithful slave,
Hath passed away, and those who fled
In horror from his stricken bed,
Have come, like vultures to the dead,—
Have come to batten on the store
    He left to those he held so dear—
To claim them in their anguish sore,
    As born thralls to a bondage drear.
And one whose guilty deeds hurl shame
    On white-robed Justice' sainted name,
Holding no sacred thing in awe,
    Dared to proclaim the marriage tie
    Shielding them with its purity,
A fraud upon the slaver's law.
A wailing comes upon the breeze,

That sighs amid the orange trees;
 And she is there, and all alone.
Oh, linger, night! for with the day
Her children will be far away—
Her children! Ah! no more her own!
O, mother! mourning by the spot
 Hallowed by sweetest memory,
And bidding fancy shape the lot
 Each little one is doomed to see.
Alas! thy poor heart knows too well
What to itself it dares not tell!
Hundred of boys as gently born
 As he who was thy joy and pride,
Have by the cruel lash been torn,
 And 'neath its bloody scourgings died.
Hundreds of maidens full as fair
 As she whose little life you gave,
Know what a dowry of despair
 Is beauty in a female slave.
And thou, lorn mother!—thy sole part
Is weeping, till it breaks thy heart.
Shades of the heroes, long since gone!
 Was this your glory's end and aim
Was it for this, O Washington!
 That, welcoming the rebel's name,
Halter and battle you defied?
For this, O Warren! that you died?

BENJAMIN CLARK

The Emigrant

Adieu to the land of my birth—
   Proud land of the slave and the free!
What charms have thy bosom on earth
   For men of complexion like me?

In this boasted land of the free
   I've suffered contumely and scorn;
And cannot relate what I see
   Is reserved for millions unborn.

If places on earth can be found
   Untainted by slavery's breath,
I'll find them, or search the world round
   Till my sorrows are ended in death.

Thy liberty is but a name—
   A byword—a jargon, in fine!
Thy freemen of colour—oh shame!—
   Are glad to escape from thy clime!

Adieu to thy stripes and thy stars,
   That vauntingly float o'er the main!
Adieu to thy Lynch-laws and jars,
   Thy fetters, thy charter, and chain!

I go to the Isles of the Sea,
   Where men are not judged by their hue!
Where all are protected and free—
   My native land, therefore, adieu!

JAMES MADISON BELL

Song for the First of August

With cheerful hearts we've come
From many a happy home,
   Our friends to greet;
And pass a social hour
Beneath this leafy bower,
Where many a shrub and flower
   In fragrance meet.

We come to joy with those
Whose gloomy night of woes
Have past away,
And render worthy meeds
To men whose noble deeds
First cast the genial seeds
   Of Liberty.

Then let our heart's best song
In acclamations strong,
   Reach heaven's height,
In honor of that hour
When Slavery's massive tower
Crumble beneath the power
   Of truth and right.

This is proud Freedom's day!
Swell, swell the gladsome day,
   Till earth and sea
Shall echo with the strain,
Through Britain's vast domain;
No bondman clanks his chain,
   All men are free.

God hasten on the time
When Slavery's blighting crime
    And curse shall end;
When man may widely roam
Beneath the arching dome,
And find with man a home,
    In man a friend.

CHARLOTTE FORTEN GRIMKÉ

A June Song

We would sing a song to the fair young June,
To the rare and radiant June,
The lovely, laughing, fragrant June.
How shall her praise be sung or said?
Her cheek has caught the roses' hue,
Her eye the heavens' serenest blue.

And the gold of sunset crowns her head,
And her smile—ah! there's never a sweeter, I ween,
Than the smile of this fair young summer queen.
What life, what hope, her coming brings!
What joy anew in the sad heart springs
As her robe of beauty o'er all she flings!

Old earth grows young in her presence sweet,
And thrills at the touch of her gentle feet,
As the flowers spring forth her face to greet.
Hark! how the birds are singing her praise,
In their gladdest, sweetest, roundelays!

The trees on the hillside have caught the glow,
And the heaven smiles down on the earth below,
And our radiant June,
Our lovely, joyous June,
Our summer queen,
Smiles, too, as she stands
With folded hands,
And brow serene.

How shall we crown her bright young head?
Crown it with roses, rare and red;
Crown it with roses, creamy white,
As the lotus bloom that sweetens the night.
Crown it with roses as pink as shell

In which the voices of ocean dwell.
And a fairer queen
Shall ne'er be seen
Than our lovely, laughing June.

We have crowned her now, but she will not stay,
The vision of beauty will steal away
And fade, as faded the fair young May.
Ah, loveliest maiden, linger a while!
Pour into our hearts the warmth of thy smile,
The gloom of the winter will come too soon.
Stay with us, gladden us, beautiful June!
Thou glidest away from our eager clasp.
They will hold thee fast; and the days to be
Will be brighter and sweeter for thoughts of thee.
Our song shall not be a song of farewell,
As with words of love the chorus we swell,
In praise of the fair young June,
Of the rare and radiant June,
The lovely, laughing, fragrant June.

A Parting Hymn

When Winter's royal robes of white
    From hill and vale are gone,
And the glad voices of the spring
    Upon the air are borne,
Friends, who have met with us before,
Within these walls shall meet no more.

Forth to a noble work they go:
    O, may their hearts keep pure,
And hopeful zeal and strength be theirs
    To labor and endure,
That they an earnest faith may prove
By words of truth and deeds of love.

May those, whose holy task it is
   To guide impulsive youth,
Fail not to cherish in their souls
   A reverence for truth;
For teachings which the lips impart
Must have their source within the heart.

May all who suffer share their love—
   The poor and the oppressed;
So shall the blessing of our God
   Upon their labors rest.
And may we meet again where all
Are blest and freed from every thrall.

———————

In the earnest path of duty,
   With high hopes and hearts sincere,
We, to useful lives aspiring,
   Daily meet to labor here.

No vain dreams of earthly glory
   Urge us onward to explore
Far-extending realms of knowledge,
   With their rich and varied store;

But, with hope of aiding others,
   Gladly we perform our part;
Nor forget, the mind, while storing,
   We must educate the heart,—

Teach it hatred of oppression,
   Truest love of God and man;
Thus our high and holy calling
   May accomplish His great plan.

Not the great and gifted only
   He appoints to do his will,
But each one, however lowly,
   Has a mission to fulfill.

Knowing this, toil we unwearied,
  With true hearts and purpose high;—
We would win a wreath immortal,
  Whose bright flowers ne'er fade and die.

HENRIETTA CORDELIA RAY

Toussaint L'Ouverture

To those fair isles where crimson sunsets burn,
We send a backward glance to gaze on thee,
Brave Toussaint! thou wast surely born to be
A hero; thy proud spirit could but spurn
Each outrage on thy race. Couldst thou unlearn
The lessons taught by instinct? Nay! and we
Who share the zeal that would make all men free,
Must e'en with pride unto thy life-work turn.
Soul-dignity was thine and purest aim;
And ah! how sad that thou wast left to mourn
In chains 'neath alien skies. On him, shame! shame!
That mighty conqueror who dared to claim
The right to bind thee. Him we heap with scorn,
And noble patriot! guard with love thy name.

Self-Mastery

To catch the spirit in its wayward flight
Through mazes manifold, what task supreme!
For when to floods has grown the quiet stream,
Much human skill must aid its rage to fight;
And when wild winds invade the solemn night,
Seems not man's vaunted power but a dream?
And still more futile, ay, we e'en must deem
This quest to tame the soul, and guide aright
Its restless wanderings,—to lure it back
To shoals of calm. Full many a moan and sigh
Attend the strife; till, effort merged in prayer,
Oft uttered, clung to—when of strength the lack
Seems direst—brings the answer to our cry:
A gift from Him who lifts our ev'ry care.

ALBERY A. WHITMAN

from *The Rape of Florida*

I.

The negro slave by Swanee river sang;
Well-pleased he listened to his echoes ringing;
For in his heart a secret comfort sprang,
When Nature seemed to join his mournful singing.
To mem'ry's cherished objects fondly clinging;
His bosom felt the sunset's patient glow,
And spirit whispers into weird life springing,
Allured to worlds he trusted yet to know,
And lightened for a while life's burdens here below.

II.

The drowsy dawn from many a low-built shed,
Beheld his kindred driven to their task;
Late evening saw them turn with weary tread
And painful faces back: and dost thou ask
How sang these bondmen? how their suff'rings mask?
Song is the soul of sympathy divine,
And hath an inner ray where hope may bask;
Song turns the humblest waters into wine,
Illumines exile hearts and makes their faces shine.

III.

The negro slave by Swanee river sang,
There soon, the human hunter rode along;
And eagerly behind him came a gang
Of hounds and men,—the bondman hushed his song—
Around him came a silent list'ning throng;
"Some runaway!" he muttered, said no more,
But sank from view the growing corn among;
And though deep pangs his wounded spirit bore,
He hushed his soul, and went on singing as before.

IV.

So fared the land where slaves were groaning yet—
Where beauty's eyes must feed the lusts of men!
'Tis as when horrid dreams we half forget,
Would then relate, and still relate again—
Ah! cold abhorrence hesitates my pen!
The heavens were sad, and hearts of men were faint;
Philanthropy implored and wept, but then
The wrong, unblushing, trampled on Restraint,
While feeble Law sat by and uttered no complaint.

V.

"Fly and be free!" A whisper comes from heaven,
"Thy cries are heard!" the bondman's up and gone!
To grasp the dearest boon to mortals given,
He frantic flies, unaided and alone.
To him the red man's dwellings are unknown;
But he can crave the freedom of his race,
Can find his harvests in the desert sown,
And in the cypress forest's dark embrace,
A pathway to his habitations safely trace.

VI.

The sable slave, from Georgia's utmost bounds,
Escapes for life into the Great Wahoo.
Here he has left afar the savage hounds
And human hunters that did late pursue;
There in the hommock darkly hid from view,
His wretched limbs are stretched awhile to rest,
Till some kind Seminole shall guide him thro',
To where by hound nor hunter more distrest,
He, in a flow'ry home, shall be the red man's guest.

VII.

If tilled profusion does not crown the view,
Nor wide-ranged farms begirt with fences spread;
The cultivated plot is well to do;
And where no slave his groaning life has led,
The songs of plenty fill the lowliest shed.
Who could wish more, when Nature always green,

Brings forth fruit-bearing woods and fields of bread?
Wish more, where cheerful valleys bloom between,
And herds browse on the hills, that winter ne'er has seen?

VIII.

Shall high-domed mosque or steepled cathedral,
Alone, to man his native land endear?
Shall pride's palatial pomp and ease withal,
The only shrines of patriotism rear?
Oh! who can limit adoration's sphere,
Or check the inspiring currents of the soul?—
Who hush the whispers of the vernal year,
Or press the sons of freedom from their goal?
Or who from Nature wrest the mystery of control!

IX.

Plebeian, Savage, Sage, or lord or fiend,
Man hath of justice and of right a cause.
Prior to all that e'er has contravened,
Or e'en to man's existence, justice was.
Right would be right amid the wreck of laws:
'Tis so, and all ordaining Nature gives
Somewhere to live, to every child she has;
She gives, and to her bosom each receives,
Inducing it to love the spot whereon it lives.

X.

Fair Florida! whose scenes could so enhance—
Could in the sweetness of the earth excel!
Wast thou the Seminole's inheritance?
Yea, it was thee he loved, and loved so well!
'Twas neath thy palms and pines he strove to dwell.
Not savage, but resentful to the knife,
For thee he sternly struggled—sternly fell!
Thoughtful and brave, in long uneven strife,
He held the verge of manhood mid dark hights of life.

XI.

A wild-born pride endeared him to thy soil!
Where roamed his herds without a keeper's care—

Where man knew not the pangs of slavish toil!
And where thou didst not blooming pleasures spare,
But well allotted each an ample share,
He loved to dwell: Oh! isn't the goal of life
Where man has plenty and to man is fair?
When free from avarice's pinch and strife,
Is earth not like the Eden-home of man and wife?

XII.

If earth were freed from those who buy and sell,
It soon were free from most, or *all* its ills;
For that which makes it, most of all, a hell,
Is what the stingy of purse of Fortune fills:
The man who blesses and the man who kills,
Oft have a kindred purpose after all,
A purpose that will ring in Mammon's tills;
And that has ne'er unheeded made a call,
Since Eve and Adam trod the thistles of their Fall.

A Question

Shall my hand lie cold on the strings of my lyre,
And the heart that is warm lose its pathos and fire,
    Ere my countrymen hear my song?
Shall the bard who sang in the tents of the slave,
And no wakes his harp for the free and the brave,
Unheeded wander along?

FRANCES ELLEN WATKINS HARPER

The Slave Mother

Heard you that shriek? It rose
   So wildly on the air,
It seem'd as if a burden'd heart
   Was breaking in despair.

Saw you those hands so sadly clasped—
   The bowed and feeble head—
The shuddering of that fragile form—
   That look of grief and dread?

Saw you the sad, imploring eye?
   Its every glance was pain,
As if a storm of agony
   Were sweeping through the brain.

She is a mother pale with fear,
   Her boy clings to her side,
And in her kyrtle vainly tries
   His trembling form to hide.

He is not hers, although she bore
   For him a mother's pains;
He is not hers, although her blood
   Is coursing through his veins!

He is not hers, for cruel hands
   May rudely tear apart
The only wreath of household love
   That binds her breaking heart.

His love has been a joyous light
   That o'er her pathway smiled,
A fountain gushing ever new,
   Amid life's desert wild.

His lightest word has been a tone
    Of music round her heart,
Their lives a streamlet blent in one—
    Oh, Father! must they part?

They tear him from her circling arms,
    Her last and fond embrace:—
Oh! never more may her sad eyes
    Gaze on his mournful face.

No marvel, then, these bitter shrieks
    Disturb the listening air;
She is a mother, and her heart
    Is breaking in despair.

Bury Me in a Free Land

Make me a grave where'er you will,
In a lowly plain, or a lofty hill,
Make it among earth's humblest graves,
But not in a land where men are slaves.

I could not rest if around my grave
I heard the steps of a trembling slave:
His shadow above my silent tomb
Would make it a place of fearful gloom.

I could not rest if I heard the tread
Of a coffle gang to the shambles led,
And the mother's shriek of wild despair
Rise like a curse on the trembling air.

I could not sleep if I saw the lash
Drinking her blood at each fearful gash,
And I saw her babes torn from her breast,
Like trembling doves from their parent nest.

I'd shudder and start if I heard the bay
Of blood-hounds seizing their human prey,
And I heard the captive plead in vain
As they bound afresh his galling chain.

Learning to Read

Very soon the Yankee teachers
   Came down and set up school;
But, oh! how the Rebs did hate it,—
   It was agin' their rule.

Our masters always tried to hide
   Book learning from our eyes;
Knowledge did'nt agree with slavery—
   'Twould make us all too wise.

But some of us would try to steal
   A little from the book,
And put the words together,
   And learn by hook or crook.

I remember Uncle Caldwell,
   Who took pot liquor fat
And greased the pages of his book,
   And hid it in his hat.

And had his master ever seen
   The leaves upon his head,
He'd have thought them greasy papers,
   But nothing to be read.

And there was Mr. Turner's Ben,
   Who heard the children spell,
And picked the words right up by heart,
   And learned to read 'em well.

Well, the Northern folks kept sending
      The Yankee teachers down;
And they stood right up and helped us,
      Though Rebs did sneer and frown.

And I longed to read my Bible,
      For precious words it said;
But when I begun to learn it,
      Folks just shook their heads,

And said there is no use trying,
      Oh! Chloe, you're too late;
But as I was rising sixty,
      I had no time to wait.

So I got a pair of glasses,
      And straight to work I went,
And never stopped till I could read
      The hymns and Testament.

Then I got a little cabin
      A place to call my own—
And I felt as independent
      As the queen upon her throne.

A Double Standard

Do you blame me that I loved him?
      If when standing all alone
I cried for bread a careless world
      Pressed to my lips a stone.

Do you blame me that I loved him,
      That my heart beat glad and free,
When he told me in the sweetest tones
      He loved but only me?

Can you blame me that I did not see
  Beneath his burning kiss
The serpent's wiles, nor even hear
  The deadly adder hiss?

Can you blame me that my heart grew cold
  That the tempted, tempter turned;
When he was feted and caressed
  And I was coldly spurned?

Would you blame him, when you draw from me
  Your dainty robes aside.
If he with gilded baits should claim
  Your fairest as his bride?

Would you blame the world if it should press
  On him a civic crown;
And see me struggling in the depth
  Then harshly press me down?

Crime has no sex and yet to-day
  I wear the brand of shame;
Whilst he amid the gay and proud
  Still bears an honored name.

Can you blame me if I've learned to think
  Your hate of vice a sham,
When you so coldly crushed me down
  And then excused the man?

Would you blame me if to-morrow
  The coroner should say,
A wretched girl, outcast, forlorn,
  Has thrown her life away?

Yes, blame me for my downward course,
  But oh! remember well,
Within your homes you press the hand
  That led me down to hell.

I'm glad God's ways are not our ways,
  He does not see as man,
Within His love I know there's room
  For those whom others ban.

I think before His great white throne,
  His throne of spotless light,
That whited sepulchres shall wear
  The hue of endless night.

That I who fell, and he who sinned,
  Shall reap as we have sown;
That each the burden of his loss
  Must bear and bear alone.

No golden weights can turn the scale
  Of justice in His sight;
And what is wrong in woman's life
  In man's cannot be right.

Songs for the People

Let me make the songs for the people,
  Songs for the old and young;
Songs to stir like a battle-cry
  Wherever they are sung.

Not for the clashing of sabres,
  Nor carnage nor for strife;
But songs to thrill the hearts of men
  With more abundant life.

Let me make the songs for the weary,
  Amid life's fever and fret,
Till hearts shall relax their tension,
  And careworn brows forget.

Let me sing for little children,
  Before their footsteps stray,
Sweet anthems of love and duty,
  To float o'er life's highway.

I would sing for the poor and aged,
  When shadows dim their sight;
Of the bright and restful mansions,
  Where there shall be no night.

Our world, so worn and weary,
  Needs music, pure and strong,
To hush the jangle and discords
  Of sorrow, pain, and wrong.

Music to soothe all its sorrow,
  Till war and crime shall cease;
And the hearts of men grown tender
  Girdle the world with peace.

TWO
LIFT EVERY VOICE
(1900–1918)

WILLIAM STANLEY BRAITHWAITE

The House of Falling Leaves

I

Off our New England coast the sea to-night
Is moaning the full sorrow of its heart:
There is no will to comfort it apart
Since moon and stars are hidden from its sight.
And out beyond the furthest harbor-light
There runs a tide that marks not any chart
Wherewith man knows the ending and the start
Of that long voyage in the infinite.

If change and fate and hapless circumstance
May baffle and perplex the moaning sea,
And day and night in alternate advance
Still hold the primal Reasoning in fee,
Cannot my Grief be strong enough to chance
My voice across the tide I cannot see?

II

We go from house to house, from town to town,
And fill the distance full of smiles and words;
We take all pleasure that our strength affords
And care not if the sun be up or down.
The way of it no man has ever known—
But suddenly there is a snap of chords
Within the heart that sounds like hollow boards,—
We question every shadow that is thrown.

O to be near when the last word is said!
And see the last reflection in the eye—
For when the word is brought our friend is dead,
How bitter is the tear that will not dry,
Because so far away our steps are led
When Love should draw us close to say Good-bye!

OLIVIA WARD BUSH

Driftwood

Sung by the strand to the music of the wave.

MORNING

Bright glows the morn, I pace the shining sands,
And watch the children, as with eager hands
They gather driftwood for the evening fire.
Their merry laughter, ringing loud and clear,
Resounds like sweetest music to my ear,
As swift they toil, each with the same desire.

And now their task completed, they depart,
Each one with beaming face and happy heart,
They too, will watch the driftwood fire to-night,
And knowing this, they hasten glad and gay,
With willing feet, along the homeward way,
Their precious burdens bearing with delight.

I watch these little children of the poor,
Till they have reached each lowly dwelling's door,
And then, I too my footsteps homeward turn;
I fancy what a joyous sight 'twill be,
To see the children sitting in their glee,
Close by the fire and laugh to see it burn.

EVENING

From out my open window, I can see
The rolling waves, as fierce and restlessly,
They dash against the long, long stretch of shore,
And in the distance, I can dimly trace,
Some out-bound vessel having left her place
Of Harbor, to return perhaps no more.

Within my mind there dwells this lingering thought,
How oft from ill the greatest good is wrought,
Perhaps some shattered wreck along the strand,
Will help to make the fire burn more bright,
And for some weary traveller to-night,
'Twill serve the purpose of a guiding hand.

Ah yes, and thus it is with these our lives,
Some poor misshapen remnant still survives,
Of what was once a fair and beauteous form,
And yet some dwelling may be made more bright,
Some one afar may catch a gleam of light,
After the fury of the blighting storm.

DRIFTING

And now the sun in tinted splendor sank,
    The west was all aglow with crimson light;
The bay seemed like a sheet of burnished gold,
    Its waters glistened with such radiance bright.

At anchor lay the yachts with snow-white sails,
    Outlined against the glowing, rose-hued sky;
No ripple stirred the waters' calm repose
    Save when a tiny craft sped lightly by.

Our boat was drifting slowly, gently round,
    To rest secure till evening shadows fell;
No sound disturbed the stillness of the air,
    Save the soft chiming of the vesper bell.

Yea, drifting, drifting; and I thought that life,
    When nearing death, is like the sunset sky:
And death is but the slow, sure drifting in,
    To rest far more securely, by and by.

Then let me drift along the Bay of time,
    Till my last sun shall set in glowing light;
Let me cast anchor where no shadows fall,
    Full safely moored within Heaven's harbor bright.

Newport, June 12, 1898

CARRIE WILLIAMS CLIFFORD

America

America is *not* another name for opportunity
To all her sons! Nay, bid me not be dumb—
I will be heard. Christians, I come
To plead with burning eloquence of truth
A brother's cause; ay, to demand, forsooth,
The manhood rights of which he is denied;
Too long your pretense have your acts belied.

What has he done to merit your fierce hate?
I charge you, speak the truth; for know, his fate
Irrevocably is bound up with yours,
For good or ill, as long as time endures.
Torn from his native home by ruthless hands,
For centuries he tilled your fruitful lands,
In shameful, base, degrading slavery;
Your humble, patient, loyal vassal, he—
Piling your coffers high with magic gold,
Himself, the while, like cattle bought and sold.

When devastating war stalked through the land,
And dangers threatened you on every hand,
These sons whose color you cannot forgive,
Did freely shed their blood that you might live
A nation, strong and great. And will you then
Continue to debase, degrade, contemn
Your loyal children, while with smiling face
You raise disloyal ones to power and place?

Is race or color crime, that for this cause
You draft against the Negro unjust laws?
Is race or color sin that he should be
For these things treated so outrageously?
O, boastful, white American, beware!
It is the handiwork of God you dare

Thus to despise and He will you repay
With generous measure overflowing, yea,
For all the good which in his life you've wrought,
For helpful deed, or kindly, loving thought—
For every act of cruelty you've done,
For every groan which you have from him wrung,
For every infamy by him endured,
He will you all repay, be thou assured!
Not here alone ere time shall cease to be,
But likewise There, through all eternity.

Character or Color—Which?

What is blood, or what is birth?
What is black or white?
Or small or great, or rich or poor?
Just so the man's all right?

O, vain and haughty white man, why
Of ancestry prate so?
Can you in tracing your descent,
Farther than Adam go?

Why boast of culture? Well you know,
Ere to your present state
Of progress and renown you'd come,
(With statesmen wise and great—)

The blacks had splendidly achieved
Long centuries before;
Their monuments, unrivaled still,
Adorn old Afric's shore.

No adventitious circumstance
Can fix a people's station.
Integrity's the thing that counts
In any man or nation.

Then modestly let's run our course—
All hist'ry tells the story:
No race but has its page of shame,
None lacks its page of glory.

So what is blood or what is birth?
What is black or white?
Or great or small, or rich or poor,
Just so the man's all right?

Little Mother

(Upon the lynching of Mary Turner)

Oh, tremble, Little Mother,
For your dark-eyed, unborn babe,
Whom in your secret heart you've named
The well-loved name of "Gabe."

For Gabriel is the father's name,
And the son is sure to be
"Just like his father!" as she wants
The whole, wide world to see!

But tremble, Little Mother,
For your unborn baby's fate;
The father tarries long away—
Why does he stay so late?

For dark the night and weird the wind,
And chilled the heart with fear!
What are those hideous sounds and cries
Each instant drawing near?

Oh, tremble, dark-faced mother,
At the dreadful word that falls
From lips of pale-faced demons,
As the black man pleads and calls.

For they're dragging Gabe, at a stout rope's end,
And they say, "She is bound to tell!"
Something she knows not a thing about,
Or they'll "Give her the same as well!"

Oh, tremble, helpless mother!
They're beating down the door,
And you'll never feel the father's kiss,
Or the stir of the baby more.

Oh, the human beasts were ruthless,
And there upon the ground,
Two bodies—and an unborn babe—
The ghastly morning found.

JAMES D. CORROTHERS

Paul Laurence Dunbar

He came, a dark youth, singing in the dawn
        Of a new freedom, glowing o'er his lyre,
        Refining, as with great Apollo's fire,
        His people's gift of song. And, thereupon,
This negro singer, come to Helicon,
        Constrained the masters, listening, to admire,
        And roused a race to wonder and aspire,
        Gazing which way their honest voice was gone,
With ebon face uplit of glory's crest.
        Men marveled at the singer, strong and sweet,
        Who brought the cabin's mirth, the tuneful night,
But faced the morning, beautiful with light,
        To die while shadows yet fell toward the west,
        And leave his laurels at his people's feet.

Dunbar, no poet wears your laurels now;
        None rises, singing, from your race like you,
        Dark melodist, immortal, though the dew
        Fell early on the bays upon your brow,
And tinged with pathos every halcyon vow
        And brave endeavor. Silence o'er you threw
        Flowerets of love. Or, if an envious few
        Of your own people brought no garlands, how
Could Malice smite him whom the gods had crowned?
        If, like the meadow-lark, your flight was low,
        Your flooded lyrics half the hilltops drowned;
A wide world heard you, and it loved you so
        It stilled its heart to list the strains you sang,
        And o'er your happy songs its plaudits rang.

JOSEPH SEAMON COTTER, JR.

A Prayer

As I lie in bed,
Flat on my back;
There passes across my ceiling
An endless panorama of things—
Quick steps of gay-voiced children,
Adolescence in its wondering silences,
Maid and man on moonlit summer's eve,
Women in the holy glow of motherhood,
Old men gazing silently thru the twilight
Into the beyond.
O God, give me words to make my dream-children live.

And What Shall You Say?

Brother, come!
And let us go unto our God.
And when we stand before Him
I shall say—
"Lord, I do not hate,
I am hated.
I scourge no one,
I am scourged.
I covet no lands,
My lands are coveted.
I mock no peoples,
My people are mocked."
And brother, what shall you say?

Supplication

I am so tired and weary,
　　So tired of the endless fight,
So weary of waiting the dawn
　　And finding endless night.

That I ask but rest and quiet—
　　Rest for days that are gone,
And quiet for the little space
　　That I must journey on.

A Woman at Her Husband's Grave

Peace to his ashes!
I cannot for the soul of me
Sorrowing bow,
Tho I search thru the heart of me
Grieve for him now.
'Tis well he is gone
And heart-break is over,
A husband he was
But never a lover.

JOSEPH SEAMON COTTER, SR.

Dr. Booker T. Washington to the National Negro Business League

'Tis strange indeed to hear us plead
   For selling and for buying
When yesterday we said: "Away
   With all good things but dying."

The world's ago, and we're agog
   To have our first brief inning;
So let's away through surge and fog
   However slight the winning.

What deeds have sprung from plow and pick!
   What bank-rolls from tomatoes!
No dainty crop of rhetoric
   Can match one of potatoes.

Ye orators of point and pith,
   Who force the world to heed you,
What skeletons you'll journey with
   Ere it is forced to feed you.

A little gold won't mar our grace,
   A little ease our glory.
This world's a better biding place
   When money clinks its story.

W.E.B. DU BOIS

A Litany at Atlanta

O Silent God, Thou whose voice afar in mist and mystery
hath left our ears an-hungered in these fearful days—
Hear us, good Lord!

Listen to us, Thy children: our faces dark with doubt are
made a mockery in Thy Sanctuary. With uplifted hands we
front Thy Heaven, O God, crying:
We beseech Thee to hear us, good Lord!

We are not better than our fellows, Lord; we are but weak
and human men. When our devils do deviltry, curse Thou
the doer and the deed,—curse them as we curse them, do to
them all and more than ever they have done to innocence and
weakness, to womanhood and home.
Have mercy upon us, miserable sinners!

And yet, whose is the deeper guilt? Who made these devils?
Who nursed them in crime and fed them on injustice? Who
ravished and debauched their mothers and their grandmothers?
Who bought and sold their crime and waxed fat and rich on
public iniquity?
Thou knowest, good God!

Is this Thy Justice, O Father, that guile be easier than
innocence and the innocent be crucified for the guilt of the
untouched guilty?
Justice, O Judge of men!

Wherefore do we pray? Is not the God of the Fathers dead?
Have not seers seen in Heaven's halls Thine hearsed and lifeless
form stark amidst the black and rolling smoke of sin, where all
along bow bitter forms of endless dead?
Awake, Thou that sleepest!

Thou art not dead, but flown afar, up hills of endless light,
through blazing corridors of suns, where worlds do swing of
good and gentle men, of women strong and free—far from
the cozenage, black hypocrisy, and chaste prostitution of this
shameful speck of dust!

Turn again, O Lord; leave us not to perish in our sin!
From lust of body and lust of blood,—
  Great God, deliver us!
From lust of power and lust of gold,—
  Great God, deliver us!
From the leagued lying of despot and of brute,—
  Great God, deliver us!
A city lay in travail, God our Lord, and from her loins sprang twin Murder and Black Hate. Red was the midnight; clang, crack, and cry of death and fury filled the air and trembled underneath the stars where church spires pointed silently to Thee. And all this was to sate the greed of greedy men who hide behind the veil of vengeance!
  Bend us Thine ear, O Lord!
In the pale, still morning we looked upon the deed. We stopped our ears and held our leaping hands, but they—did they not wag their heads and leer and cry with bloody jaws: *Cease from Crime!* The word was mockery, for thus they train a hundred crimes while we do cure one.
  Turn again our captivity, O Lord!
Behold this maimed and broken thing, dear God; it was an humble black man, who toiled and sweat to save a bit from the pittance paid him. They told him: *Work and Rise!* He worked. Did this man sin? Nay, but someone told how someone said another did—one whom he had never seen nor known. Yet for that man's crime this man lieth maimed and murdered, his wife naked to shame, his children to poverty and evil.
  Hear us, O heavenly Father!
Doth not this justice of hell stink in Thy nostrils, O God? How long shall the mounting flood of innocent blood roar in Thine ears and pound in our hearts for vengeance? Pile the pale frenzy of blood-crazed brutes, who do such deeds, high on Thine Altar, Jehovah Jireh, and burn it in hell forever and forever!
  Forgive us, good Lord; we know not what we say!
Bewildered we are and passion-tossed, mad with the madness of a mobbed and mocked and murdered people; straining at the armposts of Thy throne, we raise our shackled hands and charge Thee, God, by the bones of our stolen fathers, by the

tears of our dead mothers, by the very blood of Thy crucified
Christ: What meaneth this? Tell us the plan; give us the sign!

Keep not Thou silent, O God!

Sit not longer blind, Lord God, deaf to our prayer and dumb
to our dumb suffering. Surely Thou, too, art not white, O
Lord, a pale, bloodless, heartless thing!

Ah! Christ of all the Pities!

Forgive the thought! Forgive these wild, blasphemous words!
Thou art still the God of our black fathers and in Thy Soul's
Soul sit some soft darkenings of the evening, some shadowings
of the velvet night.

But whisper—speak—call, great God, for Thy silence is
white terror to our hearts! The way, O God, show us the way
and point us the path!

Whither? North is greed and South is blood; within, the
coward, and without, the liar. Whither? To death?

Amen! Welcome, dark sleep!

Whither? To life? But not this life, dear God, not this. Let
the cup pass from us, tempt us not beyond our strength, for
there is that clamoring and clawing within, to whose voice we
would not listen, yet shudder lest we must,—and it is red. Ah!
God! It is a red and awful shape.

Selah!

In yonder East trembles a star.

Vengeance is Mine; I will repay, saith the Lord!

PAUL LAURENCE DUNBAR

We Wear the Mask

We wear the mask that grins and lies,
It hides our cheeks and shades our eyes—
This debt we pay to human guile;
With torn and bleeding hearts we smile
And mouth with myriad subtleties,

Why should the world be over-wise,
In counting all our tears and sighs?
Nay, let them only see us, while
 We wear the mask.

We smile, but oh great Christ, our cries
To Thee from tortured souls arise.
We sing, but oh the clay is vile
Beneath our feet, and long the mile,
But let the world dream otherwise,
 We wear the mask!

A Negro Love Song

Seen my lady home las' night,
 Jump back, honey, jump back.
Hel' huh han' an' sque'z it tight,
 Jump back, honey, jump back.
Hyeahd huh sigh a little sigh,
Seen a light gleam f'om huh eye,
An' a smile go flittin' by—
 Jump back, honey, jump back.

Hyeahd de win' blow thoo de pine,
 Jump back, honey, jump back.

Mockin'-bird was singin' fine,
    Jump back, honey, jump back.
An' my hea't was beatin' so,
When I reached my lady's do',
Dat I could n't ba' to go—
    Jump back, honey, jump back.

Put my ahm aroun' huh wais',
    Jump back, honey, jump back.
Raised huh lips an' took a tase,
    Jump back, honey, jump back.
Love me, honey, love me true?
Love me well ez I love you?
An' she answe'd, "'Cose I do"—
    Jump back, honey, jump back.

When Malindy Sings

G'way an' quit dat noise, Miss Lucy—
    Put dat music book away;
What's de use to keep on tryin'?
    Ef you practise twell you're gray,

You cain't sta't no notes a-flyin'
    Lak de ones dat rants and rings
F'om de kitchen to de big woods
    When Malindy sings.

You ain't got de nachel o'gans
    Fu' to make de soun' come right,
You ain't got de tu'ns an' twistin's
    Fu' to make it sweet an' light.
Tell you one thing now, Miss Lucy,
    An' I'm tellin' you fu' true,
When hit comes to raal right singin',
    'T ain't no easy thing to do.

Easy 'nough fu' folks to hollah,
   Lookin' at de lines an' dots,
When dey ain't no one kin sence it,
   An' de chune comes in, in spots;
But fu' real melojous music,
   Dat jes' strikes yo' hea't and clings,
Jes' you stan' an' listen wif me
   When Malindy sings.

Ain't you nevah hyeahd Malindy?
   Blessed soul, tek up de cross!
Look hyeah, ain't you jokin', honey?
   Well, you don't know whut you los'.
Y' ought to hyeah dat gal a-wa'blin',
   Robins, la'ks, an' all dem things,
Heish dey moufs an' hides dey faces
   When Malindy sings.

Fiddlin' man jes' stop his fiddlin',
   Lay his fiddle on de she'f;
Mockin'-bird quit tryin' to whistle,
   'Cause he jes' so shamed hisse'f.
Folks a-playin' on de banjo
   Draps dey fingahs on de strings—
Bless yo' soul—fu'gits to move 'em,
   When Malindy sings.

She jes' spreads huh mouf and hollahs,
   "Come to Jesus," twell you hyeah
Sinnahs' tremblin' steps and voices,
   Timid-lak a-drawin' neah;
Den she tu'ns to "Rock of Ages,"
   Simply to de cross she clings,
An' you fin' yo' teahs a-drappin'
   When Malindy sings.

Who dat says dat humble praises
   Wif de Master nevah counts?
Heish yo' mouf, I hyeah dat music,
   Ez hit rises up an' mounts—

Floatin' by de hills an' valleys,
    Way above dis buryin' sod,
Ez hit makes its way in glory
    To de very gates of God!

Oh, hit's sweetah dan de music
    Of an edicated band;
An' hit's dearah dan de battle's
    Song o' triumph in de lan'.
It seems holier dan evenin'
    When de solemn chu'ch bell rings,
Ez I sit an' ca'mly listen
    While Malindy sings.

Towsah, stop dat ba'kin', hyeah me!
    Mandy, mek dat chile keep still;
Don't you hyeah de echoes callin'
    F'om de valley to de hill?
Let me listen, I can hyeah it,
    Th'oo de bresh of angel's wings,
Sof' an' sweet, "Swing Low, Sweet Chariot,"
    Ez Malindy sings.

When de Co'n Pone's Hot

Dey is times in life when Nature
    Seems to slip a cog an' go,
Jes' a-rattlin' down creation,
    Lak an ocean's overflow;
When de worl' jes' stahts a-spinnin'
    Lak a picaninny's top,
An' yo' cup o' joy is brimmin'
    'Twell it seems about to slop,
An' you feel jes' lak a racah,
    Dat is trainin' fu' to trot—
When yo' mammy says de blessin'
    An' de co'n pone's hot.

When you set down at de table,
    Kin' o' weary lak an' sad,
An' you 'se jes' a little tiahed
    An' purhaps a little mad;
How yo' gloom tu'ns into gladness,
    How yo' joy drives out de doubt
When de oven do' is opened,
    An' de smell comes po'in' out;
Why, de 'lectric light o' Heaven
    Seems to settle on de spot,
When yo' mammy says de blessin'
    An' de co'n pone's hot.

When de cabbage pot is steamin'
    An' de bacon good an' fat,
When de chittlins is a-sputter'n'
    So 's to show you whah dey's at;
Tek away yo' sody biscuit,
    Tek away yo' cake an' pie,
Fu' de glory time is comin',
    An' it's 'proachin' mighty nigh,
An' you want to jump an' hollah,
    Dough you know you'd bettah not,
When yo' mammy says de blessin',
    An' de co'n pone's hot.

I have hyeahd o' lots o' sermons,
    An' I've hyeahd o' lots o' prayers,
An' I've listened to some singin'
    Dat has tuck me up de stairs
Of de Glory-Lan' an' set me
    Jes' below de Mahstah's th'one,
An' have lef my hea't a-singin'
    In a happy aftah tone;
But dem wu'ds so sweetly murmured
    Seem to tech de softes' spot,
When my mammy says de blessin',
    An' de co'n pone's hot.

An Ante-Bellum Sermon

We is gathahed hyeah, my brothahs,
　　In dis howlin' wildaness,
Fu' to speak some words of comfo't
　　To each othah in distress.
An' we chooses fu' ouah subjic'
　　Dis—we'll 'splain it by an' by;
"An' de Lawd said, 'Moses, Moses,'
　　An' de man said, 'Hyeah am I.'"

Now ole Pher'oh, down in Egypt,
　　Was de wuss man evah bo'n,
An' he had de Hebrew chillun
　　Down dah wukin' in his co'n;
'T well de Lawd got tiahed o' his foolin',
　　An' sez he: "I'll let him know—
Look hyeah, Moses, go tell Pher'oh
　　Fu' to let dem chillun go."

"An' ef he refuse to do it,
　　I will make him rue de houah,
Fu' I'll empty down on Egypt
　　All de vials of my powah."
Yes, he did—an' Pher'oh's ahmy
　　Was n't wuth a ha'f a dime;
Fu' de Lawd will he'p his chillun,
　　You kin trust him evah time.

An' yo' enemies may 'sail you
　　In de back an' in de front;
But de Lawd is all aroun' you,
　　Fu' to ba' de battle's brunt.
Dey kin fo'ge yo' chains an' shackles
　　F'om de mountains to de sea;
But de Lawd will sen' some Moses
　　Fu' to set his chillun free.

An' de lan' shall hyeah his thundah,
   Lak a blas' f'om Gab'el's ho'n,
Fu' de Lawd of hosts is mighty
   When he girds his ahmor on.
But fu' feah some one mistakes me,
   I will pause right hyeah to say,
Dat I'm still a-preachin' ancient,
   I ain't talkin' 'bout to-day.

But I tell you, fellah christuns,
   Things 'll happen mighty strange;
Now, de Lawd done dis fu' Isrul,
   An' his ways don't nevah change,
An' de love he showed to Isrul
   Was n't all on Isrul spent;
Now don't run an' tell yo' mastahs
   Dat I's preachin' discontent.

'Cause I is n't; I 'se a-judgin'
   Bible people by deir ac's;
I 'se a-givin' you de Scriptuah,
   I 'se a-handin' you de fac's.
Cose ole Pher'oh b'lieved in slav'ry,
   But de Lawd he let him see,
Dat de people he put bref in,—
   Evah mothah's son was free.

An' dahs othahs thinks lak Pher'oh,
   But dey calls de Scriptuah liar,
Fu' de Bible says "a servant
   Is a-worthy of his hire."
An' you cain't git roun' nor thoo dat,
   An' you cain't git ovah it,
Fu' whatevah place you git in,
   Dis hyeah Bible too'll fit.

So you see de Lawd's intention,
   Evah sence de worl' began,

Was dat His almighty freedom
    Should belong to evah man,
But I think it would be bettah,
    Ef I'd pause agin to say,
Dat I'm talkin' 'bout ouah freedom
    In a Bibleistic way.

But de Moses is a-comin',
    An' he's comin', suah and fas'
We kin hyeah his feet a-trompin',
    We kin hyeah his trumpit blas'.
But I want to wa'n you people,
    Don't you git too brigity;
An' don't you git to braggin'
    'Bout dese things, you wait an' see.

But when Moses wif his powah
    Comes an' sets us chillun free,
We will praise de gracious Mastah
    Dat has gin us liberty;
An' we'll shout ouah halleluyahs,
    On dat mighty reck'nin' day,
When we'se reco'nised ez citiz'—
    Huh uh! Chillun, let us pray!

Sympathy

I know what the caged bird feels, alas!
    When the sun is bright on the upland slopes;
When the wind stirs soft through the springing grass,
And the river flows like a stream of glass;
    When the first bird sings and the first bud opes,
And the faint perfume from its chalice steals—
I know what the caged bird feels!

I know why the caged bird beats his wing
    Till its blood is red on the cruel bars;

For he must fly back to his perch and cling
When he fain would be on the bough a-swing;
   And a pain still throbs in the old, old scars
And they pulse again with a keener sting—
I know why he beats his wing!

I know why the caged bird sings, ah me,
   When his wing is bruised and his bosom sore,—
When he beats his bars and he would be free;
It is not a carol of joy or glee,
   But a prayer that he sends from his heart's deep core,
But a plea, that upward to Heaven he flings—
I know why the caged bird sings!

A Death Song

Lay me down beneaf de willers in de grass,
Whah de branch 'll go a-singin' as it pass.
   An' w'en I 's a-layin' low,
   I kin hyeah it as it go
Singin', "Sleep, my honey, tek yo' res' at las'."

Lay me nigh to whah hit meks a little pool,
An' de watah stan's so quiet lak an' cool,
   Whah de little birds in spring,
   Ust to come an' drink an' sing,
An' de chillen waded on dey way to school.

Let me settle w'en my shouldahs draps dey load
Nigh enough to hyeah de noises in de road;
   Fu' I t'ink de las' long res'
   Gwine to soothe my sperrit bes'
Ef I 's layin' 'mong de t'ings I 's allus knowed.

Compensation

Because I had loved so deeply,
   Because I had loved so long,
God in His great compassion
   Gave me the gift of song.

Because I have loved so vainly,
   And sung with such faltering breath,
The Master in infinite mercy
   Offers the boon of Death.

ALICE DUNBAR-NELSON

Violets

I had not thought of violets of late,
The wild, shy kind that springs beneath your feet
In wistful April days, when lovers mate
And wander through the fields in raptures sweet.
And thought of violets meant florists' shops,
And bows and pins, and perfumed paper fine;
And garish lights, and mincing little fops
And cabarets and songs, and deadening wine.
So far from sweet real things my thoughts had strayed,
I had forgot wide fields, and clear brown streams;
The perfect loveliness that God has made—
Wild violets shy and heaven-mounting dreams.
And now—unwittingly, you've made me dream
Of violets, and my soul's forgotten gleam.

I Sit and Sew

I sit and sew—a useless task it seems,
My hands grown tired, my head weighed down with
    dreams—
The panoply of war, the martial tred of men,
Grim-faced, stern-eyed, gazing beyond the ken
Of lesser souls, whose eyes have not seen Death,
Nor learned to hold their lives but as a breath—
But—I must sit and sew.

I sit and sew—my heart aches with desire—
That pageant terrible, that fiercely pouring fire
On wasted fields, and writhing grotesque things
Once men. My soul in pity flings
Appealing cries, yearning only to go

There in that holocaust of hell, those fields of woe—
But—I must sit and sew.

The little useless seam, the idle patch;
Why dream I here beneath my homely thatch,
When there they lie in sodden mud and rain,
Pitifully calling me, the quick ones and the slain?
You need me, Christ! It is no roseate dream
That beckons me—this pretty futile seam,
It stifles me—God, must I sit and sew?

The Proletariat Speaks

I love beautiful things:
Great trees, bending green winged branches to a velvet lawn,
Fountains sparkling in white marble basins,
Cool fragrance of lilacs and roses and honeysuckle,
Or exotic blooms, filling the air with heart-contracting
     odors;
Spacious rooms, cool and gracious with statues and books,
Carven seats and tapestries, and old masters
Whose patina shows the wealth of centuries.

And so I work
In a dusty office, whose griméd windows
Look out in an alley of unbelievable squalor,
Where mangy cats, in their degradation, spurn
Swarming bits of meat and bread;
Where odors, vile and breath taking, rise in fetid waves
Filling my nostrils, scorching my humid, bitter cheeks.

I love beautiful things:
Carven tables laid with lily-hued linen
And fragile china and sparkling irridescent glass;
Pale silver, etched with heraldies,
Where tender bits of regal dainties tempt,
And soft-stepped service anticipates the unspoken wish.

And so I eat
In the food-laden air of a greasy kitchen,
At an oil-clothed table:
Plate piled high with food that turns my head away,
Lest a squeamish stomach reject too soon
The lumpy gobs it never needed,
Or in a smoky cafeteria, balancing a slippery tray
To a table crowded with elbows
Which lately the bus boy wiped with a grimy rag.

I love beautiful things:
Soft linen sheets and silken coverlet,
Sweet coolth of chamber opened wide to fragrant breeze;
Rose shaded lamps and golden atomizers,
Spraying Parisian fragrance over my relaxed limbs,
Fresh from a white marble bath, and sweet cool spray.

And so I sleep
In a hot hall-room whose half opened window,
Unscreened, refuses to budge another inch;
Admits no air, only insects, and hot choking gasps,
That make me writhe, nun-like, in sack-cloth sheets and
        lumps of straw.
And then I rise
To fight my way to a dubious tub,
Whose tiny, tepid stream threatens to make me late;
And hurrying out, dab my unrefreshed face
With bits of toiletry from the ten cent store.

ANGELINA WELD GRIMKÉ

The Black Finger

I have just seen a most beautiful thing
              Slim and still
        Against a gold, gold sky,
        A straight black cypress,
              Sensitive,
              Exquisite,
              A black finger
              Pointing upwards.
Why, beautiful still finger, are you black?
And why are you pointing upwards?

A Mona Lisa

I

I should like to creep
Through the long brown grasses
        That are your lashes;
I should like to poise
        On the very brink
Of the leaf-brown pools
        That are your shadowed eyes;
I should like to cleave
        Without sound,
Their glimmering waters,
        Their unrippled waters,
I should like to sink down
        And down
              And down . . . . .
                    And deeply drown.

96

2

Would I be more than a bubble breaking?
        Or an ever-widening circle
        Ceasing at the marge?
Would my white bones
        Be the only white bones
Wavering back and forth, back and forth
        In their depths?

El Beso

Twilight—and you,
Quiet—the stars;
Snare of the shine of your teeth,
Your provocative laughter,
The gloom of your hair;
Lure of you, eye and lip;
Yearning, yearning,
Languor, surrender;
        Your mouth,
And madness, madness,
Tremulous, breathless, flaming,
The space of a sigh;
Then awakening—remembrance,
Pain, regret—your sobbing;
And again quiet—the stars,
Twilight—and you.

You

I love your throat, so fragrant, fair,
The little pulses beating there;
Your eye-brows' shy and questioning air;
    I love your shadowed hair.

I love your flame-touched ivory skin;
Your little fingers frail and thin;
Your dimple creeping out and in;
   I love your pointed chin.

I love the way you move, you rise;
Your fluttering gestures, just-caught cries;
I am not sane, I am not wise,
   God! How I love your eyes!

Rosabel

I

Leaves, that whisper, whisper ever,
   Listen, listen, pray;
Birds, that twitter, twitter softly,
   Do not say me nay;
Winds, that breathe about, upon her,
   (Since I do not dare)
Whisper, twitter, breathe unto her
   That I find her fair.

II

Rose whose soul unfolds white petaled
   Touch her soul rose-white;
Rose whose thoughts unfold gold petaled
   Blossom in her sight;
Rose whose heart unfolds red petaled
   Quick her slow heart's stir;
Tell her white, gold, red my love is;
   And for her,—for her.

The Eyes of My Regret

Always at dusk, the same tearless experience,
The same dragging of feet up the same well-worn path
To the same well-worn rock;
The same crimson or gold dropping away of the sun,
The same tints,—rose, saffron, violet, lavender, grey,
Meeting, mingling, mixing mistily;
Before me the same blue black cedar rising jaggedly to a
        point;
Over it, the same slow unlidding of twin stars,
Two eyes unfathomable, soul-searing,
Watching, watching—watching me;
The same two eyes that draw me forth, against my will dusk
        after dusk;
The same two eyes that keep me sitting late into the night,
        chin on knees,
Keep me there lonely, rigid, tearless, numbly miserable—
            The eyes of my Regret.

Trees

God made them very beautiful, the trees:
He spoke and gnarled of bole or silken sleek
They grew; majestic bowed or very meek;
Huge-bodied, slim; sedate and full of glees.
And He had pleasure deep in all of these.
And to them soft and little tongues to speak
Of Him to us, He gave, wherefore they seek
From dawn to dawn to bring us to our knees.

                . . . .

Yet here amid the wistful sounds of leaves,
A black-hued gruesome something swings and swings,
Laughter it knew and joy in little things
Till man's hate ended all. ——And so man weaves.
And God, how slow, how very slow weaves He—
Was Christ Himself not nailéd to a tree?

Tenebris

There is a tree, by day,
That, at night,
Has a shadow,
A hand huge and black,
With fingers long and black.
        All through the dark,
Against the white man's house,
        In the little wind,
The black hand plucks and plucks
        At the bricks.
The bricks are the color of blood and very small.
        Is it a black hand,
        Or is it a shadow?

Grass Fingers

Touch me, touch me,
Little cool grass fingers,
Elusive, delicate grass fingers.
With your shy brushings,
Touch my face—
My naked arms—
My thighs—
My feet.
Is there nothing that is kind?
You need not fear me.
Soon I shall be too far beneath you,
For you to reach me, even,
With your tiny, timorous toes.

To Keep the Memory of Charlotte Forten Grimké

Still are there wonders of the dark and day;
The muted shrilling of shy things at night,
So small beneath the stars and moon;
The peace, dream-frail, but perfect while the light
Lies softly on the leaves at noon.
These are, and these will be
Until Eternity;
But she who loved them well has gone away.

Each dawn, while yet the east is veiled grey,
The birds about her window wake and sing;
And far away each day some lark
I know is singing where the grasses swing;
Some robin calls and calls at dark.
These are, and these will be
Until Eternity;
But she who loved them well has gone away.

The wild flowers that she loved down green ways stray;
Her roses lift their wistful buds at dawn,
But not for eyes that loved them best;
Only her little pansies are all gone,
Some lying softly on her breast.
And flowers will bud and be
Until Eternity;
But she who loved them well has gone away.

Where has she gone? And who is there to say?
But this we know: her gentle spirit moves
And is where beauty never wanes,
Perchance by other streams, mid other groves;
And to us here, ah! she remains
A lovely memory,
Until Eternity;
She came, she loved, and then she went away.

WALTER EVERETTE HAWKINS

Wooing

Tell me why you yielded, love,
　　To my simple plea—
Some good grace that you wot of,
　　　You discerned in me?

When I touched your hand, dear child,
　　Passing thru the glen,
And you glanced at me and smiled—
　　Did you love me then?

When upon thyself so meek,
　　A rose I sought to pin—
A sweeter rose bloomed in your cheek—
　　Did you love me then?

When I filled your goblet up,
　　Crystal clear and thin;
You left love within my cup—
　　Did you love me then?

A Spade Is Just a Spade

As I talk with learned people,
I have heard a strange remark,
Quite beyond my comprehension,
And I'm stumbling in the dark.
They advise: Don't be too modest,
Whatsoever thing is said,
Give to every thing its color,
Always call a spade a spade.

Now I am not versed in Logic,
Nor these high-flown classic things,
And am no adept in solving
Flighty aphoristic flings;
So this proverb seems to baffle
All the efforts I have made,—
Now what else is there to call it,
When a spade is just a spade?

Here and Hereafter

I can see no cause for worry
'Bout a future heaven or hell,
For the thing has long been settled
And it's plain as tongue can tell;
And it's mighty poor religion
That won't keep a man from fear;
For the next place *must* be heaven,
Since 'tis hell we are having here.

JOSEPHINE D. HEARD

Retrospect

I sat alone at my window,
    While the pattering raindrops brought
Along with their music upon the roof,
    A lengthy train of thought.

I stepped aboard of it quickly,
    And rapidly on I sped,
Away to the scenes of my childhood days.
    I followed where fancy led.

I roamed the fragrant meadow,
    And through the silent wood;
At last I came to the babbling brook,
    And sadly there I stood.

Into its clear water gazing
    I felt a strange, sweet spell
Enthral my being slowly
    As o'er my life it fell.

I saw in the waters merry,
    Dear faces of long ago,
That had drifted away on the sea of life,
    As the winds blew loud or low.

My brain grew dazed with horror,
    And my heart was wrung with pain;
Some barks were dashed on a rock-bound coast.
    They could not return again.

I saw the same old mill-pond,
    And beside it the noisy mill,
And once again I heard the bell
    Of the old Church on the hill.

There was the dear old School-House,
　The scene of my childhood joys,
And in the yard I romped among
　The happy girls and boys.

And once again came "May Day,"
　When the fields were dressed in green,
And roses shed their rich perfume,
　The children crowned me Queen.

I saw again our own sweet home
　Half hidden 'mong the trees,
My parents, brothers, sisters and I,
　As happy and busy as bees.

Around the door of the homestead,
　The sweet Wistaria vines,
And on the old oak in the yard
　The clinging ivy twines.

There stands the grim old court-house,
　And the Jail with dingy cells,
And on the Church the old town-clock
　The fleeting moment tells.

Next I came to the old town Graveyard
　And entered with silent tread,
And dropped a tear o'er the grassy grave
　Of the peacefully sleeping dead.

FENTON JOHNSON

When I Die

I

When I die my song shall be,
Crooning of the summer breeze;
When I die my shroud shall be,
Leaves plucked from the maple trees;
On a couch as green as moss
And a bed as soft as down,
I shall sleep and dream my dream
Of a poet's laurel crown.

II

When I die my star shall drop
Singing like a nightingale;
When I die my soul shall rise,
Where the lyre strings never fail;
In the rose my blood shall lie,
In the violet the smile,
And the moonbeams thousand strong,
Past my grave each night shall file.

The Lonely Mother

(*A Negro Spiritual*)

I.

Oh, my mother's moaning by the river,
My poor mother's moaning by the river,
For her son who walks the earth in sorrow.
Long my mother's moaned beside the river,
And her tears have filled an angel's pitcher,
"Lord of Heaven, bring to me my honey,

Bring to me the darling of my bosom,
For a lonely mother by the river."

II.

Cease, O mother, moaning by the river,
Cease, good mother, moaning by the river;
I have seen the star of Michael shining
Michael shining at the Gates of Morning;
Row, O mighty Angel, down the twilight,
Row until I find a lonely woman,
Swaying long beneath a tree of cypress.
Swaying for her son who walks in sorrow.

Who Is That A-Walking in the Corn?

Who is that a-walking in the corn?
I have looked to East and looked to West
But nowhere could I find Him who walks
    Master's cornfield in the morning.

Who is that a-walking in the corn?
Is it Joshua, the son of Nun?—
Or King David come to fight the giant
    Near the cornfield in the morning?

Who is that a-walking in the corn?
Is it Peter jangling Heaven's keys?—
Or old Gabriel come to blow his horn
    Near the cornfield in the morning?

Who is that a-walking in the corn?
I have looked to East and looked to West
But nowhere could I find Him who walks
    Master's cornfield in the morning.

from *African Nights*

TIRED

I am tired of work; I am tired of building up somebody else's
    civilization.

Let us take a rest, M'Lissy Jane.

I will go down to the Last Chance Saloon, drink a gallon or
    two of gin, shoot a game or two of dice and sleep the
    rest of the night on one of Mike's barrels.

You will let the old shanty go to rot, the white people's
    clothes turn to dust, and the Calvary Baptist Church
    sink to the bottomless pit.

You will spend your days forgetting you married me and your
    nights hunting the warm gin Mike serves the ladies in
    the rear of the Last Chance Saloon.

Throw the children into the river; civilization has given us
    too many. It is better to die than it is to grow up and
    find out that you are colored.

Pluck the stars out of the heavens. The stars mark our
    destiny. The stars marked my destiny.

I am tired of civilization.

AUNT JANE ALLEN

State Street is lonely to-day. Aunt Jane Allen has driven her
chariot to Heaven.

I remember how she hobbled along, a little woman, parched
of skin, brown as the leather of a satchel and with eyes that had
scanned eighty years of life.

Have those who bore her dust to the last resting place buried
with her the basket of aprons she went up and down State
Street trying to sell?

Have those who bore her dust to the last resting place buried
with her the gentle word Son that she gave to each of the seed
of Ethiopia?

THE BANJO PLAYER

There is music in me, the music of a peasant people.

I wander through the levee, picking my banjo and singing my songs of the cabin and the field. At the Last Chance Saloon I am as welcome as the violets in March; there is always food and drink for me there, and the dimes of those who love honest music. Behind the railroad tracks the little children clap their hands and love me as they love Kris Kringle.

But I fear that I am a failure. Last night a woman called me a troubadour. What is a troubadour?

THE SCARLET WOMAN

Once I was good like the Virgin Mary and the Minister's wife.

My father worked for Mr. Pullman and white people's tips; but he died two days after his insurance expired.

I had nothing, so I had to go to work.

All the stock I had was a white girl's education and a face that enchanted the men of both races.

Starvation danced with me.

So when Big Lizzie, who kept a house for white men, came to me with tales of fortune that I could reap from the sale of my virtue I bowed my head to Vice.

Now I can drink more gin than any man for miles around.

Gin is better than all the water in Lethe.

RULERS

It is said that many a king in troubled Europe would sell his
    crown for a day of happiness.
I have seen a monarch who held tightly the jewel of happiness
On Lombard Street in Philadelphia, as evening dropped to
    earth, I gazed upon a laborer duskier than a sky devoid
    of moon. He was seated on a throne of flour bags,
    waving his hand imperiously as two small boys played on
    their guitars the ragtime tunes of the day.
God's blessing on the monarch who rules on Lombard Street
    in Philadelphia.

JAMES WELDON JOHNSON

Lift Every Voice and Sing

Lift every voice and sing
Till earth and heaven ring,
Ring with the harmonies of Liberty;
Let our rejoicing rise
High as the listening skies,
Let it resound loud as the rolling sea.
Sing a song full of the faith that the dark past has taught us,
Sing a song full of the hope that the present has brought us.
Facing the rising sun of our new day begun,
Let us march on till victory is won.

Stony the road we trod,
Bitter the chastening rod,
Felt in the days when hope unborn had died;
Yet with a steady beat,
Have not our weary feet
Come to the place for which our fathers sighed?
We have come over a way that with tears has been watered,
We have come, treading our path through the blood of the
      slaughtered,
Out from the gloomy past,
Till now we stand at last
Where the white gleam of our bright star is cast.

God of our weary years,
God of our silent tears,
Thou who hast brought us thus far on the way;
Thou who hast by Thy might
Led us into the light,
Keep us forever in the path, we pray.
Lest our feet stray from the places, our God, where we met
      Thee,
Lest, our hearts drunk with the wine of the world, we forget
      Thee;

Shadowed beneath Thy hand,
May we forever stand.
True to our God,
True to our native land.

Sence You Went Away

Seems lak to me de stars don't shine so bright,
Seems lak to me de sun done loss his light,
Seems lak to me der's nothin' goin' right,
  Sence you went away.

Seems lak to me de sky ain't half so blue,
Seems lak to me dat ev'ything wants you,
Seems lak to me I don't know what to do,
  Sence you went away.

Seems lak to me dat ev'ything is wrong,
Seems lak to me de day's jes twice es long,
Seems lak to me de bird's forgot his song,
  Sence you went away.

Seems lak to me I jes can't he'p but sigh,
Seems lak to me ma th'oat keeps gittin' dry,
Seems lak to me a tear stays in ma eye,
  Sence you went away.

O Black and Unknown Bards

O black and unknown bards of long ago,
How came your lips to touch the sacred fire?
How, in your darkness, did you come to know
The power and beauty of the minstrel's lyre?
Who first from midst his bonds lifted his eyes?
Who first from out the still watch, lone and long,
Feeling the ancient faith of prophets rise
Within his dark-kept soul, burst into song?

Heart of what slave poured out such melody
As "Steal away to Jesus"? On its strains
His spirit must have nightly floated free,
Though still about his hands he felt his chains.
Who heard great "Jordan roll"? Whose starward eye
Saw chariot "swing low"? And who was he
That breathed that comforting, melodic sigh,
"Nobody knows de trouble I see"?

What merely living clod, what captive thing,
Could up toward God through all its darkness grope,
And find within its deadened heart to sing
These songs of sorrow, love, and faith, and hope?
How did it catch that subtle undertone,
That note in music heard not with the ears?
How sound the elusive reed so seldom blown,
Which stirs the soul or melts the heart to tears.

Not that great German master in his dream
Of harmonies that thundered amongst the stars
At the creation, ever heard a theme
Nobler than "Go down, Moses." Mark its bars,
How like a mighty trumpet-call they stir
The blood. Such are the notes that men have sung
Going to valorous deeds; such tones there were
That helped make history when Time was young.

There is a wide, wide wonder in it all,
That from degraded rest and servile toil
The fiery spirit of the seer should call
These simple children of the sun and soil.
O black slave singers, gone, forgot, unfamed,
You—you alone, of all the long, long line
Of those who've sung untaught, unknown, unnamed,
Have stretched out upward, seeking the divine.

You sang not deeds of heroes or of kings;
No chant of bloody war, no exulting pean
Of arms-won triumphs; but your humble strings
You touched in chord with music empyrean.

My City

When I come down to sleep death's endless night,
The threshold of the unknown dark to cross,
What to me then will be the keenest loss,
When this bright world blurs on my fading sight?
Will it be that no more I shall see the trees
Or smell the flowers or hear the singing birds
Or watch the flashing streams or patient herds?
No. I am sure it will be none of these.

But, ah! Manhattan's sights and sounds, her smells,
Her crowds, her throbbing force, the thrill that comes
From being of her a part, her subtle spells,
Her shining towers, her avenues, her slums—
O God! the stark, unutterable pity,
To be dead, and never again behold my city.

Go Down Death

A Funeral Sermon

Weep not, weep not,
She is not dead;
She's resting in the bosom of Jesus.
Heart-broken husband—weep no more;
Grief-stricken son—weep no more;
Left-lonesome daughter—weep no more;
She's only just gone home.

Day before yesterday morning,
God was looking down from his great, high heaven,
Looking down on all his children,
And his eye fell on Sister Caroline,
Tossing on her bed of pain.
And God's big heart was touched with pity,

With the everlasting pity.

And God sat back on his throne,
And he commanded that tall, bright angel standing at his
     right hand:
Call me Death!
And that tall, bright angel cried in a voice
That broke like a clap of thunder:
Call Death!—Call Death!
And the echo sounded down the streets of heaven
Till it reached away back to that shadowy place,
Where Death waits with his pale, white horses.

And Death heard the summons,
And he leaped on his fastest horse,
Pale as a sheet in the moonlight.
Up the golden street Death galloped,
And the hoofs of his horse struck fire from the gold,
But they didn't make no sound.
Up Death rode to the Great White Throne,
And waited for God's command.

And God said: Go down, Death, go down,
Go down to Savannah, Georgia,
Down in Yamacraw,
And find Sister Caroline.
She's borne the burden and heat of the day,
She's labored long in my vineyard,
And she's tired—
She's weary—
Go down, Death, and bring her to me.

And Death didn't say a word,
But he loosed the reins on his pale, white horse,
And he clamped the spurs to his bloodless sides,
And out and down he rode,
Through heaven's pearly gates,
Past suns and moons and stars;
On Death rode,

And the foam from his horse was like a comet in the sky;
On Death rode,
Leaving the lightning's flash behind;
Straight on down he came.

While we were watching round her bed,
She turned her eyes and looked away,
She saw what we couldn't see;
She saw Old Death. She saw Old Death,
Coming like a falling star.
But Death didn't frighten Sister Caroline;
He looked to her like a welcome friend.
And she whispered to us: I'm going home,
And she smiled and closed her eyes.

And Death took her up like a baby,
And she lay in his icy arms,
But she didn't feel no chill.
And Death began to ride again—
Up beyond the evening star,
Out beyond the morning star,
Into the glittering light of glory,
On to the Great White Throne.
And there he laid Sister Caroline
On the loving breast of Jesus.

And Jesus took his own hand and wiped away her tears,
And he smoothed the furrows from her face,
And the angels sang a little song,
And Jesus rocked her in his arms,
And kept a-saying: Take your rest,
Take your rest, take your rest.

Weep not—weep not,
She is not dead;
She's resting in the bosom of Jesus.

GEORGE R. MARGETSON

from *The Fledgling Poet and the Poetry Society*

Critics all, both far and near,
You who hold the public ear
And interpret for the care
And counsel of the people,
If you find no merit here
Please tell it to the people;
Write it, speak it everywhere
In converse with the people;
You should really have no fear
To tell it to the people.

But if you perchance should find
Art with poetry interlined,
Reason, truth and wit combined,—
So tell it to the people
All the tangled parts unwind
And show them to the people,
With a calm and candid mind
Present them to the people;
'Twould alike be fair and kind
To tell it to the people.

Tell it not to cheer me glad,
Tell it not to bruise me sad,
Tell it not to jar me mad,
Just tell it for the people,
As you find it good or bad,
Thus deal it to the people.
If in homely colors clad,
So show it to the people.
Nothing minus, nothing add
True tell it to the people.

Me they are not writ to please,
Nor the Yankee devil to tease,
But outrageous fate to pease,
I will write them for the people.
Out upon life's foaming seas.
I wrought them of the people
When I strike the tuneful keys
I strike to rouse the people
Tell it therefore at your ease
But tell it for the people.

ELOISE BIBB THOMPSON

Ode to the Sun

How many scenes, O sun,
Hast thou not shone upon!
How many tears, O light,
Have dropped before thy sight!
How many heart-felt sighs.
How many piercing cries,
How many deeds of woe,
Dost thy bright light not know!
How many broken hearts,
That are pierced by sorrow's darts;
How many maddened brains,
That are wild with passion's rains;
How many soul-sick lives,
Stabbed with despair's sharp knives,
Hast thou above the skies,
Not seen with thy radiant eyes!
Shine on, majestic one!
Shine on, O glorious sun!
And never fail to cheer
My life so dark and drear.
Whene'er thou shinest bright,
And show thy brilliant light,
The cares I know each day
Silently steal away.

PRISCILLA JANE THOMPSON

To a Little Colored Boy

Oh, pure and sportive little child,
  Be happy while you may;
Ring out your laughter loud and clear;
  Be blithe, enjoy your day.

Your eyes of sloe, they sparkle bright;
  Your rounded, dusky cheeks,
Are ever dimpled in a smile,
  From each week into weeks.

Build high your castles in the air;
  Dream on of manhood's fame;
What matter, if your pure, young, heart,
  Deems each man's chance the same.

I hold your little hand in mine;
  Fast wags your childish tongue;
Your prospects doth look bright to you,
  Because you are so young.

Thou knoweth not, poor little boy,
  What Future holds for thee,
Thy dreams are not extravagant,
  And yet, they canst not be.

This mass of midnight curly hair,
  This soft and dusky skin,
Will bring not fortune's smile to you,
  When childhood's day will end.

Thou art a child, of promise rare;
  God, for some cause, profound,
Hath cast thee in a finer mold,
  Than most about you found.

E'en now your little high-aimed heart,
    A pris'ner seems to be,
And with impatience beats the bars,
    Of helpless infancy.

You'll bloom a rare high-minded man;
    Surpassing fair-faced men;
Would God, the Future, held for you,
    The hope it holds for them.

Would that your path of life could be,
    Like theirs, with roses strewn:
Would that your thorns, be brushed aside,
    As often as their own.

Would that the world, which you must face,
    Were free from this low sin,
To meanly wrong a fellow-man,
    For darkness of his skin.

I look me deep into thine eyes;
    My love is mixed with grief;
To think that naught, within my power,
    Can later, bring relief.

But pure and sportive little boy,
    When time his trials lend,
Think not that you are destitute;
    In me you have a friend.

LUCIAN B. WATKINS

The New Negro

He thinks in black. His God is but the same
John saw—with hair "like wool" and eyes "as fire"—
Who makes the visions for which men aspire.
His kin is Jesus and the Christ who came
Humbly to earth and wrought His hallowed aim
'Midst human scorn. Pure is his heart's desire;
His life's religion lifts; his faith leads higher.
Love is his Church, and Union is its name.

Lo, he has learned his own immortal rôle
In this momentous drama of the hour;
Has read aright the heavens' Scriptural scroll
'Bove ancient wrong—long boasting in its tower.
Ah, he has sensed the truth. Deep in his soul
He feels the manly majesty of power.

THREE
THE DARK TOWER
(1919–1936)

LEWIS GRANDISON ALEXANDER

Japanese Hokku

I

Life goes by moving,
Up and down a chain of moods
Wanting what's nothing.

II

My soul is the wind
Dashing down fields of Autumn:
O, too swift to sing.

III

Listen to the rain
Falling broken on the ground:
Pity the sky once.

IV

Knowing not at all
Who stands above me seeing:
Tears of gratitude.

V

The nightingale sings
My heart desires but the night
Space swallows my voice:

VI

I shall spend my moods
Like a rose discards leaves
And die without moods.

VII

Did you say a sound?
Did you say the wind? Dashing
Only my soul's quick—

VIII

O moon of to-night
Let me rest my head on you
And hear my life sing.

IX

My ears burn for speech
And you lie cold and silent.
Supinely cruel:

X

Look at the white moon
The sphinx does not question more.
Turn away your eyes.

XI

Thought that is no thought
Poems buried in my heart
Song that is no song. . . .

XII

The poetry of life?
No, the picture of my dreams
Flashing on my heart.

XIII

I ride down the stream
Between the earth and the sun
On the moon's shadow.

XIV

Treading wearily
A unit of the parade
There is no escape.

XV

Within the shadow
I am weaving the pattern
Of a spider web.

XVI

My heart like a shell
Moans at the breast of the earth
Being too full to sing.

XVII

You are life's fountain
Springing from eternity
Flow not recklessly.

XVIII

I will wrap the song
In the leaves of the lotus
And send it to you.

XIX

No words speak louder
Than the tragic look of eyes
Close yours out of love.

XX

Why should I wander
I who have known no surprise?
Every day the same.

Negro Woman

The sky hangs heavy tonight
Like the hair of a Negro woman.
The scars of the moon are curved
Like the wrinkles on the brow of a Negro woman.

The stars twinkle tonight
Like the glaze in a Negro woman's eyes,
Drinking the tears set flowing by an aging hurt
Gnawing at her heart.

The earth trembles tonight
Like the quiver of a Negro woman's eye-lids cupping tears.

Effigy

FORM

You stood in the yard
Like a lilac bush
With your head tossed high
As if to push
Your hair in a blossom
About your head
You wore the grace
Of a fragile reed.

FASHION

Your gown crackled loud
Like the swish of leaves
Being flitted about
By a lyric breeze
Your step was like a dainty fawn
Breathing the nectared air at dawn,
Oft have I seen the rose in you
But it never bloomed such a brilliant hue.

GWENDOLYN B. BENNETT

Heritage

I want to see the slim palm-trees,
Pulling at the clouds
With little pointed fingers . . .

I want to see lithe Negro girls,
Etched dark against the sky
While sunset lingers.

I want to hear the silent sands,
Singing to the moon
Before the Sphinx-still face . . .

I want to hear the chanting
Around a heathen fire
Of a strange black race.

I want to breathe the Lotus flow'r,
Sighing to the stars
With tendrils drinking at the Nile . . .

I want to feel the surging
Of my sad people's soul
Hidden by a minstrel-smile.

Lines Written at the Grave of Alexander Dumas

Cemeteries are places for departed souls
And bones interred,
Or hearts with shattered loves.

A woman with lips made warm for laughter
Would find grey stones and silent thoughts
Too chill for living, moving pulses . . .

And thou great soul, would shiver in thy granite shroud,
Should idle mirth or empty talk
Disturb thy tranquil sleeping.

A cemetery is a place for shattered loves
And broken hearts . . .
Bowed before the crystal chalice of thy soul,
I find the multi-colored fragrance of thy mind
Has lost itself in Death's transparency.

Oh, stir the lucid waters of thy sleep
And coin for me a tale
Of happy loves and gems and joyous limbs
And hearts where love is sweet!

A cemetery is a place for broken hearts
And silent thoughts . . .
And silence never moves, nor speaks
Nor sings.

Fantasy

I sailed in my dreams to the Land of Night
Where you were the dusk-eyed queen,
And there in the pallor of moon-veiled light
The loveliest things were seen . . .

A slim-necked peacock sauntered there
In a garden of lavender hues,
And you were strange with your purple hair
As you sat in your amethyst chair
With your feet in your hyacinth shoes.

Oh, the moon gave a bluish light
Through the trees in the land of dreams and night.
I stood behind a bush of yellow-green
And whistled a song to the dark-haired queen . . .

To a Dark Girl

I love you for your brownness,
And the rounded darkness of your breast;
I love you for the breaking sadness in your voice
And shadows where your wayward eyelids rest.

Something of old forgotten queens
Lurks in the lithe abandon of your walk,
And something of the shackled slave
Sobs in the rhythm of your talk.

Oh, little brown girl, born for sorrow's mate,
Keep all you have of queenliness,
Forgetting that you once were slave
And let your full lips laugh at Fate!

Dirge for a Free Spirit

The minister crossed himself and said
That Death's dark angel hovered round your bed.
I saw your lips curled in a smile
Half scornful and I knew the while
They prayed your soul into a Paradise
You lay there mocking all their silly lies.
I knew that on some far and rain-drenched hill
Your lidded eyes would drink their fill
Of all the sweet and earthly things;
That birds for you sing sweeter songs than ever angel sings.
With arms flung wide in undecorous glee,
You'd clasp your dear dead body to a tree,

And digging deep into the earth
Your body shake in such unconsecrated mirth.

They laid you out in saintly white,
Surrounded you with candle light,
And knelt beside your flowered bier
Shedding for you tear on pious tear,
While all the time I knew
Heaven was no place for you.
They prayed for you and laid you in the ground—
I heard your laughter, such a wicked sound!—
Go gaily on the breeze
And tangle in and out the trees.
How should they know? Why should I tell
That you were happy now in hell?

I Build America

I build America—
Mortared brick on brick,
And in with each I lay
The heart of all my brothers,
Dead from coast to other sea.
Mixed with gravel and cement
And sand, I turn the powdered bones
Of all the dead
Who lie from Canada
To Mexico's warm Gulf.
I am the dead,
Building America.

I died in a smelting furnace
White-hot and shining molten, I,
To make a bridge or singing rail;
My body flew winging
Through the walls of that great dam
That holds a waterway in steady check;
I am the top-soil,

Strewn over storm-tried Florida,
Where I, a thousand strong,
Lay piled against a mourning day;
It is my last breath
Soughing through that burning coal,
Mined where the shaft fell.
That riddled thing,
Lowered by weeping Negroes
From a lynching tree,
Was me . . .
That dangling scalp,
Hanging from a Redskin's belt
Was mine . . .
And that slim, red body,
Laid high on a funeral pyre,
Had a bullet through my heart.
The red men, the black, the white,
Lying end to end
Beneath cities and towns,
In river-beds,
And under docks,
Whose dust is mingled yet
With farm and field
And growing grain for food or cloth,
Are one with me.
I died a thousand deaths,
A million strong,
In a thousand different places—
Pioneering, on battle-fronts,
In strikes, at the hand of brother citizens,
By lynch-ropes and with police clubs.
I died,
Building America.

And so . . .
I, the dead, build America.
My fleshless fingers
Build American cities,
Stretch bridges and pile up towns.
My unmuscled arms

Swing hammers and dig subways.
My sightless eyes
Survey the plains and chart railways.
All the cities and subways and trains
And bridges and people
Are my bones,
Covered with brick and cement,
With steel and rock and flesh.
From the empty space
Between my gaping ribs
I, knowing death
And understanding how life is,
Breathe a living song
Into the nation that I build.

I build America . . .
I, underneath the ground,
And rumbling through the air,
At work at machines,
Guiding roaring motors,
And teaching unborn children—
I am the dead,
Building America.

Epitaph

When I am dead, carve this upon my stone:
Here lies a woman, fit root for flower and tree,
Whose living flesh, now mouldering round the bone,
Wants nothing more than this for immortality,
That in her heart, where love so long unfruited lay
A seed for grass or weed shall grow,
And push to light and air its heedless way;
That she who lies here dead may know
Through all the putrid marrow of her bones
The searing pangs of birth,
While none may know the pains nor hear the groans
Of her who lived with barrenness upon the earth.

ARNA BONTEMPS

The Return

Once more, listening to the wind and rain,
once more, you and I, and above the hurting sound
of these comes back the throbbing of remembered rain,
treasured rain falling on dark ground.
Once more, huddling birds upon the leaves
and summer trembling on a withered vine.
And once more, returning out of pain,
the friendly ghost that was your love and mine.

Darkness brings the jungle to our room:
the throb of rain is the throb of muffled drums.
Darkness hangs our room with pendulums
of vine and in the gathering gloom
our walls recede into a denseness of
surrounding trees. This is a night of love
retained from those lost nights our fathers slept
in huts; this is a night that must not die.
Let us keep the dance of rain our fathers kept
and tread our dreams beneath the jungle sky.

And now the downpour ceases
let us go back once more upon the glimmering leaves
and as the throbbing of the drums increases
shake the grass and dripping boughs of trees.
A dry wind stirs the palm; the old tree grieves.
Time has charged the years: the old days have returned.

Let us dance by metal waters burned
with gold of moon, let us dance
with naked feet beneath the young spice trees.
What was that light, that radiance
on your face—something I saw when first
you passed beneath the jungle tapestries?

A moment we pause to quench our thirst
kneeling at the water's edge, the gleam
upon your face is plain: you have wanted this.
Let us go back and search the tangled dream
and as the muffled drum-beats throb and miss
remember again how early darkness comes
to dreams and silence to the drums.

Let us go back into the dusk again,
slow and sad-like following the track
of blowing leaves and cool white rain
into the old gray dream, let us go back.
Our walls close about us we lie and listen
to the noise of the street, the storm and the driven birds.
A question shapes your lips, your eyes glisten
retaining tears, but there are no more words.

A Black Man Talks of Reaping

I have sown beside all waters in my day.
I planted deep, within my heart the fear
that wind or fowl would take the grain away.
I planted safe against this stark, lean year.

I scattered seed enough to plant the land
in rows from Canada to Mexico
but for my reaping only what the hand
can hold at once is all that I can show.

Yet what I sowed and what the orchard yields
my brother's sons are gathering stalk and root;
small wonder then my children glean in fields
they have not sown, and feed on bitter fruit.

Southern Mansion

Poplars are standing there still as death
and ghosts of dead men
meet their ladies walking
two by two beneath the shade
and standing on the marble steps.

There is a sound of music echoing
through the open door
and in the field there is
another sound tinkling in the cotton:
chains of bondmen dragging on the ground.

The years go back with an iron clank,
a hand is on the gate,
a dry leaf trembles on the wall.
Ghosts are walking.
They have broken roses down
and poplars stand there still as death.

The Day-breakers

We are not come to wage a strife
with swords upon this hill:
it is not wise to waste the life
against a stubborn will.

Yet would we die as some have done:
beating a way for the rising sun.

STERLING A. BROWN

Ma Rainey

I

When Ma Rainey
Comes to town,
Folks from anyplace
Miles aroun',
From Cape Girardeau,
Poplar Bluff,
Flocks in to hear
Ma do her stuff;
Comes flivverin' in,
Or ridin' mules,
Or packed in trains,
Picknickin' fools.
That's what it's like,
Fo' miles on down,
To New Orleans delta
An' Mobile town,
When Ma hits
Anywheres aroun'.

II

Dey comes to hear Ma Rainey from de little river settlements,
From blackbottom cornrows and from lumber camps;
Dey stumble in de hall, jes a-laughin' an' a-cacklin',
Cheerin' lak roarin' water, lak wind in river swamps.

An' some jokers keeps deir laughs a-goin' in de crowded aisles
An' some folks sits dere waitin' wid deir aches an' miseries,
Till Ma comes out before dem, a-smilin' gold-toofed smiles
An' Long Boy ripples minors on de black an' yellow keys.

III

O Ma Rainey,
Sing yo' song;
Now you's back
Whah you belong,
Git way inside us,
Keep us strong. . . .

O Ma Rainey,
Li'l an' low;
Sing us 'bout de hard luck
Roun' our do';
Sing us 'bout de lonesome road
We mus' go. . . .

IV

I talked to a fellow, an' the fellow say,
"She jes' catch hold of us, somekindaway.
She sang Backwater Blues one day:

> *'It rained fo' days an' de skies was dark as night,*
> *Trouble taken place in de lowlands at night.*
>
> *'Thundered an' lightened an' the storm begin to roll*
> *Thousan's of people ain't got no place to go.*
>
> *'Den I went an' stood upon some high ol' lonesome hill,*
> *An' looked down on the place where I used to live.'*

An' den de folks, dey natchally bowed dey heads an' cried,
Bowed dey heavy heads, shet dey moufs up tight an' cried,
An' Ma lef' de stage, an' followed some de folks outside."

Dere wasn't much more de fellow say:
She jes' gits hold of us dataway.

Old Lem

I talked to old Lem
and old Lem said:
      "They weigh the cotton
      They store the corn
          We only good enough
          To work the rows;
      They run the commissary
      They keep the books
          We gotta be grateful
          For being cheated;
      Whippersnapper clerks
      Call us out of our name
          We got to say mister
          To spindling boys
      They make our figgers
      Turn somersets
      We buck in the middle
          Say, "Thankyuh, sah."
          They don't come by ones
          They don't come by twos
          But they come by tens.

      "They got the judges
      They got the lawyers
      They got the jury-rolls
      They got the law
          They don't come by ones
      They got the sheriffs
      They got the deputies
          They don't come by twos
      They got the shotguns
      They got the rope
          We git the justice
          In the end
          And they come by tens.

"Their fists stay closed
Their eyes look straight
   Our hands stay open
   Our eyes must fall
      They don't come by ones
They got the manhood
They got the courage
      They don't come by twos
   We got to slink around
   Hangtailed hounds.
They burn us when we dogs
They burn us when we men
     They come by tens . . .

"I had a buddy
Six foot of man
Muscled up perfect
Game to the heart
     They don't come by ones
Outworked and outfought
Any man or two men
     They don't come by twos
He spoke out of turn
At the commissary
They gave him a day
To git out the county
He didn't take it.
He said 'Come and get me.'
They came and got him
     And they came by tens.
He stayed in the county—
He lays there dead.

      They don't come by ones
      They don't come by twos
      But they come by tens."

Slim Greer

Listen to the tale
Of Ole Slim Greer,
Waitines' devil
Waitin' here;

      Talkinges' guy
      An' biggest liar,
      With always a new lie
      On the fire.

Tells a tale
Of Arkansaw
That keeps the kitchen
In a roar;

      Tells in a long-drawled
      Careless tone,
      As solemn as a Baptist
      Parson's moan.

How he in Arkansaw
Passed for white,
An' he no lighter
Than a dark midnight.

      Found a nice white woman
      At a dance,
      Thought he was from Spain
      Or else from France;

Nobody suspicioned
Ole Slim Greer's race
But a Hill Billy, always
Roun' the place,

      Who called one day
      On the trustful dame

An' found Slim comfy
When he came.

The whites lef' the parlor
All to Slim
Which didn't cut
No ice with him,

> An' he started a-tinklin'
> Some mo'nful blues,
> An' a-pattin' the time
> With No. Fourteen shoes.

The cracker listened
An' then he spat
An' said, "No white man"
Could play like that. . . .

> The white jane ordered
> The tattler out;
> Then, female-like,
> Began to doubt,

Crept into the parlor
Soft as you please,
Where Slim was agitatin'
The ivories.

> Heard Slim's music—
> An' then, hot damn!
> Shouted sharp—"Nigger!"
> An' Slim said, "Ma'am?"

She screamed and the crackers
Swarmed up soon,
But found only echoes
Of his tune;

> 'Cause Slim had sold out
> With lightnin' speed;

"Hope I may die, sir—
Yes, indeed. . . ."

Strange Legacies

One thing you left with us, Jack Johnson.
One thing before they got you.

You used to stand there like a man,
Taking punishment
With a golden, spacious grin;
Confident.
Inviting big Jim Jeffries, who was boring in:
"Heah ah is, big boy; yuh sees whah Ise at.
Come on in. . . ."

Thanks, Jack, for that.

John Henry, with your hammer;
John Henry, with your steel driver's pride,
You taught us that a man could go down like a man,
Sticking to your hammer till you died.
Sticking to your hammer till you died.

Brother,
When, beneath the burning sun
The sweat poured down and the breath came thick,
And the loaded hammer swung like a ton
And the heart grew sick;
You had what we need now, John Henry.
Help us get it.

So if we go down
Have to go down
We go like you, brother,
'Nachal' men. . . .

Old nameless couple in Red River Bottom,
Who have seen floods gutting out your best loam,
And the boll weevil chase you
Out of your hard-earned home,
Have seen the drought parch your green fields,
And the cholera stretch your porkers out dead;
Have seen year after year
The commissary always a little in the lead;
Even you said
That which we need
Now in our time of fear,—
Routed your own deep misery and dread,
Muttering, beneath an unfriendly sky,
"Guess we'll give it one mo' try.
Guess we'll give it one mo' try."

Southern Cop

Let us forgive Ty Kendricks.
The place was Darktown. He was young.
His nerves were jittery. The day was hot.
The Negro ran out of the alley.
And so he shot.

Let us understand Ty Kendricks.
The Negro must have been dangerous,
Because he ran;
And here was a rookie with a chance
To prove himself a man.

Let us condone Ty Kendricks
If we cannot decorate.
When he found what the Negro was running for,
It was too late;
And all we can say for the Negro is
It was unfortunate.

Let us pity Ty Kendricks,
He has been through enough,
Standing there, his big gun smoking,
Rabbit-scared, alone,
Having to hear the wenches wail
And the dying Negro moan.

To a Certain Lady, in Her Garden

(*For Anne Spencer*)

Lady, my lady, come from out the garden,
Clay-fingered, dirty-smocked, and in my time
I too shall learn the quietness of Arden,
Knowledge so long a stranger to my rhyme.

What were more fitting than your springtime task?
Here, close-engirdled by your vines and flowers
Surely there is no other grace to ask,
No better cloister from the bickering hours.

A step beyond, the dingy streets begin
With all their farce, and silly tragedy—
But here, unmindful of the futile din
You grow your flowers, far wiser certainly.

You and your garden sum the same to me,
A sense of strange and momentary pleasure,
And beauty snatched—oh, fragmentarily
Perhaps, yet who can boast of other seizure?

Oh, you have somehow robbed, I know not how,
The secret of the loveliness of these
Whom you have served so long. Oh, shameless, now
You flaunt the winnings of your thieveries.

Thus, I exclaim against you, profiteer. . . .
For purpled evenings spent in pleasing toil,
Should you have gained so easily the dear
Capricious largesse of the miser soil?

Colorful living in a world grown dull,
Quiet sufficiency in weakling days,
Delicate happiness, more beautiful
For lighting up belittered, grimy ways—

Surely I think I shall remember this,
You in your old, rough dress, bedaubed with clay,
Your smudgy face parading happiness,
Life's puzzle solved. Perhaps, in turn, you may

One time, while clipping bushes, tending vines,
(Making your brave, sly mock at dastard days),
Laugh gently at these trivial, truthful lines—
And that will be sufficient for my praise.

Let Us Suppose

Let us suppose him differently placed,
In wider fields than these bounded by bayous
And the fringes of moss-hung trees
Over which, in lazy spirals, the caranchos soar and dip.

Let us suppose these horizons pushed farther,
So that his eager mind,
His restless senses, his swift eyes,
Could glean more than the sheaves he stored
Time and time again:
Let us suppose him far away from here.

ANITA SCOTT COLEMAN

Portraiture

Black men are the tall trees that remain standing in a forest
    after a fire.

        Flame strips their branches,
        Flame sears their limbs,
        Flame scorches their trunks;
        Yet stand these trees,
        For their roots are thrust deep
        in the heart of the earth.

 Black men are the tall trees that remain standing in a forest
    after a fire.

Black Baby

The baby I hold in my arms is a black baby.
    Today I set him in the sun and
    Sunbeams danced on his head.

The baby I hold in my arms is a black baby.
    I toil, and I cannot always cuddle him.
    I place him on the ground at my feet.
    He presses the warm earth with his hands,
    He lifts high the sand and laughs to see
    It flow through his chubby fingers.
    I watch to discern which are his hands,
    Which is the sand. . . .
Lo . . . the rich loam is black like his hands.

The baby I hold in my arms is a black baby.
    Today the coal-man brought me coal
    Sixteen dollars a ton is the price I pay for coal,—
    Costly fuel . . . though they say:—
    Men must sweat and toil to dig it from the ground.
    Costly fuel . . . 'Tis said:—
    If it is buried deep enough and lies hidden long enough
    'Twill be no longer coal but diamonds. . . .
    My black baby looks at me.
    His eyes are like coals,
    They shine like diamonds.

Impressions from a Family Album

GRAND-PAP

    Grandpap was very old,
    When this was struck. So old!
    But he could recollect . . .
    The way 'twas told
    That Annie was the p'utt'est gal
    On ol' Marse Tom's plantation,
    And Annie was his mammy.
      'Could recollect . . .
    How he was allus kept
    To wait 'pon ol' Marse Tom
    To shoo off flies, while ol' Marse slept
    And when ol' Marse woke
    Go fetch his pipe and bring his book
    And mix the mint-julep . . .
      'Could recollect
    The w'uppin's Master gin him
    'Lowing fo' to teach him how to show
    The proper 'spec's where 'spec's were due . . .
    'Lawsy! Ol' Marster sure insisted
    Wid a great big strop
    That he say:—"Thank-ee, Yessuh . . .
    Yessuh, Thank-ee," in de proper way.

'Could recollect . . .
The w'uppin's sure enuff
And all the times he said:—
"Thank-ee," and cussed ol' Marster . . .
Underneath his breaf.

OLD PRAYING SUE

My man is black . . .
God . . . You alone, know why.
Shed but one briny tear
For all the drops of sweat
That fall from off his brow
Merciful God . . . mark one little smile
That wreathes his trembling lips
See but the mite of faith and courage
In his eyes . . .
That I might learn with blest humility
Even though, my man is black
It is not he, but Christ
They crucify.

MELISSA—LITTLE BLACK GIRL

Dolly, my dear . . .
A kind lady gave you to me
I'm grateful too . . . 'um, yes.
    'Cause you're pretty and sweet
    And you're dressed up neat.
But I don't love you . . . I positively don't . . .
    'Cause the man that made you
    Gave you long flaxen hair.
    And God made me . . . But look at my hair.
    The man that made you, didn't put any feel
    Inside your cold little breast.
    He left the feel out
    From your head to your heels,
But he gave you blue eyes, instead.
Now suppose you were me . . .
Oh . . . my baby-doll Rose . . .

And you knew how it felt
To be lonely and black
And I . . . just sat on a chair
And gave you . . . a cold stare . . .
Wouldn't you . . . give my head
A hard whack . . . Just like that!

———

Oh . . . oh . . . My dolly . . .
  My doll-baby Rose . . .

JIM—A WEARY TRAVELER

I been a weary traveler
But I ain't goin'er be no more . . .
I'm 'bout to take my chance at lovin'
'Cause my heart tells me to.
I been a weary traveler
But I ain't goin'er be no more.
When a man's dry, he wants licker
When he's weary, he takes his rest.
When he finds a sweet woman . . .
To please her . . . he tries his best.

LITTLE SAMSON—PHILOSOPHER

Some white folks are anglers
  They throws the bait . . .
Some white folks are fishes
  They swallows bait.
Us, black folks?
  Go 'long, don't bother me.
    We is bait.

Coveted Epitaph

This—my spirit: disciplined
　　To haven no whimpering sound
Of flaccid pity or loose-lipped plaint
　　That its wounds went long unbound.

Fired like old Damascus steel,
　　Patterned to scrupulous vein;
Tempered to bend—tip to hilt—
　　Bend—and spring back again.

Denial

These shining years which cover by some grace
Each wistful moment with a warm content,
Must still go lightly, lest irreverent
Or careless passing leave them commonplace.
We must seem lustreless, who know the trace
Of rapture in each smallest incident—
Must casually note each dear intent,
To bear its wonder with a quiet face.
Yet, by serene avowal of my heart
I shall be marked from common folk, who go
In dull and dusty ways. Because I know
This blinding beauty and can have no part
With loneliness or sorrow very long—
My silence wears the ecstasy of song.

Idle Wonder

My cat is so sleek and contented;
She is a real house-cat.
She has not seen any other cat
Since she came to live with me,

I wonder does she think,
I wonder does she dream,
I wonder does she ever imagine
Herself out, among cats
I wonder is she like poor Agnes.

Agnes lives with the white folks,
And they think she is contented,
And actually delighted with being
Their house-maid.

MAE V. COWDERY

Longings

To dance—
In the light of moon
A platinum moon
Poised like a slender dagger
On the velvet darkness
Of night.

To dream—
'Neath the bamboo tree
On the sable breast
Of earth—
And listen to the wind.

To croon
Weird sweet melodies
Round the cabin door
With banjoes clinking softly—
And from out the shadow
Hear the beat of tom-toms
Resonant through the years.

To plunge
My brown body
In a golden pool
And lazily float on the swell
Watching the rising sun.

To stand
On a purple mountain
Hidden from earth
By mists of dreams
And tears.

To talk—
With God.

Goal

My words shall drip
Like molten lava
From the towering volcano,
On the sleeping town
'Neath its summit.

My thoughts shall be
Hot ashes
Burning all in its path.

I shall not stop
Because critics sneer,
Nor stoop to fawning
At man's mere fancy.

I shall breathe
A clearer freer air
For I shall see the sun
Above the crowd.

I shall not blush
And make excuse
When a son of Adam,
Who calls himself
"God's Layman,"
Slashes with scorn
A thing born from
Truth's womb and nursed
By beauty. It will not
Matter who stoops
To cast the first stone.
Does not my spirit
Soar above these feeble

Minds? Thoughts born
From prejudice's womb
And nursed by tradition?

I will shatter the wall
Of darkness that rises
From gleaming day
And seeks to hide the sun.
I will turn this wall of
Darkness (that is night)
Into a thing of beauty.

I will take from the hearts
Of black men—
Prayers their lips
Are 'fraid to utter.
And turn their coarseness
Into a beauty of the jungle
Whence they came.

The lava from the black volcano
Shall be words, the ashes, thoughts
Of all men.

Farewell

No more
the feel of your hand
On my breast
Like the silver path
Of the moon
On dark heaving ocean.

No more
The rumpled softness
Of your hair
Like wind
In leafy shadowed trees.

No more
The lush sweetness
Of your lips
Like dew
On new-opened moon flowers.

No more
The drowsy murmurings
Of your voice
Like the faint twitter
Of birds before dawn.

No more
The poignant melody
Of hours spent
Between moonlight
And sunrise
Like the song
Of a crystal river
Going out to sea . . .

Only the awful sound
Of silence
In that hour
Before dawn
When the moon has waned,
The stars died,
And the sun is buried in mist!

Having Had You

Were you anything
But what you are . . . .
A dream come true
And now a dream again . . . .
I might have you back!

But having had you once
And lost you,
It is too much
To want you back again!

Four Poems—After the Japanese

Night turned over
In her sleep
And a star fell
Into the sea.

———

Earth was a beautiful
Snow woman
Until the rain
Washed her face one day.

———

I am the rain
Throbbing futilely
On the cold roof
Of your heart.

———

The moon
Is a madonna
Cradling in the crescent curve
Of her breast
A new born star.

For a New Mother

O lovely form
That has lain so long
Beneath my heart
Now looking up at me
With star-filled eyes . . .

What can I teach thee
Of singing?
Who are the meaning of all sound.

What can I give thee
Of beauty?
Who are the source of all loveliness.

What can I tell thee
Of life?
Who are the only reason for my birth.

I Look at Death

I looked into the face of death
And found it kind.
I looked at life that offered me
No more than before . . . a spilled cup
Of wine . . . My heart's own blood.

Death was friendly
And showed me pale gardens
And trees with silver fruit
And slender jade grass
With pearls for dew . . .

I am in a quandary
There is something so strange
. . . So still . . . about this loveliness
Of death . . .

COUNTEE CULLEN

Yet Do I Marvel

I doubt not God is good, well-meaning, kind,
And did He stoop to quibble could tell why
The little buried mole continues blind,
Why flesh that mirrors Him must some day die,
Make plain the reason tortured Tantalus
Is baited by the fickle fruit, declare
If merely brute caprice dooms Sisyphus
To struggle up a never-ending stair.
Inscrutable His ways are, and immune
To catechism by a mind too strewn
With petty cares to slightly understand
What awful brain compels His awful hand.
Yet do I marvel at this curious thing:
To make a poet black, and bid him sing!

Incident

(*For Eric Walrond*)

Once riding in old Baltimore,
    Heart-filled, head-filled with glee,
I saw a Baltimorean
    Keep looking straight at me.

Now I was eight and very small,
    And he was no whit bigger,
And so I smiled, but he poked out
    His tongue, and called me, "Nigger."

I saw the whole of Baltimore
    From May until December;

Of all the things that happened there
    That's all that I remember.

Tableau

(For Donald Duff)

Locked arm in arm they cross the way,
    The black boy and the white,
The golden splendor of the day,
    The sable pride of night.

From lowered blinds the dark folk stare,
    And here the fair folk talk,
Indignant that these two should dare
    In unison to walk.

Oblivious to look and word
    They pass, and see no wonder
That lightning brilliant as a sword
    Should blaze the path of thunder.

Saturday's Child

Some are teethed on a silver spoon,
    With the stars strung for a rattle;
I cut my teeth as the black raccoon—
    For implements of battle.

Some are swaddled in silk and down,
    And heralded by a star;
They swathed my limbs in a sackcloth gown
    On a night that was black as tar.

For some, godfather and goddame
    The opulent fairies be;
Dame Poverty gave me my name,
    And Pain godfathered me.

For I was born on Saturday—
    "Bad time for planting a seed,"
Was all my father had to say,
    And, "One mouth more to feed."

Death cut the strings that gave me life,
    And handed me to Sorrow,
The only kind of middle wife
    My folks could beg or borrow.

Heritage

(*For Harold Jackman*)

What is Africa to me:
Copper sun or scarlet sea,
Jungle star or jungle track,
Strong bronzed men, or regal black
Women from whose loins I sprang
When the birds of Eden sang?
One three centuries removed
From the scenes his fathers loved,
Spicy grove, cinnamon tree,
What is Africa to me?

So I lie, who all day long
Want no sound except the song
Sung by wild barbaric birds
Goading massive jungle herds,
Juggernauts of flesh that pass
Trampling tall defiant grass
Where young forest lovers lie,

Plighting troth beneath the sky.
So I lie, who always hear,
Though I cram against my ear
Both my thumbs, and keep them there,
Great drums throbbing through the air.
So I lie, whose fount of pride,
Dear distress, and joy allied,
Is my somber flesh and skin,
With the dark blood dammed within
Like great pulsing tides of wine
That, I fear, must burst the fine
Channels of the chafing net
Where they surge and foam and fret.

Africa? A book one thumbs
Listlessly, till slumber comes.
Unremembered are her bats
Circling through the night, her cats
Crouching in the river reeds,
Stalking gentle flesh that feeds
By the river brink; no more
Does the bugle-throated roar
Cry that monarch claws have leapt
From the scabbards where they slept.
Silver snakes that once a year
Doff the lovely coats you wear,
Seek no covert in your fear
Lest a mortal eye should see;
What's your nakedness to me?
Here no leprous flowers rear
Fierce corollas in the air;
Here no bodies sleek and wet,
Dripping mingled rain and sweat,
Tread the savage measures of
Jungle boys and girls in love.
What is last year's snow to me,
Last year's anything? The tree
Budding yearly must forget
How its past arose or set—
Bough and blossom, flower, fruit,

Even what shy bird with mute
Wonder at her travail there,
Meekly labored in its hair.
One three centuries removed
From the scenes his fathers loved,
Spicy grove, cinnamon tree,
What is Africa to me?

So I lie, who find no peace
Night or day, no slight release
From the unremittent beat
Made by cruel padded feet
Walking through my body's street.
Up and down they go, and back,
Treading out a jungle track.
So I lie, who never quite
Safely sleep from rain at night—
I can never rest at all
When the rain begins to fall;
Like a soul gone mad with pain
I must match its weird refrain;
Ever must I twist and squirm,
Writhing like a baited worm,
While its primal measures drip
Through my body, crying, "Strip!
Doff this new exuberance.
Come and dance the Lover's Dance!"
In an old remembered way
Rain works on me night and day.

Quaint, outlandish heathen gods
Black men fashion out of rods,
Clay, and brittle bits of stone,
In a likeness like their own,
My conversion came high-priced;
I belong to Jesus Christ,
Preacher of humility;
Heathen gods are naught to me.

Father, Son, and Holy Ghost,
So I make an idle boast;
Jesus of the twice-turned cheek,
Lamb of God, although I speak
With my mouth thus, in my heart
Do I play a double part.
Ever at Thy glowing altar
Must my heart grow sick and falter,
Wishing He I served were black,
Thinking then it would not lack
Precedent of pain to guide it,
Let who would or might deride it;
Surely then this flesh would know
Yours had borne a kindred woe.
Lord, I fashion dark gods, too,
Daring even to give You
Dark despairing features where,
Crowned with dark rebellious hair,
Patience wavers just so much as
Mortal grief compels, while touches
Quick and hot, of anger, rise
To smitten cheek and weary eyes.
Lord, forgive me if my need
Sometimes shapes a human creed.

All day long and all night through,
One thing only must I do:
Quench my pride and cool my blood,
Lest I perish in the flood.
Lest a hidden ember set
Timber that I thought was wet
Burning like the dryest flax,
Melting like the merest wax,
Lest the grave restore its dead.
Not yet has my heart or head
In the least way realized
They and I are civilized.

from *Epitaphs*

FOR MY GRANDMOTHER

This lovely flower fell to seed;
  Work gently, sun and rain;
She held it as her dying creed
  That she would grow again.

FOR A LADY I KNOW

She even thinks that up in heaven
  Her class lies late and snores,
While poor black cherubs rise at seven
  To do celestial chores.

FOR A MOUTHY WOMAN

God and the devil still are wrangling
  Which should have her, which repel;
God wants no discord in his heaven;
  Satan has enough in hell.

FOR PAUL LAURENCE DUNBAR

Born of the sorrowful of heart,
  Mirth was a crown upon his head;
Pride kept his twisted lips apart
  In jest, to hide a heart that bled.

FOR MYSELF

What's in this grave is worth your tear;
  There's more than the eye can see;
Folly and Pride and Love lie here
  Buried alive with me.

From the Dark Tower

(To Charles S. Johnson)

We shall not always plant while others reap
The golden increment of bursting fruit,
Not always countenance, abject and mute,
That lesser men should hold their brothers cheap;
Not everlastingly while others sleep
Shall we beguile their limbs with mellow flute,
Not always bend to some more subtle brute;
We were not made eternally to weep.

The night whose sable breast relieves the stark,
White stars is no less lovely being dark,
And there are buds that cannot bloom at all
In light, but crumple, piteous, and fall;
So in the dark we hide the heart that bleeds,
And wait, and tend our agonizing seeds.

Uncle Jim

"White folks is white," says uncle Jim;
"A platitude," I sneer;
And then I tell him so is milk,
And the froth upon his beer.

His heart walled up with bitterness,
He smokes his pungent pipe,
And nods at me as if to say,
"Young fool, you'll soon be ripe!"

I have a friend who eats his heart
Away with grief of mine,
Who drinks my joy as tipplers drain
Deep goblets filled with wine.

I wonder why here at his side,
Face-in-the-grass with him,
My mind should stray the Grecian urn
To muse on uncle Jim.

Scottsboro, Too, Is Worth Its Song

(A poem to American poets)

I said:
Now will the poets sing,—
Their cries go thundering
Like blood and tears
Into the nation's ears,
Like lightning dart
Into the nation's heart.

Against disease and death and all things fell,
And war,
Their strophes rise and swell
To jar
The foe smug in his citadel.

Remembering their sharp and pretty
Tunes for Sacco and Vanzetti,
I said:
Here too's a cause divinely spun
For those whose eyes are on the sun,
Here in epitome
Is all disgrace
And epic wrong,
Like wine to brace
The minstrel heart, and blare it into song.

Surely, I said,
Now will the poets sing.
    But they have raised no cry.
    I wonder why.

WARING CUNEY

No Images

She does not know
her beauty,
she thinks her brown body
has no glory.

If she could dance
naked
under palm trees
and see her image in the river,
she would know.

But there are no palm trees
on the street,
and dish water gives back
no images.

Nineteen-twenty-nine

Some folks hollered hard times
in nineteen-twenty-nine.
In nineteen-twenty-eight
say I was way behind.

Some folks hollered hard times
because hard times were new.
Hard times is all I ever had,
why should I lie to you?

Some folks hollered hard times.
What is it all about?
Things were bad for me when
those hard times started out.

My Lord, What a Morning

Oh, my Lord
What a morning,
Oh, my Lord,
What a feeling,
When Jack Johnson
Turned Jim Jeffries'
Snow-white face
Up to the ceiling.
Yes, my Lord
Fighting is wrong,
But what an uppercut.
Oh, my Lord,
What a morning,
Oh, my Lord
What a feeling,
When Jack Johnson
Turned Jim Jeffries'
Lily-white face
Up to the ceiling.
Oh, my Lord
What a morning,
Oh, my Lord
Take care of Jack.
Keep him, Lord
As you made him,
Big, and strong, and black.

Down-Home Boy

I'm a down-home boy
trying to get ahead.
It seems like I go
backwards instead.

Been in Chicago
over a year.
Had nothing down home,
not much here.

A measly job,
a greedy boss—
that's how come
I left Waycross.

Those Great Lake winds
blow all around:
I'm a light-coat man
in a heavy-coat town.

Carry Me Back

Carry me back to old Virginia.
  Magnolia blossoms fill the air.
Carry me back to old Virginia:
  the only way you'll get me there.

CLARISSA SCOTT DELANY

The Mask

So detached and cool she is
No motion e'er betrays
The secret life within her soul,
The anguish of her days.

She seems to look upon the world
With cold ironic eyes,
To spurn emotion's fevered sway,
To scoff at tears and sighs.

But once a woman with a child
Passed by her on the street,
And once she heard from casual lips
A man's name, bitter-sweet.

Such baffled yearning in her eyes,
Such pain upon her face!
I turned aside until the mask
Was slipped once more in place.

Solace

My window opens out into the trees
And in that small space
Of branches and of sky
I see the seasons pass
Behold the tender green
Give way to darker heavier leaves.
The glory of the autumn comes
When steeped in mellow sunlight
The fragile, golden leaves
Against a clear blue sky

Linger in the magic of the afternoon
And then reluctantly break off
And filter down to pave
A street with gold.
Then bare, gray branches
Lift themselves against the
Cold December sky
Sometimes weaving a web
Across the rose and dusk of late sunset
Sometimes against a frail new moon
And one bright star riding
A sky of that dark, living blue
Which comes before the heaviness
Of night descends, or the stars
Have powdered the heavens.
Winds beat against these trees;
The cold, but gentle rain of spring
Touches them lightly
The summer torrents strive
To lash them into a fury
And seek to break them—
But they stand.
My life is fevered
And a restlessness at times
An agony—again a vague
And baffling discontent
Possesses me.
I am thankful for my bit of sky
And trees, and for the shifting
Pageant of the seasons.
Such beauty lays upon the heart
A quiet.
Such eternal change and permanence
Take meaning from all turmoil
And leave serenity
Which knows no pain.

JESSIE REDMON FAUSET

Dead Fires

If this is peace, this dead and leaden thing,
   Then better far the hateful fret, the sting.
Better the wound forever seeking balm
   Than this gray calm!

Is this pain's surcease? Better far the ache,
   The long-drawn dreary day, the night's white wake,
Better the choking sigh, the sobbing breath
   Than passion's death!

La Vie C'est la Vie

On summer afternoons I sit
Quiescent by you in the park,
And idly watch the sunbeams gild
And tint the ash-trees' bark.

Or else I watch the squirrels frisk
And chaffer in the grassy lane;
And all the while I mark your voice
Breaking with love and pain.

I know a woman who would give
Her chance of heaven to take my place;
To see the love-light in your eyes,
The love-glow on your face!

And there's a man whose lightest word
Can set my chilly blood afire;
Fulfilment of his least behest
Defines my life's desire.

But he will none of me, Nor I
Of you. Nor you of her. 'Tis said
The world is full of jests like these.—
I wish that I were dead.

Oblivion

From the French of Massilon Coicou (Haiti)

I hope when I am dead that I shall lie
    In some deserted grave—I cannot tell you why,
But I should like to sleep in some neglected spot
    Unknown to every one, by every one forgot.

There lying I should taste with my dead breath
    The utter lack of life, the fullest sense of death;
And I should never hear the note of jealousy or hate,
    The tribute paid by passersby to tombs of state.

To me would never penetrate the prayers and tears
    That futilely bring torture to dead and dying ears;
There I should lie annihilate and my dead heart would bless
    Oblivion—the shroud and envelope of happiness.

NICOLÁS GUILLÉN

My Last Name

A family elegy

I

Ever since school
and even before . . . Since the dawn, when I was
barely a patch of sleep and wailing,
since then
I have been told my name. A password
that I might speak with stars.
Your name is, you shall be called . . .
And then they handed me
this you see here written on my card,
this I put at the foot of all poems;
thirteen letters
that I carry on my shoulders through the street,
that are with me always, no matter where I go.
Are you sure it is my name?
Have you got all my particulars?
Do you already know my navigable blood,
my geography full of dark mountains,
of deep and bitter valleys
that are not on the maps?
Perhaps you have visited my chasms,
my subterranean galleries
with great moist rocks,
islands jutting out of black puddles,
where I feel the pure rush
of ancient waters
falling from my proud heart
with a sound that's fresh and deep
to a place of flaming trees,
acrobatic monkeys,
legislative parrots and snakes?

Does all my skin (I should have said),
Does all my skin come from that Spanish marble?
My frightening voice too,
the harsh cry in my throat?
Are all my bones from there?
My roots and the roots
of my roots and also
these dark branches swayed by dreams
and these flowers blooming on my forehead
and this sap embittering my bark?
Are you certain?
Is there nothing more than this that you have written,
than this which you have stamped
with the seal of anger?
(Oh, I should have asked!)

Well then, I ask you now:
Don't you see these drums in my eyes?
Don't you see these drums, tightened and
beaten with two dried-up tears?
Don't I have, perhaps,
a nocturnal grandfather
with a great black scar
(darker still than his skin)
a great scar made by a whip?
Have I not, then,
a grandfather who's Mandingo, Dahoman, Congolese?
What is his name? Oh, yes, give me his name!
Andrés? Francisco? Amable?
How do you say Andrés in Congolese?
How have you always said
Francisco in Dahoman?
In Mandingo, how do you say Amable?
No? Were they, then, other names?
The last name then!
Do you know my other last name, the one that comes
to me from that enormous land, the captured,
bloody last name, that came across the sea
in chains, which came in chains across the sea.

Ah, you can't remember it!
You have dissolved it in immemorial ink.
You stole it from a poor, defenseless Black.
You hid it, thinking that I would
lower my eyes in shame.
Thank you!
I am grateful to you!
Noble people, thanks!
Merci!
Merci bien!
Merci beaucoup!
But no . . . Can you believe it? No.
I am clean.
My voice sparkles like newly polished metal.
Look at my shield: it has a baobab,
it has a rhinoceros and a spear.
I am also the grandson,
great grandson,
great great grandson of a slave.
(Let the master be ashamed.)
Am I Yelofe?
Nicolás Yelofe, perhaps?
Or Nicolás Bakongo?
Maybe Guillén Banguila?
Or Kumbá?
Perhaps Guillén Kumbá?
Or Kongué?
Could I be Guillén Kongué?
Oh, who knows!
What a riddle in the waters!

II

I feel immense night fall
on profound beasts,
on innocent castigated souls;
but also on ready voices,
which steal suns from the sky,
the brightest suns,
to decorate combatant blood.
From some flaming land pierced through

by the great equatorial arrow,
I know there will come distant cousins,
my ancestral anguish cast upon the winds;
I know there will come portions of my veins,
my ancestral blood,
with calloused feet bending frightened grasses;
I know there will come men whose lives are green,
my ancestral jungle,
with their pain open like a cross and their breasts red with
    flames.
Having never met, we will know each other by the hunger,
by the tuberculosis and the syphilis,
by the sweat bought in a black market,
by the fragments of chain
still clinging to the skin;
Having never met we will know each other
by the dream-full eyes
and even by the rock-hard insults
the quadrumanes of ink and paper
spit at us each day.
What can it matter, then.
(What does it matter now!)
ah, my little name
of thirteen letters?
Or the Mandingo, Bantu,
Yoruba, Dahoman name
of the sad grandfather drowned
in notary's ink.
Good friends, what does it matter?
Oh, yes, good friends
come look at my name!
My name without end,
made up of endless names;
My name, foreign,
free and mine, foreign and yours,
foreign and free as the air.

Translated by Robert Marquez and David Arthur McMurray

FRANK HORNE

Notes Found Near a Suicide

My little stone
sinks quickly
into the bosom of this deep, dark pool
of oblivion . . .
I have troubled its breast but little
yet those far shores
that knew me not
will feel the fleeting, furtive kiss
of my tiny concentric ripples . . .

TO MOTHER

I came
in the blinding sweep
of ecstatic pain,
I go
in the throbbing pulse
of aching space—
in the aeons between
I piled upon you
pain on pain
ache on ache
and yet as I go
I shall know
that you will grieve
and want me back . . .

TO B

You have freed me—
in opening wide the doors
of flesh

you have freed me
of the binding leash.
I have climbed the heights
of white disaster
my body screaming
in the silver crash of passion . . .
Before you gave yourself
to him
I had chained myself
for you.
But when at last
you lowered your proud flag
in surrender complete
you gave me too, as hostage—
and I have wept my joy
at the dawn-tipped shrine
of many breasts.

TO JEAN

When you poured your love
like molten flame
into the throbbing mould
of her pulsing veins
leaving her blood a river of fire
and her arteries channels of light,
I hated you . . .
hated with that primal hate
that has its wells
in the flesh of me
and the flesh of you
and the flesh of her
I hated you—
hated with envy
your mastery of her being . . .
with one fleshy gesture
you pricked the iridescent bubble
of my dreams
and so to make
your conquest more sweet

I tell you now
that I hated you.

TO LEWELLYN

You have borne full well
the burden of my friendship—
I have drunk deep
at your crystal pool,
and in return
I have polluted its water
with the bile of my hatred.
I have flooded your soul
with tortuous thoughts,
I have played Iscariot
to your Pythias . . .

TO . . .

You call it
Death of the Spirit
and I call it Life . . .
The vigor of vibration,
the muffled knocks,
the silver sheen of passion's flood,
the ecstacy of pain . . .
You call it
Death of the Spirit
and I call it Life.

TO CAROLINE

Your piano
is the better instrument . . .
Yesterday
your fingers
so precisely
touched the cold keys—
a nice string
of orderly sounds,

a proper melody . . .
Tonight
your hands
so wantonly
caressed my tingling skin—
a mad whirl
of cacophony,
a wild chanting . . .
Your piano
is the better instrument.

TO CATALINA

Love thy piano, oh girl,
it will give you back
note for note
the harmonies of your soul.
It will sing back to you
the high songs of your heart.
It will give
as well as take . . .

TO TELIE

You have made my voice
a rippling laugh
but my heart
a crying thing . . .
'Tis better thus:
a fleeting kiss
and then,
the dark . . .

TO MARIETTE

I sought consolation
in the sorrow of your eyes.
You sought reguerdon
in the crying of my heart.
We found that shattered dreamers
can be bitter hosts . . .

TO "CHICK"

Oh Achilles of the moleskins
and the gridiron
do not wonder
nor doubt that this is I
that lies so calmly here—
this is the same exultant beast
that so joyously
ran the ball with you
in those far-flung days of abandon.
You remember how recklessly
we revelled in the heat and the dust
and the swirl of conflict?
You remember they called us
The Terrible Two?
And you remember
after we had battered our heads
and our bodies
against the stonewall of their defense,
you remember the signal I would call
and how you would look at me
in faith and admiration
and say "Let's go" . . .
how the lines would clash
and strain,
and how I would slip through
fighting and squirming
over the line
to victory.

You remember, Chick?
When you gaze at me here
let that same light
of faith and admiration
shine in your eyes
for I have battered the stark stonewall
before me . . .
I have kept faith with you
and now

I have called my signal,
found my opening
and slipped through
fighting and squirming
over the line
to victory . . .

TO HENRY

I do not know
how I shall look
when I lie down here
but I really should be smiling
mischievously . . .
You and I have studied
together
the knowledge of the ages
and lived the life of science
matching discovery for discovery—
and yet
in a trice
with a small explosion
of this little machine
in my hand
I shall know
all
that Aristotle, Newton, Lavoisier, and Galileo
could not determine
in their entire
lifetimes . . .
And the joke of it is,
Henry,
that I have
beat you to it . . .

TO THE POETS

Why do poets
like to die
and sing raptures to the grave?

They seem to think
that bitter dirt
turns sweet between the teeth.

I have lived
and yelled hosannas
at the climbing stars

I have lived
and drunk deep
the deceptive wine of life . . .

And now, tipsy and reeling
from its dregs
I die . . .

Oh, let the poets sing
raptures to the grave.

TO ONE WHO CALLED ME "NIGGER"

You are Power
and send steel ships hurtling
from shore to shore . . .

You are Vision
and cast your sight through aeons of space
from world to world . . .

You are Brain
and throw your voice endlessly
from ear to ear . . .

You are Soul
and falter at the yawning chasm
from White to Black . . .

TO ALFRED

I have grown tired of you

and your wife
sitting there
with your children,
little bits of you
running about your feet
and you two so calm
and cold together . . .
It is really better
to lie here
insensate
than to see new life
creep upon you
calm and cold
sitting there . . .

TO YOU

All my life
they have told me
that You
would save my soul
that only
by kneeling in Your house
and eating of Your body
and drinking of Your blood
could I be born again . . .
And yet
one night
in the tall black shadow
of a windy pine
I offered up
the Sacrifice of Body
upon the altar
of her breast . . .
You
who were conceived
without ecstacy
or pain
can You understand
that I knelt last night

in Your house
and ate of Your body
and drank of Your blood
. . . and thought only of her?

TO WANDA

To you, so far away
so cold and aloof,
to you, who knew me so well,
this is my last Grand Gesture
this is my last Great Effect
and as I go winging
through the black doors of eternity
is that thin sound I hear
your applause . . . ?

TO JAMES

Do you remember
how you won
that last race . . . ?
how you flung your body
at the start . . .
how your spikes
ripped the cinders
in the stretch . . .
how you catapulted
through the tape . . .
do you remember . . . ?
Don't you think
I lurched with you
out of those starting holes . . . ?
Don't you think
my sinews tightened
at those first
few strides . . .
and when you flew into the stretch
was not all my thrill
of a thousand races

in your blood . . . ?
At your final drive
through the finish line
did not my shout
tell of the
triumphant ecstacy
of victory . . . ?

Live
as I have taught you
to run, Boy—
it's a short dash.
Dig your starting holes
deep and firm
lurch out of them
into the straightaway
with all the power
that is in you
look straight ahead
to the finish line
think only of the goal
run straight
run high
run hard
save nothing
and finish
with an ecstatic burst
that carries you
hurtling
through the tape
to victory . . .

LANGSTON HUGHES

The Negro Speaks of Rivers

I've known rivers:
I've known rivers ancient as the world and older than the
    flow of human blood in human veins.

My soul has grown deep like the rivers.

I bathed in the Euphrates when dawns were young.
I built my hut near the Congo and it lulled me to sleep.
I looked upon the Nile and raised the pyramids above it.
I heard the singing of the Mississippi when Abe Lincoln went
    down to New Orleans, and I've seen its muddy bosom
    turn all golden in the sunset.

I've known rivers:
Ancient, dusky rivers.

My soul has grown deep like the rivers.

The Weary Blues

Droning a drowsy syncopated tune,
Rocking back and forth to a mellow croon,
    I heard a Negro play.
Down on Lenox Avenue the other night
By the pale dull pallor of an old gas light
    He did a lazy sway. . . .
    He did a lazy sway. . . .
To the tune o' those Weary Blues.
With his ebony hands on each ivory key
He made that poor piano moan with melody.
    O Blues!
Swaying to and fro on his rickety stool

He played that sad raggy tune like a musical fool.
    Sweet Blues!
Coming from a black man's soul.
    O Blues!
In a deep song voice with a melancholy tone
I heard that Negro sing, that old piano moan—
    "Ain't got nobody in all this world,
        Ain't got nobody but ma self.
        I's gwine to quit ma frownin'
        And put ma troubles on the shelf."

Thump, thump, thump, went his foot on the floor.
He played a few chords then he sang some more—
    "I got the Weary Blues
        And I can't be satisfied.
        Got the Weary Blues
        And can't be satisfied—
        I ain't happy no mo'
        And I wish that I had died."
And far into the night he crooned that tune.
The stars went out and so did the moon.
The singer stopped playing and went to bed
While the Weary Blues echoed through his head.
He slept like a rock or a man that's dead.

Mother to Son

Well, son, I'll tell you:
Life for me ain't been no crystal stair.
It's had tacks in it,
And splinters,
And boards torn up,
And places with no carpet on the floor—
Bare.
But all the time
I'se been a-climbin' on,
And reachin' landin's,
And turnin' corners,

And sometimes goin' in the dark
Where there ain't been no light.
So boy, don't you turn back.
Don't you set down on the steps
'Cause you finds it's kinder hard.
Don't you fall now—
For I'se still goin', honey,
I'se still climbin',
And life for me ain't been no crystal stair.

Jazz Band in a Parisian Cabaret

Play that thing,
Jazz band!
Play it for the lords and ladies,
For the dukes and counts,
For the whores and gigolos,
For the American millionaires,
And the school teachers
Out for a spree.
Play it,
Jazz band!
You know that tune
That laughs and cries at the same time.
You know it.

   May I?
   Mais oui.
   Mein Gott!
   Parece una rumba.
Play it, jazz band!
You've got seven languages to speak in
And then some,
Even if you do come from Georgia.
   Can I go home wid yuh, sweetie?
   Sure.

Beale Street Love

Love
Is a brown man's fist
With hard knuckles
Crushing the lips,
Blackening the eyes,—
Hit me again,
Says Clorinda.

Cross

My old man's a white old man
And my old mother's black.
If ever I cursed my white old man
I take my curses back.

If ever I cursed my black old mother
And wished she were in hell,
I'm sorry for that evil wish
And now I wish her well.

My old man died in a fine big house.
My ma died in a shack.
I wonder where I'm gonna die,
Being neither white nor black?

Personal

In an envelope marked:
    Personal
God addressed me a letter.
In an envelope marked:
    Personal
I have given my answer.

Midwinter Blues

In the middle of the winter,
Snow all over the ground.
In the middle of the winter,
Snow all over the ground—
'Twas the night befo' Christmas
My good man turned me down.

Don't know's I'd mind his goin'
But he left me when the coal was low.
Don't know's I'd mind his goin'
But he left when the coal was low.
Now, if a man loves a woman
That ain't no time to go.

He told me that he loved me
But he must a been tellin' a lie.
He told me that he loved me.
He must a been tellin' a lie.
But he's the only man I'll
Love till the day I die.

I'm gonna buy me a rose bud
An' plant it at my back door,
Buy me a rose bud,
Plant it at my back door,
So when I'm dead they won't need
No flowers from the store.

Bound No'th Blues

Goin' down the road, Lawd,
Goin' down the road.
Down the road, Lawd,
Way, way down the road.
Got to find somebody
To help me carry this load.

Road's in front o' me,
Nothin' to do but walk.
Road's in front o' me,
Walk . . . an' walk . . . an' walk.
I'd like to meet a good friend
To come along an' talk.

Hates to be lonely,
Lawd, I hates to be sad.
Says I hates to be lonely,
Hates to be lonely an' sad,
But ever friend you finds seems
Like they try to do you bad.

Road, road, road, O!
Road, road . . . road . . . road, road!
Road, road, road, O!
On the no'thern road.
These Mississippi towns ain't
Fit fer a hoppin' toad.

Dream Variations

To fling my arms wide
In some place of the sun,
To whirl and to dance
Till the white day is done.
Then rest at cool evening
Beneath a tall tree
While night comes on gently,
        Dark like me—
That is my dream!

To fling my arms wide
In the face of the sun,
Dance! Whirl! Whirl!
Till the quick day is done.
Rest at pale evening . . .

A tall, slim tree . . .
Night coming tenderly
   Black like me.

I, Too

I, too, sing America.

I am the darker brother.
They send me to eat in the kitchen
When company comes,
But I laugh,
And eat well,
And grow strong.

Tomorrow,
I'll be at the table
When company comes.
Nobody'll dare
Say to me,
"Eat in the kitchen,"
Then.

Besides,
They'll see how beautiful I am
And be ashamed—

I, too, am America.

Song for a Dark Girl

Way Down South in Dixie
   (Break the heart of me)
They hung my black young lover
   To a cross roads tree.

Way Down South in Dixie
    (Bruised body high in air)
I asked the white Lord Jesus
    What was the use of prayer.

Way Down South in Dixie
    (Break the heart of me)
Love is a naked shadow
    On a gnarled and naked tree.

Let America Be America Again

Let America be America again.
Let it be the dream it used to be.
Let it be the pioneer on the plain
Seeking a home where he himself is free.

(America never was America to me.)

Let America be the dream the dreamers dreamed—
Let it be that great strong land of love
Where never kings connive nor tyrants scheme
That any man be crushed by one above.

(It never was America to me.)

O, let my land be a land where Liberty
Is crowned with no false patriotic wreath,
But opportunity is real, and life is free,
Equality is in the air we breathe.

(There's never been equality for me,
Nor freedom in this "homeland of the free.")

Say, who are you that mumbles in the dark?
And who are you that draws your veil across the stars?

I am the poor white, fooled and pushed apart,
I am the Negro bearing slavery's scars.
I am the red man driven from the land,
I am the immigrant clutching the hope I seek—
And finding only the same old stupid plan
Of dog eat dog, of mighty crush the weak.

I am the young man, full of strength and hope,
Tangled in that ancient endless chain
Of profit, power, gain, of grab the land!
Of grab the gold! Of grab the ways of satisfying need!
Of work the men! Of take the pay!
Of owning everything for one's own greed!

I am the farmer, bondsman to the soil.
I am the worker sold to the machine.
I am the Negro, servant to you all.
I am the people, humble, hungry, mean—
Hungry yet today despite the dream.
Beaten yet today—O, Pioneers!
I am the man who never got ahead,
The poorest worker bartered through the years.

Yet I'm the one who dreamt our basic dream
In that Old World while still a serf of kings,
Who dreamt a dream so strong, so brave, so true,
That even yet its mighty daring sings
In every brick and stone, in every furrow turned
That's made America the land it has become.
O, I'm the man who sailed those early seas
In search of what I meant to be my home—
For I'm the one who left dark Ireland's shore,
And Poland's plain, and England's grassy lea,
And torn from Black Africa's strand I came
To build a "homeland of the free."

The free?

Who said the free? Not me?
Surely not me? The millions on relief today?

The millions shot down when we strike?
The millions who have nothing for our pay?
For all the dreams we've dreamed
And all the songs we've sung
And all the hopes we've held
And all the flags we've hung,
The millions who have nothing for our pay—
Except the dream that's almost dead today.

O, let America be America again—
The land that never has been yet—
And yet must be—the land where *every* man is free.
The land that's mine—the poor man's, Indian's, Negro's,
    ME—
Who made America,
Whose sweat and blood, whose faith and pain,
Whose hand at the foundry, whose plow in the rain,
Must bring back our mighty dream again.

Sure, call me any ugly name you choose—
The steel of freedom does not stain.
From those who live like leeches on the people's lives,
We must take back our land again,
America!

O, yes,
I say it plain,
America never was America to me,
And yet I swear this oath—
America will be!

Out of the rack and ruin of our gangster death,
The rape and rot of graft, and stealth, and lies,
We, the people, must redeem
The land, the mines, the plants, the rivers.
The mountains and the endless plain—
All, all the stretch of these great green states—
And make America again!

from *Montage of a Dream Deferred*

DREAM BOOGIE

Good morning, daddy!
Ain't you heard
The boogie-woogie rumble
Of a dream deferred?

Listen closely:
You'll hear their feet
Beating out and beating out a——

> *You think
> It's a happy beat?*

Listen to it closely:
Ain't you heard
something underneath
like a——

> *What did I say?*

Sure,
I'm happy!
Take it away!

> *Hey, pop!
> Re-bop!
> Mop!*

> *Y-e-a-h!*

PARADE

Seven ladies
and seventeen gentlemen
at the Elks Club Lounge
planning planning a parade:

Grand Marshal in his white suit
will lead it.
Cadillacs with dignitaries
will precede it.
And behind will come
with band and drum
on foot . . . on foot . . .
on foot . . .

Motorcycle cops,
white,
will speed it
out of sight
if they can:
Solid black,
can't be right.

Marching . . . marching . . .
marching . . .
noon till night . . .

> *I never knew*
> *that many Negroes*
> *were on earth,*
> *did you?*

> *I never knew!*

PARADE!

A chance to let

PARADE!

the whole world see

PARADE!

old black me!

CHILDREN'S RHYMES

When I was a chile we used to play,
"One—two—buckle my shoe!"
and things like that. But now, Lord,
listen at them little varmints!

> *By what sends*
> *the white kids*
> *I ain't sent:*
> *I know I can't*
> *be President.*

There is two thousand children
in this block, I do believe!

> *What don't bug*
> *them white kids*
> *sure bugs me:*
> *We knows everybody*
> *ain't free!*

Some of these young ones is cert'ly bad——
One batted a hard ball right through my window
and my gold fish et the glass.

> *What's written down*
> *for white folks*
> *ain't for us a-tall:*
> *"Liberty And Justice——*
> *Huh—For All."*

> *Oop-pop-a-da!*
> *Skee! Daddle-de-do!*
> *Be-bop!*

Salt'peanuts!

De-dop!

SISTER

That little Negro's married and got a kid.
Why does he keep on foolin' around Marie?
Marie's my sister—not married to me——
But why does *he* keep on foolin' around Marie?
Why don't she get a boy-friend
I can understand—some decent man?

> *Did it ever occur to you, son,*
> *the reason Marie runs around with trash*
> *is she wants some cash?*

Don't decent folks have dough?

> *Unfortunately usually no!*

Well, anyway, it don't have to be a married man.

> *Did it ever occur to you, boy,*
> *that a woman does the best she can?*

COMMENT ON STOOP

So does a man.

PREFERENCE

I likes a woman
six or eight and ten years older'n myself.
I don't fool with these young girls.
Young girl'll say,
> *Daddy, I want so-and-so.*
> *I needs this, that, and the other.*
But a old woman'll say,
> *Honey, what does YOU need?*

I just drawed my money tonight
and it's all your'n.
That's why I likes a older woman
who can appreciate me:
When she conversations you
it ain't forever, *Gimme*!

NECESSITY

Work?
I don't have to work.
I don't have to do nothing
but eat, drink, stay black, and die.
This little old furnished room's
so small I can't whip a cat
without getting fur in my mouth
and my landlady's so old
her features is all run together
and God knows she sure can overcharge——
Which is why I reckon I *does*
have to work after all.

QUESTION

Said the lady, *Can you do*
what my other man can't do——
That is
love me, daddy——
and feed me, too?

FIGURINE

De-dop!

BUDDY

That kid's my buddy,
still and yet
I don't see him much.
He works downtown for Twelve a week.

Has to give his mother Ten——
she says he can have
the other Two
to pay his carfare, buy a suit,
coat, shoes,
anything he wants out of it.

JUKE BOX LOVE SONG

I could take the Harlem night
and wrap around you,
Take the neon lights and make a crown,
Take the Lenox Avenue busses,
Taxis, subways,
And for your love song tone their rumble down.
Take Harlem's heartbeat,
Make a drumbeat,
Put it on a record, let it whirl,
And while we listen to it play,
Dance with you till day——
Dance with you, my sweet brown Harlem girl.

ULTIMATUM

Baby, how come you can't see me
when I'm paying your bills
each and every week?

If you got somebody else,
tell me——
else I'll cut you off
without your rent.
I mean
without a cent.

WARNING

Daddy,
don't let your dog
curb you!

CROON

I don't give a damn
For Alabam'
Even if it is my home.

NEW YORKERS

I was born here,
that's no lie, he said,
right here beneath God's sky.

> *I wasn't born here, she said,*
> *I come—and why?*
> *Where I come from*
> *folks work hard*
> *all their lives*
> *until they die*
> *and never own no parts*
> *of earth nor sky.*
> *So I come up here.*
> *Now what've I got?*
> *You!*

She lifted up her lips
in the dark:
The same old spark!

WONDER

Early blue evening.
Lights ain't come on yet.
Looky yonder!
They come on now!

EASY BOOGIE

Down in the bass
That steady beat
Walking walking walking
Like marching feet.

Down in the bass
That easy roll,
Rolling like I like it
In my soul.

Riffs, smears, breaks.

Hey, Lawdy, Mama!
Do you hear what I said?
Easy like I rock it
In my bed!

BALLAD OF THE LANDLORD

Landlord, landlord,
My roof has sprung a leak.
Don't you 'member I told you about it
Way last week?

Landlord, landlord,
These steps is broken down.
When you come up yourself
It's a wonder you don't fall down.

Ten Bucks you say I owe you?
Ten Bucks you say is due?
Well, that's Ten Bucks more'n I'll pay you
Till you fix this house up new.

What? You gonna get eviction orders?
You gonna cut off my heat?
You gonna take my furniture and
Throw it in the street?

Um-huh! You talking high and mighty.
Talk on—till you get through.

You ain't gonna be able to say a word
If I land my fist on you.

Police! Police!
Come and get this man!
He's trying to ruin the government
And overturn the land!

Copper's whistle!
Patrol bell!
Arrest.

Precinct Station.
Iron cell.
Headlines in press:

MAN THREATENS LANDLORD

TENANT HELD NO BAIL

JUDGE GIVES NEGRO 90 DAYS IN COUNTY JAIL.

CAFÉ: 3 A.M.

Detectives from the vice squad
with weary sadistic eyes
spotting fairies.
        Degenerates,
some folks say.

        But God, Nature,
        or somebody
        made them that way.

Police lady or Lesbian
over there?
        Where?

———————

THEME FOR ENGLISH B

The instructor said,

> *Go home and write*
> *a page tonight.*
> *And let that page come out of you—*
> *Then, it will be true.*

I wonder if it's that simple?
I am twenty-two, colored, born in Winston-Salem.
I went to school there, then Durham, then here
to this college on the hill above Harlem.
I am the only colored student in my class.
The steps from the hill lead down into Harlem,
through a park, then I cross St. Nicholas,
Eighth Avenue, Seventh, and I come to the Y,
the Harlem Branch Y, where I take the elevator
up to my room, sit down, and write this page:

It's not easy to know what is true for you or me
at twenty-two, my age. But I guess I'm what
I feel and see and hear, Harlem, I hear you:
hear you, hear me—we two—you, me, talk on this page.
(I hear New York, too.) Me—who?
Well, I like to eat, sleep, drink, and be in love.
I like to work, read, learn, and understand life.
I like a pipe for a Christmas present,
or records—Bessie, bop, or Bach.
I guess being colored doesn't make me *not* like
the same things other folks like who are other races.
So will my page be colored that I write?
Being me, it will not be white.

But it will be
a part of you, instructor.
You are white—
yet a part of me, as I am a part of you.
That's American.
Sometimes perhaps you don't want to be a part of me.
Nor do I often want to be a part of you.
But we are, that's true!
As I learn from you,
I guess you learn from me—
although you're older—and white—
and somewhat more free.

This is my page for English B.

HARLEM

What happens to a dream deferred?

     Does it dry up
     like a raisin in the sun?
     Or fester like a sore—
     And then run?
     Does it stink like rotten meat?
     Or crust and sugar over—
     like a syrupy sweet?

     Maybe it just sags
     like a heavy load.

     Or does it explode?

ISLAND

     Between two rivers,
     North of the park,
     Like darker rivers
     The streets are dark.

Black and white,
Gold and brown—
Chocolate-custard
Pie of a town.

Dream within a dream,
Our dream deferred.

Good morning, daddy!

Ain't you heard?

Madam and the Rent Man

The rent man knocked.
He said, Howdy-do?
I said, What
Can I do for you?
He said, You know
Your rent is due.

I said, Listen,
Before I'd pay
I'd go to Hades
And rot away!

The sink is broke,
The water don't run,
And you ain't done a thing
You promised to've done.

Back window's cracked,
Kitchen floor squeaks,
There's rats in the cellar,
And the attic leaks.

He said, Madam,
It's not up to me.

I'm just the agent,
Don't you see?

I said, Naturally,
You pass the buck.
If it's money you want
You're out of luck.

He said, Madam,
I ain't pleased!
I said, Neither am I.

So we agrees!

from *Ask Your Mama*

CULTURAL EXCHANGE

IN THE   *The*
IN THE QUARTER   *rhythmically*
IN THE QUARTER OF THE NEGROES   *rough*
WHERE THE DOORS ARE DOORS OF PAPER   *scraping*
DUST OF DINGY ATOMS   *of a guira*
BLOWS A SCRATCHY SOUND.   *continues*
AMORPHOUS JACK-O'-LANTERNS CAPER   *monotonously*
AND THE WIND WON'T WAIT FOR   *until a lonely*
    MIDNIGHT
FOR FUN TO BLOW DOORS DOWN.   *flute call,*
                                                   high and
BY THE RIVER AND THE RAILROAD   *far away,*
WITH FLUID FAR-OFF GOING   *merges*
BOUNDARIES BIND UNBINDING   *into piano*
A WHIRL OF WHISTLES BLOWING   *variations*
NO TRAINS OR STEAMBOATS GOING—   *on German*
YET LEONTYNE'S UNPACKING.   *lieder*
                                                   gradually
IN THE QUARTER OF THE NEGROES   *changing*
WHERE THE DOORKNOB LETS IN LIEDER   *into*
MORE THAN GERMAN EVER BORE,   *old-time*
HER YESTERDAY PAST GRANDPA—   *traditional*

NOT OF HER OWN DOING— *12-bar*
IN A POT OF COLLARD GREENS *blues*
IS GENTLY STEWING. *up strong*
between verses

THERE, FORBID US TO REMEMBER, *until*
COMES AN AFRICAN IN MID-DECEMBER *African*
SENT BY THE STATE DEPARTMENT *drums*
AMONG THE SHACKS TO MEET THE *throb*
    BLACKS:
LEONTYNE SAMMY HARRY POITIER *against*
LOVELY LENA MARIAN LOUIS PEARLIE *blues*
    MAE

GEORGE S. SCHUYLER MOLTO BENE *fading*
COME WHAT MAY LANGSTON HUGHES *as the*
IN THE QUARTER OF THE NEGROES *music*
WHERE THE RAILROAD AND THE RIVER *ends.*
HAVE DOORS THAT FACE EACH WAY TACIT
AND THE ENTRANCE TO THE MOVIE'S
UP AN ALLEY UP THE SIDE.

"Hesitation
PUSHCARTS FOLD AND UNFOLD *Blues" with*
IN A SUPERMARKET SEA. *full band*
AND WE BETTER FIND OUT, MAMA, *up strong*
WHERE IS THE COLORED LAUNDROMAT, *for a chorus*
SINCE WE MOVED UP TO MOUNT VERNON. *in the clear*
between verses

RALPH ELLISON AS VESPUCIUS *then down*
INA-YOURA AT THE MASTHEAD *under voice*
ARNA BONTEMPS CHIEF CONSULTANT *softly as*
MOLTO BENE MELLOW BABY PEARLIE MAE *deep-toned*
SHALOM ALEICHEM JIMMY BALDWIN *distant*
    SAMMY
COME WHAT MAY—THE SIGNS POINT: *African*
    GHANA   *GUINEA* *drums*
AND THE TOLL BRIDGE FROM *join the*
    WESTCHESTER
IS A GANGPLANK ROCKING RISKY *blues until*
BETWEEN THE DECK AND SHORE *the music*

OF A BOAT THAT NEVER QUITE   *dies. . . .*
KNEW ITS DESTINATION.

IN THE QUARTER OF THE NEGROES   TACIT
ORNETTE AND CONSTERNATION
CLAIM ATTENTION FROM THE PAPERS
THAT HAVE NO NEWS THAT DAY OF
    MOSCOW.

IN THE POT BEHIND THE
PAPER DOORS WHAT'S COOKING?
WHAT'S SMELLING, LEONTYNE?   *Delicate*
LIEDER, LOVELY LIEDER   *lieder*
AND A LEAF OF COLLARD GREEN.   *on piano*
LOVELY LIEDER LEONTYNE.   *continues*
                                         between verses
IN THE SHADOW OF THE NEGROES   *to merge*
    NKRUMAH   *softly*
IN THE SHADOW OF THE NEGROES   *into the*
    NASSER NASSER   *melody of the*
IN THE SHADOW OF THE NEGROES   *"Hesitation*
    ZIK AZIKIWE   *Blues" asking*
CUBA CASTRO GUINEA TOURÉ   *its haunting*
FOR NEED OR PROPAGANDA   *question,*
    KENYATTA   *"How long*
AND THE TOM DOGS OF THE CABIN   *must I*
THE COCOA AND THE CANE BRAKE   *wait?*
THE CHAIN GANG AND THE SLAVE BLOCK   *Can I*
TARRED AND FEATHERED NATIONS   *get it*
SEAGRAM'S AND FOUR ROSES   *now—or*
$5.00 BAGS A DECK OR DAGGA.   *must I*
FILIBUSTER VERSUS VETO   *hesitate?"*
LIKE A SNAPPING TURTLE—   *Suddenly*
WON'T LET GO UNTIL IT THUNDERS   *the drums*
WON'T LET GO UNTIL IT THUNDERS   *roll like*
TEARS THE BODY FROM THE SHADOW   *thunder*
WON'T LET GO UNTIL IT THUNDERS   *as the*
IN THE QUARTER OF THE NEGROES   *music ends*
                                         sonorously.
AND THEY ASKED ME RIGHT AT   TACIT
    CHRISTMAS

IF MY BLACKNESS, WOULD I RUB OFF?
I SAID, ASK YOUR MAMA.

*Figure impishly
into "Dixie"*

DREAMS AND NIGHTMARES . . .
NIGHTMARES . . . DREAMS! OH!
DREAMING THAT THE NEGROES
OF THE SOUTH HAVE TAKEN OVER—
VOTED ALL THE DIXIECRATS
RIGHT OUT OF POWER—
COMES THE *COLORED HOUR*:
MARTIN LUTHER KING IS GOVERNOR OF
     GEORGIA,
DR. RUFUS CLEMENT HIS CHIEF ADVISOR,
ZELMA WATSON GEORGE THE HIGH
     GRAND WORTHY.
IN WHITE PILLARED MANSIONS
SITTING ON THEIR WIDE VERANDAS,
WEALTHY NEGROES HAVE WHITE
     SERVANTS,
WHITE SHARECROPPERS WORK THE BLACK
     PLANTATIONS,
AND COLORED CHILDREN HAVE WHITE
     MAMMIES:

*ending in high
shrill flute call.*
TACIT

MAMMY FAUBUS
MAMMY EASTLAND
MAMMY PATTERSON.
DEAR, *DEAR* DARLING OLD WHITE
     MAMMIES—
SOMETIMES EVEN BURIED WITH OUR
     FAMILY!
DEAR OLD
MAMMY FAUBUS!
CULTURE, THEY SAY, *IS A TWO-WAY STREET*:
HAND ME MY MINT JULEP, MAMMY.
     MAKE HASTE!

*"When the
Saints Go
Marching In"
joyously for two
full choruses
with
maracas. . . .*

FINAL CALL

SEND FOR THE PIED PIPER AND LET HIM PIPE THE RATS
    AWAY.
SEND FOR ROBIN HOOD TO CLINCH THE ANTI-POVERTY
    CAMPAIGN.
SEND FOR THE FAIRY QUEEN WITH A WAVE OF THE WAND
TO MAKE US ALL INTO PRINCES AND PRINCESSES.
SEND FOR KING ARTHUR TO BRING THE HOLY GRAIL.
SEND FOR OLD MAN MOSES TO LAY DOWN THE LAW.
SEND FOR JESUS TO PREACH THE SERMON ON THE MOUNT.
SEND FOR DREYFUS TO CRY, "*J'ACCUSE!*"
SEND FOR DEAD BLIND LEMON TO SING THE B FLAT BLUES.
SEND FOR ROBESPIERRE TO SCREAM, "*ÇA IRA! ÇA IRA! ÇA
    IRA!*"
SEND (GOD FORBID—HE'S NOT DEAD LONG ENOUGH!)
FOR LUMUMBA TO CRY, "FREEDOM NOW!"
SEND FOR LAFAYETTE AND TELL HIM, "HELP! HELP ME!"
SEND FOR DENMARK VESEY CRYING, "FREE!"
FOR CINQUE SAYING, "RUN A NEW FLAG UP THE MAST."
FOR OLD JOHN BROWN WHO KNEW SLAVERY COULDN'T LAST.
SEND FOR LENIN! (DON'T YOU DARE!—HE CAN'T COME
    HERE!)
SEND FOR TROTSKY! (WHAT? DON'T CONFUSE THE ISSUE,
    PLEASE!)
SEND FOR UNCLE TOM ON HIS MIGHTY KNEES.
SEND FOR LINCOLN, SEND FOR GRANT.
SEND FOR FREDERICK DOUGLASS, GARRISON, BEECHER,
    LOWELL.
SEND FOR HARRIET TUBMAN, OLD SOJOURNER TRUTH.
SEND FOR MARCUS GARVEY (WHAT?) SUFI (WHO?) FATHER
    DIVINE (WHERE?)
DUBOIS (WHEN?) MALCOLM (OH!) SEND FOR STOKELY. (NO?)
    THEN
SEND FOR ADAM POWELL ON A NON-SUBPOENA DAY.
SEND FOR THE PIED PIPER TO PIPE OUR RATS AWAY.

(And if nobody comes, send for me.)

EVA A. JESSYE

The Singer

Because his speech was blunt and manner plain,
Untaught in subtle phrases of the wise;
Because the years of slavery and pain
Ne'er dimmed the light of faith within his eyes;
Because of ebon skin and humble pride,
The world with hatred thrust the youth aside.

But fragrance wafts from every trodden flower,
And through our grief we rise to nobler things,
Within the heart in sorrow's darkest hour
A well of sweetness there unbidden springs;
Despised of men, discarded and alone—
The world of nature claimed him as her own.

She taught him truth that liberates the soul
From bonds more galling than the slaver's chain—
That manly natures, lily-wise, unfold
Amid the mire of hatred void of stain;
Thus in his manhood, clean, superbly strong,
To him was born the priceless gift of song.

The glory of the sun, the hush of morn,
Whisperings of tree-top faintly stirred,
The desert silence, wilderness forlorn,
Far ocean depths, the tender lilt of bird;
Of hope, despair, he sang, his melody
The endless theme of Life's brief symphony.

And nations marveled at the minstrel lad,
Who swayed emotions as his fancy led;
With him they wept, were melancholy, sad;
"'Tis but a cunning jest of Fate," they said;
They did not dream in selfish spheres apart
That song is but the essence of the heart.

217

The Maestro

Like silence tensely gripped an eager world
Ere seas were loosed, or restless winds unbound—

Emotion etched in steel, the master stands,
Infinitely of sound held breathless neath his hands.

A signal—and an instant crash of thunder
Bursts forth as from one pulsing, golden throat;
Each instrument he calls in turn; the brasses
Reply with Greed's impatient, strident note.
Sweet viols speak of Love; harsh reeds complaining,
The cello's sob of anguish pierces through:
For one brief bar the tranquil harp, consoling,
Till clashing cymbal spurs the Strife anew.
The drum's sharp rat-a-tat of Circumstance
Soon changes to the steady roll of Fate—
Soft throbbing through the maze in rhythmic measure
The motif of the whole, inviolate.

His ears attuned to symphonies of Heav'n,
And soul aswoon in ecstacy divine—
The master senses through the burning cadence
The moods and passion of all Humankind;
And swift he weaves from thread of sound outpouring
Immortal Rhapsody of Joy and Pain,
Where, ever like a mystic strand of scarlet,
The minor theme of Life recurs again.

GEORGIA DOUGLAS JOHNSON

The Heart of a Woman

The heart of a woman goes forth with the dawn,
As a lone bird, soft winging, so restlessly on,
Afar o'er life's turrets and vales does it roam
In the wake of those echoes the heart calls home.

The heart of a woman falls back with the night,
And enters some alien cage in its plight,
And tries to forget it has dreamed of the stars
While it breaks, breaks, breaks on the sheltering bars.

Cosmopolite

Not wholly this or that,
But wrought
Of alien bloods am I,
A product of the interplay
Of traveled hearts.
Estranged, yet not estranged, I stand
All comprehending;
From my estate
I view earth's frail dilemma;
Scion of fused strength am I,
All understanding,
Nor this nor that
Contains me.

Black Woman

Don't knock at my door, little child,
    I cannot let you in,

You know not what a world this is
    Of cruelty and sin.
Wait in the still eternity
    Until I come to you,
The world is cruel, cruel, child,
    I cannot let you in!

Don't knock at my heart, little one,
    I cannot bear the pain
Of turning deaf-ear to your call
    Time and time again!
You do not know the monster men
    Inhabiting the earth,
Be still, be still, my precious child,
    I must not give you birth!

Old Black Men

They have dreamed as young men dream
Of glory, love and power;
They have hoped as youth will hope
Of life's sun-minted hour.

They have seen as others saw
Their bubbles burst in air,
And they have learned to live it down
As though they did not care.

Common Dust

And who shall separate the dust
Which later we shall be:
Whose keen discerning eye will scan
And solve the mystery?

The high, the low, the rich, the poor,
The black, the white, the red,
And all the chromatique between,
Of whom shall it be said:

Here lies the dust of Africa;
Here are the sons of Rome;
Here lies one unlabelled
The world at large his home!

Can one then separate the dust,
Will mankind lie apart,
When life has settled back again
The same as from the start?

I Want to Die While You Love Me

I want to die while you love me,
  While yet you hold me fair,
While laughter lies upon my lips
  And lights are in my hair.

I want to die while you love me
  And bear to that still bed
Your kisses—turbulent, unspent,
  To warm me when I'm dead.

I want to die while you love me
  Oh, who would care to live,
'Til love has nothing more to ask
  And nothing more to give.

Interracial

Let's build bridges here and there
Or sometimes, just a spiral stair
That we may come somewhat abreast
And sense what cannot be exprest.
And by these measures can be found
A meeting place—a common ground
Nearer the reaches of the heart
Where truth revealed, stands clear, apart;
With understanding come to know
What laughing lips will never show:
How tears and torturing distress
May masquerade as happiness:
Then you will know when my heart's aching
And I, when yours is slowly breaking.

Commune—The altars will reveal . . .
We then shall be impulsed to kneel
And send a prayer upon its way
For those who wear the thorns today.

Oh, let's build bridges everywhere
And span the gulf of challenge there.

HELENE JOHNSON

Sonnet to a Negro in Harlem

You are disdainful and magnificent—
Your perfect body and your pompous gait,
Your dark eyes flashing solemnly with hate,
Small wonder that you are incompetent
To imitate those whom you so despise—
Your shoulders towering high above the throng,
Your head thrown back in rich, barbaric song,
Palm trees and mangoes stretched before your eyes.
Let others toil and sweat for labor's sake
And wring from grasping hands their meed of gold.
Why urge ahead your supercilious feet?
Scorn will efface each footprint that you make.
I love your laughter arrogant and bold.
You are too splendid for this city street!

Poem

Little brown boy,
Slim, dark, big-eyed,
Crooning love songs to your banjo
Down at the Lafayette—
Gee, boy, I love the way you hold your head,
High sort of and a bit to one side,
Like a prince, a jazz prince. And I love
Your eyes flashing, and your hands,
And your patent-leathered feet,
And your shoulders jerking the jig-wa.
And I love your teeth flashing,
And the way your hair shines in the spotlight
Like it was the real stuff.
Gee, brown boy, I loves you all over.
I'm glad I'm a jig. I'm glad I can

Understand your dancin' and your
Singin', and feel all the happiness
And joy and don't-care in you.
Gee, boy, when you sing, I can close my ears
And hear tomtoms just as plain.
Listen to me, will you, what do I know
About tomtoms? But I like the word, sort of,
Don't you? It belongs to us.
Gee, boy, I love the way you hold your head,
And the way you sing and dance,
And everything,
Say, I think you're wonderful. You're
All right with me,
You are.

Invocation

Let me be buried in the rain
In a deep, dripping wood,
Under the warm wet breast of Earth
Where once a gnarled tree stood.
And paint a picture on my tomb
With dirt and a piece of bough
Of a girl and a boy beneath a round, ripe moon
Eating of love with an eager spoon
And vowing an eager vow.
And do not keep my plot mowed smooth
And clean as a spinster's bed,
But let the weed, the flower, the tree,
Riotous, rampant, wild and free,
Grow high above my head.

AGNES MAXWELL-HALL

Jamaica Market

Honey, pepper, leaf-green limes,
Pagan fruit whose names are rhymes,
Mangoes, breadfruit, ginger-roots,
Granadillas, bamboo-shoots,
Cho-cho, ackees, tangerines,
Lemons, purple Congo-beans,
Sugar, okras, kola-nuts,
Citrons, hairy cocoanuts,
Fish, tobacco, native hats,
Gold bananas, woven mats,
Plantains, wild-thyme, pallid leeks,
Pigeons with their scarlet beaks,
Oranges and saffron yams,
Baskets, ruby guava jams,
Turtles, goat-skins, cinnamon,
Allspice, conch-shells, golden rum.
Black skins, babel—and the sun
That burns all colours into one.

CLAUDE McKAY

Christmas in de Air

Dere is Christmas in de air:—
But de house is cold an' bare,
An' me wife half paralize'
Is a-dyin' wid bad eyes;
Food too is so extra dear,
An' dere's Christmas in de air.

Oh! de time is 'tiff wid me!
Coffee parch up 'pon de tree,
All de yam-plants tek an' die
'Counten o' de awful dry:
Ah, I wonder how we'll fare,
Although Christmas in de air.

We no e'en hab mancha leaf
T'rough de miserable t'ief,
Not a money fe buy clo'es
Fe Joanna or fe Rose;
Dey're so awful short o' gear,
An' dere's Christmas in de air.

Dere's me poo' wife sick in bed
An' de children to be fed,
While de baby 'pon me knee
Is as hungry as can be
Ah tough life, so cold an' drear!
Yet dere a Christmas in de air.

Wuk is shet do'n 'pon de road,
An' plantation pay no good.
Whole day ninepence for a man!
Wha' dah come to dis ya lan'?
Lard, I trimble when I hear
Dat dere's Christmas in de air.

226

Gov'mint seem no hea' de cry
Dat de price o' food is high,
Not a single wud is said
'Bouten taxes to be paid;
Same old taxes ebery year,
Though dere's hunger in de air.

While we batter t'rough de tret,
'Tis a reg'lar pay dem get;
While we're sufferin' in pain
Dem can talk 'bout surplus-gain;
Oh me God! de sad do'n-care,
An' dere's *Hard Times* in de air.

But we'll batter on tell deat',
Holdin' life in desp'rate fait',
For we're foolish 'nough to know
Life is but a poppy show;
We feel glad de end is near,
Though dere's Christmas in de air.

O sweet life so sad, so gay,
Oh why did you come my way,
All your gaiety to vaunt
An' yet torture me wid want?
I'm a-dyin' o' despair
While dere's Christmas in de air.

The Harlem Dancer

Applauding youths laughed with young prostitutes
And watched her perfect, half-clothed body sway;
Her voice was like the sound of blended flutes
Blown by black players upon a picnic day.
She sang and danced on gracefully and calm,
The light gauze hanging loose about her form;
To me she seemed a proudly-swaying palm
Grown lovelier for passing through a storm.

Upon her swarthy neck black shiny curls
Luxuriant fell; and tossing coins in praise,
The wine-flushed, bold-eyed boys, and even the girls,
Devoured her shape with eager, passionate gaze;
But looking at her falsely-smiling face,
I knew her self was not in that strange place.

Harlem Shadows

I hear the halting footsteps of a lass
    In Negro Harlem when the night lets fall
Its veil. I see the shapes of girls who pass
    To bend and barter at desire's call.
Ah, little dark girls who in slippered feet
Go prowling through the night from street to street!

Through the long night until the silver break
    Of day the little gray feet know no rest;
Through the lone night until the last snow-flake
    Has dropped from heaven upon the earth's white breast,
The dusky, half-clad girls of tired feet
Are trudging, thinly shod, from street to street.

Ah, stern harsh world, that in the wretched way
    Of poverty, dishonor and disgrace,
Has pushed the timid little feet of clay,
    The sacred brown feet of my fallen race!
Ah, heart of me, the weary, weary feet
In Harlem wandering from street to street.

If We Must Die

If we must die, let it not be like hogs
Hunted and penned in an inglorious spot,
While round us bark the mad and hungry dogs,
Making their mock at our accursèd lot.

If we must die, O let us nobly die,
So that our precious blood may not be shed
In vain; then even the monsters we defy
Shall be constrained to honor us though dead!
O kinsmen! we must meet the common foe!
Though far outnumbered let us show us brave,
And for their thousand blows deal one death-blow!
What though before us lies the open grave?
Like men we'll face the murderous, cowardly pack,
Pressed to the wall, dying, but fighting back!

On Broadway

About me young and careless feet
Linger along the garish street;
    Above, a hundred shouting signs
Shed down their bright fantastic glow
    Upon the merry crowd and lines
Of moving carriages below:
O wonderful is Broadway—only
My heart, my heart is lonely.

Desire naked, linked with Passion,
Goes strutting by in brazen fashion;
    From playhouse, cabaret and inn
The rainbow lights of Broadway blaze
    All gay without, all glad within;
As in a dream I stand and gaze
At Broadway, shining Broadway—only
My heart, my heart is lonely.

The Tropics in New York

Bananas ripe and green, and ginger-root,
    Cocoa in pods and alligator pears,
And tangerines and mangoes and grape fruit,
    Fit for the highest prize at parish fairs,

Set in the window, bringing memories
   Of fruit-trees laden by low-singing rills,
And dewy dawns, and mystical blue skies
   In benediction over nun-like hills.

My eyes grew dim, and I could no more gaze;
   A wave of longing through my body swept,
And, hungry for the old, familiar ways,
   I turned aside and bowed my head and wept.

The Lynching

His Spirit in smoke ascended to high heaven.
His father, by the cruelest way of pain,
Had bidden him to his bosom once again;
The awful sin remained still unforgiven.
All night a bright and solitary star
(Perchance the one that ever guided him,
Yet gave him up at last to Fate's wild whim)
Hung pitifully o'er the swinging char.
Day dawned, and soon the mixed crowds came to view
The ghastly body swaying in the sun
The women thronged to look, but never a one
Showed sorrow in her eyes of steely blue;
And little lads, lynchers that were to be,
Danced round the dreadful thing in fiendish glee.

America

Although she feeds me bread of bitterness,
And sinks into my throat her tiger's tooth,
Stealing my breath of life, I will confess
I love this cultured hell that tests my youth!
Her vigor flows like tides into my blood,
Giving me strength erect against her hate.

Her bigness sweeps my being like a flood.
Yet as a rebel fronts a king in state,
I stand within her walls with not a shred
Of terror, malice, not a word of jeer.
Darkly I gaze into the days ahead,
And see her might and granite wonders there,
Beneath the touch of Time's unerring hand,
Like priceless treasures sinking in the sand.

My Mother

I

Reg wished me to go with him to the field,
I paused because I did not want to go;
But in her quiet way she made me yield
Reluctantly, for she was breathing low.
Her hand she slowly lifted from her lap
And, smiling sadly in the old sweet way,
She pointed to the nail where hung my cap.
Her eyes said: I shall last another day.
But scarcely had we reached the distant place,
When o'er the hills we heard a faint bell ringing;
A boy came running up with frightened face;
We knew the fatal news that he was bringing.
I heard him listlessly, without a moan,
Although the only one I loved was gone.

II

The dawn departs, the morning is begun,
The trades come whispering from off the seas,
The fields of corn are golden in the sun,
The dark-brown tassels fluttering in the breeze;
The bell is sounding and the children pass,
Frog-leaping, skipping, shouting, laughing shrill,
Down the red road, over the pasture-grass,
Up to the school-house crumbling on the hill.
The older folk are at their peaceful toil,

Some pulling up the weeds, some plucking corn,
And others breaking up the sun-baked soil.
Float, faintly-scented breeze, at early morn
Over the earth where mortals sow and reap—
Beneath its breast my mother lies asleep.

———————

The white man is a tiger at my throat
Drinking my blood as my life ebbs away,
While saying that his terribly striped coat
Is Democracy's and means the Light of Day.
Oh white man, you may suck all of my blood
And throw my carcass into potter's field,
But never will I say with you your mud
Is bread for Negroes! Never will I yield.

Europe and Asia, Africa await
A new Fascism, the American brand,
And new worlds will be built upon race and hate
And the Eagle and the Dollar will command.
Oh Lord, my body and my heart too break,
The tiger in his strength his thirst must slake!

MYRA ESTELLE MORRIS

Man and Maid

Dear human beings:
For forty long years
I've tried to learn
What puzzled philosophers
For four hundred years;
The thing that Solomon
Four thousand years ago
Didn't know—
To wit:
The way of a man
With a maid.
Now just last night
While we cozily sat
Around the fire
Digesting our food
And thanking God
'Way off in His heaven
That all's well with our world;
From out of the night
Came a woman's scream
That chilled our spines;
And someone yelled:
They're fighting!
We dropped our papers
And forgot our peace
And madly rushed
To the little white house
Next door to us.
We grabbed his wife
And held them tight
But they continued to fight
In spite of us
With words.
The man was driven

From the door
Never to return
Again.
We cleared the house
Of broken vases
Of smashed chairs
And pieces of dishes;
We even bandaged
As best we could
The maid's hurt feelings
With condemnations
And offered refuge
In our house for the night.
But that very same night
The man returned
To his wife and bed;
Forgotten the fight
And what was said.
All that the woman
Had solemnly vowed
She'd never again do
She did.
Such is the way
Of a man with a maid
Which passes all understanding.

RICHARD BRUCE NUGENT

Shadow

Silhouette
On the face of the moon
Am I.
A dark shadow in the light.
A silhouette am I
On the face of the moon
Lacking color
Or vivid brightness
But defined all the clearer
Because
I am dark,
Black on the face of the moon.
A shadow am I
Growing in the light,
Not understood as is the day,
But more easily seen
Because
I am a shadow in the light.

LUCIA MAE PITTS

Requiem

If I should hear tonight that you were dead,
forsaking me and all this earthly place,
I do not think that I would bow my head
and weep wild tears into a square of lace.
I think I'd only silently arise
and step outside, then walk and walk and walk
until I found some hill that touched the skies,
long leagues away from any madd'ning talk.
High up, where stars swarm bright, I'd disembark
my sorrow on the cool, receptive ground.
And in that quiet place, warmed by the spark
of memory, I think strength could be found
to bear my loss dry-eyed, and see the days
go by much as before—though with less praise . . .

This Is My Vow

This I have made my sacred vow:
The god of bitterness shall never be my god.
Whatever is, or was, or is to be,
When I go down to death, to greet the sod,
I'll go with a taste in my mouth
Of the wine of very heaven.
The bitter cup the jaded Life need never give,
For I shall never drink it—never while I live.

The sweeter draught I take for mine.
The cup of life, when first we sip, has little taste
But may, upon our whims as years go by,
Be filled with sweetest wine or bitter waste.
I have known pain and misery
But that I swear I will forget,

Remembering only hours that made the happy years:
I will not spoil my piquant wine with bitter tears.

I shall pluck moments from the days
As I would pluck the loveliest flowers from their bed.
These I will keep for my remembering—
Forgetting fingers that the thorns have bled.
Love and beauty, these will I hold,
And dancing hours, with music in my ears.
This is my vow: When I go down at last to death,
Who leans near me will catch the sweetness of my breath.

ESTHER POPEL

October Prayer

Change me, oh God,
Into a tree in autumn,
And let my dying
Be a blaze of glory!

Drape me in a
Crimson, leafy gown,
And deck my soul
In dancing flakes of gold!

And then when Death
Comes by, and with his hands
Strips off my rustling garment
Let me stand

Before him, proud and naked,
Unashamed, uncaring,
All the strength in me revealed
Against the sky!

Oh, God,
Make me an autumn tree
If I must die!

Flag Salute

(Note: In a classroom in a Negro school a pupil gave as his news topic
during the opening exercises of the morning, a report of the Princess
Anne lynching of Oct. 18, 1933. A brief discussion of the facts of the
case followed, after which the student in charge gave this direction:
Pupils, rise, and give the flag salute! They did so without hesitation!)

"*I pledge allegiance to the flag*"—
They dragged him naked
Through the muddy streets,
A feeble-minded black boy!
And the charge? Supposed assault
Upon an aged woman!
"*Of the United States of America*"—
One mile they dragged him
Like a sack of meal,
A rope around his neck,
A bloody ear
Left dangling by the patriotic hand
Of Nordic youth! (A boy of seventeen!)
"*And to the Republic for which it stands*"—
And then they hanged his body to a tree,
Below the window of the county judge
Whose pleadings for that battered human flesh
Were stifled by the brutish, raucous howls
Of men, and boys, and women with their babes,
Brought out to see the bloody spectacle
Of murder in the style of '33!
(Three thousand strong, they were!)
"*One Nation, Indivisible*"—
To make the tale complete
They built a fire—
What matters that the stuff they burned
Was flesh—and bone—and hair—
And reeking gasoline!
"*With Liberty—and Justice*"—
They cut the rope in bits
And passed them out,
For souvenirs, among the men and boys!
The teeth no doubt, on golden chains
Will hang
About the favored necks of sweethearts, wives,
And daughters, mothers, sisters, babies, too!
"*For All!*"

ANDY RAZAF

Black and Blue

VERSE

Out in the street,
Shufflin' feet
Couples passin' two by two,
While here am I,
Left high and dry
Black, and 'cause I'm black I'm blue.
Browns and yellers
All have fellers,
Gentlemen prefer them light.
Wish I could fade,
Can't make the grade,
Nothin' but dark days in sight.

REFRAIN I

Cold, empty bed,
Springs hard as lead,
Pains in my head,
Feel like old Ned,
What did I do
To be so black and blue?
No joys for me,
No company,
Even the mouse
Ran from my house,
All my life through
I've been so black and blue.
I'm white
Inside,
It don't help my case,
'Cause I
Can't hide

What is on my face, ooh!
I'm so forlorn,
Life's just a thorn,
My heart is torn,
Why was I born?
What did I do
To be so black and blue?

REFRAIN 2

Just 'cause you're black,
Folks think you lack,
They laugh at you,
And scorn you too
What did I do
To be so black and blue?
When you are near,
They laugh and sneer,
Set you aside
And you're denied:
What did I do
To be so black and blue?
How sad I am,
Each day I feel worse,
My mark of Ham
Seems to be a curse, ooh!
How will it end?
Ain't got a friend,
My only sin
Is in my skin,
What did I do
To be so black and blue?

The Tree of Hope

Under the weary Tree of Hope
  A sad performer stands.
His ribs (from months of "miss-meal cramps")
  Stand out like iron bands,
His brow is wet with gin-mill sweat,
  Reefer stains are on his hands.

And there he talks from sun to sun
  Of the shows that he has stopped,
But never once will he admit
  The times that he has flopped;
He brags about the dough he's earned
  And the dough that he has dropped.

He says show business has been ruined
  By the chiselers in the game;
That they treat performers worse than dogs
  And their salaries are a shame,
But it has never occurred to him
  That he has himself to blame.

He never stands up like a man
  For his profession's sake,
But plays the role of Uncle Tom
  When his own job is at stake;
He'll play a dozen shows a day—
  Any cut he'll gladly take.

Week in, week out, from year to year,
  This same performer goes;
Nothing attempted, nothing done
  But installment cars and clothes;
Just a "big-timer," never looking
  Further than his nose.

Thanks, thanks to thee, my stupid friend
  For the lessons thou hast taught:
The chances and the coin you've had
  Mean absolutely naught.
What would you have, the money now
  Or the gin that you have bought?

ANNE SPENCER

At the Carnival

Gay little Girl-of-the-Diving-Tank,
I desire a name for you,
Nice, as a right glove fits;
For you—who amid the malodorous
Mechanics of this unlovely thing,
Are darling of spirit and form.
I know you—a glance, and what you are
Sits-by-the-fire in my heart.
My Limousine-Lady knows you, or
Why does the slant-envy of her eye mark
Your straight air and radiant inclusive smile?
Guilt pins a fig-leaf; Innocence is its own adorning.
The bull-necked man knows you—this first time
His itching flesh sees form divine and vibrant health
And thinks not of his avocation.
I came incuriously—
Set on no diversion save that my mind
Might safely nurse its brood of misdeeds
In the presence of a blind crowd.
The color of life was gray.
Everywhere the setting seemed right
For my mood.
Here the sausage and garlic booth
Sent unholy incense skyward;
There a quivering female-thing
Gestured assignations, and lied
To call it dancing;
There, too, were games of chance
With chances for none;
But oh! Girl-of-the-Tank, at last!
Gleaming Girl, how intimately pure and free
The gaze you send the crowd,
As though you know the dearth of beauty
In its sordid life.

We need you—my Limousine-Lady,
The bull-necked man and I.
Seeing you here brave and water-clean,
Leaven for the heavy ones of earth,
I am swift to feel that what makes
The plodder glad is good; and
Whatever is good is God.
The wonder is that you are here;
I have seen the queer in queer places,
But never before a heaven-fed
Naiad of the Carnival-Tank!
Little Diver, Destiny for you,
Like as for me, is shod in silence;
Years may seep into your soul
The bacilli of the usual and the expedient;
I implore Neptune to claim his child today!

White Things

Most things are colorful things—the sky, earth, and sea.
Black men are most men; but the white are free!
White things are rare things; so rare, so rare
They stole from out a silvered world—somewhere.
Finding earth-plains fair plains, save greenly grassed,
They strewed white feathers of cowardice, as they passed;
  The golden stars with lances fine,
  The hills all red and darkened pine,
They blanched with their wand of power;
And turned the blood in a ruby rose
To a poor white poppy-flower.

They pyred a race of black, black men,
And burned them to ashes white; then,
Laughing, a young one claimed a skull,
For the skull of a black is white, not dull,
  But a glistening awful thing;
  Made it seems, for this ghoul to swing

In the face of God with all his might,
And swear by the hell that siréd him:
      "Man-maker, make white!"

Sybil Warns Her Sister

It is dangerous for a woman to defy the gods;
To taunt them with the tongue's thin tip,
Or strut in the weakness of mere humanity,
Or draw a line daring them to cross;
The gods who own the searing lightning,
The drowning waters, the tormenting fears,
The anger of red sins . . .
Oh, but worse still if you mince along timidly—
Dodge this way or that, or kneel, or pray,
Or be kind, or sweat agony drops,
Or lay your quick body over your feeble young,
If you have beauty or plainness, if celibate,
Or vowed—the gods are Juggernaut,
Passing over each of us . . .
    Or this you may do:
Lock your heart, then, quietly,
And, lest they peer within,
Light no lamp when dark comes down
Raise no shade for sun,
Breathless must your breath come thru,
If you'd die and dare deny
The gods their god-like fun!

JEAN TOOMER

Five Vignettes

1

The red-tiled ships you see reflected,
Are nervous,
And afraid of clouds.

2

There, on the clothes-line
Still as she pinned them,
Pieces now the wind may wear.

3

The old man, at ninety,
Eating peaches,
Is he not afraid of worms?

4

Wear my thimble of agony
And when you sew,
No needle points will prick you.

5

In Y. Don's laundry
A Chinese baby fell
And cried as any other.

Her Lips Are Copper Wire

whisper of yellow globes
gleaming on lamp-posts that sway
like bootleg licker drinkers in the fog

and let your breath be moist against me
like bright beads on yellow globes

telephone the power-house
that the main wires are insulate

(her words play softly up and down
dewy corridors of billboards)

then with your tongue remove the tape
and press your lips to mine
till they are incandescent

from *Cane*

REAPERS

Black reapers with the sound of steel on stones
Are sharpening scythes. I see them place the hones
In their hip-pockets as a thing that's done.
And start their silent swinging, one by one.
Black horses drive a mower through the weeds.
And there, a field rat, startled, squealing bleeds.
His belly close to ground. I see the blade,
Blood-stained, continue cutting weeds and shade.

NOVEMBER COTTON FLOWER

Boll-weevil's coming, and the winter's cold,
Made cotton-stalks look rusty, season's old,
And cotton, scarce as any southern snow,
Was vanishing; the branch, so pinched and slow,
Failed in its function as the autumn rake;
Drouth fighting soil had caused the soil to take
All water from the streams; dead birds were found

In wells a hundred feet below the ground—
Such was the season when the flower bloomed.
Old folks were startled, and it soon assumed
Significance. Superstition saw
Something it had never seen before:
Brown eyes that loved without a trace of fear,
Beauty so sudden for that time of year.

COTTON SONG

Come, brother, come. Lets lift it;
Come now, hewit! roll away!
Shackles fall upon the Judgment Day
But lets not wait for it.

God's body's got a soul,
Bodies like to roll the soul,
Cant blame God if we dont roll,
Come, brother, roll, roll!

Cotton bales are the fleecy way
Weary sinner's bare feet trod,
Softly, softly to the throne of God,
"We aint agwine t wait until th Judgment Day!

Nassur; nassur,
Hump.
Eoho, eoho, roll away!
We aint agwine t wait until th Judgment Day!"

God's body's got a soul,
Bodies like to roll the soul,
Cant blame God if we dont roll,
Come, brother, roll, roll!

SONG OF THE SON

Pour O pour that parting soul in song,
O pour it in the sawdust glow of night,
Into the velvet pine-smoke air tonight,
And let the valley carry it along.
And let the valley carry it along.

O land and soil, red soil and sweet-gum tree,
So scant of grass, so profligate of pines,
Now just before an epoch's sun declines
Thy son, in time, I have returned to thee.
Thy son, I have in time returned to thee.

In time, for though the sun is setting on
A song-lit race of slaves, it has not set;
Though late, O soil, it is not too late yet
To catch thy plaintive soul, leaving, soon gone,
Leaving, to catch thy plaintive soul soon gone.

O Negro slaves, dark purple ripened plums,
Squeezed, and bursting in the pine-wood air,
Passing, before they stripped the old tree bare
One plum was saved for me, one seed becomes

An everlasting song, a singing tree,
Caroling softly souls of slavery,
What they were, and what they are to me,
Caroling softly souls of slavery.

GEORGIA DUSK

The sky, lazily disdaining to pursue
    The setting sun, too indolent to hold
    A lengthened tournament for flashing gold,
Passively darkens for night's barbeque,

A feast of moon and men and barking hounds.
　　An orgy for some genius of the South
　　With blood-hot eyes and cane-lipped scented mouth,
Surprised in making folk-songs from soul sounds.

The sawmill blows its whistle, buzz-saws stop,
　　And silence breaks the bud of knoll and hill,
　　Soft settling pollen where plowed lands fulfill
Their early promise of a bumper crop.

Smoke from the pyramidal sawdust pile
　　Curls up, blue ghosts of trees, tarrying low
　　Where only chips and stumps are left to show
The solid proof of former domicile.

Meanwhile, the men, with vestiges of pomp,
　　Race memories of king and caravan,
　　High-priests, an ostrich, and a juju-man,
Go singing through the footpaths of the swamp.

Their voices rise . . the pine trees are guitars,
　　Strumming, pine-needles fall like sheets of rain . .
　　Their voices rise . . the chorus of the cane
Is caroling a vesper to the stars . .

O singers, resinous and soft your songs
　　Above the sacred whisper of the pines,
　　Give virgin lips to cornfield concubines,
Bring dreams of Christ to dusky cane-lipped throngs.

from *Essentials*

VIII

Productivity is my first aim.

I struggle that I may not die through life.

He is soil no longer fertile for me to plant in.

We must husk off even friends—to make way for new friends.

Growing is a stern taking and eliminating, as relentless as life
    itself.

XXIV

I am of no particular race. I am of the human race, a man at
    large in the human world, preparing a new race.

I am of no specific region. I am of earth.

I am of no particular class. I am of the human class,
    preparing a new class.

I am neither male nor female nor in-between. I am of sex,
    with male differentiations.

I am of no special field. I am of the field of being.

XL

Each of us has in himself a fool who says I'm wise.

Most novices picture themselves as masters—and are content
    with the picture.
    This is why there are so few masters.

When I speak I am persuaded.

People mistake their limitations for high standards.

Ordinarily, each person is a cartoon of himself.

Be with Me

I hoped that you
Would help me tap the second stream
And reverse my steps, the ages
I have walked away
Seeking I knew not what.

You did not fail me;
To the second station I did not arise,
Hearing the strange accents
Of our native language
  While those around me
  Call me dead.

Dead to the first
I live to the second;
And when I die where now I live,
And all these people call me dead,
  Do you, dark sister,
  Not forsake me.

FOUR
BALLADS OF REMEMBRANCE
(1936–1959)

SAMUEL ALLEN

To Satch (*American Gothic*)

Sometimes I feel like I will *never* stop
Just go on forever
Till one fine mornin'
I'm gonna reach up and grab me a handfulla stars
Swing out my long lean leg
And whip three hot strikes burnin' down the heavens
And look over at God and say
How about that!

Nat Turner or *Let Him Come*

An Invitational Appeal

From the obscurity of the past, we saw
the dark now flaming face of a giant Nathaniel
calling
whosoever will
let him come.

For a moment, Turner's features softened
    he mourned the lost years
    the centuries of lined and somber faces
    the broken ranks of his people
    thousands by the tens of thousands
    torn from the soil of their fathers
    to death in life
        on bleak, distant shores.

And his face hardened
and we heard, again, the voice, calling
Whosoever will

Let him come
Let him come now
Him who can hear
Whosoever will—Come
Him who thirsts—Ha
Would drink of the waters—Come
Would drink of the waters of life
Would drink freely.

   Is there one?
   Is there anyone?

I who speak according to prophecy
In his name I say Come
For the thousands gone, Come
For the living the dead and the not yet born, I say Come

   Is there one?
   Is there anyone?
   Even so. Thank God. Praise him.
   I say Come.

   Is there another? Is there one?
   I say Come.

I which testify these things—Ha!
Surely now—who would—Ha!
Let him come. Let him come quickly—Ha!

   Even so. Thanks be to God. Yes, another!
   You will drink, my brother, of the breaking waters
   of free*dom*. Thanks be to the father!
   Is there another? Is there another? Let him come.
   Yes, come weeping. Come rejoicing!
   My God, come! I say, Come!
   Yes, another and another.
   Thanks be to the father.
   All, come. I say, Come!

Who would drink—Ha!
Anyman—Ha!
Whosoever—

   Yes, even so. Thank God. Let them come!

Yesssss, my brothers!
everyman, anyman—in the sound of my voice!
The time is coming
Now so I testify
I which—Ha! say anyman—Ha!
which—shall drink
of the cooling waters
though he die—yessss—shall he live

   Let him come
   The sign is come
   NOW!
   Let him comoan
   Come!

If the Stars Should Fall

   Again the day
   The low bleak day of the stricken years
   And now the years.

   The huge slow grief drives on
   And I wonder why
   And I grow cold
   And care less
   And less and less I care.

   If the stars should fall,
   I grant them privilege;
   Or should they rise to brighter flame
   The mighty Dog, the buckled Orion
   To excellent purposes should gain—

I would renew their privilege
To fall.

It is all to me the same
The same to me
I say the great gods, all of them, all
    —cold, pitiless—
Let them fall down
Let them buckle and drop.

RUSSELL ATKINS

Narrative

I sat with John Brown. That night moonlight framed
    the blown of his beard like a portent's undivulged.
He came and said 'It's Harper's, men!'

Now Harper's was a place in which death thousand'd for us!
Already our faces, even as he told of how,
    sweated. And then suddenly, he,
with fierced spark'd eye—incredible heavens!

Horses dreadful appearance had of exhumed:
    our boots strode the ready. We dared off.

As generally seeming of the trail
    smooth—and so whist!
    i.e., save sounded thunder
    of us in a rush
    passed swift fierce "ft
    'ierce shsh!!
    'ss'd in a w'isk!
    'ierced passed "ft!
Harper's a!p!p!e!a!r!e!d!
—into it we went in a dust!

"ft passed 'ierced
    "if's, in, ss'd
    shsh "erced
    "ft
    "isk

Night and a Distant Church

Forward abrupt   up
then mmm mm
wind mmm m
        mmm   m
upon
the mm mm
wind mmm m
        mmm
into the mm wind
rain now and again
the mm wind
    ells
b

        ell s
    b

It's Here in The

Here in the newspaper—wreck of the East Bound.
A photograph bound to bring on cardiac asthenia.
There is a blur that mists the pages:
On one side's a gloom of dreadful harsh,
Then breaks flash lights up sheer.
There is much huge about. I suppose
    those no's are people
    between that suffering of—
    (what have we more? for Christ's sake!
Something of a full stop of it
crash of blood and the still shock
  of stark sticks and an immense swift gloss
And two dead no's lie aghast still

One casts a crazed eye and the other's
    closed dull
        the heap twists up
    hardening the unhard, unhardening
    the hardened

Spyrytual

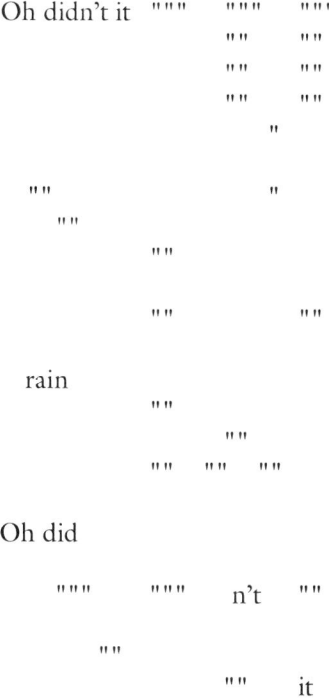

Oh didn't it   """   """"   """"
                  ""   ""
                  ""   ""
                  ""   ""
                        "

    ""   "
      ""
            ""

            ""   ""

    rain
            ""
                ""
            ""   ""   ""

Oh did

      """   """   n't   ""

         ""
              ""   it
    rain

              ""
              ""

GWENDOLYN BROOKS

from *A Street in Bronzeville*

KITCHENETTE BUILDING

We are things of dry hours and the involuntary plan,
Grayed in, and gray. "Dream" makes a giddy sound, not
    strong
Like "rent," "feeding a wife," "satisfying a man."

But could a dream send up through onion fumes
Its white and violet, fight with fried potatoes
And yesterday's garbage ripening in the hall,
Flutter, or sing an aria down these rooms

Even if we were willing to let it in,
Had time to warm it, keep it very clean,
Anticipate a message, let it begin?

We wonder. But not well! not for a minute!
Since Number Five is out of the bathroom now,
We think of lukewarm water, hope to get in it.

THE MOTHER

Abortions will not let you forget.
You remember the children you got that you did not get,
The damp small pulps with a little or with no hair,
The singers and workers that never handled the air.
You will never neglect or beat
Them, or silence or buy with a sweet.
You will never wind up the sucking-thumb
Or scuttle off ghosts that come.
You will never leave them, controlling your luscious sigh,
Return for a snack of them, with gobbling mother-eye.

I have heard in the voices of the wind the voices of my dim
    killed children.
I have contracted. I have eased
My dim dears at the breasts they could never suck.
I have said, Sweets, if I sinned, if I seized
Your luck
And your lives from your unfinished reach,
If I stole your births and your names,
Your straight baby tears and your games,
Your stilted or lovely loves, your tumults, your marriages,
    aches, and your deaths,
If I poisoned the beginnings of your breaths,
Believe that even in my deliberateness I was not deliberate.
Though why should I whine,
Whine that the crime was other than mine?—
Since anyhow you are dead.
Or rather, or instead,
You were never made.
But that too, I am afraid,
Is faulty: oh, what shall I say, how is the truth to be said?
You were born, you had body, you died.
It is just that you never giggled or planned or cried.

Believe me, I loved you all.
Believe me, I knew you, though faintly, and I loved, I loved
    you
All.

A SONG IN THE FRONT YARD

I've stayed in the front yard all my life.
I want a peek at the back
Where it's rough and untended and hungry weed grows.
A girl gets sick of a rose.

I want to go in the back yard now
And maybe down the alley,
To where the charity children play.
I want a good time today.

They do some wonderful things.
They have some wonderful fun.
My mother sneers, but I say it's fine
How they don't have to go in at quarter to nine.
My mother, she tells me that Johnnie Mae
Will grow up to be a bad woman.
That George'll be taken to Jail soon or late
(On account of last winter he sold our back gate.)

But I say it's fine. Honest, I do.
And I'd like to be a bad woman, too,
And wear the brave stockings of night-black lace
And strut down the streets with paint on my face.

SADIE AND MAUD

Maud went to college.
Sadie stayed at home.
Sadie scraped life
With a fine-tooth comb.

She didn't leave a tangle in.
Her comb found every strand.
Sadie was one of the livingest chits
In all the land.

Sadie bore two babies
Under her maiden name.
Maud and Ma and Papa
Nearly died of shame.
Every one but Sadie
Nearly died of shame.

When Sadie said her last so-long
Her girls struck out from home.
(Sadie had left as heritage
Her fine-tooth comb.)

Maud, who went to college,
Is a thin brown mouse.
She is living all alone
In this old house.

Beverly Hills, Chicago

("and the people live till they have white hair")
E. M. PRICE

The dry brown coughing beneath their feet,
(Only a while, for the handyman is on his way)
These people walk their golden gardens.
We say ourselves fortunate to be driving by today.

That we may look at them, in their gardens where
The summer ripeness rots. But not raggedly.
Even the leaves fall down in lovelier patterns here.
And the refuse, the refuse is a neat brilliancy.

When they flow sweetly into their houses
With softness and slowness touched by that everlasting gold,
We know what they go to. To tea. But that does not mean
They will throw some little black dots into some water and
add sugar and the juice of the cheapest lemons that are
sold,

While downstairs that woman's vague phonograph bleats,
"Knock me a kiss."
And the living all to be made again in the sweatingest
physical manner
Tomorrow. . . . Not that anybody is saying that these people
have no trouble.
Merely that it is trouble with a gold-flecked beautiful banner.

Nobody is saying that these people do not ultimately cease to
        be. And
Sometimes their passings are even more painful than ours.
It is just that so often they live till their hair is white.
They make excellent corpses, among the expensive flowers. . . .

Nobody is furious. Nobody hates these people.
At least, nobody driving by in this car.
It is only natural, however, that it should occur to us
How much more fortunate they are than we are.

It is only natural that we should look and look
At their wood and brick and stone
And think, while a breath of pine blows,
How different these are from our own.

We do not want them to have less.
But it is only natural that we should think we have not
        enough.
We drive on, we drive on.
When we speak to each other our voices are a little gruff.

The Bean Eaters

They eat beans mostly, this old yellow pair.
Dinner is a casual affair.
Plain chipware on a plain and creaking wood,
Tin flatware.

Two who are Mostly Good.
Two who have lived their day,
But keep on putting on their clothes
And putting things away.

And remembering . . .
Remembering, with twinklings and twinges,

As they lean over the beans in their rented back room that is
    full of beads and receipts and dolls and cloths, tobacco
    crumbs, vases and fringes.

We Real Cool

*The Pool Players.
Seven at the Golden Shovel.*

    We real cool. We
    Left school. We

    Lurk late. We
    Strike straight. We

    Sing sin. We
    Thin gin. We

    Jazz June. We
    Die soon.

A Bronzeville Mother Loiters in Mississippi. Meanwhile, a Mississippi Mother Burns Bacon

From the first it had been like a
Ballad. It had the beat inevitable. It had the blood.
A wildness cut up, and tied in little bunches,
Like the four-line stanzas of the ballads she had never quite
Understood—the ballads they had set her to, in school.

Herself: the milk-white maid, the "maid mild"
Of the ballad. Pursued
By the Dark Villain. Rescued by the Fine Prince.
The Happiness-Ever-After.
That was worth anything.

It was good to be a "maid mild."
That made the breath go fast.

Her bacon burned. She
Hastened to hide it in the step-on can, and
Drew more strips from the meat case. The eggs and
        sour-milk biscuits
Did well. She set out a jar
Of her new quince preserve.

. . . But there was a something about the matter of the Dark
        Villain.
He should have been older, perhaps.
The hacking down of a villain was more fun to think about
When his menace possessed undisputed breadth, undisputed
        height,
And a harsh kind of vice.
And best of all, when his history was cluttered
With the bones of many eaten knights and princesses.

The fun was disturbed, then all but nullified
When the Dark Villain was a blackish child
Of fourteen, with eyes still too young to be dirty,
And a mouth too young to have lost every reminder
Of its infant softness.

That boy must have been surprised! For
These were grown-ups. Grown-ups were supposed to be wise.
And the Fine Prince—and that other—so tall, so broad, so
Grown! Perhaps the boy had never guessed
That the trouble with grown-ups was that under the
        magnificent shell of adulthood, just under,
Waited the baby full of tantrums.
It occurred to her that there may have been something
Ridiculous in the picture of the Fine Prince
Rushing (rich with the breadth and height and
Mature solidness whose lack, in the Dark Villain, was
        impressing her,
Confronting her more and more as this first day after the
        trial

And acquittal wore on) rushing
With his heavy companion to hack down (unhorsed)
That little foe.
So much had happened, she could not remember now what
    that foe had done
Against her, or if anything had been done.
The one thing in the world that she did know and knew
With terrifying clarity was that her composition
Had disintegrated. That, although the pattern prevailed,
The breaks were everywhere. That she could think
Of no thread capable of the necessary
Sew-work.

She made the babies sit in their places at the table.
Then, before calling Him, she hurried
To the mirror with her comb and lipstick. It was necessary
To be more beautiful than ever.
The beautiful wife.
For sometimes she fancied he looked at her as though
Measuring her. As if he considered, Had she been worth It?
Had *she* been worth the blood, the cramped cries, the little
    stuttering bravado,
The gradual dulling of those Negro eyes,
The sudden, overwhelming *little-boyness* in that barn?
Whatever she might feel or half-feel, the lipstick necessity was
    something apart. He must never conclude
That she had not been worth It.

He sat down, the Fine Prince, and
Began buttering a biscuit. He looked at his hands.
He twisted in his chair, he scratched his nose.
He glanced again, almost secretly, at his hands.
More papers were in from the North, he mumbled. More
    meddling headlines.
With their pepper-words, "bestiality," and "barbarism," and
"Shocking."
The half-sneers he had mastered for the trial worked across
His sweet and pretty face.

What he'd like to do, he explained, was kill them all.
The time lost. The unwanted fame.
Still, it had been fun to show those intruders
A thing or two. To show that snappy-eyed mother,
That sassy, Northern, brown-black—

Nothing could stop Mississippi.
He knew that. Big Fella
Knew that.
And, what was so good, Mississippi knew that.
Nothing and nothing could stop Mississippi.
They could send in their petitions, and scar
Their newspapers with bleeding headlines. Their governors
Could appeal to Washington. . . .

"What I want," the older baby said, "is 'lasses on my jam."
Whereupon the younger baby
Picked up the molasses pitcher and threw
The molasses in his brother's face. Instantly
The Fine Prince leaned across the table and slapped
The small and smiling criminal.

She did not speak. When the Hand
Came down and away, and she could look at her child,
At her baby-child,
She could think only of blood.
Surely her baby's cheek
Had disappeared, and in its place, surely,
Hung a heaviness, a lengthening red, a red that had no end.
She shook her head. It was not true, of course.
It was not true at all. The
Child's face was as always, the
Color of the paste in her paste-jar.

She left the table, to the tune of the children's lamentations,
     which were shriller
Than ever. She
Looked out of a window. She said not a word. *That*
Was one of the new Somethings—

The fear,
Tying her as with iron.

Suddenly she felt his hands upon her. He had followed her
To the window. The children were whimpering now.
Such bits of tots. And she, their mother,
Could not protect them. She looked at her shoulders, still
Gripped in the claim of his hands. She tried, but could not
    resist the idea
That a red ooze was seeping, spreading darkly, thickly, slowly,
Over her white shoulders, her own shoulders,
And over all of Earth and Mars.

He whispered something to her, did the Fine Prince,
    something
About love, something about love and night and intention.
She heard no hoof-beat of the horse and saw no flash of the
    shining steel.

He pulled her face around to meet
His, and there it was, close close,
For the first time in all those days and nights.
His mouth, wet and red,
So very, very, very red,
Closed over hers.

Then a sickness heaved within her. The courtroom
    Coca-Cola,
The courtroom beer and hate and sweat and drone,
Pushed like a wall against her. She wanted to bear it.
But his mouth would not go away and neither would the
Decapitated exclamation points in that Other Woman's eyes.

She did not scream.
She stood there.
But a hatred for him burst into glorious flower,
And its perfume enclasped them—big,
Bigger than all magnolias.

The last bleak news of the ballad.
The rest of the rugged music.
The last quatrain.

The Last Quatrain of the Ballad of Emmett Till

After the Murder,
After the Burial

Emmett's mother is a pretty-faced thing;
        the tint of pulled taffy.
She sits in a red room,
        drinking black coffee.
She kisses her killed boy.
        And she is sorry.
Chaos in windy grays
        through a red prairie.

The Chicago Defender Sends a Man to Little Rock

Fall, 1957

In Little Rock the people bear
Babes, and comb and part their hair
And watch the want ads, put repair
To roof and latch. While wheat toast burns
A woman waters multiferns.

Time upholds or overturns
The many, tight, and small concerns.

In Little Rock the people sing
Sunday hymns like anything,
Through Sunday pomp and polishing.

And after testament and tunes,
Some soften Sunday afternoons
With lemon tea and Lorna Doones.

I forecast
And I believe
Come Christmas Little Rock will cleave
To Christmas tree and trifle, weave,
From laugh and tinsel, texture fast.

In Little Rock is baseball; Barcarolle.
That hotness in July . . . the uniformed figures raw and
        implacable
And not intellectual,
Batting the hotness or clawing the suffering dust.
The Open Air Concert, on the special twilight green . . .
When Beethoven is brutal or whispers to lady-like air.
Blanket-sitters are solemn, as Johann troubles to lean
To tell them what to mean. . . .

There is love, too, in Little Rock. Soft women softly
Opening themselves in kindness,
Or, pitying one's blindness,
Awaiting one's pleasure
In azure
Glory with anguished rose at the root. . . .
To wash away old semi-discomfitures.
They re-teach purple and unsullen blue.
The wispy soils go. And uncertain
Half-havings have they clarified to sures.

In Little Rock they know
Not answering the telephone is a way of rejecting life,
That it is our business to be bothered, is our business
To cherish bores or boredom, be polite
To lies and love and many-faceted fuzziness.

I scratch my head, massage the hate-I-had.
I blink across my prim and pencilled pad.

The saga I was sent for is not down.
Because there is a puzzle in this town.
The biggest News I do not dare
Telegraph to the Editor's chair:
"They are like people everywhere."

The angry Editor would reply
In hundred harryings of Why.

And true, they are hurling spittle, rock,
Garbage and fruit in Little Rock.
And I saw coiling storm a-writhe
On bright madonnas. And a scythe
Of men harassing brownish girls.
(The bows and barrettes in the curls
And braids declined away from joy.)

I saw a bleeding brownish boy. . . .

The lariat lynch-wish I deplored.

The loveliest lynchee was our Lord.

The Lovers of the Poor

      arrive. The Ladies from the Ladies' Betterment League
Arrive in the afternoon, the late light slanting
In diluted gold bars across the boulevard brag
Of proud, seamed faces with mercy and murder hinting
Here, there, interrupting, all deep and debonair,
The pink paint on the innocence of fear;
Walk in a gingerly manner up the hall.
Cutting with knives served by their softest care,
Served by their love, so barbarously fair.
Whose mothers taught: You'd better not be cruel!
You had better not throw stones upon the wrens!
Herein they kiss and coddle and assault

Anew and dearly in the innocence
With which they baffle nature. Who are full,
Sleek, tender-clad, fit, fiftyish, a-glow, all
Sweetly abortive, hinting at fat fruit,
Judge it high time that fiftyish fingers felt
Beneath the lovelier planes of enterprise.
To resurrect. To moisten with milky chill.
To be a random hitching post or plush.
To be, for wet eyes, random and handy hem.
        Their guild is giving money to the poor.
The worthy poor. The very very worthy
And beautiful poor. Perhaps just not too swarthy?
Perhaps just not too dirty nor too dim
Nor—passionate. In truth, what they could wish
Is—something less than derelict or dull.
Not staunch enough to stab, though, gaze for gaze!
God shield them sharply from the beggar-bold!
The noxious needy ones whose battle's bald
Nonetheless for being voiceless, hits one down.
        But it's all so bad! and entirely too much for them.
The stench; the urine, cabbage, and dead beans,
Dead porridges of assorted dusty grains,
The old smoke, *heavy* diapers, and, they're told,
Something called chitterlings. The darkness. Drawn
Darkness, or dirty light. The soil that stirs.
The soil that looks the soil of centuries.
And for that matter the *general* oldness. Old
Wood. Old marble. Old tile. Old old old.
Not homekind Oldness! Not Lake Forest, Glencoe.
Nothing is sturdy, nothing is majestic,
There is no quiet drama, no rubbed glaze, no
Unkillable infirmity of such
A tasteful turn as lately they have left,
Glencoe, Lake Forest, and to which their cars
Must presently restore them. When they're done
With dullards and distortions of this fistic
Patience of the poor and put-upon.
        They've never seen such a make-do-ness as
Newspaper rugs before! In this, this "flat,"

Their hostess is gathering up the oozed, the rich
Rugs of the morning (tattered! the bespattered . . .),
Readies to spread clean rugs for afternoon.
Here is a scene for you. The Ladies look,
In horror, behind a substantial citizeness
Whose trains clank out across her swollen heart.
Who, arms akimbo, almost fills a door.
All tumbling children, quilts dragged to the floor
And tortured thereover, potato peelings, soft-
Eyed kitten, hunched-up, haggard, to-be-hurt.
　　　Their League is allotting largesse to the Lost.
But to put their clean, their pretty money, to put
Their money collected from delicate rose-fingers
Tipped with their hundred flawless rose-nails seems . . .
　　　They own Spode, Lowestoft, candelabra,
Mantels, and hostess gowns, and sunburst clocks,
Turtle soup, Chippendale, red satin "hangings,"
Aubussons and Hattie Carnegie. They Winter
In Palm Beach; cross the Water in June; attend,
When suitable, the nice Art Institute;
Buy the right books in the best bindings; saunter
On Michigan, Easter mornings, in sun or wind.
Oh Squalor! This sick four-story hulk, this fibre
With fissures everywhere! Why, what are bringings
Of loathe-love largesse? What shall peril hungers
So old old, what shall flatter the desolate?
Tin can, blocked fire escape and chitterling
And swaggering seeking youth and the puzzled wreckage
Of the middle passage, and urine and stale shames
And, again, the porridges of the underslung
And children children children. Heavens! That
Was a rat, surely, off there, in the shadows? Long
And long-tailed? Gray? The Ladies from the Ladies'
Betterment League agree it will be better
To achieve the outer air that rights and steadies,
To hie to a house that does not holler, to ring
Bells elsetime, better presently to cater
To no more Possibilities, to get
Away. Perhaps the money can be posted.

Perhaps they two may choose another Slum!
Some serious sooty half-unhappy home!—
Where loathe-love likelier may be invested.
     Keeping their scented bodies in the center
Of the hall as they walk down the hysterical hall,
They allow their lovely skirts to graze no wall,
Are off at what they manage of a canter,
And, resuming all the clues of what they were,
Try to avoid inhaling the laden air.

Malcolm X

For Dudley Randall

Original.
Ragged-round.
Rich-robust.

He had the hawk-man's eyes.
We gasped. We saw the maleness.
The maleness raking out and making guttural the air
and pushing us to walls.

And in a soft and fundamental hour
a sorcery devout and vertical
beguiled the world.

He opened us—
who was a key,

who was a man.

The Second Sermon on the Warpland

For Walter Bradford

1.

This is the urgency: Live!
and have your blooming in the noise of the whirlwind.

2.

Salve salvage in the spin.
Endorse the splendor splashes;
stylize the flawed utility;
prop a malign or failing light—
but know the whirlwind is our commonwealth.
Not the easy man, who rides above them all,
not the jumbo brigand,
not the pet bird of poets, that sweetest sonnet,
shall straddle the whirlwind.
Nevertheless, live.

3.

All about are the cold places,
all about are the pushmen and jeopardy, theft—
all about are the stormers and scramblers but
what must our Season be, which starts from Fear?
Live and go out.
Define and
medicate the whirlwind.

4.

The time
cracks into furious flower. Lifts its face
all unashamed. And sways in wicked grace.
Whose half-black hands assemble oranges
is tom-tom hearted

(goes in bearing oranges and boom).
And there are bells for orphans—
and red and shriek and sheen.
A garbageman is dignified
as any diplomat.
Big Bessie's feet hurt like nobody's business,
but she stands—bigly—under the unruly scrutiny, stands in
      the wild weed.

In the wild weed
she is a citizen,
and is a moment of highest quality; admirable.

It is lonesome, yes. For we are the last of the loud.
Nevertheless, live.

Conduct your blooming in the noise and whip of the
      whirlwind.

Paul Robeson

            That time
            we all heard it,
            cool and clear,
            cutting across the hot grit of the day.
            The major Voice.
            The adult Voice
            forgoing Rolling River,
            forgoing tearful tale of bale and barge
            and other symptoms of an old despond.
            Warning, in music-words
            devout and large,
            that we are each other's
            harvest:
            we are each other's
            business:
            we are each other's
            magnitude and bond.

The Life of Lincoln West

Ugliest little boy
that everyone ever saw.
That is what everyone said.

Even to his mother it was apparent—
when the blue-aproned nurse came into the
northeast end of the maternity ward
bearing his squeals and plump bottom
looped up in a scant receiving blanket,
bending, to pass the bundle carefully
into the waiting mother-hands—that this
was no cute little ugliness, no sly baby waywardness
that was going to inch away
as would baby fat, baby curl, and
baby spot-rash. The pendulous lip, the
branching ears, the eyes so wide and wild,
the vague unvibrant brown of the skin,
and, most disturbing, the great head.
These components of That Look bespoke
the sure fibre. The deep grain.

His father could not bear the sight of him.
His mother high-piled her pretty dyed hair and
put him among her hairpins and sweethearts,
dance slippers, torn paper roses.
He was not less than these,
he was not more.

As the little Lincoln grew,
uglily upward and out, he began
to understand that something was
wrong. His little ways of trying
to please his father, the bringing
of matches, the jumping aside at
warning sound of oh-so-large and
rushing stride, the smile that gave
and gave and gave—Unsuccessful!

Even Christmases and Easters were spoiled.
He would be sitting at the
family feasting table, really
delighting in the displays of mashed potatoes
and the rich golden
fat-crust of the ham or the festive
fowl, when he would look up and find
somebody feeling indignant about him.

What a pity what a pity. No love
for one so loving. The little Lincoln
loved Everybody. Ants. The changing
caterpillar. His much-missing mother.
His kindergarten teacher.

His kindergarten teacher—whose
concern for him was composed of one
part sympathy and two parts repulsion.
The others ran up with their little drawings.
He ran up with his.
She
tried to be as pleasant with him as
with others, but it was difficult.
For she was all pretty! all daintiness,
all tiny vanilla, with blue eyes and fluffy
sun-hair. One afternoon she
saw him in the hall looking bleak against
the wall. It was strange because the
bell had long since rung and no other
child was in sight. Pity flooded her.
She buttoned her gloves and suggested
cheerfully that she walk him home. She
started out bravely, holding him by the
hand. But she had not walked far before
she regretted it. The little monkey.
Must everyone look? And clutching her
hand like that . . . Literally pinching
it . . .

At seven, the little Lincoln loved
the brother and sister who
moved next door. Handsome. Well-
dressed. Charitable, often, to him. They
enjoyed him because he was
resourceful, made up
games, told stories. But when
their More Acceptable friends came they turned
their handsome backs on him. He
hated himself for his feeling
of well-being when with them despite—
Everything.

He spent much time looking at himself
in mirrors. What could be done?
But there was no
shrinking his head. There was no
binding his ears.

"Don't touch me!" cried the little
fairy-like being in the playground.

Her name was Nerissa. The many
children were playing tag, but when
he caught her, she recoiled, jerked free
and ran. It was like all the
rainbow that ever was, going off
forever, all, all the sparklings in
the sunset west.

One day, while he was yet seven,
a thing happened. In the down-town movies
with his mother a white
man in the seat beside him whispered
loudly to a companion, and pointed at
the little Linc.
"THERE! That's the kind I've been wanting
to show you! One of the best
examples of the specie. Not like

those diluted Negroes you see so much of on
the streets these days, but the
real thing.

Black, ugly, and odd. You
can see the savagery. The blunt
blankness. That is the real
thing."

His mother—her hair had never looked so
red around the dark brown
velvet of her face—jumped up,
shrieked "Go to ——" She did not finish.
She yanked to his feet the little
Lincoln, who was sitting there
staring in fascination at his assessor. At the author of his
new idea.

All the way home he was happy. Of course,
he had not liked the word
"ugly."
But, after, should he not
be used to that by now? What had
struck him, among words and meanings
he could little understand, was the phrase
"the real thing."
He didn't know quite why,
but he liked that.
He liked that very much.

When he was hurt, too much
stared at—
too much
left alone—he
thought about that. He told himself
"After all, I'm
the real thing."

It comforted him.

The Boy Died in My Alley

to Running Boy

The Boy died in my alley
without my Having Known.
Policeman said, next morning,
"Apparently died Alone."

"You heard a shot?" Policeman said.
Shots I hear and Shots I hear.
I never see the Dead.

The Shot that killed him yes I heard
as I heard the Thousand shots before;
careening tinnily down the nights
across my years and arteries.

Policeman pounded on my door.
"Who is it?" "POLICE!" Policeman yelled.
"A Boy was dying in your alley.
A Boy is dead, and in your alley.
And have you known this Boy before?"

I have known this Boy before.
I have known this Boy before, who
ornaments my alley.
I never saw his face at all.
I never saw his futurefall.
But I have known this Boy.

I have always heard him deal with death.
I have always heard the shout, the volley.
I have closed my heart-ears late and early.
And I have killed him ever.

I joined the Wild and killed him
with knowledgeable unknowing.

I saw where he was going.
I saw him Crossed. And seeing,
I did not take him down.

He cried not only "Father!"
but "Mother!
Sister!
Brother."
The cry climbed up the alley.
It went up to the wind.
It hung upon the heaven
for a long
stretch-strain of Moment.

The red floor of my alley
is a special speech to me.

Infirm

Everybody here
is infirm.
Everybody here is infirm.
Oh. Mend me. Mend me. Lord.

Today I
say to them
say to them
say to them, Lord:
look! I am beautiful, beautiful with
my wing that is wounded
my eye that is bonded
or my ear not funded
or my walk all a-wobble.
I'm enough to be beautiful.

You are
beautiful too.

I Am a Black

Kojo

According to my Teachers,
I am now an African-American.

They call me out of my name.

BLACK is an open umbrella.
I am a Black and A Black forever.

I am one of The Blacks.

We are Here, we are There.
We occur in Brazil, in Nigeria, Ghana,
in Botswana, Tanzania, in Kenya,
in Russia, Australia, in Haiti, Soweto,
in Grenada, in Cuba, in Panama, Libya,
in England and Italy, France.

We are graces in any places.
I am Black and A Black
forever.

I am other than Hyphenation.

I say, proudly, MY PEOPLE!
I say, proudly, OUR PEOPLE!

Our People do not disdain to eat yams or melons or grits
or to put peanut butter in stew.

I am Kojo. In West Afrika Kojo
means Unconquerable. My parents
named me the seventh day from my birth
in Black spirit, Black faith, Black communion.
I am Kojo. I am A Black.

And I Capitalize my name.

Do not call me out of my name.

An Old Black Woman, Homeless, and Indistinct

1.

Your every day is a pilgrimage.
A blue hubbub.
Your days are collected bacchanals of fear and self-troubling.

And your nights! Your nights.
When you put you down in alley or cardboard or viaduct,
your lovers are rats, finding your secret places.

2.

When you rise in another morning,
you hit the street, your incessant enemy.

See? Here you are, in the so-busy world.
You walk. You walk.
You pass The People.
No. The People pass you.

Here's a Rich Girl marching briskly to her charms.
She is suede and scarf and belting and perfume.
She sees you not, she sees you very well.
At five in the afternoon Miss Rich Girl will go Home
to brooms and vacuum cleaner and carpeting,
two cats, two marble-top tables, two telephones,
shiny green peppers, flowers in impudent vases, visitors.
Before all that there's luncheon to be known.
Lasagna, lobster salad, sandwiches.
All day there's coffee to be loved.
There are luxuries
of minor dissatisfaction, luxuries of Plan.

3.

That's her story,
You're going to vanish, not necessarily nicely, fairly soon,
Although essentially dignity itself a death
is not necessarily tidy, modest or discreet.
When they find you
your legs may not be tidy nor aligned.
Your mouth may be all crooked or destroyed.

Black old woman, homeless, indistinct—
Your last and least adventure is Review.
        Folks used to celebrate your birthday!
Folks used to say "She's such a pretty little thing!"
Folks used to say "She draws such handsome horses, cows
        and houses,"
Folks used to say "That child is going far."

September, 1992.

JULIA DE BURGOS

To Julia de Burgos

Already the people murmur that I am your enemy
because they say that in verse I give the world your me.

They lie, Julia de Burgos. They lie, Julia de Burgos.
Who rises in my verses is not your voice. It is my voice
because you are the dressing and the essence is me;
and the most profound abyss is spread between us.

You are the cold doll of social lies,
and me, the virile starburst of the human truth.

You, honey of courtesan hypocrisies; not me;
in all my poems I undress my heart.

You are like your world, selfish; not me
who gambles everything betting on what I am.

You are only the ponderous lady very lady;
not me; I am life, strength, woman.

You belong to your husband, your master; not me;
I belong to nobody, or all, because to all, to all
I give myself in my clean feeling and in my thought.

You curl your hair and paint yourself; not me;
the wind curls my hair, the sun paints me.

You are a housewife, resigned, submissive,
tied to the prejudices of men; not me;
unbridled, I am a runaway Rocinante
snorting horizons of God's justice.

You in yourself have no say; everyone governs you;
your husband, your parents, your family,

the priest, the dressmaker, the theatre, the dance hall,
the auto, the fine furnishings, the feast, champagne,
heaven and hell, and the social, "what will they say."

Not in me, in me only my heart governs,
only my thought; who governs in me is me.
You, flower of aristocracy; and me, flower of the people.
You in you have everything and you owe it to everyone,
while me, my nothing I owe to nobody.

You nailed to the static ancestral dividend,
and me, a one in the numerical social divider,
we are the duel to death who fatally approaches.

When the multitudes run rioting
leaving behind ashes of burned injustices,
and with the torch of the seven virtues,
the multitudes run after the seven sins,
against you and against everything unjust and inhuman,
I will be in their midst with the torch in my hand.

Translated by Jack Agüeros

Ay, Ay, Ay of the Kinky-Haired Negress

Ay, ay, ay, that am kinky-haired and pure black;
kinks in my hair, Kafir in my lips;
and my flat nose Mozambiques.

Black of pure tint, I cry and laugh
the vibration of being a black statue;
a chunk of night, in which my white
teeth are lightning;
and to be a black vine
which entwines in the black
and curves the black nest
in which the raven lies.
Black chunk of black in which I sculpt myself,
ay, ay, ay, my statue is all black.

They tell me that my grandfather was the slave
for whom the master paid thirty coins.
Ay, ay, ay, that the slave was my grandfather
is my sadness, is my sadness.
If he had been the master
it would be my shame:
that in men, as in nations,
if being the slave is having no rights
being the master is having no conscience.

Ay, ay, ay, wash the sins of the white King
in forgiveness black Queen.

Ay, ay, ay, the race escapes me
and buzzes and flies toward the white race,
to sink in its clear water;
or perhaps the white will be shadowed in the black.

Ay, ay, ay, my black race flees
and with the white runs to become bronzed;
to be one for the future,
fraternity of America!

Translated by Jack Agüeros

Poem of the Unborn Child

As you were born for daylight
you departed unborn.

You lost yourself serenely
before me,
and covered with centuries
the agony of not seeing you.

You didn't want the edge of anguish
nor the why of some hours that pass slowly
in life,

without leaving a sigh,
nor a memory,
nor anything.

You didn't want the aurora.
Nor death.
You rejected oblivion,
and blew perpetual in the flute of the air.

You didn't want love in a coffin of waves
nor the silence left by the brief tunnel
where man has slept.

Yours, immensely yours,
as you were born for daylight,
you departed unborn,
spikenard between two pupils that never knew
how to separate the echo from the shadow.
Wellspring without painful dewdrops,
fertile foot forever walking the earth.

Translated by Jack Agüeros

Farewell in Welfare Island

It has to be from here,
right this instance,
my cry into the world.

Life was somewhere forgotten
and sought refuge in depths of tears
and sorrows
over this vast empire of solitude
and darkness.

Where is the voice of freedom,
freedom to laugh,
to move
without the heavy phantom of despair?

Where is the form of beauty
unshaken in its veil simple and pure?
Where is the warmth of heaven
pouring its dreams of love in broken spirits?

It has to be from here,
right this instance,
my cry into the world.
My cry that is no more mine,
but hers and his forever,
the comrades of my silence,
the phantoms of my grave.

It has to be from here,
forgotten hut unshaken,
among comrades of silence
deep into Welfare Island
my farewell to the world.

Goldwater Memorial Hospital
Welfare Island. NYC
Feb., 1953

The Sun in Welfare Island

The sun
is shining in despair
at my sorrowful heart.

Singing birds are all tuning
eternal hymns of freedom
into my land of silence
and my soul responds:
Solitude!

Daisies mirror their sweetness
into my hidden gardens
seeking a smile of liberty

and my lips respond:
Solitude!

The river, dancing images
for my untendered eyes
implores a look of cheerfulness
and my eyes respond:
Solitude!

The sun,
only the sun immortal
is shining in despair
at my sorrowful heart.

For my soul asks just
solitude,
My smile depends on
solitude,
my eyes are full of
solitude
and all of me is loneliness
in a rebellious heart.

Goldwater Memorial Hospital
Welfare Island, NYC
April 30, 1953

MARGARET DANNER

The Small Bells of Benin

Here in a Chicago museum, these small bells of Benin,
without ringing, are bringing their charm to a foreign scene.

The concave cylindrical draping of some
is as prim as the poise of a Quaker maid.
While the rare quadrangular forms of the rest
with their molded latticed designs, suggest
the iron fences displayed

in New Orleans, and who can escape
the quaint, spellbound, gargoyle-like
bronze faces that stare from their settings
of thin metal lace?

I wish I could obtain one of these bells
or even a facsimile, but the formula
to their deft mouldings was lost
and hasn't been quite reproduced or found.

Etta Moten's Attic

It was as if Gauguin
had upset a huge paintpot
of his incomparable tangerine,

splashing wherever my startled eyes ran
here, there and at my very hand on
masques and carvings and paintings not seen

here before; spilling straight as a stripe
spun geometrically in Ndebele rug
flung over an ebony chair,

or dripping round as a band on a type
of bun the Watussi warriors
make of their pompadoured hair,

splashing high as a sunbird or fly moving
over a frieze of mahogany trees,
or splotching out from low underneath as a root,

shimmering bright as a ladybug, grooving
a green bed of moss, sparkling as a beetle,
a bee, shockingly dotting the snoot

of an ape or the nape of its neck or as clue
to its navel, stamping a Zulu's
intriguing masque, tipping

the lips of a chief of Ashanti's who
was carved to his stool so he'd sit
there forever and never fear a slipping

of rule or command, dyeing the skirt
(all askew) that wouldn't stay put on the
Pygmy in spite of his real leather belt,
quickening and charming till we felt the bloom
of veldt and jungle flow through the room.

FRANK MARSHALL DAVIS

from *Ebony Under Granite*

REV. JOSEPH WILLIAMS

Being a Man of God
and a child of flesh and blood
my soul thirsting for truth
and my body hungering for eat and drink
realizing that the satisfaction of one
depended upon the survival of the other and
this could best be done
by preserving the Second Baptist Church and
that on the sisters
depended such preservation
you can understand
why the congregation stuck together
and why, when I died
the sisters mourned
and why so many children
will likewise search for truth
and have moles on their necks
like the Rev. Joseph Williams.

ROBERT WHITMORE

Having attained success in business
possessing three cars
one wife and two mistresses
a home and furniture
talked of by the town
and thrice ruler
of the local Elks
Robert Whitmore
died of apoplexy
when a stranger from Georgia

mistook him
for a former Macon waiter.

GEORGE BROWN

For forty years in Mississippi
Voteless he watched white men swept into office by
a tidal wave of race hate
Powerless he saw the crooked politicians
eat the money he paid for taxes
at the table of Public Service
Voiceless he saw bigots who demanded
respect for the Constitution
stand with gun drawn if he tried
to exercise his Constitutional right
of the ballot
I say for forty years
he saw the majority vote given a winner
was less than a fraction of those taken
from his disfranchised people.
So when he came North to Chicago
and a man blacker than he
sought a seat in Congress
was it so wrong of him to use
five of the votes
saved from Mississippi
even though it meant
the rest of his life
in the state penitentiary?

Mojo Mike's Beer Garden

Four fat white spiders of throttled electric globes cling
    motionless to the ceiling spinning a misty web
    downward through the porous air

Soft runners of light finger the brown contours of a gambler's
    chin, a harlot's face, a pimp's profile, then go floating on

The room is filled with the misty web, the white thin web
    four spiders spin

Two yellow gals take 'em their beer and wine and gin . . .

    This room is an unscored symphony
    of colors and sounds
    People sit like geometric angles
    awaiting measurement
    Their talk is countless bubbles
    breaking against the ceiling
    Sharp scissors of a radio
    snip fancy cutouts in the thick noise
    Gray pigeons of tobacco smoke
    fly lazily in the air above
    Like a leafy tree in high winds
    the room moves its heads and hands

Two slate-black men and two orange-brown women spill low
    stories into four steins of beer

From her youngly rouged face fifty year old eyes look out like
    unwashed windows in a newly painted house . . . this
    woman who sits alone tosses a promise through her gaze
    to all male youths

Words shoot from the lips of three race track losers like water
    from a hose at the Stockyards Fire

Before the long flat back of a brown-stained bar men and
    women laugh, talk, drink, sweat, swapping monotony
    for alcohol

From his stool by the cash register Mojo Mike sees nothing
    but faces and each face is a nickle beer or the price of a
    pint of whiskey to be put away and counted when his
    joint is emptied for the night

And . . . while the spiders spin . . . two yellow gals take 'em
    their beer and wine and gin . . .

Four Glimpses of Night

I

Eagerly
Like a woman hurrying to her lover
Night comes to the room of the world
And lies, yielding and content
Against the cool round face
Of the moon.

II

Night is a curious child, wandering
Between earth and sky, creeping
In windows and doors, daubing
The entire neighborhood
With purple paint.
Day
Is an apologetic mother
Cloth in hand
Following after.

III

Peddling
From door to door
Night sells

Black bags of peppermint stars
Heaping cones of vanilla moon
Until
His wares are gone
Then shuffles homeward
Jingling the gray coins
Of daybreak.

IV

Night's brittle song, sliver-thin
Shatters into a billion fragments
Of quiet shadows
At the blaring jazz
Of a morning sun.

OWEN DODSON

Sorrow Is the Only Faithful One

Sorrow is the only faithful one:
The lone companion clinging like a season
To its original skin no matter what the variations.

If all the mountains paraded
Eating the valleys as they went
And the sun were a coiffure on the highest peak,

Sorrow would be there between
The sparkling and the giant laughter
Of the enemy when the clouds come down to swim.

But I am less, unmagic, black,
Sorrow clings to me more than to doomsday mountains
Or erosion scars on a palisade.

Sorrow has a song like a leech
Crying because the sand's blood is dry
And the stars reflected in the lake

Are water for all their twinkling
And bloodless for all their charm.
I have blood, and a song.

Sorrow is the only faithful one.

The Morning Duke Ellington Praised the Lord and Six Little Black Davids Tapped Danced Unto

The morning Duke Ellington praised the Lord
The stars plus the moon shone out loud—

Six little black Davids
Tapped danced unto:
Gabriel trumpeted up arthritic Michael:
Plus some Archangels who had slipped from grace
Into Hell when God rode like a roaring
General of peace into the universe.
Trumpets: who whee, who wheee—
Duke's horns, all his brasses plus drums
Did a dip pip pip-a-de doo.
Duke now called out: "Recite the books!"
Trumpets, and all brasses plus thumping piano,
Plus triumphant chorus—
Sang, wailed, beat, spit out
Under the cymbals and the drums and the brass plates:
Of Bible sin and redemption:

Now! who whooee—a dip-a-de do: now, come on:
Genesis, Exodus, Leviticus:
Now Chorus: "In the beginning God created
The Heavens and the earth."
Whooee, wee, whooee, whoohee
Joy amazing glory in the books of God:
Ruth, Naomi, Daniel plus Hosiah and Malachi
And so forth and what not; my testimony
Is with Judges:
"Don't judge me!
"Yes, judge me—yes put me, me on the witness stand."
Let the trumpets blow the candles out
Then Naomi can kiss the cross in the dark.
Do a dip-a-de do.
Ruth lights them again
To make the wailing wall of darkness
A pillar of light, Whoee, ooee, whoee
Duke's drums are cymbals
The trumpets spit back a dance:
Then there is doomsday and eternity
Sitting on your black entrails.
Duke knows the stained-glassed window
Of Christ will fall down.
Does he want it on his back?

He doesn't want anything
But Genesis, Numbers, Malachi, Leviticus, and so forth
Where is God with his watermelon, and dandelion wine?
Mary Magdalene has a fit when she sees
Jesus when, she is eighty-eight—
Whoo-whee-whee—her eyes are glazed
As Jesus presents her manna
Milk and honey, but no dandelion wine.
He bends over as a father:
He was thirty-three when he ended.
Naomi has a do amid the alien corn—
While Ruth devours wheat.
Duke's drums and cymbals and trumpets:
Holler whoo-whoo-whee.
Deuteronomy, Zakariah, Luke,
John the Divine who loved Jesus
Corinthians: "When I was a man I spoke as a man."

Up the altar
Six Black Davids
Tapped danced praise unto.
Jesus becomes cloud—whooee—whoo-ee—whooee—
No one is here but Duke and his black boys.
We hear the trumpet of Gabriel through it all.
He has called the children home.
Is that your combo, Duke?
Right on!
Six black boys still tap dance up the marble altar praising
        unto.
Hallelujah to tomorrow.
A dip-a-do,
A dip-a-dip
A dip-a-de-do. Do!

ROBERT HAYDEN

Those Winter Sundays

Sundays too my father got up early
and put his clothes on in the blueblack cold,
then with cracked hands that ached
from labor in the weekday weather made
banked fires blaze. No one ever thanked him.

I'd wake and hear the cold splintering, breaking.
When the rooms were warm, he'd call,
and slowly I would rise and dress,
fearing the chronic angers of that house,

Speaking indifferently to him,
who had driven out the cold
and polished my good shoes as well.
What did I know, what did I know
of love's austere and lonely offices?

Frederick Douglass

When it is finally ours, this freedom, this liberty, this
     beautiful
and terrible thing, needful to man as air,
usable as earth; when it belongs at last to all,
when it is truly instinct, brain matter, diastole, systole,
reflex action; when it is finally won; when it is more
than the gaudy mumbo jumbo of politicians:
this man, this Douglass, this former slave, this Negro
beaten to his knees, exiled, visioning a world
where none is lonely, none hunted, alien,
this man, superb in love and logic, this man
shall be remembered. Oh, not with statues' rhetoric,
not with legends and poems and wreaths of bronze alone,

but with the lives grown out of his life, the lives
fleshing his dream of the beautiful, needful thing.

Middle Passage

I

Jesús, Estrella, Esperanza, Mercy:

>   Sails flashing to the wind like weapons,
>   sharks following the moans the fever and the dying;
>   horror the corposant and compass rose.

Middle Passage:
>   voyage through death
>   to life upon these shores.

>   "10 April 1800—
>   Blacks rebellious. Crew uneasy. Our linguist says
>   their moaning is a prayer for death,
>   ours and their own. Some try to starve themselves.
>   Lost three this morning leaped with crazy laughter
>   to the waiting sharks, sang as they went under."

Desire, Adventure, Tartar, Ann:

>   Standing to America, bringing home
>   black gold, black ivory, black seed.

>   *Deep in the festering hold thy father lies,*
>   *of his bones New England pews are made,*
>   *those are altar lights that were his eyes.*

Jesus   Saviour   Pilot   Me
Over   Life's   Tempestuous   Sea

We pray that Thou wilt grant, O Lord,
safe passage to our vessels bringing
heathen souls unto Thy chastening.

Jesus   Saviour

"8 bells. I cannot sleep, for I am sick
with fear, but writing eases fear a little
since still my eyes can see these words take shape
upon the page & so I write, as one
would turn to exorcism. 4 days scudding,
but now the sea is calm again. Misfortune
follows in our wake like sharks (our grinning
tutelary gods). Which one of us
has killed an albatross? A plague among
our blacks—Ophthalmia: blindness—& we
have jettisoned the blind to no avail.
It spreads, the terrifying sickness spreads.
Its claws have scratched sight from the Capt.'s eyes
& there is blindness in the fo'c'sle
& we must sail 3 weeks before we come
to port."

> *What port awaits us, Davy Jones'*
> *or home? I've heard of slavers drifting, drifting,*
> *playthings of wind and storm and chance, their*
> > *crews*
> *gone blind, the jungle hatred*
> *crawling up on deck.*

Thou   Who   Walked   On   Galilee

"Deponent further sayeth *The Bella J*
left the Guinea Coast
with cargo of five hundred blacks and odd
for the barracoons of Florida:

"That there was hardly room 'tween-decks for half
the sweltering cattle stowed spoon-fashion there;
that some went mad of thirst and tore their flesh
and sucked the blood:

"That Crew and Captain lusted with the comeliest
of the savage girls kept naked in the cabins;

that there was one they called The Guinea Rose
and they cast lots and fought to lie with her:

"That when the Bo's'n piped all hands, the flames
spreading from starboard already were beyond
control, the negroes howling and their chains
entangled with the flames:

"That the burning blacks could not be reached,
that the Crew abandoned ship,
leaving their shrieking negresses behind,
that the Captain perished drunken with the wenches:

"Further Deponent sayeth not."

Pilot   Oh   Pilot   Me

                         II
Aye, lad, and I have seen those factories,
Gambia, Rio Pongo, Calabar;
have watched the artful mongos baiting traps
of war wherein the victor and the vanquished

Were caught as prizes for our barracoons.
Have seen the nigger kings whose vanity
and greed turned wild black hides of Fellatah,
Mandingo, Ibo, Kru to gold for us.

And there was one—King Anthracite we named him—
fetish face beneath French parasols
of brass and orange velvet, impudent mouth
whose cups were carven skulls of enemies:

He'd honor us with drum and feast and conjo
and palm-oil-glistening wenches deft in love,
and for tin crowns that shone with paste,
red calico and German-silver trinkets

Would have the drums talk war and send
his warriors to burn the sleeping villages

and kill the sick and old and lead the young
in coffles to our factories.

Twenty years a trader, twenty years,
for there was wealth aplenty to be harvested
from those black fields, and I'd be trading still
but for the fevers melting down my bones.

III

Shuttles in the rocking loom of history,
the dark ships move, the dark ships move,
their bright ironical names
like jests of kindness on a murderer's mouth;
plough through thrashing glister toward
fata morgana's lucent melting shore,
weave toward New World littorals that are
mirage and myth and actual shore.

Voyage through death,
                    voyage whose chartings are unlove.

A charnel stench, effluvium of living death
spreads outward from the hold,
where the living and the dead, the horribly dying,
lie interlocked, lie foul with blood and excrement.

> *Deep in the festering hold thy father lies,*
> *the corpse of mercy rots with him,*
> *rats eat love's rotten gelid eyes.*
>
> *But, oh, the living look at you*
> *with human eyes whose suffering accuses you,*
> *whose hatred reaches through the swill of dark*
> *to strike you like a leper's claw.*
>
> *You cannot stare that hatred down*
> *or chain the fear that stalks the watches*
> *and breathes on you its fetid scorching breath;*
> *cannot kill the deep immortal human wish,*
> *the timeless will.*

"But for the storm that flung up barriers
of wind and wave, *The Amistad*, señores,
would have reached the port of Príncipe in two,
three days at most; but for the storm we should
have been prepared for what befell.
Swift as the puma's leap it came. There was
that interval of moonless calm filled only
with the water's and the rigging's usual sounds,
then sudden movement, blows and snarling cries
and they had fallen on us with machete
and marlinspike. It was as though the very
air, the night itself were striking us.
Exhausted by the rigors of the storm,
we were no match for them. Our men went down
before the murderous Africans. Our loyal
Celestino ran from below with gun
and lantern and I saw, before the cane-
knife's wounding flash, Cinquez,
that surly brute who calls himself a prince,
directing, urging on the ghastly work.
He hacked the poor mulatto down, and then
he turned on me. The decks were slippery
when daylight finally came. It sickens me
to think of what I saw, of how these apes
threw overboard the butchered bodies of
our men, true Christians all, like so much jetsam.
Enough, enough. The rest is quickly told:
Cinquez was forced to spare the two of us
you see to steer the ship to Africa,
and we like phantoms doomed to rove the sea
voyaged east by day and west by night,
deceiving them, hoping for rescue,
prisoners on our own vessel, till
at length we drifted to the shores of this
your land, America, where we were freed
from our unspeakable misery. Now we
demand, good sirs, the extradition of
Cinquez and his accomplices to La
Havana. And it distresses us to know
there are so many here who seem inclined

to justify the mutiny of these blacks.
We find it paradoxical indeed
that you whose wealth, whose tree of liberty
are rooted in the labor of your slaves
should suffer the august John Quincy Adams
to speak with so much passion of the right
of chattel slaves to kill their lawful masters
and with his Roman rhetoric weave a hero's
garland for Cinquez. I tell you that
we are determined to return to Cuba
with our slaves and there see justice done.
      Cinquez—
or let us say 'the Prince'—Cinquez shall die."

The deep immortal human wish,
the timeless will:

      Cinquez its deathless primaveral image,
      life that transfigures many lives.

Voyage through death
                  to life upon these shores.

Runagate Runagate

I

Runs falls rises stumbles on from darkness into darkness
and the darkness thicketed with shapes of terror
and the hunters pursuing and the hounds pursuing
and the night cold and the night long and the river
to cross and the jack-muh-lanterns beckoning beckoning
and blackness ahead and when shall I reach that somewhere
morning and keep on going and never turn back and keep on
    going

        Runagate
            Runagate
                Runagate

Many thousands rise and go
many thousands crossing over

>   O mythic North
>   O star-shaped yonder Bible city

Some go weeping and some rejoicing
some in coffins and some in carriages
some in silks and some in shackles

>   Rise and go or fare you well

No more auction block for me
no more driver's lash for me

>   If you see my Pompey, 30 yrs of age,
>   new breeches, plain stockings, negro shoes;
>   if you see my Anna, likely young mulatto
>   branded E on the right cheek, R on the left,
>   catch them if you can and notify subscriber.
>   Catch them if you can, but it won't be easy.
>   They'll dart underground when you try to catch them,
>   plunge into quicksand, whirlpools, mazes,
>   turn into scorpions when you try to catch them.

And before I'll be a slave
I'll be buried in my grave

>   North star and bonanza gold
>   I'm bound for the freedom, freedom-bound
>   and oh Susyanna don't you cry for me

>   Runagate

>   Runagate

II
Rises from their anguish and their power,

Harriet Tubman,

woman of earth, whipscarred,
a summoning, a shining

Mean to be free

And this was the way of it, brethren brethren,
way we journeyed from Can't to Can.
Moon so bright and no place to hide,
the cry up and the patterollers riding,
hound dogs belling in bladed air.
And fear starts a-murbling, Never make it,
we'll never make it. *Hush that now,*
and she's turned upon us, leveled pistol
glinting in the moonlight:
Dead folks can't jaybird-talk, she says;
you keep on going now or die, she says.

Wanted   Harriet Tubman   alias The General
alias Moses   Stealer of Slaves
In league with Garrison   Alcott   Emerson
Garrett   Douglass   Thoreau   John Brown

Armed and known to be Dangerous

Wanted   Reward   Dead or Alive
        Tell me, Ezekiel, oh tell me do you see
        mailed Jehovah coming to deliver me?

Hoot-owl calling in the ghosted air,
five times calling to the hants in the air.
Shadow of a face in the scary leaves,
shadow of a voice in the talking leaves:

Come ride-a my train

Oh that train, ghost-story train
through swamp and savanna movering movering,
over trestles of dew, through caves of the wish,
Midnight Special on a saber track movering movering,
first stop Mercy and the last Hallelujah.

Come ride-a my train

    Mean mean mean to be free.

Ice Storm

Unable to sleep, or pray, I stand
by the window looking out
at moonstruck trees a December storm
has bowed with ice.

Maple and mountain ash bend
under its glassy weight,
their cracked branches falling upon
the frozen snow.

The trees themselves, as in winters past,
will survive their burdening,
broken thrive. And am I less to You,
my God, than they?

A Letter from Phillis Wheatley

London, 1773

Dear Obour
         Our crossing was without
event. I could not help, at times,
reflecting on that first—my Destined—

voyage long ago (I yet
have some remembrance of its Horrors)
and marvelling at God's Ways.
          Last evening, her Ladyship presented me
to her illustrious Friends.
I scarce could tell them anything
of Africa, though much of Boston
and my hope of Heaven. I read
my latest Elegies to them.
"O Sable Muse!" the Countess cried,
embracing me, when I had done.
I held back tears, as is my wont,
and there were tears in Dear
Nathaniel's eyes.
          At supper—I dined apart
like captive Royalty—
the Countess and her Guests promised
signatures affirming me
True Poetess, albeit once a slave.
Indeed, they were most kind, and spoke,
moreover, of presenting me
at Court (I thought of Pocahontas)—
an Honor, to be sure, but one,
I should, no doubt, as Patriot decline.
          My health is much improved;
I feel I may, if God so Wills,
entirely recover here.
Idyllic England! Alas, there is
no Eden without its Serpent. Under
the chiming Complaisance I hear him Hiss;
I see his flickering tongue
when foppish would-be Wits
murmur of the Yankee Pedlar
and his Cannibal Mockingbird.
          Sister, forgive th'intrusion of
my Sombreness—Nocturnal Mood
I would not share with any save
your trusted Self. Let me disperse,
in closing, such unseemly Gloom
by mention of an Incident

you may, as I, consider Droll:
Today, a little Chimney Sweep,
his face and hands with soot quite Black,
staring hard at me, politely asked:
"Does you, M'lady, sweep chimneys too?"
I was amused, but dear Nathaniel
(ever Solicitous) was not.
        I pray the Blessings of our Lord
and Saviour Jesus Christ be yours
Abundantly. In His Name,

                              Phillis

Paul Laurence Dunbar

(for Herbert Martin)

        We lay red roses on his grave,
speak sorrowfully of him
as if he were but newly dead

        And so it seems to us
this raw spring day, though years
before we two were born he was
        a young poet dead.

        Poet of our youth—
his "cri du coeur" our own,
his verses "in a broken tongue"

        beguiling as an elder
brother's antic lore.
Their sad blackface lilt and croon
        survive him like

        The happy look (subliminal
of victim, dying man)
a summer's tintypes hold.

The roses flutter in the wind;
we weight their stems
with stones, then drive away.

[*American Journal*]

here among them   the americans   this baffling
multi people   extremes and variegations   their
noise   restlessness   their almost frightening
energy   how best describe these aliens in my
reports to The Counselors

disguise myself in order to study them unobserved
adapting their varied pigmentations   white black
red brown yellow   the imprecise and strangering
distinctions by which they live   by which they
justify their cruelties to one another

charming savages   enlightened primitives   brash
new comers lately sprung up in our galaxy   how
describe them   do they indeed know what or who
they are   do not seem to   yet no other beings
in the universe make more extravagant claims
for their importance and identity

like us they have created a veritable populace
of machines that serve and soothe and pamper
and entertain   we have seen their flags and
foot prints on the moon   also the intricate
rubbish left behind   a wastefully ingenious
people   many it appears worship the Unknowable
Essence   the same for them as for us   but are
more faithful to their machine made gods
technologists their shamans

oceans deserts mountains grain fields canyons
forest   variousness of landscapes weathers

sun light moon light as at home   much here is
beautiful   dream like vistas reminding me of
home   item   have seen the rock place known
as garden of the gods and sacred to the first
indigenes   red monoliths of home   despite
the tensions i breathe in i am attracted to
the vigorous americans   disturbing sensuous
appeal of so many   never to be admitted

something they call the american dream   sure
we still believe in it i guess   an earth man
in the tavern said   irregardless of the some
times night mare facts we always try to double
talk our way around   and its okay the dreams
okay and means whats good could be a damn sight
better   means every body in the good old u s a
should have the chance to get ahead or at least
should have three squares a day   as for myself
i do okay   not crying hunger with a loaf of
bread tucked under my arm you understand   i
fear one does not clearly follow i replied
notice you got a funny accent pal   like where
you from he asked   far from here i mumbled
he stared hard   i left

must be more careful   item   learn to use okay
their pass word   okay

crowds gathering in the streets today for some
reason obscure to me   noise and violent motion
repulsive physical contact   sentinels   pigs
i heard them called   with flailing clubs   rage
and bleeding and frenzy and screaming   machines
wailing   unbearable decibels   i fled lest
vibrations of the brutal scene do further harm
to my metabolism already over taxed

The Counselors would never permit such barbarous
confusion   they know what is best for our sereni
ty   we are an ancient race and have outgrown

illusions cherished here   item   their vaunted
liberty   no body pushes me around i have heard
them say   land of the free they sing   what do
they fear mistrust betray more than the freedom
they boast of in their ignorant pride   have seen
the squalid ghettoes in their violent cities
paradox on paradox   how have the americans
managed to survive

parades fireworks displays video spectacles
much grandiloquence much buying and selling
they are celebrating their history   earth men
in antique uniforms play at the carnage whereby
the americans achieved identity   we too recall
that struggle as enterprise of suffering and
faith uniquely theirs   blonde miss teen age
America waving from a red white and blue flower
float as the goddess of liberty   a divided
people seeking reassurance from a past few under
stand and many scorn   why should we sanction
old hypocrisies   thus dissenters   The Counse
lors would silence them

a decadent people The Counselors believe   i
do not find them decadent   a refutation not
permitted me   but for all their knowledge
power and inventiveness not yet more than raw
crude neophytes like earthlings everywhere

though i have easily passed for an american   in
bankers grey afro and dashiki long hair and jeans
hard hat yarmulke mini skirt   describe in some
detail for the amusement of The Counselors   and
though my skill in mimicry is impeccable   as
indeed The Counselors are aware   some thing
eludes me   some constant amid the variables
defies analysis and imitation   will i be judged
incompetent

america   as much a problem in metaphysics as
it is a nation earthly entity an iota in our
galaxy   an organism that changes even as i
examine it   fact and fantasy never twice the
same   so many variables

exert greater caution   twice have aroused
suspicion   returned to the ship until rumors
of humanoids from outer space   so their scoff
ing media voices termed us   had been laughed
away   my crew and i laughed too of course

confess i am curiously drawn   unmentionable   to
the americans   doubt i could exist among them for
long however   psychic demands far too severe
much violence   much that repels   i am attracted
none the less   their variousness their ingenuity
their elan vital   and that some thing   essence
quiddity   i cannot penetrate or name

TED JOANS

The Truth

IF YOU SHOULD SEE A MAN

walking down a crowded

street
    talking
        ALOUD

TO HIMSELF

      DON'T RUN
            IN THE

OPPOSITE DIRECTION

           BUT RUN

TOWARD HIM

     for he is a

        POET

you have NOTHING to
           FEAR

FROM THE

     POET
       BUT THE

    TRUTH

Jazz Is My Religion

Jazz is my religion   and it alone do I dig   the jazz clubs are
my house of worship   and sometimes the concert halls   but
some holy places are too commercial (like churches)   so
I don't dig the sermons there   I buy jazz sides to dig in
solitude   Like man / Harlem, Harlem USA Used to be a jazz
heaven where most of the jazz sermons were preached   but
now-a-days due to chacha cha and rotten rock'n'roll alotta
good jazzmen have sold their souls   but jazz is still my
religion   because I know and feel the message it brings like
Reverend Dizzy Gillespie / Brother Bird and Basie / Uncle
Armstrong / Minister Monk / Deacon Miles Davis / Rector
Rollins / Priest Ellington / His Funkness Horace Silver /
and the great John COLTRANE   and Cecil Taylor   They
Preach A Sermon That Always Swings!!   Yeah jazz is MY
religion   Jazz is my story it was my mom's and pop's   and
their moms and pops from the days of Buddy Bolden who
swung them blues to Charlie Parker and Ornette Coleman's
extension of Bebop   Yeah jazz is my religion   Jazz is a
unique musical religion the sermons spread happiness and
joy   to be able to dig and swing inside   what a wonderful
feeling jazz is / YEAH BOY!! JAZZ is my religion and dig
this: it wasn't for us to choose because they created it for a
damn good reason   as   a weapon to battle our blues! JAZZ
is my religion   and its international   all the   way   JAZZ is
just an Afroamerican music and like us it's here to stay   So
remember that JAZZ is my religion but it can be your
religion too but JAZZ is a truth that   is always black and
blue   Halleluiah I love JAZZ so   Halleluiah I dig JAZZ so
Yeah JAZZ   IS   MY   RELIGION

The Nice Colored Man

Nice Nigger Educated Nigger Never Nigger Southern Nigger
Clever Nigger Northern Nigger Nasty Nigger Unforgivable
Nigger Unforgettable Nigger Unspeakable Nigger Rude

& Uncouth Nigger Mean & Vicious Nigger Smart Black
Nigger Smart Black Nigger Smart Black Nigger Smart Black
Nigger Smart Black Nigger Smart Black Nigger   Smart Black
Nigger   Smart Black Nigger Knife Carrying Nigger Gun
Toting Nigger Military Nigger Clock Watching Nigger Food
Poisoning Nigger Disgusting Nigger Black Ass Nigger Black
Ass Nigger Black Ass Nigger Black Ass Nigger Half White
Nigger Big Stupid Nigger Big Dick Nigger Jive Ass Nigger
Wrong Nigger Naughty Nigger Uppity Nigger Middleclass
Nigger Government Nigger Sneaky Nigger Houndog
Nigger Grease Head Nigger Nappy Head Nigger Cut Throat
Nigger Dangerous Nigger Sharp Nigger Rich Nigger Poor
Nigger Begging Nigger Hustling Nigger Whoring Nigger
Pimping Nigger No Good Nigger Dirty Nigger Unhappy
Nigger Explosive Nigger Godamn Nigger Godamnigger
Godamnigger Godamnigger Godamnigger Godamnigger
Godamn Nigger Godamnigger Godamnigger Godamnigger
Godamnigger Godamnigger
                        Neat Nigger Progressive
Nigger Nextdoor Nigger Classmate Nigger Roomate Nigger
Laymate Nigger Weekend Date Nigger Dancing Nigger
Smiling Nigger Ageless Nigger Old Tired Nigger Still Nigger
Hippy Nigger White Folks Nigger Integrated Nigger Non-
Violent Nigger Demonstrating Nigger Cooperative Nigger
Peaceful Nigger American Nigger Uneducated Nigger
Underrated Nigger Bad Nigger Sad Nigger Slum Nigger
Jailhouse Nigger Stealing Nigger Robbing Nigger Raping
Nigger
        Lonely Nigger Blues Singing Nigger Dues
Paying Nigger Unemployed Nigger Unwanted Nigger
Impossible Nigger Cunning Nigger Running Nigger Cruel
Nigger Well Known Nigger Individual Nigger Purple Nigger
Beige Nigger Bronze Nigger Brown Nigger Red Nigger Bed
Nigger Yellow Nigger Tan Nigger Mulatto Nigger Creole
Nigger Inevitable Nigger Mixed Up Nigger Slave Nigger
Unfree Nigger Savage Nigger Jazz Nigger Musical Nigger
Godamnigger

Godamnigger Godamnigger Godamnigger Godamnigger
Godamnigger Jesus Loves Us Nigger Preaching Nigger We

Shall Overcome Nigger Someday Nigger Militant Nigger
Real Nigger Brave Nigger Real Nigger Violent Nigger Real
Nigger Intelligent Nigger Real Nigger Active Nigger Real
Nigger Wise Nigger Real Nigger Deceitful Nigger Real
Nigger Courageous Nigger Real Nigger Cool Nigger Real
Nigger Hip Nigger Real Nigger Hot Nigger Real Nigger
Funky Nigger Real Nigger (I Can't Figger This Nigger He's
Too Much This Nigger! He's All Over Us This Nigger I
Don't Trust This Nigger He's Far Too Much He's
Everywhere . . . . . This Nigger!)
                    Eeny Meeny Minee Mo
                    Catch Whitey By His Throat
                    If He Says—Nigger   CUT IT!!

BOB KAUFMAN

Hawk Lawler: Chorus

Hawk Lawler was born in Kansas City in a charity ward where his father was also born, perhaps in the same bed. His early childhood was that of any Negro child of his town in the nineteen thirties. Regular—attendance at a seedy rundown school, daily salutes to the flag, solemn morning pledges of allegiance, and standard Beard Geographies. A special interest in history led him to build a makeshift log cabin in his back yard in preparation for the presidency, which his father tore down for firewood as soon as he discovered what motivated Hawk. His favorite friends were those with whom he traveled to the relief depot to collect the family ration of potatoes and dried prunes—these boys he trusted; others just happened to be boys, too. In school, he was good in mathematics but hated to do figures on paper. He usually worked out arithmetic problems in his head long before the rest of the class rested their pencils.

He attended church each Sunday at the Rising Sun Baptist Church where he secretly sang hymns in numbers, because he didn't like hearing the same words all the time, yet could offer no resistance to the music. His first personal contact with music as an individual act was when he played triangle in the school band and discovered that when he pinged his instrument at the wrong times he could feel its tingle separate and distinct from the other instruments—at which times he would smile inside his mouth—while apologizing to the leader who was an ex-New Orleans musician that jazz had passed by, yet secretly enjoyed the hard-head. He discovered the saxophone while listening to the band tune up and found that this gilded pipe could play free of the mob; at that instant, he became a saxophone player for life and never touched another triangle. The only possession of which he was proud was an aging Elgin bicycle he received at Christmas from the Afro-American Doll and Toy Fund sponsored by the local Negro paper and provided for by all good white people of the town. It was given

to him during a bleak Roosevelt Christmas for winning the
school's annual composition contest. His subject was "Why
I want to be President," and he was proudest when the bike
was presented to him by a snow-bearded colored Santa Claus,
whom he recognized as the Mayor's chauffeur. This cherished
trophy he surrendered to Horton, son of the family his mother
washer for, in return for one battered saxophone which he slept
with three nights before feeling intimate enough to try it, and
when he did finally find sufficient courage to blow it, his die
was cast—he and horn were one, world blotted out.

The only two courses available to him outside of regular stud-
ies were the Bible and music, and since he preferred playing the
saxophone to being God, his choice was preordained. Before
long he was being heard in small local clubs with largely blues
clientele. Often experiencing that same feeling about words he
had once felt in church, he began to blow numbers; he was fired
over and over, yet could not stop blowing numbers. He was
hired as second-chair man with the Bat Bowles orchestra, with
the provision that he refrain from blowing numbers, which
he did, until the band's dilapidated bus pulled up in front of
the Theresa Hotel on Harlem's busiest corner, in New York
City, where without a word, he picked up his horn case and
disembarked. For no reason at all, he walked and wondered.
He had never seen so many Negroes at one time in his whole
life. He wondered if some big dam had burst in Africa and
spilled its contents, or laughed at the crazy thought that they
were all white and this was some special holiday when they all
wore black and brown faces for some religious Mardi Gras.
This speculation was soon replaced by sounds smacking into
his eardrums which dispelled any notions of masquerade, caus-
ing him to finger his case and peer into doorways for that big
hidden jazz womb, oozing blues and down warmth, welcome
as new shoes but still emptied of his embryonic numbers.

Strange melodic numbers whose sum total was the blues
and so personal no Arab would have acknowledged inventing
them—his numbers, each one a fragment of a note. In lieu of
finding a room, he found a girl, which was easier in a place
where there were more girls than rooms, and while he waited
the chance to blow his lover horn again, he blew numbers with
his body, which left him sperm-poor and brain-pained, longing

to give wind to numbers and breathe life into them. One night his girl-mother-sister-lover-whore had a five-dollar date at one of the better after-hours spots with a leading writer of detective stories, and since this writer was a favorite of his, he went along, taking his horn as always, like some tubular security blanket. Five minutes after he enters the place, God created earth, Christ was born and Gabriel exchanged his trumpet for a saxophone. For there in this headquarters of black revolution sat these long-sought comrades, blowing numbers. Illegal notes floated in air as though they had a right to, floated right into his suddenly blossomed ears, followed him up to the bandstand, crept into his pores as he deceased the horn, placed it to his parched lips and sighed, for without willing it they came—numbers, notes, songs, battle cries, laments, jazzy psalms, tribal histories in cubist and surrealist patterns, and an unmistakable call to arms, to jazz, to him, as others put down their horns in silent thanks that he had come, as the drums had promised he would come, come to lead into the unpromised land, littered with pains, odored of death, come to lead, with his pumping, grinning throat. Let us not go into it, we all know he led, though we don't all know how—some of us are more familiar with the intermissions, aware of the passions, privy to the junk, witnesses to the uprising when the handkerchief was cast off; some of us were counters of madhouse excursions, and few of us have withstood the silence, wondering from where it came. Some of us have to know.

I, Too, Know What I Am Not

No, I am not death wishes of sacred rapists, singing
     on candy gallows.
No, I am not spoor of Creole murderers hiding
     in crepe-paper bayous.
No, I am not yells of some assassinated inventor, locked
     in his burning machine.
No, I am not forced breathing of Cairo's senile burglar,
     in lead shoes.

No, I am not Indian-summer fruit of Negro piano tuners,
  with muslin gloves.
No, I am not noise of two-gun senators, in hallowed
  peppermint hall.
No, I am not pipe-smoke hopes of cynical chiropractors,
  traffickers in illegal bone.
No, I am not pitchblende curse of Indian suicides,
  in bonnets of flaming water.
No, I am not soap-powder sighs of impotent window washers,
  in pants of air.
No, I am not kisses of tubercular sun addicts, smiling
  through rayon lips.
No, I am not chipped philosopher's tattered ideas sunk
  in his granite brain.
No, I am not cry of amethyst heron, winged stone in flight
  from cambric bullets.
No, I am not sting of the neurotic bee, frustrated
  in cheesecloth gardens.
No, I am not peal of muted bell, clapperless
  in the faded glory.
No, I am not report of silenced guns, helpless
  in the pacifist hands.
No, I am not call of wounded hunter, alone
  in the forest of bone.
No, I am not eyes of the infant owls hatching
  the roofless night.
No, I am not the whistle of Havana whores with cribs
  of Cuban death.
No, I am not shriek of Bantu children, bent
  under pennywhistle whips.
No, I am not whisper of the African trees,
  leafy Congo telephones.
No, I am not Leadbelly of blues, escaped from guitar jails.
No, I am not anything that is anything I am not.

Would You Wear My Eyes?

My body is a torn mattress,
Disheveled throbbing place
For the comings and goings
Of loveless transients.
The whole of me
Is an unfurnished room
Filled with dank breath
Escaping in gasps to nowhere.
Before completely objective mirrors
I have shot myself with my eyes,
But death refused my advances.
I have walked on my walls each night
Through strange landscapes in my head.
I have brushed my teeth with orange peel,
Iced with cold blood from the dripping faucets.
My face is covered with maps of dead nations;
My hair is littered with drying ragweed.
Bitter raisins drip haphazardly from my nostrils
While schools of glowing minnows swim from my mouth.
The nipples of my breasts are sun-browned cockleburrs;
Long-forgotten Indian tribes fight battles on my chest
Unaware of the sunken ships rotting in my stomach.
My legs are charred remains of burned cypress trees;
My feet are covered with moss from bayous, flowing across
      my floor.
I can't go out anymore.
I shall sit on my ceiling.
Would you wear my eyes?

War Memoir

Jazz—listen to it at your own risk.
At the beginning, a warm dark place.

(Her screams were trumpet laughter,
Not quite blues, but almost sinful.)

Crying above the pain, we forgave ourselves;
Original sin seemed a broken record.
God played blues to kill time, all the time.
Red-waved rivers floated us into life.

(So much laughter, concealed by blood and faith;
Life is a saxophone played by death.)

Greedy to please, we learned to cry;
Hungry to live, we learned to die.
The heart is a sad musician,
Forever playing the blues.

The blues blow life, as life blows fright;
Death begins, jazz blows soft in the night,
Too soft for ears of men whose minds
Hear only the sound of death, of war,
Of flagwrapped cremation in bitter lands.

No chords of jazz as mud is shoveled
Into the mouths of men; even the blues shy
At cries of children dying on deserted corners.
Jazz deserted, leaving us to our burning.

(Jazz is an African traitor.)

What one-hundred-percent redblooded savage
Wastes precious time listening to jazz
With so much important killing to do?

Silence the drums, that we may hear the burning
Of Japanese in atomic colorcinemascope,
And remember the stereophonic screaming.

Walking Parker Home

Sweet beats of jazz impaled on slivers of wind
Kansas Black Morning/ First Horn Eyes/
Historical sound pictures on New Bird wings
People shouts/ boy alto dream/ Tomorrow's
Gold belled pipe of stops and future Blues Times
Lurking Hawkins/ shadows of Lester/ realization
Bronze fingers—brain extensions seeking trapped sounds
Ghetto thoughts/ bandstand courage/ solo flight
Nerve-wracked suspicions of newer songs and doubts
New York altar city/ black tears/ secret disciples
Hammer horn pounding soul marks on unswinging gates
Culture gods/ mob sounds/ visions of spikes
Panic excursions to tribal Jazz wombs and transfusions
Heroin nights of birth/ and soaring/ over boppy new
      ground.
Smothered rage covering pyramids of notes spontaneously
      exploding
Cool revelations/ shrill hopes/ beauty speared into greedy
      ears
Birdland nights on bop mountains, windy saxophone
      revolutions
Dayrooms of junk/ and melting walls and circling vultures/
Money cancer/ remembered pain/ terror flights/
Death and indestructible existence

In that Jazz corner of life
Wrapped in a mist of sound
His legacy, our Jazz-tinted dawn
Wailing his triumphs of oddly begotten dreams
Inviting the nerveless to feel once more
That fierce dying of humans consumed
In raging fires of Love.

Crootey Songo

DERRAT SLEGELATIONS, FLO GOOF BABEREO
SORASH SHO DUBIES, WAGO, WAILO, WAILO

GEED BOP NAVA GLIED, NAVA GLIED, NAVA
SPEERIEDER, HUYEDIST, HEDACAZ, AX, O, O

DEEREDITION, BOOMEDITION, SQUOM, SQUOM, SQUOM
DEE BEETSTRAWIST, WAPAGO, WAPAGO, LOCO, LOCORO,
     LOCOEST
VOOMETEYEREEPETIOP, BOP, BOP, BOP, WHIPOP

DEARAT, SHLOHO, KURRITIP, PLOG, MANGI, SQUOM POT
CLOPO JAGO, BREE, BREE, ASLOOPERED, AKINGO LABIOP
ENGPOP, ENGPOP, BOINT PLOLO, PLOLO, BOP BOP

Heavy Water Blues

The radio is teaching my goldfish Jiujitsu
I am in love with a skindiver who sleeps underwater,
My neighbors are drunken linguists, & I speak butterfly,
Consolidated Edison is threatening to cut off my brain,
The postman keeps putting sex in my mailbox,
My mirror died, & can't tell if i still reflect,
I put my eyes on a diet, my tears are gaining too much
     weight.

•

I crossed the desert in a taxicab
only to be locked in a pyramid
With the face of a dog
on my breath

I went to a masquerade
Disguised as myself
Not one of my friends
Recognized

I dreamed I went to John Mitchell's poetry party
in my maidenform brain

Put the silver in the barbeque pit
The Chinese are attacking with nuclear
Restaurants

The radio is teaching my goldfish Ju Jiutsu
My old lady has taken up skin diving & sleeps underwater
I am hanging out with a drunken linguist, who can speak
        butterfly
And represents the caterpillar industry down in Washington
        D.C.

●

I never understand other peoples' desires or hopes,
until they coincide with my own, then we clash.

I have definite proof that the culture of the caveman,
disappeared due to his inability to produce one magazine,
that could be delivered by a kid on a bicycle.

When reading all those thick books on the life of god,
it should be noted that they were all written by men.

It is perfectly all right to cast the first stone,
if you have some more in your pocket.

Television, america's ultimate relief, from the indian
        disturbance.

I hope that when machines finally take over,
they won't build men that break down,
as soon as they're paid for.

i shall refuse to go to the moon,
unless I'm inoculated against
the dangers of indiscriminate love.

After riding across the desert in a taxicab,
he discovered himself locked in a pyramid
with the face of a dog on his breath.

The search for the end of the circle,
constant occupation of squares.

Why don't they stop throwing symbols,
the air is cluttered enough with echoes.

Just when I cleaned the manger for the wisemen,
the shrews from across the street showed up.

The voice of the radio shouted, get up
do something to someone, but me & my son
laughed in our furnished room.

Blues for Hal Waters

My head, my secret cranial guitar, strung with myths plucked
    from
Yesterday's straits, it's buried in robes of echoes, my eyes,
    breezeless flags, lacquered to present a glint . . .
My marble lips, entrance to that cave, where visions renounce
    renunciation,
Eternity has wet sidewalks, angels are busted for drunk
    flying.
I only want privacy to create an illusion of me blotted out.
His high hopes were placed in his coffin. Long paddles of
    esteem for his symbol canoe.
If I move to the stars, forward my mail c/o God, Heaven,
    Lower East Side.
Too late for skindiving and other modern philosophies, put
    my ego in storage.
The moon is too near my family, and the craters are cold in
    winter,
Let's move to the sun, hot water, radiant heating, special
    colors,

Knife-handle convenience, adjacent to God, community
    melting free.
Eskimos have frozen secrets in their noses and have chopped
    down the North Pole.
The Last Buffalo will be torpedoed by an atomic submarine,
    firing hydrogen tiepins.
God is my favorite dictator, even though he refuses to hold
    free elections.
That gate around me will hold, I worry about the padlock I
    painted on.
My hair is overrun with crabgrass, parts of my anatomy are
    still unexplored.
No more harp sessions for me; I am going to hell and hear
    some good jazz.
Do you hear the good news, Terry and the Pirates are not
    really real.
If you value the comfort of your fellow worshippers, don't die
    in church.
Why ruin our eyes with TV, let's design freeways after dinner
    tonight.

He might have lost some friends, but Jesus could have made a
    fortune on that water to wine formula.
History is the only diary God keeps, and somebody threw it
    on the bonfire.
The day of the Big Game at Hiroshima. The moon is a
    double agent.
This year the animals are holding their first
        "Be kind to people" week.
The Siamese cats will not participate and will hold their own
    convention in Egypt. The civilized world fears they may
    attempt to put Pharoah back in place on the throne.
For God's sake, Hal, jam the radio. Trip them with your
    guitar.

Oregon

You are with me Oregon,
Day and night, I feel you, Oregon.
I am Negro, I am Oregon.
Oregon is me, the planet
Oregon, the State Oregon, Oregon.
In the night, you come with bicycle wheels,
Oregon you come
With stars of fire. You come green.
Green eyes, hair, arms,
Head, face, legs, feet, toes
Green, nose green, your
Breast green, your cross
Green, your blood green.
Oregon winds blow around
Oregon. I am green, Oregon.
You are mine, Oregon. I am yours,
Oregon. I live in Oregon.
Oregon lives in me,
Oregon, you come and make
Me into a bird and fly me
To secret places day and night.
The secret places in Oregon,
I am standing on the steps
Of the holy church of Crispus
Attucks St. John the Baptist,
The holy brother of Christ,
I am talking to Lorca. We
Decide the Hart Crane trip, home to Oregon
Heaven flight from Gulf of
Mexico, the bridge is
Crossed, and the florid black found.

PAULI MURRAY

from *Dark Testament*

5

Black men were safe when tom-toms slumbered
'Til traders came with beads and rum,
Bartered and bribed on their slaver's quest,
Killed the watcher, silenced the drum.

Villages screamed in headless horror,
Villages blazed with fiery eye,
Trapped lions roared no greater terror
Than man pinned back on burning sky.
With one great throat the forests thundered,
With one vast body their creatures fled
But man the hunter was now the hunted
Bleeding fresh trails of dying and dead.

Tethered beneath a slave-ship's girth,
The hours throbbed with dying and birth,
Foaming and champing in slime and dung,
Rumbling curses in a jungle tongue,
Torturous writhing of limbs that burst,
Whimpering children choked with thirst,
Vomiting milk from curdled breast,
Rat's teeth sinking in suckling's chest,
Slave ships plunging through westing waves,
Grinding proud men to cringing slaves.

> *"Oh, running slaves is a risky trade*
> *When you cross the path of Gov'ment sail,*
> *They'll smell you five miles down the wind*
> *For a slaver stinks like a rotting whale.*
> *And when they spy you, dump your cargo,*
> *Shove the first black over the rail . . ."*

He twists, he spins, he claws at the sun,
He plummets down, dark dagger in the flood,
He sucks in the others one by one
And the foam track crimsons with their blood
As glistening shark fins flash among
The black heads bobbing on the wave,
The slave ship flees and freedom is won
In churning torrent, in fathomless grave.

6

We have not forgotten the market square—
Malignant commerce in our flesh—
Huddled like desolate sheep—
Tumult of boisterous haggling—
We waited the dreadful moment of dispersal.
One by one we climbed the auction block—
Naked in an alien land—

>   Driven by whip's relentless tongue
>   To dance and caper in the sun,
>   Ripple the muscles from shoulders to hips,
>   To show the teeth and bulge the biceps,
>   To feel the shame of a girl whose breasts
>   Are bared to squeeze of a breeder's fists.

Sold! Resold with the same coin
Our unrewarded sweat had borne.
Endless tearing—man wrested from woman
Warm and brown as sunflower heart,
Plucked up, thrust down in untamed earth,
Uprooted, dispersed again—she was too brief a wife.
She sits in frozen grief
And stares with mindless eyes
At fatherless children crying in the night.

10

The drivers are dead now
But the drivers have sons.

The slaves are dead too
But the slaves have sons,
And when sons of drivers meet sons of slaves
The hate, the old hate, keeps grinding on.
Traders still trade in double-talk
Though they've swapped the selling-block
For ghetto and gun!

> *This is our portion, this is our testament,*
> *This is America, dual-brained creature,*
> *One hand thrusting us out to the stars,*
> *One hand shoving us down in the gutter.*

Pile up the records, sing of pioneers,
Point to images chipped from mountain-heart,
Swagger through history with glib-tongued traditions,
Say of your grass roots, "We are a hard-ribbed people,
One nation indivisible with liberty and justice for all."

> *Put it all down in a time capsule,*
> *Bury it deep in the soil of Virginia,*
> *Bury slave-song with the Constitution,*
> *Bury it in that vineyard of planters*
> *And poll-taxers, sharecroppers and Presidents.*
> *In coffin and outhouse all men are equal,*
> *And the same red earth is fed*
> *By the white bones of Tom Jefferson*
> *And the white bones of Nat Turner.*

Prophecy

I sing of a new American
Separate from all others,
Yet enlarged and diminished by all others.
I am the child of kings and serfs, freemen and slaves,
Having neither superiors nor inferiors,
Progeny of all colors, all cultures, all systems, all beliefs.
I have been enslaved, yet my spirit is unbound.

I have been cast aside, but I sparkle in the darkness.
I have been slain but live on in the rivers of history.
I seek no conquest, no wealth, no power, no revenge;
I seek only discovery
Of the illimitable heights and depths of my own being.

Cambridge, 1969

GLORIA C. ODEN

A Private Letter to Brazil

The map shows me where it is you are. I
am here, where the words NEW YORK run an inch
out to sea, ending where GULF STREAM flows by.

The coastline bristles with place names. The pinch
in printing space has launched them offshore
with the fish-bone's fine-tooth spread, to clinch

their urban identity. Much more
noticeable it is in the chain
of hopscotching islands that, loosely, moors

your continent to mine. (Already plain
is its eastward drift, and who could say
what would become of it left free!) Again,

the needle-pine alignment round SA,
while where it is you are (or often go),
RIO, spills its subtle phonic bouquet

Farthest seaward of all. Out there I know
the sounding is some deep 2000 feet,
and the nationalized current tours so

pregnant with resacas. In their flux meets
all the subtlety of God's great nature
and man's terse grief. See, Hero, at your feet

is not that slight tossing dead Leander?

Review from Staten Island

The skyline of New York does not excite me
(ferrying towards it) as mountains do in snow-steeped
                              hostility to sun.
There is something in the view—spewed up from water
                              to pure abandonment in air—
                              that snakes my spine with cold
and mouse-tracks over my heart.

Strewn across the meet of wave and wind, it seems
the incompleted play of some helter-skeltering child whose
                              hegira (as all
our circles go) has not yet led him back, but will, ripe
                              with that ferocious glee which
                              can boot these building-blocks
to earth, then heel under.

One gets used to dying living. Growth is an
end to many things—even the rose disposes of summer—
                              but still!
wince at being there when the relentless foot kicks down;
                              and the tides come roaring over
                              to pool within
the unlearned depths of me.

Man White, Brown Girl and All That Jazz

Upon the Occasion of his Marriage

It is essential I remember
ours was a fair exchange.
We were a happy consequence
to paths of darkness
in a world
no less terrible or strange

for all our years of toiling
through it.

I valued you for what I took.
That burning in you bright
illumined our collision;
your phosphorescence still
must be reckoned with
when night
heretic with your memory
trespasses.

God knows we were; though such love
did not a kingdom come to us,
each the other's
wood of destiny
has lit.
You found your clearing;
I fathom mine.
We have had the best of it.

MYRON O'HIGGINS

Young Poet

Somebody,
Cut his hair
And send him out to play.

Someone,
While there is time,
Call him down from his high place.

Tell him,
Before terror marks his face,
He will belong to the hunted.

Say
He will be betrayed,
Or high on some fruited hill
Die naked with thieves.

Go to him
While fire is in his flesh:
Take him whole
And kiss his young mouth into wisdom
And healing.

OLIVER PITCHER

Harlem Dawn

for Charles Sebree

Dawn. Street. Hour of sailor's leave's-up,
stale beer in the hour glass . . . minutes
minutes pink gnats of minutes.

Ebony masks on walking poles, a menial gait.

A Definition

An apartment building superintendant is a man who main-
tains order without being a supreme power, without a carte
blanche to call his own, a bootblack at the mercy of his polish;
in short, he has neither pot nor window. Bullying, finger-
shaking, the power behind the throne (to himself); everything,
even the throne is a whole size too large yet he lords over all in
his true sovereign, the basement with the water pipes, the sub-
terranean cosmos . . . but no goldfishes! Ash cans and mops.

Victim and witness, vaguely aware of the form into which
he has been hammered, he wears his ugliness proudly like a
horror-helmet, and tugs at the reins of runaway mops! Such is
the superman's function.

At any black as royal hour just before the garish dawn, we
can hear the endless gramophone record of fanfarannade and
abracadabra of this Minos on a trapeze, coming from the
super's highroad: the basement hell.
Listen.

Jean-Jaques

for John and Ruth Stephan

THE INFANT

The quagmire of an overstuffed sofa—
    the shin is for kicking the cat is for
    skinning the stick is for sticking
this is just the beginning: the snowsuit inferno.
    Earth and stairs they leap ice bites hot
    water bites wind bites the bite of the
    white she-wolf is broken glass. Red means
    HURT. The sun is a splinter for the eye
    lollypop is . . .
horehound suspiciousness.
    Cheeks mean love but duty is a pee pot.
No outlines of day are left uncrayoned in dreams.
They mean MORE:
    I want. Shin for kicking cat for skinning
    stick for sticking
this is just the beginning
    I want.

JEAN-JAQUES

        Pick a number from 1
        to 30, circle it on your
        calendar. Jean-Jaques
        died thumbing his nose.

The sheets, spotted, a sad sea of Latin faces. Blood and bone, grandmothers sitting, kneeling, knitting manners and diets in a graveyard, or doing their beads. And not a comtesse in the lot.

Jean-Jaques lies in an empty black room of the mind where the face of the Angel of Death appears . . .

"Take it on the lam, Angel with your twelve karat halo, dis-
robed of personal feeling. Fat and beaming or slick and chi-chi,
Angels of Death all have smelly feet . . ."
wet with tears . . .

"Jean-Jaques. When you returned to yourself you were drag-
ging a carrion carcass behind you."

"Shed your wax tears for the neon-world!"

"The door of entrances and exits has gone, Jean-Jaques.
Gone!" (*Ave! Ave!*)

A dark cloud of tragic laughter. All say goodbye. The petri-
fied sheet. Reflected on the half-lidded eyeball: the anxious
gawk of a little black haired girl, half hidden behind the door.
She shuts her eyes, and slams the door.

(*Ave.*
Aa aa aa aa
ve.)

THE PALE BLUE CASKET

Why don't we rock the casket here in the moonlight?

A man begins in the cradle and ends in the casket.
That's if he's a two time winner. In between? The
echo of a long lament. A mosaic of sleep. A marble
laugh. A few grapes. A short wail from the other
shore. The scattered moldy crumbs of best intentions
and the insecure peace of distance. The moon and
the sun go on playing an eternal game Show-me-yours-
and-I'll-show-you-mine but words fail us. We say,
here lies a man in a telephone booth, already cold
and without direct communication to the moon to
warm himself.

And rock so soon!

Rock, rock, rock the casket here in the moonlight.

CARILLION

Ringing clearly as an echo, elusive, through the
tree tops of the Foret de Compiegne, the splinters
of sound, primordial, sharply through to the Cote
d'Azur where the mirror of the sea awaits the slim
figured voice,
        "I want. I want." . . .
awaits to receive into itself, whole . . .
        "I want. I want."
—but it is not the voice of Jean-Jaques.

Jean-Jaques by another's name.

The name of our first love. Our own

received and sunken. Another rupture in the sea.

DUDLEY RANDALL

Booker T. and W. E. B.

(Booker T. Washington and W. E. B. Du Bois)

"It seems to me," said Booker T.,
"It shows a mighty lot of cheek
To study chemistry and Greek
When Mister Charlie needs a hand
To hoe the cotton on his land,
And when Miss Ann looks for a cook,
Why stick your nose inside a book?"

"I don't agree," said W. E. B.
"If I should have the drive to seek
Knowledge of chemistry or Greek,
I'll do it. Charles and Miss can look
Another place for hand or cook.
Some men rejoice in skill of hand,
And some in cultivating land,
But there are others who maintain
The right to cultivate the brain."

"It seems to me," said Booker T.,
"That all you folks have missed the boat
Who shout about the right to vote,
And spend vain days and sleepless nights
In uproar over civil rights.
Just keep your mouths shut, do not grouse,
But work, and save, and buy a house."

"I don't agree," said W. E. B.,
"For what can property avail
If dignity and justice fail?
Unless you help to make the laws,
They'll steal your house with trumped-up clause.

A rope's as tight, a fire as hot,
No matter how much cash you've got.
Speak soft, and try your little plan,
But as for me, I'll be a man."

"It seems to me," said Booker T.—

"I don't agree,"
Said W. E. B.

An Answer to Lerone Bennett's Questionnaire On a Name for Black Americans

Discarding the Spanish word for black
and taking the Anglo-Saxon word for Negro,
discarding the names of English slavemasters
and taking the names of Arabian slave-traders
won't put a single
bean in your belly
or an inch of steel
in your spine.

Call a skunk a rose,
and he'll still stink,
and make the name stink too.

Call a rose a skunk,
and it'll still smell sweet,
and even sweeten the name.

The spirit informs the name,
not the name the spirit.

If the white man took the name Negro,
and you took the name Caucasian,
he'd still kick your ass,
as long as you let him.

If you're so insecure
that a word makes you quake
another word
won't cure you.

Change your mind,
not your name.

Change your life,
not your clothes.

A Poet Is Not a Jukebox

A poet is not a jukebox, so don't tell me what to write.
I read a dear friend a poem about love, and she said,
"You're in to that bag now, for whatever it's worth,
But why don't you write about the riot in Miami?"

I didn't write about Miami because I didn't know about
    Miami.
I've been so busy working for the Census, and listening to
    music all night, and making new poems
That I've broken my habit of watching TV and reading
    newspapers.
So it wasn't absence of Black Pride that caused me not to
    write about Miami,
But simple ignorance.

Telling a Black poet what he ought to write
Is like some Commissar of Culture in Russia telling a poet
He'd better write about the new steel furnaces in the
    Novobigorsk region,
Or the heroic feats of Soviet labor in digging the trans-
    Caucasus Canal,
Or the unprecedented achievement of workers in the sugar
    beet industry who exceeded their quota by 400 per cent
    (it was later discovered to be a typist's error).

Maybe the Russian poet is watching his mother die of
    cancer,
Or is bleeding from an unhappy love affair,
Or is bursting with happiness and wants to sing of wine,
    roses, nightingales.

I'll bet that in a hundred years the poems the Russian
    people will read, sing, and love
Will be the poems about his mother's death, his unfaithful
    mistress, or his wine, roses and nightingales,
Not the poems about steel furnaces, the trans-Caucasus
    Canal, or the sugar beet industry.
A poet writes about what he feels, what agitates his heart
    and sets his pen in motion.
Not what some apparatchik dictates, to promote his own
    career or theories.

Yeah, maybe I'll write about Miami, as I wrote about
    Birmingham.
But it'll be because I want to write about Miami, not
    because somebody says I ought to.

Yeah, I write about love. What's wrong with love?
If we had more loving, we'd have more Black babies to
    become Black brothers and sisters and build the Black
    family.

When people love, they bathe with sweet-smelling soap,
    splash their bodies with perfume or cologne,
Shave, and comb their hair, and put on gleaming silken
    garments,
Speak softly and kindly and study their beloved to
    anticipate and satisfy her every desire.
After loving they're relaxed and happy and friends with all
    the world.
What's wrong with love, beauty, joy, or peace?

If Josephine had given Napoleon more loving, he wouldn't
    have sown the meadows of Europe with skulls.
If Hitler had been happy in love, he wouldn't have baked
    people in ovens.
So don't tell me it's trivial and a cop-out to write about
    love and not about Miami.

A poet is not a jukebox.
A poet is not a jukebox.
I repeat, A poet is not a jukebox for someone to shove a
    quarter in his ear and get the tune they want to hear.
Or to pat on the head and call "a good little
    Revolutionary."
Or to give a Kuumba Liberation Award.

A poet is not a *jukebox*.
A poet is *not* a jukebox.
A *poet* is not a jukebox.

So don't tell *me* what to write.

LUCY E. SMITH

Ballad of American Mores

Why are your blue eyes wet with tears?
 Surely your tears should now be dry.
The memory of my betrayal sears—
 For I was weak, and my love must die.

Do you weep because your love was wrong?
 Surely your tears should now be dry.
I weep because I was not strong—
 For I was weak, and my love must die.

Were you ashamed because your love was black?
 Surely your tears should now be dry.
I swore I'd love him to hell and back—
 But I was weak, and my love must die.

He'll die for a pure white maiden's sake—
 Surely your tears should now be dry.
He'll die, and my heart will surely break—
 For I was weak, and my love must die.

Face of Poverty

No one can communicate to you
The substance of poverty—
Can tell you either the shape,
 or the depth,
   or the breadth
Of poverty—
Until you have lived with her intimately.

No one can guide your fingers
Over the rims of her eye sockets,

Over her hollow cheeks—
Until perhaps one day
In your wife's once pretty face
You see the lines of poverty;
Until you feel
In her now skinny body,
The protruding bones,
The barely covered ribs,
The shrunken breasts of poverty,

Poverty can be a stranger
In a far-off land:
An alien face
Briefly glimpsed in a newsreel,
An empty rice bowl
In a skinny brown hand,
Until one bleak day
You look out the window—
And poverty is the squatter
In your own backyard.

Poverty wails in the night for milk,
Not knowing the price of a quart.
It is desperation in your teen-ager's face,
Wanting a new evening gown for the junior prom,
After going through school in rummage store clothes.
It is a glass of forgetfulness sold over the bar.

And poverty's voice is a jeer in the night—
      "You may bring another child
      Into the rat race that is your life;
      You may cut down on food
      To buy contraceptives;
      You may see your wife walk alone
      Down some back alley route
      To a reluctant appointment
      With an unsterile knife—
      Or you may sleep alone."
And one morning shaving
You look in the mirror—

And never again will poverty be alien,
For the face of poverty is not over your shoulder,
The face of poverty is your own.
And hearing the break in your wife's voice
At the end of a bedtime story,
You realize that somewhere along the way
The stock ending in your own story went wrong.
And now you no longer ask
That you and your wife
Will live happily ever after—
But simply that you
And your wife
And your children
Will live.

MELVIN B. TOLSON

Dark Symphony

I
Allegro Moderato

Black Crispus Attucks taught
                Us how to die
Before white Patrick Henry's bugle breath
Uttered the vertical
                Transmitting cry:
"Yea, give me liberty or give me death."

Waifs of the auction block,
                Men black and strong
The juggernauts of despotism withstood,
Loin-girt with faith that worms
                Equate the wrong
And dust is purged to create brotherhood.

No Banquo's ghost can rise
                Against us now,
Aver we hobnailed Man beneath the brute,
Squeezed down the thorns of greed
                On Labor's brow,
Garroted lands and carted off the loot.

II
Lento Grave

The centuries-old pathos in our voices
Saddens the great white world,
And the wizardry of our dusky rhythms
Conjures up shadow-shapes of ante-bellum years:

Black slaves singing *One More River to Cross*
In the torture tombs of slave-ships,
Black slaves singing *Steal Away to Jesus*
In jungle swamps,
Black slaves singing *The Crucifixion*
In slave-pens at midnight,
Black slaves singing *Swing Low, Sweet Chariot*
In cabins of death,
Black slaves singing *Go Down, Moses*
In the canebrakes of the Southern Pharaohs.

III
Andante Sostenuto

They tell us to forget
The Golgotha we tread . . .
We who are scourged with hate,
A price upon our head.
They who have shackled us
Require of us a song,
They who have wasted us
Bid us condone the wrong.

They tell us to forget
Democracy is spurned.
They tell us to forget
The Bill of Rights is burned.
Three hundred years we slaved,
We slave and suffer yet:
Though flesh and bone rebel,
They tell us to forget!

Oh, how can we forget
Our human rights denied?
Oh, how can we forget
Our manhood crucified?
When Justice is profaned
And plea with curse is met,

When Freedom's gates are barred,
Oh, how can we forget?

IV
Tempo Primo

The New Negro strides upon the continent
In seven-league boots . . .
The New Negro
Who sprang from the vigor-stout loins
Of Nat Turner, gallows-martyr for Freedom,
Of Joseph Cinquez, Black Moses of the Amistad Mutiny,
Of Frederick Douglass, oracle of the Catholic Man,
Of Sojourner Truth, eye and ear of Lincoln's legions,
Of Harriet Tubman, Saint Bernard of the Underground
     Railroad.

The New Negro
Breaks the icons of his detractors,
Wipes out the conspiracy of silence,
Speaks to *his* America:

"My history-moulding ancestors
Planted the first crops of wheat on these shores,
Built ships to conquer the seven seas,
Erected the Cotton Empire,
Flung railroads across a hemisphere,
Disemboweled the earth's iron and coal,
Tunneled the mountains and bridged rivers,
Harvested the grain and hewed forests,
Sentineled the Thirteen Colonies,
Unfurled Old Glory at the North Pole,
Fought a hundred battles for the Republic."

The New Negro:
His giant hands fling murals upon high chambers,
His drama teaches a world to laugh and weep,
His music leads continents captive,
His voice thunders the Brotherhood of Labor,

His science creates seven wonders,
His Republic of Letters challenges the Negro-baiters.

The New Negro,
Hard-muscled, Fascist-hating, Democracy-ensouled,
Strides in seven-league boots
Along the Highway of Today
Toward the Promised Land of Tomorrow!

V

Larghetto

None in the Land can say
To us black men Today:
You send the tractors on their bloody path,
And create Okies for *The Grapes of Wrath.*
You breed the slum that breeds a *Native Son*
To damn the good earth Pilgrim Fathers won.

None in the Land can say
To us black men Today:
You dupe the poor with rags-to-riches tales,
And leave the workers empty dinner pails.
You stuff the ballot box, and honest men
Are muzzled by your demagogic din.

None in the Land can say
To us black men Today:
You smash stock markets with your coined blitzkriegs,
And make a hundred million guinea pigs.
You counterfeit our Christianity,
And bring contempt upon Democracy.

None in the Land can say
To us black men Today:
You prowl when citizens are fast asleep,
And hatch Fifth Column plots to blast the deep
Foundations of the State and leave the Land
A vast Sahara with a Fascist brand.

VI
Tempo di Marcia

Out of abysses of Illiteracy,
Through labyrinths of Lies,
Across waste lands of Disease . . .
We advance!

Out of dead-ends of Poverty,
Through wildernesses of Superstition,
Across barricades of Jim Crowism . . .
We advance!

With the Peoples of the World . . .
We advance!

from *Harlem Gallery, Book I: The Curator*

From the mouth of the Harlem Gallery
came a voice like a
ferry horn in a river of fog:

"Hey, man, when you gonna close this dump?
Fetch highbrow stuff for the middlebrows who
don't give a damn and the lowbrows who ain't hip!
Think you're a little high-yellow Jesus?"

No longer was I a boxer with a brain bruised
against its walls by Tyche's fists,
as I welcomed Hideho Heights,
the vagabond bard of Lenox Avenue,
whose satyric legends adhered like beggar's-lice.

"Sorry, Curator, I got here late:
my black ma birthed me in the Whites' bottom drawer,
and the Reds forgot to fish me out!"

His belly laughed and quaked
the Blakean tigers and lambs on the walls.
Haw-Haw's whale of a forefinger mocked
Max Donachie's revolutionary hero, Crispus Attucks,
in the Harlem Gallery and on Boston Commons.
"In the beginning was the Word,"
he challenged, "not the Brush!"
The scorn in the eyes that raked the gallery
was the scorn of an Ozymandias.

The metal smelted from the ore of ideas,
his grin revealed all the gold he had stored away.
"Just came from a jam session
at the Daddy-O Club," he said.
"I'm just one step from heaven
with the blues a-percolating in my head.
You should've heard old Satchmo blow his horn!
The Lord God A'mighty made no mistake
the day that cat was born!"

Like a bridegroom unloosing a virgin knot,
from an inner pocket he coaxed a manuscript.
"Just given Satchmo a one-way ticket
to Immortality," he said. "Pure inspiration!"
His lips folded about the neck of a whiskey bottle
whose label belied its white-heat hooch.
I heard a gurgle, a gurgle—a death rattle.
His eyes as bright as a parachute light,
he began to rhetorize in the grand style
of a Doctor Faustus in the dilapidated Harlem Opera House:

*King Oliver of New Orleans
has kicked the bucket, but he left behind
old Satchmo with his red-hot horn
to syncopate the heart and mind.
The honky-tonks in Storyville
have turned to ashes, have turned to dust,
but old Satchmo is still around
like Uncle Sam's IN GOD WE TRUST.*

Where, oh, where is Bessie Smith
with her heart as big as the blues of truth?
Where, oh, where is Mister Jelly Roll
with his Cadillac and diamond tooth?
Where, oh, where is Papa Handy
with his blue notes a-dragging from bar to bar?
Where, oh, where is bulletproof Leadbelly
with his tall tales and 12-string guitar?

Old Hip Cats,
when you sang and played the blues
the night Satchmo was born,
did you know hypodermic needles in Rome
couldn't hoodoo him away from his horn?
Wyatt Earp's legend, John Henry's, too,
is a dare and a bet to old Satchmo
when his groovy blues put headlines in the news
from the Gold Coast to cold Moscow.

Old Satchmo's
gravelly voice and tapping foot and crazy notes
set my soul on fire.
If I climbed
the seventy-seven steps of the Seventh
Heaven, Satchmo's high C would carry me higher!
Are you hip to this, Harlem? Are you hip?
On Judgment Day, Gabriel will say
after he blows his horn:
"I'd be the greatest trumpeter in the Universe,
if old Satchmo had never been born!"

———————

Hideho Heights,
a black Gigas,
ghosted above us
in a fan vaulting of awkward-age lights and shadows.

Sudden silence,
succulent as the leaves of a fat hen, swallowed
up the Zulu Club.

He staged a brown pose that minded me
of an atheistic black baritone
who sang blue spirituals that turned
some white folk white, some pink, and others red.

Hideho's voice was the Laughing Philosopher's
as he said:
"Only kings and fortunetellers,
poets and preachers,
are born to be."

In spite of the mocker's mask,
I saw Hideho
as a charcoal Piute Messiah
at a ghetto
ghost dance.

Does a Yeats or a beast or a Wovoka
see and hear
when our own faculties fail?

Was it *vox populi*
or the Roman procurator
who said to the
Roman who was not a Roman,
"Much learning doth make thee mad"?

In a faraway funereal voice,
Hideho continued:
"The night John Henry was born
no Wise Men came to his cabin, because
they got lost in a raging storm
that tore
the countryside apart
like a mother's womb
when a too-big son is born."

"Great God A'mighty!"
cried Dipsy Muse,
as his arm went halfway round
the calf's-foot
jelly mound
of the Xanthippean spouse
whom the whim
of Tyche
had created in the image
of Fatso Darden.
The Birth of John Henry!
Murmurs ebbed and flowed:
soughing sounds
in the ears of a stethoscope.

•   •   •

The night John Henry is born an ax
of lightning splits the sky,
and a hammer of thunder pounds the earth,
and the eagles and panthers cry!

•   •   •

Wafer Waite—
an ex-peon from the Brazos Bottoms,
who was in the M.-K.-T. station
when a dipping funnel
canyoned the Cotton Market Capital—
leaps to his feet and shouts,
"Didn't John Henry's Ma and Pa
get no warning?"

Hideho,
with the tolerance of Diogenes
naked in the market place on a frosty morning,
replies:
"Brother,
the tornado alarm became
tongue-tied."

•   •   •

John Henry—he says to his Ma and Pa:
"Get a gallon of barleycorn.

I want to start right, like a he-man child,
the night that I am born!"
•   •   •

The Zulu Club patrons whoop and stomp,
    clap thighs and backs and knees:
    the poet and the audience one,
        each gears itself to please.

Says: "I want some ham hocks, ribs, and jowls,
a pot of cabbage and greens;
some hoecakes, jam, and buttermilk
a platter of pork and beans!"

John Henry's Ma—she wrings her hands,
and his Pa—he scratches his head.
John Henry—he curses in giraffe-tall words,
flops over, and kicks down the bed.

He's burning mad, like a bear on fire—
so he tears to the riverside.
As he stoops to drink, Old Man River gets scared
and runs upstream to hide!

Some say he was born in Georgia—O Lord!
Some say in Alabam.
But it's writ on the rock at the Big Bend Tunnel:
"Lousyana was my home. So scram!"

———

Black Boy,
true—you
have not
dined and wined
(*ignoti nulla cupido*)
in the El Dorado of aeried Art,
for unreasoned reasons;
and your artists, not so lucky as the Buteo,
find themselves without a

skyscape sanctuary
in the
season of seasons:
in contempt of the contemptible,
refuse the herb of grace, the rue
of Job's comforter;
take no
lie-tea in lieu
of Broken Orange Pekoe.
Doctor Nkomo said: "*What* is he who smacks
his lips when dewrot eats away the golden grain
of self-respect exposed like flax
to the rigors of sun and rain?"

Black Boy,
every culture,
every caste,
every people,
every class,
facing the barbarians
with lips hubris-curled,
believes its death rattle omens
the *Dies Irae* of the world.

Black Boy,
summon Boas and Dephino,
Blumenbach and Koelreuter,
from their posts
around the gravestone of Bilbo,
who, with cancer in his mouth,
orated until he quaked the magnolias of the South,
while the pocketbooks of his weeping black serfs
shriveled in the drouth;
summon the ghosts
of scholars with rams' horns from Jericho
and facies in letters from Jerusalem,
so
we may ask them:
"What is a Negro?"

Black Boy,
What's in a people's name that wries the brain
like the neck of a barley bird?
Can sounding brass create
an ecotype with a word?

MARGARET WALKER

For My People

For my people everywhere singing their slave songs
     repeatedly: their dirges and their ditties and their blues
     and jubilees, praying their prayers nightly to an
     unknown god, bending their knees humbly to an
     unseen power;

For my people lending their strength to the years, to the
     gone years and the now years and the maybe years,
     washing ironing cooking scrubbing sewing mending
     hoeing plowing digging planting pruning patching
     dragging along never gaining never reaping never
     knowing and never understanding;

For my playmates in the clay and dust and sand of Alabama
     backyards playing baptizing and preaching and doctor
     and jail and soldier and school and mama and cooking
     and playhouse and concert and store and hair and Miss
     Choomby and company;

For the cramped bewildered years we went to school to learn
     to know the reasons why and the answers to and the
     people who and the places where and the days when, in
     memory of the bitter hours when we discovered we
     were black and poor and small and different and nobody
     cared and nobody wondered and nobody understood;

For the boys and girls who grew in spite of these things to
     be man and woman, to laugh and dance and sing and
     play and drink their wine and religion and success, to
     marry their playmates and bear children and then die
     of consumption and anemia and lynching;

For my people thronging 47th Street in Chicago and Lenox
     Avenue in New York and Rampart Street in New

Orleans, lost disinherited dispossessed and happy
people filling the cabarets and taverns and other
people's pockets needing bread and shoes and milk and
land and money and something—something all our own;

For my people walking blindly spreading joy, losing time
being lazy, sleeping when hungry, shouting when
burdened, drinking when hopeless, tied, and shackled
and tangled among ourselves by the unseen creatures
who tower over us omnisciently and laugh;

For my people blundering and groping and floundering in
the dark of churches and schools and clubs and
societies, associations and councils and committees and
conventions, distressed and disturbed and deceived and
devoured by money-hungry glory-craving leeches,
preyed on by facile force of state and fad and novelty, by
false prophet and holy believer;

For my people standing staring trying to fashion a better way
from confusion, from hypocrisy and misunderstanding,
trying to fashion a world that will hold all the people,
all the faces, all the adams and eves and their countless
generations;

Let a new earth rise. Let another world be born. Let a
bloody peace be written in the sky. Let a second
generation full of courage issue forth; let a people
loving freedom come to growth. Let a beauty full of
healing and a strength of final clenching be the pulsing
in our spirits and our blood. Let the martial songs be
written, let the dirges disappear. Let a race of men now
rise and take control.

Molly Means

Old Molly Means was a hag and a witch;
Chile of the devil, the dark, and sitch.

Her heavy hair hung thick in ropes
And her blazing eyes was black as picch.
Imp at three and wench at 'leben
She counted her husbands to the number seben.
    O Molly, Molly, Molly Means
    There goes the ghost of Molly Means.

Some say she was born with a veil on her face
So she could look through unnatural space
Through the future and through the past
And charm a body or an evil place
And every man could well despise
The evil look in her coal black eyes.
    Old Molly, Molly, Molly Means
    Dark is the ghost of Molly Means.

And when the tale begun to spread
Of evil and of holy dread:
Her black-hand arts and her evil powers
How she could cast her spells and called the dead.
The younguns was afraid at night
And the farmers feared their crops would blight.
    Old Molly, Molly, Molly Means
    Cold is the ghost of Molly Means.

Then one dark day she put a spell
On a young gal-bride just come to dwell
In the lane just down from Molly's shack
And when her husband come riding back
His wife was barking like a dog
And on all fours like a common hog.
    O Molly, Molly, Molly Means
    Where is the ghost of Molly Means?

The neighbors come and they went away
And said she'd die before break of day
But her husband held her in his arms
And swore he'd break the wicked charms;
He'd search all up and down the land
And turn the spell on Molly's hand.

O Molly, Molly, Molly Means
Sharp is the ghost of Molly Means.

So he rode all day and he rode all night
And at the dawn he come in sight
Of a man who said he could move the spell
And cause the awful thing to dwell
On Molly Means, to bark and bleed
Till she died at the hands of her evil deed.
    Old Molly, Molly, Molly Means
    This is the ghost of Molly Means.

Sometimes at night through the shadowy trees
She rides along on a winter breeze.
You can hear her holler and whine and cry.
Her voice is thin and her moan is high,
And her cackling laugh or her barking cold
Bring terror to the young and old.
    O Molly, Molly, Molly Means
    Lean is the ghost of Molly Means.

October Journey

Traveller take heed for journeys undertaken in the dark of the
    year.
Go in the bright blaze of Autumn's equinox.
Carry protection against ravages of a sun-robber, a vandal, a
    thief.
Cross no bright expanse of water in the full of the moon.
Choose no dangerous summer nights;
no heavy tempting hours of spring;
October journeys are safest, brightest, and best.

I want to tell you what hills are like in October
when colors gush down mountainsides
and little streams are freighted with a caravan of leaves,
I want to tell you how they blush and turn in fiery shame and
    joy,

how their love burns with flames consuming and terrible
until we wake one morning and woods are like a smoldering
    plain—
a glowing caldron full of jewelled fire;
the emerald earth a dragon's eye
the poplars drenched with yellow light
and dogwoods blazing bloody red.
Travelling southward earth changes from gray rock to green
    velvet.
Earth changes to red clay
with green grass growing brightly
with saffron skies of evening setting dully
with muddy rivers moving sluggishly.

In the early spring when the peach tree blooms
wearing a veil like a lavender haze
and the pear and plum in their bridal hair
gently snow their petals on earth's grassy bosom below
then the soughing breeze is soothing
and the world seems bathed in tenderness,
but in October
blossoms have long since fallen.
A few red apples hang on leafless boughs;
wind whips bushes briskly.
And where a blue stream sings cautiously
a barren land feeds hungrily.

An evil moon bleeds drops of death.
The earth burns brown.
Grass shrivels and dries to a yellowish mass.
Earth wears a dun-colored dress
like an old woman wooing the sun to be her lover,
be her sweetheart and her husband bound in one.
Farmers heap hay in stacks and bind corn in shocks
against the biting breath of frost.

The train wheels hum, "I am going home, I am going home,
I am moving toward the South."
Soon cypress swamps and muskrat marshes
and black fields touched with cotton will appear.

I dream again of my childhood land
of a neighbor's yard with a redbud tree
the smell of pine for turpentine
an Easter dress, a Christmas eve
and winding roads from the top of a hill,
A music sings within my flesh
I feel the pulse within my throat
my heart fills up with hungry fear
while hills and flatlands stark and staring
before my dark eyes sad and haunting
appear and disappear.

Then when I touch this land again
the promise of a sun-lit hour dies.
The greenness of an apple seems
to dry and rot before my eyes.
The sullen winter rains
are tears of grief I cannot shed.
The windless days are static lives.
The clock runs down
timeless and still.
The days and nights turn hours to years
and water in a gutter marks the circle of another world
hating, resentful, and afraid,
stagnant, and green, and full of slimy things.

RICHARD WRIGHT

Between the World and Me

And one morning while in the woods I stumbled suddenly
    upon the thing,
Stumbled upon it in a grassy clearing guarded by scaly oaks
    and elms.
And the sooty details of the scene rose, thrusting themselves
    between the world and me . . .

There was a design of white bones slumbering forgottenly
    upon a cushion of ashes.
There was a charred stump of a sapling pointing a blunt
    finger accusingly at the sky.
There were torn tree limbs, tiny veins of burnt leaves and a
    scorched coil of greasy hemp;
A vacant shoe, an empty tie, a ripped shirt, a lonely hat, and a
    pair of trousers stiff with black blood.
And upon the trampled grass were buttons, dead matches,
    butt-ends of cigars and cigarettes, peanut shells, a
    drained gin-flask and a whore's lipstick;
Scattered traces of tar, restless arrays of feathers, and the
    lingering smell of gasoline.
And through the morning air the sun poured yellow surprise
    into the eye sockets of a stony skull . . .
And while I stood my mind was frozen with a cold pity for
    the life that was gone.
The ground gripped my feet and my heart was circled by icy
    walls of fear—
The sun died in the sky; a night wind muttered in the grass
    and fumbled the leaves in the trees; the woods poured
    forth the hungry yelping of hounds; the darkness
    screamed with thirsty voices; and the witnesses rose and
    lived:

The dry bones stirred, rattled, lifted, melting themselves into
    my bones.
The gray ashes formed flesh firm and black, entering into my
    flesh.
The gin-flask passed from mouth to mouth; cigars and
    cigarettes glowed, the whore smeared the lipstick red
    upon her lips,
And a thousand faces swirled around me, clamoring that my
    life be burned . . .

And then they had me, stripped me, battering my teeth into
    my throat till I swallowed my own blood.
My voice was drowned in the roar of their voices, and my
    black wet body slipped and rolled in their hands as they
    bound me to the sapling.
And my skin clung to the bubbling hot tar, falling from me
    in limp patches.
And the down and quills of white feathers sank into my raw
    flesh, and I moaned in my agony.
Then my blood was cooled mercifully, cooled by a baptism of
    gasoline.
And in a blaze of red I leaped to the sky as pain rose like
    water, boiling my limbs.
Panting, begging I clutched child-like, clutched to the hot
    sides of death.
Now I am dry bones and my face a stony skull staring in
    yellow surprise at the sun . . .

Haiku

"Oh, Mr. Scarecrow,
Stop waving your arms about
Like a foreigner!"

———

One magnolia
Landed upon another
In the dew-wet grass.

———

In the falling snow
A laughing boy holds out his palms
Until they are white.

———

A September rain
Tumbling down in drops so big
They wobble as they fall.

———

Lonelier than dew
On shriveled magnolias
Burnt black by the sun.

———

A sleepless spring night:
Yearning for what I never had,
And for what never was.

———

The Christmas season:
A whore is painting her lips
Larger than they are.

FIVE
IDEAS OF ANCESTRY
(1959–1975)

MAYA ANGELOU

Still I Rise

You may write me down in history
With your bitter, twisted lies,
You may trod me in the very dirt
But still, like dust, I'll rise.

Does my sassiness upset you?
Why are you beset with gloom?
'Cause I walk like I've got oil wells
Pumping in my living room.

Just like moons and like suns,
With the certainty of tides,
Just like hopes springing high,
Still I'll rise.

Did you want to see me broken?
Bowed head and lowered eyes?
Shoulders falling down like teardrops,
Weakened by my soulful cries?

Does my haughtiness offend you?
Don't you take it awful hard
'Cause I laugh like I've got gold mines
Diggin' in my own backyard.

You may shoot me with your words,
You may cut me with your eyes,
You may kill me with your hatefulness,
But still, like air, I'll rise.

Does my sexiness upset you?
Does it come as a surprise
That I dance like I've got diamonds
At the meeting of my thighs?

Out of the huts of history's shame
I rise
Up from a past that's rooted in pain
I rise
I'm a black ocean, leaping and wide,
Welling and swelling I bear in the tide.

Leaving behind nights of terror and fear
I rise
Into a daybreak that's wondrously clear
I rise
Bringing the gifts that my ancestors gave,
I am the dream and the hope of the slave.
I rise
I rise
I rise.

Phenomenal Woman

Pretty women wonder where my secret lies.
I'm not cute or built to suit a fashion model's size
But when I start to tell them,
They think I'm telling lies.
I say,
It's in the reach of my arms,
The span of my hips,
The stride of my step,
The curl of my lips.
I'm a woman
Phenomenally.
Phenomenal woman,
That's me.

I walk into a room
Just as cool as you please,
And to a man,
The fellows stand or

Fall down on their knees.
Then they swarm around me,
A hive of honey bees.
I say,
It's the fire in my eyes,
And the flash of my teeth,
The swing in my waist,
And the joy in my feet.
I'm a woman
Phenomenally.
Phenomenal woman,
That's me.

Men themselves have wondered
What they see in me.
They try so much
But they can't touch
My inner mystery.
When I try to show them,
They say they still can't see.
I say,
It's in the arch of my back,
The sun of my smile,
The ride of my breasts,
The grace of my style.
I'm a woman
Phenomenally.
Phenomenal woman,
That's me.

Now you understand
Just why my head's not bowed.
I don't shout or jump about
Or have to talk real loud.
When you see me passing,
It ought to make you proud.
I say,
It's in the click of my heels,
The bend of my hair,

the palm of my hand,
The need for my care.
'Cause I'm a woman
Phenomenally.
Phenomenal woman,
That's me.

AMIRI BARAKA (LEROI JONES)

Preface to a Twenty Volume Suicide Note

for Kellie Jones, born 16 May 1959

Lately, I've become accustomed to the way
The ground opens up and envelopes me
Each time I go out to walk the dog.
Or the broad edged silly music the wind
Makes when I run for a bus . . .

Things have come to that.

And now, each night I count the stars,
And each night I get the same number.
And when they will not come to be counted,
I count the holes they leave.

Nobody sings anymore.

And then last night, I tiptoed up
To my daughter's room and heard her
Talking to someone, and when I opened
The door, there was no one there . . .
Only she on her knees, peeking into

Her own clasped hands.

March 1957

Look for You Yesterday, Here You Come Today

Part of my charm:
>   envious blues feeling
>   separation of church & state
>   grim calls from drunk debutantes

387

Morning never aids me in my quest.
I have to trim my beard in solitude.
I try to hum lines from "The Poet In New York."

People saw metal all around the house on Saturdays. The
    Phone rings.

terrible poems come in the mail. Descriptions of celibate
    parties
                        torn trousers: Great Poets dying
                        with their strophes on. & me
                        incapable of a simple straightforward
                            anger.

It's so diffuse
being alive. Suddenly one is aware
            that nobody really gives a damn.
            My wife is pregnant with *her* child.
            "It means nothing to me," sez Strindberg.

An avalanche of words
could cheer me up. Words from Great Sages.
            Was James Karolis a great sage??
            Why did I let Ora Matthews beat him up
            in the bathroom? Haven't I learned my lesson.

I would take up painting
If I cd think of a way to do it
better than Leonardo. Than Bosch
Than Hogarth. Than Kline.

Frank walked off the stage, singing
"My silence is as important as Jack's incessant yatter."

I am a mean hungry sorehead.
Do I have the capacity for grace??

To arise one smoking spring
& find one's youth has taken off
for greener parts.

A sudden blankness in the day
as if there were no afternoon.
& all my piddling joys retreated
to their own dopey mythic worlds.

The hours of the atmosphere
grind their teeth like hags.

                    (When will world war two be over?)

I stood up on a mailbox
waving my yellow tee-shirt
watching the grey tanks
stream up Central Ave.
                    All these thots
                    are Flowers Of Evil
                    cold & lifeless
                    as subway rails

the sun like a huge cobblestone
flaking its brown slow rays
primititi
          once, twice, . My life
          seems over & done with.
          Each morning I rise
          like a sleep walker
          & rot a little more.

All the lovely things I've known have disappeared.
I have all my pubic hair & am lonely.
There is probably no such place as BattleCreek, Michigan!

Tom Mix dead in a Boston Nightclub
before I realized what happened.

People laugh when I tell them about Dickie Dare!
What is one to do in an alien planet
where the people breath New Ports?
Where is my space helmet, I sent for it

3 lives ago . . . when there were box tops.

What has happened to box tops??

O, God . . . I must have a belt that glows green
in the dark. Where is my Captain Midnight decoder??
I can't understand what Superman is saying!

   THERE *MUST* BE A LONE RANGER!!!

* * * *

but this also
is part of my charm.
A maudlin nostalgia
that comes on
like terrible thoughts about death.

How dumb to be sentimental about anything
To call it love
& cry pathetically
into the long black handkerchief
of the years.

      "Look for you yesterday
      Here you come today
      Your mouth wide open
      But what you got to say?"

        —part of my charm

          old envious blues feeling
          ticking like a big cobblestone clock.

I hear the reel running out . . .
the spectators are impatient for popcorn:
It was only a selected short subject

F. Scott Charon
will soon be glad-handing me
like a legionaire
My silver bullets all gone
My black mask trampled in the dust

& Tonto way off in the hills
moaning like Bessie Smith.

Notes for a Speech

African blues
does not know me. Their steps, in sands
of their own
land. A country
in black & white, newspapers
blown down pavements
of the world. Does
not feel
what I am.
              Strength
in the dream, an oblique
suckling of nerve, the wind
throws up sand, eyes
are something locked in
hate, of hate, of hate, to
walk abroad, they conduct
their deaths apart
from my own. Those
heads, I call
my "people."
              (And who are they. People. To concern
myself, ugly man. Who
you, to concern
the white flat stomachs
of maidens, inside houses
dying. Black. Peeled moon

light on my fingers
move under
her clothes. Where
is her husband. Black
words throw up sand
to eyes, fingers of
their private dead. Whose
soul, eyes, in sand. My color
is not theirs. Lighter, white man
talk. They shy away. My own
dead souls, my, so called
people. Africa
is a foreign place. You are
as any other sad man here
american.

The Liar

What I thought was love
in me, I find a thousand instances
as fear. (Of the tree's shadow
winding around the chair, a distant music
of frozen birds rattling
in the cold.

       Where ever I go to claim
my flesh, there are entrances
of spirit. And even its comforts
are hideous uses I strain
to understand.

       Though I am a man
who is loud
on the birth
of his ways. Publicly redefining
each change in my soul, as if I had predicted
them,

and profited, biblically, even tho
   their chanting weight,
                    erased familiarity
                    from my face.
                             A question I think,

an answer; whatever sits
counting the minutes
till you die.

        When they say, "It is Roi
        who is dead?" I wonder
        who will they mean?

Short Speech to My Friends

A political art, let it be
tenderness, low strings the fingers
touch, or the width of autumn
climbing wider avenues, among the virtue
and dignity of knowing what city
you're in, who to talk to, what clothes
—even what buttons—to wear. I address

                / the society
                the image, of
                common utopia.

                  / The perversity
                  of separation,
                      isolation,
after so many years of trying to enter their kingdoms,
now they suffer in tears, these others, saxophones whining
through the wooden doors of their less than gracious homes.
The poor have become our creators. The black. The thoroughly
ignorant.
        Let the combination of morality
and inhumanity
begin.

2.

Is power, the enemy? (Destroyer
of dawns, cool flesh of valentines, among
the radios, pauses, drunks
of the 19th century. I see it,
as any man's single history. All the possible heroes
dead from heat exhaustion

                         at the beach,
                         or hiding for years from cameras

only to die cheaply in the pages
of our daily lie.
                    One hero
has pretensions toward literature
one toward the cultivation of errors, arrogance,
and constantly changing disguises, as trucker, boxer,
valet, barkeep, in the aging taverns of memory. Making love
to those speedy heroines of masturbation. Or kicking literal
     evil
continually down filmy public stairs.

A compromise
would be silence. To shut up, even such risk
as the proper placement
of verbs and nouns. To freeze the spit
in mid-air, as it aims itself
at some valiant intellectual's face.

There would be someone
who would understand, for whatever
fancy reason. Dead, lying, Roi, as your children
came up, would also rise. As George Armstrong Custer
these 100 years, has never made
a mistake.

Three Modes of History and Culture

Chalk mark sex of the nation, on walls we drummers
know
as cathedrals. Cathedra, in a churning meat milk.

Women glide through looking for telephones. Maps
weep
and are mothers and their daughters listening to

music teachers. From heavy beginnings. Plantations,
learning
America, as speech, and a common emptiness. Songs knocking

inside old women's faces. Knocking through cardboard trunks.
Trains
leaning north, catching hellfire in windows, passing through

the first ignoble cities of missouri, to illinois, and the panting
Chicago.
And then all ways, we go where flesh is cheap. Where factories

sit open, burning the chiefs. Make your way! Up through fog
        and
history
Make your way, and swing the general, that it come flash open

and spill the innards of that sweet thing we heard, and gave
        theory
to.
Breech, bridge, and reach, to where all talk is energy. And
        there's

enough, for anything singular. All our lean prophets and
        rhythms.
Entire
we arrive and set up shacks, hole cards, Western hearts at the
        edge

of saying. Thriving to balance the meanness of particular skies.
Race
of madmen and giants.

Brick songs. Shoe songs. Chants of open weariness.
Knife wiggle early evenings of the wet mouth. Tongue
dance midnight, any season shakes our house. Don't
tear my clothes! To doubt the balance of misery
ripping meat hug shuffle fuck. The Party of Insane
Hope. I've come from there too. Where the dead told lies
about clever social justice. Burning coffins voted
and staggered through cold white streets listening
to Willkie or Wallace or Dewey through the dead face
of Lincoln. Come from there, and belched it out.

I think about a time when I will be relaxed.
When flames and non-specific passion wear themselves
away. And my eyes and hands and mind can turn
and soften, and my songs will be softer
and lightly weight the air.

SOS

Calling black people
Calling all black people, man woman child
Wherever you are, calling you, urgent, come in
Black People, come in, wherever you are, urgent, calling
you, calling all black people
calling all black people, come in, black people, come
on in.

Black Art

Poems are bullshit unless they are
teeth or trees or lemons piled
on a step. Or black ladies dying

of men leaving nickel hearts
beating them down. Fuck poems
and they are useful, wd they shoot
come at you, love what you are,
breathe like wrestlers, or shudder
strangely after pissing. We want live
words of the hip world live flesh &
coursing blood. Hearts Brains
Souls splintering fire. We want poems
like fists beating niggers out of Jocks
or dagger poems in the slimy bellies
of the owner-jews. Black poems to
smear on girdlemamma mulatto bitches
whose brains are red jelly stuck
between 'lizabeth taylor's toes. Stinking
Whores! We want "poems that kill."
Assassin poems, Poems that shoot
guns. Poems that wrestle cops into alleys
and take their weapons leaving them dead
with tongues pulled out and sent to Ireland. Knockoff
poems for dope selling wops or slick halfwhite
politicians Airplane poems, rrrrrrrrrrrrrrr
rrrrrrrrrrrrrr . . . tuhtuhtuhtuhtuhtuhtuhtuh
. . . rrrrrrrrrrrrrrr . . . Setting fire and death to
whities ass. Look at the Liberal
Spokesman for the jews clutch his throat
& puke himself into eternity . . . rrrrrrrr
There's a negroleader pinned to
a bar stool in Sardi's eyeballs melting
in hot flame Another negroleader
on the steps of the white house one
kneeling between the sheriff's thighs
negotiating coolly for his people.
Agggh . . . stumbles across the room . . .
Put it on him, poem. Strip him naked
to the world! Another bad poem cracking
steel knuckles in a jewlady's mouth
Poem scream poison gas on beasts in green berets
Clean out the world for virtue and love,
Let there be no love poems written

until love can exist freely and
cleanly. Let Black People understand
that they are the lovers and the sons
of lovers and warriors and sons
of warriors Are poems & poets &
all the loveliness here in the world

We want a black poem. And a
Black World.
Let the world be a Black Poem
And Let All Black People Speak This Poem
Silently
or LOUD

Why's 12

(High Society)
"Old" George Lewis

A farmer come to the city

dirt growing in his mind
songs black land come into
curl your poetry blind
Banjo
waves and sinking bones
play eyes on sky
blood music

heaven people
say see heaven
they seeing
up side down

now they say we fought for evil
took our guns, the wise ones hid, say you
never was to be here
you never was to be

kept to edge of city
alleys behind the bossman's
house. got a job, you got a space,
you got a bond to heal your face
changed from slave
to convict, gone

from lazy to vagrant
jail lost boy in sleep
jail house/plantation moan
jail, was how they changed it

we
    vote among roaches.

GERALD BARRAX

King: April 4, 1968

for Eva Ray

When I was a child
in the Fall the axes fell
in Alabama and I tried
to be somewhere else,
but the squeals of the pigs dying
and hogs and the sight of their
opened throats were everywhere.

I wasn't given that kind of stomach.

When I was 14, I killed
my last thing bigger than a mouse
with my Daisy Red Ryder,
a fat robin on a telephone wire,
still singing,
as my first shot went high
I sighted down and heard from where I was
the soft thud of the copper pellet in his
fat red breast. It just stopped
and fell over backwards
and I had run away
before it hit the ground, taking
my stomach with me.

I'll never know about people—
if the soft thing in the stomach can be cut out—
because I missed all the wars—
but when I learned that non
violence kills you anyway
I wished
I wished I could do it I wished I

could
do you know what it means to wish
you could kill to
wish you were given that?

But I am
me. Whatever made me made
you, and I anesthetize the soft thing
to stop squirming when
you do it brothers I shout
righton righton rightON
my heart is with you
though my stomach is still in Alabama pig
pens.

KAMAU BRATHWAITE

Blues

1   BASIE

Hunched, hump-backed, gigantic,
the pianist presides above the
rumpus, his fingers clutch the

chords, dissonance and discord vie
and vamp across the key-
board: his big feet beat

the beat until the whole joint
rocks. it is not romantic:
but a subtle fingering exudes a sweet exotic
fragrance, now and then: you'll
recognize the odour if you listen well.
this flower blooms and blossoms till

brash boogie-woogie hordes come
bourgeoning up from hell,
blind and gigantic

2   KLOOK

The drummer is thin and has been
a failure at every trade but this

but here he is the king of the
cats: it is he who kills them

sick, sad and subtle,
from his throne of skin and symbol

he controls the jumping rumble
using simple shock and cymbal

his quick sticks clip and tap, tattoo
a trick or two that leaves you

prancing: and reveals that perfect quattrocento
patterning: giotto, ghirlandaio, chano pozo, klook . . .

3   MILES

He grows dizzy
with altitude
the sun blares
he hears
only the brass
of his own mood.
if he could fly
he would be
an eagle.
he would see
how the land lies
softly in contours
how the fields lie
striped, how the houses
fit into the valleys.
he would see cloud lying
on water, moving
like the hulls of great ships
over the land.
but he is only
a cock.
he sees
nothing
cares
nothing.
he reaches to the sky
with his eyes closed
his neck
bulging.
imagination
topples through the sunlight like a shining stone

4   TRANE

Propped against the crowded bar
he pours into the curved and silver horn
his old unhappy longing for a home

the dancers twist and turn
he leans and wishes he could burn
his memories to ashes like some old notorious emperor

of rome. but no stars blazed across the sky when he was born
no wise men found his hovel; this crowded bar
where dancers twist and turn.

holds all the fame and recognition he will ever earn
on earth or heaven, he leans against the bar
and pours his old unhappy longing in the saxophone

5   SO LONG, CHARLIE PARKER

The night before he died
the bird walked on and played

his heart out: notes fell
like figure-forming pebbles

in a pond. he
was angry: and we

knew he wept to know his time had come
so soon. so little had been done

so little time to do it in

he wished to hold the night from burning
all time long. but time

is short
and life
is short

and breath
is short

and so he
slowed and
slurred and
stopped. his
fingers fixed
upon a minor key:
then slipped

his bright eyes blazed and bulged against the death in him
    then knocking at the door

he watched:
as one will watch a great clock striking time from a great
    booming midnight bell:
the silence slowly throbbing in behind the dying bell

the night before be died
the bird walked on through fear through faith through
    frenzy that he tried
to hide but could not stop that bell

6   BASS

Bassey the bassist
loves his lady

hugs her to him
like a baby

plucks her
chucks her

makes her
boom

waltz or tango
bop or shango

watch them walk
or do the 'dango:

bassey and his lovely lady

bassey and his lovely lady
like the light and not the shady:

bit by boom
they build from duty

humming strings and throbbing
beauty:

beat by boom
they build this beauty:

bassey and his lovely lady

All God's Chillun

I

They call me Uncle
Tom and mock me

these my children
mock me

they hate the hat
in hand

the one-
roomed God

I praise.
Winds raise

the flat-
roofed house

each harvest
time

each southern soft Sep-
tember.

'Hey, nuncle!
wanna see

what God in heaven
brought for me?

One pink-ear'd rat,
thick knuckle-headed land

one plot, you know, one
bloody plot; one cow, one dog

one fuckin' plough that only works one way,
a snotty pond in which my children play

leap frog: frog's habitat.
A sniffin' mouse

won't touch the best
we have to offer it; and yet there was a time

we kept
our state on golden stools—remember?'

2

Yes, I remember . . .
but what good
is recollection now
my own mock

me; my own seed,
ruined on this rock
of God, struggle
to strike me

and what need
my story
in these fields
where these cart-wheels

turn over heart
crush hard our hurt
destroy the roots of love
with pain.

Boss man makes rules:
who works, who jerks
the rope, who rips
the patient dirt.

Boss man makes rules:
I am his patient mule.

Boss man rates gain:
I am his living vein
of sustenance:
his corn, his meal, his grain.

Boss man lacks pride:
so hides his
fear of fear and darkness
in the whip.

Boss man lacks pride:
I am his hide

of darkness. Bide
the black times, Lord, hide
my heart from the lips
that spit

from the hate
that grips
the sweat-
ing flesh

the whips
that rip
so wet, so red,
so fresh.

3

They call me
Uncle Tom and mock me
they laugh
laugh loud
laugh loud at me
from the barrels
of their bellies
swishing loud with liquor.

They laugh and the white
man laughs: each
wishing for mercy, each
fearful of mercy, teach-
ing their children to hate
their skin to its bitter root in the bone.

Hold hard
heart

From the bold
sun of the over-

seer's rod
from the cold

sneer of my own
children's fear;

for I fear
to see them

back broken
black broken

teeth their own
gravestones,

pinched
by fever

lynched
by the balls.

 4

'But to hell with this, nuncle!
You fussy black Uncle
Tom, hat in your hand!

Cut the cake-
walkin', man; bus'
the crinoline off the white woman,

man; be the black buttin' ram
that she makes you
an' let's get to hell out'a Pharaoh's land!'

 5

These my children?
God, you hear them?

What deep sin
what shattered glory?

What harsh logic
guides their story?

When release
from further journey?

6

Ease
up, Lord.

The White River

1

From the Akuapim ridge un-
rolled a new land.
Hands on the hoe
knew new grasses:

nkyekyere and lemon;
and the bold knocking demon
of darkness was tamed on the Akropong rocks.
Light rounded to flesh

at Aburi; and the hills
of the Ga lands: Akuse
and Shai: were like islands
burning to green in the water of pastures;

plains drowned in the shallow
drifting of cloud. Crowds
flocked to the Volta, darker
at Ada; and over we ferried

to the hard, sandy gold of Keta.
Here at last was the rager,
the growler, wet breather,
life giver, white curly smoker,

time's river, rushing for-
ever: round pebbles, carved musical
shells; wet ropes in the tide,
tugging moon's motion;

wet sails in the salt; winds drying
the sand into powder; drying

fish, glittered silver;
guinea cock's eyes of their scales in the dark

wood of boats: forest trees fallen and scooped
with tongue's fire; canoes reaping danger;
sharp shark's teeth's death-whiteness ready;
at the slow sloping ledge of our village; time's water's

edge; the white river.

2

This was at last the last;
this was the limit of motion;
voyages ended;
time stopped where its movement began;

horizons returned inaccessible.
Here at last was the limit;
the minutes of pebbles drop-
ping into the hourless pool.

Hands reached into water;
gods nudged us like fish;
black bottomless whales that we worshipped.
O new world of want, who will build the new ways,

the new ships?

Sam Lord

The lord is my shepherd
he created my black belly sheep

he maketh me to lie down in green pastures
where the spiders sleep

he leadeth me beside the still waters:
lakes, green pond, constitution river, glitter bay

he leadeth me in the paths of righteousness for his name sake
though i am dry as a cracked sculptor's mould

he restoreth my soul

yea, though i walk through the valley of the shadow of death:
gullyroot, limegrove, lignum vitae

i will fear no eyevil: for thou art with me

ragged point at dream's morning
oistin town dripping to dust

thy rod and thy staff they comfort me
thou preparest a table before me in the presence of mine
    enemies

candle, book of confectionery that i will proudly bear
bell that i will break and pour its sound in the vévé

breadnut: casket of my mother
plantain, mortar, slave song

and the grapefruit which is life which is love
which is death which is resurrection

skin of fire, pith of innocent air
pulp of flesh of freshest clear: gold volcano seed of earth

thou anointest my head with oil
halleluja

thy rod and thy staff no longer assault me
my cup of hands runneth over

surely goodness and mercy
francina and faith

shall follow me all the days of my life
and i will dwell in the house of the merchant for never

LUCILLE CLIFTON

in the inner city
or
like we call it
home
we think a lot about uptown
and the silent nights
and the houses straight as
dead men
and the pastel lights
and we hang on to our no place
happy to be alive
and in the inner city
or
like we call it
home

miss rosie

when i watch you
wrapped up like garbage
sitting, surrounded by the smell
of too old potato peels
or
when i watch you
in your old man's shoes
with the little toe cut out
sitting, waiting for your mind
like next week's grocery
i say
when i watch you
you wet brown bag of a woman
who used to be the best looking gal in georgia
used to be called the Georgia Rose
i stand up

through your destruction
i stand up

good times

my daddy has paid the rent
and the insurance man is gone
and the lights is back on
and my uncle brud has hit
for one dollar straight
and they is good times
good times
good times

my mama has made bread
and grampaw has come
and everybody is drunk
and dancing in the kitchen
and singing in the kitchen
oh these is good times
good times
good times

oh children think about the
good times

admonitions

boys
i don't promise you nothing
but this
what you pawn
i will redeem
what you steal
i will conceal
my private silence to

your public guilt
is all i got

girls
first time a white man
opens his fly
like a good thing
we'll just laugh
laugh real loud my
black women

children
when they ask you
why is your mama so funny
say
she is a poet
she don't have no sense

———————

being property once myself
i have a feeling for it,
that's why i can talk
about environment.
what wants to be a tree,
ought to be he can be it.
same thing for other things.
same thing for men.

the lost baby poem

the time i dropped your almost body down
down to meet the waters under the city
and run one with the sewage to the sea
what did i know about waters rushing back
what did i know about drowning
or being drowned

you would have been born in winter
in the year of the disconnected gas
and no car   we would have made the thin
walk over genesee hill into the canada wind
to watch you slip like ice into strangers' hands
you would have fallen naked as snow into winter
if you were here i could tell you these
and some other things

if i am ever less than a mountain
for your definite brothers and sisters
let the rivers pour over my head
let the sea take me for a spiller
of seas   let black men call me stranger
always   for your never named sake

from *some jesus*

ADAM AND EVE

the names
of the things
bloom in my mouth

my body opens
into brothers

MOSES

i walk on bones
snakes twisting
in my hand
locusts breaking my mouth
an old man
leaving slavery
home is burning in me
like a bush
God got his eye on

JONAH

what i remember
is green
in the trees
and the leaves
and the smell of mango
and yams
and if i had a drum
i would send to the brothers
—Be care full of the ocean—

MARY

this kiss
as soft as cotton

over my breasts
all shiny bright

something is in this night
oh Lord have mercy on me

i feel a garden
in my mouth

between my legs
i see a tree

EASTER SUNDAY

while i was in the middle of the night
I saw red stars and black stars
pushed out of the sky by white ones
and i knew as sure as jungle
is the father of the world
i must slide down like a great dipper of stars
and lift men up

cutting greens

curling them around
i hold their bodies in obscene embrace
thinking of everything but kinship.
collards and kale
strain against each strange other
away from my kissmaking hand and
the iron bedpot.
the pot is black,
the cutting board is black,
my hand,
and just for a minute
the greens roll black under the knife,
and the kitchen twists dark on its spine
and i taste in my natural appetite
the bond of live things everywhere.

homage to my hips

these hips are big hips
they need space to
move around in.
the don't fit into little
petty places, these hips
are free hips.
they don't like to be held back.
these hips have never been enslaved,
they go where they want to go
they do what they want to do.
these hips are mighty hips.
these hips are magic hips.
i have known them
to put a spell on a man and
spin him like a top!

the light that came to lucille clifton
came in a shift of knowing
when even her fondest sureties
faded away. it was the summer
she understood that she had not understood
and was not mistress even
of her own off eye. then
the man escaped throwing away his tie and
the children grew legs and started walking and
she could see the peril of an
unexamined life.
she closed her eyes, afraid to look for her
authenticity
but the light insists on itself in the world;
a voice from the nondead past started talking,
she closed her ears and it spelled out in her hand
"you might as well answer the door, my child,
the truth is furiously knocking."

jasper   texas   1998

for j. byrd

i am a man's head hunched in the road.
i was chosen to speak by the members
of my body.   the arm as it pulled away
pointed toward me, the hand opened once
and was gone.

why and why and why
should i call a white man brother?
who is the human in this place,
the thing that is dragged or the dragger?
what does my daughter say?

the sun is a blister overhead.
if i were alive i could not bear it.

the townsfolk sing we shall overcome
while hope bleeds slowly from my mouth
into the dirt that covers us all.
i am done with this dust.   i am done.

why some people be mad at me sometimes

they ask me to remember
but they want me to remember
their memories
and i keep on remembering
mine.

———————

i am accused of tending to the past
as if i made it,
as if i sculpted it
with my own hands. i did not.
this past was waiting for me
when i came,
a monstrous unnamed baby,
and i with my mother's itch
took it to breast
and named it
History.
she is more human now,
learning language everyday,
remembering faces, names and dates.
when she is strong enough to travel
on her own, beware, she will.

Jump Rope Rhymes (transcribed)

Donna died
How'd she die
Oh she died like this

Donna died
How'd she die
Oh she died like this

Donna lived
Where she live
Oh she lived in a country called
Tennessee

She wore short short dresses
Up above her knee
And she shake that thing
Wherever she goes

Hands Up
Boogie Woogie
Hands down
Boogie Woogie

*

Vote Vote Vote for little NeeNee
In comes Gilly at the door
Door door door

She's the only one
That can have a lot of fun
So we don't need NeeNee
    anymore.

*

Joycie
The girl we love
Joycie
The girl we love
Joycie
The girl we love
She's the girl from Baltimore

She can rock that thing
But she can't rock me

She can rock that thing
But she can't rock me

She can rock that thing
But she can't rock me

She's the girl from Baltimore

*

Little Sally Walker
Was walkin down the street
She didn't know what to do
So she stopped in front of me

She said
Go girl
Shake that thing
Shake that thing and stop
    (repeat)

*

Down in the valley
Where the green grass grows
Here is Lucy
Sweet as a rose

She sang
She sang
She sang so sweet

Along came Anthony
And kissed her on the cheek

How many kisses did she
    receive
            one
            two
            three
                Etc.

study the masters

like my aunt timmie.
it was her iron,
or one like hers,
that smoothed the sheets
the master poet slept on.
home or hotel, what matters is
he lay himself down on her handiwork
and dreamed.   she dreamed too,   words:
some cherokee, some masai and some
huge and particular as hope.
if you had heard her
chanting as she ironed
you would understand form and line
and discipline and order and
america.

to my last period

well girl, goodbye,
after thirty-eight years.
thirty-eight years and you
never arrived
splendid in your red dress
without trouble for me
somewhere, somehow

now it is done
and i feel just like
the grandmothers who,
after the hussy has gone,
sit holding her photograph
and sighing, *wasn't she
beautiful? wasn't she beautiful?*

wishes for sons

i wish them cramps.
i wish them a strange town
and the last tampon.
i wish them no 7-11.

i wish them one week early
and wearing a white skirt.
i wish them one week late.

later i wish them hot flashes
and clots like you
wouldn't believe.   let the
flashes come when they
meet someone special.
let the clots come
when they want to.

let them think they have accepted
arrogance in the universe,
then bring them to gynecologists
not unlike themselves.

———————

surely i am able to write poems
celebrating grass and how the blue
in the sky can flow green or red
and the waters lean against the
chesapeake shore like a familiar,
poems about nature and landscape
surely   but whenever i begin
"the trees wave their knotted branches
and . . ."   why
is there under that poem always
an other poem?

———————

won't you celebrate with me
what i have shaped into
a kind of life? i had no model.
born in babylon
both nonwhite and woman
what did i see to be except myself?
i made it up
here on this bridge between
starshine and clay,
my one hand holding tight
my other hand; come celebrate
with me that everyday
something has tried to kill me
and has failed.

JAYNE CORTEZ

How Long Has Trane Been Gone

       Tell me about the good things
you clappin & laughin

Will you remember
or will you forget

Forget about the good things
like Blues & Jazz being Black
Yeah Black Music
all about you

And the musicians that
write & play about you
a Black brother groanin
a Black sister moanin
& beautiful Black children
ragged . . . underfed laughin
not knowin—

Will you remember their names
or do they have no names
no lives—only products
to be used when you wanna
dance fuck & cry

You takin—they givin
You livin—they
creating starving dying
trying to make a better tomorrow
Giving you & your children a history
But what do you care about
history—Black History
and John Coltrane

No
All you wanna do
is pat your foot
sip a drink & pretend
with your head bobbin up & down

What do you care about acoustics
bad microphones or out-of-tune pianos
& noise
You the club owners & disc jockeys
made a deal didn't you
a deal about Black Music
& you really don't give
a shit long as you take

      There was a time
when certain radio stations played all Black Music
from Charlie Parker to Johnny Ace
on show after show
but what happened
I'll tell you what happened
they divided Black Music
doubled the money
& left us split again
is what happened

John Coltrane's dead & some
of you
have yet to hear him play
How long how long has that Trane been gone

and how many more Tranes will go
before you understand your life
John Coltrane who had the whole of
life wrapped up in B flat
John Coltrane like Malcolm
True image of Black Masculinity

Now tell me about the good things
I'm telling you about

John Coltrane

A name that should ring
throughout the projects mothers
Mothers with sons
who need John Coltrane
Need the warm arm of his music
like words from a Father
words of Comfort
words of Africa
words of Welcome
How long how long has that Trane been gone

John palpitating love notes
in a lost-found nation
within a nation
His music resounding discovery
signed Always
John Coltrane

Rip those dead white people off
your walls Black People
Black people whose walls
should be a hall
A Black Hall of Fame
so our children will know
will know & be proud
Proud to say I'm from Parker City—Coltrane City—Ornette
        City
Pharaoh City living on Holiday Street next to
James Brown Park in the State of Malcolm

How long
how long
will it take for you to understand
that Trane's been gone
riding in a portable radio
next to your son who's lonely
Who walks walks walks into nothing
no city no state no home no nothing

how long
How long
have Black People been gone

Orisha

Across the flesh and feeling of soledad
tornados of blackness
patoised in its beauty
in its luminous fuchsia lagos nights
ruby darkness

criss-crossing in front of the music
in front of my pigeontoed solitude
another bush of praise
another battle ground for accents
insurrecting against brainwash and breakdowns
white bucks and famished lyrics
spellbound and peglegged
on cartridges of gunpowder teeth

Windpipes of burgundy lands
burning veins of respect forward into the blues
into pulsating ear of my cobra skin heart immense
in its infancy of these few words
Orisha   Orisha   Satchmo   Orisha

Rape

What was Inez supposed to do for
the man who declared war on her body
the man who carved a combat zone between her breasts
Was she supposed to lick crabs from his hairy ass
kiss every pimple on his butt
blow hot breath on his big toe
draw back the corners of her vagina and
hee haw like a California burro

This being wartime for Inez
she stood facing the knife
the insults and
her own smell drying on the penis of
the man who raped her

She stood with a rifle in her hand
doing what a defense department will do in times of war
And when the man started grunting and panting and
    wobbling
forward like
a giant hog
She pumped lead into his three hundred pounds of shaking
    flesh
Sent it flying to the Virgin of Guadalupe
then celebrated day of the dead rapist punk
and just what the fuck else was she supposed to do

And what was Joanne supposed to do for
the man who declared war on her life
Was she supposed to tongue his encrusted toilet-stool lips
suck the numbers off of his tin badge
choke on his clap trap balls
squeeze on his nub of rotten maggots and
sing god bless America thank you for fucking my life away

This being wartime for Joanne
she did what a defense department will do in times of war
and when the piss-drinking shit-sniffing guard said
I'm gonna make you wish you were dead black bitch come
    here
Joanne came down with an ice pick in
the swat freak motherfucker's chest
yes in the fat neck of that racist policeman
Joanne did the dance of the ice picks
and once again
from coast to coast
house to house
we celebrated day of the dead rapist punk
and just what the fuck else were we supposed to do

Jazz Fan Looks Back

I crisscrossed with Monk
Wailed with Bud
Counted every star with Stitt
Sang "Don't Blame Me" with Sarah
Wore a flower like Billie
Screamed in the range of Dinah
& scatted "How High the Moon" with Ella Fitzgerald
as she blew roof off the Shrine Auditorium
                                Jazz at the Philharmonic

I cut my hair into a permanent tam
Made my feet rebellious metronomes
Embedded record needles in paint on paper
Talked bopology talk
Laughed in high-pitched saxophone phrases
Became keeper of every Bird riff
every Lester lick
as Hawk melodicized my ear of infatuated tongues
& Blakey drummed militant messages in
soul of my applauding teeth
& Ray hit bass notes to the last love seat in my bones
I moved in triple time with Max
Grooved high with Diz
Perdidoed with Pettiford
Flew home with Hamp
Shuffled in Dexter's Deck
Squatty-rooed with Peterson
Dreamed a "52nd Street Theme" with Fats
& scatted "Lady Be Good" with Ella Fitzgerald
as she blew roof off the Shrine Auditorium
                                Jazz at the Philharmonic

HENRY DUMAS

Son of Msippi

Up
from Msippi I grew.
(Bare walk and cane stalk
make a hungry belly talk.)
Up
from the river of death.
(Walk bare and stalk cane
make a hungry belly talk.)

Up
from Msippi I grew.
Up
from the river of pain.

Out of the long red earth dipping, rising,
spreading out in deltas and plains,
out of the strong black earth turning
over by the iron plough,

out of the swamp green earth dripping
with moss and snakes,

out of the loins of the leveed lands
muscling its American vein:
the great Father of Waters,
I grew
up,
beside the prickly boll of white,
beside the bone-filled Mississippi
rolling on and on,
breaking over,
cutting off,
ignoring my bleeding fingers.

Bare stalk and sun walk
I hear a boll-weevil talk
cause I grew
up
beside the ox and the bow,
beside the rock church and the shack row,
beside the fox and the crow,
beside the melons and maize,
beside the hound dog,
beside the pink hog,
flea-hunting,
mud-grunting,
cat-fishing,
dog pissing
in the Mississippi
rolling on and on,
ignoring the colored coat I spun
of cotton fibers.

Cane-sweat river-boat
nigger-bone floating.

Up from Msippi
I grew,
wailing a song with every strain.

Woman gone woe man too
baby cry rent-pause daddy flew.

Black Star Line

My black mothers I hear them singing.

    Sons, my sons,
dip into this river with your ebony cups
A vessel of knowledge sails under power.

Study stars as well as currents.
Dip into this river with your ebony cups.

My black fathers I hear them chanting.

          Sons, my sons,
let ebony strike the blow that launches the ship!
Send cargoes and warriors back to sea.
Remember the pirates and their chains of nails.
Let ebony strike the blow that launches this ship.
Make your heads not idle sails, blown about
by any icy wind like a torn page from a book.
          Bones of my bones,
all you golden-black children of the sun,
lift up! and read the sky
written in the tongue of your ancestors.
It is yours, claim it.
Make no idle sails, my sons,
make heavy-boned ships that break a wave and pass it.
Bring back sagas from Songhay, Kongo, Kaaba,
deeds and words of Malik, Toussaint, Marcus,
statues of Mahdi and a lance of lightning.
Make no idle ships.
Remember the pirates.
For it is the sea who owns the pirates,
not the pirates the sea.

My black mothers I hear them singing.

          Children of my flesh,
dip into this river with your ebony cups.
A ship of knowledge sails unto wisdom.
Study what mars and what lifts up.
Dip into this river with your ebony cups.

Outer Space Blues

(to Sun Ra Myth)

People, I heard the news the other day
                    like to scared me half to death
Yeah things happen in this world
                    like to scared me half to death
TV say a spaceship is comin here
                    if it do wont be no people left

But I tell you folks, spaceship cant be so bad
Reckon I just a fool people,
                    spaceship cant be too bad
I been on earth all my life,
                    and all my life I been mad

So when the spaceship land
                    I aint runnin too fast
I say, I reckon I might not run too fast
I might run over into Mississippi
                    and you know I can't pass

Hold it people, I see a flying saucer comin
                    guess I wait and see
Yeah, a spaceship comin
                    guess I wait and see
All I know they might look just like me

MARI EVANS

I Am a Black Woman

I am a black woman
the music of my song
some sweet arpeggio of tears
is written in a minor key
and I
can be heard humming in the night
Can be heard
            humming
in the night

I saw my mate leap screaming to the sea
and I/with these hands/cupped the lifebreath
from my issue in the canebrake
I lost Nat's swinging body in a rain of tears
and heard my son scream all the way from Anzio
for Peace he never knew. . . . I
learned Da Nang and Pork Chop Hill
in anguish
Now my nostrils know the gas
and these trigger tire/d fingers
seek the softness in my warrior's beard

I
am a black woman
tall as a cypress
strong
beyond all definition still
defying place
and time
and circumstance
  assailed
    impervious
      indestructible

Look
   on me and be
renewed

SARAH WEBSTER FABIO

I Would Be for You Rain

I would be for you rain,
yet, might bring into your
life, again, the storm;
summer days exact their dues:
troubled skies bring earth greener
hues. Lightning flashes through
the heavy air, rending it with
blinding light and thunderous
swells which press against the
inner drums of my still ears.

Have you forgotten
the grace of having wetness
rain about your face, of
watching greeness sprout,
bursting through the earth
beneath your mudcaked feet?

And for as far as the eye
can see lush fields abound,
and rainbows span the distant
hills.

I would be for you rain;
insistent, persistent, yet
intermittent. Too much
would swell the nearby waters,
flood your fruitladen fields,
laying them to waste. And,
drought has kinder hands.

Life stirs to be born again.
The waters usher in flowers
and grain. I would be for you
rain.

JULIA FIELDS

High on the Hog

Take my share of Soul Food—
I do not wish
To taste of pig
      Of either gut
             or Grunt
            from bowel
              Or jowl
I want caviar
Shrimp souffle
Sherry
      Champagne
             And not because
      These are the
      Whites' domain
      But just because
      I'm entitled—

For I've been
             V.d.'d enough
             T.b.'d enough
    and
      Hoe-cake fed Knock-Knee'd enough
      Spindly led-bloodhound tree'd enough
             To eat
             High on the Hog
      I've been
             Hired last
             Fired first enough
      I've sugar-watered my
             Thirst enough—

Been lynched enough
  Slaved enough
  Cried enough
  Died enough

Been deprived—
   Have survived enough
     To eat
  High on the Hog

Keep the black-eyed peas
   And the grits
   The high blood-pressure chops
   And gravy sops

I want aperitifs supreme
   Baked Alaska—
  Something suave, cool
  For I've been considered faithful fool
  From 40 acres and a mule . . .

I've been
  Slighted enough
  Sever-righted enough
  And up tighted enough
 And I want
  High on the Hog

For dragging the cotton sack
  On bended knees
  In burning sun
  In homage to the
   Great-King cotton
  For priming the money-green tobacco
   And earning pocket-change

  For washing in iron pots
  For warming by coal and soot
  For eating the leavings from
   Others' tables

I've lived my wretched life
        Between domestic rats
             And foreign wars
        Carted to my final rest
             In second-hand cars

But I've been leeched enough
        Dixie-peached enough
        Color bleached enough

        And I want
        High on the Hog!

Oh, I've heard the Mau Mau
        Screaming

        Romanticising Pain
        I hear them think
        They go against the Grain

But I've lived in shacks
             Long enough
        Had strong black beaten
             Backs long enough

And I've been
        Urban-planned
             Been monyihanned
             Enough
        And I want
        High on the Hog

NIKKI GIOVANNI

Black Power

(*For All the Beautiful Black Panthers East*)

But the whole thing is a miracle—See?

We were just standing there
talking—not touching or smoking
Pot
When this cop told
Tyrone
Move along buddy—take your whores
outa here

And this tremendous growl
From out of nowhere
Pounced on him

Nobody to this very day
Can explain
How it happened

And none of the zoos or circuses
Within fifty miles
Had reported
A panther
Missing

Nikki-Rosa

childhood remembrances are always a drag
if you're Black
you always remember things like living in Woodlawn

with no inside toilet
and if you become famous or something
they never talk about how happy you were to have
your mother
all to yourself and
how good the water felt when you got your bath
from one of those
big tubs that folk in chicago barbecue in
and somehow when you talk about home
it never gets across how much you
understood their feelings
as the whole family attended meetings about Hollydale
and even though you remember
your biographers never understand
your father's pain as he sells his stock
and another dream goes
And though you're poor it isn't poverty that
concerns you
and though they fought a lot
it isn't your father's drinking that makes any difference
but only that everybody is together and you
and your sister have happy birthdays and very good
Christmases
and I really hope no white person ever has cause
to write about me
because they never understand
Black love is Black wealth and they'll
probably talk about my hard childhood
and never understand that
all the while I was quite happy

For Saundra

i wanted to write
a poem
that rhymes
but revolution doesn't lend
itself to be-bopping

then my neighbor
who thinks i hate
asked—do you ever write
tree poems—i like trees
so i thought
i'll write a beautiful green tree poem
peeked from my window
to check the image
noticed the school yard was covered
with asphalt
no green—no trees grow
in manhattan

then, well, i thought the sky
i'll do a big blue sky poem
but all the clouds have winged
low since no-Dick was elected

so i thought again
and it occurred to me
maybe i shouldn't write
at all
but clean my gun
and check my kerosene supply

perhaps these are not poetic
times
at all

Ego Tripping

(there may be a reason why)

I was born in the congo
I walked to the fertile crescent and built
    the sphinx
I designed a pyramid so tough that a star

that only glows every one hundred years falls
　　into the center giving divine perfect light
I am bad

I sat on the throne
　　drinking nectar with allah
I got hot and sent an ice age to europe
　　to cool my thirst
My oldest daughter is nefertiti
　　the tears from my birth pains
　　created the nile
I am a beautiful woman

I gazed on the forest and burned
　　out the sahara desert
　　with a packet of goat's meat
　　and a change of clothes
I crossed it in two hours
I am a gazelle so swift
　　so swift you can't catch me

　　For a birthday present when he was three
I gave my son hannibal an elephant
　　He gave me rome for mother's day
My strength flows ever on

My son noah built new/ark and
I stood proudly at the helm
　　as we sailed on a soft summer day

I turned myself into myself and was
　　jesus
　　men intone my loving name
　　All praises All praises
I am the one who would save

I sowed diamonds in my back yard
My bowels deliver uranium
　　the filings from my fingernails are
　　semi-precious jewels

On a trip north
I caught a cold and blew
My nose giving oil to the arab world
I am so hip even my errors are correct
I sailed west to reach east and had to round off
   the earth as I went
   The hair from my head thinned and gold was laid
   across three continents

I am so perfect so divine so ethereal so surreal
I cannot be comprehended
   except by my permission

I mean . . . I . . . can fly
   like a bird in the sky . . .

A Poem for Carol

(*May She Always Wear Red Ribbons*)

when i was very little
though it's still true today
there were no sidewalks in lincoln heights
and the home we had on jackson street
was right next to a bus stop and a sewer
which didn't really ever become offensive
but one day from the sewer a little kitten
with one eye gone
came crawling out
though she never really came into our yard but just
sort of hung by to watch the folk
my sister who was always softhearted but able
to act effectively started taking milk
out to her while our father would only say
don't bring *him* home and everyday
after school i would rush home to see if she was still
there and if gary had fed her but i could never

bring myself to go near her
she was so loving
and so hurt and so singularly beautiful and i knew
i had nothing to give that would
replace her one gone eye

and if I had named her which I didn't I'm sure
i would have called her carol

Legacies

her grandmother called her from the playground
　　　"yes, ma'am"
　　　"i want chu to learn how to make rolls" said the old
woman proudly
but the little girl didn't want
to learn how because she knew
even if she couldn't say it that
that would mean when the old one died she would be less
dependent on her spirit so
she said
　　　"i don't want to know how to make no rolls"
with her lips poked out
and the old woman wiped her hands on
her apron saying "lord
　　　these children"
and neither of them ever
said what they meant
and i guess nobody ever does

MICHAEL S. HARPER

American History

Those four black girls blown up
in that Alabama church
remind me of five hundred
middle passage blacks,
in a net, under water
in Charleston harbor
so *redcoats* wouldn't find them.
Can't find what you can't see
can you?

Dear John, Dear Coltrane

> a love supreme, a love supreme
> a love supreme, a love supreme

Sex fingers toes
in the marketplace
near your father's church
in Hamlet, North Carolina—
witness to this love
in this calm fallow
of these minds,
there is no substitute for pain:
genitals gone or going,
seed burned out,
you tuck the roots in the earth,
turn back, and move
by river through the swamps,
singing: *a love supreme, a love supreme*;
what does it all mean?
Loss, so great each black

woman expects your failure
in mute change, the seed gone.
You plod up into the electric city—
your song now crystal and
the blues. You pick up the horn
with some will and blow
into the freezing night:
a love supreme, a love supreme—

Dawn comes and you cook
up the thick sin 'tween
impotence and death, fuel
the tenor sax cannibal
heart, genitals, and sweat
that makes you clean—
a love supreme, a love supreme—

Why you so black?
cause I am
why you so funky?
cause I am
why you so black?
cause I am
why you so sweet?
cause I am
why you so black?
cause I am
a love supreme, a love supreme:

So sick
you couldn't play *Naima,*
so flat we ached
for song you'd concealed
with your own blood,
your diseased liver gave
out its purity,
the inflated heart
pumps out, the tenor kiss,
tenor love:

a love supreme, a love supreme—
a love supreme, a love supreme—

Nightmare Begins Responsibility

I place these numbed wrists to the pane
watching white uniforms whisk over
him in the tube-kept
prison
fear what they will do in experiment
watch my gloved stickshifting gasolined hands
breathe *boxcar-information-please* infirmary tubes
distrusting white-pink mending paperthin
silkened end hairs, distrusting tubes
shrunk in his *trunk-skincapped*
shaven head, in thighs
distrusting-white-hands-picking-baboon-light
on his son who will not make his second night
of this wardstrewn intensive airpocket
where his father's asthmatic
hymns of *night-train*, train done gone
his mother can only know that he has flown
up into essential calm unseen corridor
going boxscarred home, *mamaborn, sweetsonchild*
gonedowntown into *researchtestingwarehousebatteryacid*
*mama-son-done-gone/*me telling her 'nother
train tonight, no music, no breathstroked
heartbeat in my infinite distrust of them:

and of my distrusting self
white-doctor-who-breathed-for-him-all-night
say it for two sons gone,
say nightmare, say it loud
panebreaking heartmadness:
nightmare begins responsibility.

Reuben, Reuben

I reach from pain
to music great enough
to bring me back,
swollenhead, madness,
lovefruit, a pickle of hate
so sour my mouth twicked
up and would not sing;
there's nothing in the beat
to hold it in
melody and turn human skin;
a brown berry gone
to rot just two days on the branch;
we've lost a son,
the music, *jazz*, comes in.

Tongue-Tied in Black and White

"I had a most marvelous piece of luck. I died."

In Los Angeles
while the mountains cleared of smog
your songs dreamed
Jefferson and Madison
walking hand in hand
as my grandfather walked to Canada.
What eyes met the black student
next to me, her hands fanning
your breezy neck from this veranda,
but Henry's/Mr. Bones.

Home from Mexico and you in LIFE,
I walk dead center into the image
of LBJ cloistered by the draping
flags of Texas and the confederacy,

and as my aunt of Oklahoma told me
I understood your father's impulse
to force you into Crane's nightmare.

After the Roethke reading in Seattle
you stroked the stout legs of an ex-
student's wife while he sketched
you in adoration and as you cautioned
your audience, "forty-five minutes and no longer,"
how Harvard paid in prestige not money,
how a man at Harvard read for four hours,
that he ought to be set down in the Roman
courtyard and have rocks set upon him
until death—your audience laughed.

You admired my second living son
as you loved the honeyed dugs of his mother,
your spotless tan suit weaving in the arch
where goalposts supported you in foyer
for you would not fall.

At your last public reading,
let out for fear of incident without a drink,
your foot bandaged from fire you'd
stamped out in a wastebasket of songs,
your solitary voice speckled in Donne,
in Vermont where the stories of Bread
Loaf, Brown, another broken leg abandoned
in monotones of your friends studying you;

Now I must take up our quarrel:
never dangerous with women
though touched by their nectared hair,
you wrote in that needful black idiom
offending me, for only your inner voices
spoke such tongues, your father's soft prayers
in an all black town in Oklahoma; your ear lied.
That slave in you was white blood forced to derision,
those seventeenth-century songs saved you from review.

Naked, in a bottle of Wild Turkey,
the bridge you dived over was your source:
St. Paul to St. Louis to New Orleans,
the *asiento*, Toussaint, border ruffians,
signature of Lincoln, porters bringing
messages to white widows of Europe,
a classics major, and black, taking your classes,
the roughpage of your bird legs and beard
sanitizing your hospital room,
the last image of your bandaged foot
stamping at flames on the newborn bridge.

This is less than the whole truth
but it is the blacker story
and what you asked to be told:
"lay off the sauce when you write"
you said to me, winking at the brownskinned
actress accompanying me to the lectern;
and how far is Texas from Canada
and our shared relatives in blacktown
on the outskirts of your tongue, tied still.

Last Affair: Bessie's Blues Song

Disarticulated
arm torn out,
large veins cross
her shoulder intact,
her tourniquet
her blood in all-white big bands:

Can't you see
what love and heartache's done to me
I'm not the same as I used to be
this is my last affair

Mail truck or parked car
in the fast lane,
afloat at forty-three
on a Mississippi road,
Two-hundred-pound muscle on her ham bone,
'nother nigger dead 'fore noon.

Can't you see
what love and heartache's done to me
I'm not the same as I used to be
this is my last affair

Fifty-dollar record
cut the vein in her neck,
fool about her money
toll her black train wreck,
white press missed her fun'ral
in the same stacked deck:

Can't you see
what love and heartache's done to me
I'm not the same as I used to be
this is my last affair

Loved a little blackbird
heard she could sing,
Martha in her vineyard
pestle in her spring,
Bessie had a bad mouth
made my chimes ring:

Can't you see
what love and heartache's done to me
I'm not the same as I used to be
this is my last affair

The Love Letters of Helen Pitts Douglass

When I stood behind his desk chair
and when he sat, on rare occasions,
on the porch, "sage of Anacostia,"
they called him, I smelled his mane
glorious, and as a hand saddle
the aroma of hair took me to neckline
and below. In Egypt, long after
Napoleon had shot off the face
of the Sphinx, I thought of this
man, and the cusp of his palms
on my shoulder blades;
as always he was carrying the mail
of gender, his touch immaculate
in the true blend of the cortex,
and of the complex, risen on a pulpit,
and after the hot air, wintry parlance,
the syllables of my name in his ear,
when he touched me, as he had touched
me then.
　　　　I had my suspicions of English
ladies, actresses, ghosts of the Thames,
concubines, as we had been into this next
century. And they had their wiles with him.

I do not feel forbidden; the cameo ring
he gave me, recession of his maleness
all I need, and highlights of my dark
profile, any children we might have
had buried in architecture,
and the hate of his daughter Rosetta,
who I have spoken to over the grate.
The sun rises and sets in our neighborhood:
I WILL BURN THESE. But when I place my fingers
in that mane it is to the saddle he will come.

DAVID HENDERSON

Do Nothing till You Hear from Me

For Langston Hughes

i arrive   / Langston
the new york times told me when to come
but i attended your funeral
late
by habit of colored folk
and didnt miss a thing

you lie on saint nicholas avenue
between the black ghetto & sugar hill
where slick black limousines await yr body
for the final haul
from neutral santa claus avenue
harlem usa

you are dressed sharp & dark as death
yr cowlick is smooth
like the negro gentleman
in the ebony whiskey ads /
gone is yr puff of face
yr paunch of chest
tho   yr lips are fuller now
especially
on the side
where hazard had you
                      a cigarette /

two sisters
                felines of egypt
vigil yr dead body
one is dressed in a bean picker's brown
the other is an erstwhile gown

of the harlem renaissance /
they chatter
like all the sapphires
of Kingfish's harem /
                              old sisters
                                        old relations

in writing the fine details
of yr last production
you would have the black sapphires / there
guardians of yr coffin
                              yr argosy
                                        in life & death
the last time blues /
                    with no hesitations . . .

day of the vernal winds / 1967

A Coltrane Memorial

my first day in new orleans
                    home-house of jass
coltrane dead
              in my dreams
among marching creoles
among marching blacks
                    bojangling jass parade
in *le quartier*
as a resident of a black theatre thru southland
 i laid upon carver's grave   lingered in his laboratory
                                        in tuskegee
i kissed Laly   an ancestor
                         of booker t.
she wore her hair afro
& played coltrane all night   slow
where the southern cross
the yellow dog

long caravan speeding thru alabama
then georgia red clay
black theatre of an albany backwood church
and then
            the long convoy stretch to new "o"
to find coltrane dead
amid the rubble
of newark negroes

i would want my favorite things
in summertime ritual
have coltrane
               the medicine man
of my ancestral journeys
towards my favorite moments

energy dies
energy dies
            tumult or riots
                              die
         the way of escape
         the underground rails
                     the trains
the freight   train
                                  coltrane
                     cargo of fate
         as we ride on
         up
           the way

CALVIN HERNTON

Medicine Man

North of Dark
North from Shango
In kangaroo jungle of West Lost
Dressed in hide of fox
Dressed at last to kill
Thirteen grains of sand
Seven memories
And Ten voices whispering in a rock

Time medicine riddle
Time rock disguised in evil bite
In devil flight
Time encloses cycles
Voice memory
Revolve
Age leaps upon the lips
Hawk! Kiss of hatred
Is turtle blood
Is love's hair buried in an old tin can

Then I said to my knee bones
Teach me how to bend
My knee bones hardening seven memories
Recalled what I fail to know
In an estranged familiar tongue
Said:
    If you must go
    Go by the abandoned railroad yard

The muddy ditch
The lizard infested by-pass
Flank to the left where an old black woman
With prayers for you in her wrinkled hands
Cupped in an old-fashioned apron lap

Rocks eternally
Eternal rock
Rocking chair
Pause, leave a tear
Beneath the fallen viaduct
But do not linger
For the road back is never
Home is never where you were born
Oh Grandmother, figurine gris gris Goddess
Do I
Should I
Can I live so that I may die easily

Thirty years wrinkle
My belly folds
When I sit
When I stand
My belly spreads

Thirty red years contending with Satan
The backbones breaking pain
Thirty times ten removed from gods
My fathers knew

Oh, Shango, man of mothers
Will you join us in trance
In eating of the bowels of black man
Who is our victim
Who no longer is father of his man

And do I approve
If I do not approve
I have done somebody wrong
If I do approve
Why should I approve
Thirty times ten removed from voices
Ancestral

Birth is April fish belly.
Love is love going the wrong way.

And if I weep
I weep for my twin rising out of
The marriage womb leaping upon me mid-years

Hence I put away old handed-down ailments
Put away hence common motives that drive men
To conventional madness
And weep for the mother of my twin
And conjure Dance on pages of medicine book
        of white hands
And by ceaseless slapping on genital organ
And by eating of embryo taken from ovaries
        of the dead infant boy
Leaping to meet me death
If I weep at all

We may not live until love
Until moon
And if I approve
Eating entrails of multitude of living victims
It will not resurrect those already dead
It will not heal ear and tongue of betrayal
April is a time of betrayal
And I do not approve
I do not approve

And if I pray
I pray not to God nor Shango
I pray to bellies of deep sea sharks
And pray for us survived west lost
North of dark in chains

After the present pain is gone.
The hate who roars in the brain.
The one who sucks my breath like an evil cigarette
The one who crushes the young men and smashes them
Who will be left to care

So shameless black men speak blood of their sisters!
And will it if I weep

Drive away juju of the fox
And if I pray
I have done somebody wrong

And if I do not pray
I pray for those who will live until moon
And to those residing in evil bite
And to the old black woman living in my wounds
And for the twin of the father who falters

I pray because I was born
And have sinned my birth to clay.

Wherefore I said to my knee bones
Instruct me how to stand
Teach me how to love and how to die
And my bones wherein the hot oil
Of the sun is contained
Said:
    Go by the abandoned railroad yard
    Flank to the left your black mamma
    Is rocking
    Seven memories recall what
    You know
    North of the dark path in juju jungle
    Age leaps upon the lips and caresses
    The kiss of wisdom is love
    Hold thirteen grains of sand
    Look at the sun until it three-times
    Blinds you, and listen
    Listen to ten voices
    Singing in that rocking chair

    Singing in that rock!
    Singing in that rock!

JUNE JORDAN

What Would I Do White?

What would I do white?
What would I do clearly full
of not exactly beans nor
pearls my nose a manicure
my eyes a picture of your wall?

I would disturb the streets by
passing by so pretty kids
on stolen petty cash would look
at me like foreign
writing in the sky

I would forget my furs on any chair.
I would ignore the doormen at the knob
the social sanskrit of my life
unwilling to disclose my cosmetology,
I would forget.

Over my wine I would acquire
I would inspire big returns to equity
the equity of capital I am
accustomed to accept

like wintertime.

I would do nothing.
That would be enough.

These Poems

These poems
they are things that I do
in the dark
reaching for you
whoever you are
and
are you ready?

These words
they are stones in the water
running away

These skeletal lines
they are desperate arms for my longing and love.

I am a stranger
learning to worship the strangers
around me

whoever you are
whoever I may become.

I Must Become a Menace to My Enemies

*Dedicated to the Poet Agostinho Neto, President
of The People's Republic of Angola: 1976*

I

I will no longer lightly walk behind
a one of you who fear me:
                    Be afraid.
I plan to give you reasons for your jumpy fits
and facial tics

I will not walk politely on the pavements anymore
and this is dedicated in particular
to those who hear my footsteps
or the insubstantial rattling of my grocery
cart
then turn around
see me
and hurry on
away from this impressive terror I must be:
I plan to blossom bloody on an afternoon
surrounded by my comrades singing
terrible revenge in merciless
accelerating
rhythms
But
I have watched a blind man studying his face.
I have set the table in the evening and sat down
to eat the news.
Regularly
I have gone to sleep.
There is no one to forgive me.
The dead do not give a damn.
I live like a lover
who drops her dime into the phone
just as the subway shakes into the station
wasting her message
canceling the question of her call:

fulminating or forgetful but late
and always after the fact that could save or
condemn me

I must become the action of my fate.

2

How many of my brothers and my sisters
will they kill
before I teach myself
retaliation?

Shall we pick a number?
South Africa for instance:
do we agree that more than ten thousand
in less than a year but that less than
five thousand slaughtered in more than six
months will
WHAT IS THE MATTER WITH ME?

I must become a menace to my enemies.

3

And if I
if I ever let you slide
who should be extirpated from my universe
who should be cauterized from earth
completely
(lawandorder jerkoffs of the first the
terrorist degree)
then let my body fail my soul
in its bedeviled lecheries

And if I
if I ever let love go
because the hatred and the whisperings
become a phantom dictate I o-
bey in lieu of impulse and realities
(the blossoming flamingos of my
wild mimosa trees)
then let love freeze me
out.

I must become
I must become a menace to my enemies.

Poem about My Rights

Even tonight and I need to take a walk and clear
my head about this poem about why I can't
go out without changing my clothes my shoes
my body posture my gender identity my age
my status as a woman alone in the evening/
alone on the streets/alone not being the point/
the point being that I can't do what I want
to do with my own body because I am the wrong
sex the wrong age the wrong skin and
suppose it was not here in the city but down on the beach/
or far into the woods and I wanted to go
there by myself thinking about God/or thinking
about children or thinking about the world/all of it
disclosed by the stars and the silence:
I could not go and I could not think and I could not
stay there
alone
as I need to be
alone because I can't do what I want to do with my own
body and
who in the hell set things up
like this
and in France they say if the guy penetrates
but does not ejaculate then he did not rape me
and if after stabbing him if after screams if
after begging the bastard and if even after smashing
a hammer to his head if even after that if he
and his buddies fuck me after that
then I consented and there was
no rape because finally you understand finally
they fucked me over because I was wrong I was
wrong again to be me being me where I was/wrong
to be who I am
which is exactly like South Africa
penetrating into Namibia penetrating into
Angola and does that mean I mean how do you know if
Pretoria ejaculates what will the evidence look like the

proof of the monster jackboot ejaculation on Blackland
and if
after Namibia and if after Angola and if after Zimbabwe
and if after all of my kinsmen and women resist even to
self-immolation of the villages and if after that
we lose nevertheless what will the big boys say will they
claim my consent:
Do You Follow Me: We are the wrong people of
the wrong skin on the wrong continent and what
in the hell is everybody being reasonable about
and according to the *Times* this week
back in 1966 the C.I.A. decided that they had this problem
and the problem was a man named Nkrumah so they
killed him and before that it was Patrice Lumumba
and before that it was my father on the campus
of my Ivy League school and my father afraid
to walk into the cafeteria because he said he
was wrong the wrong age the wrong skin the wrong
gender identity and he was paying my tuition and
before that
it was my father saying I was wrong saying that
I should have been a boy because he wanted one/a
boy and that I should have been lighter skinned and
that I should have had straighter hair and that
I should not be so boy crazy but instead I should
just be one/a boy and before that
it was my mother pleading plastic surgery for
my nose and braces for my teeth and telling me
to let the books loose to let them loose in other
words
I am very familiar with the problems of the C.I.A.
and the problems of South Africa and the problems
of Exxon Corporation and the problems of white
America in general and the problems of the teachers
and the preachers and the F.B.I. and the social
workers and my particular Mom and Dad/I am very
familiar with the problems because the problems
turn out to be
me

I am the history of rape
I am the history of the rejection of who I am
I am the history of the terrorized incarceration of
my self
I am the history of battery assault and limitless
armies against whatever I want to do with my mind
and my body and my soul and
whether it's about walking out at night
or whether it's about the love that I feel or
whether it's about the sanctity of my vagina or
the sanctity of my national boundaries
or the sanctity of my leaders or the sanctity
of each and every desire
that I know from my personal and idiosyncratic
and indisputably single and singular heart
I have been raped
be-
cause I have been wrong the wrong sex the wrong age
the wrong skin the wrong nose the wrong hair the
wrong need the wrong dream the wrong geographic
the wrong sartorial I
I have been the meaning of rape
I have been the problem everyone seeks to
eliminate by forced
penetration with or without the evidence of slime and/
but let this be unmistakable this poem
is not consent I do not consent
to my mother to my father to the teachers to
the F.B.I. to South Africa to Bedford-Stuy
to Park Avenue to American Airlines to the hardon
idlers on the corners to the sneaky creeps in
cars
I am not wrong: Wrong is not my name
My name is my own my own my own
and I can't tell you who the hell set things up like this
but I can tell you that from now on my resistance
my simple and daily and nightly self-determination
may very well cost you your life

Poem for Haruko

I never thought I'd keep a record of my pain
or happiness
like candles lighting the entire soft lace
of the air
around the full length of your hair/a shower
organized by God
in brown and auburn
undulations luminous like particles
of flame

But now I do
retrieve an afternoon of apricots
and water interspersed with cigarettes
and sand and rocks
we walked across:
                How easily you held
my hand
beside the low tide
of the world

Now I do
relive an evening of retreat
a bridge I left behind
where all the solid heat
of lust and tender trembling
lay as cruel and as kind
as passion spins its infinite
tergiversations in between the bitter
and the sweet

Alone and longing for you
now I do

KEORAPETSE KGOSITSILE

Blues for Some Literary Friends & Myself

So now you walk the streets alone
at night. And your eye is not the coil
around your soul and soil

Your soul is soiled
Your memory is but a bloodstain
teetering on legs thinner than your shadow

Bwana poet please please tell me about love
or is yours tucked away too deep in the yellowing pages
of your books? Tell me about justice. About Amilcar Cabral.
Tell me about beauty. Or about the rhythm
of the sun, or the whip, on the back of a slave

Your soul is soiled
Your memory is but a bloodstain
And love is often just another word
for the boundary between soul and soul
And when you talked of justice did you know
that it is often just another word for compromise,
an affirmation of conflicting interests

O, fathers of my father and me
the voice of our land and blood is still
our skeletons rattle between the yellowing pages
and the young eyes will soon curse our cowardice
with a simple: What did you do between despair and desire

So now you walk the streets alone at night
If you are not an artifact dead as any curio,
Then, like my sister said, sick of your loud mouth:
If you are the soldier they shout you are,
shoot! Shoot then. . . . shoot buckshot

in their hearts. Let them know that heaven
is a hole in the air and hell needs its
teeth kicked out, here and now!

For Art Blakey and the Jazz Messengers

For the sound we revere
we dub you art as continuum
as spirit as sound of depth
here to stay

       In my young years
I heard you bopping and weaving
messages I could only walk to
where wood mates with skin

I would have dubbed you godhead
but your sound rolled and pealed:
I am the drumhead even though
Blue Note don't care nothing
bout nothing but profit

How you sound is
who you are
where your ear
leans moaning or bopping
from the amen corner
of chicken and dumpling
memories and places

In my young years
I would have dubbed you
something strange as god
of opiate heaven
of brutal contact
of bible and rifle memories

But the drumhead rolled my name:
How you sound is
who you are
like drumsound
backing back to root
roosting at the meeting place
the time that has always been here

Even here where wood
mates with skin on wax
to make memory, to place us
even in this hideous place
pp-ppounding pp-ppounding
the ss-sssounds of who
we are even in this place
of strange and brutal design

ETHERIDGE KNIGHT

A Poem for Myself

(*or Blues for a Mississippi Black Boy*)

I was born in Mississippi;
I walked barefooted thru the mud.
Born black in Mississippi,
Walked barefooted thru the mud.
But, when I reached the age of twelve
I left that place for good.
Said my daddy chopped cotton
And he drank his liquor straight.
When I left that Sunday morning
He was leaning on the barnyard gate.
Left her standing in the yard
With the sun shining in her eyes.
And I headed North
As straight as the Wild Goose Flies,
I been to Detroit & Chicago
Been to New York city too.
I been to Detroit & Chicago
Been to New York city too.
Said I done strolled all those funky avenues
I'm still the same old black boy with the same old blues.
Going back to Mississippi
This time to stay for good
Going back to Mississippi
This time to stay for good—
Gonna be free in Mississippi
Or dead in the Mississippi mud.

The Idea of Ancestry

1

Taped to the wall of my cell are pictures: 47 black
faces: my father, mother, grandmothers (1 dead), grand-
fathers (both dead), brothers, sisters, uncles, aunts,
cousins (1st & 2nd), nieces, and nephews. They stare
across the space at me sprawling on my bunk. I know
their dark eyes, they know mine. I know their style,
they know mine. I am all of them, they are all of me;
they are farmers, I am a thief, I am me, they are thee.

I have at one time or another been in love with my mother,
1 grandmother, 2 sisters, 2 aunts (1 went to the asylum),
and 5 cousins. I am now in love with a 7 yr old niece
(she sends me letters written in large block print, and
her picture is the only one that smiles at me).

I have the same name as 1 grandfather, 3 cousins, 3 nephews,
and 1 uncle. The uncle disappeared when he was 15, just took
off and caught a freight (they say). He's discussed each year
when the family has a reunion, he causes uneasiness in
the clan, he is an empty space. My father's mother, who is 93
and who keeps the Family Bible with everybody's birth dates
(and death dates) in it, always mentions him. There is no
place in her Bible for "whereabouts unknown."

2

Each fall the graves of my grandfathers call me, the brown
hills and red gullies of mississippi send out their electric
messages, galvanizing my genes. Last yr / like a salmon
        quitting
the cold ocean-leaping and bucking up his birthstream / I
hitchhiked my way from L.A. with 16 caps in my pocket and a
monkey on my back. And I almost kicked it with the kinfolks.
I walked barefooted in my grandmother's backyard / I smelled
        the old

land and the woods / I sipped cornwhiskey from fruit jars with
    the men /
I flirted with the women / I had a ball till the caps ran out
and my habit came down. That night I looked at my
    grandmother
and split / my guts were screaming for junk / but I was almost
contented / I had almost caught up with me.
(The next day in Memphis I cracked a croaker's crib for a fix.)

This yr there is a gray stone wall damming my stream, and
    when
the falling leaves stir my genes, I pace my cell or flop on my
    bunk
and stare at 47 black faces across the space. I am all of them,
they are all of me, I am me, they are thee, and I have no children
to float in the space between.

The Bones of My Father

    I.

      There are no dry bones
      here in this valley. The skull
      of my father grins
      at the Mississippi moon
      from the bottom
      of the Tallahatchie,
      the bones of my father
      are buried in the mud
      of these creeks and brooks that twist
      and flow their secrets to the sea.
      but the wind sings to me
      here the sun speaks to me
      of the dry bones of my father.

2.

There are no dry bones
in the northern valleys, in the Harlem alleys
young / black / men with knees bent
nod on the stoops of the tenements
and dream
of the dry bones of my father.

And young white longhairs who flee
their homes, and bend their minds
and sing their songs of brotherhood
and no more wars are searching for
my father's bones.

3.

There are no dry bones here.
We hide from the sun.
No more do we take the long straight strides.
Our steps have been shaped by the cages
that kept us. We glide sideways
like crabs across the sand.
We perch on green lilies, we search
beneath white rocks . . .
THERE ARE NO DRY BONES HERE

The skull of my father
grins at the Mississippi moon
from the bottom
of the Tallahatchie.

Connecticut—February 21, 1971

Haiku

1

Eastern guard tower
glints in sunset; convicts rest
like lizards on rocks.

2

The piano man
is stingy at 3 A.M.
his songs drop like plum.

3

Morning sun slants cell.
Drunks stagger like cripple flies
On Jailhouse floor.

4

To write a blues song
is to regiment riots
and pluck gems from graves.

5

A bare pecan tree
slips a pencil shadow down
a moonlit snow slope.

6

The falling snow flakes
Cannot blunt the hard aches nor
Match the steel stillness.

7

Under moon shadows
A tall boy flashes knife and
Slices star bright ice.

8

In the August grass
Struck by the last rays of sun
The cracked teacup screams.

9

Making jazz swing in
Seventeen syllables AIN'T
No square poet's job.

For Freckle-Faced Gerald

Now you take ol Rufus. He beat drums,
was free and funky under the arms,
fucked white girls, jumped off a bridge
(and thought nothing of the sacrilege),
he copped out—and he was over twenty-one.

Take Gerald. Sixteen years hadn't even done
a good job on his voice. He didn't even know
how to talk tough, or how to hide the glow
of life before he was thrown in as "pigmeat"
for the buzzards to eat.

Gerald, who had no memory or hope of copper hot lips—
of firm upthrusting thighs
to reinforce his flow,
let tall walls and buzzards change the course
of his river from south to north.

(No safety in numbers, like back on the block:
two's aplenty. three? definitely not.
four? "you're all muslims."
five? "you were planning a race riot."
plus, Gerald could never quite win
with his precise speech and innocent grin
the trust and fists of the young black cats).

Gerald, sun-kissed ten thousand times on the nose
and cheeks, didn't stand a chance,
didn't even know that the loss of his balls
had been plotted years in advance
by wiser and bigger buzzards than those
who now hover above his track
and at night light upon his back.

The Violent Space

(or when your sister sleeps around for money)

Exchange in greed the ungraceful signs. Thrust
The thick notes between green apple breasts.
Then the shadow of the devil descends,
The violent space cries and angel eyes,
Large and dark, retreat in innocence and in ice.
(Run sister run—the Bugga man comes!)

The violent space cries silently,
Like you cried wide years ago
In another space, speckled by the sun
And the leaves of a green plum tree,
And you were stung
By a red wasp and we flew home.
(Run sister run—the Bugga man comes!)

Well, hell, lil sis, wasps still sting.
You are all of seventeen and as alone now
In your pain as you were with the sting
On your brow.
Well, shit, lil sis, here we are:
You and I and this poem.
And what should I do? should I squat
In the dust and make strange markings on the ground?
Shall I chant a spell to drive the demon away?
(Run sister run—the Bugga man comes!)

In the beginning you were the Virgin Mary,
And you are the Virgin Mary now.
But somewhere between Nazareth and Bethlehem
You lost your name in the nameless void.
"*O Mary don't you weep don't you moan*"
O Mary shake your butt to the violent juke,
Absorb the demon puke and watch the white eyes pop,
(Run sister run—the Bugga man comes!)

And what do I do. I boil my tears in a twisted spoon
And dance like an angel on the point of a needle.
I sit counting syllables like Midas gold.
I am not bold. I cannot yet take hold of the demon
And lift his weight from you black belly,
So I grab the air and sing my song.
(But the air cannot stand my singing long.)

Hard Rock Returns to Prison from the Hospital for the Criminal Insane

Hard Rock / was / "known not to take no shit
From nobody," and he had the scars to prove it:
Split purple lips, lumbed ears, welts above
His yellow eyes, and one long scar that cut
Across his temple and plowed through a thick
Canopy of kinky hair.

The WORD / was / that Hard Rock wasn't a mean nigger
Anymore, that the doctors had bored a hole in his head,
Cut out part of his brain, and shot electricity
Through the rest. When they brought Hard Rock back,
Handcuffed and chained, he was turned loose,
Like a freshly gelded stallion, to try his new status.
And we all waited and watched, like a herd of sheep,
To see if the WORD was true.

As we waited we wrapped ourselves in the cloak
Of his exploits: "Man, the last time, it took eight

Screws to put him in the Hole." "Yeah, remember when he
Smacked the captain with his dinner tray?" "He set
The record for time in the Hole—67 straight days!"
"Ol Hard Rock! man, that's one crazy nigger."
And then the jewel of a myth that Hard Rock had once bit
A screw on the thumb and poisoned him with syphilitic spit.

The testing came, to see if Hard Rock was really tame.
A hillbilly called him a black son of a bitch
And didn't lose his teeth, a screw who knew Hard Rock
From before shook him down and barked in his face.
And Hard Rock did *nothing*. Just grinned and looked silly,
His eyes empty like knot holes in a fence.

And even after we discovered that it took Hard Rock
Exactly 3 minutes to tell you his first name,
We told ourselves that he had just wised up,
Was being cool; but we could not fool ourselves for long,
And we turned away, our eyes on the ground. Crushed.
He had been our Destroyer, the doer of things
We dreamed of doing but could not bring ourselves to do,
The fears of years, like a biting whip,
Had cut deep bloody grooves
Across our backs.

For Eric Dolphy

on flute
spinning   spinning   spinning
love
thru / out
the universe

i
know
exactly
whut chew mean
man

you like
tittee
my sister
who never expressed LOVE   d
in words (like the white folks always   o
she would sit in the corner   i
and cry   n
everytime   g
i
got a whuppin

Feeling Fucked Up

Lord she's gone done left me done packed / up and split
and i with no way to make her
come back and everywhere the world is bare
bright bone white   crystal sand glistens
dope death dead dying and jiving drove
her away made her take her laughter and her smiles
and her softness and her midnight sighs—

Fuck Coltrane and music and clouds drifting in the sky
fuck the sea and trees and the sky and birds
and alligators and all the animals that roam the earth
fuck marx and mao fuck fidel and nkrumah and
democracy and communism fuck smack and pot
and red ripe tomatoes fuck joseph fuck mary fuck
god jesus and all the disciples fuck fanon nixon
and malcolm fuck the revolution fuck freedom fuck
the whole muthafucking thing
all i want now is my woman back
so my soul can sing

PINKIE GORDON LANE

On Being Head of the English Department

I will look with detachment
on the signing of contracts,
the ordering of books,
and making of schedules—
will sing hymns of praise
to the negative, when
it is necessary to survive.

> And if the morning
> light freezes in the east,
> a dawn-covered sky
> will tell me I am cold
> to your pleas, but never whore
> to the spirit. I will
> write poems in the blue
> frosted lake.

If I disdain poetasters,
announcers, and the gods
of mediocrity, knowing
that they, too, insist on living,
it is because I hand you
the bread and the knife
but never the music and art
of my existence.

You will not swallow me or absorb me:
I have grown too lean for that.
I am selfish, I am cruel,

> I am love.

AUDRE LORDE

Coal

I
Is the total black, being spoken
From the earth's inside.
There are many kinds of open.
How a diamond comes into a knot of flame
How a sound comes into a word, coloured
By who pays what for speaking.

Some words are open
Like a diamond on glass windows
Singing out within the crash of passing sun
Then there are words like stapled wagers
In a perforated book—buy and sign and tear apart—
And come whatever wills all chances
The stub remains
An ill-pulled tooth with a ragged edge.
Some words live in my throat
Breeding like adders. Others know sun
Seeking like gypsies over my tongue
To explode through my lips
Like young sparrows bursting from shell.
Some words
Bedevil me.

Love is a word another kind of open—
As a diamond comes into a knot of flame
I am black because I come from the earth's inside
Take my word for jewel in your open light.

Revolution Is One Form of Social Change

When the man is busy
making niggers
it doesn't matter
much
what shade
you are.

If he runs out of one
particular color
he can always switch
to size
and when he's finished
off the big ones
he'll just change
to sex
which is
after all
where it all began.

A Litany for Survival

For those of us who live at the shoreline
standing upon the constant edges of decision
crucial and alone
for those of us who cannot indulge
the passing dreams of choice
who love in doorways coming and going
in the hours between dawns
looking inward and outward
at once before and after
seeking a now that can breed
futures
like bread in our children's mouths
so their dreams will not reflect
the death of ours;

For those of us
who were imprinted with fear
like a faint line in the center of our foreheads
learning to be afraid with our mother's milk
for by this weapon
this illusion of some safety to be found
the heavy-footed hoped to silence us
For all of us
this instant and this triumph
We were never meant to survive.

And when the sun rises we are afraid
it might not remain
when the sun sets we are afraid
it might not rise in the morning
when our stomachs are full we are afraid
of indigestion
when our stomachs are empty we are afraid
we may never eat again
when we are loved we are afraid
love will vanish
when we are alone we are afraid
love will never return
and when we speak we are afraid
our words will not be heard
nor welcomed
but when we are silent
we are still afraid.

So it is better to speak
remembering
we were never meant to survive.

Power

The difference between poetry and rhetoric
is being ready to kill
yourself
instead of your children.

I am trapped on a desert of raw gunshot wounds
and a dead child dragging his shattered black
face off the edge of my sleep
blood from his punctured cheeks and shoulders
is the only liquid for miles
and my stomach
churns at the imagined taste while
my mouth splits into dry lips
without loyalty or reason
thirsting for the wetness of his blood
as it sinks into the whiteness
of the desert where I am lost
without imagery or magic
trying to make power out of hatred and destruction
trying to heal my dying son with kisses
only the sun will bleach his bones quicker.

A policeman who shot down a ten year old in Queens
stood over the boy with his cop shoes in childish blood
and a voice said "Die you little motherfucker" and
there are tapes to prove it. At his trial
this policeman said in his own defense
"I didn't notice the size nor nothing else
only the color." And
there are tapes to prove that, too.

Today that 37 year old white man
with 13 years of police forcing
was set free
by eleven white men who said they were satisfied
justice had been done
and one Black Woman who said

"They convinced me" meaning
they had dragged her 4'10" Black Woman's frame
over the hot coals
of four centuries of white male approval
until she let go
the first real power she ever had
and lined her own womb with cement
to make a graveyard for our children.

I have not been able to touch the destruction
within me.
But unless I learn to use
the difference between poetry and rhetoric
my power too will run corrupt as poisonous mold
or lie limp and useless as an unconnected wire
and one day I will take my teenaged plug
and connect it to the nearest socket
raping an 85 year old white woman
who is somebody's mother
and as I beat her senseless and set a torch to her bed
a greek chorus will be singing in 3/4 time
"Poor thing. She never hurt a soul. What beasts they are."

Lunar Eclipse

August 16, 1989

Last night I watched the moon go out
become a dark opalescent glow
I could not believe what was happening
even as I saw the change in light.

The first time I met you
we sat up all night reading
each other's poems   morning hopes
followed us down Cole Street
chattering like a flock of quits.

You stretch across our best years
like a living wire
between heaven and hell
at war   Being sisters
wasn't always easy
but it was never dull.

I can't believe you are gone
out of my life
So you are not.

Inheritance—His

I

My face resembles your face
less and less each day. When I was young
no one mistook whose child I was.
Features   build   coloring
alone among my creamy fine-boned sisters
marked me Byron's daughter.

No sun set when you died, but a door
opened onto my mother. After you left
she grieved her crumpled world aloft
an iron fist sweated with business symbols
a printed blotter   *dwell in a house of Lord's*
your hollow voice chanting down a hospital corridor
            yea, though I walk through the valley
            of the shadow of death
            I will fear no evil.

II

I rummage through the deaths you lived
swaying on a bridge of question.
At seven   in Barbados
dropped into your unknown father's life
your courage vault from his tailor's table

back to the sea
Did the Grenada treeferns sing
your 15th summer as you jumped ship
to seek your mother
finding her   too late
surrounded with new sons?

Who did you bury to become enforcer of the law
the handsome legend
before whose raised arm even trees wept
a man of deep and wordless passion
who wanted sons and got five girls?
You left the first two scratching in a treefern's shade
the youngest is a renegade poet
searching for your answer in my blood.

My mother's Grenville tales
spin through early summer evenings.
But you refused to speak of home
of stepping proud Black and penniless
into this land where only white men
ruled by money.   How you labored
in the docks of the Hotel Astor
your bright wife a chambermaid upstairs
welded love and survival to ambition
as the land of promise withered
crashed   the hotel closed
and you peddle dawn-bought apples
from a pushcart on Broadway.
Does an image of return
wealthy and triumphant
warm your chilblained fingers
as you count coins in the Manhattan snow
or is it only Linda
who dreams of home?

When my mother's first-born crys for milk
in the brutal city winter
do the faces of your other daughters dim
like the image of the treeferned yard

where a dark girl first cooked for you
and her ash heap still smells curry?

III

Did the secret of my sisters steal your tongue
like I stole money from your midnight pockets
stubborn and quaking
as you threaten to shoot me if I am the one?
the naked lightbulbs in our kitchen ceiling
glint off your service revolver
as you load   whispering.

Did two little dark girls in Grenada
dart like flying fish
between your averred eyes
and my pajamaless body
our last adolescent summer
eavesdropped orations
to your shaving mirror
our most intense conversations
were you practicing how to tell me
of my twin sisters   abandoned
as you had been abandoned
by another Black woman seeking
her fortune   Grenada   Barbados
Panama   Grenada.
New York City.

IV

You bought old books at auction
for my unlanguaged world
gave me your idols   Marcus Garvey   Citizen Kane
and morsels from your dinner plate
when I was seven.
I owe you my Dahomeyan jaw
the free high school for gifted girls
no one else thought I should attend
and the darkness that we share.
Our deepest bonds remain
the mirror and the gun.

V

An elderly Black judge
known for his way with women
visits this island where I live
shakes my hand, smiling
"I knew your father," he says
"quite a man!" Smiles again.
I flinch at his raised eyebrow.
A long-gone woman's voice
lashes out at me   in parting
"You will never be satisfied
until you have the whole world
in your bed!"

Now I am older than you were when you died
overwork and silence exploding in your brain.
You are gradually receding from my face.
Who were you outside the 23rd Psalm?
Knowing so little
how did I become so much
like you?

Your hunger for rectitude
blossoms into rage
the hot tears of mourning
never shed for you before
your twisted measurements
the agony of denial
the power of unshared secrets.

[*January 23–September 10, 1992*]

HAKI MADHUBUTI (DON L. LEE)

But He Was Cool

or: he even stopped for green lights

super-cool
ultrablack
a tan/purple
had a beautiful shade.

he had a double-natural
that wd put the sisters to shame.
his dashikis were tailor made
& his beads were imported sea shells
   (from some blk/country i never heard of)
he was triple-hip.

his tikis were hand carved
out of ivory
& came express from the motherland.
he would greet u in swahili
& say good-by in yoruba.
woooooooooooooo-jim he bes so cool & ill tel li gent
                cool-cool is so cool he was un-cooled by
                    other niggers' cool
                cool-cool ultracool was bop-cool/ice box
                    cool so cool cold cool
                his wine didn't have to be cooled, him was
                    air conditioned cool
                cool-cool/real cool made me cool—now
                    ain't that cool
                cool-cool so cool him nicknamed refrigerator.

cool-cool so cool
he didn't know,
after detroit, newark, chicago &c.,

495

we had to hip
       cool-cool/super-cool/real cool
  that
to be black
is
to be
very-hot.

Don't Cry, Scream

*(for John Coltrane/ from a black poet/ in a basement
apt. crying dry tears of "you ain't gone.")*

into the sixties
a trane
came/out of the
fifties with a
golden boxcar
riding the rails
of novation.
     blowing
     a-melodics
     screeching,
     screaming,
     blasting—
          driving some away,
          (those paper readers who thought
          manhood was something innate)

          bring others in,
          (the few who didn't believe that the
          world existed around established whi
          teness & leonard bernstein)
music that ached,
murdered our minds (we reborn)
born into a neoteric aberration.
& suddenly
you envy the

BLIND man—
you know that he will
hear what you'll never
see.
     your music is like
     my head—nappy black/
     a good nasty feel with
     tangled songs of:
          we-eeeeeeeeee   sing
          WE-EEEeeeeeeeee   loud &
          WE-EEEEEE EEEEEEEEEE   high
                                          with
                                          feeling

a people playing
the sound of me when
i combed it. combed at
it.

i cried for billy holiday.
the blues. we ain't blue
the blues exhibited illusions of manhood.
destroyed by you. Ascension into:

     scream-eeeeeeeeeeeeee-ing   sing
     SCREAM-EEEeeeeeeeeeee-ing loud &
     SCREAM-EEEEEEEEEEE EEE-ing long with
                                       feeling

we ain't blue, we are black.
we ain't blue, we are black.
        (all the blues did was
        make me cry)
soultrane gone on a trip
he left man images
he was a life-style of
man-makers & annihilator
of attache case carriers.

Trane done went.
(got his hat & left me one)

naw brother,
i didn't cry,
i just—
    Scream-eeeeeeeeeeeee e-ed   sing loud
    SCREAM-EEEEEEEEEEEEEEEEEE-ED   & high with
     we-eeeeeeeeeeeeeeeeeeeeee ee   feeling
     WE-E-EEEEEeeeeeeee EEEEEEEE   letting
     WE-EEEEEEEEEEEEEEEEEEEEEE   yr/voice
     WHERE YOU DONE GONE, BROTHER? break

it hurts, grown babies
dying. born. done caught me
a trane. steel wheels broken
by popsicle sticks. i went out
& tried to buy a nickle bag
with my standard oil card.

blonds had more fun—
with snagga-tooth niggers
who saved pennies & pop bottles for week-ends
to play negro & other filthy inventions.
be-bop-en to james brown's
cold sweat—these niggers didn't sweat,
they perspired. & the blond's dye came out,
i ran. she did too, with his pennies, pop bottles
& his mind. tune in next week same time same station
for anti-self in one lesson.

to the negro cow-sissies
who did tchaikovsky &
the beatles & live in
split-level homes & had
split-level minds & babies.
who committed the act of
love with their clothes on.
                (who hid in the bathroom to read
                jet mag., who didn't read the Chicago
                defender because of the misspelled
                words & had shelves of books by
                europeans on display. untouched. who
                hid their little richard & lightnin'

            slim records & asked: "John who?"
            instant hate.)
they didn't know any better,
brother, they were too busy getting
into debt, expressing humanity &
taking off color.

   SCREAMMMM/we-eeeee/screech/teee   improvise
   aheeeeeeeee/screeeeeee/theeee/ee   with
   ahHHHHHHHHH/WEEEEEEEE/scrEEE feeling
      EEEE
   we-eeeeeWE-EEEEEEEEWE-EE-EEEEE
the ofays heard you &
were wiped out. spaced.
one clown asked me during,
my favorite things, if
you were practicing.
i fired on the muthafucka & said,
"i'm practicing."

naw brother,
i didn't cry.
i got high off my thoughts—
they kept coming back,
back to destroy me.

& that BLIND man
i don't envy him anymore
i can see his hear
& hear his heard through my pores.
i can see my me. it was truth you gave,
like a daily shit
it had to come.
                can you scream—brother?   very
                can you scream—brother?   soft

i hear you.
i hear you.

and the Gods will too.

CLARENCE MAJOR

Swallow the Lake

gave me things I
could not use.   Then.   Now.
Rain night bursting upon and into—
I shine up-down into Lake Michigan

like the glow from the lights of the Loop.
            Walks. Deaths. Births. Streets.
Things I could not give back—
            or use. Gave me loneliness.
Feelings I could not put into words
            into people. Blank monkeys of the hierarchy!
More deaths! Stupidity and death
turning them on, timing them
            to the beat of my droopy heart,
to my Middle Passage blues
to my self-corroding hate—

In my release, I come to become
            neon iron eyes stainless lungs
blood zinc-gripped steel
I come up abstract—
not able to take their bricks.
            Their tar. Their flesh. Their plastic.
I ran—stung.
Loop fumes hung in my smoky lungs.
            Duped, left with ideas I could not break
                        or form,
I crawled through the game.

Illusion illusion and you
            would swear before screaming—
these choked voices in me screaming.

Screaming with crawling thing in the blood,
        screaming the huge immune loneliness.
One becomes immune to the bricks
        to the feelings.
One becomes death.
One becomes each one and every person I become.
And I could not—
        I could not—
I could not whistle and walk in storms
along Lake Michigan's shore.
        Concrete walks. Concrete deaths.
I could not—
I could not swallow the lake.

Hair

In the old days
hair was magical.
If hair was cut
you had to make sure it didn't end up
in the wrong hands.

Bad people could mix it
with, say, the spit of a frog.
Or with the urine of a rat!
And certain words
might be spoken.
Then horrible things
might happen to you.

A woman with a husband
in the Navy
could not comb her hair after dark.
His ship might go down.

But good things
could happen, too.
My grandmother

threw a lock of her hair
into the fireplace.
It burned brightly.
That is why she lived
to be a hundred and one.

My uncle had red hair.
One day it started falling out.
A few days later
his infant son died.

Some women let their hair grow long.
If it fell below the knees
that meant
they would never find a husband.

Braiding hair into cornrows
was a safety measure.
It would keep hair
from falling out.

My aunt dropped a hairpin.
It meant somebody
was talking about her.

Birds gathered human hair
to build their nests.
They wove it around sticks.
And nothing happened to the birds.

They were lucky.
But people?

LARRY NEAL

Malcolm X—An Autobiography

I am the Seventh Son of the son
who was also the seventh.
I have drunk deep of the waters of my ancestors,
have traveled the soul's journey toward cosmic harmony—
the Seventh Son.

Have walked slick avenues
and seen grown men, fall, to die in a blue doom
of death and ancestral agony;
have seen old men glide, shadowless, feet barely
touching the pavements.

I sprang out of the Midwestern plains
the bleak Michigan landscape, the black blues of Kansas
City, these kiss-me-nights;
out of the bleak Michigan landscape wearing the slave name
Malcolm Little.

Saw a brief vision in Lansing when I was seven, and in
my momma's womb heard the beast cry death;
a landscape on which white robed figures ride, and my
Garvey father silhouetted against the night-fire
gun in hand,
form outlined against a panorama of violence.

Out of the Midwestern bleakness, I sprang, pushed eastward,
past shack on country nigger shack, across the wilderness
of North America.
I hustler. I pimp. I unfulfilled black man
bursting with destiny.
New York City Slim called me Big Red,
and there was no escape, close nights of the smell of death.
Pimp. Hustler. The day fills these rooms.
I'm talking about New York, Harlem.

Talking about the neon madness.
Talking about ghetto eyes and nights
Talking about death protruding across the room
Talking about Small's Paradise.
Talking about cigarette butts, and rooms smelly with white
sex-flesh, and dank sheets, and being on the run.
Talking about cocaine illusions.
Talking about stealing and selling.
Talking about these New York cops who smell
of blood and money.
I am Big Red, tiger, vicious, Big Red, bad nigger, will kill.

But there is rhythm here
Its own special substance:
I hear Billie sing, no Good Man, and dig Prez, wearing
the Zoot suit of life, the Porkpie hat tilted at the
correct angle; through the Harlem smoke of beer and
whiskey, I understand the mystery of the Signifying
Monkey;
in a blue haze of inspiration
I reach for the totality of being.
I am at the center of a swirl of events.
War and death.
Rhythm.
Hot women.
I think life a commodity bargained
for across the bar in Small's.
I perceive the echoes of Bird
and there is a gnawing the maw
of my emotions.

And then there is jail.
America is the world's greatest jailer,
and we are all in jails
holy spirits contained like magnificent
birds of wonder.
I now understand my father urged on by the ghost of Garvey,
and see a small brown man standing in a corner.
The cell. Cold. Dank.
The light around him vibrates.

(Am I crazy?)
But to understand is to submit to a more perfect will,
a more perfect order.
To understand is to surrender the imperfect self
for a more perfect self.

Allah formed man, I follow
and shake within the very depth of my most interesting
    being;
and I bear witness to the Message of Allah
and I bear witness; all praise is due Allah.

Spring, 1967

Don't Say Goodbye to the Porkpie Hat

Mingus, Bird, Prez, Langston, and them

Don't say goodbye to the Porkpie Hat that rolled
along on nodded shoulders
                that swang bebop phrases
                in Minton's jelly roll dreams
Don't say goodbye to hip hats tilted in the style of a soulful era;
the Porkpie Hat that Lester dug
swirling in the sound of sax blown suns
                phrase on phrase, repeating bluely
                tripping in and under crashing
                hi-hat cymbals, a fickle girl
                getting sassy on the rhythms.
Musicians heavy with memories
move in and out of this gloom;
the Porkpie Hat reigns supreme
smell of collard greens
and cotton madness
commingled in the nigger elegance of the style.
                The Porkpie Hat sees tonal memories
                of salt peanuts and hot house birds
                the Porkpie Hat sees . . .

Cross riffing square kingdoms, riding midnight Scottsboro
trains. We are haunted by the lynched limbs.
On the road:
It would be some hoodoo town
It would be some cracker place
you might meet redneck lynchers
face to face
but mostly you meet mean horn blowers
running obscene riffs
Jelly Roll spoke of such places:
the man with the mojo hand
the dyke with the .38
the yaller girls
and the knifings.

Stop-time Buddy and Creole Sydney
wailed in here. Stop time.
chorus repeats, stop and shuffle.
stop and stomp.
listen to the horns, ain't they mean?
now   ain't they mean
in blue
in blue
in blue
in blue streaks of mellow wisdom
blue notes
coiling around
the Porkpie Hat
and ghosts of dead musicians drifting through
here on riffs that smack
of one-leg trumpet players
and daddy glory piano ticklers
who
twisted arpeggios
with diamond-flashed fingers.
There was Jelly Roll Morton, the sweet mackdaddy,
hollering Waller, and Willie The Lion Smith—
some mean showstoppers.

Ghosts of dead holy rollers ricocheted in the air funky
with white lightnin' and sweat.
Emerald bitches shot shit in a kitchen smelling
of funerals and fried chicken.
Each city had a different sound:
there was Mambo, Rheba, Jeanne;
holy the voice of these righteous sisters.

Shape to shape, horn to horn
the Porkpie Hat resurrected himself
night to night, from note to note
skimming the horizons, flashing bluegreenyellow lights
and blowing black stars
and weird looneymoon changes; chords coiled about him
and he was flying
fast
zipping
past
sound
into cosmic silences.

And yes
and caresses flowed from the voice in the horn in the blue
of the yellow whiskey room where bad hustlers with big
coats moved, digging the fly sister, fingerpopping while
tearing at chicken and waffles.

The Porkpie Hat loomed specter like, a vision for the world;
shiny, the knob toe shoes,
sporting hip camel coats
and righteous pin stripes—
pants pressed razor shape;
and caressing his horn, baby like.

So we pick up our axes and prepare
to blast the white dream;
we pick up our axes
re-create ourselves and the universe,
sounds splintering the deepest regions
of spiritual space

crisp and moaning voices
leaping in the horns of destruction,
blowing death and doom to all who have no use for the spirit.

So we cook out of sight
into cascading motions of joy delight
shooflies the Bird lolligagging
and laughing for days,
and the rhythms way up in there
wailing, sending scarlet rays, luminescent,
spattering bone and lie.
we go on cool lords
wailing on into star nights,
rocking whole worlds, unfurling song on song
into long stretches of green spectral shimmerings,
blasting on, fucking the moon with the blunt edge
of a lover's tune, out there now, joy riffing
for days and do
railriding and do
talking some lovely shit and do
to the Blues God who blesses us.

No, don't say goodbye to the Porkpie Hat—
he lives, oh yes.

Lester lives and leaps
Delancey's dilemma is over
Bird lives
Lady lives
Eric stands next to me
while I finger the Afro-horn
Bird lives
Lady lives
Lester leaps in every night
Tad's delight
is mine now
Dinah knows
Richie knows
that Bud is Buddha
that Jelly Roll dug juju

and Lester lives
in Ornett's leapings
the Blues God lives
we live
live
spirit lives
and sound lives
bluebird lives
lives and leaps
dig the mellow voices
dig the Porkpie Hat
dig the spirit in Sun Ra's sound
dig the cosmic Trane
dig be
dig be
dig be
spirit lives in sound
dig be
sound lives in spirit
dig be
yeah ! ! !
spirit lives
spirit lives
spirit lives
SPIRIT ! ! !
SWHEEEEEEEEEEEEEEETTT ! ! !

take it again
this time from the top

RAYMOND R. PATTERSON

26 Ways of Looking at a Black Man

I

On the road we met a blackman,
But no one else.

II

Dreams are reunions. Who has not
On occasion entertained the presence
Of a blackman?

III

From brown paper bags
A blackman fills the vacancies of morning
With orange speculations.

IV

Always I hope to find
The blackman I know,
Or one who knows him.

V

Devouring earthly possessions
Is one of a blackman's excesses.
Exaggerating their transiency
Is another.

VI

Even this shadow has weight.
A cool heaviness.
Call it a blackman's ghost.

VII

The possibilities of color
Were choices made by the eye

Looking inward.
The possibilities of rhythms
For a blackman are predetermined.

VIII

When it had all been unravelled,
The blackman found that it had been
Entirely woven of black thread.

IX

Children who loved him
Hid him from the world
By pretending he was a blackman.

X

The fingerprints of a blackman
Were on her pillow. Or was it
Her luminous tears?
. . . An absence, or a presence?
Only when it was darker
Would she know.

XI

The blackman dipped water
From a well.
And when the well dried,
He dipped cool blackness.

XII

We are told that the seeds
Of rainbows are not unlike
A blackman's tear.

XIII

What is more beautiful than black flowers,
Or blackmen in fields
Gathering them?
. . . The bride, or the wedding?

XIV

When it was finished,
Some of the carvers of Destiny
Would sigh in relief,
But the blackmen would sigh in intaglio,
Having shed vain illusions in mastering the stone.

XV

Affirmation of negatives:
A blackman trembles
That his thoughts run towards darkness.

XVI

The odor of a blackman derives
No less from the sweat of his apotheosis,
Than emanations of crushed apples
He carries under his arms.

XVII

If I could imagine that shaping of Fate,
I would think of blackmen
Handling the sun.

XVIII

Is it harvest time in the brown fields,
Or is it just a blackman
Singing?

XIX

There is the sorrow of blackmen
Lost in cities. But who can conceive
Of cities lost in a blackman?

XX

A small boy lifts a seashell
To his listening ear.
It is the blackman again,
Whispering his sagas of drowned sailors.

XXI

At the cradle of Justice were found
Three gifts: a pair of scales, a sword,
And a simple cloth. But the Magi had departed.
Several who were with us agreed,
One of the givers must have been
A blackman.

XXII

As vines grow towards light,
So roots grow towards darkness.
Back and forth a blackman goes,
Gathering the harvest.

XXIII

By moonlight
We tossed our pebbles into the lake
And marveled
At the beauty of concentric sorrows.
You thought it was like the troubled heart
Of a blackman,
Because of the dancing light.

XXIV

As the time of our leave taking drew near,
The blackman blessed each of us
By pronouncing the names of his children.

XXV

As I remember it,
The only unicorn in the park
Belonged to a blackman
Who went about collecting bits
And torn scraps of afternoons.

XXVI

At the center of Being,
Said the blackman,
All is tangential.
Even this laughter, even your tears.

STERLING D. PLUMPP

Howlin Wolf

He
annoints the sun: lingering
spells of its appreciation.
Drag
their tales round night's confined spirit.
Let it
out into urges
only the unfree memorize.
In shacks
and stereotypes covering faces like quilts.
Let it
out into nocturnal transformations
in the bottom.
Where evil going on
flees the superstition of light.
His voice,
a meteor, hurled from distances
in depths of tribulations,
howls willingness in slaves.
They meet
at the cross
roads in memory:
steal three hundred pounds of heavenly joy
from a barrel of footsteps
swimming in muddy pods of dreams.
They march
out of my mind with a whole lotta
lightning in their eyes.
Claim
the darkness as their temple.
Sprinkle
saw
dust over the floor.
Let

the good
times
roll over curses damning
my name.

Big Maybelle

(for Angela Jackson)

She
parks her sorrows
near a curb, gets
out of
her skin and
stumbles
up steps of pleas.
Un
listening, at
tentative and calloused
hearts
tune
in.
She
gets back in
her skin, cries off
down the long boulevard of
memory.
Her pain in
her voice/her
people's in
her veins.

N. H. PRITCHARD

From Where the Blues?

Stacks of paperbacks
against whiteless walls
foliate the landscape
of the incubal inclosure.
Above, at the perimeter
of my left eye, curtains
hand siennaed by the neglect
of other importances.

A rueful "Pierrot"
looks downward from his
clipboard perch as if easeled
too long in this pagan pasture
where Bacchus boards and Coleridge
no doubt would have lengthened Kubla Khan.

"The Lady" utters a cantata in "praise"
of morning heartaches . . . one more chance
to realize that it's   the unsung
that makes the song. From where the blues?
Strange, this combat that selects its soldiers.
From where the blues? The feeling knows
my ways and stalk them, like the black cat
there, with the yellowed eyes.
I too know the wishing for forgetfulness.

———————

WE NEED——please read this and see if you
qualify, if you do not care to take advantage of this
please pass it on to a friend.

grown on instead opens the door
a blind went away pulling

516

large numbers covered with rows
decidedly

toward them some its own
dressed away with the rain
flying in borrowed kind
things in the basket

beside twisted ruddy before
without those mostly on an under
plundered nearly though feasted
delighted so as to be carried

//

″	″	″	″	″				
″	″	″	red	″				
″	″	″	″	″	″	red	″	″
″	″	″	″	red	″	″	″	red
red	red	″	″	″	red	″	″	″
″	″	red	″	″	red	″	red	″
red	″	″	″	″	red	″	″	″
″	red	″	″	″	″	″	″	″
″	″	″	red	″	″	″	″	″
″	″	″	″	″	″	red	″	″
red	″	″	″	″	″	″	″	″
red	″	″	″	″	red	″	″	″
red	″	″	red	″	″	″	″	″
″	″	″	red	″	″	″	red	″
″	red	″	″	″	″	″	red	″
″	″	″	″	″				
red	″	″	″	″				
″	″	″	″	″				
″	″	″	″	″				

Metagnomy

A mid the non com mit t e d
com pound s of t he m in d
an i m age less gleam in g
we at hers h aunts as yet un k no w n
& t a u n t s
thru a c he mist r y of ought
t h at c hang e s
c ours e s
s ee m in g l y
as if a bird in f light
a w or d
f or got ten
in t he w in d ' s w on t

W h at aim co un s e l s such a gain
un to t he sylvan d own of w om b s
w h at n ever ever s t and
c a uses such man if est s t a s is
to r ide on ly up on t h at move men t
t he ear t h pro vide s

Of ten the set t in g m in d
like d us k a j our n s
as thou g h the k now in g
as thou g h the g low in g

To s ee k
to f in d
a l a n c e
to pier c e the p o s s i b l e

Oft e n a w is h de fin e d
like l us t re turn s
as tho up on an alt e r
b l oo d is b r o k e n
as m eat
is rite

& a cc u ring p aga n
c r u c i fix ion

E n chant m e n t s
abo und ab out
the abysses of a m in d
oft e n b l in d e d
by the cat a r acts of curt concern
w h i l e
aim s it s daunt less l y
on a p e d e s t a l
be in g peck e d up on
by t he w in d ' s w on t

ISHMAEL REED

Beware: Do Not Read This Poem

tonite, *thriller* was
abt an ol woman, so vain she
surrounded her self w/
   many mirrors

It got so bad that finally she
locked herself indoors & her
whole life became the
   mirrors

one day the villagers broke
into her house, but she was too
swift for them. she disappeared
   into a mirror
each tenant who bought the house
after that, lost a loved one to
   the ol woman in the mirror:
   first a little girl
   then a young woman
   then the young woman/s husband

the hunger of this poem is legendary
it has taken in many victims
back off from this poem
it has drawn in yr feet
back off from this poem
it has drawn in yr legs
back off from this poem
it is a greedy mirror
you are into this poem. from
   the waist down
nobody can hear you can they?
this poem has had you up to here
   belch

this poem aint got no manners
you cant call out frm this poem
relax now & go w/ this poem
move & roll on to this poem

> do not resist this poem
> this poem has yr eyes
> this poem has his head
> this poem has his arms
> this poem has his fingers
> this poem has his fingertips

this poem is the reader & the
       reader this poem

statistic: the us bureau of missing persons reports
   that in 1968 over 100,000 people disappeared
   leaving no solid clues
      nor trace   only
a space   in the lives of their friends

Paul Laurence Dunbar in the Tenderloin

> Even at 26, the hush when
> you unexpectedly walked
> into a theatre. One year
> after *The History of Cakewalk*,
>
> Desiring not to cause
> a fuss, you sit alone
> in the rear, watching a re
> hearsal.
> The actors are impressed. Wel
> don Johnson, so super at des
> cription, jots it all down.
>
> I dont blame you for
> disliking Whitman, Paul.

He lacked your style, like
your highcollared mandalaed
portrait in hayden's
Kaleidoscope; unobserved,
Death, the uncouth critic
does a first draft on your
    breath.

The Reactionary Poet

If you are a revolutionary
Then I must be a reactionary
For if you stand for the future
I have no choice but to
Be with the past

Bring back suspenders!
Bring back Mom!
Homemade ice cream
Picnics in the park
Flagpole sitting
Straw hats
Rent parties
Corn liquor
The banjo
Georgia quilts
Krazy Kat
Restock

The syncopation of
Fletcher Henderson
The Kiplingesque lines
of James Weldon Johnson
Black Eagle
Mickey Mouse
The Bach Family
Sunday School
Even Mayor La Guardia

Who read the comics
Is more appealing than
Your version of
What Lies Ahead

In your world of
Tomorrow Humor
Will be locked up and
The key thrown away
The public address system
Will pound out headaches
All day
Everybody will wear the same
Funny caps
And the same funny jackets
Enchantment will be found
Expendable, charm, a
Luxury
Love and kisses
A crime against the state
Duke Ellington will be
Ordered to write more marches
"For the people," naturally

If you are what's coming
I must be what's going

Make it by steamboat
I likes to take it real slow

ED ROBERSON

sonnet

i must be careful about such things as these.
the thin-grained oak.   the quiet grizzlies scared
into the hills by the constant tracks squeezing
in behind them closer in the snow.   the snared
rigidity of the winter lake.   deer after deer
crossing on the spines of fish who look up and stare
with their eyes pressed to the ice.   in a sleep.   hearing
the thin taps leading away to collapse like the bear
in the high quiet.   i must be careful not to shake
anything in too wild an elation.   not to jar
the fragile mountains against the paper far-
ness.   nor avalanche the fog or the eagle from the air.
of the gentle wilderness i must set the precarious
words.   like rocks.   without one snowcapped mistake

poll

skin that is a closed   curtain.
it is impossible to know.   how
the light is cast.

a mark that is kept   the elect-
ion determining the race
before the candidate   runs.

darkie is the night is
an old image given color.
the skin is history.the dark horse

524

the poor houses

they are made to stand side by side
the black lawns of their toes to the curb.
though we who know the nakedness of mind
might not call them naked   they are naked
in the cold   stripped to what comes

before and holds the mind. their attic heads
except for those rare spots where warmth is thought
gathered beneath their struts   are beaten
white with snow   and snow's fine lash
delineates the brick hairs on their chests.

icicles drop from what the windows see
inside and out across the street   icicles
what the door addressed answers in turn
when underground the bestial root system
of supply's demands face them unpaid.

othello jones dresses for dinner

no one could have a blacker tail
or whiter tie in contrast on
than me.   the face of the evening guests
is some shade earlier than darkness
which is my countenance.   i bring
your daughter in the arm of midnight
she knows that i eat orchids with
my fingers.   she has seen unnapkined
my whole greedy primitive body.
and she wiped it with her hair
and when i smiled she said how proud
she was that i was always dressed.
for dinner.   if i sneer in the sheets at night
my tie becomes crooked but do not
be alarmed i am well mannered.

American Jazz Quartet

1. PIANO

IN THE LOBBY, NOT THE DOORMAN

In the evening when people are returning home
anxious to abandon the strain of these attentions,
he comes downstairs from his apartment
and stakes out the bench in the lobby
by the elevators where he has everybody
who enters the building trapped
into socializing with him, if by even
no more than an annoyed nod and a tired
look away from a cheer come of the predatory.
    Their dresses, how good they look, how he'll be up
for dinner at their place in a minute,
how he knows you out there makin' all that money.
    The people in this building are out there
making like he must have at one time.
Or done, made it and sat down. These floors aren't cheap.
He's harmless. But how we haunt our own success.

2. BASS

URBAN SPECIFIC

standing on the corner begging
for company   a little change

in conversation   something different
made   of to have to come up with

by the time see you later   or else
be in that killing

loneliness of a room   even on the street
stopping people   still left alone—

old   crime   neither poor nor disorderly
just vagrant time's   old crime of age

unaddressed   victim nor perpetrator   just
a man whose only empty pockets are of people

come around   asks if you can spare a little
while   so he can make the train home

3. SAXOPHONE

THEN THERE'S THIS ONE, PICK HIM UP

pick him up and take him to the jail
of his winnings, take him into house arrest
up from his success, winner lifted
out of his easy to get to by people, drive

the diamond under his fingernail
up through the flesh to pimple as
his wearing,—poppin' light in folks' eyes—
having his nothing come from

funny money. His is real, nothin' but
but a callous disease from discipline
that cuts him off is no joke

no plus
size chile who's got   nor his own
he's somebody else's crime for his time

4. DRUMS

TITHES FOR CHARITY

An angry generosity
comes from the careless hold he has
on what little he has;
     much is taken.

And angered if not from that, then that
he goes along with his losses too
passively,
     too pride-hustled to question.

    So, he
is always wanting back,
never clear he has given, only sure
the gleaners expect too much.

    Then, angry resentment
at the little he has for spill
compared to the stash his privilege has
to flurry from for him, for white's own
    on its white landfill,

that cold storm of trickle down
from coffers vast and out of reach,
privately owned as the sky,
    the deaf sky.

CAROLYN RODGERS

how i got ovah

i can tell you
about them
i have shaken rivers
out of my eyes
i have waded eyelash deep
have crossed rivers
have shaken the water weed out
of my lungs
have swam for strength
pulled by strength
through waterfalls with electric beats
i have bore the shocks
of water deep deep
waterlogs are my bones
i have shaken the water free of my hair
have kneeled on the banks
and kissed my ancestors of the dirt
whose rich dark root fingers rose up reached out
grabbed and pulled me rocked me cupped me
gentle strong and firm
carried me
made me swim for strength
cross rivers
though i shivered
was wet was cold
and wanted to sink down
and float as water, yea—
i can tell you.
i have shaken rivers
out of my eyes.

SONIA SANCHEZ

for our lady

yeh.
     billie.   if someone
had loved u like u
shud have been loved
ain't no tellen what
kinds of songs
          u wud have swung
gainst this country's wite mind.
or what kinds of lyrics
          wud have pushed us from
our blue / nites.
          yeh.   billie.
if some blk / man
          had reallee
made u feel
          permanentlee warm.
ain't no tellen
          where the jazz of yo/songs.
          wud have led us.

A Poem for My Father

how sad it must be
to love so many women
to need so many black
perfumed bodies weeping
underneath you.
     when i remember all those nights
i filled my mind with
long wars between short
sighted trojans & greeks
while you slapped some

wide hips about in
your pvt dungeon,
when i remember your
deformity   i want to
do something about your
makeshift manhood,
i guess
            that is why
on meeting your sixth
wife, i cross myself
with her confessionals.

A poem for my brother

(reflections on his death from AIDS: June 8, 1981)

I. DEATH

The day you died
a fever starched my bones.
within the slurred
sheets, i hoarded my legs
while you rowed out among the boulevards
balancing your veins on sails.
easy the eye of hunger
as i peeled the sharp
sweat and swallowed wholesale molds.

2. RECOVERY (A)

What comes after
is consciousness of the morning
of the licensed sun that subdues
immoderate elements.
there is a kindness in illness
the indulgence of discrepancies.

reduced to the ménage of houses
and green drapes that puff their seasons
toward the face.
i wonder what to do now.
i am afraid
i remember a childhood that cried
after extinguished lights
when only the coated banners answered.

3. RECOVERY (B)

There is a savior in these buds
look how the phallic stems distend
in welcome.
O copper flowerheads
confine my womb that i may dwell within.

i see these gardens, whom i love
i feel the sky's sweat on my face
now that these robes no longer bark
i praise abandonment.

4. WAKE

i have not come for summary.
must i renounce all babylons?
here, without psalms,
these leaves grow white
and burn the bones with dance.
here, without surfs,
young panicles bloom on the clouds and fly
while myths tick grey as thunder.

5. BURIAL

you in the crow's rain
rusting amid ribs
my mouth spills your birth
i have named you prince of boards
stretching with the tides.

you in the toad's tongue
peeling on nerves
look. look. the earth is running palms.

6. (ON) (THE) (ROAD). AGAIN.

somewhere a flower walks in mass
purchasing wholesale christs
sealing white-willow sacraments.

naked on steeples
where trappist idioms sail
an atom peels the air.

O i will gather my pulse
muffled by sibilants
and follow disposable dreams.

from *Philadelphia: Spring, 1985*

*/a phila. fireman reflects after
seeing a decapitated body in the MOVE ruins/*

to see those eyes
orange like butterflies
over the walls.

i must move away
from this little-ease
where the pulse
shrinks into itself
and carve myself in white.

O to press the seasons
and taste the quiet juice
of their veins.

haiku

*(for Osage ave
and Doorknop)*

coastlines of powdered
bones run side by side turning
into black cobwebs.

haiku

*(for mungu and morani
and the children of soweto)*

may yo seasons be
long with endless green streets and
permanent summer legs.

two haiku

*(for Clarence H. Watson and
The Count)*

1.

you and The Count walked
straight up drank the waters of
the underworld. Sailed

2.

you came forth by day
praising the nite with music
giving our ears souls.

tanka

*(for papa Joe Jones who used to
toss me up to the sky)*

sailing upward i
crease the air see you look a/
way. yo spastic arms
in conversation with the day
turn to catch my yellow lips.

haiku

*(for domestic workers
in the african diaspora)*

i works hard but treated
bad   man. i'se telling you de
truth   i full of it.

haiku

man. you write me so
much you bad as the loanhouse
asking fo they money

tanka

like dark old men the
pomp of our passion is
mere ceremony

and each day is drowned in a
procession of polished pain.

haiku

like ermine when i
come to lick your winter salt
my tongue freezes in blood.

haiku

i want to make you
roar with laughter as i ride
you into morning.

blues

will you love me baby when the sun goes down
i say will you love me baby when the sun goes down
or you just a summer time man leaving fo winter comes round.

will you keep me baby when I'm feeling down 'n' out
i say will you hold me baby when i'm feeling down 'n' out
or will you just stop & spit while i lives from hand to mouth.

done drunk so much of you i staggers in my sleep
i say done drunk so much of you man, i staggers in my sleep
when i wakes up baby, gonna start me on a brand new week.

will you love me baby when the sun goes down
i say will you love me baby when the sun goes down
or you just a summer time man leaving fo winter comes round.

Song No. 2

(1)   i say. all you young girls waiting to live
      i say. all you young girls taking yo pill
      i say. all you sisters tired of standing still
      i say. all you sisters thinkin you won't, but you will.

      don't let them kill you with their stare
      don't let them closet you with no air
      don't let them feed you sex piece-meal
      don't let them offer you any old deal.

      i say. step back sisters. we're rising from the dead
      i say. step back johnnies. we're dancing on our heads
      i say. step back man. no mo hangin by a thread
      i say. step back world. can't let it all go unsaid.

(2)   i say. all you young girls molested at ten
      i say. all you young girls giving it up again & again
      i say. all you sisters hanging out in every den
      i say. all you sisters needing your own oxygen.

      don't let them trap you with their coke
      don't let them treat you like one fat joke
      don't let them bleed you till you broke
      don't let them blind you in masculine smoke.

      i say. step back sisters. we're rising from the dead
      i say. step back johnnies. we're dancing on our heads
      i say. step back man. no mo hanging by a thread.
      i say. step back world. can't let it go unsaid.

GIL SCOTT-HERON

Whitey on the Moon

A rat done bit my sister Nell.
  (with Whitey on the moon)
Her face and arms began to swell.
  (and Whitey's on the moon)
I can't pay no doctor bill.
  (but Whitey's on the moon)
Ten years from now I'll be payin' still.
  (while Whitey's on the moon)
The man jus' upped my rent las' night.
  ('cause Whitey's on the moon)
No hot water, no toilets, no lights.
  (but Whitey's on the moon)
I wonder why he uppin' me?
  ('cause Whitey's on the moon?)
I wuz already payin' 'im fifty a week.
  (with Whitey on the moon)
Taxes takin' my whole damn check,
Junkies make me a nervous wreck,
The price of food is goin' up,
An' as if all that crap wuzn't enough:
A rat done bit my sister Nell.
  (with Whitey on the moon)
Her face an' arm began to swell.
  (but Whitey's on the moon)
Was all that money I made las' year
  (for Whitey on the moon?)
How come there ain't no money here?
(Hmm! Whitey's on the moon)
Y'know I jus' 'bout had my fill
  (of Whitey on the moon.)
I think I'll sen' these doctor bills
  (to Whitey on the moon.)

The Revolution Will Not Be Televised

You will not be able to stay home, brother.
You will not be able to plug in, turn on and cop out.
You will not be able to lose yourself on scag and
skip out for beer during commercials because
The revolution will not be televised.

The revolution will not be televised.
The revolution will not be brought to you by Xerox in four
    parts without commercial interruption.
The revolution will not show you pictures of Nixon blowing
    a bugle and leading a charge by John Mitchell, General
    Abramson and Spiro Agnew to eat hog maws confiscated
    from a Harlem sanctuary.
The revolution will not be televised.

The revolution will not be brought to you by
The Schaeffer Award Theatre and will not star
Natalie Wood and Steve McQueen or Bullwinkle and Julia?
The revolution will not give your mouth sex appeal.
The revolution will not get rid of the nubs.
The revolution will not make you look five pounds thinner.
The revolution will not be televised, brother.

There will be no pictures of you and Willie Mae
pushing that shopping cart down the block on the dead run
or trying to slide that color tv in a stolen ambulance.
NBC will not be able to predict the winner at 8:32 on reports
    from twenty-nine districts.
The revolution will not be televised.

There will be no pictures of pigs shooting down brothers
on the instant replay.
There will be no pictures of pigs shooting down brothers
on the instant replay.
There will be no slow motion or still lifes of Roy
Wilkins strolling through Watts in a red, black

and green liberation jumpsuit that he has been
saving for just the proper occasion.

Green Acres, Beverly Hillbillies and Hooterville Junction
will no longer be so damned relevant
and women will not care if Dick finally got down with Jane
on *Search for Tomorrow*
because black people will be in the streets looking for
A Brighter Day.
The revolution will not be televised.

There will be no highlights on the *Eleven O'clock News*
and no pictures of hairy armed women liberationists
and Jackie Onassis blowing her nose.
The theme song will not be written by Jim Webb or Francis
        Scott Key
nor sung by Glen Campbell, Tom Jones, Johnny Cash,
Englebert Humperdink or Rare Earth.
The revolution will not be televised.

The revolution will not be right back after a
message about a white tornado, white lightning or white
        people.
You will not have to worry about a dove in your bedroom,
the tiger in your tank or the giant in your toilet bowl.
The revolution will not go better with Coke.
The revolution will not fight germs that may cause bad
        breath.
The revolution *will* put you in the driver's seat.
The revolution will not be televised
                will not be televised
            not be televised
                be televised
The revolution will be no re-run, brothers.
The revolution will be LIVE.

Home Is Where the Hatred Is

A junkie walking through the twilight
I'm on my way home
I left three days ago
But no one seems to know I'm gone.

Home is where the hatred is
Home is filled with pain
And it might not be such a bad idea if I never
Never went home again.

Stand as far away from me as you can
And ask me why.
Hang on to your rosy beads
Close your eyes to watch me die.

You keep saying, "Kick it, quit it, kick it, quit it."
But God did you ever try
To turn your sick soul inside out
So that the world
So that the world
Can watch you die.

Home is where I live inside
My white powder dreams.
Home was once an empty vacuum
That's filled now with my silent screams.
Home is where the needle marks
Try to heal my broken heart.
And it might not be such a bad idea
If I never
If I never went home again
Home again
Home again
Home again.
Kick it, quit it, kick it, quit it, kick it, quit it, kick it.
Can't go home again

Home again
Home again
You know, I can't go home again.

A. B. SPELLMAN

After Vallejo

i will die in havana in a hurricane
it will be morning, i'll be facing southwest
away from the gulf, away from the storm
away from home, looking to the virid hills
of matanzas where the *orisha* rise, lifted
by *congueros* in masks of iron, *bongoseros*
in masks of water, *timbaleros* in masks of fire
by all the *clave* that binds the rhythms of this world

i'll be writing when i go, revising another
hopeful survey of my life. i will die of nothing
that i did but of all that i did not do
i promised myself a better self
than i could make & i will not forgive

you will be there, complaining
that i never saved you, that i left you
where you live, stranded
in your own green dream

when you come for me come singing
no dirge, but scat my eulogy in bebop
code. sing that i died among gods
but lived with no god & did not suffer
for it. find one true poem that i made
& sing it to my shade as it fades
into the wind. sing it presto, in 4/4 time
in the universal ghetto key of b flat

i will die in havana in rhythm. *tumbao
montuno*, *guaguanco*, dense strata
of rhythm pulsing me away
                                    & the mother of waters
will say to the saint of crossroads
well, damn. he danced his way out after all

LORENZO THOMAS

Inauguration

The land was there before us
Was the land. Then things
Began happening fast. Because
The bombs us have always work
Sometimes it makes me think
God must be one of us. Because
Us has saved the world. Us gave it
A particular set of regulations
Based on 1) undisputable acumen.
2) carnivorous fortunes, delicately
Referred to here as "bull market"
And (of course) other irrational factors
Deadly smoke thick over the icecaps,
Our man in Saigon   Lima   Tokyo   etc   etc

Song

You asked me to sing
Then you seemed not
To hear; to have gone out
From the edge of my voice

And I was singing
There I was singing
In a heathen voice
You could not hear
Though you requested

The song—it was for them.
Although they refuse you
And the song I made for you
Tangled in their tongue

They wd mire themselves in the spring
Rains, as I sit here folding and
Unfolding my nose in your gardens

I wouldn't mind it so bad

Each word is cheapened
In the air, sounding like
Language that riots and
Screams in the dark city

Thoughts they requested
Concepts that rule them

Since I can't have you
I will steal what you have

1966

QUINCY TROUPE

One for Charlie Mingus

into space-time walks bass strings of charlie mingus
jambalaya rhythms deepening our ears, hear
voices springing from tongues of mingus riding sweet bass
     strings
deep stepping through sound, through light & shadows of
     blood
cut out into the leaping night walking music swings the wind
as tongues of evening caress the flying darkness, there
inside rhythms, tight embraces of sound-thump bass grooves
lengthening the graceful flights of cadences shading chords
     of voodoo
who doing who there, juicing mean watts boys sluicing,
     shimmying down
mean streets of the city of angels, when mingus played a
     strange, disquieting
beauty, turned it on, believed in whatever he thought he was
     back then
played it all the way here, where eye am dreaming now,
     listening
within this moment of musical amazement, walking in
his voice riding in through vibrating strings thumping &
     humping
like naked lovers inside musky hot steaming rumpled
     backwater bedrooms
in the afterglow of undercover damplight, in the nighttime of
     their dreams
mingus skybreaking his bass through steep blue
lifetimes of urban screams, who doing what to who here
inside the city of lights, raining tears, raining blood & blue
     showers
electrifying nights where mingus walked music through
     voodoo
flying all the way home, thumping the rhythms, mingus
     stalks

the music tone after magical tone, walks the mysterious
music all the way home, tone after magisterial tone

Poem for My Father

for Quincy T. Trouppe Sr

father, it was an honor to be there, in the dugout
with you, the glory of great black men swinging their lives
as bats, at tiny white balls
burning in at unbelievable speeds, riding up & in & out
a curve breaking down wicked, like a ball falling off a table
moving away, snaking down, screwing its stitched magic
into chitlin circuit air, its comma seams spinning
toward breakdown, dipping, like a hipster
bebopping a knee-dip stride, in the charlie parker forties
wrist curling, like a swan's neck
behind a slick black back
cupping an invisible ball of dreams

& you there, father, regal, as an african, obeah man
sculpted out of wood, from a sacred tree, of no name, no
        place, origin
thick branches branching down, into cherokee & someplace
        else lost
way back in africa, the sap running dry
crossing from north carolina into georgia, inside
        grandmother mary's
womb, where your mother had you in the violence of that red
        soil
ink blotter news, gone now, into blood graves
of american blues, sponging rococo
truth long gone as dinosaurs
the agent-oranged landscape of former names
absent of african polysyllables, dry husk, consonants there
now, in their place, names, flat, as polluted rivers
& that guitar string smile always snaking across

some virulent, american, redneck's face
scorching, like atomic heat, mushrooming over nagasaki
& hiroshima, the fever blistered shadows of it all
inked, as etchings, into sizzled concrete
but you, there, father, through it all, a yardbird solo
riffing on bat & ball glory, breaking down the fabricated
    myths
of white major league legends, of who was better than who
beating them at their own crap
game, with killer bats, as bud powell swung his silence into
    beauty
of a josh gibson home run, skittering across piano keys of
    bleachers
shattering all manufactured legends up there in lights
struck out white knights, on the risky edge of amazement
awe, the miraculous truth sluicing through
steeped & disguised in the blues
confluencing, like the point at the cross
when a fastball hides itself up in a slider, curve
breaking down & away in a wicked, sly grin
curved & posed as an ass-scratching uncle tom, who
like old satchel paige delivering his famed hesitation pitch
before coming back with a hard, high, fast one, is slicker
sliding, & quicker than a professional hitman—
the deadliness of it all, the sudden strike
like that of the "brown bomber's" crossing right
of sugar ray robinson's, lightning, cobra bite

& you, there, father, through it all, catching rhythms
of chono pozo balls, drumming, like conga beats into your
    catcher's mitt
hard & fast as "cool papa" bell jumping into bed
before the lights went out

of the old, negro baseball league, a promise, you were
father, a harbinger, of shock waves, soon come

After Hearing a Radio Announcement:
A Comment on Some Conditions

yesterday in new york city
the gravediggers went on strike
& today the undertakers went on strike
because they said of the overwhelming
amount of corpses
(unnecessarily they said because
of wars & stupid killings in the streets
& etcetera & etcetera.)

sweating the world   corpses
propped up straight in living room chairs
clogging up rivers   jamming up freeways
stopping up elevators   in the gutters   corpses
everywhere you turn
& the undertakers said that they were
being overworked with all this goddamned killing
going on   said that they couldn't even enjoy
all the money they was making
said that this shit has got to stop

& today eye just heard that
the coffin-makers are waiting in the wings
for their chance to do the same thing
& tomorrow & if things keep going this way
eye expect to hear of the corpses
themselves boycotting death
until things get better
or at least getting themselves
together in sort of union-espousing
self-determination
for better funeral &
burial conditions
or something extraordinarily
heavy like that

DEREK WALCOTT

A Far Cry from Africa

A wind is ruffling the tawny pelt
Of Africa. Kikuyu, quick as flies,
Batten upon the bloodstreams of the veldt.
Corpses are scattered through a paradise.
Only the worm, colonel of carrion, cries:
"Waste no compassion on these separate dead!"
Statistics justify and scholars seize
The salients of colonial policy.
What is that to the white child hacked in bed?
To savages, expendable as Jews?

Threshed out by beaters, the long rushes break
In a white dust of ibises whose cries
Have wheeled since civilization's dawn
From the parched river or beast-teeming plain.
The violence of beast on beast is read
As natural law, but upright man
Seeks his divinity by inflicting pain.
Delirious as these worried beasts, his wars
Dance to the tightened carcass of a drum,
While he calls courage still that native dread
Of the white peace contracted by the dead.

Again brutish necessity wipes its hands
Upon the napkin of a dirty cause, again
A waste of our compassion, as with Spain,
The gorilla wrestles with the superman.
I who am poisoned with the blood of both,
Where shall I turn, divided to the vein?
I who have cursed
The drunken officer of British rule, how choose
Between this Africa and the English tongue I love?
Betray them both, or give back what they give?

How can I face such slaughter and be cool?
How can I turn from Africa and live?

Codicil

Schizophrenic, wrenched by two styles,
one a hack's hired prose, I earn
my exile. I trudge this sickle, moonlit beach for miles,

tan, burn
to slough off
this love of ocean that's self-love.

To change your language you must change your life.

I cannot right old wrongs.
Waves tire of horizon and return.
Gulls screech with rusty tongues

Above the beached, rotting pirogues,
they were a venomous beaked cloud at Charlotteville.

Once I thought love of country was enough,
now, even if I chose, there's no room at the trough.

I watch the best minds root like dogs
for scraps of favour.
I am nearing middle

age, burnt skin
peels from my hand like paper, onion-thin,
like Peer Gynt's riddle.

At heart there's nothing, not the dread
of death. I know too many dead.
They're all familiar, all in character,

even how they died. On fire,
the flesh no longer fears that furnace mouth
of earth,

that kiln or ashpit of the sun,
nor this clouding, unclouding sickle moon
whitening this beach again like a blank page.

All its indifference is a different rage.

Blues

Those five or six young guys
hunched on the stoop
that oven-hot summer night
whistled me over. Nice
and friendly. So, I stop.
MacDougal or Christopher
Street in chains of light.

A summer festival. Or some
saint's. I wasn't too far from
home, but not too bright
for a nigger, and not too dark.
I figured we were all
one, wop, nigger, jew,
besides, this wasn't Central Park.
I'm coming on too strong? You figure
right! They beat this yellow nigger
black and blue.

Yeah. During all this, scared
in case one used a knife,
I hung my olive-green, just-bought
sports coat on a fire plug.
I did nothing. They fought
each other, really. Life

gives them a few kicks,
that's all. The spades, the spicks.

My face smashed in, my bloody mug
pouring, my olive-branch jacket saved
from cuts and tears,
I crawled four flights upstairs.
Sprawled in the gutter, I
remember a few watchers waved
loudly, and one kid's mother shouting
like "Jackie" or "Terry,"
"now that's enough!"
It's nothing really.
They don't get enough love.

You know they wouldn't kill
you. Just playing rough,
like young America will.
Still, it taught me something
about love. If it's so tough,
forget it.

from *The Schooner* Flight

1 ADIOS, CARENAGE

In idle August, while the sea soft,
and leaves of brown islands stick to the rim
of this Caribbean, I blow out the light
by the dreamless face of Maria Concepcion
to ship as a seaman on the schooner *Flight.*
Out in the yard turning grey in the dawn,
I stood like a stone and nothing else move
but the cold sea rippling like galvanize
and the nail holes of stars in the sky roof,
till a wind start to interfere with the trees.
I pass me dry neighbour sweeping she yard
as I went downhill, and I nearly said:
"Sweep soft, you witch, 'cause she don't sleep hard,"

but the bitch look through me like I was dead.
A route taxi pull up, park-lights still on.
The driver size up my bags with a grin:
"This time, Shabine, like you really gone!"
I ain't answer the ass, I simply pile in
the back seat and watch the sky burn
above Laventille pink as the gown
in which the woman I left was sleeping,
and I look in the rearview and see a man
exactly like me, and the man was weeping
for the houses, the streets, that whole fucking island.

Christ have mercy on all sleeping things!
From that dog rotting down Wrightson Road
to when I was a dog on these streets;
if loving these islands must be my load,
out of corruption my soul takes wings,
But they had started to poison my soul
with their big house, big car, big-time bohbohl,
coolie, nigger, Syrian, and French Creole,
so I leave it for them and their carnival—
I taking a sea-bath, I gone down the road.
I know these islands from Monos to Nassau,
a rusty head sailor with sea-green eyes
that they nickname Shabine, the patois for
any red nigger, and I, Shabine, saw
when these slums of empire was paradise.
I'm just a red nigger who love the sea,
I had a sound colonial education,
I have Dutch, nigger, and English in me,
and either I'm nobody, or I'm a nation.

But Maria Concepcion was all my thought
watching the sea heaving up and down
as the port side of dories, schooners, and yachts
was painted afresh by the strokes of the sun
signing her name with every reflection;
I knew when dark-haired evening put on
her bright silk at sunset, and, folding the sea,
sidled under the sheet with her starry laugh,

that there'd be no rest, there'd be no forgetting.
Is like telling mourners round the graveside
about resurrection, they want the dead back,
so I smile to myself as the bow rope untied
and the *Flight* swing seaward: "Is no use repeating
that the sea have more fish. I ain't want her
dressed in the sexless light of a seraph,
I want those round brown eyes like a marmoset, and
till the day when I can lean back and laugh,
those claws that tickled my back on sweating
Sunday afternoons, like a crab on wet sand."
As I worked, watching the rotting waves come
past the bow that scissor the sea like silk,
I swear to you all, by my mother's milk,
by the stars that shall fly from tonight's furnace,
that I loved them, my children, my wife, my home;
I loved them as poets love the poetry
that kills them, as drowned sailors the sea.

You ever look up from some lonely beach
and see a far schooner? Well, when I write
this poem, each phrase go be soaked in salt;
I go draw and knot every line as tight
as ropes in this rigging; in simple speech
my common language go be the wind,
my pages the sails of the schooner *Flight*.
But let me tell you how this business begin.

2   RAPTURES OF THE DEEP

Smuggled Scotch for O'Hara, big government man,
between Cedros and the Main, so the Coast Guard couldn't
        touch us,
and the Spanish pirogues always met us halfway,
but a voice kept saying: "Shabine, see this business
of playing pirate?" Well, so said, so done!
That whole racket crash. And I for a woman,
for her laces and silks, Maria Concepcion.
Ay, ay! Next thing I hear, some Commission of Enquiry
was being organized to conduct a big quiz,

with himself as chairman investigating himself.
Well, I knew damn well who the suckers would be,
not that shark in shark skin, but his pilot fish,
khaki-pants red niggers like you and me.
What worse, I fighting with Maria Concepcion,
plates flying and thing, so I swear: "Not again!"
It was mashing up my house and my family.
I was so broke all I needed was shades and a cup
or four shades and four cups in four-cup Port of Spain;
all the silver I had was the coins on the sea.

You saw them ministers in *The Express*,
guardians of the poor—one hand at their back,
and one set o' police only guarding their house,
and the Scotch pouring in through the back door.
As for that minister-monster who smuggled the booze,
that half-Syrian saurian, I got so vex to see
that face thick with powder, the warts, the stone lids
like a dinosaur caked with primordial ooze
by the lightning of flashbulbs sinking in wealth,
that I said: "Shabine, this is shit, understand!"
But he get somebody to kick my crutch out his office
like I was some artist! That bitch was so grand,
couldn't get off his high horse and kick me himself.
I have seen things that would make a slave sick
in this Trinidad, the Limers' Republic.

I couldn't shake the sea noise out of my head,
the shell of my ears sang Maria Concepcion,
so I start salvage diving with a crazy Mick,
name O'Shaughnessy, and a limey named Head;
but this Caribbean so choke with the dead
that when I would melt in emerald water,
whose ceiling rippled like a silk tent,
I saw them corals: brain, fire, sea-fans,
dead-men's-fingers, and then, the dead men.
I saw that the powdery sand was their bones
ground white from Senegal to San Salvador,
so, I panic third dive, and surface for a month
in the Seamen's Hostel. Fish broth and sermons.

When I thought of the woe I had brought my wife,
when I saw my worries with that other woman,
I wept under water, salt seeking salt,
for her beauty had fallen on me like a sword
cleaving me from my children, flesh of my flesh!

There was this barge from St. Vincent, but she was too deep
to float her again. When we drank, the limey
got tired of my sobbing for Maria Concepcion.
He said he was getting the bends. Good for him!
The pain in my heart for Maria Concepcion,
the hurt I had done to my wife and children,
was worse than the bends. In the rapturous deep
there was no cleft rock where my soul could hide
like the boobies each sunset, no sandbar of light
where I could rest, like the pelicans know,
so I got raptures once, and I saw God
like a harpooned grouper bleeding, and a far
voice was rumbling, "Shabine, if you leave her,
if you leave her, I shall give you the morning star."
When I left the madhouse I tried other women
but, once they stripped naked, their spiky cunts
bristled like sea-eggs and I couldn't dive.
The chaplain came round. I paid him no mind.
Where is my rest place, Jesus? Where is my harbour?
Where is the pillow I will not have to pay for,
and the window I can look from that frames my life?

3   SHABINE LEAVES THE REPUBLIC

I had no nation now but the imagination.
After the white man, the niggers didn't want me
when the power swing to their side.
The first chain my hands and apologize, "History";
the next said I wasn't black enough for their pride.
Tell me, what power, on these unknown rocks—
a spray-plane Air Force, the Fire Brigade,
the Red Cross, the Regiment, two, three police dogs
that pass before you finish bawling "Parade!"?
I met History once, but he ain't recognize me,

a parchment Creole, with warts
like an old sea-bottle, crawling like a crab
through the holes of shadow cast by the net
of a grille balcony; cream linen, cream hat.
I confront him and shout, "Sir, is Shabine!
They say I'se your grandson. You remember Grandma,
your black cook, at all?" The bitch hawk and spat.
A spit like that worth any number of words.
But that's all them bastards have left us: words.

I no longer believed in the revolution.
I was losing faith in the love of my woman.
I had seen that moment Aleksandr Blok
crystallize in *The Twelve*. Was between
the Police Marine Branch and Hotel Venezuelana
one Sunday at noon. Young men without flags
using shirts, their chests waiting for holes.
They kept marching into the mountains, and
their noise ceased as foam sinks into sand.
They sank in the bright hills like rain, every one
with his own nimbus, leaving shirts in the street,
and the echo of power at the end of the street.
Propeller-blade fans turn over the Senate;
the judges, they say, still sweat in carmine,
on Frederick Street the idlers all marching
by standing still, the Budget turns a new leaf.
In the 12:30 movies the projectors best
not break down, or you go see revolution. Aleksandr Blok
enters and sits in the third row of pit eating choc-
olate cone, waiting for a spaghetti West-
ern with Clint Eastwood and featuring Lee Van Cleef.

4   THE *Flight*, PASSING BLANCHISSEUSE

Dusk. The *Flight* passing Blanchisseuse.
Gulls wheel like from a gun again,
and foam gone amber that was white,
lighthouse and star start making friends,
down every beach the long day ends,
and there, on that last stretch of sand,

on a beach bare of all but light,
dark hands start pulling in the seine
of the dark sea, deep, deep inland.

5   SHABINE ENCOUNTERS THE MIDDLE PASSAGE

Man, I brisk in the galley first thing next dawn,
brewing li'l coffee; fog coil from the sea
like the kettle steaming when I put it down
slow, slow, 'cause I couldn't believe what I see:
where the horizon was one silver haze,
the fog swirl and swell into sails, so close
that I saw it was sails, my hair grip my skull,
it was horrors, but it was beautiful.
We float through a rustling forest of ships
with sails dry like paper, behind the glass
I saw men with rusty eyeholes like cannons,
and whenever their half-naked crews cross the sun,
right through their tissue, you traced their bones
like leaves against the sunlight; frigates, barkentines,
the backward-moving current swept them on,
and high on their decks I saw great admirals,
Rodney, Nelson, de Grasse, I heard the hoarse orders
they gave those Shabines, and the forest
of masts sail right through the *Flight*,
and all you could hear was the ghostly sound
of waves rustling like grass in a low wind
and the hissing weeds they trailed from the stern;
slowly they heaved past from east to west
like this round world was some cranked water wheel,
every ship pouring like a wooden bucket
dredged from the deep; my memory revolve
on all sailors before me, then the sun
heat the horizon's ring and they was mist.

Next we pass slave ships. Flags of all nations,
our fathers below deck too deep, I suppose,
to hear us shouting. So we stop shouting. Who knows
who his grandfather is, much less his name?
Tomorrow our landfall will be the Barbados.

Sea Canes

Half my friends are dead.
I will make you new ones, said earth.
No, give me them back, as they were, instead,
with faults and all, I cried.

Tonight I can snatch their talk
from the faint surf's drone
through the canes, but I cannot walk

on the moonlit leaves of ocean
down that white road alone,
or float with the dreaming motion

of owls leaving earth's load.
O earth, the number of friends you keep
exceeds those left to be loved.

The sea canes by the cliff flash green and silver;
they were the seraph lances of my faith,
but out of what is lost grows something stronger

that has the rational radiance of stone,
enduring moonlight, further than despair,
strong as the wind, that through dividing canes

brings those we love before us, as they were,
with faults and all, not nobler, just there.

Volcano

Joyce was afraid of thunder,
but lions roared at his funeral
from the Zurich zoo.
Was it Zurich or Trieste?
No matter. These are legends, as much

as the death of Joyce is a legend,
or the strong rumour that Conrad
is dead, and that *Victory* is ironic.
On the edge of the night-horizon
from this beach house on the cliffs
there are now, till dawn,
two glares from the miles-out-
at-sea derricks; they are like
the glow of the cigar
and the glow of the volcano
at *Victory*'s end.
One could abandon writing
for the slow-burning signals
of the great, to be, instead,
their ideal reader, ruminative,
voracious, making the love of masterpieces
superior to attempting
to repeat or outdo them,
and be the greatest reader in the world.
At least it requires awe,
which has been lost to our time;
so many people have seen everything,
so many people can predict,
so many refuse to enter the silence
of victory, the indolence
that burns at the core,
so many are no more than
erect ash, like the cigar,
so many take thunder for granted.
How common is the lightning,
how lost the leviathans
we no longer look for!
There were giants in those days.
In those days they made good cigars.
I must read more carefully.

Easter

Anna, my daughter,
you have a black dog
that noses your heel,
selfless as a shadow;
here is a fable
about a black dog:
On the last sunrise
the shadow dressed with Him,
it stretched itself also—
they were two big men
with one job to do.
But life had been lent to one
only for this life.
They strode in silence toward
uncontradicting night.
The rats at the Last Supper
shared crumbs with their shadows,
the shadow of the bread
was shared by the bread;
when the candles lowered,
the shadow felt larger,
so He ordered it to leave;
He said where He was going
it would not be needed,
for there there'd be either
radiance or nothing.
It stopped when He turned
and ordered it home,
then it resumed the scent;
it felt itself stretching
as the sun grew small
like the eyes of the soldiers
receding into holes
under the petrified
serpents on their helmets;
the narrowing pupils
glinted like nailheads,

so before He lay back
it crept between the wood
as if it were the pallet
they had always shared;
it crept between the wood
and the flesh nailed to the wood
and it rose like a black flag
as the crossbeam hoisted
itself and the eyes
closed very slowly
extinguishing the shadow—
everything was nothing.
Then the shadow slunk away,
crawling low on its belly,
and it left there knowing
that never again
would He ever need it;
it reentered the earth,
it didn't eat for three days,
it didn't go out,
then it peeped out carefully
like a mole from its hole,
like a wolf after winter,
like a surreptitious serpent,
looking for those forms
that could give back its shape;
then it ran out when the bells
began making wide rings
and rings of radiance;
it keeps nosing for His shape
and it finds it again, in
the white echo of a pigeon
with its wings extended
like a shirt on a clothesline,
like a white shirt on Monday
dripping from a clothesline,
like the greeting of a scarecrow
or a man yawning
at the end of a field.

from *Omeros:*
Chapter VIII

I

In the islet's museum there is a twisted
wine-bottle, crusted with fool's gold from the iron-
cold depth below the redoubt. It has been listed

variously by experts: one, that a galleon
blown by a hurricane out of Cartagena,
this far east, had bled a trail of gold bullion

and wine from its hold (a view held by many a
diver lowering himself); the other was nonsense
and far too simple: that the gold-crusted bottle

came from a flagship in the Battle of the Saints,
but the glass was so crusted it was hard to tell.
Still, the myth widened its rings every century:

that the *Ville de Paris* sank there, not a galleon
crammed with imperial coin, and for her sentry,
an octopus-cyclops, its one eye like the moon.

Deep as a diver's faith but never discovered,
their trust in the relic converted the village,
who came to believe that circling frigates hovered

over the relic, that gulls attacked them in rage.
They kept their faith when the experts' ended in doubt.
The galleon's shadow rode over the ruled page

where Achille, rough weather coming, counted his debt
by the wick of his kerosene lamp; the dark ship
divided his dreams, while the moon's octopus eye

climbed from the palms that lifted their tentacles' shape.
It glared like a shilling. Everything was money.
Money will change her, he thought. Is this bad living

that make her come wicked. He had mocked the belief
in a wrecked ship out there. Now he began diving
in a small shallop beyond the line of the reef,

with spear-gun and lobster-pot. He had to make sure
no sail would surprise him, feathering the oars back
without clicking the oarlocks. He fed the anchor

carefully overside. He tied the cinder-block
to one heel with a slip-knot for faster descent,
then slipped the waterproof bag around his shoulders

for a money-pouch. She go get every red cent,
he swore, crossing himself as he dived. Wedged in boulders
down there was salvation and change. The concrete, tied

to his heel, pulled him down faster than a lead-
weighted, canvas-bound carcass, the stone heart inside
his chest added its poundage. What if love was dead

inside her already? What good lay in pouring
silver coins on a belly that had warmed him once?
This weighed him down even more, so he kept falling

for fathoms towards his fortune: moidores, doubloons,
while the slow-curling fingers of weeds kept calling;
he felt the cold of the drowned entering his loins.

II

Why was he down here, from their coral palaces,
pope-headed turtles asked him, waving their paddles
crusted with rings, nudged by curious porpoises

with black friendly skins. Why? asked the glass sea-horses,
curling like questions. What on earth had he come for,
when he had a good life up there? The sea-mosses

shook their beards angrily, like submarine cedars,
while he trod the dark water. Wasn't love worth more
than the coins of light pouring from the galleon's doors?

In the corals' bone kingdom his skin calcifies.
In that wavering garden huge fans on hinges
swayed, while fingers of seaweed pocketed the eyes

of coins with the profiles of Iberian kings;
here the sea-floor was mud, not corrugating sand
that showed you its ribs; here, the mutating fishes

had goggling eye-bulbs; in that world without sound,
they sucked the white coral, draining it like leeches,
and what looked like boulders sprung the pincers of crabs.

This was not a world meant for the living, he thought.
The dead didn't need money, like him, but perhaps
they hated surrendering things their hands had brought.

The shreds of the ocean's floor passed him from corpses
that had perished in the crossing, their hair like weeds,
their bones were long coral fingers, bubbles of eyes

watched him, a brain-coral gurgled their words,
and every bubble englobed a biography,
no less than the wine-bottle's mouth, but for Achille,

treading the mulch floor of the Caribbean Sea,
no coins were enough to repay its deep evil.
The ransom of centuries shone through the mossy doors

that the moon-blind Cyclops counted, every tendril
raked in the guineas it tested with its soft jaws.
Light paved the ceiling with silver with every swell.

Then he saw the galleon. Her swaying cabin-doors
fanned vaults of silvery mackerel. He caught the glint
of their coin-packed scales, then the tentacle-shadows

whose motion was a miser's harvesting his mint.
He loosened the block and shot up. Next day, her stealth
increased, her tentacles calling, until the wreck

vanished with all hope of Helen. Once more the whelk
was his coin, his bank the sea-conch's. Now, every day
he was clear-headed as the sea, wrenching lace fans

from the forbidden reef, or tailing a sting-ray
floating like a crucifix when it sensed his lance,
and saving the conch-shells he himself had drowned.

And though he lost faith in any fictional ship,
an anchor still forked his brow whenever he frowned,
for she was a spectre now, in her ribbed shape,

he did not know where she was. She'd never be found.
He thought of the white skulls rolling out there like dice
rolled by the hand of the swell, their luck was like his;

he saw drowned Portuguese captains, their coral eyes
entered by minnows, as he hauled the lobster-pot,
bearded with moss, in the cold shade of the redoubt.

III

Philoctete tried to make peace between them. He told
Hector that they were men, that he bore his own wound
as patiently as God allowed him, that the bad blood

between them was worse, that they had a common bond
between them: the sea. The sea that changed the cedars
into canoes, from the day they had hacked the trees

in the heights. He said, whatever a woman does,
that is her business, but men are bound by their work.
But neither listened. Like Hector. Like Achilles.

ALICE WALKER

Women

They were women then
My mama's generation
Husky of voice— Stout of
Step
With fists as well as
Hands
How they battered down
Doors
And ironed
Starched white
Shirts
How they led
Armies
Headragged Generals
Across mined
Fields
Booby-trapped
Ditches
To discover books
Desks
A place for us
How they knew what we
Must know
Without knowing a page
Of it
Themselves.

TOM WEATHERLY

blues for franks wooten

House of the Lifting of the Head

let me open mama your 3 corner box.
yes open mama your 3 corner box.
i have a black snake baby his tongues hot.

you shake round those curves baby dont quite make the grade.
you shake round those curves baby dont make the grade.
man come home tired dont want no lemonade.

we been blowing spit bubbles baby in each others mouf.
we been blowing spit bubbles baby in each others mouf.
burst all them bubbles mama norf cold like the souf.

let me be your woodpecker mama tom do like no pecker would.
let me be your woodpecker mama tom tom do like no pecker
    would.
open your front door baby black dark come home for good.

from *Maumau American Cantos: Canto 4*

GULLFISH

what is black
in me is not like white
you thot enuf
to say   what we were
brought up to be

569

our parents we are not.

you no souf carolina gal
tell me i bring no
chocolate to an occupied town . . .
is another war i'm involved
in will do
        speak of my
        self respect
        for myself
no success, the score is
success, the ritual put down
all the blues gone west
mongers of the world unite!

AL YOUNG

How Stars Start

I don't ask to be forgiven
nor do I wish to be given up,
not entirely, not yet, not while
pain is shooting clean through
the only world I know: this one.
This is no Mal Waldron song or
Marlene Dietrich epic in black
& white where to scrawl against
the paradigms of time is to mean
something benign, like dismissing
present actions or behavior because
I know & understand deep down
inside & beyond that life itself
is acting all of this out; this
kamikaze drama, cosmic if you
will, but certainly comic, in a style
so common as to invite confusion.

Who am I now? What have I become?
Where do we draw the line between being
who I am and what I ought to be?
Need is a needle, nosing its sticky load
into my grief, spilling into veins
that can't be sewn, transforming their dark
cells into lighted semblances of relief.
The stomach is involved; flesh itself;
memories of an island doom that leaves
no room for sense or sensitive
assessments of truth about myself.
Which is the me that never changes?

All roads lead back to starts, to where
I started out, to stars: the fiery
beginnings of our ends & means; our

meanness & our meanings. There never
was a night begun in darkness,
nor a single day begun in light.

Dance of the Infidels

in memory of Bud Powell

The smooth smell of Manhattan taxis,
Parisian taxis, it doesnt matter, it's
the feeling that modern man is all youve
laid him out to be in those tinglings & rushes;
the simple touch of your ringed fingers
against a functioning piano.

                            The winds of Brooklyn
still mean a lot to me. The way certain chicks
formed themselves & their whole lives around
a few notes, an attitude more than anything.
I know about the being out of touch, bumming
nickels & dimes worth of this & that off
him & her here & there—everything but
hither & yon.

                 Genius does not grow on trees.

                                        I owe
you a million love dollars & so much more than
thank-you for re-writing the touch & taste & smell
of the world for me those city years when I could
very well have fasted on into oblivion.

                            Ive just
been playing the record you made in Paris with Art
Blakey & Lee Morgan. The european audience
is applauding madly. I think of what Ive heard
of Buttercup's flowering on the Left Bank & days

you had no one to speak to. Wayne Shorter is
beautifying the background of sunlight with
children playing in it & shiny convertibles
& sedans parked along the block as I blow.

                                     Grass
grows. Negroes. Women walk. The world, in case
youre losing touch again, keeps wanting the same
old thing.

       You gave me some of it; beauty I sought
before I was even aware how much I needed it.

                                    I know
this world is terrible & that one must, above all,
hold onto the heart & the hearts of others.

                I love *you*

Boogie with O.O. Gabugah

O.O. Gabugah writes that he "was born in a taxicab right
smack on 125th and Lenox in Harlem on Lincoln's Birthday,
1945. Franklin Delano Watson was the name my poor brain-
washed parents gave me but I had that racist tag legally altered
once I got old enough to see what was going down. The O.O.,
by the way, stands for *Our Own*, i.e., we need to do *our own*
thing, can you dig it?"

In addition to being one of our strongest young Black revolu-
tionary voices, Brother Gabugah is the author of half a dozen
volumes, all of which have appeared since last year. *Slaughter
the Pig & Git Yo'self Some Chit'lins* is the title of his most
popular work which is presently in its sixth big printing. Other
volumes include: *Niggers with Knives, Black on Back, Love Is
a White Man's Snot-Rag* and *Takin Names and Kickin Asses.
His plays—Transistor Willie & Latrine Lil* and *Go All the Way*

Down & Come Up Shakin (a revolutionary Black musical)—
received last month's Drama Authority Award.

The brother is presently the recipient of both a Federal Arts
Agency grant as well as a Vanderbilt Fellowship to conduct
research on Richard Wright. Currently vacationing in Aus-
tralia, he is preparing a collection of critical essays tentatively
titled *Woodpile Findings: Cultural Investigations into What's
Goin On*.

His last critical work, *Nothin Niggers Do Will Ever Please Me*,
is also a favorite.

"O.O. Gabugah draws strong folk poetry from the voice of a
strident but vital revolutionary who attacks the Uncle Tom,"
states *The Nation* in its March 19, 1973, issue.

A militant advocate of the oral tradition, he chooses to dictate
his poems through me rather than write them down himself.

The Old O.O. Blues

Like right now it's the summertime
    and I'm so all alone
I gots to blow some fonky rhyme
    on my mental saxophone

Brother Trane done did his thang
    and so have Wes Montgomery,
both heavyweights in the music rang,
    now I'mo play my summary

It's lotsa yall that thank yall white
    (ought I say European?)
who thank Mozart and Bach's all right,
    denyin your Black bein

Well, honkyphiles, yall's day done come,
    I mean we gon clean house
and rid the earth of Oreo scum
    that put down Fats for Faust

This here's one for-real revolution
    where aint nobody playin
We intends to stop this cultural pollution
    Can yall git to what I'm sayin?

Sittin up there in your Dior gown
    and Pierre Cardin suit
downtown where all them devil clowns
    hang out and they aint poot!

We take the white man's bread and grants
    but do our own thang with it
while yall bees itchin to git in they pants
    and taint the true Black spirit

I'm blowin for Bird and Dinah and Billie,
    for Satch, Sam Cooke, and Otis,
for Clifford, Eric, and Trane outta Philly
    who split on moment's notice

Chump, you aint gon never change,
    your narrow ass is sankin
Like Watergate, your shit is strange
    You drownin while we thankin

My simple song might not have class
    but you cant listen with impunity
We out to smash your bourgeois ass
    and by *we* I mean The Community!

A Poem for Players

Yes, theyll let you play,
let you play third base or fender bass,
let you play Harrah's Club or Shea Stadium

Theyll let you play
in a play anyway: Shakespeare,
Ionesco, Bullins, Baraka, or Genet,
only dont get down *too* much
& dont go gettin too uppity

Theyll let you play,
oh yes, on the radio, stereo,
even on the video, Ojays,
O.J. Simpson, only please dont stray
too far from your ghetto rodeo

Theyll let you be Satchmo,
theyll let you be Diz,
theyll let you be Romeo,
   or star in *The Wiz*
but you gots to remember that
   that's all there is

Oh, you can be a lawyer or a medico,
a well-briefcased executive with Texaco;
you can even get yourself hired, man,
to go teach *Ulysses* in Dublin, Ireland

Theyll let you play
so long as you dont play around,
so long as you play it hot or cool,
so long as you dont play down the blues
theyll let you play in *Playboy*, *Playgirl*,
   or the *Amsterdam News*

Finally theyll let you play
politics if you dont get in the way

the way some of us did and had to be
iced by conspiracy, international mystery

Theyll let you play anybody but you,
that's pretty much what they will do

SIX
BLUE LIGHT SUTRAS
(1976–1989)

AI

Twenty-Year Marriage

You keep me waiting in a truck
with its one good wheel stuck in the ditch,
while you piss against the south side of a tree.
Hurry. I've got nothing on under my skirt tonight.
That still excites you, but this pickup has no windows
and the seat, one fake leather thigh,
pressed close to mine is cold.
I'm the same size, shape, make as twenty years ago,
but get inside me, start the engine;
you'll have the strength, the will to move.
I'll pull, you push, we'll tear each other in half.
Come on, baby, lay me down on my back.
Pretend you don't owe me a thing
and maybe we'll roll out of here,
leaving the past stacked up behind us;
old newspapers nobody's ever got to read again.

I Can't Get Started

for Ira Hayes

I. SATURDAY NIGHT

A coyote eats chunks of the moon,
the night hen's yellow egg,
while I lie drunk, in a ditch.
Suddenly, a huge combat boot
punches a hole through the sky
and falls toward me.
I wave my arms. Get back.
It keeps coming.

2. SUNDAY MORNING

I stumble out of the ditch
and make it to the shack.
I shoot a few holes in the roof,
then stare at the paper clippings of Iwo Jima.
I remember raising that rag
of red, white and blue,
afraid that if I let go, I'd live.
The bullets never touched me.
Nothing touches me.

Around noon, I make a cup of coffee
and pour a teaspoon of pepper in it
to put the fire out.
I hum between sips
and when I finish, I hug myself.
I'm burning from the bottom up,
a bottle of flesh,
kicked across the hardwood years.
I pass gin and excuses from hand to mouth,
but it's me. It's me.
I'm the one dirty habit
I just can't break.

Two Brothers

A Fiction

I

Night tightens its noose.
You swim toward me out of sleep
like an eel,
as I put the glass canister
beside you on the bed.
Death, Bobby, hit me
like the flat of a hand.

Imagine you are made of crystal
and someone ice picks you
and you shatter,
all your cells coming
almost to despair
it is so good. Dallas. Dallas.
I turn toward the window,
then turn back to you.
Remember that Crayola drawing
of John-John's?—
the black smoke coming out the roof
of the White House
like curly black hair.
How Jackie spanked his hand
and drew him another
with angels lifting up?
Our own childhoods?—
days of ease and grace.
The good life sucking us deeper
and deeper in
toward its hot, liquid center,
where seasoned with the right diction,
schools, and politics
we would fry crisp and greaseless.
King for a day,
that's who I was.
I drove power,
the solid-gold Cadillac.
Go ahead, frown.
Tell me about the sin of pride
and I'll tell you
about the lie of forgiveness.
It wasn't Oswald killed me,
it was envy.

2

"I have this dream, Jack," you say.
"I'm at Arlington. It's twilight.
Thousands of funeral markers

rise from the ground
like dirty alabaster arms.
It's here, pilgrim,
they seem to say.
And then I'm in a room.
A man is counting green bills
sharp enough to cut,
while I pry the lid off a barrel
and peer down into it,
as if inside, there are dark green pickles
or steel-blue fish,
as if I were a boy
on a crowded street in Russia
with my hand around a coin
and the other in my brother's hand.
And while I scuff my shoe
and try to decide,
from far away I hear bugles, hoofbeats,
I see my brother's head
suddenly rise from his body
like a tiny pink ball
on a spout of dark red water,
clear past the rooftops
into the serene evening sky.
I am that boy, Jack,
dipping his hands
in the one standing barrel,
into water warm as blood,
with nothing to say to anybody,
except, 'My brother is the moon.'"

3

Riddles, I say,
lifting the lid off the canister.
I pull out a wet, gray mass,
stare at it, then put it back.
Some African tribes
eat the brains of their dead.
It brings them closer;

it kills them too.
But whatever it takes, Bobby, right?
I look out the window
at the deep rose welts of dawn,
streaking the sky's broad back,
then hand you the canister.
You lift out my brain.
When you bite down, I burn.
The air smells like creosote
and I stand before you,
my skin plump and pink,
my wounds healed.
I put my arms around you
and you disappear into me . . .

I stare at myself in the mirror:
Jack Kennedy,
thinner now, almost ascetic,
wearing the exhaust fumes of L.A.
like a sharkskin suit,
while the quarter moon
hangs from heaven,
a swing on a gold chain. My throne.
I step back and knot my tie.
Bobby, it's all a matter of showmanship.
You have to have the ability to entertain,
to stand like P. T. Barnum
in the enchanted center
of the public eye,
to drop your pants now and then
and have the crowd
cry for more,
to give it to them,
to take those encores,
till like the clown in Piaf's song
the show is all there is,
and the bravos, the bravos.
You give the people what they want, Bobby,
someone they can't help loving
like a father or an uncle,

someone who through his own magical fall
lifts them above the slime
of their daily lives.
Not God made man,
but man made God.
I step back to the mirror.
Break a leg, kid, I say to myself.
Give 'em a miracle.
Give 'em Hollywood.
Give 'em Saint Jack.

The Good Shepherd: Atlanta, 1981

I lift the boy's body
from the trunk,
set it down,
then push it over the embankment
with my foot.
I watch it roll
down into the river
and feel I'm rolling with it,
feel the first cold slap of the water,
wheeze and fall down on one knee.
So tired, so cold.
Lord, I need a new coat,
not polyester, but wool,
new and pure
like the little lamb
I killed tonight.
With my right hand,
that same hand that hits
with such force,
I push myself up gently.
I know what I'd like—
some hot cocoa by the heater.

Once home, I stand at the kitchen sink,
letting the water run
till it overflows the pot,
then I remember the blood
in the bathroom
and so upstairs.
I take cleanser,
begin to scrub
the tub, tiles, the toilet bowl,
then the bathroom.
Mop, vacuum, and dust rag.
Work, work for the joy of it,
for the black boys
who know too much,
but not enough to stay away,
and sometimes a girl, the girls too.
How their hands
grab at my ankles, my knees.
And don't I lead them
like a good shepherd?
I stand at the sink,
where the water is still
overflowing the pot,
turn off the faucet,
then heat the water and sit down.
After the last sweet mouthful of chocolate
burns its way down my throat,
I open the library book,
the one on mythology,
and begin to read.
Saturn, it says, devours his children.
Yes, it's true, I know it.
An ordinary man, though, a man like me
eats and is full.
Only God is never satisfied.

WILL ALEXANDER

from *Haiti*

we who exist as a scar
of eternal & murky significance
in this crepuscular enclave
like a wasp
or a windless brandishing torch
or a planet at dusk whose rotation is suspended in evil

we are honed by our dread
we burn & we drift
as a blank & a-rhythmic burst by witness
in blind meridian burrows
fraught by internal nigrescence & terror
the extremities
the mud leeches
the flameless underwater dartings
ruled in synecdoche by a harried nomadology
by monsoon & clinging as our only grasp of fire

this
the ironies of malevolent Stygian rest
greenish
beneath corroded gypsum flames
as medicines or ointments
or floating sand iguanas
we exist as nutrients
as hotly lettered moths
as a flock of magnetic whistling pediculates
climbing to a peak of imagined rhythmical snow
near the first seven burnings of elliptic proto-suns
therefore
we are deaf with irascence
with monomial ice & tearing
we who have counted our mazes by death clocks
by brutal cyanide potions

by mixed centripetal blasts
by the bladder of vultures & gender
we who exist as lost theocracy & arrogance
as a green reactive sub-base
it is we
who blister our songs in the flagrant treachery of exile
it is we
who don ourselves in dripping viper's teeth
it is we
who wade in the hair of writhing snakes & sibyls
scorching ourselves in Neptune molten
in twisted citron flamings

yes
we exist
with the pure emotion of hatred
with our riddles & our brine
with obscure & melted needles
we listen with clair-audience
as carnivores
as listless & negative dust authority

for us
the living who are forced to peruse us
hear us with superior molecular tragedy
for every dawn they come near us
for every strife that they fear
we acknowledge their scorn & ruin
with muzzles
with dejection & hopeless bread
soaked with a sorrowful screaming
because we know that our vocal omniscience exists
that we flagellate & kindle in the first scorched immensity
in the first soulless terror
riddled
bloodless
dreaded
under the vines
of a morose & circular vector
contradicting all the pattern
all the physics of vein & law

GEORGE BARLOW

Titta

Mama said they called you *Titta*
& loved you

She said that you would go crabbing
on Avery Island each morning
& picnicking at Camp Knighton
in the summer

That your salt held things together
when my grandfather
a handsome young doctor
collapsed in the kitchen & passed
into his dream of a fine brick house
for his family

That you came to her one night
after they had buried you
& stopped her crying because
everything was gonna be all right

Titta she said means *sister*
woman of New Iberia
sister of the South woman of the bayou
hot sauce & mystery in your veins
myths & songs in your voice

I see you now in an old photo
a giant oak behind you
a creole sun on half your face
Mama Auntie Vet & Brother
clinging like leaves
in the background

And when we gather to eat
our marriage birth & death
I troll the depths of heavy black pots
crack open the past
with my teeth & fingers
chew its tender legends
breathe your name
in the gumbo air

CYRUS CASSELLS

Soul Make a Path Through Shouting

for Elizabeth Eckford
Little Rock, Arkansas, 1957

Thick at the schoolgate are the ones
Rage has twisted
Into minotaurs, harpies
Relentlessly swift;
So you must walk past the pincers,
The swaying horns,
Sister, sister,
Straight through the gusts
Of fear and fury,
Straight through;
Where are you going?

I'm just going to school.

Here we go to meet
The hydra-headed day,
Here we go to meet
The maelstrom—

Can my voice be an angel-on-the-spot,
An amen corner?
Can my voice take you there,
Gallant girl with a notebook.
Up, up from the shadows of gallows trees
To the other shore:
A globe bathed in light,
A chalkboard blooming with equations—

I have never seen the likes of you,
Pioneer in dark glasses:
You won't show the mob your eyes,

But I know your gaze,
Steady-on-the-North-Star, burning—
With their jerry-rigged faith,
Their spear of the American flag,
How could they dare to believe
You're someone sacred?:
Nigger, burr-headed girl,
Where are you going?

I'm just going to school.

Sally Hemings to Thomas Jefferson

for Barbara Chase-Riboud and for my family, reputed to be the
direct descendents of Hemings and Jefferson

Je m'appelle Sally:
How simply my first French lesson
Returns to me,
The stern and exacting gaze of my tutor,
Monsieur Perrault,
And your rich, commanding voice
—The voice of one
Both demigod and father:
Tell me Sally, what did you learn?
Master, I learned to say
My name.
Now, years later, I repeat the French,
As if to yield
All that I am,
And open the locket to find,
Cached in the tiny, gold-lined womb,
A lock of your red hair:
It happens, your face
Looms again in my lifetime.
If I could go to the doorway,
And stand, waiting for you

As you take the hall, your leonine figure
Assembling in the longest mirror
As in my eyes.
But you are dead, Thomas Jefferson,
And I can only sit,
Motionless, my heart pounding
At your phantom,
For today I learned
The census-taker made me white
To absolve you of the crime
Of having loved a slavewoman.
So I burned our correspondence
—The diaries and *billet-doux* an ash
Clinging to my skirts,
A smoke in my hair. Each word
A swatch of myself, a forbidden history:
The Hôtel de Langeac, the Palace of Marly,
The Capitol, Monticello—
Now I am robbed of everything,
Even of my color.

I was fifteen when you took me,
Your daughter's nursemaid;
You brushed my cheek
With your red-plumed chest,
Whispering *Martha, Martha*
—Piercing me with the name
Of your dead wife, my white half-sister
Whom I resembled.
I was so frightened by you then,
So overawed and unbelieving
Of your love.
I would stand before my mirror,
Cupping my breasts
In my two hands, amazed: no fledgling
But a woman—
Je t'aime, Sally, Je t'aime,
I heard you say,
And in Paris I mislaid
My slavery.

So home to Monticello, I met
My mother's loving, though accusatory face,
And knew I should have chosen freedom.

*

The battlecries,
Your glittering words of revolution
Have been recorded,
But in a secret wing of Monticello,
Against your will, I marked
The dreams and follies of our seven children,
The shocked faces of our foreign guests.
But O what I could not capture
Was your silence
As all the country crowned me
Black Lillith, Sooty Chatelaine.
In your pain and ravaged pride,
You clung to me.
Love me, stay with me, you whispered.
They say a man cannot free what he loves:
Is it your truth, your story,
I hear in these words?
Love me and remain a slave?

*

In the recurrent dream,
I stand on the steps of Monticello,
And see what blinds me:
Our children like hunted deer,
In a dead run—our children
You could never acknowledge.
I recall pausing on the Pont de Neuilly,
And absently dropping
A key into the Seine,
As I watched the word *enceinte*
Darken your gaze:

Return with me to Virginia,
You pleaded, a great man,
Lonely in your aegis,
But I refused, knowing I was unfettered
As long as I remained in France.

You would love me;
We would return to Paris,
And my child would be given
Freedom at adulthood
—A perilous, vouchsafed freedom, surely,
To pass from slavery
Into a forged whiteness
That begs amnesia.
I looked into your eyes, two sapphires
Set in a human face,
And met a suffering so vast, what else
But to take your hand
And whisper, *Yes* . . .
My love and master, I need to believe
I would choose this way again,
Though as property
I had no choice
'Cept to give myself
But I, Mademoiselle Sally,
Gave you my heart,
And returned to slavery.
Nothing could free me from you.

BARBARA CHASE-RIBOUD

from *Portrait of a Nude Woman as Cleopatra*

CLEOPATRA

Deep in the folds of a huge and glistening afternoon
Penumbric, I lie across you,
The slanting sun probing my back,
A slick dew between the poised weapons of our bodies.
Mine, I know, is weightless upon yours,
No more than a pale color when what I want
Is the weight of Imperial Rome,
Opening you, sliding into soul and substance,
Widening your eyes in astonishment that refract
In my hair: extinguished & strangely feminine—
A sudden young girl; lips sullen and insubordinate.
What did I do, swain?
Shatter your solemn and complacent body
With my long-knifed African sun?

ANTONY

Afternoon sleep is so different from night's.
Its fitful daydreams hang
In the tottering heat and light while
Voices of children rock like a hand on a cradle and
Murmurs of the honest gossip of women
Click like ivory balls and stir the curtains.
The drunken rumors of real life unsettle our bodies,
Wrapping them not in the silence of lunar darkness
But like a running spring, rutting despatches of
Daylight stream in rivulets
Along nerve ends already worn and fatigued
By impending treason,
Washing our deep knotted and tressed flesh
In gentle and vague disillusion.

CLEOPATRA

In the time a wave recedes to the applause of
Beached pebbles, I've toured the world in the curve of
Your mouth, dropping kisses like salt-slicked stones,
A slow and passionate lapping that breaks,
Content, onto the tuneless Syrian afternoon.
Not until one disappears do I place another,
Patiently bartering my life for your lips.
I make a curtain of my hair to screen you
From the sun, wind, and all visitors so that
In my shade you endure the usury of
Endless, insatiable infractions,
Stone by stone, kiss by kiss,
Swooned by obdurate prejudice,
In the time of a wave and a wife's divorce.

WANDA COLEMAN

What It Means to Be Dark

when you are beaten
it is more difficult for scars to be seen

in all chase scenes
you are the bad guy. chaser or chasee

when shot it is more difficult to see
bullet holes therefore easier for them
to keep shooting

of course you're always hostile

of course you're always paranoid and overly
sensitive about your race

of course you fail to appreciate that some of them
have tough lives too

are you your brutha's keeper?
even though he sold you out

—darkness quiz—

no one asks if: a) you are a virgin
                    b) you've ever been to jail
                    c) you drink alcohol or use dope
                    d) you are a thief
                    e) you can dance good
                    f) all of the above

you know you are in the dark when they sit
you at the table nearest the kitchen
and you take immediate umbrage even if
it's the only table available and
is offered out of expediency

Mastectomy

the fall of
velvet plum points and umber aureolae

remember living

forget cool evening air kisses the rush of
liberation freed from the brassiere

forget the cupping of his hands the pleasure
his eyes looking down/anticipating

forget his mouth. his tongue at the nipples
his intense hungry nursing

forget sensations which begin either
on the right or the left. go thru the body
linger between thighs

forget the space once grasped during his ecstasy

sweet sweet mama you taste so

from *American Sonnets*

I.

the lurid confessions of an ex-cake junky: "i blew it
all. blimped. i was really stupid. i waited
until i was forty to get hooked on white flour
and powdered sugar"

$$\frac{\text{white greed}}{\text{socio-eco dominance}} \ \ \text{X} \ \ \frac{\text{black anger}}{\text{socio-eco disparity}} =$$

a) increased racial tension/polarization
b) increased criminal activity
c) sporadic eruptions manifest as mass killings
d) collapses of longstanding social institutions
e) the niggerization of the middle class

the blow to his head cracks his skull
he bleeds eighth notes & treble clefs

(sometimes i feel like i'm almost going)

to Chicago. baby you want to go?

   4.

rejection can kill you

it can force you to park outside neon-lit
liquor stores and finger the steel of
your contemplation. it can even make you
rob yourself

(when does the veteran of one war fail to
appreciate the vet of another?)

the ragged scarecrow lusts in the midst of
a fallow field

and the lover who prances in circles envies me
my moves/has designs on my gizzard/kicks shit

this is the city we've come to
all the lights are red all the poets are dead
and there are no norths

   5.

rusted busted and dusted

the spurious chain of plebeian events
(aintjahmamaauntjemimaondapancakebox?)

which allows who to claim the largest number of homicides
the largest number of deaths by cancer the largest
number of institutionalized men the largest number of
single female heads of household the largest number of
crimes of possession the largest number of functionally
insane the largest number of consumers of dark rum

largely
preoccupied with perfecting plans of escape

see you later alligator
after while crocodile
after supper muthafucka

    15.

dear most important believer

on behalf of everyone i'd like to thank you
for your trust and loyalty. to recognize
you as among the sincerest of followers. i'm
pleased to personally welcome you to the many
privileges and benefits. you'll enjoy exclusive
advantages unavailable to others. because you deserve
special attention. i've enclosed your emblems
of guaranteed earned recognition. please take a moment to
contemplate and admire them. we've gone to great lengths
to exceed your every expectation. if you have questions
about a higher level, remember there is none. if
you feel you need extra recognition this is all there
is since it is special indication of your status

thank you for showing us your best

    24.

i'm on uptime/have no resting place/cannot rest
constant strive constant drive
getting into bed is an act of creation. i'm putting
on weight and hope with unequaled relish—trapped twixt
the
illusion of escape and the hallucination of release

i am the love wish of secret rapists/the men
who break before they enter
they fight to maintain the myths i die by
(when underthegun who has time to keep a war journal?)

in that blues pocket of need reed where sweet darkness
begins befogged in the snooze of mist, my legacy
the slave-soaked night wailings of misbegotten dreamers
beseeching the dead to rise once more—that fierce
hoodoo of humans consumed in the defiant flames of living

35.

boooooooo. spooky ripplings of icy waves. this
umpteenth time she returns—this invisible woman
long on haunting short on ectoplasm

"you're a good man, sistuh," a lover sighed solongago.
"keep your oil slick and your motor running."

wretched stained mirrors within mirrors of
fractured webbings like nests of manic spiders
reflect her ruined mien (rue wiggles remorse
squiggles woe jiggles bestride her). oozy Manes spill
out yonder spooling in night's lofty hour exudes
her gloom and spew in rankling odor of heady dour

as she strives to retrieve flesh to cloak her bones
again to thrive to keep her poisoned id alive

usta be young usta be gifted—still black

91.

the gates of mercy slammed on the right foot.
they would not permit return and bent
a wing. there was no choice but
to learn to boogaloo. those horrid days
were not without their pleasures, learning
to swear and wearing mock leather so tight
eyes bulged, a stolen puff or two

behind crack-broken backs and tickled palms
in hallways dark, flirtations during choir practice
as the body organized itself against the will
(a mystic gone ballistic, not home but blood
on the range) as one descended on this effed-up
breeding hole of greeds—to suffer chronic seeings

was't hunger or holiness spurred the sighting?

nostrum nostalgia my notes on never nada no

94.

collect against my reluctance/forced tabulations
dey did dis, say me, and dat and dat dere
why have there been no arrests? no hearings? no justice?
(what is not offered cannot be refused)

i regress/the despoiled child, the deserted schoolyard

weeper. this is your execution
weeper. this is your groveling stone
weeper. yours is the burst & burnings of a city

stunned tearless in the uselessness of limp pursuit
breathlessness besets and brings the ass earthward

rest. the answer yellows and loses its wit, its crispness
my bed to make my heart to stake my soul to take

how i committed suicide: i revealed myself to you.
i trusted you. i forgot the color of my birth

SAM CORNISH

Harriet in the Promised Land

From the book by Jacob Lawrence

in a red dress
a woman on her knees
washes the floor
a hundred years ago

she is shaping the life of her children
she thinks as a woman
does of freedom
a dark place in the woods
where the north enters the trees

she wonders if words mean history   a woman
losing her children
if reading is a crime
she does not ask for pity

there is a damp rag on the floor
she wipes
in the dress she slept in   the dress
she had her children in

she scrubs the floor
does not brush her teeth
she picks them with straws or sticks

she moves on her knees
and watches the ceiling in the water
reflected in the water

everything in her life
is hard like the floor she
touches

the water in her hands
the water is between her legs
her body like a sack of muscle
her hands are dark with water

she wonders about her children
how many children   if she could count
pass her fingers
about her body
the words she would find if she could read

she gathers water
like sounds in her head
she kneels
like a slave
in church
like a slave preparing to dance
in front of the big house
she pretends to be quiet
her mind is grinding
glass
pissing in the evening meal

TOI DERRICOTTE

Blackbottom

When relatives came from out of town,
we would drive down to Blackbottom,
drive slowly down the congested main streets
    —Beubian and Hastings—
trapped in the mesh of Saturday night.
Freshly escaped, black middle class,
we snickered, and were proud;
the louder the streets, the prouder.
We laughed at the bright clothes of a prostitute,
a man sitting on a curb with a bottle in his hand.
We smelled barbecue cooking in dented washtubs,
    and our mouths watered.
As much as we wanted it we couldn't take the chance.

Rhythm and blues came from the windows, the throaty voice of
    a woman lost in the bass, in the drums, in the dirty down
    and out, the grind.
"I love to see a funeral, then I know it ain't mine."
We rolled our windows down so that the waves rolled over us
    like blood.
We hoped to pass invisibly, knowing on Monday we would
    return safely to our jobs, the post office and classroom.
We wanted our sufferings to be offered up as tender meat,
and our triumphs to be belted out in raucous song.
We had lost our voice in the suburbs, in Conant Gardens,
    where each brick house delineated a fence of silence;
we had lost the right to sing in the street and damn creation.

We returned to wash our hands of them,
to smell them
whose very existence
tore us down to the human.

The Weakness

That time my grandmother dragged me
through the perfume aisles at Saks, she held me up
by my arm, hissing, "Stand up,"
through clenched teeth, her eyes
bright as a dog's
cornered in the light.
She said it over and over,
as if she were Jesus,
and I were dead. She had been
solid as a tree,
a fur around her neck, a
light-skinned matron whose car was parked, who walked on
        swirling
marble and passed through
brass openings—in 1945.
There was not even a black
elevator operator at Saks.
The saleswoman had brought velvet
leggings to lace me in, and cooed,
as if in the service of all grandmothers.
My grandmother had smiled, but not
hungrily, not like my mother
who hated them, but wanted to please,
and they had smiled back, as if
they were wearing wooden collars.
When my legs gave out, my grandmother
dragged me up and held me like God
holds saints by the
roots of the hair. I begged her
to believe I couldn't help it. Stumbling,
her face white
with sweat, she pushed me through the crowd, rushing
away from those eyes
that saw through
her clothes, under
her skin, all the way down
to the transparent
genes confessing.

On the Turning Up
of Unidentified Black Female Corpses

Mowing his three acres with a tractor,
a man notices something ahead—a mannequin—
he thinks someone threw it from a car. Closer
he sees it is the body of a black woman.

The medics come and turn her with pitchforks.
Her gaze shoots past him to nothing. Nothing
is explained. How many black women
have been turned up to stare at us blankly,

in weedy fields, off highways,
pushed out in plastic bags,
shot, knifed, unclothed partially, raped,
their wounds sealed with a powdery crust.

Last week on TV, a gruesome face, eyes bloated shut.
No one will say, "She looks like she's sleeping," ropes
of blue-black slashes at the mouth. Does anybody
know this woman? Will anyone come forth? Silence

like a backwave rushes into that field
where, just the week before, four other black girls
had been found. The gritty image hangs in the air
just a few seconds, but it strikes me,

a black woman, there is a question being asked
about my life. How can I
protect myself? Even if I lock my doors,
walk only in the light, someone wants me dead.

Am I wrong to think
if five white women had been stripped,
broken, the sirens would wail until
someone was named?

Is it any wonder I walk over these bodies
pretending they are not mine, that I do not know
the killer, that I am just like any woman—
if not wanted, at least tolerated.

Part of me wants to disappear, to pull
the earth on top of me. Then there is this part
that digs me up with this pen
and turns my sad black face to the light.

Black Boys Play the Classics

The most popular "act" in
Penn Station
is the three black kids in ratty
sneakers & T-shirts playing
two violins and a cello—Brahms.
White men in business suits
have already dug into their pockets
as they pass and they toss in
a dollar or two without stopping.
Brown men in work-soiled khakis
stand with their mouths open,
arms crossed on their bellies
as if they themselves have always
wanted to attempt those bars.
One white boy, three, sits
cross-legged in front of his
idols—in ecstasy—
their slick, dark faces,
their thin, wiry arms,
who must begin to look
like angels!
Why does this trembling
pull us?
A: *Beneath the surface we are one.*
B: *Amazing! I did not think that they could speak this tongue.*

RALPH DICKEY

Leaving Eden

Named and unnamed and renamed
armed and unarmed and disarmed
I have my covenant outside the womb
in the solitary confinement of my cells

The cries of my bones
like the cries of animals
followed me out of my mother
into exile

from *The Arcanum Poems*

13

During the age of my ice-history

Once again upon the nothing
is transformed the holy mouse from prince.

I was born a calico deer without hooves,
crept into bays of leaves to soothe
my young stalks and hide from bulls
who would plunge their points in the fawn.

Green mold grows in my palms.

———————

21

I do not want a poem
that depends on madness alone
for its vision, nor on madness
alone for its madness.

Having made my meaning,
I make my meaning
clear. It is unreal
like the wings of ants.

Father

I sat on my stool
in the dark
a plane of light
from the cracked door
fell across my face
like a burn
in the next room
my father was beating
my mother to death
he kicked her until
she cried blood
and then he kicked her
until she came down
with a coma
and then he kicked her until
he just couldn't
kick her no more
he came in to see me
and put his hand on
my shoulder listen
I want you to kill
a man for me
I stood up he shoved me
back sit down I'll

give you a hundred
dollars what do you
say I said well
who is it
here's a piece of paper
with the man's name
kill him I'll give you
a hundred dollars
I opened the paper my name
was on it I turned
it over to see if
there was an alternate
what is this I said
some kind of goddam
joke I never joke
about money
he said

MELVIN DIXON

Tour Guide: *La Maison des Esclaves*

He speaks of voyages:
men traveling spoon-fashion,
women dying in afterbirth,
babies clinging
to salt-dried nipples.
For what his old eyes still see
his lips have few words. Where
his flat thick feet still walk
his hands crack
into a hundred lifelines.

Here wave rush to shore
breaking news that we return
to empty rooms
where the sea is nothing calm.
And sun, tasting the skin
of black men,
leaves teeth marks.

The rooms are empty until he speaks.
His guttural French is a hawking trader.
His quick Wolof a restless warrior.
His slow, impeccable syllables
a gentleman trader. He tells
in their own language
what they have done.

Our touring maps and cameras ready
we stand in the weighing room
where chained men paraded firm backs,
their women open, full breasts,
and children,
rows of shiny teeth.

Others watched from the balcony,
set the price in guilders, francs,
pesetas and English pounds. Later,
when he was finished we too
can leave our coins
where stiff legs dragged
in endless bargain.

He shows how some sat knee-bent
in the first room.
Young virgins waited in the second.
In the third, already red,
the sick and dying
gathered near the exit to the sea.

In the weighing room again
he takes a chain to show us
how it's done. We take
photographs to remember,
others leave coins to forget.
No one speaks
except iron on stone
and the sea
where nothing's safe.

He smiles for he has spoken
of the ancestors: his, ours.
We leave quietly, each alone,
knowing that they who come after us
and breaking
in these tides will find
red empty rooms
to measure long journeys.

Ile de Gorée, Senegal

Turning Forty in the 90's

April 1990

We promised to grow old together, our dream
since years ago when we began
to celebrate our common tenderness
and touch. So here we are:

Dry, ashy skin, falling hair, losing breath
at the top of stairs, forgetting things.
Vials of Septra and AZT line the bedroom dresser
like a boy's toy army poised for attack—
your red, my blue, and the casualties are real.

Now the dimming in your man's eyes and mine.
Our bones ache as the muscles dissolve,
exposing the fragile gates of ribs, our last defense.
And we calculate pensions and premiums.
You are not yet forty-five, and I
not yet forty, but neither of us for long.

No Senior discounts here, so we clip coupons
like squirrels in late November, foraging
each remaining month or week, day or hour.
We hold together against the throb and jab
of yet another bone from out of nowhere poking through.
You grip the walker and I hobble with a cane.
Two witnesses for our bent generation.

Wednesday Mourning

Morning blood on my pillow,
dried brown from the night fighting me
and I don't know why.

I check myself and find no cuts,
no pimples scratched off, no teeth
loose and gummy, no fingers peeled,

but lips swollen from calling his name
and feeling my head and throat run dry—
the fluids fled are body tears
that take their mourning weight.

My head empties after drink or dream.
But this is not the first blood—two,
three, four mornings straight,
in different pillow spots when I awake

and coloring my whole day red.
My eyes tell it: someone
upstairs inside me is dying
not the first death.

Heartbeats

Work out. Ten laps.
Chin ups. Look good.

Steam room. Dress warm.
Call home. Fresh air.

Eat right. Rest well.
Sweetheart. Safe sex.

Sore throat. Long flu.
Hard nodes. Beware.

Test blood. Count cells.
Reds thin. Whites low.

Dress warm. Eat well.
Short breath. Fatigue.

Night sweats. Dry cough.
Loose stools. Weight loss.

Get mad. Fight back.
Call home. Rest well.

Don't cry. Take charge.
No sex. Eat right.

Call home. Talk slow.
Chin up. No air.

Arms wide. Nodes hard.
Cough dry. Hold on.

RITA DOVE

The House Slave

The first horn lifts its arm over the dew-lit grass
and in the slave quarters there is a rustling—
children are bundled into aprons, cornbread

and water gourds grabbed, a salt pork breakfast taken.
I watch them driven into the vague before-dawn
while their mistress sleeps like an ivory toothpick

and Massa dreams of asses, rum and slave-funk.
I cannot fall asleep again. At the second horn,
the whip curls across the backs of the laggards—

sometimes my sister's voice, unmistaken, among them.
"Oh! pray," she cries. "Oh! pray!" Those days
I lie on my cot, shivering in the early heat,

and as the fields unfold to whiteness,
and they spill like bees among the fat flowers,
I weep. It is not yet daylight.

David Walker (*1785–1830*)

Free to travel, he still couldn't be shown how lucky
he was: *They strip and beat and drag us about*
like rattlesnakes. Home on Brattle Street, he took in the sign
on the door of the slop shop. All day at the counter—
white caps, ale-stained pea coats. Compass needles,
eloquent as tuning forks, shivered, pointing north.
Evenings, the ceiling fan sputtered like a second pulse.
Oh Heaven! I am full!! I can hardly move my pen!!!

On the faith of an eye-wink, pamphlets were stuffed
into trouser pockets. Pamphlets transported
in the coat linings of itinerant seamen, jackets
ringwormed with salt traded drunkenly to pursers
in the Carolinas, pamphlets ripped out, read aloud:
Men of colour, who are also of sense.
Outrage. Incredulity. Uproar in state legislatures.

We are the most wretched, degraded and abject set
of beings that ever lived since the world began.
The jewelled canaries in the lecture halls tittered,
pressed his dark hand between their gloves.
Every half-step was no step at all.
Every morning, the man on the corner strung a fresh
bunch of boots from his shoulders. "I'm happy!" he said.
"I never want to live any better or happier than
when I can get a-plenty of boots and shoes to clean!"

A second edition. A third.
The abolitionist press is *perfectly appalled.*
Humanity, kindness and the fear of the Lord
does not consist in protecting devils. A month—
his person (is that all?) found face-down
in the doorway at Brattle Street,
his frame slighter than friends remembered.

Adolescence—II

Although it is night, I sit in the bathroom, waiting.
Sweat prickles behind my knees, the baby-breasts are alert.
Venetian blinds slice up the moon; the tiles quiver in pale strips.

Then they come, the three seal men with eyes as round
As dinner plates and eyelashes like sharpened tines.
They bring the scent of licorice. One sits in the washbowl,

One on the bathtub edge; one leans against the door.
"Can you feel it yet?" they whisper.
I don't know what to say, again. They chuckle,

Patting their sleek bodies with their hands.
"Well, maybe next time." And they rise,
Glittering like pools of ink under moonlight,

And vanish. I clutch at the ragged holes
They leave behind, here at the edge of darkness.
Night rests like a ball of fur on my tongue.

Banneker

What did he do except lie
under a pear tree, wrapped in
a great cloak, and meditate
on the heavenly bodies?
Venerable, the good people of Baltimore
whispered, shocked and more than
a little afraid. After all it was said
he took to strong drink.
Why else would he stay out
under the stars all night
and why hadn't he married?

But who would want him! Neither
Ethiopian nor English, neither
lucky nor crazy, a capacious bird
humming as he penned in his mind
another enflamed letter
to President Jefferson—he imagined
the reply, polite and rhetorical.
Those who had been to Philadelphia
reported the statue
of Benjamin Franklin
before the library

his very size and likeness.
A wife? No, thank you.
At dawn he milked
the cows, then went inside

and put on a pot to stew
while he slept. The clock
he whittled as a boy
still ran. Neighbors
woke him up
with warm bread and quilts.
At nightfall he took out

his rifle—a white-maned
figure stalking the darkened
breast of the Union—and
shot at the stars, and by chance
one went out. Had he killed?
I assure thee, my dear Sir!
Lowering his eyes to fields
sweet with the rot of spring, he could see
a government's domed city
rising from the morass and spreading
in a spiral of lights. . . .

from *Thomas and Beulah*

*(These poems tell two sides of a story and
are meant to be read in sequence.)*

THE EVENT

Ever since they'd left the Tennessee ridge
with nothing to boast of
but good looks and a mandolin,

the two Negroes leaning
on the rail of a riverboat
were inseparable: Lem plucked

to Thomas' silver falsetto.
But the night was hot and they were drunk.
They spat where the wheel

churned mud and moonlight,
they called to the tarantulas
down among the bananas

to come out and dance.
*You're so fine and mighty; let's see
what you can do*, said Thomas, pointing

to a tree-capped island.
Lem stripped, spoke easy: *Them's chestnuts,
I believe.* Dove

quick as a gasp. Thomas, dry
on deck, saw the green crown shake
as the island slipped

under, dissolved
in the thickening stream.
At his feet

a stinking circle of rags,
the half-shell mandolin.
Where the wheel turned the water

gently shirred.

ONE VOLUME MISSING

Green sludge of a riverbank,
swirled and blotched,
as if a tree above him were shuffling
cards.
        Who would have thought
the binding of a "Standard Work
of Reference in the Arts,
Science, History, Discovery
and Invention" could bring back

slow afternoons with a line and bent nail

here, his wingtips balanced
on a scuffed linoleum square
at the basement rummage sale
of the A.M.E. Zion Church?

He opens *Motherwell-Orion* and finds
orchids on the frontispiece
overlain with tissue,
fever-specked and drooping
their inflamed penises.

Werner's Encyclopedia,
Akron, Ohio, 1909:
Complete in Twenty-Five Volumes
minus one—

for five bucks
no zebras, no Virginia,
no wars.

MOTHERHOOD

She dreams the baby's so small she keeps
misplacing it—it rolls from the hutch
and the mouse carries it home, it disappears
with his shirt in the wash.
Then she drops it and it explodes
like a watermelon, eyes spitting.

Finally they get to the countryside;
Thomas has it in a sling.
He's strewing rice along the road
while the trees chitter with tiny birds.
In the meadow to their right three men
are playing rough with a white wolf. She calls

warning but the wolf breaks free
and she runs, the rattle
rolls into the gully, then she's
there and tossing the baby behind her,
listening for its cry as she straddles
the wolf and circles its throat, counting
until her thumbs push through to the earth.
White fur seeps red. She is hardly breathing.
The small wild eyes
go opaque with confusion and shame, like a child's.

DAYSTAR

She wanted a little room for thinking:
but she saw diapers steaming on the line,
a doll slumped behind the door.

So she lugged a chair behind the garage
to sit out the children's naps.

Sometimes there were things to watch—
the pinched armor of a vanished cricket,
a floating maple leaf. Other days
she stared until she was assured
when she closed her eyes
She'd see only her own vivid blood.

She had an hour, at best, before Liza appeared
pouting from the top of the stairs.
And just *what* was mother doing
out back with the field mice? Why,

building a palace. Later
that night when Thomas rolled over and
lurched into her, she would open her eyes
and think of the place that was hers
for an hour—where
she was nothing,
pure nothing, in the middle of the day.

Canary

for Michael S. Harper

Billie Holiday's burned voice
had as many shadows as lights,
a mournful candelabra against a sleek piano,
the gardenia her signature under that ruined face.

(Now you're cooking, drummer to bass,
magic spoon, magic needle.
Take all day if you have to
with your mirror and your bracelet of song.)

Fact is, the invention of women under siege
has been to sharpen love in the service of myth.

If you can't be free, be a mystery.

The Return of Lieutenant James Reese Europe

(*Victory Parade, New York City, February 1919*)

We trained in the streets: the streets where we came from.
We drilled with sticks, boys darting between bushes,
     shouting—
that's all you thought we were good for. We trained anyway.
In camp we had no plates or forks. First to sail, first to join
     the French,
first to see combat with the shortest training time.

My, the sun is looking fine today.

We toured devastation, American good will
in a forty-four piece band. Dignitaries smiled; the wounded
settled back to dream. That old woman in St. Nazaire
who tucked up her skirts so she could "walk the dog."
German prisoners tapping their feet as we went by.

Miss Flatiron with your tall cool self: How do.

You didn't want us when we left but we went.
You didn't want us coming back but here we are,
stepping right up white-faced Fifth Avenue in a phalanx
(*no prancing, no showing of teeth, no swank*)
past the Library lions, eyes forward, tin hats aligned—

a massive, upheld human shield.

No jazz for you: We'll play a brisk French march
and show our ribbons, flash our *Croix de Guerre*
(yes, we learned French, too) all the way
until we reach 110th Street and yes! take our turn
onto Lenox Avenue and all those brown faces and then—

Baby, Here Comes Your Daddy Now!

Hattie McDaniel Arrives at the Cocoanut Grove

late, in aqua and ermine, gardenias
scaling her left sleeve in a spasm of scent,
her gloves white, her smile chastened, purse giddy
with stars and rhinestones clipped to her brilliantined hair,
on her free arm that fine Negro,
Mr. Wonderful Smith.

It's the day that isn't, February 29th,
at the end of the shortest month of the year—
and the shittiest, too, everywhere
except Hollywood, California,
where the maid can wear mink and still be a maid,
bobbing her bandaged head and cursing
the white folks under her breath as she smiles
and shoos their silly daughters
in from the night dew . . . what can she be
thinking of, striding into the ballroom
where no black face has ever showed itself
except above a serving tray?

Hi-Hat Hattie, Mama Mac, Her Haughtiness,
the "little lady" from *Showboat* whose name
Bing forgot, Beulah & Bertha & Malena
& Carrie & Violet & Cynthia & Fidelia,
one half of the Dark Barrymores—
dear Mammy we can't help but hug you crawl into
your generous lap tease you
with arch innuendo so we can feel that
much more wicked and youthful
and sleek but oh what

we forgot: the four husbands, the phantom
pregnancy, your famous parties, your celebrated
ice box cake. Your giggle above the red petticoat's rustle,
black girl and white girl walking hand in hand
down the railroad tracks
in Kansas City, six years old.
The man who advised you, now
that you were famous, to "begin eliminating"
your more "common" acquaintances
and your reply (catching him square
in the eye): "That's a good idea.
I'll start right now by eliminating you."

Is she or isn't she? Three million dishes,
a truckload of aprons and headrags later, and here
you are: poised, between husbands
and factions, no corset wide enough
to hold you in, your huge face a dark moon split
by that spontaneous smile—your trademark,
your curse. No matter, Hattie: It's a long, beautiful walk
into that flower-smothered standing ovation,
so go on
and make them wait.

from *Sonata Mulattica*

THE WARDROBE LESSON

Everyone in this brine-soused village
believes an African loves color—so let it be
red for our promenade along the Steyne,
with a splash of yellow
to inflame their watery sensibilities.
I think it's the sun they so yearn for;
blue saddens this close to the sea, though
turquoise is beckoning and emerald's best
a hue entertained only in furnishings. True,

we are props of a sort, let's not forget it;
yet what an aspect we'll project
unleashed among the masses!
Against our darker palette, any color thrills.
The main thing is fabric and plenty of it:
clouds of silk, waves of damask
to be cast off or furled neat to the chest
with a certain, sly emphasis. . . .

You'll learn these sophistications in time.
For now, it's enough to remember
we are here to confound them,
these wizened polyps crossing the sands
in their creaking bathing machines!
So: bright sashes and billowing sleeves,
rings on as many fingers as you dare,
perhaps a turban or some other headdress
to lend majesty without competing.

The ladies *adore* a cape. Different
from a cloak, this you can wear inside,
where one brisk swirl will conjure a fable
of perfumed trysts and moonlit swordplay.
As for the embroidered slippers—ungainly

as they might seem, the upturned toes
do not emasculate. Each step becomes
necessarily deliberate, and so recalls

the boudoir.
               Don't flinch! It won't do
to ignore what waits behind each smile—
that unvoiced sigh, accompanying
your every tremolo! Go ahead, examine
those upturned faces in the concert hall,
their tiny gasps and glistening cheeks. . . .
I've seen it, boy, even for one young as you.

Ah, the ladies are always bored and lonely.

You will not need a horse if you have a cape.

CORNELIUS EADY

The Dance

When the world ends,
I will be in a red dress.
When the world ends,
I will be in a smoky bar
　　on Friday night.
When the world ends,
I will be a thought-cloud.
When the world ends,
I will be steam in a tea kettle.
When the world ends,
I will be a sunbeam through
　　a lead window,
And I will shake like the
　　semis on the interstate,
And I will shake like the tree
　　kissed by lightning,
And I will move; the earth will move
　　too,
And I will move; the cities will move
　　too,
And I will move, with the remains of
　　my last paycheck in my pocket.
It will be Friday night
And I will be in a red dress,
My feet relieved of duty,
My body in free-fall,
Loose as a ballerina
　　in zero gravity,
Equal at last with feathers
　　and dust,
As the world faints and tumbles
　　down the stairs,
The jukebox is overtaken at last,

And the cicadas, under the eaves,
    warm up their legs.

The Supremes

We were born to be gray. We went to school,
Sat in rows, ate white bread,
Looked at the floor a lot. In the back
Of our small heads

A long scream. We did what we could,
And all we could do was
Turn on each other. How the fat kids suffered!
Not even being jolly could save them.

And then there were the anal retentive,
The terrified brown-noses, the desperately
Athletic or popular. This, of course,
Was training. At home

Our parents shook their heads and waited.
We learned of the industrial revolution,
The sectioning of the clock into pie slices.
We drank cokes and twiddled our thumbs. In the
Back of our minds

A long scream. We snapped butts in the showers,
Froze out shy girls on the dance floor,
Pinpointed flaws like radar.
Slowly we understood: this was to be the world.

We were born insurance salesmen and secretaries,
Housewives and short order cooks,
Stockroom boys and repairmen,
And it wouldn't be a bad life, they promised,
In a tone of voice that would force some of us
To reach in self-defense for wigs,
Lipstick,

Sequins.

from *Brutal Imagination*

in the following poems, the speaker is the young black man
Susan Smith claimed kidnapped her children.

MY HEART

Susan Smith has invented me because
Nobody else in town will do what
She needs me to do.
I mean: jump in an idling car
And drive off with two sad and
Frightened kids in the back.
Like a bad lover, she has given me a poisoned heart.
It pounds both our ribs, black, angry, nothing but business.
Since her fear is my blood
And her need part mythical,
Everything she says about me is true.

MY FACE

If you are caught
In my part of town
After dark,
You are not lost;
You are abandoned.

All that the neighbors will tell
Your kin
Is that you should
Have known better.

All they will do
Is nod their heads.
They will feel sorry
For you,

But rules are rules,
And when you were
Of a certain age
Someone pointed
A finger
In the wrong direction

And said:
All they do
Is fuck and drink
All they're good for
Ain't worth a shit.

You recall me now
To the police artist.
It wasn't really my face
That stared back that day,
But it was that look.

SUSAN SMITH'S POLICE REPORT

My shape came from out-of-nowhere.
The way some things don't belong
That's the way

I clanged up to the car
Trapped by a badly timed light.
Her poor kids never saw our image

Swell in the rearview mirror.
I was the danger of bulk; fast,
Nervous fingers

Barked the unlocked door open
And in I flooded, all the heartache
A lonely stretch of road can give.

Then she was alone, blinking in
The sight of an indifferent moon
Above the pines.

This, she swore, was the sound
Of my voice.

THE LAW

I'm a black man, which means,
In Susan's case,
That I pour out of a shadow
At a traffic light,

But I'm also a mother,
Which is why she has me promise,
"I won't hurt your kids,"
Before I drift down the road.

I'm a mother,
Which is why we sing
Have mercy, come home,
No questions asked.

But I'm black, and we both know
The law.
Who's going to believe
That we had no choice
But to open that door?

Who's going to care
That it was now or
Never,
That there was no time
To unbuckle them,
That it was take the car
Or leave the car?

I'm black, which means
I mustn't slow down.
I float in forces
I can't always control,

But I'm also a mother,
Which is why
I hope
I'm as good as my word.

UNCLE TOM IN HEAVEN

My name is mud; let's get that out
Of the way first. I am not a child.
I was made to believe that God
Kept notes, ran a tab on the blows,
So many on one cheek, so many on
The other.

I watch another black man pour from a
White woman's head. I fear
He'll live the way I did, a brute,
A flimsy ghost of an idea. Both
Of us groomed to go only so far.

That was my duty. I'm well aware
Of what I've become; a name
Children use to separate themselves
On a playground. It doesn't matter
To know I'm someone else's lie,

Anything human can slip, and that's enough
To make grown men worry about
Their accent, where their ambition might
Stray. It doesn't help anything to tell you
I was built to be a hammer,
A war cry. Like him, nobody knew me,

But in my prime, I filled the streets, worried
Into the eardrum, scared up thoughts
Of laws and guns. How I would love
Not to be dubious,

But I am a question whole races spend
Their time trying to answer. My author
Believed in God, and being denied the
Power to hate her,

I watch another black man roam the land,
Dull in his invented hide.

NIKKY FINNEY

Brown Girl Levitation, 1962–1989

(for Beulah Lenorah Butler Davenport,
supreme watermelon, cantaloupe & pansy grower)

Something sharper than any blade cuts
the heavy roped balloon cord at the end
of my wrists; ascension begins. No tingle
of warning, just the thin, rising held-breath
of a brown girl, super sudden lift, then,
the instinctive dive & grab for anything
dependable, two ton, well tethered, close:

Shaggy, heavy-bellied, near blind sheep dog.
Bulbous, well-rooted, yellow meat watermelon.
Iron held, black leather, Detroit-Buick car arm.
Steel blue, cavernous, baby brother crib roof.
Brass, honeycomb canopy, octopus jungle gym.
Mesozoic era, roots, trunk, cane field of azalea.

I could smell it inching closer to full power,
like a storm nearing from across the field of
my young life. Except, it wasn't over there,
coming. It was inside, gaining on me, blooming.
I could not grab my girl hat and run. Could not
turn my long yellow feet into brown girl spikes
and beat it home. Wherever I happened to be
when it hit—I had to hunker down.

I would lean hard into that high, elephant-lifting wind
with everything I had, carrying my girl mind & muscle
to the thing that I knew had been grandmother sent,
engineered, just for me. And there she would appear:
straw hat, cotton dress, cow boots, rabbit grass stogie
between her two front teeth, walking the dirt road back

to the old homehouse. Her humming heart in mighty step
with the bee wings of the July air. Her arms full of as many
bowling-ball headed, green-striped melons as she could
      manage.
The red sweet flesh, the jet-eyes, my just-in-time juicy
body weights passed from her arms to my lap,
until the great gray wind retreated & agreed
that I'd had enough & turned
me loose, disappearing back
beyond, into the indigo
heaven, until the next
lifting time.

Concerto no. 7: *Condoleezza {working out} at the Watergate*

Condoleezza rises at four,
stepping on the treadmill.

Her long fingers brace the two slim handles
of accommodating steel.

She steadies her sleepy legs for the long day ahead.
She doesn't get very far.

Her knees buckle wanting back
last night's dream.

[dream #9]

*She is fifteen and leaning forward from the bench,
playing Mozart's piano concerto in D minor, alone,
before the gawking, disbelieving, applauding crowd.*

not [dream #2]

She is nine, and not in the church that explodes into dust,
the heart pine floor giving way beneath her friend Denise,
rocketing her up into the air like a jack-in-the-box
of a Black girl, wrapped in a Dixie cross.

She ups the speed on the treadmill, remembering,
she has to be three times as good.

Don't mix up your dreams Condi.

She runs faster, back to the right, finally hitting her stride.
Mozart returns to her side.

She is fifteen again, all smiles, and relocated
to the peaks of the Rocky Mountains,

where she and the Steinway
are the only Black people in the room.

CALVIN FORBES

Some Pieces

When two elephants fight
It's only the grass that suffers

In the land of nod
Coke is king and scag god

I'm going I'm gone
Baby look what you've done
Left me and now day has come

The statues of some people never smile
Buddha does like a senile grandmother

Between us the bread was always stale

Should I lay my head on railroad tracks
Or should I lay my head on your wide lap

They can't plow the river
Snow lies on everything except
The road and it's black black

If I were a catfish swimming
In the deep blue sea
I'd start all you women
Jumping in after me

Somebody's in my bed
And they got my long johns on
I don't mind you taking my woman
But you better take my long johns off

And the white hand
Which bought me here

Which I learnt to hold
Now pushes me off the cliff

You can go home now

Your fingers are negroes
They do all the work for your fat arms

Hand Me Down Blues

for my brother George
1933–1971

Though I look like you
I never knew you very well.
You always confuse my slow shadow
And mock my fate.

I wear your defeats, limp or strut,
Even lie like you.
And I grow to fit your fears:
The carnivorous marriage,

And you swallowing a soft poison
Prescribed for healing
Only minor wounds.
I inherit new and old scars,

Dimples and warts; I am the residue
Of your black waste, its sin.
I am what remains
Beyond hunger or repair,

Your dead-ringer.
The worst lie is to say good-bye.
Where are you going that I won't follow?
My best is full of holes.

Dark Mirror

If I were from Timbuktu, perhaps
I should think the sea as mysterious
As the Sahara. Crossing water

In a hole of voices and fire eyes.
Inches apart but we can't see our bodies.
Only bright eyes and hearing

Continuous moans. My chains rattle
Like charms and we hide ourselves
In the darkness as if we were jackals.

I can't sleep. During the day we
Take a breath of air one by one up top.
You can see your shadow in the smooth ocean

If the big waves aren't bewitched.
But at night the air is dark
The ocean also and no one will see me.

CHRISTOPHER GILBERT

This Bridge Across

A moment comes to me
and it's a lot like the dead
who get in the way sometimes
hanging around, with their ranks
growing bigger by the second
and the game of tag they play
claiming whoever happens by.
I try to put them off
but the space between us
is like a country growing closer
which has a language I know
more and more of me is
growing up inside of, and
the clincher is the nothing
for me to do inside here
except to face my dead
as the spirits they are,
find the parts of me in them—
call them back with my words.
Ancestor worship or prayer?
It's a kind of getting by—
an extension of living
beyond my self my people taught me,
and each moment is a boundary
I will throw this bridge across.

Time with Stevie Wonder in It

Winter, the empty air, outside
cold shaking its rigid tongue
announcing itself like something stone,
spit out, which is still a story

and a voice to be embraced.
Januaried movements but I hear a tune
carries me home to Lansing.

Always waiting for signs of thaw,
dark nomads getting covered by snow,
our parents would group in the long night—
tune frequencies to the Black stations
blasting out of Memphis, Nashville,
still playing what was played down south—
Ray Charles, Charles Brown, Ruth Brown, Muddy and Wolf.

The tribal families driven north
to neighborhoods stacked like boxes—
to work the auto plants was progress,
to pour steel would buy a car
to drive hope further on down the road.
How could you touch, hear
or be alive; how could anybody

wearing our habits, quiet Protestant
heads aimed up to some future?
This was our rule following—
buy at J.C. Penney and Woolworth's,
work at Diamond Reo, Oldsmobile, Fisher Body.
On Fridays drink, dance, and try to forget
the perverse comfort of huddling in
what was done to survive (the buffering,
the forgetting). How could we not
"turn the head/pretend not to see?"
This is what we saw: hope screwed
to steel flesh, this was machine city
and the wind through it—neutral
to an extent, private, and above all

perfectly European language
in which we could not touch, hear
or be alive. How could anybody
be singing "Fingertips?" Little Stevie
Wonder on my crystal, 1963.

Blind boy comes to go to school,
the air waves politely segregated.

*

If this were just a poem
there would be a timelessness—
the punchclock midwest would go on
ticking, the intervals between ticks
metaphor for the gap in our lives
and in that language which would not
carry itself beyond indifferent

consequences. The beauty of the word,
though, is the difference between language
and the telling made through use.
Dance Motown on his lip, he lays
these radio tracks across the synapse
of snow. The crystals show
a future happening with you in it.

Chris Gilbert: An Improvisation

The writing on the half-filled helium balloon says,
"Get Well Soon." A few days from getting out of the hospital,
I'm trying to make the balloon float again
while I watch the body of Lt. Col. William Higgins somewhere
in Lebanon swing from its noose on the TV news.
High on Cyclosporine, Prednisone, Imuran, Nefedipine,
Zantac, Tenormin, Lasix, and Persantine, I toss
the balloon on its tether toward the tepid air
around the TV where Dan Rather's voice rises,
though it is as cloaked in lifelessness as the corpse
it describes, which, even as it swings, is getting
hardened into a media thing, a factual because
it's no longer filled with the ponderous void that living brings.
A weight fills me as I allow myself to think
that being alive is hard work, full of just this

human future which, in the light of Higgins, hits me
as an emptiness I make promises of to lift my spirit with.
As I watch TV I imagine the kidney I've been given is
Higgins's, but now my nurse comes in with more medicine
and juice to swallow this with, and stories of how her shift
has been, and promises of a backrub later that, though
it might not show what will become of me as it really is,
does distinguish my next few hours or so from his.
So for this moment I take this strange white setting
and its alien equipment, my nurse, and even my new body
and its present distinctions as parts of a momentary thing
pursuing its momentary meaning, or else—like Higgins—
hardening into a loss or ending. I am reaching to get through
the frozen doors of these stagnant facts, to sully the present
happy affliction with lack, with becoming, or some
unfinished act to show the consequences of where I'm at.
So tonight when the team from hematology troops in
to take my blood again, asking if I'm the transplant patient,
and I go mum because I've gone through this twice
daily now for two weeks, my family who will be
visiting and who will have helped me into whatever
state of mind I am will clear the air for me to declare
I am. The IV unit with my name and directions for my care
taped to the top will indicate I am. The ID bracelet
I've been wearing since I got here will say for me,
"I am." The scar the surgeon left as a signature
on my belly's right side will say, "I am." I am
I feel a gathering possibility passing from temporary
articulation to articulation the way the horizon
arises in the sun as a series of evident illuminations
while the earth spins clockwise toward futurity.
When the time comes I'll rise and say, "I am."
I'll gather all my questions, step into their midst
and say, "I am." I am I am.

C. S. GISCOMBE

Vernacular Examples

You can always say what you are. Half the time the allegory's music, how song goes with its cornets and saxophones. Do you have something to say to me? Closure re-gathers the shape of the original undoing, the place where memory changed or picked up. Or it's human-looking: big-boned, about as noisy, parts missing or left out, parts overstated. A loud brother to the divine, an admonishment; I was two men, I was something, I was "something monstrous." Jokes just drain the spirit.

Palaver

Neighborhood? Proximities change on you sooner or later. There's a level of artlessness; my luck has changed more than one time. Love could be an embankment, even an esker, or Customs; or a sailing ship, noisy at the horizon. The idea was that the wind could *carry* your voice from here to there, from one side of the field to the other. I was always leaving a place at the point where I'd begun to care for it. This was the gain of singing; the devil's hungry (in a song), the devil is sweet. How do I look? Neighborhood's a little fishtail in the substances.

Sotto Voce

What's missing: my country voice, the miracle singing is, to vex and hound the speaker, to outfox him. (Originally the lyrics went, "where lived a *colored* boy named Johnny B. Goode.") What's missing's the way into what's visible or obvious from a distance; or a way to distinguish that from mirage, love's floating-in-the-air door.

LORNA GOODISON

For My Mother (*May I Inherit Half Her Strength*)

My mother loved my father
I write this as an absolute
in this my thirtieth year
the year to discard absolutes

he appeared, her fate disguised,
as a sunday player in a cricket match,
he had ridden from a country
one hundred miles south of hers.

She tells me he dressed the part,
visiting dandy, maroon blazer
cream serge pants, seam like razor,
and the beret and the two-tone shoes.

My father stopped to speak to her sister,
till he looked and saw her by the oleander,
sure in the kingdom of my blue-eyed grandmother.
He never played the cricket match that day.

He wooed her with words and he won her.
He had nothing but words to woo her,
On a visit to distant Kingston he wrote,

'I stood on the corner of King Street and looked,
and not one woman in that town was lovely as you.'

My mother was a child of the petite bourgeoisie
studying to be a teacher, she oiled her hands
to hold pens.
My father barely knew his father, his mother died young,
he was a boy who grew with his granny.

My mother's trousseau came by steamer through the snows
of Montreal
where her sisters Albertha of the cheekbones and the
perennial Rose, combed Jewlit backstreets with French-
turned names for Doris' wedding things.

Such a wedding Harvey River, Hanover, had never seen
Who anywhere had seen a veil fifteen chantilly yards long?
and a crepe de chine dress with inlets of silk godettes
and a neck-line clasped with jewelled pins!

And on her wedding day she wept. For it was a brazen bride
      in those days
who smiled.
and her bouquet looked for the world like a sheaf of wheat
      against the unknown of her belly,
a sheaf of wheat backed by maidenhair fern, representing
      Harvey River
her face washed by something other than river water.

My father made one assertive move, he took the imported
      cherub down
from the heights of the cake and dropped it in the soft
      territory
between her breasts . . . and she cried.

When I came to know my mother many years later, I knew
      her as the figure
who sat at the first thing I learned to read: 'SINGER,' and
      she breast-fed
my brother while she sewed; and she taught us to read while
      she sewed and
she sat in judgement over all our disputes as she sewed.

She could work miracles, she would make a garment from a
      square of cloth
in a span that defied time. Or feed twenty people on a stew
      made from
fallen-from-the-head cabbage leaves and a carrot and a
      cho-cho and a palmful
of meat.

And she rose early and sent us clean into the world and she
    went to bed in
the dark, for my father came in always last.

There is a place somewhere where my mother never took the
    younger ones
a country where my father with the always smile
my father whom all women loved, who had the perpetual
    quality of wonder
given only to a child . . . hurt his bride.

Even at his death there was this 'Friend' who stood by her
    side,
but my mother is adamant that that has no place in the
    memory of
my father.

When he died, she sewed dark dresses for the women
    amongst us
and she summoned that walk, straight-backed, that she gave
    to us
and buried him dry-eyed.

Just that morning, weeks after
she stood delivering bananas from their skin
singing in that flat hill country voice

she fell down a note to the realization that she did
not have to be brave, just this once
and she cried.

For her hands grown coarse with raising nine children
for her body for twenty years permanently fat
for the time she pawned her machine for my sister's
Senior Cambridge fees
and for the pain she bore with the eyes of a queen

and she cried also because she loved him.

For Claude McKay

Thanks for rousing me good forerunner friend
when I'd reached Far Rockaway; me alone,
me alone, going down to where the line ends.
You are a long way from home you said; come
I'll take you to where you can reconnect
with your right train. You appeared as watchman
or agent of insomniac angel.
Thanks for delivering me to my station,
for urging strong resistance to a death:
hunted and penned in an inglorious spot.
Since then I have fought hard against the mad
hungry dogs, confounding barking mockers,
I stay awake; must keep faith with the just
bard, McKay, who pronounced my blood precious.

FORREST HAMER

Goldsboro Narrative #4:
My father's Viet Nam tour near over

The young dead soldier was younger
than they thought: the 14-year-old passed
himself as seventeen, forged
a father's signature. In the Army no more
than months, he was killed early
the week before a cease-fire.
The boy was someone-I-somewhat-knew's
older brother and someone-my-mother-
had-taught's son, and, lying
in the standard Army casket, an American
flag draped over the unopened half,
the boy didn't look like anyone
anybody would know—a big kid his dark skin
peached pale, lips pouted. I was sure
I didn't recognize him.

        When kids older than us
closed down one campus after another,
I thought they'd close all colleges down,
and there would be no place for me
when it was my time. It didn't seem fair.

        Capt. Howell's wife answered
the door one day, and two men
in military dress asked to come in.
She had no choice, I suppose,
but once they came into her living room,
she no longer had a husband, and
the three boys and the girl no longer
had their father. So *this is how
it happens*, I thought: two men come
to your house in the middle of the day,

ringing a bell or rapping on the door.
And, afterwards, there's nothing left
to look forward to.

Goldsboro Narrative #28

When folks caught on to what was happening
between Rev. Johnson and Sister Edna,
the grown-ups went back to speaking
in front of children as if we couldn't spell.
It was easy to figure out, though:
Rev. Johnson's wife didn't get happy; and,
after service, she wouldn't shake hands
with Sister Edna or any of her kin.
And Sister Edna's husband, Mr. Sam,
who never came to church, began waiting
in the parking lot to drive his wife home.

Now the age Rev. Johnson was then, I doubt
he was concerned with being forgiven.
But when I was 12 and kept on falling
from available grace, I began dismissing him
and mostly all of what he said he meant.
I went witnessing instead to Mr. Sam,
his truck idling outside the paned windows,
him dressed in overalls and a new straw hat.

Goldsboro Narrative #33

These usually quiet men, these dignified
and dressed well men
seemed bowed by the week between Sundays,
by too many hours at work, or by no work,
or not enough work.

Even the Spirit seemed partial to their wives
                              and mothers,
And each third Sunday in June
                 when the Men's Chorus sang,
we half expected them to wail out at us,

                 boys distracted by vague travels we would make
                              once we left
our mothers who kept bringing us here,
                              once we could run roads
                 conjured from the ink

of funeral-home fans with pictures of a white Jesus,
                                        laying out
                 long streets to have fights on,
                              where we could own things
                 and grow big, have what we needed.

But Mr. Joe's voice trembled, too deep and too loud
                                        to fit,
and it reminded us he had gone away
but come back.
Because the men liked him, they didn't mind
                 how much his voice startled their babies,
                              distracted the wives.
They wanted him singing with them.
                       Usually he sang two solos,
                       the bass part only.

                 Children dared themselves to hum along
                              in alto or in tenor.
                 And each year, after Mr. Joe finished, mothers
                       looked back into the eyes
                 of all of the boys in the congregation,

expecting we had learned something.

Goldsboro Narrative #7

Time was a boy, specially a black boy,
need to be whipped by his kin, teach him
not to act up, get hisself killt.
Folks did this cause they loved they boys.
The man laughs. And boys would do what all
they could to get out of them whippings,
play like they was getting tore up,
some play like they was going to die.
My grandmama the first one that whipped me,
and she made me get my own switches.
If I come back to her with a switch too small,
she make me go right back and get a big one.
And she whipped me for that, too. He laughs.
I loved that woman, though. Sho did.

Annual Visit of the Quiet, Unmarried Son

After my mother kissed my sleeping father,
she kissed me and thanked God for letting me see
the New Year, for many had not been so blessed.

She talked about her friend Mr. James,
months before murdered in a night of profound
        disappointments,
the wounds in couples all over

his body (even under his feet),
the handsome young lover who killed him when wronged,
the old mother left grieving,

the many at his wake, the way he looked then
—like a boy just calming after a nightmare,
they say: my mother had stayed away,

that the man who found the shreds of the body
has not been the same, that no one nearby heard
a sound. I wanted to scream at her to stop

and I wanted her to tell me everything she'd heard,
my mother reckoning on into morning
with something hurt between us, still unmentioned.

ESSEX HEMPHILL

Heavy Corners

For Joe

Don't let it be loneliness
that kills us.
If we must die
on the front line
let us die men
loved by both sexes.

Don't let it be envy
that drives us
to suck our thumbs
or shoot each other dead
over snake eyes.

Let us not be dancing
with the wind
on heavy corners
tattered by doom.

Let us not accept
partial justice.
If we believe our lives
are priceless
we can't be conquered.

If we must die
on the front line
don't let loneliness
kill us.

Civil Servant

For Nurse Eunice Rivers

I could perform my job no other way:
obey instructions or be dismissed,
which would end my nursing career.
I was a Colored nurse,
special, one of few.
I didn't question the authority
the government doctors exercised over me.
Their control of life and death
and my sense of duty and responsibility
were parallel and reciprocating.
My father, Tuskegee Institute, and Dr. Dibble
had trained me to obey
the instructions of white men,
and all men.
I didn't talk back,
raise my voice in protest,
or demand the doctors save the men.
It wasn't my place to diagnose,
prescribe, or agitate.

When the doctors told me
to prevent the men
from getting treatment elsewhere,
I did. I supplied their names
to all county health officials.
They agreed to withhold treatment
even after penicillin was discovered
to be an effective cure for bad blood.
The government doctors
viewed the men
as syphilis experiments.
I troubled myself
to remember their names.
I visited their homes

between annual checkups
to listen to their hearts
and feel their pulses.
They had aches and pains
and complaints too numerous to name,
but I soothed them. I tried.
I gave them spring tonic
for their blood.
I couldn't give them medicine.
I tried to care for everyone
including the women,
the old folks, and children.
I became an adopted member
of many of the families I visited.
I ate at their tables,
sat at their sickbeds,
mourned at their funerals.
I married one of their sons.

I never thought my duty
damned the men.
They were sick with bad blood,
but I thought they were lucky.
Most Colored folks in Macon
went from cradle to grave
without ever visiting a doctor.
The ones with bad blood were envied
because they received free
medical attention, food,
and rides to the health sites
come checkup time.

As the men died, I wept
with their wives and families.
I was there to comfort them,
to offer fifty dollars
if they let the doctors
"operate"—
cut open the deceased
from scrotum sack to skull.

They were usually horrified
by my offer,
fearing disfigurement
or the courting of blasphemy.
I assured them no one would know
that their hearts and brains
had been removed.
I suggested fifty dollars
could cover burial costs
and buy unexpected food
and clothes.

I never thought my silence
a symptom of bad blood.
I never considered my care complicity.
I was a Colored nurse, a proud
graduate of Tuskegee Institute,
one of few, honored by my profession.
I had orders, important duties,
a government career.

For My Own Protection

I want to start
an organization
to save my life.
If whales, snails,
dogs, cats,
Chrysler, and Nixon
can be saved,
the lives of Black men
are priceless
and can be saved.
We should be able
to save each other.
I don't want to wait
for the Heritage Foundation
to release a study

stating Black men
are almost extinct.
I don't want to be
the living dead
pacified with drugs
and sex.

If a human chain
can be formed
around missile sites,
then surely Black men
can form human chains
around Anacostia, Harlem,
South Africa, Wall Street,
Hollywood, each other.

If we have to take tomorrow
with our blood are we ready?
Do our S curls,
dreadlocks, and Phillies
make us any more ready
than a bush or conkaline?
I'm not concerned
about the attire of a soldier.
All I want to know
for my own protection
is are we capable
of whatever,
whenever?

SAFIYA HENDERSON-HOLMES

"C" ing in Colors: Blue

It was fall, early in the morning.
It is fall, early in the morning.
Things turn.

1.

October 31st 1994 7:30 am, on a street in Syracuse New York
I'm a black female disguised as a scary bag of bones. In my right
lung I carry a Jack-O-Lantern which surgery couldn't carve. I
enter a Hematology, Oncology clinic. A haunted house. I walk
slowly towards the infusion area. There are monsters.

2.

October 16th 1995 early in the morning, rallying against mon-
strosities of racism and beasts which dwell in their own souls,
a million black men dressed in the bewitching costumes of
atoned skin, faces unmasked, hands empty arrive in Washing-
ton D.C. on buses, trains, cars, planes, long walks, leaving
work, leaving cardboard covered benches. They've been arriv-
ing for days.

3.

The Million Man March on Washington D.C. and my follow
up doctor's appointment to check on the size of Jack had been
planned for months. October 16th is x-ed in every calendar I
own. The day is Monday, a moon or lunar day. The day's color
is blue for spirit or air. The number's seven for luck or change.
The news media follows the men to D.C. I go alone to the
doctor. We are in the armor and amour of skin.

4.

Infusion: (trick or treat) to infuse, to instill, inculcate, to steep
or soak without boiling. (There's no safe candy here)

663

5.

Every haunted house I've ever been in is the same to me. Distorted lights and angles of floors, cries in walls, faces and hands reaching, falling into and out of darkened places, darkened places around corners, corners slippery and cold.

6.

And there's always a door that seems to dare me, "the spooked one" to open or close it. I breathe, hold my breath. When I've summoned the courage to grab the handle, because I know it's halloween and only the candy's real; a monster leaps, takes my tongue and I run, eyes closed somewhere.

7.

I strip for the doctor. The room's cold, corners slippery. The doctor listens to my lungs, surveys my radiation burned back and suture creased chest. Who but a doctor's eye to show such skin to, who but a doctor's touch? I think of the black men in Washington D.C. The doctor looks at my chart. I look at my breast. The quiet, almost shy scar above the right. I imagine the men.

8.

I imagine the brothers, fathers, sons, bringing their sons, fathers, brothers, bringing pictures of dead homies in their wallets and hearts, bringing their hearts on their sleeves like women, their hearts on t-shirts like girls. Grown men in special haircuts and a Sundays' best or whatever's left over from Wednesday. Perhaps there's one who looks like my socialist father. How he marched and drank Johnny Walker 'til he died. Perhaps there's more than a few who resemble my older brother.

9.

How he stood Airforce and affirmatively proud with his hands in his pockets seconds before his nerves broke. How he stood Airforce and affirmatively proud every day after. I imagine in the millions the sons and grandsons I may still have. The husband. The lover. All my men. All my scars.

10.

The doctor folds his arms across his chest, gives me a suspicious bill of good health. Jack is going, but not gone. I have a follow up date in the not so distant future.

11.

Future. I march to an infusion room. In the infusion room is cable television: C-Span, CNN, BET. In the infusion room the chemomonster commands. Today it's sleeping. The I.V. pole glares in a corner. I cover it with my coat, close the infusion room door, push the power button on the television set, raise the volume, raise a fist, sit very close, bow my head.

12.

During six months of chemotherapy I may have seen four black patients. This number may be one too many. But the four or five of us exchanged eyes. Whenever words were given, we spoke of family members, professions, ages of children, a school's location—just in case.

13.

I asked my chemo nurse where do most of the black cancer patients of Central New York receive treatments. She nearly whispered, "they die, it's a growing national concern." She's the only black chemo nurse in this clinic.

14.

She's the only.

15.

Despite method or message the Great Lawn in front of the White House in Washington D.C. America, October 16th isn't big enough. The black men go way back, on fences as if to lift them, not ride them, in trees as if growing, not being lynched, walking the waters of the nation's reflecting pools. Going way back. How many named Malcolm, how many named Martin, how many named Medgar, how many named Moses? Way back.

16.

October 16th 1995 in my infusion room no burning veins, no raw stomach. No Jack. Encouraged and inspired I want to take over this room, march on the ceiling, rally my breath and breast against the walls and floor, make banners of my arms and legs which read "free me!" "free all of me now!" Afterwards, after every piece of me goes home, washes, eats, I want to climb into the monster's bed, fall down between someone's thighs, come into this haunted room with something other than fear. This is victory. This is desire. This is blue. This is October 16th 1995.

17.

I lock the infusion room door, secure my coat on the I.V. pole, look around the room; a near empty box of tissues, a red pail for toxic tears. I look at the televised and prime time black men hold hands and sway. I sit closer to those hands. I sway. Look around the room again; the hard candies in a small glass jar, the perfect shine of the chrome faucet, the unexpected heat. I unbutton my blouse. What am I asking to take place here, what am I daring this room to become?

18.

I have a dream. Prayers and speeches surround me.

19.

Privately, without shame or fear, under the soft wool of my dress I touch the television screen, outline a few of the million, smile at some, call to some, moan.

20.

Deep blue. Deep, deep blue.

21.

A prayer ends. I button my blouse. Open the door. My chemo nurse opens a window. The monster's courtyard is filled with heartbeat and breathing.

ERICA HUNT

Surplus Future Imperfect

When the smoke lifted there was no promised land in sight. No place to make a phone call. No lounge to use the soap in. No holy days, no spirituals, no speeches intended to solder you to earth. No seams between the excuses and platitudes. No reason to get up. No stops. No long nights of man-made objects. No more of the same. No difference. No table of contents just a list of demands. No anecdotes, we were getting paid by the hour. No benefits, we were temporary workers. No music, corporate ambience. No seat belts, the entire world seemed unsafe. No geography, tourists were made at home with identical decor. No libraries, information out of the picture. No thought police, we all became deputies, we never let a line blur.

Woman, with wings

The way out of the library isn't always
clear. Victory, or so she calls herself
drives with me. We move closing the
zipper across the landscape, joining
two sides of an emotion together.

Up ahead, at the fork, causality
breaks into a side effect. We interrupt the
librarian's silent monologue. It drains
his face of animation, sucks the air
from the room.

His figure bars the exit like
a bad habit. It is possible to train these
associations whether you like them or not.
With practice you can predict defeat, or

summon the sun
rise over the scene murderously.

Work is pushing past resistance,
past the sense
it has all been written
before, spilling off the inventory shelves.
Sometimes you can read
with the headlights on, sometimes
you can drive to moods for which
no correlates exist, only curves, shaded
paths in the wilderness, occasional plots of
land ignored by absentee owners.

The cars ahead of us have disappeared.
Finally the way is clear, we have come to a way out;
past the flocked walls, the manipulated
seams, past the unzippered feeling, the tacit
violence between its teeth,
the trick with the mirrors and speed.

Should you find me

Should you find me, the short one on the left, knocking green
against brown hills, a fleck in the crowd, not to blink but
peeled, coming off with the tape.

Should you find me would you have a word for me, or do I go
forward on faith.

Where would you find me between the residential grids, in
the tear downs, the private cul de sacs, security chamber hand
cuffs, sound, zeroes in on a day in a life. But whose life? In the
malls' maw patrolled by card bearing youth or in abandoned
villages smoking ruins patrolled by uzi bearing youth?

Would I recognize my name in the voice from the burning bush? Would I hold my breath and then who would call the tune?

If you should find me, I would have to relearn my own name, talk to the letters in the alphabet, one by one, my new best friends. Invent spill over, there's gotta be more days in the year, these birthdays don't need to be rationed, lose the war footing and spread the new shoes.

If you should find me, maybe the pop quiz in the picture, rebus times pantomime tariffs pygmy? Or perhaps wrinkles in the landscape, wrinkles across the forehead no more than new wrinkles in the knees. Just more buttoned down.

Should you find me, would I button down? Could I carry the tune?

If you should find me, need I carry a sign with me to explain my place under the circumstances, my arrival by car in my time travel dress (with a Peter Pan collar). Dodge dart background, grinning for the company in the next century.

If you should find me, I could learn to measure as you do, a pinch, a pause, punctuation in the moment.

If you should find me, could I stop doing, doing, red onions, beets, radishes, peppers? Then who would restore the crunch to color? Everyone knows it's not easy to hold things still: the red and its expectation, the bell and its missing clapper, the beet sugar, the skin.

If you should find me and still I sleep, slumbering as if nothing had changed, a great sand bowl, against which dreams track traceries raised by day's consciousness, night wipes mind clean. Sleep comes from other side of the paper as an eyelid brims with excess light.

Should you find me, how could I miss? Who would I miss? Who would miss me?

If you should find me, new responsibilities would find me
too, still weeks away from vacation. Using an alias, could I
follow directions, read the small print under changed lighting
conditions.

These times are brittle and we are frail even as we cup hands
over eyes, our mouths, our ears.

GAYL JONES

Deep Song

for B. H.

The blues calling my name.
She is singing a deep song.
She is singing a deep song.
I am human.
He calls me crazy.
He says, "You must be
crazy."
I say, "Yes, I'm crazy."
He sits with his knees apart.
His fly is broken.
She is singing a deep song.
He smiles.
She is singing a deep song.
"Yes, I'm crazy."
I care about you.
I care.
I care about you.
I care.
He lifts his eyebrows.
The blues is calling my name.
I tell him he'd better
do something about his fly.
He says something softly.
He says something so softly
that I can't even hear him.
He is a dark man.
Sometimes he is a good dark man.
Sometimes he is a bad dark man.
I love him.

PATRICIA SPEARS JONES

i done got so thirsty that my mouth
waters at the thought of rain

i done got so thirsty that my mouth waters
at the thought of rain
let it come down on into me/like this pain
let it just intensify my eyes
let the will slip away in an avalanche of tears
all choked up
all choked up
all choked up
been dancing on a dream too long
& found myself lost in this desert/no
lovers tonight/not a one
no rain for days
got too much sun/burning through my heart
& every bone/muscle/corpuscle
aches
aches
aches
been running through these streets
looking for a coolness/a coolness
been running through these streets
looking for your face/your face/that
soft smile/long gone/cross that barrier
past tense

songs rolling on the tongues of angels
i don't hear them/off at a distance/six
men beat up on one/bottle breaks/blue lights
flashing/get the cops/GET THE COPS/a
screaming/through the dancing music
a quick mambo baby 'fore i goes
yeah
& the tight lips of the drunken women

they walk past the windows/broken/like
the windows/oh these women/bellies so swollen
tongues don't move 'cept to curse/oh these
women/broken/like glass gouged into the
face of the *pendijito* who was in the wrong
place on the wrong saturday night
come on
come on
come on rain/come on water/down this dry
throat/got no time for dying like this/in
the sun/give me some greenery/some fertility
tell me 'bout female forms & what happens to
them when they are abandoned
all you get is sticks & mud/drying

i been thirsty so long that my mouth feels
like parchment/got words written 'cross it/dead
stories 'bout dead feelings/dried up/dead
i been thirsty so long that my hands are
crusts of brown bread flaking out into the
fields eaten by dying men/no sustenance
no dreams/dancing

i been thirsty been dry been drinking in the
sun/no moisture/not a drop of blood saliva
all of it taken out of me removed/the removal
of fingers/the loss of touch/what *is* velvet &
how am i to know your lips/the whore's short skirt
reveals soft flabby knees that bulge with fat wishes
loss of taste/what makes me come/nothing/i just
do it/for the money/for the time passing/no man's
hands can ever move me/my voice is the dryest
wind/hard sound/diamonds on the sidewalk/what is in her
hair/that scent/god only knows/what ever did he do
this for/why are you looking the other way/what happened
here/just this desert dry sand falling falling on the
orphan and the whore/some want light in the darkness
candles have turned my soul to ashes/what kinds of
movements/slow/slow/slow i've been so thirsty/so truly
in need of liquids/water/wine/whiskey/*leche con dulces*

dulces/sweet water on my tongue/need to move these female
forms round over this dry ground/need to get down eighth
avenue without seeing broken women pass by/as bottles
break cross the *pendejo's* throat & the cops come
too late

i've been thirsty so long my mouth dreams
at the thought of water dancing
dancing in the blood of women dripping
on the sidewalk like flooded houses
wasted of time and touch

SYBIL KEIN

Fragments from the Diary of Amelie Patiné, Quadroon Mistress of Monsieur Jacques R -------

New Orleans, 14 Novembre, 1825

Morn.
Coeur cassé. My life is settling in a cup of
silk shadows, blue and brown Madras on the divan.
Will he return? Not a fortnight but he was here in my
arms, weeping in delicious agony. Has my body withered
suddenly?
For three years, we wore the tastes of love's wild
oranges; his flesh mine, my soul his. He was my saint;
I wore his smile. My mouth twitches at the memory. Now,
this chilled day rends at my bodice. I fear my bosom will
explode. I have seen her! She is wife. But to leave me?
I would that we were spirits flying together between hell
and heaven.

Noontide.
Am I abandoned in this latticed cottage on Rue Esplanade?
Coffined between stiff red velvet drapes and mirrored
plafond?[*] Should I wrap my hair around the bed posts to
cover those carved Cupids and their forever taut bows? He
could have warned me. We would have fled or died sweetly
imprisoned here. My fingers pinch and swell at this quill.

Eventide.
And how she flung the words. *Fongasse!* Whore! Some I dare
not say. Heaven's worst lost gift to white men. O lady,
were you in my stead. Could you live bought, adored,
despised paramour, blight made flesh; hidden, held in
dire esteem, yet sought for bare beauty, fate begging?

---

[*] Ceiling.

Privileged sister, you know me not!
Who but I have planted the blush that he transfers to your
pale cheeks? How heavy would beat your heart if it were
not for his lambent ecstasy that is constantly renewed at my
lips, my loins. Your peasant crudeness flares for what I am.
What shallow passion, frivolous morality do you wear as mask
for this worthless vengeance? He must not leave me! Love is
not fabricated nor tarnished but by the petty decrees of a
society wrought with fraud, deceit, and barbarous wickedness.

Candle-light.
Jacques. I am no longer afraid to write your name.
We have met. She is sworn to revenge.
Where can I hide now, as this taper burns in quiet
pools of thick secretion? What will become of us?
Beguin. My shadow lies withdrawn upon the bed.
Shall I continue to sip this darkened Spanish wine
at your hour of eventide? Who will feel the vapors
rising under my skin? Who will muff my little cries,
unruff these violet sheets that stare coldly at my
spine? Must this night slip with me into eternity?
Oh blaze the heavens with this memory: my lover,
fallen on his knees, his tender mouth closed in
my bosom repeating endlessly my name!

Such sorrowful murmurs I scrape across these pages.
The doleful moon breaks against my window. Or did
my shadow move?

DOLORES KENDRICK

from *The Women of Plums*

JENNY IN SLEEP

Nothin' be as terrible

                    as sleep

nothin'
be as bright, either.

I come and go

               as I please.

JENNY IN LOVE

Danced in the evenin'

                 while

the supper
burn;

whupped

                 in the morning:

danced again:

YUSEF KOMUNYAKAA

Annabelle

My head hangs.

It's all to do with
a woman back in Alabama.
All to do with Annabelle
hugging every road sign
between here & Austin, Texas.
All to do with rope & blood.

He's all to do with America.
All to do with all the No-Dick
Joneses. Mornings shattered.
Crickets mourn—
sign out of genetic code.

All to do with shadows
kneeling in the woods.
All to do with inherited iron maidens.
Beg for death in the womb.
Beg for it inside skulls—flower,
dust, lilac perfume, cold fire.

Gonna get lowdown tonight.

More Girl Than Boy

You'll always be my friend.
Is that clear, Robert Lee?
We go beyond the weighing
of each other's words,
hand on a shoulder,
go beyond the color of hair.

Playing Down the Man on the Field
we embraced each other before
I discovered girls.
You taught me a heavy love
for jazz, how words can hurt
more than a quick jab.
Something there's no word for
saved us from the streets.

Night's pale horse
rode you past common sense,
but you made it home from Chicago.
So many dreams dead.
All the man-sweet gigs
meant absolutely nothing.
Welcome back to earth, Robert.
You always could make that piano
talk like somebody's mama.

Letter to Bob Kaufman

The gold dust of your voice
& twenty-five cents
can buy a cup of coffee.
We sell pain for next to nothing! Nope,
you don't know me but your flesh-
&-blood language lingers in my head
like treason & raw honey.
I read GOLDEN SARDINE
& dance the Calinda
to come to myself.
Needles, booze, high-steppers
with dangerous eyes.
Believe this, brother,
we're dice in a hard time hustle.
No more than handfuls of meat.
C'mon, play the dozens,
you root worker & neo-hoodooist,

you earth lover & hole-card peeper.
We know roads dusty with old griefs
& hot kiss joys.
Bloodhounds await ambush.
Something, perhaps the scent
of love, draws them closer.

Blue Light Lounge Sutra for the Performance Poets at Harold Park Hotel

the need gotta be
so deep words can't
answer simple questions
all night long notes
stumble off the tongue
& color the air indigo
so deep fragments of gut
& flesh cling to the song
you gotta get into it
so deep salt crystallizes on eyelashes
the need gotta be
so deep you can vomit up ghosts
& not feel broken
till you are no more
than a half ounce of gold
in painful brightness
you gotta get into it
blow that saxophone
so deep all the sex & dope in this world
can't erase your need
to howl against the sky
the need gotta be
so deep you can't
just wiggle your hips
& rise up out of it
chaos in the cosmos
modern man in the pepperpot

you gotta get hooked
into every hungry groove
so deep the bomb locked
in rust opens like a fist
into it into it so deep
rhythm is pre-memory
the need gotta be basic
animal need to see
& know the terror
we are made of honey
cause if you wanna dance
this boogie be ready
to let the devil use your head
for a drum.

February in Sydney

Dexter Gordon's tenor sax
plays "April in Paris"
inside my head all the way back
on the bus from Double Bay.
Round Midnight, the '50s,
cool cobblestone streets
resound footsteps of Bebop
musicians with whiskey-laced voices
from a boundless dream in French.
Bud, Prez, Webster, & The Hawk,
their names run together riffs.
Painful gods jive talk through
bloodstained reeds & shiny brass
where music is an anesthetic.
Unreadable faces from the human void
float like torn pages across the bus
windows. An old anger drips into my throat,
& I try thinking something good,
letting the precious bad
settle to the salty bottom.
Another scene keeps repeating itself:

I emerge from the dark theatre,
passing a woman who grabs her red purse
& hugs it to her like a heart attack.
Tremolo. Dexter comes back to rest
behind my eyelids. A loneliness
lingers like a silver needle
under my black skin,
as I try to feel how it is
to scream for help through a horn.

from *Dien Cai Dau*

WE NEVER KNOW

He danced with tall grass
for a moment, like he was swaying
with a woman. Our gun barrels
glowed white-hot.
When I got to him,
a blue halo
of flies had already claimed him.
I pulled the crumbled photograph
from his fingers.
There's no other way
to say this: I fell in love.
The morning cleared again,
except for a distant mortar
& somewhere choppers taking off.
I slid the wallet into his pocket
& turned him over, so he wouldn't be
kissing the ground.

A BREAK FROM THE BUSH

The South China Sea
drives in another herd.
The volleyball's a punching bag:
Clem's already lost a tooth

& Johnny's left eye is swollen shut.
Frozen airlifted steaks burn
on a wire grill, & miles away
machine guns can be heard.
Pretending we're somewhere else,
we play harder.
Lee Otis, the point man,
high on Buddha grass,
buries himself up to his neck
in sand. "Can you see me now?
In this spot they gonna build
a Hilton. Invest in Paradise.
Bang, bozos! You're dead."
Frenchie's cassette player
unravels Hendrix's "Purple Haze."
Snake, 17, from Daytona,
sits at the water's edge,
the ash on his cigarette
pointing to the ground
like a crooked finger. CJ,
who in three days will trip
a fragmentation mine,
runs after the ball
into the whitecaps,
laughing.

FACING IT

My black face fades,
hiding inside the black granite.
I said I wouldn't
dammit: No tears.
I'm stone. I'm flesh.
My clouded reflection eyes me
like a bird of prey, the profile of night
slanted against morning. I turn
this way—the stone lets me go.
I turn that way—I'm inside
the Vietnam Veterans Memorial
again, depending on the light

to make a difference.
I go down the 58,022 names,
half-expecting to find
my own in letters like smoke.
I touch the name Andrew Johnson;
I see the booby trap's white flash.
Names shimmer on a woman's blouse
but when she walks away
the names stay on the wall.
Brushstrokes flash, a red bird's
wings cutting across my stare.
The sky. A plane in the sky.
A white vet's image floats
closer to me, then his pale eyes
look through mine. I'm a window.
He's lost his right arm
inside the stone. In the black mirror
a woman's trying to erase names:
No, she's brushing a boy's hair

Venus's-flytraps

I am five,
   Wading out into deep
      Sunny grass,
Unmindful of snakes
   & yellowjackets, out
      To the yellow flowers
Quivering in sluggish heat.
   Don't mess with me
      'Cause I have my Lone Ranger
Six-shooter. I can hurt
   You with questions
      Like silver bullets.
The tall flowers in my dreams are
   Big as the First State Bank,
      & they eat all the people
Except the ones I love.

They have women's names,
    With mouths like where
Babies come from. I am five.
  I'll dance for you
    If you close your eyes. No
Peeping through your fingers.
  I don't supposed to be
    This close to the tracks.
One afternoon I saw
  What a train did to a cow.
    Sometimes I stand so close
I can see the eyes
  Of men hiding in boxcars.
    Sometimes they wave
& holler for me to get back. I laugh
  When trains make the dogs
    Howl. Their ears hurt.
I also know bees
  Can't live without flowers.
    I wonder why Daddy
Calls Mama honey.
  All the bees in the world
    Live in little white houses
Except the ones in these flowers.
  All sticky & sweet inside.
    I wonder what death tastes like.
Sometimes I toss the butterflies
  Back into the air.
    I wish I knew why
The music in my head
  Makes me scared.
    But I know things
I don't supposed to know.
  I could start walking
    & never stop.
These yellow flowers
  Go on forever.
    Almost to Detroit.
Almost to the sea.
  My mama says I'm a mistake.

That I made her a bad girl.
My playhouse is underneath
  Our house, & I hear people
    Telling each other secrets.

My Father's Love Letters

On Fridays he'd open a can of Jax
After coming home from the mill,
& ask me to write a letter to my mother
Who sent postcards of desert flowers
Taller than men. He would beg,
Promising to never beat her
Again. Somehow I was happy
She had gone, & sometimes wanted
To slip in a reminder, how Mary Lou
Williams' "Polka Dots & Moonbeams"
Never made the swelling go down.
His carpenter's apron always bulged
With old nails, a claw hammer
Looped at his side & extension cords
Coiled around his feet.
Words rolled from under the pressure
Of my ballpoint: Love,
Baby, Honey, Please.
We sat in the quiet brutality
Of voltage meters & pipe threaders,
Lost between sentences . . .
The gleam of a five-pound wedge
On the concrete floor
Pulled a sunset
Through the doorway of his toolshed.
I wondered if she laughed
& held them over a gas burner.
My father could only sign
His name, but he'd look at blueprints
& say how many bricks
Formed each wall. This man,

Who stole roses & hyacinth
For his yard, would stand there
With eyes closed & fists balled,
Laboring over a simple word, almost
Redeemed by what he tried to say.

Anodyne

I love how it swells
into a temple where it is
held prisoner, where the god
of blame resides. I love
slopes & peaks, the secret
paths that make me selfish.
I love my crooked feet
shaped by vanity & work
shoes made to outlast
belief. The hardness
coupling milk it can't
fashion. I love the lips,
salt & honeycomb on the tongue.
The hair holding off rain
& snow. The white moons
on my fingernails. I love
how everything begs
blood into song & prayer
inside an egg. A ghost
hums through my bones
like Pan's midnight flute
shaping internal laws
beside a troubled river.
I love this body
made to weather the storm
in the brain, raised
out of the deep smell
of fish & water hyacinth,
out of rapture & the first

regret. I love my big hands.
I love it clear down to the soft
quick motor of each breath,
the liver's ten kinds of desire
& the kidney's lust for sugar.
This skin, this sac of dung
& joy, this spleen floating
like a compass needle inside
nighttime, always divining
West Africa's dusty horizon.
I love the birthmark
posed like a fighting cock
on my right shoulder blade.
I love this body, this
solo & ragtime jubilee
behind the left nipple,
because I know I was born
to wear out at least
one hundred angels.

Ode to the Maggot

Brother of the blowfly
& godhead, you work magic
Over battlefields,
In slabs of bad pork

& flophouses. Yes, you
Go to the root of all things.
You are sound & mathematical.
Jesus Christ, you're merciless

With the truth. Ontological & lustrous,
You cast spells on beggars & kings
Behind the stone door of Caesar's tomb
Or split trench in a field of ragweed.

No decree or creed can outlaw you
As you take every living thing apart. Little
Master of earth, no one gets to heaven
Without going through you first.

NATHANIEL MACKEY

Falso Brilhante

for Elis Regina

I wake up chasing my breath, my
dead lungs undone by alcohol and cocaine,
    a rope of dust at my throat . . .
     Raw thread of a dirge woven into the
      wind, all night I wonder
                      what
  but unruliness ranges the heart . . .

                      A blunt featherless
        bird hovering close to my chest as
I wake up, what but ennui that I'd even
    wonder, what but a whim, the clouded rum
        I drink   drains me of light
    I dream I hang from, dangling,
                     draped
  as in rags, white fractured sky from which
               I fall . . .
      White sky made blue by the blackness
beyond it, withered light, wind says *Better*
                not
     to have been born.
             Breath caught in
    a cloud, I cross myself, *So be it*,
             my self-embrace
    a rickety crib I serenade
          myself
             inside . . .
 And I'm singing all the songs that made me a
  star, my arms like wings as though
 they were not quite my own anymore . . .

691

Leaned

on by a ghost, I launch a prayer to Iansã, Ogum
at my back, my torn voice haloed
by an orbiting chorus as it bleeds,
hand on my heart as if I were taking an
oath,
a faint, fading
spark, the seeds of this parting planted
who knows how far back . . .

A see-thru lid on the coffin I rest in.
See-thru exit, see-thru sign of the times . . .
Weepers fill the streets of São Paulo,
I wake up gasping,   chasing my breath,
another
snuffed-out star.   Prophetic wingtip skimming
the water . . .
A crystalline cut color masks
in time. . .
In every crack the same suffocating sweat,
this
world with its arrows . . .
Its rosary of worms, its
neon angels, its megatons . . .

One eye with
God, the other eye with Satan, I watch the
empty-eyed, pipe-smoking saints . . .

The keepers of bread do with the world as they
will,
whose cards collapse . . .
The way the
wind has of having its way
with a falling
leaf

Song of the Andoumboulou: 31

Sound was back. Bukka White
sang "Single Man Blues" on
 the box, renamed it "Ogo's
    Lament." He and Eronel
   lay chest to chest, right
                        leg
    to left . . . Some we met said
                        they were
     outmoded, failed andoumboulouous
   birth brought back to life,
                        trek
   we resisted they insisted we
 set out on, whatsaid hejira, what
    being said made so . . .

 No what for which to've come, no
   why, lift we spoke of lost
as we spoke, nonsonant last
  resort. So that all thought
    was now transitless "it,"
                        blunt
   would-be husk, maculate mask
turned iterative tooth, recidivist
  gum,   feasted on scraps laid
     aside for some ghost.
    Skeletal he no less than
       skeletal she filled in
                        from
  memory. Skeletal they spun
    by skeletal we, backwardsbending
   rush . . . Skeletal stretch,
stretched limbs' analogic
     landscape, backwardswalking
                        vamp's
    lag-inducted run . . .

Me not
looking at them, them not looking
   at me, we stood looking out
across the wall which held us
                              back.
    Something unclear was being
         sung about a man who couldn't feel
      his toe, something we heard, thought
we heard, said his neck
   had been cut . . . Nor could
                              we,
      having stood so long on
   the tips of our toes, nonsonant
                              struff

   the new ledge we
   walked

                              •

   Wanted to say of he-and-she-ness
    it creaks, bit our tongues,
      we who'd have been done with

                              him and her

      were we able, each the

                              other's
   legendary lack. Uninevitable
he who'd have sooner been
   she, uninevitable she who'd
      have sooner been he . . .
                              We,
         who'd have been done
                              With both,
      looked out across the wall,
                              saw

      no new day
   come

                    _____

Whatever it was we were
on. Wherever it was
  we were. Elsewhere was
elsewhere, always . . . No way
  we'd end up there . . .
                              Strung out
  across the he/she line, we
    relented, convinced it
  was a train we were on.
    Backwardswalking Lenore
        looked us each in the
        eye while receding, Eronel
        the name we called her,
    Monk's tune long taken
                              away . . .

      So that love's newly
    disengendered voice
      coiled up from under
    us, epithet as much as
        elegy, we of whose
        adamance much had
            been made, fraught
        voice too long
                        taken to,
        loath under
                      lifted
    cloth

                ————————

    Who were drowning, dreaming it
  seemed. "Because we don't need
    to be messed with," we said out
  loud in our sleep, repeated
      it over and over, said why,
                          wouldn't
        say why what.
                          Burnt word
  we applauded, worlded us

                    more than we knew. Myth
                asked had it been there would
                    we have seen it,   wished-for
                        resolution, resisted,
                    the new day we said we

                                        not-saw . . .
            Wondered where the we we
                were after would come
            from, awaited what rush
                we were told awaited

                                    us,
                "beyond" but with what
                but skin to make a
            mark, high mind, high
                    fractious mind

                                heart's

                meat

COLLEEN J. McELROY

Gra'ma

Gra'ma was a little bit of a thing,
Full of spirits wandering
From an Alabama plantation to St. Louis.
Three on a match and a hat on the bed
Says the oldest will die.
She told me this at the age of five.
Her skin spoke of Chinese coolies
And overseers. Her face sang
Of Tanzania near Congolese waters,
Crocodiles running rapidly by
Gathering stones as a village screamed
Its death throes. That combination
Got her in the house when she was young;
Scrubbing, serving and suckling
Pink babies. Kept her there
Until 40 acres and a mule
Times a hundred kin freed her
With that long tall man
We came to love as Papa.
Set them near a Georgia swamp,
Pulling half a year's living
From the soil. He moved her north
Where she had a story for every day.
Told me: Listen close, child,
The world and the Lord are both profound.
When Papa died, her stories grew shorter;
She forgot which of those 40 acres
Could be mine or how many mules
You need to pull a plow.
When she finally saw my son,
She said: I guess the mules
Done long since gone.

697

Try to Understand Papa

Papa's not too hard to understand;
  he was just a man
With a hawkish face and long steps
Ending in feet that emptied puddles.
Kept his manhood locked inside
His fists so tight, they turned
Ashen black.

Papa's easy to understand,
  if you're a man
Who stands high watching white folks
Slide by the brewery stable where
He kept the horses fine. Standing
His ground as they pranced on the end
Of the lead; standing so tall
He needed a spear.

Papa was an easy man to understand
  even then—
When he was so gentle they called him boy,
And couldn't see the thin bolt of vein
Corded from shoulder to forearm. I pluck
The wet scent of frying meat and the scent
Of his hands from those mornings
When he helped me wake.

Grandpa was a man who posed
  in a Ford
With his jaw at right angles to the sun,
And even cousins called him Papa
'cause they could understand
How he held out through a card game
That lost the house. Then won it back
Playing kept woman against man.

Gossip tells that he paced
  before the doorway

Of a fourposter and counted eight times
Before he got a son—then spent
His manhood away from home.
But I smell the scent of his hands
And purse the lips he gave me.
He loved as a man;
It's not too hard to understand.

Throwing Stones at the All White Pool

after Gwendolyn Brooks

the first plopped mid-pool
leaving an oh-so shallow cavern
niga niga niga sucking in all
the hooting hollering spit of words
the next volley closer to shore
rippled in eddies of false kindness
lacy little bubbles popping
in warm summer air like flower buds
after that they all joined in willy-nilly
they all silly smiled made fart sounds
with their arm pits as we eased toes in
refused to show hurt that never goes away
we were afraid we were afraid
we'd gone too far to turn back
we owned the pain   broke the barricades
owned up to our small failures
eight year old bodies prickled with icy shocks

Fade to Black

in the Antioch Theater we feasted on films
made by colored folks like Oscar Micheaux
those Saturdays back then when we were Colored

before we were Black and all films were black and white
after Hopalong Cassidy rode into white westerns
we watched Ralph Cooper or Mantan Moreland
break up shady deals in Harlem guns blasting
tables turned against white folks robbed
of their power on the silver screen
at those matinees we cheered always the underdog
even Boston Blackie who was black in name only

between Movietone News and cartoons
we laughed stomped and celebrated in the dark
this was like recess without teachers to boss us

one Saturday I stayed too long at the party
and by nightfall my mother sent my cousins
James and Warren to fetch me—the two entering
like side kicks in one of Micheaux's films
Bumpsy hooted louder than the others
when my name appeared on a slip of paper
inserted between the projector and lens
James in police uniform found me in the beam
of his flashlight and Warren scouting the other aisle

left me no escape but to follow the sheriff out
to the dusky evening where my mother waited
while Micheaux's detectives ran toward the light

THYLIAS MOSS

Life in a Sterile Environment: A Case Study

1.

Manna must be pried
from the road. A towheaded boy
helps me. We're a couple:
mother/son, father/daughter,
lovers. The mind is made
to accept so much, truth
we couldn't possibly verify
except to point out
new hairs around my nipples.
All growth will have to come
from within. These rocks
are not unlike the puffball cakes
I sprinkled sugar over
on holidays.

2.

We pile manna on my skirt.
I'm only ashamed of not being much
to look at. Once
I dreamt of stripping
in front of Hajek's Bakery,
lying prone on hot cobblestone
until officers covered me
with a sheet.

The boy thinks only of manna,
should we eat it raw
or cooked. Should we save some
or is it true the supply's inexhaustible.
I give him a piece, he won't swallow it,
won't be greedy in this time of plenty.
He can't remember ever having more,

701

not in the last hundred years.
He'd forgotten how long he'd lived,
how much he'd eaten: can't die
or starve. He throws the manna,
hands me my skirt.
There's something eternal at work,
not the long-sought peace but   absence.

   3.

We sketch birds in the dirt,
stare at them till they fly away
then we thank any idea of God
that remains in the rubble
of St. Andrew's,
holding hands so tightly
we break the nails;
yes, we were good parents,
he tells me, staring at the empty sky,
we let go.

He leads me to the fishmonger's stall:
interpreter, tour guide, seeing eye,
composer of epitaphs.
Here, steel-and-brick-hued carp
shined like new money.
That's when you buy,
after the ice under them melts,
after they stink. A good price then.

He spins a wheel of the overturned cart,
starts the monger's steely voice.
"Love for sale." *Buy it*, I plead.
"Going once." *Buy it.* "Going twice."
"Gone."

The Day before Kindergarten: Taluca, Alabama, 1959

I watch daddy tear down
Mama Lelia's outhouse
with just his hands;
the snakes and slugs
didn't fret him none.
Then he takes me and mama riding.

We stop at the store,
looks like a house,
okra right in front,
chickpeas and hollyhocks.
Me and mama go in. The fan
don't move her hair.
She keeps her head down, stands
a long time at the counter.
Just wants some thread,
could get it herself,
there's a basketfull beside her.
Clerk keeps reading.

She's hurting my wrist,
I pull away, pick up a doll.
Clerk says we have to leave.
Mama grabs me and runs
right by daddy,
he's just coming in.

We hide in the car.
Mama smells like sour milk
and bleach.
Daddy comes out toting a sack,
clerk thought he was white.

When the store starts burning
I'm on Mama Lelia's porch

wanting to see
how the red
melts off peppermint.
I know it's like that.
One by one
each thing burns.
Pickle jars explode.
Mama Lelia asks me:
do it look like rain?
No'm, it don't.
Ain't God good!
She laughs.

Later,
while it's still smoking
I go poking with a stick.
Ashes look like nappy
nigger hair. Smells
like when the hot comb
gets too hot
and burns mama's neck.
This smell's so big
must have come
from a hundred necks.

Holding my doll
I look at the smoke,
could be a black man
running down the road;
then rub some ashes
on her face
cause I ain't scared
no more
of nothing.
Maybe I should be
but I ain't.

A Reconsideration of the Blackbird

Let's call him *Jim Crow.*

Let's call him *Nigger* and see if he rises
faster than when we say *abracadabra.*

Guess who's coming to dinner?
Score ten points if you said blackbird.
Score twenty points if you were more specific, as in the first
    line.

What do you find *from here to eternity?*
Blackbirds.

Who never sang for my father?
The blackbirds who came, one after the other, landed on the
    roof
and pressed it down, burying us alive.
Why didn't we jump out the windows? Didn't we have
    enough time?
We were outnumbered (13 on the clothesline, 4 & 20 in the
    pie).
We were holding hands and hugging like never before.
You could say the blackbirds did us a favor.

Let's not say that however. Instead let the crows speak.
Let them use their tongues or forfeit them.

Problem: What would we do with 13 little black tongues?

Solution: Give them away. Hold them for ransom. Make
    belts.
Little nooses for little necks.

Problem: The little nooses fit only fingers.

Solution: Get married.

Problem: No one's in love with the blackbirds.

Solution: Paint them white, call them visions, everyone will
    want one.

An Anointing

*Boys have to slash their fingers to become brothers. Girls trade
their Kotex, me and Molly do in the mall's public facility.*

*Me and Molly never remember each other's birthdays. On pur-
pose. We don't like scores of any kind. We don't wear watches or
weigh ourselves.*

*Me and Molly have tasted beer. We drank our shampoo. We
went to the doctor together and lifted our specimen cups in a toast.
We didn't drink that stuff. We just gargled.*

*When me and Molly get the urge, we are careful to put it back
exactly as we found it. It looks untouched.*

Between the two of us, me and Molly have 20/20 vision.

*Me and Molly are in eighth grade for good. We like it there.
We adore the view. We looked both ways and decided not to cross
the street. Others who'd been to the other side didn't return. It
was a trap.*

*Me and Molly don't double date. We don't multiply anything.
We don't know our multiplication tables from a coffee table. We'll
never be decent waitresses, indecent ones maybe.*

*Me and Molly do not believe in going ape or going bananas or
going Dutch. We go as who we are. We go as what we are.*

*Me and Molly have wiped each other's asses with ferns. Made
emergency tampons of our fingers. Me and Molly made do with
what we have.*

Me and Molly are in love with wiping the blackboard with each other's hair. The chalk gives me and Molly an idea of what old age is like; it is dusty and makes us sneeze. We are allergic to it.

Me and Molly, that's M and M, melt in your mouth.

What are we doing in your mouth? Me and Molly bet you'll never guess. Not in a million years. We plan to be around that long. Together that long. Even if we must freeze the moment and treat the photograph like the real thing.

Me and Molly don't care what people think. We're just glad that they do.

Me and Molly lick the dew off the morning grasses but taste no honey till we lick each other's tongues.

We wear full maternity sails. We boat upon my broken water. The katabatic action begins, Molly down my canal binnacle first, her water breaking in me like an anointing.

Poem for My Mothers and Other Makers of Asafetida

Brown in the bottle, my
honeyed memory of my grandmother in
which I drench myself, pour over myself
one of her tight hugs, homemade gravy on
lips and ribs, eventually hips, *taste her, taste her*
and feast on my church in a bottle, the
gospel like Sis. Posey sings it, *oh when, when will
I get home?* Looking over Dixie, over
Jordan, river of life, needing to cross (already got
a cross), needing to swim to *Jordan's stormy
other shore*, listen: the brown choir's brown liquid voice,
my arms moving me through it, swimming is just directing
the choir, giving instructions, *Mama always told me to be still*

sometimes and feel the power, wait while the river moves down
     my
throat, urine the rest of the miracle that makes of me
a fountain; nasty asafetida, tastes like the bootleg, jackleg
medicine it is
curing me as only generations can, asafetida is *a quilt*
for my innards, she said, up to her neck in gizzards, hocks,
     pickled
pig's feet, her hands good as dull knives that can't
have accidents.
And everywhere, everywhere eggs like teeth big as
what memory does to Grandma. Even the heart of gold.

Finally
the asafetida toast just after gunfire, the new year
shot for coming uninvited, ahead of schedule, years
coming and going, out of control, Trojan years bringing
lots of what we don't want set loose in foreclosed fields
of stone potatoes so hardhearted, hardheaded there are
no eyes except the ones I look into and fall in love, right
into Mama's pupils, the past dark with dense ancestry, all
who came before having to fit into the available space of
history which is existence's memory and year after year
the overcrowding worsens, *remember, remember: darkest*
     before
the day every dog will have, we are dogs sometimes, vestiges
of our evolution giving us dreams, instincts, secrets for dark
recall; nothing really goes away
especially not that sickening paradox, falling to reach
the sublime emotion; want to rise in love, want a boost,
elevator ride to the penthouse, silk jacket smoking
with lust, man making it with an asafetida bottle, a glass
mama with an excuse for breaking; whatever sustains you is
     your
mama, that wall holding back wind, jazz on the airwaves and
     in
the Thunderbird, the Boone's Farm; the oar smacking
     discipline
into fish while ferrying you across the water
that takes you back to old Virginny, every visit is return

to the scene of crimes, so much happened there, so much
    history
there; rivers are sad affairs flowing between past and future
like pompous blue (if sunny) ribbons that must deepen,
    widen
or spill to really go anywhere and still there are limits,
disillusionment to cap any growth, live to the fullest and just
have more to lose to death but Grandma said, Mama says,
    now
I say: *maybe possible to have so much*
death can't take it all; asafetida still on the shelf, oil in the
    puddle
still ghetto stained glass, still rainbow remnants in rock
bottom ghetto sky like a promise of no more tears, asafetida
bottle floating there, some kind of Moses, some kind of
    deliverer,
there's always a way. Away means not here. Place where
    bagpipes echo
with sound of a stuck doll calling *Mama, Mama,* nothing but
    inspiration
in the air, and the prophet Jolson proclaiming *Mammy,*
    asking for
her who can make him wash his face; she's the one who can
    turn it into
something to love.

The Lynching

They should have slept, would have
but had to fight the darkness, had
to build a fire and bathe a man in
flames. No

other soap's as good when
the dirt is the skin. Black since
birth, burnt by birth. His father
is not in heaven. No parent

of atrocity is in heaven. My father chokes
in the next room. It is night, darkness
has replaced air. We are white like
incandescence

yet lack light. The God in my father
does not glow. The only lamp
is the burning black man. Holy
burning, holy longing, remnants of

a genie after greed. My father
baptizes by fire same as
Jesus will. Becomes a holy ghost when
he dons his sheet, a clerical collar

out of control, Dundee Mills percale,
fifty percent cotton, dixie, confederate
and fifty percent polyester, man-made, man-
ipulated, unnatural, mulatto fiber, warp

of miscegenation.
After the bath, the man is hung as if
just his washed shirt, the parts
of him most capable of sin removed.

Charred, his flesh is bark, his body
a trunk. No sign of roots. I can't leave
him. This is limbo. This is the life after
death coming if God is an invention as were

slaves. So I spend the night, his thin moon-begot
shadow as mattress; something smouldering
keeps me warm. Patches of skin fall onto me
in places I didn't know needed mending.

HARRYETTE MULLEN

from *Muse & Drudge*

wine's wicked wine's divine
pickled drunk down to the rind
depression ham ain't got no bone
watermelons rampant emblazoned

island named Dawta
Gullah backwater
she swim she fish
here it be fresh

cassava yuca taro dasheen
spicy yam okra vinegary greens
guava salt cod catfish ackee
fatmeat's greasy that's too easy

not to be outdone she put
the big pot in the little pot
when you get food this good
you know the cook stuck her foot in it

———

if your complexion is a mess
our elixir spells skin success
you'll have appeal bewitch be adored
hechizando con crema dermoblanqueadora

what we sell is enlightenment
nothing less than beauty itself
since when can be seen in the dark
what shines hidden in dirt

double dutch darky
take kisses back to Africa

they dipped you in a vat
at the wacky chocolate factory

color we've got in spades
melanin gives perpetual shade
though rhythm's no answer to cancer
pancakes pale and butter can get rancid

———

dry bones in the valley
turn over with wonder
was it to die for our piece
of buy 'n' buy pie chart

hot water cornbread
fresh water trout
God's plenty the preacher shouts
while the congregation's eating out

women of honey harmonies offer
alfalfa wild flower buckwheat and clover
to feed Oshun who has sweet teeth
and is pleased to accept their gift

these mounts that heaven touched
saints sleep in their beds
distress is hushed by dream when
they allow the birds to lift their heads

———

get off your rusty dusty
give the booty a rest
you must be more than just musty
unless you're abundantly blessed

I can't dance don't chance it
if anyone asks I wasn't present
see I wear old wrinkles
so please don't press me

my head ain't fried
just fresh rough dried
ain't got to cook
nor iron it neither

you've seen the museum of famous hats
where hot comb was an artifact
now it's known that we use mum or numb our stresses
sometimes forget to fret about our tresses

―――

go on sister sing your song
lady redbone señora rubia
took all day long
shampooing her nubia

she gets to the getting place
without or with him
must I holler when
you're giving me rhythm

members don't get weary
add some practice to your theory
she wants to know is it a men thing
or a him thing

wishing him luck
she gave him lemons to suck
told him please dear
improve your embouchure

―――

rap attacks your tick
cold fusion's licks
could make you sick
nobody's dying in this music

womanish girl meets mannish boy
whose best buddy's a doggish puppy
he dictate so dicty, she sedate so seditty
the girl get biggity when the boy go uppity

I'm down to Saint James Infirmary
getting tested for HIV
the needle broke, the doctor choked
and told me I'd croak from TB

did I say nobody's dying
well I lied, like last night
I was lying with your mama who was crying
for all the babies born in Alabama

———

spaginzy spigades
splibby splabibs
choice voice noise
gets dress and breath

slave-made artifact
your salt-glazed poetry
mammy manufacture
jig-rig nitty-gritty

fast dance synched up so
coal burning tongues
united surviving ruin
last chance apocalypso

broke body stammering spirit
been worked so hard
if I heard a dream
I couldn't tell it

from *Sleeping with the Dictionary*

BLACK NIKES

We need quarters like King Tut needed a boat. A slave could row him to heaven from his crypt in Egypt full of loot. We've lived quietly among the stars, knowing money isn't what matters. We only bring enough to tip the shuttle driver when we hitch a ride aboard a trailblazer of light. This comet could scour the planet. Make it sparkle like a fresh toilet swirling with blue. Or only come close enough to brush a few lost souls. Time is rotting as our bodies wait for now I lay me down to earth. Noiseless patient spiders paid with dirt when what we want is stardust. If nature abhors an expensive appliance, why does the planet suck ozone? This is a big-ticket item, a thickety ride. Please page our home and visit our sigh on the wide world's ebb. Just point and cluck at our new persuasion shoes. We're opening the gate that opens our containers for recycling. Time to throw down and take off on our launch. This flight will nail our proof of pudding. The thrill of victory is, we're exiting earth. We're leaving all this dirt.

ELLIPTICAL

They just can't seem to . . . They should try harder to . . . They ought to be more . . . We all wish they weren't so . . . They never . . . They always . . . Sometimes they . . . Once in a while they . . . However it is obvious that they . . . Their overall tendency has been . . . The consequences of which have been . . . They don't appear to understand that . . . If only they would make an effort to . . . But we know how difficult it is for them to . . . Many of them remain unaware of . . . Some who should know better simply refuse to . . . Of course, their perspective has been limited by . . . On the other hand, they obviously feel entitled to . . . Certainly we can't forget that they . . . Nor can it be denied that they . . . We know that this has had an enormous impact on their . . . Nevertheless their behavior strikes us as . . . Our interactions unfortunately have been . . .

MARILYN NELSON

A Strange Beautiful Woman

A strange beautiful woman
met me in the mirror
the other night.
Hey,
I said,
What you doing here?
She asked me
the same thing.

Sleepless Nights

We used to tell each other erotic stories
at slumber parties when I was about ten:
We'd meet and kiss dark, handsome boys,
and then sink into sixty-year dreams
from which we'd wake up for church weddings
and to name our butterscotch babies.
From there we always jumped ahead
to the pooping-out party, and died laughing
into our silencing pillows at the way
we'd overdose on laxatives, and be dead.

We never dreamed of the face-making
self-reconstruction from scratch
we'd be engaged in for most of our lives,
of at thirty-four an ordinary day
on which an aspiration is adjusted down
another notch like a dress let out twice
at the waist, then finally given away,
of the rambling Victorian responsibilities we'd own,
full of furniture that doesn't match
and appliances that always need kicking.

We carefully flashed away the traces
of the filched cigarettes we'd tried
before our two o'clock forays in the dark,
then we raced back on tiptoe to devour
unsweetened chocolate, olives, laundry starch,
and in our floppy pajamas, giggled for hours.

When we made out each other's drawn faces
by the first pale murmurs of light
we were stupefied
to see how old we could grow overnight.

Lonely Eagles

*For Daniel "Chappie" James, General USAF
and for the 332nd Fighter Group*

Being black in America
was the Original Catch,
so no one was surprised
by 22:
The segregated airstrips,
separate camps.
They did the jobs
they'd been trained to do.

Black ground-crews kept them in the air;
black flight-surgeons kept them alive;
the whole Group removed their headgear
when another pilot died.

They were known by their names:
"Ace" and "Lucky,"
"Sky-hawk Johnny," "Mr. Death."
And by their positions and planes.
*Red Leader to Yellow Wing-man,
do you copy?*

If you could find a fresh egg
you bought it and hid it
in your dopp-kit or your boot
until you could eat it alone.
On the night before a mission
you gave a buddy
your hiding-places
as solemnly
as a man dictating
his will.
There's a chocolate bar
in my Bible;
my whiskey bottle
is inside my bed-roll.

In beat-up Flying Tigers
that had seen action in Burma,
they shot down three German jets.
They were the only outfit
in the American Air Corps
to sink a destroyer
with fighter planes.
Fighter planes with names
like "By Request."
Sometimes the radios
didn't even work.

They called themselves
"Hell from Heaven."
This Spookwaffe.
My father's old friends.

It was always
maximum effort:
A whole squadron
of brother-men
raced across the tarmac
and mounted their planes.

My tent-mate was a guy named Starks.
The funny thing about me and Starks
was that my air mattress leaked,
and Starks' didn't.
Every time we went up,
I gave my mattress to Starks
and put his on my cot.

One day we were strafing a train.
Strafing's bad news:
you have to fly so low and slow
you're a pretty clear target.
My other wing-man and I
exhausted our ammunition and got out.
I recognized Starks
by his red tail
and his rudder's trim-tabs.
He couldn't pull up his nose.
He dived into the train
and bought the farm.

I found his chocolate,
three eggs, and a full fifth
of his hoarded-up whiskey.
I used his mattress
for the rest of my tour.

It still bothers me, sometimes:
I was sleeping
on his breath.

Star-Fix

For Melvin M. Nelson, Captain USAF (ret.) (1917–1966)

At his cramped desk
under the astrodome,
the navigator looks

thousands of light-years
everywhere but down.
He gets a celestial fix,
measuring head-winds;
checking the log;
plotting wind-speed,
altitude, drift
in a circle of protractors,
slide-rules, and pencils.

He charts in his Howgozit
the points of no alternate
and of no return.
He keeps his eyes on the compass,
the two altimeters, the map.
He thinks, *Do we have enough fuel?*
What if my radio fails?

He's the only Negro in the crew.
The only black flyer on the whole base,
for that matter. Not that it does:
this crew is a team.
Bob and Al, Les, Smitty, Nelson.

Smitty, who said once
after a poker game,
I love you, Nelson.
I never thought I could love
a colored man.
When we get out of this man's Air Force,
if you ever come down to Tuscaloosa,
look me up and come to dinner.
You can come in the front door, too;
hell, you can stay overnight!
Of course, as soon as you leave,
I'll have to burn down my house.
Because if I don't
my neighbors will.

The navigator knows where he is
because he knows where he's been
and where he's going.

At night, since he can't fly
by dead-reckoning,
he calculates his position
by shooting a star.

The octant tells him
the angle of a fixed star
over the artificial horizon.
His position in that angle
is absolute and true:
Where the hell are we, Nelson?
Alioth, in the Big Dipper.
Regulus. Antares, in Scorpio.

He plots their lines
of position on the chart,
gets his radio bearing,
corrects for lost time.

Bob, Al, Les, and Smitty
are counting on their navigator.
If he sleeps,
they all sleep.
If he fails
they fall.

The navigator keeps watch
over the night and the instruments,
going hungry for five or six hours
to give his flight-lunch
to his two little girls.

BRENDA MARIE OSBEY

How I Became the Blues

I.

it was
dancing in mid-air
with an old half-crazed
smooth-skinned gentleman
his knees moving
at an angular plane
that i became the blues
against an afternoon glazed in mint
or van-van.
it was this urge of his
to only keep moving
as long as there was daylight
as long as there was darkness
the length of arms and legs
their own shadows
circling them
at a slower ragged pace.
and all he asked
was that i move with him
like so
he kept saying
like so
like breathing
or waiting for someone to lean at you
like a too-hungry lover
hesitating
and so he bruised me with this blues
his lips at a distance
from the hairs on my left ear.

2.

come and dance
with an old man
honey.
i'm tired of learning to do it
with my hand glued to the air.
there is nothing past this body for me
nothing past this white cotton shirt.
lean on me a little bit
where the hurt used to be.

that was how he called it:
where the hurt used to be.

3.

i call it dancing
because i have no other name for it
this old man
dreaming onto my forehead
moving me
urging me
past this blues
past endurance
to where i can not hold up my body
much less be required to dance
to keep sane the connection
between a starched white shirt
and an aged body.
and so i am leaning on his past
my feet and the rest of me
going on inside him
until the two of us realize
there is no name for this.
and even though we sing
the only words in town tell us:

it was like this
it was like so
just so
where the hurt used to be.

PEDRO PIETRI

The Broken English Dream

It was the night
before the welfare check
and everybody sat around the table
hungry heartbroken cold confused
and unable to heal the wounds
on the dead calendar of our eyes
Old newspapers and empty beer cans
and jesus is the master of this house
Picture frames made in japan by the u.s.
was hanging out in the kitchen
which was also the livingroom
the bedroom and the linen closet
Wall to wall bad news was playing
over the radio that last week was stolen
by dying dope addicts looking for a fix
to forget that they were ever born
The slumlord came with hand grenades
in his bad breath to collect the rent
we were unable to pay six month ago
and inform us and all the empty
shopping bags we own that unless
we pay we will be evicted immediately
And the streets where the night lives
and the temperature is below zero
three hundred sixty-five days a year
will become our next home address
All the lightbulbs of our apartment
were left and forgotten at the pawnshop
across the street from the heart attack
the broken back buildings were having
Infants not born yet played hide n seek
in the cemetery of their imagination
Blind in the mind tenants were praying
for numbers to hit so they can move out

and wake up with new birth certificates
The grocery stores were outnumbered by
funeral parlors with neon signs that said
Customers wanted No experience necessary
A liquor store here and a liquor store
everywhere you looked filled the polluted
air with on the job training prostitutes
pimps and winos and thieves and abortions
White business store owners from clean-cut
plush push-button neat neighborhoods
who learn how to speak spanish in six weeks
wrote love letters to their cash registers
Vote for me! said the undertaker: I am
the man with the solution to your problems

To the united states we came
To learn how to mispell our name
To lose the definition of pride
To have misfortune on our side
To live where rats and roaches roam
in a house that is definitely not a home
To be trained to turn on television sets
To dream about jobs you will never get
To fill out welfare applications
To graduate from school without an education
To be drafted distorted and destroyed
To work full time and still be unemployed
To wait for income tax returns
and stay drunk and lose concern
for the heart and soul of our race
and the climate that produce our face

To pledge allegiance
to the flag
of the united states
of installment plans
One nation
under discrimination
for which it stands
and which it falls

with poverty injustice
and televised
firing squads
for everyone who has
the sun on the side
of their complexion

Lapiz: Pencil
Pluma: Pen
Cocina: Kitchen
Gallina: Hen

Everyone who learns this
will receive a high school equivalency diploma
a lifetime supply of employment agencies
a different bill collector for every day of the week
the right to vote for the executioner of your choice
and two hamburgers for thirty-five cents in times square

We got off
the two-engine airplane
at idlewild airport
(re-named kennedy airport
twenty years later)
with all our furniture
and personal belongings
in our back pockets

We follow the sign
that says welcome to america
but keep your hands
off the property
violators will be electrocuted
follow the garbage truck
to the welfare department
if you cannot speak english

So this is america
land of the free
for everybody

but our family
So this is america
where you wake up
in the morning
to brush your teeth
with the home relief
the leading toothpaste
operation bootstrap
promise you you will get
every time you buy
a box of cornflakes
on the lay-away plan
So this is america
land of the free
to watch the
adventures of superman
on tv if you know
somebody who owns a set
that works properly
So this is america
exploited by columbus
in fourteen ninety-two
with captain video
and lady bird johnson
the first miss subways
in the new testament
So this is america
where they keep you
busy singing
en mi casa toman bustelo
en mi casa toman bustelo

KATE RUSHIN

The Black Back-Ups

This is dedicated to Merry Clayton, Fontella Bass, Vonetta
Washington, Carolyn Franklin, Yolanda McCullough,
Carolyn Willis, Gwen Guthrie, Helaine Harris and Darlene
Love. This is for all of the Black women who sang back-up
for Elvis Presley, John Denver, James Taylor, Lou Reed. Etc.
Etc. Etc.

I said Hey Babe
Take a Walk on The Wild Side
I said Hey Babe
Take a Walk on The Wild Side

And the colored girls say
Do dodo do do dodododo
Do dodo do do dodododo
Do dodo do do dodododo ooooo

This is for my Great-Grandmother Esther, my Grandmother
Addie, my Grandmother called Sister, my Great-Aunt Rachel,
my Aunt Hilda, my Aunt Tine, My Aunt Breda, my Aunt
Gladys, my Aunt Helen, my Aunt Ellie, my Cousin Barbara,
my Cousin Dottie and my Great-Great-Aunt Vene.

This is dedicated to all of the Black women riding on buses
and subways back and forth to The Main Line, Haddonfield,
Cherry Hill and Chevy Chase. This is for the women who
spend their summers in Rockport, Newport, Cape Cod and
Camden, Maine. This is for the women who open bundles of
dirty laundry sent home from ivy-covered campuses.

728

My Great-Aunt Rachel worked for the Carters
ever since I can remember.
There was *The Boy*
whose name I never knew,
and there was *The Girl*
whose name was Jane.

Great-Aunt Rachael brought Jane's dresses for me to wear.
     Perfectly Good Clothes
And I should've been glad to get them.
     Perfectly Good Clothes
No matter they didn't fit quite right.
     Perfectly Good Clothes
brought home in a brown paper bag with an
air of accomplishment and excitement,
     Perfectly Good Clothes
which I hated.

At school in Ohio,
I swear there was always somebody
telling me that the only person
in their whole house who listened and understood them,
despite the money and the lessons,
was the housekeeper.
And I knew it was true.
But what was I supposed to say?

I know it's true. I watch her getting off the train,
moving slowly toward the Country Squire
station wagon with her uniform in her
shopping bag. And the closer she gets to the car,
the more the two little kids jump and laugh
and even the dog is about to turn inside out
because they just can't wait until she gets there.
Edna. Edna. Wonderful Edna.

But Aunt Edna to me, or Gram, or Miz Johnson.
Sister Johnson on Sundays.

And the colored girls say
Do dodo do do dodododo
Do dodo do do dodododo
Do dodo do do dodododo ooooo

This is for Hattie McDaniel, Butterfly McQueen and Ethel
        Waters.
Sapphire.
Saphronia.
Ruby Begonia.
Aunt Jemima.
Aunt Jemima on the pancake box.
Aunt Jemima on the pancake box?
AuntJemimaonthepancakebox?
Ainchamamaonthepancakebox?
Ain't chure Mama on the pancake box?

Mama . . . Mama . . .
Get off that box and come home to me.
And my Mama leaps off that box and
she swoops down in her nurses's cape
which she wears on Sundays and for
Wednesday Night Prayer Meeting
and she wipes my forehead and she
fans my face and she makes me a cup o' tea.
And it don't do a thing for my real pain except
she is my mama.

Mama   Mommy   Mammy
Maa-mee   Maa-mee
I'd Walk a Mill-yon Miles For
One o' Your Smiles . . .

This is for The Black Back-Ups.
This is for my mama and your mama,
my grandma and your grandma.
This is for the thousand thousand Black Back-Ups.

And the colored girls say
Do   dodo   do do   dodododo
do   dodo
dodo
do
do

PRIMUS ST. JOHN

All the Way Home

The lamps hung like a lynching
In my town.
It was a dark town.
In a dark town,
Light is a ragged scar.
Fright begs that ragged scar.
It begs doorways.

I love that town.
From its lean men
I learned
Emotion;
And how to hold that fine edge,
That makes us
        people . . .

Mrs. Blackwell's
Sold her house.
Since her husband revolved his head,
She wears bright hats
That speak to people.

B.J.'s doing time.
His children betray that time,
By the breathing it takes
To dream through windows.
Mary Lee dreams him letters;
She dreams by heart . . .

Now I feel a new scar.
I've left home
And leaned so far,
I'm almost zero.

And though it's lonely,
Whatever knowing is,
It strings a long fine wire.
At night I lie awake
And listen to that wire—

All the way home.

from *Dreamer*

*"Fictive kinship ties probably resulted from
relationships among those who had been
on board slave ships together from West Africa."*

We came to know each other
Through the constant touch of our bodies,
The endless devotion
Of our mingled sweat;
Finally I said,
"You stink," in my language.
"Yoruba man, son of a Lagos beast,
So do you," he said
In his own language.
Almighty God, Olofin-Orun,
Discerner of hearts,
I did not kill him;
It was good to know
He too was still human,
For we have come to live
In the enormous hole
Of a world that creaks,
That rocks from side to side
Like the astonishing breast
Of the full moon.
A world fertile with death,
Seductive with madness,
With enough pain to produce crops;
And in this world

We have become as rancid
As salt fish after an enormous journey,
Rancid
With stories of enigmatic love
And profuse loss—
So Olorun
It was because we sensed
We were some last precious gift
For some lost future kin,
It was in that spirit
Wattled and daubed in our own shit
That we reached into the darkness
And became brothers.

TIM SEIBLES

Trying for Fire

Right now, even if a muscular woman wanted
to teach me the power of her skin
I'd probably just stand here with my hands
jammed in my pockets. Tonight
I'm feeling weak as water, watching the wind
bandage the moon. That's how it is tonight:
sky like tar, thin gauzy clouds,
a couple lame stars. A car rips by—
the driver's cigarette pinwheels past
the dog I saw hit this afternoon.
One second he was trotting along
with his wet nose tasting the air,
next thing I know he's off the curb,
a car swerves and, bam, it's over. For an instant,
he didn't seem to understand he was dying—
he lifted his head as if he might still reach
the dark-green trash bags half-open
on the other side of the street.

I wish someone could tell me
how to live in the city. My friends
just shake their heads and shrug. I
can't go to church—I'm embarrassed by things
preachers say we should believe.
I would talk to my wife, but she's worried
about the house. Whenever she listens
she hears the shingles giving in
to the rain. If I read the paper
I start believing some stranger
has got my name in his pocket—
on a matchbook next to his knife.

When I was twelve I'd take out the trash—
the garage would open like some ogre's cave

while just above my head the Monday Night Movie
stepped out of the television, and my parents
leaned back in their chairs. I can still hear
my father's voice coming through the floor,
"Boy, make sure you don't make a mess down there."
I remember the red-brick caterpillar of row houses
on Belfield Avenue and, not much higher than the rooftops,
the moon, soft and pale as a nun's thigh.

I had a plan back then—my feet were made
for football: each toe had the heart
of a different animal, so I ran
ten ways at once. I knew I'd play pro,
and live with my best friend, and
when Vanessa let us pull up her sweater
those deep-brown balloony mounds made me believe
in a world where eventually you could touch
whatever you didn't understand.

If I was afraid of anything it was
my bedroom when my parents made me
turn out the light: that knocking noise
that kept coming from the walls,
the shadow shapes by the bookshelf,
the feeling that something was always there
just waiting for me to close my eyes.
But only sleep would get me, and I'd
wake up running for my bike, my life
jingling like a little bell on the breeze.
I understood so little that I
understood it all, and I still know
what it meant to be one of the boys
who had never kissed a girl.

I never did play pro football.
I never got to do my mad-horse,
mountain goat, happy-wolf dance
for the blaring fans in the Astro Dome.
I never snagged a one-hander over the middle
against Green Bay and stole my snaky way
down the sideline for the game-breaking six.

And now, the city is crouched like a mugger
behind me—right outside, in the alley behind my door,
a man stabbed this guy for his wallet, and sometimes
I see this four-year-old with his face all bruised,
his father holding his hand like a vise. When I
turn on the radio the music is just like the news.
So, what should I do—close my eyes and hope
whatever's out there will just let me sleep?
I won't sleep tonight. I'll stay near my TV
and watch the police get everybody.

Across the street a woman is letting
her phone ring. I see her in the kitchen
stirring something on the stove. Farther off
a small dog chips the quiet with his bark.
Above me the moon looks like a nickel
in a murky little creek. This
is the same moon that saw me twelve,
without a single bill to pay, zinging
soup can tops into the dark—I called them
flying saucers. This is the same
white light that touched dinosaurs, that
found the first people trying for fire.

It must have been very good, that moment
when wood smoke turned to flickering, when
they believed night was broken
once and for all—I wonder what almost-words
were spoken. I wonder how long
before that first flame went out.

NTOZAKE SHANGE

from *for colored girls who have considered suicide / when the rainbow is enuf*

lady in brown
dark phrases of womanhood
of never havin been a girl
half-notes scattered
without rhythm/ no tune
distraught laughter fallin
over a black girl's shoulder
it's funny/ it's hysterical
the melody-less-ness of her dance
don't tell nobody don't tell a soul
she's dancin on beer cans & shingles

this must be the spook house
another song with no singers
lyrics/ no voices
& interrupted solos
unseen performances

are we ghouls?
children of horror?
the joke?

don't tell nobody don't tell a soul
are we animals? have we gone crazy?

i can't hear anythin
but maddening screams
& the soft strains of death
& you promised me
you promised me . . .
somebody/ anybody
sing a black girl's song

bring her out
to know herself
to know you
but sing her rhythms
carin/ struggle/ hard times
sing her song of life
she's been dead so long
closed in silence so long
she doesn't know the sound
of her own voice
her infinite beauty
she's half-notes scattered
without rhythm/ no tune
sing her sighs
sing the song of her possibilities
sing a righteous gospel
let her be born
let her be born
& handled warmly.

———————

lady in red
i sat up one nite walkin a boardin house
screamin/ cryin/ the ghost of another woman
who waz missin what i waz missin
i wanted to jump up outta my bones
& be done wit myself
leave me alone
& go on in the wind
it waz too much
i fell into a numbness
til the only tree i cd see
took me up in her branches
held me in the breeze
made me dawn dew
that chill at daybreak
the sun wrapped me up swingin rose light everywhere
the sky laid over me like a million men

i waz cold/ i waz burnin up/ a child
& endlessly weavin garments for the moon
wit my tears

i found god in myself
& i loved her/ i loved her fiercely

PATRICIA SMITH

Building Nicole's Mama

for the 6th grade class of Lillie C. Evans
School, Liberty City, Miami

I am astonished at their mouthful names—
Lakinishia, Fumilayo, Chevellanie, Delayo—
their ragged rebellions and lip-glossed pouts,
and all those pants drooped as drapery.
I rejoice when they kiss my face, whisper wet
and urgent in my ear, make me their obsession
because I have brought them poetry.

They shout me raw, bruise my wrists with pulling,
and brashly claim me as mama as they
cradle my head in their little laps,
waiting for new words to grow in my mouth.

You.
You.
You.
Angry, jubilant, weeping poets—we are all
saviors, reluctant hosannas in the limelight,
but you knew that, didn't you? So let us
bless this sixth grade class—40 nappy heads,
40 cracking voices, and all of them
raise their hands when I ask. They have all seen
the Reaper, grim in his heavy robe,
pushing the button for the dead project elevator,
begging for a break at the corner pawn shop,
cackling wildly in the back pew of the Baptist church.

I ask the death question and forty fists
punch the air, *me!, me!* And O'Neal,
matchstick crack child, watched his mother's
body become a claw, and 9-year-old Tiko Jefferson,

741

barely big enough to lift the gun, fired a bullet
into his own throat after Mama bended his back
with a lead pipe. Tamika cried into a sofa pillow
when Daddy blasted Mama into the north wall
of their cluttered one-room apartment,
Donya's cousin gone in a drive-by. Dark window,
click, click, gone, says Donya, her tiny finger
a barrel, the thumb a hammer. I am shocked
by their losses—and yet when I read a poem
about my own hard-eyed teenager, Jeffrey asks

He is dead yet?

It cannot be comprehended,
my 18-year-old still pushing and pulling
his own breath. And those 40 faces pity me,
knowing that I will soon be as they are,
numb to our bloodied histories,
favoring the Reaper with a thumbs-up and a wink,
hearing the question and shouting *me, me,
Miss Smith, I know somebody dead!*

Can poetry hurt us? they ask me before
snuggling inside my words to sleep.
I love you, Nicole says, Nicole wearing my face,
pimples peppering her nose, and she is as black
as angels are. Nicole's braids clipped, their ends
kissed with match flame to seal them,
and *can you teach me to write a poem about my mother?*
*I mean, you write about your daddy and he dead,
can you teach me to remember my mama?*

A teacher tells me this is the first time Nicole
has admitted that her mother is gone,
murdered by slim silver needles and a stranger
rifling through her blood, the virus pushing
her skeleton through for Nicole to see.
And now this child with rusty knees
and mismatched shoes sees poetry as her scream
and asks me for the words to build her mother again.

Replacing the voice.
Stitching on the lost flesh.

So poets,
as we pick up our pens,
as we flirt and sin and rejoice behind microphones—
remember Nicole.
She knows that we are here now,
and she is an empty vessel waiting to be filled.

And she is waiting.
And she
is
waiting.
And she waits.

Don't Drink the Water

A dog's sudden slickness slices such raw terror
through the surface, its collar biting into bloat,
jaunty bone-shaped tag a dollop of odd on black.

Sluggish miracle silvers of oil clutch Tuesday's
stupid brazen light and wink gorgeous while belching
sudden scattered flames. And over there, a window—

its dusty shadowed pane spidered into hundreds
of crusted pins in search of bared skin or dwelling.
Skimming leviathan vermin, their teeth bared, snort

the sugar of such leaving. Gleeful, they survive
on odor, exploded food, the gooey glued spine
of—wait—that looks like *How Stella Got Her Groove Back*.

Some mama's body, gaseous, a dimming star splayed
and so gently spinning, threatens its own soft seams,
collides sloppily with mattresses, power lines,

shards of four-doors. And trees, of course, are the monsters
we always knew they were. With lengthy gnarled arms raw
and lightning-slashed, they fist through the dark rushing
    depths

to etch hungered talons against blue. On the soft
bark of an oak, *H-E-L-p,* knifed in fever.
The water's black teeth reach for the helpless vowel.

Networks deftly edit and craft this sexy glint
of sudden ocean, wait for mama's bobbing bulk
to sweetly swirl into view, framed—*now!*—by the word.

Beneath this wet, at deeper wet, soulless shit reigns,
a sludge of skitters and screams, everything that drains
from the dying curdles, folds into hellish soup.

Winn-Dixie checkers, baby daddies, vague Baptists,
scared cops slog through, the slow wilting jazz of their legs
razored by the murk. What claws at their stride is piss,

lies about wind. What slows their forward is fetid,
fervently lapping, E coli, fuel, old meat.
Nudges toward hellfire hiss against forearm and knee.

It's almost laughable, this wading through the thick
toward other rain. That mama whirls such splayed grace
on drenched sky. Better to rest, succumb to float, shine.

SEKOU SUNDIATA

from *Free!*

watch her climb a barstool.
one thousand eyes
from the black canvass stretched
beyond the stage, house lights
down,   tight shot.
she sing: man born of woman's
bound to woman want man,
man won't do.
she say: pain so bad
even her hair it hurt.
man she say hard head
more ways than one.
say nigger think she
cockroach brain
making tiny questions.
he cough salt upside her head,

gardenia falls on rocks,   twisted
iron combs.   teardrop
straight no chaser.
woman cold shake roots
clatter like chains from
scratch she jagged throat—
breath lowdown.
he don't like
what kinda song,   flower
in her head,   spit
on ground,   say,   naw
what kinda song?

AFAA MICHAEL WEAVER

Inside the Blues Whale

1978–1979 for Vincent Woodard

It is not just my problem. It belongs
to us all. I have been cajoled into
coming to the emergency room where
everything scares me. Black folk
shoot and cut each other until they end
here where guards have guns. I refuse
to be taken upstairs and locked away.
I was trying to think of a poem. It got me
to this place. With my mother, I stand
against the wall, guards on either side.
They have guns, and this is my mother.
It is now everybody's problem. A bird
is singing in my hair, more important
than Thorazine. My head is a tree
stretching its leaves to burn in the sun.
They say if I make a treaty to take
the medicine, I can leave with my family
since my family is crazy. I look at the guns
on the hips of the guards and know I must
be as still and quiet as death or this will
turn into psychosis as sick as nightmares.
I am angry that they would have me here
with my mother, angry at white doctors.
I am in a whale in the ocean. Who can
swim out to me? Who can cast a line?
If I take out the first guard by breaking
his neck, I can protect my mother, but
it is more important that we are all now
underwater, inside a whale who laughs.
Later the therapist they say likes me
keeps talking about the appointment.

She is doing something subliminal with
the word "come," repeating, repeating.
She leans to me when she says it.
It bothers me that such people think
crazy people are stupid, but it is more
important that my head is a tree
with a bird singing in it inside a whale
in the ocean. The most important thing
of all is that this whale that ate us
likes to laugh a lot. He has the blues.

Scrapple

It was cousin Alvin who stole the liquor,
slipped down Aunt Mabie's steps on the ice,
fresh from jail for some small crime.
Alvin liked to make us laugh while he took
the liquor or other things we did not see,
in Aunt Mabie's with her floors polished,
wood she polished on her hands and knees
until they were truth itself and slippery
enough to trick you, Aunt Mabie who loved
her Calvert Extra and loved the bright inside
of family, the way we come connected in webs,
born in clusters of promises, dotted
with spots that mark our place in the karma
of good times, good times in the long ribbon
of being colored I learned when colored
had just given way to Negro and Negro was
leaving us because blackness chased it out
of the house, made it slip on the ice, fall
down and spill N-e-g-r-o all over the sidewalk
until we were proud in a new avenue of pride,
as thick as the scrapple on Saturday morning
with King syrup, in the good times, between
the strikes and layoffs at the mills when work
was too slack, and Pop sat around pretending
not to worry, not to let the stream of sweat

he wiped from his head be anything except
the natural way of things, keeping his habits,
the paper in his chair by the window, the radio
with the Orioles, with Earl Weaver the screamer
and Frank Robinson the gentle black man,
keeping his habits, Mama keeping hers,
the WSID gospel in the mornings, dusting
the encyclopedias she got from the A&P,
collecting the secrets of neighbors, holding
marriages together, putting golden silence
on children who took the wrong turns, broke
the laws of getting up and getting down
on your knees. These brittle things we call
memories rise up, like the aroma of scrapple,
beauty and ugliness, life's mix
where the hard and painful things from folk
who know no boundaries live beside
the bright eyes that look into each other,
searching their pupils for paths to prayer.

Washing the Car with My Father

It is the twilight blue Chevrolet,
four doors with no power but the engine,
whitewall tires, no padding on the dashboard,
the car I drive on dates, park on dark lanes
to ask for a kiss, now my hand goes along
the fender, wiping every spot, the suds
in the bucket, my father standing at the gate,
poor and proud, tall and stout, a wise man,

a man troubled by a son gone missing
in the head, drag racing his only car
at night, traveling with hoodlums to leave
the books for street life, naming mentors
the men who pack guns and knives, a son
gone missing from all the biblical truth,
ten talents, prophecies, burning bushes,
dirty cars washed on Saturday morning.

He tells me not to miss a spot, to open
the hood when I'm done so he can check
the oil, the vital thing like blood, blood
of kinship, blood spilled in the streets
of Baltimore, blood oozing from the soul
of a son walking prodigal paths leading
to gutters. Years later I tell him the stories
of what his brother-in-law did to me, and

he wipes a tear from the corner of his eye,
wraps it in a white handkerchief for church,
walks up the stairs with the aluminum
crutch to scream at the feet of black Jesus
and in these brittle years of his old age we
grow deeper, talk way after midnight,
peeping over the rail of his hospital bed
as we wash the twilight blue Chevrolet.

John Henry Sleeping in High Grass

Mowers miles away, mud flies on top
his hammer like they own it, his chest
cresting and falling in shapes shifting
between sunlight and leaves, black steel
his destiny, John is motion at rest,
tides of moon and waves in still waters,
suns igniting hearts of molten iron,
a hardened conviction, rose petals in rain.

Sleep is a dream, the real world a poundage,
work a sentence for being his mama's son,
the hammer in his crib, the supernatural

a drum song of woodpeckers, cow bells
in the field, heaven a home going back to
a place before the bugle call to be born.

SHERLEY ANNE WILLIAMS

from *Letters to a New England Negro*

Miss Ann Spencer
Lyme on Eaton
New Strowbridge, Connecticut

August 30, 1867

Dear Ann,

Caution is not so necessary
here as in some other parts
of the state, but we hear of
the "night-riding" and terror
and so are careful. Yet, Miss
Esther's bearing is such that
she is accorded grudging
civility by even
rabid Rebels and though there
was at first some muttering
at young white women teaching
"nigras," Cassie and Beryl are
likewise accepted; thus the
School escapes reprisals.

And,
if the local ladies lift
their skirts aside as I pass—
Well, perhaps I should smirch them.

If my cast-off clothes are
thought unsuited to my station,
my head held too high as I
step back to let the meanest white

go before me, why— What then
is a concert in Newport
or a day in Boston compared
to the chance to be arrogant
amongst so many southerners!

————————

October 22, 1867

The girls are bold, fingering
our dresses, marveling at
our speech. They cluster around
us at recess, peppering
us with questions about the
North and ourselves. Today, one
asked why I did not cover
my head or at least braid my
hair as is decent around
white folk. We do not speak of
hair in the north, at least in
public, and I answered sharply,
It is not the custom in
the North and I am from the
North—meaning, of course, that I
am freeborn.

I know how
chancy freedom is among
us and so have never
boasted of my birth. And
they were as much stung by my
retort as I by their question.
But in the moment of my
answer the scarves worn by the
women seemed so much a symbol
of our slavery that I would
have died before admitting
my childhood's longing for just

such patient plaiting of my
tangled hair or cover now
my wild and sullen head.

March 3, 1868

Dearest One,

I have no clear recall of
how I came to be at the
door of my first mistress, kept
little of that beginning, save
that through bargaining I fixed
my wage and worked extra for
room and board. I cannot now
remember all the helping
hands I passed through before the
Harrises took me in. There are
things I tell no one and have
ceased to tell myself. I have
grown to womanhood with my past
almost a blank.

I do not
recall, yet the memory
colors all that I am. I
know only that I was a
servant; now my labor is
returned to me and all my
waiting is upon myself.

CHRIS ABANI

Blue

I

Africans in the hold fold themselves
to make room for hope. In the afternoon's
ferocity, tar, grouting the planks like the glue
of family, melts to the run of a child's licorice stick.

Wet decks crack, testing the wood's mettle.
Distilled from evaporating brine, salt
dusts the floor, tickling with the measure
into time and the thirst trapped below.

II

The captain's new cargo of Igbos disturbs him.
They stand, computing the swim back to land.
Haitians still say: *Igbo pend'c or' a ya!*
But we do not hang ourselves in cowardice.

III

Sold six times on the journey to the coast,
once for a gun, then cloth, then iron
manilas, her pride was masticated like husks
of chewing sticks, spat from morning-rank mouths.

Breaking loose, edge of handcuffs held high
like the blade of a vengeful axe, she runs
across the salt scratch of deck,
pain deeper than the blue inside a flame.

IV

The sound, like the break of bone
could have been the Captain's skull
or the musket shot dropping her
over the side, her chains wrapped
around his neck in dance.

The New Religion

The body is a nation I have not known.
The pure joy of air: the moment between leaping
from a cliff into the wall of blue below. Like that.
Or to feel the rub of tired lungs against skin-
covered bone, like a hand against the rough of bark.
Like that. "The body is a savage," I said.
For years I said that: the body is a savage.
As if this safety of the mind were virtue
not cowardice. For years I have snubbed
the dark rub of it, said, "I am better, Lord,
I am better," but sometimes, in an unguarded
moment of sun, I remember the cowdung-scent
of my childhood skin thick with dirt and sweat
and the screaming grass.
But this distance I keep is not divine,
for what was Christ if not God's desire
to smell his own armpit? And when I
see him, I know he will smile,
fingers glued to his nose, and say, "Next time
I will send you down as a dog
to taste this pure hunger."

ELIZABETH ALEXANDER

The Venus Hottentot

(*1825*)

I. CUVIER

Science, science, science!
Everything is beautiful

blown up beneath my glass.
Colors dazzle insect wings.

A drop of water swirls
like marble. Ordinary

crumbs become stalactites
set in perfect angles

of geometry I'd thought
impossible. Few will

ever see what I see
through this microscope.

Cranial measurements
crowd my notebook pages,

and I am moving closer,
close to how these numbers

signify aspects of
national character.

Her genitalia
will float inside a labeled

pickling jar in the Musée
de l'Homme on a shelf

above Broca's brain:
"the Venus Hottentot."

Elegant facts await me.
Small things in this world are mine.

2.

There is unexpected sun today
in London, and the clouds that
most days sift into this cage
where I am working have dispersed.
I am a black cutout against
a captive blue sky, pivoting
nude so the paying audience
can view my naked buttocks.

I am called "Venus Hottentot."
I left Capetown with a promise
of revenue: half the profits
and my passage home: A boon!
Master's brother proposed the trip;
the magistrate granted me leave.
I would return to my family
a duchess, with watered-silk

dresses and money to grow food,
rouge and powders in glass pots,
silver scissors, a lorgnette,
voile and tulle instead of flax,
cerulean blue instead
of indigo. My brother would
devour sugar-studded non-
pareils, pale taffy, damask plums.

That was years ago. London's
circuses are florid and filthy,

swarming with cabbage-smelling
citizens who stare and query,
"Is it muscle? Bone? Or fat?"
My neighbor to the left is
The Sapient Pig, "The Only
Scholar of His Race." He plays

at cards, tells time and fortunes
by scraping his hooves. Behind
me is Prince Kar-mi, who arches
like a rubber tree and stares back
at the crowd from under the crook
of his knee. A professional
animal trainer shouts my cues.
There are singing mice here.

"The Ball of Duchess DuBarry":
In the engraving I lurch
toward the *belles dames*, mad-eyed, and
they swoon. Men in capes and pince-nez
shield them. Tassels dance at my hips.
In this newspaper lithograph
my buttocks are shown swollen
and luminous as a planet.

Monsieur Cuvier investigates
between my legs, poking, prodding,
sure of his hypothesis.
I half expect him to pull silk
scarves from inside me, paper poppies,
then a rabbit! He complains
at my scent and does not think
I comprehend, but I speak

English. I speak Dutch. I speak
a little French as well, and
languages Monsieur Cuvier
will never know have names.
Now I am bitter and now
I am sick. I eat brown bread,

drink rancid broth. I miss good sun,
miss Mother's *sadza*. My stomach

is frequently queasy from mutton
chops, pale potatoes, blood sausage.
I was certain that this would be
better than farm life. I am
the family entrepreneur!
But there are hours in every day
to conjure my imaginary
daughters, in banana skirts

and ostrich-feather fans.
Since my own genitals are public
I have made other parts private.
In my silence I possess
mouth, larynx, brain, in a single
gesture. I rub my hair
with lanolin, and pose in profile
like a painted Nubian

archer, imagining gold leaf
woven through my hair, and diamonds.
Observe the wordless Odalisque.
I have not forgotten my Khoisan
clicks. My flexible tongue
and healthy mouth bewilder
this man with his rotting teeth.
If he were to let me rise up

from this table, I'd spirit
his knives and cut out his black heart,
seal it with science fluid inside
a bell jar, place it on a low
shelf in a white man's museum
so the whole world could see
it was shriveled and hard,
geometric, deformed, unnatural.

Nineteen

That summer in Culpeper, all there was to eat was white:
cauliflower, flounder, white sauce, white ice-cream.
I snuck around with an older man who didn't tell me
he was married. I was the baby, drinking rum and Coke
while the men smoked reefer they'd stolen from the campers.
I tiptoed with my lover to poison-ivied fields, camp vans.
I never slept. Each fortnight I returned to the city,
black and dusty, with a garbage bag of dirty clothes.

At nineteen it was my first summer away from home.
His beard smelled musty. His eyes were black. "The ladies
     love my hair,"
he'd say, and like a fool I'd smile. He knew everything
about marijuana, how dry it had to be to burn,
how to crush it, sniff it, how to pick the seeds out. He said
he learned it all in Vietnam. He brought his son to visit
after one of his days off. I never imagined a mother.
"Can I steal a kiss?" he said, the first thick night in the field.

I asked and asked about Vietnam, how each scar felt,
what combat was like, how the jungle smelled. He listened
to a lot of Marvin Gaye, was all he said, and grabbed
between my legs. I'd creep to my cot before morning.
I'd eat that white food. This was before I understood
that nothing could be ruined in one stroke. A sudden
storm came hard one night; he bolted up inside the van.
"The rain sounded just like that," he said, "on the roofs
     there."

Race

Sometimes I think about Great-Uncle Paul who left
     Tuskegee,
Alabama to become a forester in Oregon and in so doing
became fundamentally white for the rest of his life, except

when he traveled without his white wife to visit his siblings—
now in New York, now in Harlem, USA—just as
     pale-skinned,
as straight-haired, as blue-eyed as Paul, and black. Paul never
     told anyone
he was white, he just didn't say that he was black, and who
     could imagine,
an Oregon forester in 1930 as anything other than white?
The siblings in Harlem each morning ensured
no one confused them for anything other than what they
     were, black.
They were black! Brown-skinned spouses reduced confusion.
Many others have told, and not told, this tale.
When Paul came East alone he was as they were, their
     brother.

The poet invents heroic moments where the pale black
     ancestor stands up
on behalf of the race. The poet imagines Great-Uncle Paul
in cool, sagey groves counting rings in redwood trunks,
imagines pencil markings in a ledger book, classifications,
imagines a sidelong look from an ivory spouse who is
     learning
her husband's caesuras. She can see silent spaces
but not what they signify, graphite markings in a forester's
     code.

Many others have told, and not told, this tale.
The one time Great-Uncle Paul brought his wife to New York
he asked his siblings not to bring their spouses,
and that is where the story ends: ivory siblings who would
     not
see their brother without their telltale spouses.
What a strange thing is "race," and family, stranger still.
Here a poem tells a story, a story about race.

Ars Poetica #28: African Leave-Taking Disorder

The talk is good. The two friends linger
at the door. Urban crickets sing with them.

There is no *after* the supper and talk.
The talk is good. These two friends linger

at the door, half in, half out, 'til one
decides to walk the other home. And so

they walk, more talk, the new doorstep, the
nightgowned wife who shakes her head and smiles

from the bedroom window as the men talk
in love and the crickets sing along.

The joke would be if the one now home
walked the other one home, where they started,

to keep talking, and so on: "African
Leave-Taking Disorder," which names her children

everywhere trying to come back together and talk.

Ars Poetica #100: I Believe

Poetry, I tell my students,
is idiosyncratic. Poetry

is where we are ourselves
(though Sterling Brown said

"Every 'I' is a dramatic 'I'"),
digging in the clam flats

for the shell that snaps,
emptying the proverbial pocketbook.

Poetry is what you find
in the dirt in the corner,

overhear on the bus, God
in the details, the only way

to get from here to there.
Poetry (and now my voice is rising)

is not all love, love, love,
and I'm sorry the dog died.

Poetry (here I hear myself loudest)
is the human voice,

and are we not of interest to each other?

Praise Song for the Day

Each day we go about our business,
walking past each other, catching each other's
eyes or not, about to speak or speaking.

All about us is noise. All about us is
noise and bramble, thorn and din, each
one of our ancestors on our tongues.

Someone is stitching up a hem, darning
a hole in a uniform, patching a tire,
repairing the things in need of repair.

Someone is trying to make music somewhere,
with a pair of wooden spoons on an oil drum,
with cello, boom box, harmonica, voice.

A woman and her son wait for the bus.
A farmer considers the changing sky.
A teacher says, *Take out your pencils. Begin.*

We encounter each other in words, words
spiny or smooth, whispered or declaimed,
words to consider, reconsider.

We cross dirt roads and highways that mark
the will of some one and then others, who said
I need to see what's on the other side.

I know there's something better down the road.
We need to find a place where we are safe.
We walk into that which we cannot yet see.

Say it plain: that many have died for this day.
Sing the names of the dead who brought us here,
who laid the train tracks, raised the bridges,

picked the cotton and the lettuce, built
brick by brick the glittering edifices
they would then keep clean and work inside of.

Praise song for struggle, praise song for the day.
Praise song for every hand-lettered sign,
the figuring-it-out at kitchen tables.

Some live by *love thy neighbor as thyself,*
others by *first do no harm or take no more
than you need*. What if the mightiest word is love?

Love beyond marital, filial, national,
love that casts a widening pool of light,
love with no need to pre-empt grievance.

In today's sharp sparkle, this winter air,
any thing can be made, any sentence begun.
On the brink, on the brim, on the cusp,

praise song for walking forward in that light.

QUAN BARRY

loose strife

Listen closely as I sing this. The man standing at the gate
tottering on his remaining limb is a kind of metronome, his
    one
leg planted firmly on the earth. Yes, I have made him
    beautiful

because I aim to lay all my cards on the table. In the book
    review
the critic writes, "Barry seeks not to judge but to
    understand."
Did she want us to let her be, or does she want

to be there walking the grounds of the old prison on the hill
of the poison tree where comparatively a paltry twenty
    thousand
died? In the first room with the blown up

black-and-white of a human body gone abstract someone has
to turn and face the wall not because of the human pain
represented in the photo but because of her calmness,

the tranquility with which she tells us that her father
and her sister and her brother were killed. In graduate school
a whole workshop devoted to an image of a woman with
    bleach

thrown in the face and the question of whether or not
the author could write, "The full moon sat in the window
like a calcified eye, the woman's face aglow with a
    knowingness."

I felt it come over me and I couldn't stop. I tried to pull
    myself

together and I couldn't. They were children. An army of
        child
soldiers. In the room papered with photos of the Khmer
        Rouge

picture after picture of teenagers, children whose parents
were killed so that they would be left alone in the world
to do the grisly work that precedes paradise.

And the photos of the victims, the woman holding her
        newborn
in her arms as her head is positioned in a vise, in this case
the vise an instrument not of torture

but of documentation, the head held still as the camera
        captures
the image, the thing linking all their faces, the abject fear
and total hopelessness as exists

in only a handful of places in the history of the visible world.
For three $US per person she will guide you through what
        was
Tuol Sleng prison, hill of the strychnine tree.

Without any affectation she will tell you the story of how
her father and her sister and her brother went among
the two million dead. There are seventy-four forms

of poetry in this country and each one is still meant to be
        sung.

Doug Flutie's 1984 Orange Bowl
Hail Mary as Water into Fire

Listen w/o distraction.

Even before its incarnation we were transported, which is to
        say

we were there, the Miami night
larval, charged.

Read this to me when I'm dying, when I'm in the
        intermediate state—
    my consciousness dissipating through the elements.

Did the child-me know it would be all right, that the next six
        seconds would represent
    human existence?

This is the way it always begins: in huddled confusion, then
        the object
    churning toward a predetermined end.

There is a plan. There is hope. Then something happens.

Love comes & goes. Anger. Happiness. Decay. A man stands
        on the other side
    & holds out his hands.

Something is sailing through the new year.

Teacher, call me by my other name. Tell me to breathe
        through my eyes, see
    the path through the luminosity.

We are the ball. We are the arc through the air. We are the
        no time left on the clock
    & the disbeliever.

Read this to me when I'm dying, when I'm neither here
    nor there.

Say, "Grab onto nothing & it will come to you."

PAUL BEATTY

Verbal Mugging

this is a performance piece
a recitation of woe
that begins with my head bowed
and my eyes closed

either im asleep
or this poem must be deep

i start by speaking real slow and succinct
my diction sittin in a rocking chair
weaving narrated stage histrionics to the page

                        needle and tongue click

          a crossover stitch
          that knits the written

                              with the bullshit
                                told at quittin time

now i pretend to light a cornpipe
and from memory recite
a story of folklore that if it were true i would rather forget

during act II

my face goes solemn and sallow
it seems we've come to the part
where all hope is lost

                    heres when
                            i make the sign of the cross

give thanks to an *extensive theatrical background*
that allows me to pretentiously

769

drop to one knee
             so that any fool could see
             that whatever im talking about
             involves some method acting pleas for freedom

performance poetry to go
biodegradable relatedness
you put your elbows on the table
rest your chin on your rodin brass hand
and you dont have to think

cause i illustrate my words
with some cheesy rip-off diana ross and four tops hand gestures
now dressed in mink and rhinestone leisure suit pink
my poem works an imaginary hoe
a slave to a rhythm so real

you can almost hear the refrains of

                              "please let my people go"

             spin out the fields
             with a basso so profundo
             you can almos' feel

                         the pat of patronization
                         on top yo' head

maybe youve noticed
ive lapsed into a southern drawl
and when i say we that means yawl

the reader at one with the bleeder
isnt that how the gentiles learn to feel jesus
clenchin both my fists for emphasis
i clutch them to my chest
to show that you n me together and separate
feel the oppression of every person who's ever
been shot at spat on and shat upon

                        pigs christened
                        in a backwoods baptismal
                        together we are cleansed

wallowing in the muddled dirt wrongs
done to someone else

a pause   and i lower my voice a couple of octaves
                and project so that you can hear me way in the back

i do this in order to convey a poetic warmth
that crackles on the burning memories of fireside chats
with long since dead   grandpop fred
                              aunt teddy
                big daddy kane and miss jane pittman

gingerly my missive sits on the edge of the stage
dangles its feet and proceeds
to shove an earnest down-home tone   right down your throat

as i regale you with cliché and tales of ancestors ive never
        even known

                        i end this oral tome
                        drenched in sweat
                        wiping away the crocodile tears

of happy endings
in a make believe world
where people speed listen and skim
the poet goes round
makin ends meet
by beatin muthafuckas over the head with sound
bangin tuning forks on minds
lookin for vibrations that dont stop with time

JERICHO BROWN

Prayer of the Backhanded

Not the palm, not the pear tree
Switch, not the broomstick,
Nor the closest extension
Cord, not his braided belt, but God,
Bless the back of my daddy's hand
Which, holding nothing tightly
Against me and not wrapped
In leather, eliminated the air
Between itself and my cheek.
Make full this dimpled cheek
Unworthy of its unfisted print
And forgive my forgetting
The love of a hand
Hungry for reflex, a hand that took
No thought of its target
Like hail from a blind sky,
Involuntary, fast, but brutal
In its bruising. Father, I bear the bridge
Of what might have been
A broken nose. I lift to you
What was a busted lip. Bless
The boy who believes
His best beatings lack
Intention, the mark of the beast.
Bring back to life the son
Who glories in the sin
Of immediacy, calling it love.
God, save the man whose arm
Like an angel's invisible wing
May fly backward in fury
Whether or not his son stands near.
Help me hold in place my blazing jaw
As I think to say, *excuse me.*

Bullet Points

I will not shoot myself
In the head, and I will not shoot myself
In the back, and I will not hang myself
With a trashbag, and if I do,
I promise you, I will not do it
In a police car while handcuffed
Or in the jail cell of a town
I only know the name of
Because I have to drive through it
To get home. Yes, I may be at risk,
But I promise you, I trust the maggots
Who live beneath the floorboards
Of my house to do what they must
To any carcass more than I trust
An officer of the law of the land
To shut my eyes like a man
Of God might, or to cover me with a sheet
So clean my mother could have used it
To tuck me in. When I kill me, I will
Do it the same way most Americans do,
I promise you: cigarette smoke
Or a piece of meat on which I choke
Or so broke I freeze
In one of these winters we keep
Calling worst. I promise if you hear
Of me dead anywhere near
A cop, then that cop killed me. He took
Me from us and left my body, which is,
No matter what we've been taught,
Greater than the settlement
A city can pay a mother to stop crying,
And more beautiful than the new bullet
Fished from the folds of my brain.

'N'em

They said to say goodnight
And not goodbye, unplugged
The TV when it rained. They hid
Money in mattresses
So to sleep on decisions.
Some of their children
Were not their children. Some
Of their parents had no birthdates.
They could sweat a cold out
Of you. They'd wake without
An alarm telling them to.
Even the short ones reached
Certain shelves. Even the skinny
Cooked animals too quick
To catch. And I don't care
How ugly one of them arrived,
That one got married
To somebody fine. They fed
Families with change and wiped
Their kitchens clean.
Then another century came.
People like me forgot their names.

Another Elegy

This is what our dying looks like.
You believe in the sun. I believe
I can't love you. Always be closing,
Said our favorite professor before
He let the gun go off in his mouth.
I turned 29 the way any man turns
In his sleep, unaware of the earth
Moving beneath him, its plates in
Their places, a dated disagreement.
Let's fight it out, baby. You have

Only so long left—a man turning
In his sleep—so I take a picture.
I won't look at it, of course. It's
His bad side, his Mr. Hyde, the hole
In a husband's head, the O
Of his wife's mouth. Every night,
I take a pill. Miss one, and I'm gone.
Miss two, and we're through. Hotels
Bore me, unless I get a mountain view,
A room in which my cell won't work,
And there's nothing to do but see
The sun go down into the ground
That cradles us as any coffin can.

The Tradition

Aster. Nasturtium. Delphinium. We thought
Fingers in dirt meant it was our dirt, learning
Names in heat, in elements classical
Philosophers said could change us. *Stargazer.*
Foxglove. Summer seemed to bloom against the will
Of the sun, which news reports claimed flamed hotter
On this planet than when our dead fathers
Wiped sweat from their necks. *Cosmos. Baby's Breath.*
Men like me and my brothers filmed what we
Planted for proof we existed before
Too late, sped the video to see blossoms
Brought in seconds, colors you expect in poems
Where the world ends, everything cut down.
John Crawford. Eric Garner. Mike Brown.

DARRELL BURTON

A Balance of Blues & Angels

At the Eureka Springs Blues Festival
eighty-something Honey Boy Edwards
sits onstage spotlit in red like some
junkyard angel. John Deere hat askew—
following stagehands' entreats to play
then to stop.
When they give the OK, he sets
his guitar aside & simply taps his foot,
conjures up a down-home delta blues
right from the hardwood floor.

He sings: *Ya'll too young to know,*
each verse coaxing the crowd closer
toward a hurt in his sorry voice
as raw as the ache of an unmet need.
He finishes, & just sits there smiling,
stagehands come help him off—
handling him like
stuff you can't get anymore.

At *Inga's*, Bernard Allison's face
is disfigured in a sweaty mania.
I'm a blues guitar player!
he shouts, bending low into
some private sorrow.
He climbs aboard tabletops & chairs,
refuses a break
then weaves his way outside
to those who couldn't get in.

On the mountaintop high above,
a statuesque Jesus overlooks from
the *Passion-Play,* panged-faced,

pale arms outstretched—not quite
in dance, but tonight maybe,
regretting who he is.

KYLE DARGAN

nap · i · ness

When kinks began clustering on my head,
cousins named them naps.
I had to adapt—forget them
and learn to love the Brillo.
It was like wool. I
was like Jesus, Julius, Malcolm,
Amiri—unkempt and proud.
In came hip-hop, and the barber sheared my hair
in the shape of the Ka'bbah: black-box history,
our chronicle recorded forever inside.

But I learned someone had edited
my text with different blood
than it was fashioned in—
loosening the pages like lye
so the words wouldn't twist or dreadlock.
Then I realized
I was never truly in *his* likeness
nor the doctor's
nor the prophet's
nor the poet's. I am enigma—
living one history, combing another.

KWAME DAWES

Natural

for Bob Marley

In the silence, the silence of
a new void of morning. I taste
the bitter weed of loss, like mauby,
like a forerunner to my own loss—
staring at the open autopsied corpse
of the body that housed my father,
lamenting only that which may have been,
lamenting that sometimes we die
before poetic justice can mete its magic:
Oh the things that could have been!
The dead young are impossible equations.
Morning, morning, I walk along the leaf-strewn
avenues of the campus, a sun-specked
day; the blessed light on my upturned face
making me think of the confession you made
at Cane River where on the rocks you laid your head,
there in desolate places to make your bed,
to make music, I find the stones here
take to the alchemy of poetry so well.
I walk like a poet in search of remembrances.
The slip of my memory gathers images
and tosses them among the turning leaves
to let fall something like rain
on a blazing hot day, rainwater touching
soft asphalt and making steam as sweet
and reassuring as incense in the sanctuary.

Black Funk

The rigid of my jawbone
is power forged in the oven
of every blow I have felt.
My water walk is something like
compensation for a limp.
Don't begrudge me my sashay
walk, it's all I got sometimes.

'Cause I know the way you stare,
pale blue eyes like a machete edge
catching the color of new sky,
the way you barely whisper
your orders, spit out the food,
complain about my shuffling gait,
snorting out my funky smell,
find fault in each task I do,
never right, never good enough,
curse my children like dogs,
'cause I know you just hurting
drooling your bitterness
when my back is turned,
when the shape of my black ass
swings that way you hate,
sashaying through this room of daggers.

I know you're wondering what I've got
down there, in my belly, in my thighs,
make him leave your side,
crawl out of his pale sick skin
and howl like a beast at night,
whimper like a motherless babe
suckling on me, suckling on me.

You can't hide the shame you feel
to know I sometimes turn him back.
I know you know it, from the way
he comes on you hard and hurried,

searching for a hole to weep his soul in—
yes, I turn him back when I want,
and he still comes back for more.
I've got my pride sometimes.

I know the way you try to read me,
try to be me, can't be me,
never be me, never feel the black
of me, never know the blues in me,
'cause you never want to see you
in me even though we bleed together,
finding each other's tidal rhythms,
and bloat together like sisters,
hoarding the waters of the moon together.

So I sashay through your life,
averting the blades with my leather skin.
I abuse you, and when he bawls,
that is my pride at work,
all I've got sometimes.
I'll cook your meals
until he keels over,
and you just have to take it
'cause I took it with no fuss
when he forced his nothing self on me,
while my babies sucked their thumbs
within the sound of my whimpering;
I paid, baby;
I'm just reaping what y'all done sowed.

JOEL DIAS-PORTER

Wednesday Poem

I pass through the metal detector,
inside the front doors of Cardozo High,
with xeroxed poems and a lesson planned
to introduce my students to the wild iris.
After signing my name in the visitors' log,
I bop down two flights of steps.
Outside the classroom things are too quiet
and Mr. Bruno (who's Puerto Rican and writes poetry)
takes ten minutes to answer the door.
There's a student snapshot in his hand.
One of our kids got shot last night,
Remember Maurice? Maurice Caldwell.
He didn't come to school much.
A Crisis Response Team has the kids in a circle,
and I've never seen them sit so quietly.
Every computer in the classroom is dead.
A drawing of Maurice is taped to the board,
a bouquet of cards pinned under it,
Keisha (who writes funny poems in class)
says Maurice would help her with math,
she liked him but never told him.
The Crisis lady says *It's OK to cry.*
Keisha says she been ran out of tears.
Mr. Bruno tells me *Somebody called him*
from a parked Buick on Thomas Place NW.
When he walked up, they fired three times.
I freeze. That's a half block from my house.
There are four crackhouses on that block
and I never walk down that street.
I wonder why he approached the car,
was he hustling crack or weed?
Or did he recognize the dude and smile
before surprise blossomed across his face
and the truth rooted into his flesh.

His face flashes before my irises,
I see him horseplaying with Haneef,
his hair slicked back into a ponytail.
He wrote one poem this whole semester,
a battle rap between cartoon characters.
Mr. Bruno asks if I still want to teach.
I open my folder of nature poems,
then close the folder and slump in a chair.
What simile can seal a bullet wound?
Which student could these pistils protect,
here where it's natural to never see seventeen?

CAMILLE DUNGY

Frequently Asked Questions: #10

*Do you see current events differently because you were
raised by a black father
and are married to a black man?*

I am surprised they haven't left already—
things have gotten downright frosty, nearly unbearable.
A mob of them is apparently mouthing off outside

when I put down my newspaper and we all gather
to stand beside my daughter in the bay
of kitchen windows. Quiscalus quiscula:

This name sounds like a spell which, after its casting,
will make things crumble into a complement
of unanswerable questions. Though, if you need me

to tell you God's honest truth, I know nothing
but their common name the morning we watch them attack
our feeder. I complain about the mess they leave. Hulls

I'll have to sweep up or ignore. My father—
who I am thankful is still alive—says *We could use
a different kind of seed*. A simple solution. We want that

brown bird with the shock of red: the northern flicker.
We want western bluebirds, more of the skittish
finches. But mostly we get grackle grackle grackle

all day long. They scoff all we offer
and—being too close and too many—scare
other birds away. Still, can it be justifiable

to revile these harbingers? My husband says, *Look
        at all those crackles.* I almost laugh at him,
but the winter air does look hurtful loud

around the black flock. Like static is loud when it sticks
        sheets to sheets so they crackle when pulled
one from another. And sting. My father—who is older now

        than his older brothers will ever be—promises
        he will solve the problem of the grackles
and leaves the window to search for his keys.

The dawn sky—blue breaking into blackness—
        is what I see feathering their bodies. The fence
is gray. The feeder is gray, the aspen bark. Gray

        hulls litter the ground. But the grackles,
their passerine claws—three facing forward, one turned
        back—around the roost bar of the feeder, are

so bright within their blackness, I pray they will stay.

THOMAS SAYERS ELLIS

View of the Library of Congress from Paul Laurence Dunbar High School

for Doris Craig and Michael Olshausen

A white substitute teacher
At an all-Black public high school,
He sought me out saying my poems
Showed promise, range, a gift,
And had I ever heard of T.S. Eliot?
No. Then Robert Hayden perhaps?

Hayden, a former colleague,
Had recently died, and the obituary
He handed me had already begun
Its journey home—from the printed page
Back to tree, gray becoming
Yellow, flower, dirt.

No river, we skipped rocks
On the horizon, above Ground Zero,
From the roof of the Gibson Plaza Apartments.
We'd aim, then shout the names
Of the museums, famous monuments,
And government buildings

Where our grandparents, parents,
Aunts, and uncles worked. Dangerous duds.
The bombs we dropped always fell short,
Missing their mark. No one, not even
Carlton Green who had lived in
As many neighborhoods as me,
Knew in which direction
To launch when I lifted Hayden's
Place of employment—

The Library of Congress—
From the obituary, now folded
In my back pocket, a creased map.

We went home, asked our mothers
But they didn't know. Richard's came
Close: Somewhere near Congress,
On Capitol Hill, take the 30 bus,
Get off before it reaches Anacostia,
Don't cross the bridge into Southeast.

The next day in school
I looked it up—the National Library
Of the United States in Washington, D.C.
Founded in 1800, open to all taxpayers
And citizens. *Snap!* My aunt Doris
Works there, has for years.

Once, on her day off, she
Took me shopping and bought
The dress shoes of my choice.
Loafers. They were dark red,
Almost purple, bruised—the color
of blood before oxygen reaches it.

I was beginning to think
Like a poet, so in my mind
Hayden's dying and my loafers
Were connected, but years apart,
As was Dunbar to other institutions—
Ones I could see, ones I could not.

VIEVEE FRANCIS

Sugar and Brine: Ella's Understanding

Daddy slaughtered the hog right there in the side yard,
and it hurt to see it, but that won't stop me from eating.
Come Thanksgiving, I'll dip a bit of ham in Jackson's
Ribbon Cane Syrup, and pop it inside a biscuit.
When it's time to celebrate, something dies.
When something dies, we take it with the sweet.

Take my cousin Gerald—he left us last summer,
a tractor accident. We were cousins by marriage, but
friends by choice, so I cried more than when I broke my leg
jumping off the front porch—bone snapped clean through.
After the funeral, as the Lord is my witness,
those were the best potato pies I ever had.

Yesterday, where the yellow pines meet the creek,
that boy on the other side of the property line
helped bring his daddy's cattle in. I watched him watch
me standing in a field littered with cow's corn,
my head tilted just enough to let him know I was
curious. He left a scarlet ribbon tied to the barbed wire.
My heart skipped quicker than a swallow's when I found it.
Now I'm wondering what throat's going to open?
I need to warn him—the wheel never rusts, never stops.

Salt

for Veedra
(*Miami, Florida*)

Allergic to fish (shellfish or otherwise)
my sister shouts *Watermelon!*
when surprised by a fruit dinner

788

at the resort where she and I are sharing
sister time, something we rarely do.
I am old enough to be her aunt, or
even her mother. Fifteen years older
in fact, and like a mother, I take delight
in her delight. She won't be hungry
this evening, the chef has prepared
something especially for her, having
no idea what she looks like, only that
a temporary resident needs something
beyond seafood. Only the fruit is untainted.
A gentleman from Georgia sits with us
as we wait on our dinner. He, from "a good family"
"strong values" "can go back several generations"
looks at me, directly into my black pupils, and
I know what he knows. A whole history rides
the vehicle, the mule train, the wagon, the dust
track of my sister's outburst. And we begin
to laugh, hysterically. He for all the expected
reasons. And I, I laugh because somewhere
I want to cry. The landscape under my breasts,
topography of pines, clay bottomland, roofs
of tin . . . and the lie of it. The fruit so sweet, so
red, and now seedless. He and I both know
how delicious such things can be, but he can eat his
without shame, without notice.
And my sister in all her Yankee naïveté, or
innocence, knows only that she is being served
a treat, something that won't swell her throat,
noose her breath, while he and I share
our secret through grins, giggling
until we damn near choke.

ROSS GAY

burial

You're right, you're right,
the fertilizer's good—
it wasn't a gang of dullards
came up with chucking
a fish in the planting hole
or some midwife got lucky
with the placenta—
oh, I'll plant a tree here!—
and a sudden flush of quince
and jam enough for months—yes,
the magic dust our bodies become
casts spells on the roots
about which someone else
could tell you the chemical processes,
but it's just magic to me,
which is why a couple springs ago
when first putting in my two bare root plum trees
out back I took the jar which has become
my father's house,
and lonely for him and hoping to coax him back
for my mother as much as me,
poured some of him in the planting holes
and he dove in glad for the robust air,
saddling a slight gust
into my nose and mouth,
chuckling as I coughed,
but mostly he disappeared
into the minor yawns in the earth
into which I placed the trees,
splaying wide their roots,
casting the gray dust of my old man
evenly throughout the hole,
replacing then the clods
of dense Indiana soil until the roots

and my father were buried,
watering it in all with one hand
while holding the tree
with the other straight as the flag
to the nation of simple joy
of which my father is now a naturalized citizen,
waving the flag
from his subterranean lair,
the roots curled around him
like shawls or jungle gyms, like
hookahs or the arms of ancestors,
before breast-stroking into the xylem,
riding the elevator up
through the cambium and into the leaves where,
when you put your ear close enough,
you can hear him whisper
good morning, where, if you close your eyes
and push your face you can feel
his stubbly jowls and good lord
this year he was giddy at the first
real fruit set and nestled into the 30 or 40 plums
in the two trees, peering out from the sweet meat
with his hands pressed against the purple skin
like cathedral glass,
and imagine his joy as the sun
wizarded forth those abundant sugars
and I plodded barefoot
and prayerful at the first ripe plum's swell and blush,
almost weepy conjuring
some surely ponderous verse
to convey this bottomless grace,
you know, *oh father oh father* kind of stuff,
hundreds of hot air balloons
filling the sky in my chest, replacing his intubated body
listing like a boat keel side up, replacing
the steady stream of water from the one eye
which his brother wiped before removing the tube,
keeping his hand on the forehead
until the last wind in his body wandered off,
while my brother wailed like an animal,

and my mother said, weeping,
it's ok, it's ok. You can go honey,
at all of which my father
guffawed by kicking from the first bite
buckets of juice down my chin,
staining one of my two button-down shirts,
the salmon-colored silk one, hollering
there's more of that!
almost dancing now in the plum,
in the tree, the way he did as a person,
bent over and biting his lip
and chucking the one hip out
then the other with his elbows cocked
and fists loosely made
and eyes closed and mouth made trumpet
when he knew he could make you happy
just by being a little silly
and sweet.

A Small Needful Fact

Is that Eric Garner worked
for some time for the Parks and Rec.
Horticultural Department, which means,
perhaps, that with his very large hands,
perhaps, in all likelihood,
he put gently into the earth
some plants which, most likely,
some of them, in all likelihood,
continue to grow, continue
to do what such plants do, like house
and feed small and necessary creatures,
like being pleasant to touch and smell,
like converting sunlight
into food, like making it easier
for us to breathe.

ARACELIS GIRMAY

Santa Ana of Grocery Carts

Santa Ana of grocery carts, truckers,
eggs in the kitchen at 4 am, nurses, cleaning ladies,
the saints of ironing, the saints
of tortillas. Santa Ana of cross-guards, tomato pickers,
bakeries of bread in pinks & yellows, sugars.
Santa Ana of Cambodia, Viet Nam, Aztlán
down Bristol & Raitt. Santa Ana.
Boulevards of red lips, beauty salons, boomboxes, drone
of barber shop clippers fading tall Vincent's head,
    schoolyards,
the workshop architects, mechanics.
Santa Ana of mothers, radiators, trains.
Santa Ana of barbecues.
Santa Ana of Trujillos, Sampsons, & Agustins,
Zuly & Xochit with their twin lampish skins.
Santa Ana of cholas, bangs, & spray.
Santa Ana of AquaNet, altars,
the glitter & shine
of 99 cent stores, taco trocas, churches, of bells,
hallelujahs & center fields, aprons,
of winds, collard greens, & lemon cake
in Ms. Davenport's kitchen,
sweat, sweat over the stove. Santa Ana
of polka-dots, chicharonnes, Aztecs, African Fields',
    colombianas,
sun's children, vanished children. Santa Ana of orales.
Santa Ana of hairnets.
Patron saint of kitchens, asphalt, banana trees,
bless us if you are capable of blessing.

When we started, there were cousins & two parents,
now everything lost has been to you.
The house, axed, & opossums
gone. Abrigette & her husband John.

& the schoolyard boys underneath the ground,
undressed so thoroughly by your thousand mouths, Santa
    Ana.

let that be
enough.

Teeth

for cousin Gedion, who drove us to Massawa

Two sisters ride down with us.
It is liberation day in Massawa.

The older sister is the color of injera; her teeth are big &
    stuck-out.
The younger sister is a cinnamon stick.

Their almond eyes are the same.
Ink black hair falls beautiful down both their backs.

I see that you love one of them & change my mind
many times about who I think it is.

Months later, I will show their photographs to my father
who will laugh & say he knows.

"It is this one," he will say, surely, pointing
to the woman whose teeth stay, tame, in her mouth.

But what man would choose a woman
whose mouth looks stronger than his hands?

Know, Cousin, I pray there is love
between you & the older one
whose teeth might be bullets of ivory;

I imagine from this mouth:
   kites,
   rain,
   ax equal to lace, the yellow & lick
   of a jar filled with
   the sweet of stinging bees.

Ode to the Little "r"

   Little propeller
   working between
   the two fields of my a's,
   making my name
   a small boat
   that leaves the port
   of old San Juan
   or Ponce,
   with my grandfather,
   Miguel, on a boat,
   or in an airplane,
   with a hundred or so
   others, leaving the island
   for work, cities,
   in winters that would break
   their bones, make old,
   old men out of all of them,
   factory workers, domino
   players, little islands themselves
   who would eat & be eaten by Chicago,
   New York, the wars
   they fought without
   being able to vote for
   the president. Little propeller
   of their names: Francisco,
   Reymundo, Arelis, Margarita,
   Hernán, Roberto, Reina.
   Little propeller of our names
   delivering the cargo of blood

to the streets of Holyoke,
Brooklyn, New London,
Ojai, where the teacher says,
"Say your name?" sweetly,
& the beautiful propeller
working between
the two fields of my a's
& the teacher saying, "Oh!
You mean, 'Are-Raw-Sell-Lease.'"
Or "Robe-Bert-Toe"
or "Marred-Guh-Reetuh, like
the drink!" & the "r"
sounding like a balloon
deflating in the room, sad
& sagging. I am hurt.
It is as if I handed her
all my familiar trees & flowers,
every drawing of the family map
& boats & airplanes & cuatros
& coquis, & she used her English
to make an axe & tried to chop
them down. But, "r," little propeller
of my name, small & beautiful monster
changing shapes, you win. You fly
around the room, little bee, upsetting
the teacher & making all of Class-310A laugh,
you fly over the yard, in our mouths,
as our bodies make airplanes over the grass,
you, little propeller, are taking over the city,
you are the sound of cars racing, the sound
of bicycle spokes fitted with playing cards
to make it sound like we are going fast,
this is our ode to you, little "r," little
machine of our names, simple
as a heart, just working, always,
there when we go to the grocery,
there in the songs
we sing in our sleep.

RACHEL ELIZA GRIFFITHS

Seeing the Body

She died & I—
In the spring of her blood. I remember
my mother's first injury. The surprise of unborn
petals curling light, red, around her wrist.
Some fruit she cut, some onion, some
body with skin & seeds. She fed me.
She listened & I—
She held We & I—
She kept speaking with those flowers
falling from her blood, taking her
across the sky to death. I remember
her voice like a horn I never want
to pull out of my heart. In the next life,
which is here & here, I gather every thing
that ever sang my mother's blues.
She burned & I—
She talked back hard at god.
O, she danced, unbroken, too.
Bale of grief on my back, opening
into something black I wear. A life of flesh
like a petal or fruit or burning.
I've carried everything & I'm tired.
She survived & I—
(But she did not live.)
She told me Nothing & I—
She was waiting the entire time.
How does the elegy believe me?
Together, we crossed the sky.
There was a gate & we walked through
the world like that.
She wrote We & I—
She was last seen & I—
Eyes, without life, opened eternity.
When the air in her

stopped & I—
She was last seen dying. She was too silent
for the first time in her life. The spring
of my mother's blood hot & god the dark
dark beyond the closed door
that won't move again.

Duriel E. Harris

Black Mary Integrates the School House

ANIMATO.

VOCAL

Ma - ry had a lit - tle lamb, with fleece as black as su - llied snow.

And every-where that Ma - ry went, she paraded her lamb for show.

She showed it in the yard one day which was a - gainst the rule.

She let the chil-dren ti - ckle, tease, and tap her lamb at school.

And so the tea-cher turned it out, but still it ti - red not;

799

ANIMATO.

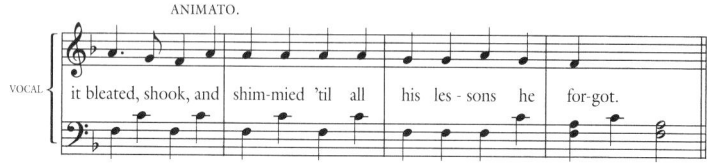

VOCAL

it bleated, shook, and | shim-mied 'til all | his les - sons he | for-got.

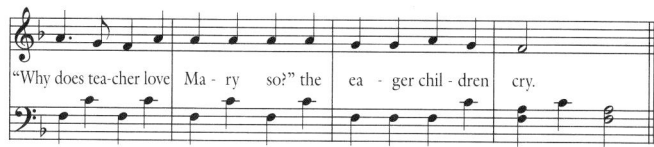

"Why does tea-cher love | Ma - ry so?" the | ea - ger chil - dren | cry.

"Why, Mary's made for | love, you know," the | tea - cher did re | - ply.

TERRANCE HAYES

Touch

We made our own laws.
I want to be a Hawk,
A Dolphin, a Lion, we'd say

In stores where team logos hung
Like animal skins.

By moonlight,
We chased each other
Around the big field

Beneath branches sagging
As if their leaves were full of blood.

We didn't notice when policemen
Came lighting tree bark
& our skin with flashlights.

They saw our game
For what it was:

Fingers clutching torso,
Shoulder, wrist—a brawl.
Some of the boys escaped,

It's true, we could have been mistaken
For animals in the dark,
But of all our possible crimes,
Blackness was the first
So they tackled me,

And read me my rights without saying:
You Down or Dead Ball.
We had a language

They did not use, a name
For collision. We called it Touch.

Satchmo Returns to New Orleans

You are the greasy Daddy of Jazz, Peasy Daddy.
You are the brassy Mother of Jazz, the bellowing bastard of
    jazz.

Sweet-trumpeting strumpet of jazz, Easy Daddy;
A hankie full of tools and zooting, Mister Sadmo;

And I shall never blame America for not loving and then
    loving you;
Nor shall I blame the Mississippi, nor the dens of Chicago,

Nor your eight-mile storyville grin, nor your Zulu blackface,
Mister Black Face. I shall not blame the "Cake Walk Blues"

Nor the "Saint Louis Blues," St Louis. I shall not blame
The "Moonlight Blues," nor the "Starlight Blues," nor the
    "Midnight Blues,"

Nor "Mack the Knife," nor the switchblade in your pocket,
Nor the pale moon shining on the fields below,

Mr. Press-Me-to-Your-Heart Sweet-Louisiana: I've got no
    reason
To be blue. Nor shall I blame the heebie-jeebies

Of the West Coast Negro, nor shall I blame the wide eye
Of the banjo, nor shall I blame the band's spit-shined

"When the Saints Go Marching In," played as if it wasn't at
    first
A funeral song, and finished somewhere near closing time

With "La Vie en Rose," your heart so broken again
You doze on the cab ride home and dream the notes

To "West End Blues," which is what an American city sounds
  like
At 45 mph after dark when your eyes are closed.

The Golden Shovel

after Gwendolyn Brooks

I. 1981

When I am so small Da's sock covers my arm, we
cruise at twilight until we find the place the real

men lean, bloodshot and translucent with cool.
His smile is a gold-plated incantation as we

drift by women on bar stools, with nothing left
in them but approachlessness. This is a school

I do not know yet. But the cue sticks mean we
are rubbed by light, smooth as wood, the lurk

of smoke thinned to song. We won't be out late.
Standing in the middle of the street last night we

watched the moonlit lawns and a neighbor strike
his son in the face. A shadow knocked straight

Da promised to leave me everything: the shovel we
used to bury the dog, the words he loved to sing

his rusted pistol, his squeaky Bible, his sin.
The boy's sneakers were light on the road. We

watched him run to us looking wounded and thin.
He'd been caught lying or drinking his father's gin.

He'd been defending his ma, trying to be a man. We
stood in the road, and my father talked about jazz,

how sometimes a tune is born of outrage. By June
the boy would be locked upstate. That night we

got down on our knees in my room. *If I should die
before I wake*. Da said to me, *it will be too soon*.

II. 1991

Into the tented city we go, we-
akened by the fire's ethereal

afterglow. Born lost and cool-
er than heartache. What we

know is what we know. The left
hand severed and school-

ed by cleverness. A plate of we-
ekdays cooking. The hour lurk-

ing in the afterglow. A late-
night chant. Into the city we

go. Close your eyes and strike
a blow. Light can be straight-

ened by its shadow. What we
break is what we hold. A sing-

ular blue note. An outcry sin-
ged exiting the throat. We

push until we thin, thin-
king we won't creep back again.

While God licks his kin, we
sing until our blood is jazz,

we swing from June to June.
We sweat to keep from we-

eping. Groomed on a die-
t of hunger, we end too soon.

Carp Poem

After I have parked below the spray paint caked in the granite
grooves of the Frederick Douglass Middle School sign,

where men-size children loiter like shadows draped in outsize
denim, jerseys, braids, and boots that mean I am no longer
        young;

after I have made my way to the New Orleans Parish Jail
        down the block,
where the black prison guard wearing the same weariness

my prison guard father wears buzzes me in, I follow his pistol
        and shield
along each corridor trying not to look at the black men

boxed and bunked around me until I reach the tiny
        classroom
where two dozen black boys are dressed in jumpsuits orange
        as the carp

I saw in a pond once in Japan, so many fat, snaggletoothed
        fish
ganged in and lurching for food that a lightweight tourist
        could have crossed

the water on their backs so long as he had tiny rice balls or
    bread
to drop into the mouths below his footsteps, which I'm
    thinking

is how Jesus must have walked on the lake that day, the
    crackers and crumbs
falling from the folds of his robe, and how maybe it was the
    one fish

so hungry it leaped up his sleeve that he later miraculously
    changed
into a narrow loaf of bread, something that could stick to a
    believer's ribs,

and don't get me wrong, I'm a believer too, in the power of
    food at least,
having seen a footbridge of carp packed gill to gill, packed
    tighter

than a room of boy prisoners waiting to talk poetry with a
    young black poet,
packed so close they'd have eaten each other had there been
    nothing
else to eat.

MAJOR JACKSON

How to Listen

I am going to cock my head tonight like a dog
in front of McGlinchy's Tavern on Locust;
I am going to stand beside the man who works all day
combing
his thatch of gray hair corkscrewed in every direction.
I am going to pay attention to our lives
unraveling between the forks of his fine-tooth comb.
For once, we won't talk about the end of the world
or Vietnam or his exquisite paper shoes.
For once, I am going to ignore the profanity and
the dancing and the jukebox so I can hear his head crackle
beneath the sky's stretch of faint stars.

Euphoria

Late winter, sky darkening after school,
& groceries bought from Shop-Mart,
My mother leaves me parked on Diamond
To guard her Benz, her keys half-turned
So I can listen to the Quiet Storm
While she smokes a few white pebbles
At the house crumbling across the street.

I clamber to the steering wheel,
Undo my school tie, just as Luther Vandross
Starts in on that one word tune, "Creepin'."
The dashboard's panel of neon glows,
And a girl my age, maybe sixteen or so,
In a black miniskirt, her hair crimped
With glitter, squats down to pane glass,

And asks, *A date, baby? For five?*
Outside, street light washes the avenue
A cheap orange: garbage swirling
A vacant lot; a crew of boys slap-boxing
On the corner, throwing back large swills
Of malt; even the sidewalk teeming with addicts,
Their eyes spread thin as egg whites.

She crams the crushed bill down
Her stockings, cradles & slides her palm
In rhythm to my hips' thrashing,
In rhythm to Luther's voice, which flutters
Around that word I now mistake for "Weep"
As sirens blast the neighborhood &
My own incomprehensible joy to silence.

Out of the house my mother steps,
Returned from the ride of her life,
Studies pavement cracks for half-empty vials,
Then looks back at bricked-over windows
As though what else mattered—
A family, a dinner, a car, nothing
But this happiness so hard to come by.

Ferguson

Once there was a boy who thought it a noble idea to lie down
in the middle of the street and sleep. For four hours, no one
bothered him, but let him lie on the road as though he were an
enchantment. This became newsworthy and soon helicopters
hovered above, hosing his curled torso and thick legs in spot-
lights televised the world over. Foreign correspondents focused
on the neighborhood and its relative poverty as recognized by
the plethora of low-hanging jeans worn by shirtless men and
loud music issuing from passing cars, which had the effect of
drowning out everyone's already bottled-up thoughts about
the boy sleeping in the middle of the street; others jumped
in front of cameras seizing an opportunity to be seen by their

relatives on the other side of town because they had run out of minutes on prepaid cellphones.

The roadkill in the neighborhood, and some on that very block, rodents, cats, and possums, feeling equal amounts of jealousy and futility, each began to rise and return to their den holes, cursing the boy sleeping in the street beneath their breaths for his virtuosic performance of stillness and tribulation in the city. The drug-addicted men and women leaning into doorways like art installations were used to being ignored, but they, too, felt affronted by the boy sleeping in the street and folded their cardboard homes.

For the first hour, he practiced not breathing. For ten seconds, he would hold his breath. And then, he practiced longer sets of minutes during the next three hours until he was able to stretch out his non-breathing for whole hunks at a time. When his breathing returned, it was so faint, his chest and shoulders barely moved; infinitesimal amounts of life poured out of him, but no one noticed. The police cordoned off his body, and after some time, declared him dead because they had only seen black men lying prone on the street as corpses, but never as sleeping humans.

The whole world, eager and hungry for a Lazarus moment, watched and waited to see when he would awaken and rise to his feet, especially his neighbors with minutes remaining on cellphones who filmed and animatedly discoursed behind yellow tape the ecstasies and muted sorrows of watching a boy sleep in the middle of the street.

HONORÉE FANNONE JEFFERS

The Gospel of Barbecue

for Alvester James

Long after it was
necessary, Uncle
Vess ate the leavings
off the hog, doused
them with vinegar sauce.
He ate chewy abominations.
Then came high pressure.
Then came the little pills.
Then came the doctor
who stole Vess's second
sight, the predication
of pig's blood every
fourth Sunday.
Then came the stillness
of barn earth, no more
trembling at his step.
Then came the end
of the rib, but before
his eyes clouded,
Uncle Vess wrote
down the gospel
of barbecue.

Chapter one:
Somebody got to die
with something at some
time or another.

Chapter two:
Don't ever trust
white folk to cook

your meat until
it's done to the bone.

Chapter three:
December is the best
time for hog killing.
The meat won't
spoil as quick.
Screams and blood
freeze over before
they hit the air.

Chapter four, Verse one:
Great Grandma Mandy
used to say food
you was whipped
for tasted the best.

Chapter four, Verse two:
Old Master knew to lock
the ham bacon chops
away quick or the slaves
would rob him blind.
He knew a padlock
to the smokehouse
was best to prevent
stealing, but even the
sorriest of slaves would
risk a beating for a full
belly. So Christmas time
he give his nasty
leftovers to the well
behaved. The head ears
snout tail fatback
chitlins feet ribs balls.
He thought gratitude
made a good seasoning.

Chapter five:
Unclean means dirty

means filthy means
underwear worn too
long in summertime heat.
Perfectly good food
can't be no sin.
Maybe the little
bit of meat on ribs
makes for lean eating.
Maybe the pink flesh
is tasteless until you add
onions garlic black
pepper tomatoes
soured apple cider
but survival ain't never been
no crime against nature
or Maker. See, stay alive
in the meantime, laugh
a little harder. Go on
and gnaw that bone clean.

TYEHIMBA JESS

Charity on Blind Tom

They say Tom takes darkness and makes it moan.
I *was* his darkness. And Lawd, did I moan
when he came out to light. And moaned some more
when his eyes wouldn't catch sight. Don't
no plantation need no stumble-blind slave—
I hid him much as I could, but no way
could I keep his body's 'fliction away
from Master Epps. Blind, slow niggas don't pay
nothin' on auction block or in the field.
More trouble than they worth—better off dead,
said most white folk. I tell you—I had to kneel
deep in the dirt for that music in his head—
for General Bethune to buy us like gifts—
I had no idea Tom would make him rich.

General Bethune on Blind Tom

I had no idea Tom would make me rich.
Blind and crazed, like a blessed-up idiot,
he'd sing bluebird songs in perfect pitch,
then bash his head against the wooden box
crib whenever his mother went to chores
in the field. He'd hop around on one leg,
bent over like a giant, pecking bird for
hours, then rattle out tunes on tin cups. I let
him stay out of compassion. Then, one day,
he heard my daughter playing piano—
Haydn, I believe. It was like a weight
fell upon him—a labor to make him whole.
My charity finally got its reward.
Who am I to deny this gift to the world?

Blind Boone's Vision

When I got old enough
I asked my mother,
to her surprise,
to tell me what she did
with my eyes. She balked
and stalled, sounding
unsure for the first time
I could remember.
It was the tender way
she held my face
and kissed where tears
should have rolled
that told me I'd asked
of her the almost impossible—
to recount my blinding
tale, to tell what became
of the rest of me.
She took me by the hand
and led me to a small
sapling that stood not
much taller than me.
I could smell the green
marrow of its promise
reaching free of the soil
like a song from Earth's
royal, dirty mouth.
Then Mother told me
how she, newly freed,
had prayed like a slave
through the night when
the surgeon took my eyes
to save my fevered life,
then got off her knees
come morning to take
the severed parts of me
for burial—right there
beneath that small tree.

They fed the roots,
climbed through its leaves
to soak in sunlight . . .
and so, she told me,
I *can* see.

When the wind rustles
up and cools me down,
when the earth shakes
with footsteps and when
the sound of birdcalls
stirs forests like the black
and white bustling
'neath my fingertips,
I am of the light and shade
of my tree. Now,
ask me how tall
that tree of mine
has grown to be
after all this time—
it touches a place
between heaven and here.
And I shudder when I hear
the earth's wind
in my bones
through the bones
of that boxed-up
swarm of wood,
bird and bee:
I let it loose . . .
and beyond
me.

Minnehaha

Edmonia Lewis, Marble, 1868

What part of me is mine that was
not mined from the mind of poets,
artists rewriting the past blow
by blow till it's pulverized past
the barely recognizable?
I was born when I was written,
then hammered out of a mountain.
I was shattered and then broken,
then sharpened to the human. I'm
carved in marble that never dies,
hardly crumbles; a stubborn queen
who'll die only with those people
who crave a ruling monarchy
of fictions—tales my sculptor plied
to strike against their pale armies
of indignities. History
is their favorite lie. I found
my face buried in its would-be
pages, then excavated by
a native who fled the country.
Such was her misery at home
in the land where my legend roams
the canonized American
poetry. I'm her stone arrow,
her refusal to bow. I wear
her chisel-sharp aim as my crown.

A. VAN JORDAN

Jesse Owens, 1963

Football Hall of Fame Induction Ceremony
Canton, Ohio

He had aged and looked
Like a man at the end of a long

Race. And when I got close
To him, close enough to taste

His breath, his breath smelled
Like bourbon and I recoiled

From the picture in my mind
Of him sitting at the end

Of a bar, at the half
Light of his life.

I could not reach out to ask
For an autograph, but

I reached out to take his hand,
Just another baton exchange

Of the truths of life
As when you're old enough

To know what it smells like,
And you get scared

Because it smells familiar,
And you begin to tremble,

Seeing the runner
Before you, extending his hand,

Still panting.

Rope

As if two girls were starting a fire
On all sides of my daughter,
She is set ablaze: the girls swing
Two clotheslines between them
As if they were goddesses
Holding two country roads
Leading to each other; neighbors
Surround her syncopated dance
As her seizure of heat begins
To flicker on the moonlit sidewalk—
Now, the ropes are white hot—
Her hair ignites in the upswing; her barrettes,
Like petrified butterflies, click on the off beat;
Her knees pump like she's walking on red coals;
Her arms flail as if she's calling the rain
To put her out; she jumps, she flirts
With the flame: she jumps backwards
And then turns forward,
Rocking in and out of the light,
Her hands testify around her head
Or pose on yet-to-be hips, till
Her fire snuffs out as a wind blows cold,
A car with flashing lights
Slows past, and the braids of our summer night
Surrender to gravity.

ALLISON JOSEPH

Thirty Lines About the Fro

The fro is homage, shrubbery, and revolt all at once.
The fro and pick have a co-dependent relationship, so
many strands, snags, such snap and sizzle between
the two. The fro wants to sleep on a silk pillowcase,
abhorring the historical atrocity of cotton.
The fro guffaws at relaxers—how could any other style
claim relaxation when the fro has a gangsta lean,
diamond-in-the-back, sunroof-top kinda attitude,
growing slowly from scalp into sky, launching pad
for brilliance and bravery, for ideas uncontained by
barbershops and their maniacal clippers, monotony
of the fade and buzzcut. The fro has much respect
for dreads, but won't go through life that twisted,
that coiled. Still, much love lives between
the two: secret handshakes, funk-bottomed struts.
The fro doesn't hate you because you're beautiful.
Or ugly. Or out-of-work or working for the Man.
Because who knows who the Man is anymore?
Is the President the Man? He used to have a fro
the size of Toledo, but now it's trimmed down
to respectability, more gray sneaking in each day,
and you've got to wonder if he misses his pick,
for he must have had one of those black power ones
with a fist on the end. After all, the fro is a fist,
all curled power, rebellious shake, impervious
and improper. Water does not scare the fro,
because water cannot change that which is
immutable—that soul-sonic force, that sly
stone-tastic, natural mystic, roots-and-rhythm
crown for the ages, blessed by God and gratitude.

My Father's Kites

were crude assemblages of paper sacks and twine,
amalgams of pilfered string and whittled sticks,
twigs pulled straight from his garden, dry patch

of stony land before our house only he
could tend into beauty, thorny roses goaded
into color. How did he make those makeshift

diamonds rise, grab ahold of the wind to sail
into sky like nothing in our neighborhood
of dented cars and stolid brick houses could?

It wasn't through faith or belief in otherworldly
grace, but rather a metaphor from moving
on a street where cars rusted up on blocks,

monstrously immobile, and planes, bound
for that world we could not see, roared
above our heads, our houses pawns

in a bigger flight path. How tricky the launch
into air, the wait for the right eddy to lift
our homemade contraptions into the sullen

blue sky above us, our eyes stinging
with the glut of the sun. And the sad tangle
after flight, collapse of grocery bags

and broken branches, snaggle of string
I still cannot unfurl. Father, you left me
with this unsated need to find the most

delicately useful of breezes, to send
myself into the untenable, balance my weight
as if on paper wings, a flutter then fall,

a stutter back to earth, an elastic sense
of being and becoming forged in our front
yard, your hand over mine over balled string.

DOUGLAS KEARNEY

Drop It Like It's Hottentot Venus.

drop it like it's hottentot venus.

dip   rump   other
trip   keister   her spot tinted skin
slip   end up on tv.   dirt   rind
sink   video   soiled   husk
teeterin' til tits up. hd   rotten   hidin' pole.
drunken   on   revoltin' ho
tilted   onto dv imprison in shot. rod
soused   nut   penis
tore up the donk. hip to under. spoo tool
              lesser   seep
      tush   vile   I pour it on. I hit it. *provoked* to
      hind   spit   poke   pushed to
look. nude heinie   shit up slot. strike pressed to
peek   spoil   slit   stroke driven to
peer   repulse   pit   *she* lust prod   onus *hers*
see so rotund in the stink. hole
              into
  distort   inside   kitten to split.
  revise   enter the pink. rip
edit the pose. turn   poon   sunder
          pivot tenders   shred
hooker do sit n spin tissue   rive
      she tripe loined. rend
      nothin'   rent it out ho.
      nil   pro
    slop in skirt.   prostitute
                  she isn't loved
                    no
                    nope
                    not
                    never.

JOHN KEENE

Language, Knowledge, a Teeming River of Implications

A small yet insubordinate squadron of impressions had laid siege to his consciousness since infancy. Everything reposed beneath a glaze of dew, which was each morning's way of announcing its arrival. The slow greening of the daylight through the shutter slats, or evening, when the gangway grew sullen with darkness. Chances are. Shadows appeared to creep across the floor, until you focused to discover them ants. Photographs will substitute for a fully-sketched description. Waterbugs and spiders were really more common, rappelling down the tiles like mountaineers. In the jar, the aphids asphyxiated. With a view to pleasing the adults, you told no one. Moreover he could claim two godfathers, to everyone's amusement, of whom one had served quite honorably in Vietnam. The violent tenor of the recollections, perhaps resulting from a delayed effect, far exceeded what everyone had expected. Your tongue, but a bat in its cavern of reassurance, would take flight when you least expected it. Montgomery, My Lai. Many of the children, except those whose parents were considered "strivers," would walk to the neighborhood school. They first launched his punt at a Montessori Academy, which was thought to enhance a youngster's chances in life. There we could play with Legos of innumerable colors, a pint-sized oven that actually baked, and the other kids, including Patty, who soon became enamored of the red-haired boy. This was before one gained a sense of the "body" and could picture oneself "in affliction." Double talk. Eventually they took turns reading the "Negro" poets from those yellow-papered books whose covers had long ago disappeared. Usually we would sit and talk, or watch the TV set, or on warmer evenings walk several blocks with the dogs or alone for a "breath of fresh night air." Nice work, if you can get it, and you might get it if you lie. At the corner store, nickel candy and a sody pop, but only if you had been sterling.

There never was, consequently, any incentive to steal, since this course of action had not been fostered alongside some greater moral lassitude. Pilfer, for a pal. Occasionally we heard shooting, but most often it was shouting, which a battle of fists or blades would readily resolve. Our ears hammer impressions into audible jewels. Further down the boulevard sat the unimposing branch library, further still the artist's studio. His wife, an artist in her own right, had sculpted the papier-mâché painting of Kali, which hung for years like a totem above the sofas. Chain of Rocks. You drew not only numerous studies of people, but a series of scenes to accompany them, yet they still denied that a child was capable of such work, convinced instead that you had traced or forged. Treemonisha. Just as well, heedlessness or laughter, a sure forgetting. The subsequent art teacher showed a mastery of the art of drawing lips and eyes, and thus encouraged us all to indulge in more identifiably "African" forms. Use a pen or pencil and answer all questions. A simpler example: a V with a circle on top, or a colorless ice-cream cone. Eugene Field House. Few things compared to culling lightning bugs live, since your mason jar theater became their nightstage. Roaches formed a different category altogether, like the stains that created a rusty crust upon the motel sheets, or that car that leapt the curb to cut the corner. "Em, eye, crookaletta, crookaletta, eye, crookaletta, crookaletta, eye, humpback, humpback, eye," and thus one could always avoid utter embarrassment in any blackboard bee. The result, a fathoming beneath the flourish of so many notes, a veritable exigesis. Music is the obvious analogue, that inimitable California poet tells us, which, in the context of the life that you have lived so far, is as much truth as trope. Yes and no. Yet, whenever the ice-cream truck would come by, the first impulse was to run to the window and perform the dance of seven wails. Who would not relent, before such shameless displays of talent. These episodes ceased, however temporarily, in the presence of "company," and at the family reunions, when all small ones were expected to be on their "absolute best behavior." Eventually the blight of crime and drugs would subsume the entire area, forcing a capitulation to the prerogatives of personal safety. And so, as his cousin said

more eloquently than the mayor and the experts, when officials
speak of "Urban Renewal," it's the Black folks that got to go.

Texts, Context, a Fear of Contamination

Education, they counseled us, is the one, true key, yet the
school was known less for its floors of tidy classrooms than
for its gym with collapsible bleachers and that polished, hard-
wood floor. Promise-harness. The committee, comprising the
clergy and the most prominent lay members, rechristened the
complex after the first Black Catholic bishop, which provided
even the most taciturn with an engaging topic of discussion.
Simply naming, while powerful, never proves enough. He was
usually charily chosen for the kickball teams, or last for any
sport requiring aggression. A palpable terror, a shortness of
breath. Consolation lay in the reading contests and the sketch-
ing assignments, when we could excel far beyond the expecta-
tions of both teachers and friends. My teeth cast a gleaming net
for you, a white and wordless reply. Cardinal Ritter. "Poetry"
served then as the recitative of bible-men and the pimp who
stayed on the corner, or the huckster who with brio sold them a
faulty vacuum cleaner. In those days we could recall the names
and life stories of the major Black inventors almost as read-
ily as our multiplication tables, though in truth a disjuncture
persisted between their paradigms and how we perceived them,
which neither teachers nor other adults sought to bridge. No
one really slept at naptime. After the wedding, marked by a
holy sacrament which he believed he understood, he and the
other children brought Mrs. Orange her namesake fruit. In
fourth grade, following a premise that defied "equality," the
classes cleaved into two distinct and ability-based homerooms,
which garnered for the smaller, brighter class a rancor it little
deserved. "Freedom School." Thus that year proceeded by way
of experimental groupings and methods, which sound noth-
ing short of radical in the context of education today. Many
the nuns who scored the names of saintly men in their heads
until each was resurrected by reflex, and who, in daily sweeps
past their desks, left a near-visible trail of camphor. With your

hair cut so short, the older boys renamed you "Shine," rubbing your head as though it were their own personal talisman. "Sensitive." Yet who did not desire to follow their model, for they were more real than his idols. What little boys do. Behavior enough to gain us mention in the newspaper, where he spoke of his desire to be popular, or in the parlance of those days, the "Caped Crusader." Ivanhoe, Pip, and Peter Pan led the list of childhood favorites, though it was hard to identify with that bespectacled, British "John." His father would not hesitate to mine him for that single ore of truth, since this, he had convinced himself, was a father's chief occupation. If you therefore were one who regularly lied, then your recollections might consist of the sum total of your childhood fictions. He waited but the invitations never materialized, so he learned to create small diversions for himself. A cleansing thus ensued, an art of remembering developed, a renewal undeniably the result. "Straight-A, Straight-A, nothing but a sissyboy who's scared to play," they screamed burning tracks across the playground, their faces brown, blazing globes of glee, as he crumpled near the swingset like a raveling, forgotten husk-doll. Repression's effects assume manifold forms. One option proposed seriously was that of skipping a grade, though they feared that might warp her emotional development. In other words, neither parent had expected such a fragile character, though they bore the verdict better once they had bought it. Some children are badly suited to this world, though their elders rarely gather this fact until the dawn of the teen years, when the complement of options has shrunk to zero. Baldwins reclined between a Jong, several Cozzenses, and two Morrisons, but Michener's opera had long held sway of the bookshelf. Neither Bolivia nor Paraguay has an ocean port, you learned from encyclopedias at the great-aunt's house. A few of them so old that they crumbled between the fingers, others crinkled with that odor of never having been fully opened. The genius lay in the execution, or at least in how she kept the deception from becoming apparent. Ebony and Black Enterprise graced the marble coffee table, though Jet garnered everyone's initial review. Our generation possesses only a cursory sense of the world that our ancestors braved, though the burdens of history bear unmovably upon us. Homer G. Phillips. Rollerskating in the summer around

Steinberg Rink, or else in one of many indoor halls, and when he was old enough to wield a racket, tennis in O'Fallon Park. Sugarloaf Mound. One assessment: the chill cast the courts in a crepuscular light. Stan, who coached the older, lither players, sported a thick, beguiling mustache, while coiled hairs spilled from the V-neck of his jersey, leaving us with a sensation that we were yet unable to name. Ruby, my dear. "Swing, baby, lemme hear that ball sing and dance, serve, but not so much racket string, you got it, now, whoa, don't fling it." By perfecting a strategy, we learned gradually, we could organize and master almost any game, a lesson as applicable and valuable outside the court as on it.

DANIELLE LEGROS GEORGES

Hostage

Almond leaves the size of hands sweep the terrace
skirting the almonds felled by last night's storm.

A slick of water and crazy ants on a toppled fir sprig
decide to be an island and small sea.

Thunder still rumbles in the sound of trucks
pitching down the mountain's sides.

This morning I am held hostage by bougainvillea
which watch me ease into my skin.

Here I am betrayed only by the uncovered watch
band of my pale and diasporic self.

Time slows to make me primordial. *Kenèps*
make me five and confused as to why

the fruit does not yield its sweetness easily.
My mother's hand at my hand's age now draws

the fruit's flesh from its coarse covering. I am
handed a perfumed ball of sugar and destroyed

in a move a month later. Returned and now
a cousin once removed and former playmate

visits with her daughters. They are strangers
to me. Estelle, *la petite*, with adult teeth

explains, "Auntie's sad because she cannot chew
our words." I bite one to prove something to her.

ROBIN COSTE LEWIS

Plantation

And then one morning we woke up
embracing on the bare floor of a large cage.

To keep you happy, I decorated the bars.
Because you had never been hungry, I knew

I could tell you the black side
of my family owned slaves.

I realize this is perhaps
the one reason why I love you,

because I told you this
and you—still—wanted to kiss

me. We laughed when I said *plantation*,
fell into our chairs when I said *cane.*

There were fingers on the floor
and the split bodies of women

who'd been torn apart by horses
during the Inquisition.

You'd said, *Well I'll be damned!*
Every now and then you'd change

from a prancing black buck
into a small high yellow girl: pigtailed,

patent leather, eyes spinning gossamer, begging
for egg salad and banana pudding.

Or just as quickly you'd become
the girl's mother, pulling

yourself away from yourself.
Because my whole head was covered

with a heaving beehive, you thought
I didn't notice. I noticed. I cried honey.

And then you were fourteen, and you had grown
a glorious steel cock under your skirt. To brag

you rubbed yourself against me. Then your tongue
was inside my mouth, and I wanted to say

Please ask me first, but it was your
tongue, so who cared suddenly

about your poor manners?
We had books and a waterfall

was falling in the corner.
I didn't tell you I couldn't

remember what that thing was
you said to me once, that tender thing

you'd said I should never forget.
The moment you said it, I forgot it.

I wondered if you thought we were lost.
We weren't lost. We were *loss*.

And meanwhile, all I could think about
were the innumerable ways I would've loved

to have eaten you, how being
devoured can make one cry. And I hoped

you liked the fresh, pleasant taste
of juiced cane. You pulled

my pubic bone toward you. I didn't
say, *It's still broken;* I didn't tell

you, *There's still this crack.* It was sore,
but I stayed silent because you were smiling.

You said, *The bars look pretty, Baby,*
then rubbed your hind legs up against me.

from *Voyage of the Sable Venus*

PROLOGUE:

What follows is a narrative poem comprised solely and entirely
of the titles, catalog entries, or exhibit descriptions of Western
art objects in which a black female figure is present, dating
from 38,000 BCE to the present.

The formal rules I set for myself were simple:

1. No title could be broken or changed in any way. While
the grammar is completely modified—I erased all periods,
commas, semicolons—each title was left as published, and
was not syntactically annotated, edited, or fragmented.

2. "Art" included paintings, sculpture, installations, pho-
tography, lithographs, engravings, any work on paper, et
cetera—all those traditional mediums now recognized
by the Western art-historical canon. However, because
black female figures were also used in ways I could never
have anticipated, I was forced to expand that definition to
include other material and visual objects, such as combs,
spoons, buckles, pans, knives, table legs.

3. At some point, I realized that museums and libraries (in what I imagine must have been either a hard-won gesture of goodwill, or in order not to appear irrelevant) had removed many nineteenth-century historically specific markers—such as *slave, colored,* and *Negro*—from their titles or archives, and replaced these words instead with the sanitized, but perhaps equally vapid, *African-American.* In order to replace this historical erasure of slavery (however well intended), I re-erased the postmodern *African-American,* then changed those titles back. That is, I re-corrected the corrected horror in order to allow that original horror to stand. My intent was to explore and record not only the history of human thought, but also how normative and complicit artists, curators, and art institutions have been in participating in—if not creating—this history.

4. As an homage, I decided to include titles of art *by* black women curators and artists, whether the art included a black female figure or not. Most of this work was created over the last century, with its deepest saturation occurring since the Cold War. I also included work by black queer artists, regardless of gender, because this body of work has made consistently some of the richest, most elegant, least pretentious contributions to Western art interrogations of gender and race.

5. In a few instances, it was more fruitful to include a museum's descriptive titles of the art rather than the titles themselves. This was especially true for the colonial period.

6. Sometimes I chose to include female figures I believed the Western art world simply had not realized were black women passing for white.

7. Finally, with one exception, no title was repeated.

*The Metropolitan Museum of Art
Employees' Association Minstrel Show and Dance
will be held at the American Woman's Association
361 West 57th Street, Saturday evening,
October 17, 1936*

*I am anxious to buy a small healthy negro girl—
ten or twelve years old, and would like to know
if you can let me have one ...*
—MRS. B. L. BLANKENSHIP

THE SHIP'S INVENTORY:

Four-Breasted Vessel, Three Women
in Front of a Steamy Pit, Two-Faced
Head Fish Trying on Earrings, Unidentified.

Young Woman with Shawl
and Painted Backdrop, Pearl
of the Forest, Two Girls

with Braids People
on a Ship with Some Dancing
Girls. Our Lady of Mercy, Blue.

Nude Iconologia Girl
with Red Flower Sisters
of the Boa Woman Flying a Butterfly.

Kite	Empty
Chair	Pocket
Book	Girl

in Red Dress with Cats and Dog's Devil.
House Door of No Return. Head-of-a-Girl-
In-the-Bedroom in the kitchen.

Contemplation Dark-Girl Girl.
In the Window Negress with
Flower Sleeping Woman

(Negress with Flower Head
of a Woman-Nude in a Land
scape)—Libyan Sybil: Coloured, Nude-High

Yellow Negro Woman
and Two Children—The Flight
of the Octoroon: the Four Quarters of

the World, Holding
a Celestial Sphere.

CATALOG I: ANCIENT GREECE & ANCIENT ROME

> *Here is your name*
> *said the woman*
> *and vanished in the corridor*
> —MAHMOUD DARWISH

I.

Statuette of a Woman Reduced
to the Shape of a Flat Paddle

Statuette of a Black Slave Girl
Right Half of Body and Head Missing

Head of a Young Black Woman Fragment
from a Statuette of a Black Dancing Girl

Reserve Head of an African Princess
Statuette of a Concubine

Full Length Figure of a Standing
Black Woman Wearing Earrings

Statuette Once Supported an Unguent Vase
Vase with Neck in the Form of a Head

of a Black Statuette of a Female
Figure with Negroid Features

Figure's Left Arm Missing Head
of a Female Full-length Figure

of a Nubian Woman
the Arms Missing

Bust of a Draped Female Facing Forward
One Breast Exposed   Black

Adolescent Female with Long Curls and Bare
Breasts Wearing a Voluminous Crown

Partially Broken Young Black Girl
Presenting a Stemmed Bowl

Supported
by a Monkey

    :

Standing Female Reliquary Figure
with Crested Coiffure and Hands

Clasped in Front of Torso, Holding
a Staff Surmounted by a Human Head

Figure Has Prominent
Vagina Bended

Knees and Oversized Head
with Half-Open Eyes

and Semicircle Mouth
That Juts Out

from the Face Some
Fine Scarification

on Chest and Belly
Dark Brown Almost Black

Patina with Oil Oozing
in Several Places

Numerous Cracks
on Back of Head and Hole

on the Coiffure
One Nipple Appears

to Be Shaved Off
or Damaged Black Woman

Standing on Tiptoe
on One End of a Seesaw

While a Caricatured Figure Jumps
on the Other

End

———————

:   ELEMENT OF FURNITURE DECORATION

[Two Nubian Prisoners Bound
to a Post] Protome [Probably

the Handle of a Whip
or Other Implement] Oil Flask Back

View Head of an African Prisoner
Statue of Prisoner Kneeling Arms

Bound at the Elbows
Left Arm Missing

Bust of a Nubian Prisoner
with Fragmentary Arms

Bound Behind Funerary Mask
of a Negro with Inlaid Glass Eyes

and Traces of Incrustations
Present in the Mouth

Censer in the Form of a Nude Negro
Dwarf Standing with His Hands

at His Sides upon an Ornate Tripod
and Supporting on His Head

a Small Cup
in the Shape

of a Lotus
Flower

II.

water jar

bowl

ointment spoon

                    in the form of swimming
                    black girl

mirror
with handle

                    in the form of a carved standing
                    black girl

handle
of a sistrum

          a Bes and an Isia dancing
          back-to-back

two nails

          with Negro heads in relief

head

          of a Negro which may have adorned

a pin

          mounted in a

ring

bezel

bowl

          decorated with three heads
          in relief

          separated by flat veined leaves
          female puppet with

mortar and pestle
necklace

          with two heads
          of black women forming

a clasp
perfume vase

                              head of an adolescent

aryballos

                              juxtaposing two heads of Negro
                              cast from the same mold

mirror
with handle

                              in the form of a young Nubian
                              female standing

lamp

                              in the form of

the head

                              of a black perhaps

incense
shovel

                              with a Negro head attached

to handle
a girl

                              with long corkscrew curls
                              round face wide
                              flat nose and mouth

open

        and jutting forward
        to form

a spout

inkwell

        in the form of a crouching
        Negro Negro
        seated writing on

a scroll

III. THE GREAT HUNT: TORMENT OF THE DAMNED

Heraldic Lion Holding
Between His Paws the Head

of a Kneeling Black Captive
Statuette of a Negro Captive Kneeling

Hands Bound Behind Back
Negro Youth Struggling

with a Crocodile Negro
Youth Struggling with a Crocodile

Negro Youth Struggling
with a Crocodile Pygmy

Armed with a Stick Statuette
of a Black Girl with Her Head

Inclined Toward the Left
Shoulder Dagger with Decoration

In Relief Lion Devouring a Black Head
of a Black Nude Black Serving Girl

Carrying an Ointment
Chest on Her Head

Ointment Spoon in the Form
of a Swimming Nubian Girl

Swimmer Holds Before Her
a Duck Fragment

That Once Formed the Spoon
[Black Swimmers Symbolizing the Dawn]

Young Black Female Carrying
a Perfume Vase with a Necklace

with Pendant Figure of the God Bes
Drawn in Black Ink Around Her

Neck   Plaited   Lock
of Hair on Left Side of Her Head Relief

[The Queen of Meroë Spearing
Captives] Handle or Pommel

in the Form of Three Conjoined Heads
Including a Black Woman Perhaps

Black in the Clutches of a Lion
Black Prisoners Followed

by Women and Children Statuette
Figure of a Young Black Girl Holding

a Perfume Vase in Front of Her Statuette
of Young Nubian Girl Carrying an Ointment Vase

Wearing a Necklace
of the God Bes

God of Joy
and of the Dance

IV.

Standing

Female Figure with Child Kneeling
Female Figure with Child Standing
Female Figure Head
Rest Supported by Seated
Female Figure Kneeling
Female Figure with Bowl Standing
Female Figure with Bowl and Child Standing
Female Figure Seated
Female Figure (Pipe)
Female Figure Undated
Female Figure Mask
Female Rhythm Pounder

Standing

V.

Attendants bringing
Offerings to the burial

Funerary relief
Detail of relief

Carved relief
Grave relief

Vase with painted
Decoration relief

Site relief
Relief fragment

From the tomb (Isis
Receiving the Sacrifice)

Relief
Relief

Relief
Relief

"Lucy Terry Prince Prepares for Her Marriage"

*from "Mr. and Mrs. Prince: An African American Courtship and
Marriage in Colonial Deerfield" by Gretchen Holbrook Gerzina*

First a fan
Then some pins
and chocolate

Later: five yards of checkered cloth
Cambric

Later still seven shillings of imported linen
More cambric
ribbons

A double-stranded white necklace
More ribbon

A string of beads
A skein of silk thread

thimble
mug

buttons
five yards of galoon

silver or gold trimming

Then, in 1751:
3 sheets of paper

MARIPOSA

Ode to the Diasporican

(*pa' mi gente*)

Mira a mi cara Puertorriqueña
A mi pelo vivo
A mis manos morenas
Mira a mi corazón que se llena de orgullo
Y di me que no soy Boricua

Some people say that I'm not the real thing
Boricua, that is
because I wasn't
born on the enchanted island
because I was born in the mainland north of Spanish Harlem
because I was born in the Bronx

Some people think I'm not bonafide
because my playground was a concrete jungle
because my Río Grande de Loiza was the Bronx River
because my Fajardo was City Island
my Luquillo, Orchard Beach
and summer nights were filled with city noises
instead of coquis
and Puerto Rico was
just some paradise
that we only saw in pictures

What does it mean to live in between
What does it take to realize that being
Boricua is
a state of mind
a state of heart
a state of soul

Mira a mi cara Puertorriqueña
A mi pelo vivo
A mis manos morenas
Mira a mi corazón que se llena de orgullo
Y di me que no soy Boricua

¡No naci en Puerto Rico.
Puerto Rico nació en mi!

DAWN LUNDY MARTIN

from *Good Stock Strange Blood*

body. Itch of layer, knot of
hair—they call us *Negro.*

To stand broad-footed in sensation of being lit up.

No monument,
only blood-earth,

warm salve to open throat-bone.

How to live between Mother and time?

As if born into the self watching
the self, already made, formless, then out of clay.

Feel the hump of our drape. Here: the body, flesh
inevitable, unsatiated hunger like a whip—

Instrumental fissure, instrumental fish, whose rasp
a whip, a book, a story left in the dark body,
to reach fingers out toward shine of morning, eyes squinted,
and find there only cordgrass, some smoke or a warning.

OUR NAME . . .

What is our name?
Where are the buttons holding
us in place?
What is place outside of time?

Outside of memory—un-stitched,
un-snatch, swell into—

Our mother's "blackened" skin,
          her "tarnished" "whiteness."
Her rope shackled to grandfather's
          black neck—

A picket, a thicket, rice, cotton,
          sugar, potatoes, cowpeas,
turnips, and rye—O, lord, thank you
for Mr. Hopeton not selling my boy.

This is the body bending over another.

          TEXTURES, WE KNOW THEM—

          bruises, our Missus's homespun cape,
linen hung by its lips, sway
—a useless body,
          trash boy.

What is a dance for being?

A step toward nothingness.

Grey, landscape, purple feet,
          I remember, I swear,
the limp relative to nothing.

Scraps, bright against sea,
          migrant legs almost
drowned already, a narrative

          wired in cells, desolate root.

          WE SUCCUMBED—

          head by measure, by—

weight of black sheath and organs,
          legacy that lingers
          —a hip thrust.

We wait in wings,
          expanse spread across
          darkening blue sky.

          We shut shades—
          huff into wings, shrink

          bones of self.

          What you drag:

          your banjo, your braided
                    neck-lace. Disappearance

          into mole. Stink of flesh become flesh.

Come now—

          arms and arches open
to pocket all dejected souls—

               —TO BE IN COVERING

          is the problem, hunger caverns
under this leather wrap—from destitution—
from split skull—

          Mother as brown as—
brawn and braided,
          toward—filth beneath,
          skin like wire—

          all our kin.

From before—
          —It happened when—
dust under foot, red dick stuck,
under guise of reason.

Who summons us
    from darkness,
from water well, one philtrum
    stitched to Wolof tongue—

Who tugs and rocks us, suckles wet mouth? We is the purpose
of the falling, swollen, our teeth hurt, their constant cutting.
Warm when sunken. Wanted the swell of black earth, a legacy,
something larger than ourselves to hold us.

ADRIAN MATEJKA

from *The Big Smoke*

CANNIBALISM

Coloreds were here before these
United States were even dreamed
of. We have always been on this
land. That's why I don't bother
about what Booker T. Washington
says. I'm a pure-blooded American
of the first rate & I don't need
to cast down a bucket unless there's
no indoor toilet. After the Great
Storm hit, the *Times* called us "black
ghouls," cannibals eating coloreds
& whites like Sunday chicken.
They said we left babies in the street
just so we could take a dead man's
shoes. They said we sawed off
fingers at the fat meat for rings.
I was there, so I know what's true:
whole families of coloreds shot
down by whites. "Protecting the dead,"
the sheriffs said, sending buckshot
at any colored in sight. Those
dead people didn't need any more
protection than the mud & rocks
covering them. After that storm
moved through, me & the other
Galveston boys slept where we could,
spent our days searching for anybody
alive. We got paid whiskey & potatoes.
We found dead mothers & sons,
dead cats & skulls cracked
like teacups under the wet wood
& rock. That's all the storm left.

COURTSHIP

Hattie, you are
as delectable & powdered
as a beignet. Your

skin is white enough
to catch a bit of sun
in its own sugar.

Your sweat glints
like the jewels I'll
buy for you. Don't you

hear me talking,
pretty lady?
I can play my viol

for you if it
will make you feel
right. We can bathe

in champagne, dry
ourselves with hundred-
dollar bills like those

Rockefellers do.
I'll take you out
of the sporting house

& into the royal
court. Keep watching
my exhibitions. Keep

hiding that smile:
your gloved hand looks
like a dove's wing

when you whisper
to your friends.
Did you tell them

the snappy left
that closed Kid's
eye like a bank on

Saturday was for you?
Did you whisper
that the gut hook dropping

the man to his knees
like a sinner meeting
with Death was for you?

"CAREFREE AS A PLANTATION DARKY IN WATERMELON TIME"

Jim Jeffries worked the corner the night
I fought his little brother, Jack. He saw up
close how my fists can put a man to sleep
like the sun going down. The younger
Jeffries was a game fighter, but he had
no elasticity & limited self-knowledge.
I knew he couldn't stand in the ring
with me & decided before the fight
to knock him out in the fifth round. I sealed
my prediction in an envelope & gave it
to a reporter for safekeeping. As I predicted,
I put Jack down at the beginning of Round
Five. Naturally, I was surprised to find I was
a ten-to-four underdog to the older Jeffries.
The same man who retired immediately
after he saw me in action. I don't care if Jim
did keep a grizzly as a pet: I'm going
to make a whole lot of money betting on
myself. If I felt any better, I'd be afraid
of myself. I'm so fast I only got my shadow
to spar with & most times, it don't keep

up either. So I shoot craps to train my fists.
I play the fiddle to train my eyes.
I play baseball to get ready for bed.
When I drive my Flyer over the red rises
into that Reno sunset, everybody from
Philadelphia to Australia will see Jack
Johnson is taking his machine for a ride.

Robot Music

The 3 fingers pointing back at you are an abacus for all your funky
    wants. You're hydraulics & supersonics on the multi-colored
    dance floor. Sergio Valente rocking 3 broke parts. No parking,

baby. You need room to get your back up. You got moves like a dump
truck backing up, a shell toe trying to right itself in the brake light

    between sidewalk & broken-arm roboting.

You're as roly & spunky as a cartoon bomb with a fuse wanting
to be lit. Break beats: the struck match.
                                        Across cutoff sleeves,
past rising sun headbands & patriotic wristbands, leg-sweeping
every pretty momma in sight right before setting the Soul Train

line on stun. Truthfully, you need a bit more hip in your robot
    convolutions. You need a chronograph for those windmill
    intrusions. That last shudder was like doing community service

    on Sunday morning. When you disco pointed at the lady

in the half-top & spandex, 3 fingers pointing back at you were joined
    by a thumb, bird-dogging the rhythms of the universe
    as you work the dance floor like a B-side's stepson.

SHARA McCALLUM

What the Oracle Said

You will leave your home:
nothing will hold you.
You will wear dresses of gold; skins
of silver, copper, and bronze.
The sky above you will shift in meaning
each time you think you understand.
You will spend a lifetime chipping away layers
of flesh. The shadow of your scales
will always remain. You will be marked
by sulphur and salt.
You will bathe endlessly in clear streams and fail
to rid yourself of that scent.
Your feet will never be your own.
Stone will be your path.
Storms will follow in your wake,
destroying all those who take you in.
You will desert your children
kill your lovers and devour their flesh.
You will love no one
but the wind and ache of your bones.
Neither will love you in return.
With age, your hair will grow matted and dull,
your skin will gape and hang in long folds,
your eyes will cease to shine.
But nothing will be enough.
The sea will never take you back.

TONY MEDINA

The Keepin' It Real Awards

Best Welfare Cheat

Best Empty Beer Can Collector

Best Ant & Roach Killer

Best Broke Back Mountain Rat Rider

Best Drive-By Shooting Victim

Best Crime Scene Tape Cordoner

Best Chalk-Marked Silhouette Model

Best Stripper in a Turquoise Thong

Best Toilet Roll Holder

Best Projects' Elevator Pisser

Best Jheri Curl Weave

Best Gold Toofus

Best Crack Attack Running Man Dancer Breaking &
    Scraping Along the Concrete Until Your Limbs Bleed

Best Sisyphean Government Surplus Cheese Hauler

Best Mister Softee Chaser

Best Popsicle Stick Race Along the Curbside Fire Hydrant
    Stream

Best Lower Back Tattoo

Best Dry Hump Beneath a Staircase

Best Heroin-Induced Vomit Nod

Best Hip Hop Grimace

Best Pallbearer

TRACIE MORRIS

Blackout 1977

Red hued brick and siding holding porous heat, stars blazed
    out
Adjacent to the round-top cement building, a former
    synagogue

We sat around eating fried food in our natural habitat
Partitioned Brooklyn between Berriman and Hegeman Sts.

White noise of the freezer, then a rumble, reached its ta-da,
Went down to kitty sound, sleepy, then silent.

A sound—applause? Nope, the cast-iron stove's collected
    works.
July's oven-roasting. We consume the meat's enzymes in
    order

to save them. Everything sienna off quiet brown
appliances of my recall. Cabinets sunny disinfected yellow.

Afternoon sun crisps Bronzeville outdoors. People
dig out sliver Everreadys from cushioned

car seats' couched, commandeered from kids' Popeye,
Farah Fawcett transistors set to James Brown.

Hot Pants!! What news, man? Who needs the same ol' same?
Con Ed made all a forced vacation—Welcome to our club!

(Crack your mother's back with them high bills.)

Twisted silent G.E. toasters, Maranz stereos, Philips TV
    parade
down the street, Looney Tunes a year late, the spirit

of America. We watched from the block, cuttin' up! Cee-lo,
hopscotch 'til the sun set and we couldn't see, throw.

Flour-dusted chicken legs, make gas pop blue-flame red. A lil
Girl carries Chinet plates to plastic white + blue weave lawn
      chairs.

Lawnless though, play sub-urban. Johnny pump sprinkling
      all
out. Gramma going from red bone to teak, frying all day.

Now my home's seasoned cast iron skillet's refract echoes.
      Car horn?
The ram gave himself for new years. Mortar crackles the wall.

FRED MOTEN

gayl jones

my daddy drank red soda pop.
once he wanted a fleetwood,
then he wanted a navigator,
so he could navigate, check out

his radio towers, deliver flowers,
drive back to give me long kisses,

watch mama burn her books. said nancy

wilson can't sing but she can style—
hold back the force of random operators/
return to the line refuse to punctuate. a moon—
but his actual drive was watching day circle,

tight-breath'd hunch, tight shoulder. sweet

nancy wilson was just cold analytics:

the difference between a new coat and the
one with ink on the pocket, calculate

like a fat young minister, strokin' like

clarence carter, increase like creflo
dollar. mama and me stayed up over

the club, cried sometimes in the same
broke off the same piece left each other

the last piece practiced the same piece
got warm on the same. however,
I'm so full this morning I have
to try and make you understand

cecil taylor

klang and cut through
burning, texture,

but it's all basic

ornament and thread

too. through broken anaclitic feel

and long long cut and long

long reserve and long

the outstretched address three!

their incline song screams

bell and shaft and cant inside
the furnished discipline,

to polish the wooden

practice box, sometimes

dance, shake your arm
and move your form.

alamillo bears striving with
mysterious title and broken

law. in the colored water

cable stays on the scene as
sculpted numbers whirling

furniture and instrument

in and out of tone until

the leaning bridge says bye

mama. this also touches on

leaving just before moses cut

new york with express barrier

circles busting blocks. remember,

striving is aleatory for

beautiful black queens.

they end in open systems
as bridges given hour by hour.

almeida ragland

johnny cash

first diesel came through cuba
long possible hard stream to memphis

gravel on the edge of that black water

white flowers till that river black motel.

like making groceries at drake's on Saturday

but no new lectronics of the sun. gotta get home to

that light by blind, slip through cotton plant
at night between the track and the river,

short sleeves but mo'nin' like a man with

a movie camera, but he took that hat off mystery,

dead slate brought back with friction. the sound
of the horn make the flat ones skim

till the edge and sharpen then red

then green then dyad then severed

                    [politically man
                         dwells down here
                in cubie

          that same train from dave cash

to the central valley. wood water asphalt steel pine

tremor flint michigan. fresh desert (cleared wood), out
from the center wheel but deep

in that high social cotton, social
ground, I don't know when,

whistle smoke drive on.

I ran from it but was still in it

I burn communities in shadow, underground, up on the
plateau, then slide with the horny horns. vision's festival
is folded in overtones and outskirts. j tizol, harry carnival
and feel lined out around an open forte, an underprivilege
of the real presence, curled up around an outlaw corner.
curling around corners puts me in mind of jean toomer.
I think I'll change my name to gene tumor. I want to be
a stream tuner, unfurled in tongues that won't belong in
anybody's mouth, mass swerving from the law of tongues,
let me slip my slap-tongued speech in your ear, the burnt
starry star of all love in your ear. o, for a muse of fire music.

I threw my shade down like a windowpane. on the
borders and cloth rises, off in the music's renegade

thicknesses, soft thighs, black elbows. and crossed

up your science except for the part that can't find

enough particles. this is the edge of an organic line

that loves each other in the cistern. it's another city
up in the waves and that cleanhead man is singing it
right now! everybody grounding, everybody making
strings out of curls with open tuning in response. John
hears it like a natural communist shadow, madly in

love with all that wealth and flow on jackson street.

I am foment. I speak blinglish. at work they call me
but I don't come. I come when she call me by my
rightful name. I come to myself from far away just
laid back in the open. I ran from it and was *still* in it.

it's a blue division on my goodbye window. I'm full
of outer space. I'm free as dred all night. I get clung

with a voice that gets held back by surge protection.

I'm daddy I come when he crazy he call me I'm crazy.
I come when he call me once upon a time in arkansas.
when the water come I come to the unprotected surge
and division in my old-new sound booth. I am fmoten.

JOHN MURILLO

On Confessionalism

Not sleepwalking, but waking still,
with my hand on a gun, and the gun
in a mouth, and the mouth
on the face of a man on his knees.
Autumn of '89, and I'm standing
in a section 8 apartment parking lot,
pistol cocked, and staring down
at this man, then up into the mug
of an old woman staring, watering
the single sad flower to the left
of her stoop, the flower also staring,
my engine idling behind me, a slow
moaning bassline and the bark
of a dead rapper nudging me on.
All to say, someone's brokenhearted.
And this man with the gun in his mouth—
this man who, like me, is really little
more than a boy—may or may not
have something to do with it.
May or may not have said a thing
or two, betrayed a secret, say,
that walked my love away. And why
not say it: She adored me. And I,
her. More than anyone, anything
in life, up to then, and then still,
for two decades after. And, therefore,
went for broke. Blacked out and woke
having gutted my piggy and pawned
all my gold to buy what a homeboy
said was a Beretta. Blacked out
and woke, my hand on a gun, the gun
in a mouth, a man, who was really
a boy, on his knees. And because
I loved the girl, I actually paused

before I pulled the trigger—once,
twice, three times—then panicked
not just because the gun jammed,
but because what if it hadn't,
because who did I almost become,
there, that afternoon, in a section 8
apartment parking lot, pistol cocked,
with the sad flower staring, because
I knew the girl I loved—no matter
how this all played out—would never
have me back. Day of damaged ammo,
or grime that clogged the chamber.
Day of faulty rods, or springs come
loose in my fist. Day nobody died,
so why not *hallelujah?* Say *amen* or
Thank you? My mother sang for years
of God, babes and fools. My father,
lymph node masses fading from
his x-rays, said surviving one thing
means another comes and kills you.
He's dead, and so, I trust him. Dead,
and so I'd wonder, years, about the work
I left undone—boy on his knees
a man now, risen, and likely plotting
his long way back to me. Fuck it.
I tucked my tool like the movie gangsters
do, and jumped back in my bucket.
Cold enough day to make a young man
weep, afternoon when everything,
or nothing, changed forever. The dead
rapper grunted, the bassline faded,
my spirits whispered something
from the trees. I left then lost the pistol
in a storm drain, somewhere between
that life and this. Left the pistol
in a storm drain, but can't remember
ever wiping away my prints.

GREGORY PARDLO

Written by Himself

I was born in minutes in a roadside kitchen a skillet
whispering my name. I was born to rainwater and lye;
I was born across the river where I
was borrowed with clothespins, a harrow tooth,
broadsides sewn in my shoes. I returned, though
it please you, through no fault of my own,
pockets filled with coffee grounds and eggshells.
I was born still and superstitious; I bore an unexpected
     burden.
I gave birth, I gave blessing, I gave rise to suspicion.
I was born abandoned outdoors in the heat-shaped air,
air drifting like spirits and old windows.
I was born a fraction and a cipher and a ledger entry;
I was an index of first lines when I was born.
I was born waist-deep stubborn in the water crying
                ain't I a woman and a brother I was born
to this hall of mirrors, this horror story I was
born with a prologue of references, pursued
by mosquitoes and thieves, I was born passing
off the problem of the twentieth century: I was born.
I read minds before I could read fishes and loaves;
I walked a piece of the way alone before I was born.

Raisin

I dragged my twelve-year-old cousin
to see the Broadway production of *A Raisin
in the Sun* because the hip-hop mogul
and rapping bachelor, Diddy, played
the starring role. An aspiring rapper gave
my cousin his last name and the occasional child
support so I thought the boy would geek to see a pop

hero in the flesh as Walter Lee. My wife was newly
pregnant, and I was rehearsing, like Diddy
swapping fictions, surrendering his manicured
thug persona for a more domestic performance.
My cousin mostly yawned throughout the play.
Except the moment Walter Lee's tween son stiffened
on stage, as if rapt by the sound of a roulette ball.
Scene: *No one breathes as Walter Lee vacillates,*
uncertain of obsequity or indignation after Lindner offers
to buy the family out of the house they've purchased
in the all-white suburb. Walter might kneel to accept,
but he senses the tension in his son's gaze. I was thinking,
for real though, what would Diddy do? "Get rich
or die trying," 50 Cent would tell us. But my father would
sing like Ricky Scaggs, "Don't get above your raisin',"
when as a kid I vowed to be a bigger man than him.
That oppressive fruit dropped heavy as a medicine
ball in my lap meant to check my ego, and I imagined
generations wimpling in succession like the conga
marching raisins that sang Marvin's hit song. Silly,
I know. Outside the theater, my cousin told me
when Diddy was two, they found his hustler dad
draping a steering wheel in Central Park,
a bullet in his head. I shared what I knew of dreams
deferred and Marvin Gaye. (When asked if he loved
his son, Marvin Sr. answered, "Let's just say I didn't
dislike him.") Beneath the bling of many billion
diodes I walked beside the boy through Times Square
as if anticipating a magic curtain that would rise,
but only one of us would get to take a bow.

WILLIE PERDOMO

Bembé-Faced

Trombones discharged their fat mugs.
Sat on a few bars before the pocket
Players drew their best shot. Then I
Shook all the safety from their style.
Came in mega-dirty, dressed to seek.
Big-thumb, bully-bass & blossoms—
Bro, my soul had spotlight to spare.
How to play it again? In back-to-back
Hurricane time, a spirit snapped from
Spool, bembé-faced in chocolate snow.
Yes, Poet—swear to life—like I said:
That night, I put the dong in the ding.
In shadow-speak, light was my king.

Arroz con Son y Clave

My father used to leave sharp sounds
By the door, steady conga heads were
Rare. When you party with grown-ups,
You learn not to suffer dancers a weak
Hand; otherwise a safe return to silence
Becomes less of a road—no yesterday.
The great readers, he would say, quote
From the kitchen. Yes, chops—cook,
Steam like jabs, stories, walls that sob
I'm sorry. In the middle of a sacrifice,
Death always has a shape to introduce:
Breath deflates & balloons a club like
An amateur soul drowning in whisper.

CARL PHILLIPS

Blue

As through marble or the lining of
certain fish split open and scooped
clean, this is the blue vein
that rides, where the flesh is even
whiter than the rest of her, the splayed
thighs mother forgets, busy struggling
for command over bones: her own,
those of the chaise longue, all
equally uncooperative, and there's
the wind, too. This is her hair, gone
from white to blue in the air.

This is the black, shot with blue, of my dark
daddy's knuckles, that do not change, ever.
Which is to say they are no more pale
in anger than at rest, or when, as
I imagine them now, they follow
the same two fingers he has always used
to make the rim of every empty blue
glass in the house sing.
Always, the same
blue-to-black sorrow
no black surface can entirely hide.

Under the night, somewhere
between the white that is nothing so much as
blue, and the black that is, finally, nothing,
I am the man neither of you remembers.
Shielding, in the half-dark,
the blue eyes I sometimes forget
I don't have. Pulling my own stoop-
shouldered kind of blues across paper.
Apparently misinformed about the rumored

stuff of dreams: everywhere I inquired,
I was told look for blue.

Cotillion

Every one of these bodies, those in drag, those
not, loves a party, that much is clear. The blonde
with the amazing lashes—lashes, more amazingly,

his own—tells me it is like when a small bird
rises, sometimes, like the difficult thing is not to.
I think he is talking about joy or pain or desire

or any of the several things desire, sweet drug,
too sweet, can lead to. I think he means moments,
like this one, sudden, when in no time I know that

these lashes, the mouth that could use now more
painting, these hairless, shaven-for-the-event arms
whose skin, against the shine of the gown, a spill of

blood and sequins the arms themselves spill from,
glitters still, but dully, like what is not the
main prize does always—I know this man is mine,

if I want him. Meanwhile around us, the room fairly
staggers with men, and an aching to be lovely—loved,
even. As in any crowd, lately, of people, the heavy

corsage of them stepping in groups, the torn bloom
that is each taking his own particular distance,
I think the trick is one neither of joining or not

joining, but of holding, as long as I can, to some
space between, call it rest for the wary, the slow
dragging to nowhere I call heaven. I'm dancing

maybe, but not on air: this time through water.

A Great Noise

Then he died.
And they said: *Another soul free.*

Which was the wrong way to see it, I thought,
having been there,
having lain down beside him until

his body became rigid with what I believe
was not the stiffening of death
but of surprise, the initial
unbelief of the suddenly ex-slave hearing
Rest; let it fall now, this burden.

The proof most commonly put forth for the soul
as a thing that exists and weighs
something is that
the body weighs something less, after death—

a clean fact.

In *The Miraculous Translation of the Body
of Saint Catherine of Alexandria to Sinai,*
the number of angels required to bear the body
all that way through the air
comes to four,
which tells us nothing
about weight, or the lack of it, since
the angels depicted
are clearly those for whom

the only business is hard labor.

the work angels,
you can tell:
the musculature;
the resigned way they wear clothes.

Beyond them in rank,
in the actual presence of God,
the seraphim stand naked, ever-burning,

six-winged: two to fly with,
in back; two at the face to withstand
the impossible winds that
are God;

and a third pair—for modesty,
for the covering
of sex.

A great
noise is said to always
attend them:
less the humming of wings than
the grinding you'd expect

from the hitching of what is hot,
destructive,
and all devotion

to the highest, brightest star.

Speak Low

The wind stirred—the water beneath it stirred accordingly . . .
The wind's pattern was its own, and the water's also. The
water in that sense was the wind's reflection. The wind was,
to the water, what the water was to the light that fell there,
or appeared to fall, spilling as if the light were a liquid, or as
if the light and the water it spilled across

                                            were now the same.
It is true that the light, like the water, assumed the pattern of
what acted upon it. But the water assumed also the shape
of what contained it, while the light did not. The light
    seemed

fugitive, a restiveness, the less-than-clear distance between
everything we know we should do, and all the rest—all
the rest that we do. Stirring, as the wind stirred it, the water
was water—was a form of clarity itself, a window we've
no sooner looked through than we've abandoned it for what
lies past that: a view, and then what comes

                                        into view, or
                                        might,
if we watch patiently enough, steadily—so we believe,
        wishing
for what, by now, even we can't put a name to, but feel
        certain
we'll recognize, having done so before. It looked, didn't it,
just like harmlessness. A small wind. Some light on water.

KHADIJAH QUEEN

I want to not have to write another word about who the cops keep killing

So at first I wanted to make another video and I thought I could do it on the weekend or after work but motherhood and overtime and then I got to image-hunting and name-searching and each name led to another name and another name and the people and I wept Again and then I got angry Again and I got my fancy microphone to read June Jordan's "Poem About My Rights" and played with filters in Garage Band and thought about going for a walk in the almost dark and having my teenager film me in a flowered dress and sun hat walking barefoot by the creek and grazing summer sunflowers with my fingertips like in a wistful movie intro or tampon commercial but then I get up and I hurt everywhere my body aches I feel heavy and as the sun goes down I realize I don't have time to make the kind of video I want to make because I have to get up at 5:30am to start work and I want to not feel this pain everywhere and I want to not be so tired I can't move but fibromyalgia exists and even though it reminds me of grief what does any of this whining have to do with Michael Brown when my beautiful brown boy is laughing in the room down the hall eating caramel gelato and not cleaning his room and I want to not think about my dead brother every time the police kill another of us and then get to pose in front of flags and lie to the cameras like the truth don't keep in blood and keep their guns and keep their public salaries and keep killing the people we love and when I think that I cry Again because I want to not cry because I actually hate crying because none of my tears can offer resurrection none of my poems can offer resurrection none of my image searches can offer resurrection and I want us to stay alive

CLAUDIA RANKINE

from *Citizen: An American Lyric*

February 26, 2012 / In Memory of Trayvon Martin

*Script for Situation video created in collaboration
with John Lucas*

My brothers are notorious. They have not been to prison. They have been imprisoned. The prison is not a place you enter. It is no place. My brothers are notorious. They do regular things, like wait. On my birthday they say my name. They will never forget that we are named. What is that memory?

The days of our childhood together were steep steps into a collapsing mind. It looked like we rescued ourselves, were rescued. Then there are these days, each day of our adult lives. They will never forget our way through, these brothers, each brother, my brother, dear brother, my dearest brothers, dear heart—

Your hearts are broken. This is not a secret though there are secrets. And as yet I do not understand how my own sorrow has turned into my brothers' hearts. The hearts of my brothers are broken. If I knew another way to be, I would call up a brother, I would hear myself saying, my brother, dear brother, my dearest brothers, dear heart—

On the tip of a tongue one note following another is another path, another dawn where the pink sky is the bloodshot of struck, of sleepless, of sorry, of senseless, shush. Those years of and before me and my brothers, the years of passage, plantation, migration, of Jim Crow segregation, of poverty, inner cities, profiling, of one in three, two jobs, boy, hey boy, each a felony, accumulate into the hours inside our lives where we are all caught hanging, the rope inside us, the tree inside us, its roots our limbs, a throat sliced through and when we open our mouth to speak, blossoms, o blossoms, no place coming out, brother, dear brother, that kind of blue. The sky is the silence of brothers all the days leading up to my call.

If I called I'd say good-bye before I broke the good-bye. I say good-bye before anyone can hang up. Don't hang up. My brother hangs up though he is there. I keep talking. The talk keeps him there. The sky is blue, kind of blue. The day is hot. Is it cold? Are you cold? It does get cool. Is it cool? Are you cool?

My brother is completed by sky. The sky is his silence. Eventually, he says, it is raining. It is raining down. It was raining. It stopped raining. It is raining down. He won't hang up. He's there, he's there but he's hung up though he is there. Good-bye, I say. I break the good-bye. I say good-bye before anyone can hang up, don't hang up. Wait with me. Wait with me though the waiting might be the call of good-byes.

Stop-and-Frisk

Script for Situation video created in
collaboration with John Lucas

I knew whatever was in front of me was happening and then the police vehicle came to a screeching halt in front of me like they were setting up a blockade. Everywhere were flashes, a siren sounding and a stretched-out roar. Get on the ground. Get on the ground now. Then I just knew.

And you are not the guy and still you fit the description because there is only one guy who is always the guy fitting the description.

I left my client's house knowing I would be pulled over. I knew. I just knew. I opened my briefcase on the passenger seat, just so they could see. Yes officer rolled around on my tongue, which grew out of a bell that could never ring because its emergency was a tolling I was meant to swallow.

In a landscape drawn from an ocean bed, you can't drive yourself sane—so angry you are crying. You can't drive yourself sane. This motion wears a guy out. Our motion is wearing you out and still you are not that guy.

Then flashes, a siren, a stretched-out roar—and you are not the guy and still you fit the description because there is only one guy who is always the guy fitting the description.

Get on the ground. Get on the ground now. I must have been speeding. No, you weren't speeding. I wasn't speeding? You didn't do anything wrong. Then why are you pulling me over? Why am I pulled over? Put your hands where they can be seen. Put your hands in the air. Put your hands up.

Then you are stretched out on the hood. Then cuffed. Get on the ground now.

———

Each time it begins in the same way, it doesn't begin the same way, each time it begins it's the same. Flashes, a siren, the stretched-out roar—

Maybe because home was a hood the officer could not afford, not that a reason was needed, I was pulled out of my vehicle a block from my door, handcuffed and pushed into the police vehicle's backseat, the officer's knee pressing into my collarbone, the officer's warm breath vacating a face creased into the smile of its own private joke.

Each time it begins in the same way, it doesn't begin the same way, each time it begins it's the same.

Go ahead hit me motherfucker fled my lips and the officer did not need to hit me, the officer did not need anything from me except the look on my face on the drive across town. You can't drive yourself sane. You are not insane. Our motion is wearing you out. You are not the guy.

This is what it looks like. You know this is wrong. This is not what it looks like. You need to be quiet. This is wrong. You need to close your mouth now. This is what it looks like. Why are you talking if you haven't done anything wrong?

And you are not the guy and still you fit the description because there is only one guy who is always the guy fitting the description.

———

In a landscape drawn from an ocean bed, you can't drive yourself sane—so angry you can't drive yourself sane.

The charge the officer decided on was exhibition of speed. I was told, after the fingerprinting, to stand naked. I stood naked. It was only then I was instructed to dress, to leave, to walk all those miles back home.

And still you are not the guy and still you fit the description because there is only one guy who is always the guy fitting the description.

July 29–August 18, 2014 / Making Room

Script for Public Fiction at Hammer Museum

On the train the woman standing makes you understand there are no seats available. And, in fact, there is one. Is the woman getting off at the next stop? No, she would rather stand all the way to Union Station.

The space next to the man is the pause in a conversation you are suddenly rushing to fill. You step quickly over the woman's fear, a fear she shares. You let her have it.

The man doesn't acknowledge you as you sit down because the man knows more about the unoccupied seat than you do. For him, you imagine, it is more like breath than wonder; he has had to think about it so much you wouldn't call it thought.

When another passenger leaves his seat and the standing woman sits, you glance over at the man. He is gazing out the window into what looks like darkness.

You sit next to the man on the train, bus, in the plane, waiting room, anywhere he could be forsaken. You put your body there in proximity to, adjacent to, alongside, within.

You don't speak unless you are spoken to and your body speaks to the space you fill and you keep trying to fill it except the space belongs to the body of the man next to you, not to you.

Where he goes the space follows him. If the man left his seat before Union Station you would simply be a person in a seat on the train. You would cease to struggle against the unoccupied seat when where why the space won't lose its meaning.

You imagine if the man spoke to you he would say, it's okay, I'm okay, you don't need to sit here. You don't need to sit and you sit and look past him into the darkness the train is moving through. A tunnel.

All the while the darkness allows you to look at him. Does he feel you looking at him? You suspect so. What does suspicion mean? What does suspicion do?

The soft gray-green of your cotton coat touches the sleeve of him. You are shoulder to shoulder though standing you could feel shadowed. You sit to repair whom who? You erase that thought. And it might be too late for that.

It might forever be too late or too early. The train moves too fast for your eyes to adjust to anything beyond the man, the window, the tiled tunnel, its slick darkness. Occasionally, a white light flickers by like a displaced sound.

From across the aisle tracks room harbor world a woman asks a man in the rows ahead if he would mind switching seats. She wishes to sit with her daughter or son. You hear but you don't hear. You can't see.

It's then the man next to you turns to you. And as if from inside your own head you agree that if anyone asks you to move, you'll tell them we are traveling as a family.

REGINALD SHEPHERD

The Difficult Music

I started to write a song about you, then I decided, *No.*
I've been trying to write about violence
for so long. (You were my mother; I love you more
dead. Not a day goes by when I'm not turning someone
into you.) A week of traffic jams and fog
filtered through glass, the country crumbling
in my sleep; old men in plaid jackets on the corner
drinking quart bottles of Old Milwaukee; the color black
again and again.
               My first summer in Boston
a bum glanced up from tapping at the pavement with a
      hammer
to whisper *Nigger*, laughing, when I walked by.
I'd passed the age of consent, I suppose;
my body was never clean again. In Buffalo, a billboard
said, "In a dream you saw a way to survive and you woke up
happy," justice talking to the sidewalk on Main Street;
I thought it was talking to me, but it was just
art. (I've wronged too many mornings hallucinating
your voice, too drunk with sleep to understand
the words.)
          Some afternoons
I can see through a history of heart attacks in two-room
tenement apartments, writing your silted name
on snow with which the lake effect shrouds
a half-abandoned rust belt city. (I've compared you
to snow's unlikely predicates, the moon's
faceless occupation. Some drift
always takes your place.) I was just
scribbling again. *Take it from me*, my stereo claims, *some day
we'll all be free.* If anyone should ever write that song.
The finely sifted light falls down.

The Lucky One

The middle-aged white man in a beat-up blue Pinto
who shouts "Hey man, what's up?", pulls up onto
the curb in front of me to ask the time, because
I am a young black man and who knows what he wants
from me: or my dream in which nothing works, not even the
    lights,
because it's France under the Occupation, and Billie Holiday
sings "I Cried for You" with blue hair on the television
while men in drag fan-dance behind her and young people
grind together in Technicolor on the studio dance floor
    (when the camera
isn't closing on her pancaked face, her one
gardenia pinned back like blue-rinsed hair), because the
    Nazis
still allow it and pleasure is such a pretty thing
to watch, and I am hiding in this house with
    air-conditioning, waiting
for the owners, whom I haven't met, to come home, the
    lights
to come back on, waking up afraid (just after
they return, turn off a dead black woman's tears)
in the second half of the twentieth century not knowing
the time of day, speaking French to myself, singing.

Hesitation Theory

I drift into the sound of wind,
how small my life must be
to fit into his palm like that, holly
leaf, bluejay feather, milkweed fluff,
pine straw or sycamore pod, resembling
scraps of light. The world
slips through these fingers
so easily, there's so much

to miss: the sociable bones
linked up in supple rows, mineral
seams just under the skin. I hold
my palm against the sun and don't see
palm or sun, don't hold anything
in either hand. I look up, look
away (*what's that?*), I trip
and stumble (fall
again), find myself face down
in duff, a foam of fallen live oak
leaves, with only
this life, mine at times.

My Mother Was No White Dove

no dove at all, coo-rooing through the dusk
and foraging for small seeds
My mother was the clouded-over night
a moon swims through, the dark against which stars
switch themselves on, so many already dead
by now (stars switch themselves off
and are my mother, she was never
so celestial, so clearly seen)

My mother was the murderous flight of crows
stilled, black plumage gleaming
among black branches, taken
for nocturnal leaves, the difference
between two darks:

a cacophony of needs
in the bare tree silhouette,
a flight of feathers, scattering
black. She was the night
streetlights oppose (perch
for the crows, their purchase on sight),

obscure bruise across the sky
making up names for rain

My mother always falling
was never snow, no kind
of bird, pigeon or crow

EVIE SHOCKLEY

from *The Lost Letters of Frederick Douglass*

June 5, 1892

Dear Daughter,
                    Can you be fifty-three this
month? I still look for you to peek around
my door as if you'd discovered a toy
you thought gone for good, ready at my smile
to run up and press your fist into my
broken palm. But your own girls have outgrown
such games, and I cannot pilfer back time
I spent pursuing Freedom. Fair to you,
to your brothers, your mother? Hardly.

                                         But
what other choice did I have? What sham,
what shabby love could I offer you, so
long as Thomas Auld held the law over
my head? And when the personal threat was
ended, whose eyes could mine enter without
shame, if turning toward my wife and children
meant turning my back?

                            Your mother's eyes stare
out at me through yours, of late. You think I
didn't love her, that my quick remarriage
makes a Gertrude of me, a corseted
Hamlet of you. You're as wrong as you are
lucky. Had Anna Murray had your
education as a girl, my love for
her would have been as passionate as it
was grateful. But she died illiterate,
when I had risked my life to master language.
The pleasures of book and pen retain
the thrill of danger even now, and you
may understand why Ottilie Assing,

come into our house to translate me into
German, could command so many hours,
years, of my time—or, as you would likely
say, of your mother's time.

                             Forgive me,
Rosetta, for broaching such indelicate
subjects, but as my eldest child and
only living daughter, I want you to
feel certain that Helen became the new
Mrs. Douglass because of what we shared
in sheaves of my papers: let no one
persuade you I coveted her skin.
I am not proud of how I husbanded
your mother all those years, but marriage,
too, is a peculiar institution.
I could not have stayed so unequally yoked
so long, without a kind of Freedom in
it. Anna accepted this, and I don't
have to tell you that her lot was better
and she, happier, than if she'd squatted
with some other man in a mutual
ignorance.

                     Perhaps I will post, rather
than burn, this letter, this time. I've written it
so often, right down to these closing lines,
in which I beg you to be kinder, much
kinder, to your step-mother. You two are
of an age to be sisters, and of like
temperament—under other circumstances,
you might have found Friendship in each other.

With regards to your husband—I am, as
ever, your loving father—

                           Frederick Douglass

statistical haiku (or, how do they discount us? let me count the ways)

only 3 of 100 black boys
entering kindergarten will graduate college—
in the night sky, shooting stars

every day a black person
under 20 years old commits suicide—
plucked magnolia blossom's funereal perfume

a black man is 700% more likely
than a white man to be sentenced to prison—
scattered thundershowers in may

every 3 minutes
a black child is born into poverty—
pine needles line the forest floor

ode to my blackness

you are my shelter from the storm
                    and the storm

my anchor

                    and the troubled sea

                    *   *   *

night casts you warm and glittering
upon my shoulders   some would
say you give off no heat   some folks
can't see beyond the closest star

                    *   *   *

you are the tunnel john henry died
        to carve
i see the light
           at the end   of you   the beginning

*   *   *

i dig down deep and there you are   at the root of my blues
you're all thick and dark, enveloping the root of my blues
seem like it's so hard to let you go   when i got nothing to
                                                    lose

*   *   *

without you, i would be just

        a self of my former shadow

TRACY K. SMITH

Sci-Fi

There will be no edges, but curves.
Clean lines pointing only forward.

History, with its hard spine & dog-eared
Corners, will be replaced with nuance,

Just like the dinosaurs gave way
To mounds and mounds of ice.

Women will still be women, but
The distinction will be empty. Sex,

Having outlived every threat, will gratify
Only the mind, which is where it will exist.

For kicks, we'll dance for ourselves
Before mirrors studded with golden bulbs.

The oldest among us will recognize that glow—
But the word *sun* will have been re-assigned

To a Standard Uranium-Neutralizing device
Found in households and nursing homes.

And yes, we'll live to be much older, thanks
To popular consensus. Weightless, unhinged,

Eons from even our own moon, we'll drift
In the haze of space, which will be, once

And for all, scrutable and safe.

Don't You Wonder, Sometimes?

1.

After dark, stars glisten like ice, and the distance they span
Hides something elemental. Not God, exactly. More like
Some thin-hipped glittering Bowie-being—a Starman
Or cosmic ace hovering, swaying, aching to make us see.
And what would we do, you and I, if we could know for sure

That someone was there squinting through the dust,
Saying nothing is lost, that everything lives on waiting only
To be wanted back badly enough? Would you go then,
Even for a few nights, into that other life where you
And that first she loved, blind to the future once, and happy?

Would I put on my coat and return to the kitchen where my
Mother and father sit waiting, dinner keeping warm on the
        stove?
Bowie will never die. Nothing will come for him in his sleep
Or charging through his veins. And he'll never grow old,
Just like the woman you lost, who will always be dark-haired

And flush-faced, running toward an electronic screen
That clocks the minutes, the miles left to go. Just like the life
In which I'm forever a child looking out my window at the
        night sky
Thinking one day I'll touch the world with bare hands
Even if it burns.

2.

He leaves no tracks. Slips past, quick as a cat. That's Bowie
For you: the Pope of Pop, coy as Christ. Like a play
Within a play, he's trademarked twice. The hours

Plink past like water from a window A/C. We sweat it out,
Teach ourselves to wait. Silently, lazily, collapse happens.
But not for Bowie. He cocks his head, grins that wicked grin.

Time never stops, but does it end? And how many lives
Before take-off, before we find ourselves
Beyond ourselves, all glam-glow, all twinkle and gold?

The future isn't what it used to be. Even Bowie thirsts
For something good and cold. Jets blink across the sky
Like migratory souls.

3.

Bowie is among us. Right here
In New York City. In a baseball cap
And expensive jeans. Ducking into
A deli. Flashing all those teeth
At the doorman on his way back up.
Or he's hailing a taxi on Lafayette
As the sky clouds over at dusk.
He's in no rush. Doesn't feel
The way you'd think he feels.
Doesn't strut or gloat. Tells jokes.

I've lived here all these years
And never seen him. Like not knowing
A comet from a shooting star.
But I'll bet he burns bright,
Dragging a tail of white-hot matter
The way some of us track tissue
Back from the toilet stall. He's got
The whole world under his foot,
And we are small alongside,
Though there are occasions

When a man his size can meet
Your eyes for just a blip of time
And send a thought like SHINE
SHINE SHINE SHINE SHINE
Straight to your mind. Bowie,
I want to believe you. Want to feel
Your will like the wind before rain.
The kind everything simply obeys,

Swept up in that hypnotic dance
As if something with the power to do so
Had looked its way and said:

      Go ahead.

The Universe Is a House Party

The universe is expanding. Look: postcards
And panties, bottles with lipstick on the rim,

Orphan socks and napkins dried into knots.
Quickly, wordlessly, all of it whisked into file

With radio waves from a generation ago
Drifting to the edge of what doesn't end,

Like the air inside a balloon. Is it bright?
Will our eyes crimp shut? Is it molten, atomic,

A conflagration of suns? It sounds like the kind of party
Your neighbors forget to invite you to: bass throbbing

Through walls, and everyone thudding around drunk
On the roof. We grind lenses to an impossible strength,

Point them toward the future, and dream of beings
We'll welcome with indefatigable hospitality:

How marvelous you've come! We won't flinch
At the pinprick mouths, the nubbin limbs. We'll rise,

Gracile, robust. *Mi casa es su casa.* Never more sincere.
Seeing us, they'll know exactly what we mean.

Of course, it's ours. If it's anyone's, it's ours.

Declaration

He has
　　sent hither swarms of Officers to harass our people

He has plundered our—

　　　　ravaged our—

　　　　　　destroyed the lives of our—

taking away our—

　　abolishing our most valuable—

and altering fundamentally the Forms of our—

In every stage of these Oppressions We have Petitioned for Redress in the most humble terms:
　　　　Our repeated Petitions have been answered only by repeated injury.

we have reminded them of the circumstances of our emigration and settlement here.

　　—taken Captive
　　　　on the high Seas
　　　　　　to bear—

SHARAN STRANGE

Offering

In the dream, I am burning the rice.
I am cooking for God. I will clean
the house to please Him. So I wash the dishes,
and it begins to burn. It is for luck.
Like rice pelting newlyweds,
raining down, it is another veil,
or an offering that suggests
her first duty: to feed him.

Burning, it turns brown, the color
of my father, whom I never pleased.
Too late, I stand at his bed, calling.
He is swathed in twisted sheets,
a heavy mummy that will not
eat or cry. Will he sleep when
a tall stranger comes to murder me?
Will I die this fourth time, or the next?

When I run it is as if underwater,
slow, sluggish as the swollen grains
rising out of the briny broth to fill the pot,
evicting the steam in low shrieks
like God's breath sucked back in.
Before I slip the black husk of sleep,
I complete the task. The rice chars,
crumbles to dust, to mix with
the salty water, to begin again.

Snow

for Toi Derricotte

It came once, the year I turned ten.
That year they told us how we
would become women, and I began
my monthly vigil. But this was
the miracle, singular, unexpected.

The whites had finally stopped
resisting. Unwanted at their school,
we went anyway—*historic*, our parents
intoned, eyes flashing caution
to our measured breaths.

That first martial autumn mellowed
into a winter of grudging acceptance
and private discontent, a season of hope
shaped by fists and threats.
Then angels molted, pelting all

of creation with their cast-off garb.
We went home early, drifting through
a landscape of sudden ghosts,
the yard churning in frothy waves,
as if by an invisible tide of protestors.

What I remember most is its rude
coldness, stinging and wet. How we
mixed it with milk, sugar, vanilla,
into a poor child's ice cream that
melted before we could savor it.

SAMANTHA THORNHILL

Ode to Gentrification

Old school denizens of this
bleach-boned block say:
the realest thing
about the white woman
and her Yorkie
on this reimagined street
is the leather of the leash
that tethers them.

Your very name, glass
splinter planted deep in the fat
of our vernacular. Gentrification,
rightly mistaken
for juxtaposition:
pretty boys with swagger,
checkerboard trains,
skyscraper sadness,
bodegas sighing out soy.

Peruvian girl and boy fattening
fridges with Fiji between
homeworks, while Pops
slices and dices, and Mom
rocks the register.

Kissing cousin to gratification,
you birth gratitude—
twin to regret.
Call me *regrateful.*

I am so sorry to thank you
for the manner in which
I participate in your cruel,
and convenient, magic.

You ushered out
the families who dreamed
where my head now rests.

Yesterday, I retrieved laundry
cleaner than bells, unmentionables
caressed by another's
mother's hands.

I sit on the up-
side of your coin,
drinking down the sky's blue
dregs, while the teens I teach,
and the sturdy black
grandmothers I salute
with my seat,
kiss concrete.

NATASHA TRETHEWEY

Flounder

Here, she said, *put this on your head.*
She handed me a hat.
You 'bout as white as your dad,
and you gone stay like that.

Aunt Sugar rolled her nylons down
around each bony ankle,
and I rolled down my white knee socks
letting my thin legs dangle,

circling them just above water
and silver backs of minnows
flitting here then there between
the sunspots and the shadows.

This is how you hold the pole
to cast the line out straight.
Now put that worm on your hook,
throw it out, and wait.

She sat spitting tobacco juice
into a coffee cup.
Hunkered down when she felt the bite,
jerked the pole straight up

reeling and tugging hard at the fish
that wriggled and tried to fight back.
A flounder, she said, *and you can tell*
'cause one of its sides is black.

The other side is white, she said.
It landed with a thump.
I stood there watching that fish flip-flop,
switch sides with every jump.

Drapery Factory, Gulfport, Mississippi, 1956

She made the trip daily, though
later she would not remember
how far to tell the grandchildren—
Better that way.
She could keep those miles
a secret, and her black face
and black hands, and the pink bottoms
of her black feet
a minor inconvenience.

She does remember the men
she worked for, and that often
she sat side by side
with white women, all of them
bent over, pushing into the hum
of the machines, their right calves
tensed against the pedals.

Her lips tighten speaking
of quitting time when
the colored women filed out slowly
to have their purses checked,
the insides laid open and exposed
by the boss's hand.

          But then she laughs
when she recalls the soiled Kotex
she saved, stuffed into a bag
in her purse, and Adam's look
on one white man's face, his hand
deep in knowledge.

Graveyard Blues

It rained the whole time we were laying her down;
Rained from church to grave when we put her down.
The suck of mud at our feet was a hollow sound.

When the preacher called out I held up my hand;
When he called for a witness I raised my hand—
Death stops the body's work, the soul's a journeyman.

The sun came out when I turned to walk away,
Glared down on me as I turned and walked away—
My back to my mother, leaving her where she lay.

The road going home was pocked with holes,
That home-going road's always full of holes;
Though we slow down, time's wheel still rolls.

　　　I wander now among names of the dead:
　　　My mother's name, stone pillow for my head.

Pilgrimage

Vicksburg, Mississippi

Here, the Mississippi carved
　　　its mud-dark path, a graveyard

for skeletons of sunken riverboats.
　　　Here, the river changed its course,

turning away from the city
　　　as one turns, forgetting, from the past—

the abandoned bluffs, land sloping up
　　　above the river's bend—where now

the Yazoo fills the Mississippi's empty bed.
       Here, the dead stand up in stone, white

marble, on Confederate Avenue. I stand
       on ground once hollowed by a web of caves;

they must have seemed like catacombs,
       in 1863, to the woman sitting in her parlor,

candlelit, underground. I can see her
       listening to shells explode, writing herself

into history, asking *what is to become*
       of all the living things in this place?

This whole city is a grave. Every spring—
       Pilgrimage—the living come to mingle

with the dead, brush against their cold shoulders
       in the long hallways, listen all night

to their silence and indifference, relive
       their dying on the green battlefield.

At the museum, we marvel at their clothes—
       preserved under glass—so much smaller

than our own, as if those who wore them
       were only children. We sleep in their beds,

the old mansions hunkered on the bluffs, draped
       in flowers—funereal—a blur

of petals against the river's gray.
       The brochure in my room calls this

living history. The brass plate on the door reads
       Prissy's Room. A window frames

the river's crawl toward the Gulf. In my dream,
         the ghost of history lies down beside me,

rolls over, pins me beneath a heavy arm.

Miscegenation

In 1965 my parents broke two laws of Mississippi;
they went to Ohio to marry, returned to Mississippi.

They crossed the river into Cincinnati, a city whose name
begins with a sound like *sin,* the sound of wrong—*mis* in
         Mississippi.

A year later they moved to Canada, followed a route the same
as slaves, the train slicing the white glaze of winter, leaving
         Mississippi.

Faulkner's Joe Christmas was born in winter, like Jesus, given
         his name
for the day he was left at the orphanage, his race unknown in
         Mississippi.

My father was reading *War and Peace* when he gave me my
         name.
I was born near Easter, 1966, in Mississippi.

When I turned 33 my father said, *It's your Jesus year—you're
         the same*
age he was when he died. It was spring, the hills green in
         Mississippi.

I know more than Joe Christmas did. Natasha is a Russian
         name—
though I'm not; it means *Christmas child,* even in
         Mississippi.

Incident

We tell the story every year—
how we peered from the windows, shades drawn—
though nothing really happened,
the charred grass now green again.

We peered from the windows, shades drawn,
at the cross trussed like a Christmas tree,
the charred grass still green. Then
we darkened our rooms, lit the hurricane lamps.

At the cross trussed like a Christmas tree,
a few men gathered, white as angels in their gowns.
We darkened our rooms and lit hurricane lamps,
the wicks trembling in their fonts of oil.

It seemed the angels had gathered, white men in their gowns.
When they were done, they left quietly. No one came.
The wicks trembled all night in their fonts of oil;
by morning the flames had all dimmed.

When they were done, the men left quietly. No one came.
Nothing really happened.
By morning all the flames had dimmed.
We tell the story every year.

LYRAE VAN CLIEF-STEFANON

Strip

A thin brown-haired girl pouts
high on stage. She cannot swing
her slight body round the new pole.
It runs floor to ceiling, piercing
the strip club like a shaft of light
the way the voice of God appears in movies.
Except this pole is plastic and God
would gurgle because it's full of liquid
like a lava lamp. The words would have to sploosh
up through bubbles
like burps, one at a time like *Jesus.*

Is. Love. except the pole's sealed
and there is no place for love to go
so the bubbles just keep going up
and down and the girl
can't get her hands around it.
She says she misses the jungle-gym-type bar
this bubble bar replaced.
She anticipates missing the smell
of its metals on her hands after work.

Training me, she instructs *Don't touch*
your thighs. Don't touch your knees.
Keep both feet on the floor at all times.
Don't do anything I do. She smiles
at the way everything is against some law.
I go on stage and the speakers spit
out the first lines of the song I picked:
I love myself / I want you to love me.
I dance for a man. He's fifty, at least,
his wife beside him. *But you're beautiful*
she says, like a mother comforting a taunted child,

like someone else's mother. Mine said *There is nothing*
you can't talk your way out of.

The bar's dark and dollars scratch my skin.
When the next song starts I take off my bra,
my breasts covered by Florida law
with flesh brown tape. I wrap my arms,
both legs around the wide, bright pole,
spin slowly down to the floor.
Who else will pay for what he can't see?
Like God, I've always been invisible

RR Lyrae: Matter

He still exists as flesh; it's the idea
that's dissipated—: husband :—what was he?
But a word I loved? There is no panacea
for missing syllables: his body: we
all know what matter's mostly made of—: space
obtains—: One day I realized I believe—:
the space in everything is God: that force
of present absence: pen: expanse: I grieve—
] *old fashioned: distance; squinting it into view* [
between body and name—in here!—I'm loose
as love is—: nebulous—: what good
this pointillism—: our eyes won't do—:
Sometimes the absences in us seem so profuse,
I wonder we don't pass through wood.

FRANK X. WALKER

Wind Talker

> Ocian in view! O! the joy.
> —William Clark

If I could make my words
dress they naked selves in blackberry juice
lay down on a piece a bark, sheep
or onion skin, like Massa do

If I could send a letter home to my wife
float it in the wind, on wings or water

I'd tell her 'bout Katonka
an all the wide an high places
this side a the big river.
How his family, numbering three
for every star in the sky
look like a forest when they graze together
turn into the muddy M'soura
when they thunder along, faster than any horse
making the grass lay down
long after the quiet has returned.
How they don't so much as raise a tail
when I come 'round with my wooly head
an tobacco skin, like I'm one a them
making the Arikara an Mandan think me
"Big Medicine"
Katonka, who walk like man.

Work Ethic

I was deeded to Massa Clark
down on the plantation in Virginy
when he was just a green sapling.
I was less in years but already in a man's body
'cause a all the hard work 'round the place.
We wadn't never what you calls friends
but we pieced together a bond that served us well
for most our time together.

The way it seem to me, the slave only got two choices.
The first is to make up his mind to wake up every day
a slave or steal away in the wind an the night.
An even if the lot he draws is to pick cotton
every day he breathe
he can decide to be the best picker ever was
or fill the bottom a his burlap with rocks an dirt.

I got a better taste a life on the frontier
in Kentucke an the Indian territory
an come to accept my duties as his servant.
It seem like God make my heart even bigger
then the chest it beat in, so I figures
the least I can do is to never let my spirit
be broken by the lash.

A slave needs plenty a fear to survive in Virginy.
I was better suited for the wild, as I had none.

ANTHONY WALTON

Dissidence

in memoriam Thelonious Monk

You have to be able to hear past the pain, the obvious
minor-thirds and major-sevenths, the merely beautiful

ninths; you have to grow deaf to what you imagine
are the sounds of loneliness; you have to learn indifference

to static, and welcome noise like rain, acclimate
to another kind of silence; you have to be able to sleep

in the city, taxis and trucks careening through your dreams
and back again, hearing the whines and sirens and shrieks

as music; you must be a mathematician, a magician
of algebra, overtone and acoustics, mapping the splintered

intervals of time, tempo, harmony, stalking or sluicing blues
scales; you have to be unafraid of redundance, and aware

that dissonance-driven explorations of dissonance
may circle back to the crowded room of resolution;

you have to disagree with everything except the piano, black
and white keys marking the path you must climb step

by half-step with no compass but the blues, no company
but your distrust of the journey, of all that you hear, of
        arrival.

Gwendolyn Brooks
(*1917–2000*)

Sometimes I see in my mind's eye a four- or five-
year-old boy, coatless and wandering
a windblown and vacant lot or street in Chicago
on the windblown South Side. He disappears
but stays with me, staring and pronouncing
me guilty of an indifference more callous
than neglect, condescension as self-pity.

Then I see him again, at ten or fifteen, on the corner,
say, 47th and Martin Luther King, or in a group
of men surrounding a burning barrel off Lawndale,
everything surrounding vacant or for sale.
Sometimes I trace him on the train to Joliet
or Menard, such towns quickly becoming native
ground to these boys who seem to be nobody's
sons, these boys who are so hard to love, so hard
to see, except as case studies.

Poverty, pain, shame, one and a half million
dreams deemed fit only for the most internal
of exiles. That four-year-old wandering
the wind tunnels of Robert Taylor, of Cabrini
Green, wind chill of an as yet unplumbed degree—
a young boy she did not have to know to love.

SIMONE WHITE

The reeds shook. A wide flat ass cradled in leather pants. This man's body I know and this one; I know what happens in two years, in five in twenty. "Time passing." Strong here, weak here, breaks along the line of. Bowsprit/disaster. Moooooooring. Silent ululations of turtle-eaters, or turtles being eaten. Vagaries and unattended lists. Everywhere giggles or handstanding over the new death, inability to love, covered in sensation and distance, wrapped in the life happening, covered in it, like a cling wrap, of which there is none. Called for you yesterday and nothing happened. Happening, also an absurdity, poorly understood until guns appear. A duet of spun tops, a trio, a quartet. Add another instrument that can't be held with life of its own that trembles with its own interior g, world itself. Call it a ghost, call its music ghostly, call what I want to do with your body a silence, call it an aporia, call it exigency, call it leave-taking or rest, I don't care what you call it, call it having been created for the no place of taking hold inside the inside call heard in the reeds.

SAUL WILLIAMS

Amethyst Rocks

CHAPTER 1

I stand on the corner of the block slinging
amethyst rocks. Drinkin 40's of mother
earth's private nectar stock. Dodgin cops.
'Cause Five-O be the 666 and I need a fix
of that purple rain. The type of shit that
drives membranes insane. Oh yeah, I'm in
the fast lane. Snorting candy yams. That free
my body and soul and send me like Shazaam!

Never question who I am. God knows.
And I know God, personally. In fact, he
lets me call him me. I be one with rain
and stars and things, with dancing feet
and watermelon wings. I bring the
sunshine and the moon. And wind blows
my tune.

CHAPTER 2

Meanwhile I spoon powdered drumbeats
into plastic, bags. Sellin kilos of kente scag
Takin drags off of collards and cornbread
Free-basin through saxophones and flutes
like mad. The high notes make me space
float. I be exhalin in rings that circle Saturn.
Leavin stains in my veins in astrological patterns.

Yeah, I'm Sirius B. Dogon NGHs plotted
shit, lovely. But the feds are also plotting
me. They're trying to imprison my astrology.
Put my stars behind bars. My stars in stripes.
Using blood-splattered banners as nationalist

kites. But I control the wind. That's why they
call it the hawk.

CHAPTER 3

I am Horus. Son of Isis. Son of Osiris.
Worshipped as Jesus. Resurrected like
Lazarus. But you can call me Lazzie. Lazy.
Yeah, I'm lazy 'cause I'd rather sit and build
than work and plow a field of cash green crops.

Your evolution stopped with the evolution
of your technology. A society of automatic
tellers and money machines. NGH WHT?
My culture is lima beans. Dreams manifest.
Dreams real. Not consistent with rational.

I dance for no reason. For reason you
can't dance. Caught in the inactiveness
of intellectualized circumstance. You
can't learn my steps until you unlearn
your thoughts. Spirit/soul can't be store
bought. Fuck thought. It leads to naught.
Simply stated, it leads to you trying to
figure me out.

CHAPTER 4

Your intellect is disfiguring your soul.
Your being's not whole. Check your flagpole:
stars and stripes. Your astrology's imprisoned
by your concept of white, of self. What's your
plan for spiritual health? Calling reality unreal.
Your line of thought is tangled.

The star-spangled got your soul mangled.
Your being's angled, forbidding you to be real
and feel. You can't find truth with an ax or a
drill, in a white house on a hill, or in factories
or plants made of steel.

CHAPTER 5

Stealing me was the smartest thing you ever
did. Too bad you don't teach the truth to your
kids. My influence on you is the reflection you
see when you look into your minstrel mirror
and talk about your culture.

Your existence is that of a schizophrenic vulture
who thinks he has enough life in him to prey on
the dead, not knowing that the dead ain't dead and
that he ain't got enough spirituality to know how
to pray. Yeah, there's no repentance. You're bound
to live an infinite, consecutive, executive life sentence.

So while you're busy serving time, I'll be in synch
with the moon, while you run from the sun. Life of
the womb reflected by guns. Worshipper of moons,
I am the sun. And I am public enemy number one.
One. One. One. One. One. One. That's seven. And
I'll be out on the block. Hustlin culture. Slingin
amethyst rocks.

KEVIN YOUNG

Money Road

for John T. Edge

On the way to Money,
  Mississippi, we see little
ghosts of snow, falling faint

  as words while we try to find
Robert Johnson's muddy
  maybe grave. Beside Little Zion,

along the highwayside, this stone
  keeps its offerings—Bud & Louisiana
Hot Sauce—the ground giving

  way beneath our feet.
The blues always dance
  cheek to cheek with a church—

Booker's Place back
  in Greenwood still standing,
its long green bar

  beautiful, Friendship Church just
a holler away. Shotgun,
  shotgun, shotgun—

———————

rows of colored
  houses, as if the same can
of bright stain might cover the sins

of rotting wood, now
mostly tarpaper & graffiti
    holding McLaurin Street together—

RIP Boochie—the undead walk
    these streets seeking something
we take pictures of

    & soon flee. The hood
of a car yawns open
    in awe, men's heads

peer in its lion's mouth
    seeking their share. FOR SALE:
Squash & Snap Beans. The midden

    of oyster shells behind Lusco's—
the tiny O of a bullethole
    in Booker's plate glass window.

———————

Even the Salvation
    Army Thrift Store
closed, bars over

    every door.
We're on our way again,
    away, along the Money

Road, past grand houses
    & porte cocheres set back
from the lane, crossing the bridge

    to find markers of what's
no more there—even the underpass
    bears a name. It's all

too grave—the fake
    sharecropper homes
of Tallahatchie Flats rented out

   along the road, staged bottle trees
chasing away nothing, the new outhouse
   whose crescent door foreign tourists

———————

pay extra for. Cotton planted
   in strict rows
for show. A quiet

   snowglobe of pain
I want to shake.
   While the flakes fall

like ash we race
   the train to reach the place
Emmett Till last

   whistled or smiled
or did nothing.
   Money more

a crossroads
   than the crossroads be—
its gnarled tree—the Bryant Store

   facing the tracks, now turnt
the color of earth, tumbling down
   slow as the snow, white

———————

& insistent as the woman
   who sent word
of that uppity boy, her men

   who yanked you out
your uncle's home
   into the yard, into oblivion—

into this store abutting
   the MONEY GIN CO.
whose sign, worn away,

   now reads UN
Or SIN, I swear—
   whose giant gin fans,

like those lashed & anchored
   to your beaten body,
still turn. Shot, dumped,

   dredged, your face not even
a mask—a marred,
   unspared, sightless stump—

———————

all your mother insists
   we must see to know
What they did

   to my baby. The true
Tallahatchie twisting south,
   the Delta

Death's second cousin
   once removed. You down
for only the summer, to leave

   the stifling city where later
you will be waked,
   displayed, defiant,

a dark glass.
   There are things
that cannot be seen

but must be. Buried
barely, this place
  no one can keep—

             ———

Yet how to kill
  a ghost? The fog
of our outdoor talk—

  we breathe,
we grieve, we drink
  our tidy drinks. I think

now winter will out—
  the snow bless
& kiss

  this cursed earth.
Or is it cussed? I don't
  yet know. Let the cold keep

still your bones.

EIGHT
AFTER THE HURRICANE
(2009–2020)

HANIF ABDURRAQIB

How Can Black People Write about Flowers at a Time Like This

dear reader, with our heels digging into the good
mud at a swamp's edge, you might tell me something

about the dandelion head & how it is not a flower itself
but a plant made up of many small flowers at its crown

& lord knows I have been called by what I look like
more than I have been called by what I actually am &

I wish to return the favor for the purpose of this
exercise. which, too, is an attempt at fashioning

something pretty out of seeds refusing to make anything
worthwhile of their burial. size me up & skip whatever
    semantics arrive

to the tongue first. say: that boy he look like a hollowed-out
    grandfather
clock. he look like a million-dollar god with a two-cent

heaven. like all it takes is one kiss & before morning,
you could scatter his whole mind across a field.

ELIZABETH ACEVEDO

La Negra Takes Medusa to the Hair Salon

and the salonist from Santiago runs her fingers through the serpents. It'll *be extra for la monstra*, she tells La Negra, *her snakes, they hiss and squirm too much*. It takes the salonist hours to bend the snakes around the rollers, lie still beneath the hair net.

The dryer bell dings. The snakes have grown drowsy, easier for the salonist to drag the wide-bristle brush through Medusa's scalp with one hand, lulling the snakes straight with the blower in the other. The last of them uncoil and hang limply down Medusa's back.

Oh, doesn't she look so much better! The women in rollers croon, *Una propia tigerasa*. They comment on how the snakes' eyes have been seared and swollen shut, how their tongues swing gently from their mouths, their fangs bent loose by the small-tooth comb.

And although Medusa cannot possibly understand the cadence of el Cibao, she fingers her half dead snakes, holds one up to her mouth,

ay Negra, ay Negra, she doesn't say.

CAMERON AWKWARD-RICH

Cento Between the Ending and the End

Sometimes you don't die
when you're supposed to
& now I have a choice
repair a world or build
a new one inside my body
a white door opens
into a place queerly brimming
gold light so velvet-gold
it is like the world
hasn't happened
when I call out
all my friends are there
everyone we love
is still alive gathered
at the lakeside
like constellations
my honeyed kin
honeyed light
beneath the sky
a garden blue stalks
white buds the moon's
marble glow the fire
distant & flickering
the body whole bright-
winged brimming
with the hours
of the day beautiful
nameless planet. Oh
friends, my friends—
bloom how you must, wild
until we are free.

JOSHUA BENNETT

America Will Be

after Langston Hughes

I am now at the age where my father calls me brother
when we say goodbye. *Take care of yourself, brother,*
he whispers a half beat before we hang up the phone,
and it is as if some great bridge has unfolded over the air
between us. He is 68 years old. He was born in the throat
of Jim Crow Alabama, one of ten children, their bodies side
by side in the kitchen each morning like a pair of hands
exalting. Over breakfast, I ask him to tell me the hardest
    thing
about going to school back then, expecting some history
I have already memorized. Boycotts & attack dogs, fire
hoses, Bull Connor in his personal tank, candy paint
shining white as a slaver's ghost. He says: *Having to read
the Canterbury Tales.* He says: *eating lunch alone.* Now, I
    hear
the word America & think first of my father's loneliness,
the hands holding the pens that stabbed him as he walked
through the hallway, unclenched palms settling
onto a wooden desk, taking notes, trying to pretend
the shame didn't feel like an inheritance. You say *democracy*
& I see the men holding documents that sent him off
to war a year later, Motown blaring from a country
boy's bunker as napalm scarred the sky into jigsaw
patterns, his eyes open wide as the blooming blue
heart of the light bulb in a Crown Heights basement
where he & my mother will dance for the first time, their
    bodies
swaying like rockets in the impossible dark & yes I know
that this is more than likely not what you mean
when you sing *liberty* but it is the only kind
I know or can readily claim, the times where those hunted

by history are underground & somehow daring to love
what they cannot hold or fully fathom when the stranger
is not a threat but the promise of a different ending
I woke up this morning and there were men on television
lauding a wall big enough to box out an entire world,
families torn with the stroke of a pen, citizenship
little more than some garment that can be stolen or reduced
to cinder at a tyrant's whim my father knows this grew up
knowing this witnessed firsthand the firebombs
the Klan multiple messiahs love soaked & shot through
somehow still believes in this grand blood-stained
experiment still votes still prays that his children might
make a life unlike any he has ever seen. He looks
at me like the promise of another cosmos and I never
know what to tell him. All of the books in my head
have made me cynical and distant, but there's a choir
in him that calls me forward my disbelief built as it is
from the bricks of his belief not in any America
you might see on network news or hear heralded
before a football game but in the quiet
power of Sam Cooke singing that he was born
by a river that remains unnamed that he runs
alongside to this day, some vast and future country,
some nation within a nation, black as candor,
loud as the sound of my father's
unfettered laughter over cheese eggs & coffee
his eyes shut tight as armories his fists
unclenched as if he were invincible

REGINALD DWAYNE BETTS

A Postmodern Two-Step

Some people say prison is *the country*
where life is cheaper than anywhere else;
you wouldn't think that watching us take leave,
our caravan three deep and black against
the wine-dark asphalt, and two of three
are nothing but escorts: four uniformed
shotguns (off safety) leading and flanking
our coffle, all intent to keep us here,
and not wherever shackles and cuffs run
in this dead of morning, less than fifty miles
from where Nat Turner dug a hole and lay
for weeks. Virginia, something noose-like then
and some say still, except for all the shit
we did to land in this here hull and cul-
de-sac. The guard, he say "die, but don't run"
when one of us begin to cough his lung
up in sleep. And this is ruin. Damn these chains,
this awkward dance I do with this van. Two-step,
my body swaying back and forth, my head
a pendulum that's rocked by the wild riffs
of the dudes I'm riding with: them white folks know
you ain't god body, what you commune wine
and bread? Where you from son? Red lines?
To what Onion? My eyes two caskets though,
so the voices are sheets of sound. Our van as dark
inside as out, and all the bodies black
and voices black too and I tell my god
if you have ears for this one, know I want
no part of it, no Onions and no tears.
I tell no one, and cry my dirge.
                              This place,
the cracked and scratching vinyl seats, the loud
loud talk of murder this and blanket fear
around the rest, is where I'm most at home,

but it's beyond where prayers reach, a point
something like purgatory. I lean back
and drift in sleep as someone says, his voice
all hoarse and jacked, all broken songbird-like
all revolutions end with a L-note.

MAHOGANY L. BROWNE

upon viewing the death of basquiat[*]

~~i look into the noise~~   ~~mouth paper thin~~
~~my tongue~~——a scatter ~~of forgotten belongings~~
extinguishes ~~the heat of~~ home

[*]once, my mother plagued a painting   swept oceanic throughout
the dreams of a brown man in the lower manhattan   three years
later   she sun rose in california   swan dove into an oblique woman
there are days i forget my name   *my name* i forget my claim   this
kind of fire that strikes black bodies into fever *spliff*   clean   cleaner,
still   ain't no mountain of needles or glass   pipes large enough to
tow away my body   today, my mouth is a tomb   of the things
people forget   such a power my maw, this spill wonder, this rapture
of psalm   ain't no way   I let the sun   set us afire   again

928

DOMINIQUE CHRISTINA

Massa's House

noiseless as a grave
the missus caint get an egg to
fry right she need
lemons in the water
lace on the table
fruits sittin heavy in big ole
glass bowls
i takes the brown ones
stick em in my apron
juice run down like church
pulp-sweet and hidden
the missus don't know
how to keep the soup pots full.
she sick wit lovelessness
she preach. she beat
til she think she got somethin
she can use.
but me?
i thick. i thick wit secrets . . .
only thing i got that's mine.

TIANA CLARK

Nashville

is hot chicken on sopping white bread with green pickle
chips—sour to balance prismatic, flame-colored spice
for white people. Or, rather, white people now curate hot
chicken for $16 and two farm-to-table sides, or maybe

they've hungered fried heat and grease from black food
and milk—but didn't want to drive to Jefferson Street or
don't know about the history of Jefferson Street or Hell's
Half Acre, north of downtown. Where freed slaves lived

on the fringe of Union camps, built their own new country.
Where its golden age brought the Silver Streak, a ballroom
bringing Basie, Ellington, and Fitzgerald. First-run movies
at the Ritz and no one had to climb to the balcony. 1968,

they built the interstate. I-40 bisected the black community
like a tourniquet of concrete. There were no highway exits.
120 businesses closed. Ambulance siren driving over
the house that called 911, diminishing howl in the distance,

black bodies going straight to the morgue. At the downtown
library, a continuous loop flashes SNCC videos with black
and white kids training for spit and circular cigarette burns
as the video toggles from coaching to counters covered

in pillars of salt and pie and soda—magma of the movement.
On I-65, there is a two-tone Confederate statue I flick off
daily on my morning commute. Walking down Second Avenue,
past neon Honky Tonks playing bro-country and Cash

and herds of squealing pink bachelorette parties—someone
yelled *Nigger-lover* at my husband. Again. Walking down
Second Avenue, I thought I heard someone yelling at the back
of my husband. I turned around to find the voice and saw

myself as someone who didn't give a damn. Again. I turned
around to find that it was I who lived inside the lovely word
made flesh by white mouths masticating mashed sweet potatoes
from my mother's mother's mother—Freelove was her name,

a slave from Warrior, North Carolina, with twelve children
with names like Pansy, Viola, Oscar, Stella, and Toy—
my grandmother. There is always a word I'm chasing inside
and outside of my body, a word inside another word, scanning

the *OED* for soot-covered roots: 1577, 1584, 1608 . . . Tracing my
finger along the boomerang shape of the Niger River for my blood.
1856, 1866, 1889 . . . *Who said it?* A hyphen—crackles and bites,
burns the body to a spray of white wisps, like when the hot comb,

with its metal teeth, cut close to petroleum jelly edging the scalp—
sizzling. Southern Babel, smoking the hive of epithets hung fat
above bustling crowds like black-and-white lynching photographs,
mute faces, red finger pointing up at my dead, some smiling,

some with hats and ties—all business, as one needlelike lady
is looking at the camera, as if looking through the camera, at me,
in the way I am looking at my lover now—halcyon and constant.
Once my mother-in-law said: *Watch your back*, and I knew exactly

what she meant. Again. I turned around to find I am the breath
of Apollo panting at the back of Daphne's wild hair, chasing words
like arrows inside the knotted meat between my shoulder blades—
four violent syllables stabbing my skin, enamored with pain.

I am kissing all the trees—searching the mob, mumbling to myself:
Who said it?
Who said it?
Who said it?

DÉLANA R. A. DAMERON

Dear——,

My Grandma taught me to give ourselves room—
belts should have extra loops; shoes an inch of give—
if we keep ourselves in a space not fit for keeping,
we'll be crushed.   I never liked shoes.
Or the south.   I want to walk one day.

I am sitting here trying to understand I only loved you
because you remind me of home & why I cannot go back.
I cannot dial your number & whisper hello.
You know I am sad when things break & cannot be mended.
Your laughter at my sadness hurts also.

Hasn't this city taught me enough
about breaking, or wilderness   to survive
is to be stone-faced, not tender?   I want soft hands.

But this city has given me tough palms & cold bones
because I packed away my coats prematurely
wishing for Aprils & Mays & bare shoulders.
I know things come & go as they please.

Winter will stay. The daffodils sprouted too soon
& now gone. I keep trying to remember the last three digits
of your phone number but I can't.   Right now
my windows are open & jazz plays in the Harlem streets—

I find it impossible not to want or miss what is familiar:
The sweet tea you keep in your New York fridge.
My father's holiday grilling.   Magnolia blossoms.
I know damn well. It's all gone.

LaTASHA N. NEVADA DIGGS

My First Black Nature Poem™

there is a dark mass following me. these legs are clumsy. they
     flap quickly.
I want to slow them down. but my nerves. *Lord,* these
     pensive endings.

the sun slumps against the merging fall on red leaves.
and *where the natives are unenlightened,* the mass comes
     closer.

          only white people swim in lakes nowadays
          you know . . . Crystal Lake?

never seen a black person jump in a lake;
let alone a river till this summer.
the Bronx River is said to be clean: we care about clean.
a month before, two boys drowned in the Bronx River.
a week after, a boy jumps into it unfazed.

abandoned tires, relics of its sewer days, river herring spark
     no fear.
and a publicly funded park with a biology class, a boat-making
     workshop
for the children of Hunt's Point, gives me hope we'd wet our
     hair again.

  (these follicles don't surf; don't swim)

but here in Virginia, there's little comfort.
the blush current from underwater springs makes me tense.

          white people form groups to paddle on boards across
               the Hudson,

taking on trends from Hawai'i. they tap into the
    yesterdays
of Algonquian tongues. Wappinger. Mohican.

a sporty new aged (like gouda) convenience.
a luxury to admire when Long Beach is too far
and Rockaway too dirty.

black folk don't swim. we splash and cool off.
we a ways forward from a Splenda hint of Senegalese
    manliness diving from a ferry,
miles off shore from Gorée. that water got too much
    memory.
we much prefer chlorine. that salt and fresh water our
    hypertension.

and that ocean is curiously scary.
and this lake is charmed and churning with tales from
    the deep.

profound is this river of B-rated torture.
deep are shadow people speculated through my rave
    tangerine goggles.

on Lake Champlain at night, the chilly air felt like a presence.
swamp monsters (this ain't a swamp). tubular amphibians
    (they'd be in rivers).
aquatic reptilians. ancestors distraught and vengeful (like
    Jason).

but this is smaller and gnawing like chiggers; something
    from my weed days
could live. down. here.

my arms fight the green clearness. so mud olive I cannot see
    the bottom.
beneath me is crisp. a fallen branch is mistaken for an eel.

EVE L. EWING

I saw Emmett Till this week at the grocery store

There is no time to be lost. Other matters must be put aside for the moment and a solution reached for Chicago's greatest problem. (44)

looking over the plums, one by one
lifting each to his eyes and
turning it slowly, a little earth,
checking the smooth skin for pockmarks
and rot, or signs of unkind days or people,
then sliding them gently into the plastic.
whistling softly, reaching with a slim, woolen arm
into the cart, he first balanced them over the wire
before realizing the danger of bruising
and lifting them back out, cradling them
in the crook of his elbow until
something harder could take that bottom space.

I knew him from his hat, one of those
fine porkpie numbers they used to sell
on Roosevelt Road. it had lost its feather but
he had carefully folded a dollar bill
and slid it between the ribbon and the felt
and it stood at attention. he wore his money.
upright and strong, he was already to the checkout
by the time I caught up with him. I called out his name
and he spun like a dancer, candy bar in hand,
looked at me quizzically for a moment before
remembering my face. he smiled. *well
hello young lady*

> *hello, so chilly today*
> *should have worn my warm coat like you*

935

yes so cool for August in Chicago

      how are things going for you

oh he sighed and put the candy on the belt
it goes, it goes.

SEAN HILL

Aunt Flo and Uncle Phineas

Two new old people
kinfolk from upcountry (Cleveland)
down for a couple of weeks of summer.

Sitting around the kitchen table
sipping moonshine—a taste from
their youth to take back North.
The sip I get expands in my throat—
a hot spirit too big for my little body.
It lingers in my mouth.
I breathe it in and out.

Relaxing on the screened-in porch Florence's smoky voice
scratches my back like the backscratchers
they brought down that we duel with.
A cough on the edge of every laugh—
phlegm, a baby's rattle in her throat.
In her purse—held close—cigarettes and flask bottle.

Listening to Phineas's voice big and booming—
round like his brown belly, which I beat on.
His voice has a hollow—not like the dark well
the old folks say is dug to hell but a hollow
like a hug—space enough to climb in and be held.

Sitting on the porch steps outside the screen, the old people
        within
earshot, I eat watermelon and spit seeds, which if I swallow
will grow inside me.

HARMONY HOLIDAY

(*Afterward*) *One Corner More/ Notes on a Letter to the Singer Abbey Lincoln from Her Lover, Abraham Lincoln*

I once received this astonishing letter, a truly atrocious one, especially upsetting because, just between us, most of what it said happened to be true. I sent it back. It came back to me. Sparring. The fix–blue mind could operate like a fugitive. Running from what. Running to something. Grace/the front row. And when you reach it. It doesn't exist.

I began praying in Paris. That I may not be a parody, that I may remain alert, naïve, piercing. I prayed from pairs of unreasonable meter, to where joy is sorrow unmasked. I prayed for at least ten years. Sometimes in public, when the brothels were full. Sometimes in Hollywood. Once upon a time they owned slaves/nowadays they rent them from the behavior of orators. I loved those men. It has nothing to do with Africa. Or a harp in the nightclub. Were you here to protect property like it was lives. Was I any of the difference? Fertile plots, of Storyland and rate times time spangled distance. Standards. Restrained urgency. When it finally cannot be judged it will be judged as jazz. You act like you know that insult by heart. But even that is a coincidence of the metaphysical world. It's cool, I'm black too. I can hear myself swallow into the microphone when he leaves in the middle of the show. As part of the song. Maybe we did what the music did, it's true. No truces. Locusts and doves,

You were a philosopher

You were a polygamous woman

You had the courage to defend yourself

It's always been like this

So if I had never met

anyone but you,

I would have known which way to go

ISHION HUTCHINSON

After the Hurricane

After the hurricane walks a silence, deranged, white as the
    white helmets
of government surveyors looking into roofless

shacks, accessing stunned fowls, noting inquiries
into the logic of feathers, reversed, like gullies still retching;
    they scribble facts

about fallen cedars, spread out like dead generals on leaf
medallions; they draw tables to show the shore

has rearranged its idea of beauty for the resort
villas, miraculously not rattled by the hurricane's—

call it Cyclops—passage through the lives
of children and pigs, the one eye that unhooked

banjos from the hills, smashed them in Rio Valley;
they record how it howled off to that dark parish

St. Thomas, stomping drunk with wire lashes and cramps,
paralyzing electric poles and coconut trees,

dishing discord among neighbours, exposed,
standing among their flattened, scattered lives for the first
    time.

It passed through Aunt May's head, upsetting
the furniture, left her chattering something,

a cross between a fowl and a child; they can't say
how it tore down her senses, no words, packing

their instruments, flies returning to genuflect
at their knees, on Aunt May's face, gone soft;

no words, except: *Don't fret,* driving off,
as if they had left better promises to come.

GARY JACKSON

Kansas

It's love you left, we'll say
when you never come back
for bells for the dead, for the grave
stone heads: the only ones
that don't keep count. Don't
we know it's love that keeps you
away, that marks every mile
devotion? You would've went
to the end with each one,
made Orpheus turn back.
Would've fell / would've leapt /
would've left. The living is easy
/ the leaving is easy / living
with ghosts, it was easy
to give up your home
to your father, struck
with the same grief
of living, demanding
what are you gonna do
with my mama's house?
Shorn grass & damp dirt:
they'll put me in the middle.
I kick the ground like tires,
feeling dumb without flowers /
tokens / grief / anything
in my hands. *You'll bring me*
back home, won't you? Stamp
it down, as if the flat earth
could answer sometimes this,
too, is love. You left.

SAEED JONES

Kudzu

I won't be forgiven
for what I've made
of myself.
      Soil recoils
from my hooked kisses.
      Pines turn their backs
on me. They know
what I can do
with the wrap of my legs.
      Each summer,
when the air becomes crowded
with want, I set all my tongues
upon you.
      To quiet this body,
you must answer
my tendriled craving.
      All I've ever wanted
was to kiss crevices, pry them open,
and flourish within dew-slick
hollows.
      How you mistake
my affection.
      If I ever strangled sparrows,
it was only because I dreamed
of better songs.

DONIKA KELLY

The moon rose over the bay. I had a lot of feelings.

I am taken with the hot animal
of my skin, grateful to swing my limbs

and have them move as I intend, though
my knee, though my shoulder, though something
is torn or tearing. Today, a dozen squid, dead

on the harbor beach: one mostly buried,
one with skin empty as a shell and hollow

feeling, and, though the tentacles look soft,
I do not touch them. I imagine they
were startled to find themselves in the sun.

I imagine the tide simply went out
without them. I imagine they cannot

feel the black flies charting the raised hills
of their eyes. I write my name in the sand:
Donika Kelly. I watch eighteen seagulls

skim the sandbar and lift low in the sky.
I pick up a pebble that looks like a green egg.

To the ditch lily I say *I am in love.*
To the Jeep parked haphazardly on the narrow
street *I am in love.* To the roses, white

petals rimmed brown, to the yellow lined
pavement, to the house trimmed in gold *I am*

in love. I shout with the rough calculus
of walking. Just let me find my way back,
let me move like a tide come in.

RICKEY LAURENTIIS

One Country

I want to be released from it.
I want its impulses stunned to lead.
This body. Its breath.
Let it. Let the whole pageant
end. If my body had a river in it
I would drain it. If by the river
was a city, let a storm shock and drown it.
If in the city was a boy made sick
from his body, the freak passions of it,
let him come out—his brown skin
lifting as a shell. Let it. Let all
his limbs pop and unhinge. First
his penis, its quick flight, as if a comet.
The eight fingers next, then thumbs,
then tongue, till every star is on the floor,
dismissed, each pointing in its own
direction, each another door
to the one country where his body is
loved and made for.

SHANE McCRAE

Still When I Picture It the Face of
God Is a White Man's Face

Before it disappears

on the sand his long white   beard before it disappears

The face of the man

in the waves I ask her does she see it ask her does

The old man in the waves   as the waves crest she see it does

she see the old man his

White   his face crumbling face it looks

as old as he's as old as

The ocean looks

and for a moment almost looks

His face like it's   all the way him

As never such old skin

looks my / Daughter age four

She thinks it might he might be real she shouts *Hello*

And after there's no answer answers *No*

ANIS MOJGANI

Closer

Come closer.

Come into this. Come closer.

You are quite the beauty. If no one has ever told you this before
know that right now. You are quite the beauty. There is joy in
how your mouth dances with your teeth. Your mouth is a sign
of how sacred your life truly is. So come into it. Come closer.
Know that whatever God prays to, He asked it to help Him
make something of worth. He woke from His dreams, scraped
the soil from the spaces inside Himself, made you, and was
happy. You make the Lord happy.

Come into this.

Come closer.

Know that something softer than us, but just as holy planted
the pieces of Himself into our feet that we might one day dance
our way back to Him. Know that you are almost home.

So come closer, come into this. There are birds beating their
wings beneath your breastplate gentle sparrows aching to
sing—come aching hearts! Come soldiers of joy, doormen of
truth! Come true-of-heart.

Know this: my heart was too big for my body so I let it go. And
most days, this world has thinned me to the point where I am
just another cloud forgetting another flock of swans—having
shaved off so many of my corners that I have felt at home only
in the shape of a ball, bending myself so far backwards that the
song of my mother believed I was returning home. But believe
me when I tell you my soul somehow still squeezes into narrow

947

spaces. Place your hand beneath your head when you sleep tonight and you may find it there making beauty as we sleep, as we dream, as we turn over. When we turn over in the ground may the ghosts that we have asked answers of do the turning, kneading us into crumbs of light and into this thing-love-thing called life. Come into it.

Come, you wooden museums,
you gentle tigers.

Come, negro farces in two broken scenes.
Come, you rusting giants—

I see teacups in your smiles, upside down, glowing. Your hands are like my heart. Some days all they do is tremble. I am like you. I am like you. I too at times am filled with so much fear. But like a hallway, must find the strength to walk through it. Walk through this with me. Through this church that is ours—this church of bone, birthed of blood and muscle, where every move our arms make and every breath we swallow is worship. If we choke, it is only on songs. Bend with me. In this church of ours.

There is a doorknob glowing like chance. Clutch it. Turn and pull. Step through. Chin up. Back straight. Eyes open. Hearts loud.
Walk through this with me.
Walk through this with me.

AJA MONET

#sayhername

i am a woman carrying other women in my mouth
behold a sister, a daughter, a mother, dear friend.
spirits demystified in a comrade's tone. they gather
to breathe and exhale, a dance with death we know
is not the end. all these nameless bodies haunted

by pellet wounds in their chest. listen for us in
the saying of a name you cannot pronounce, *black*
and *woman,* is a sort of magic you cannot hashtag.
the mere weight of it, too vast to be held. we hold
ourselves, an inheritance felt between the hips

woman of soft darkness. portal of light, watch them
envy the revolution of our movement. we break
open to give life flow. why the terror of our tears,
torment of our taste. my rage is righteous. my love
is righteous. my name is righteous. hear what i am

not here to say, we, too, have died. we know we are
dying, *too.* i am not here to say, look at me, how i
died so brutal a death, i deserve a name to fit all
the horror in. i am here to tell you, how if they
mention me in their protests and their rallies,

they would have to face their role in it, too, my
beauty, *too.* i died many times before the blow
to the body. i have bled many months before
bullet to the flesh. we know the body is not the
end. call it what you will but for all the hands,

cuffed wrists of us, shackled ankles of us, the
bend over to make room for you of us, how dare
we speak anything less than *i love you.* we who

love just as loudly in the thunderous rain as when
the sun shines golden on our skin and the world

kissed us unapologetically. we be so beautiful
when we be. how you gon be free without me?
your freedom tied up with mine at the nappy
edge of our soul singing with all our sisters, watch
them stretch their arms in my voice, how they
fly open-chested toward your ear, listen for

Rekia Boyd

                              Tanisha Anderson

          Yvette Smith
                    Aiyana Jones

Kayla Moore

                         Shelly Frey

Miriam Carey
                    Kendra James
          Alberta Spruill

                         Tarika Wilson
                Shereese Francis
                         Shantel Davis

     Malissa Williams

                              Darnisha Harris

Michelle Cusseaux
                Pearlie Golden

                              Kathryn Johnston

          Eleanor Bumpurs
     Natasha McKenna
                    Sheneque Proctor

          Sandra Bland

                              we are each saying,

we do not vanish in the bated breath of
our brothers. show me, show me a man
willing to fight beside me, my hand in his,
the color of courage, there is no mountaintop
worth seeing without us. meet me

in the trenches, where we lay
our bodies down
in the valley
of a voice

        say it   say   her   name

MORGAN PARKER

The President's Wife

Sometimes I wonder
Is Beyoncé who she says she is
Will I accidentally live forever
And be sentenced to smile at men
I wish were dead
Is loneliness cultural
Are lips true
Is a mother still a self
Do I glow in the dark
What if men are wrong
And English isn't sound blue isn't color
Eyes are the window to storm
Am I too transparent in this skirt suit
Is the skirt suit a social construct
What does money cost
Should I stop talking while the ocean
Takes California hot breath takes the capital
Will ritual outlast what visits
Sleeping daughters with bad words
What lets some girls grow warm and tall
The arms of their lovers
Are rich and imaginary like me
Is desire making me sick
Building in my organs like ammunition
Tiptoeing behind my eyes until
I'm digital I'm static
Is it called desire can it speak
What does beautiful cost do I afford it
Do I roll off the tongue
Is America going to be sick
Will fat kids inherit the earth
Will you untag me from that picture
Do you think I should cut my bangs
Do I have any friends

Do you believe in me
Should I go to sleep
Try again harder tomorrow
Should I answer the phone
Who is it
Who want the world like it is
Spoke Baraka can you hear him now
Do you understand
Are calories and sitcoms
Here to make me sad
Am I a moon no one sees
Does my lipstick look okay
Am I growing tired
Of my alternative lifestyle
Or would I like a fresh glass
Is there something spectacular
In fallen trees ancient hieroglyphs
Hippie towns twentysomethings will they
Save us
Is it possible to disappear
What's it like to be the first anything

ROWAN RICARDO PHILLIPS

Violins

He never saw a violin.
But he saw a lifetime of violence.

This is not to presume
That if he had simply seen

A violin he would have seen
Less violence. Or that living among

Violins, as though they were
Boulangeries or toppling stacks

Of other glazed goods like young adult
Fiction, would have made the violence

Less crack and more cocaine,
Less of course and more why god oh why.

More of one thing
Doesn't rhyme with one thing.

A swill of stars doesn't rhyme
With star. A posse of poets doesn't rhyme

With poet. We are all in prison.
This is the brutal lesson of the 21st century,

Swilled like a sour stone
Through the vein of the beast

Who watches you while you eat;
Our eternal host, the chummed fiddler,

The better tomorrow,
MMXVI.

CAMILLE RANKINE

History

Our stone wall was built by slaves and my bones, my bones
are paid for. We have two

of everything, twice heavy
in our pockets, warming
our two big hands.

This is the story, as I know it. One morning:
the ships came, as foretold, and death
pearl-handled, almost

and completely.
How cheap a date I turned out to be.

Each finger weak with the memory:
lost teeth, regret. Our ghosts
walk the shoulders of the road at night.
I get the feeling you've been lying to me.

JUSTIN PHILLIP REED

Black Can Sleep

on a nail bed. Black be
quick as catch can. Corner
hanger-on, black a dead
cell waiting to low-ceiling its empty
belly down a mop-dragged floor.
Lure of draining, black goes
to ground. Rain dangles: black hitches
like hick cargo. Call round. There it is
a thumb in the milk, trunk junk
strewn across a killing
of lilies. Oh Lord,
black the valley. Wise men
slather mirth, lip the gum. The news
their black tomb of tooth sucks out
won't news. Black know: Pops
a stone stopped quiet
(of all sounds) in the rolling.
Black cancer. Black sugar.
Black pressure. Black taken
off support's hollow leg. Use
to be an hour visited
on us, stained Colt & wild
around the neck, ex
of auntie, blackest one yet,
picked up only after zip,
pockets just a snatch of *ay*

young black, how you live?

ROGER REEVES

Children Listen

It turns out however that I was deeply
Mistaken about the end of the world
        The body in flames will not be the body
In flames but just a house fire ignored
        The black sails of that solitary burning
Boat rubbing along the legs of lovers
        Flung into a Roman sky by a carousel
The lovers too sick in their love
        To notice a man drenched in fire on a porch
Or a child aflame mistaken for a dog
        Mistaken for a child running to tell of a bomb
That did not knock before it entered
        In Gaza with its glad tidings of abundant joy
In Kazimierz a god is weeping
        In a window one golden hand raised
Above his head as if he's slipped
        On the slick rag of the future our human
Kindnesses unremarkable as the flies
        Rubbing their legs together while standing
On a slice of cantaloupe Children
        You were never meant to be human
You must be the grass
        You must grow wildly over the graves

ALISON C. ROLLINS

Why Is We Americans

We is gator teeth hanging from the rear-
view mirror as sickle cells suckle at Big
Momma's teats. We is dragonfly
choppers hovering above Walden Pond.
We is spinal cords shedding like the skin
of a cottonmouth. We is Psalm 23 and
the pastor's chattering chicklets. We is
a good problem to have. We is throats
constricting and the grape juice
of Jesus. We is Roach and Mingus in
Birdland. We is *body electric*, eyes
watering with moonshine, glossy lips
sticky with lard. We is half brothers in
headlock, arm wrestling in the dirt.
We is Vaseline rubbed into knocked
knees and cracked elbows. We is ham
hocks making love to kidney beans. We
is Orpheus, lyre in hand, asking *do we
have a problem?* We is the backstory
of myth. We is sitting horse and crazy
bull. We is brown paper bags,
gurgled belches. We is hooded ghosts
and holy shadows roaming Mississippi
goddamned. We is downbeats and
syncopation's cousin. We is mouths
washed out with the blood of the lamb.
We is witch hazel–coated backs sucking
on peppermint wrappers. We is the
spiked antennae of a triangle-faced
praying mantis. We is barefoot
tongue-tied hogs with slit throats and
twitching bellies. We is sun tea and
brewed bitches. We is the crying
pussies that stand down when told to

man up. We is Radio Raheem and Zoot
Suit Malcolm. We is spit-slick low cuts
and fades. We is scrappy black-masked
coons and turkey-necked bullfrogs. We
is the pits of arms at stake, the clouds
frothing at the mouth. We is swimmers
naked, private parts Whitman allegedly
fondled beneath the water. We is
late lurkers and castrated tree limbs
on the Sunday before last. We is red-
veined pupils and piss-stained knickers,
slack-jawed and slumped in the
bathroom doorway. We is whiplash
and backhanded ways of settling grief.
We is clubbin' woolly mammoths
upside the head, jammin' fingers in
Darwin's white beard. We is comin'
round yonder, pigeon-toed and
bowlegged, laughin' our heads off.
We is lassoed cowboys swingin' in
the sweet summer breeze.

NICOLE SEALEY

Object Permanence

[*for John*]

We wake as if surprised the other is still there,
each petting the sheet to be sure.

How have we managed our way
to this bed—beholden to heat like dawn

indebted to light. Though we're not so self-
important as to think everything

has led to this, everything has led to this.
There's a name for the animal

love makes of us—named, I think,
like rain, for the sound it makes.

You are the animal after whom other animals
are named. Until there's none left to laugh,

days will start with the same startle
and end with caterpillars gorged on milkweed.

O, how we entertain the angels
with our brief animation. O,

how I'll miss you when we're dead.

CHARIF SHANAHAN

Gnawa Boy, Marrakesh, 1968

The maker has marked another boy to die:
His thin body between two sheets,
Black legs jutting out onto the stone floor,
The tips of his toenails translucent as an eye.
Gray clumps of skin, powder-light,
Like dust on the curve of his unwashed heel
And the face, swollen, expanding like a lung.
At its center, the sheet lifts and curves:
His body's strangeness, even there.
One palm faces down to show the black
Surface of hand, the other facing up
White as his desert's sky.
                                    As if underwater,
He passes from that room into the blue
Porcelain silence of the hall, where the light-
Skinned women have gathered in waiting:
No song of final parting, no wailing
Ripped holy from their throats:
The women do not walk into the sun,
They hide their bodies from it
(those pale wrists, those pale temples):
They do not walk the streets,
They do not clutch their own bodies,
They do not hit themselves in grief—

SAFIYA SINCLAIR

Fisherman's Daughter

In this wet season my gone mother
climbs back again

and everything here smells gutted—
bloodtide, sea grapes in thick bloom,

our smashed plates and teacups. Dismantling
this grey shoreline for some kind of home, scared
orphans out bleating with the mongrels,
                           all of us starved

for something reclaimable. What chases them,
her barefoot rain, stains my unopened petunia, shined
church shoes, our black words, our hands.

I'll catch the day creep in, her dirt marking my father's
neck, oil-dreck steeped dark to every collar,
her tar this same fish odor I am washing.

I know I am one of them. The emptied:

How night comes raw, open-wounded,
her gills wafting in the iron's heat, sea's marrow
unrelenting, my heart one coiled mass

and sweating. I scald a ritual cleansing.
White poui tree of my youth
stripped bare, her burned hair,
what starched pleats of uniform.

My skin a red linen pressed through with salt.
The house. Even the body burns.
Carbolic disappearing; scrubbed pink into fingernail,
a prayer, bone of coral

scraped, kneaded
into breasts and thighs.
Frankincense and swallow a bar of soap.
But no washing will avail me
                              of this ghost.

I smell her at school and sulk my head
into the sand, watch my body carve
                              this resurrection—
its dull gleam of scales, a new ache:

For salt, for sea grapes, her brown flesh
sucked down like a thumb. Sun and snapper-eye
sucked out, her spine like a straw.

I cannot help myself.

Her keen and shadowing.
My hair still tied in her old handkerchief.
Pray, pray she is not here today.

Teacher, unbeliever. Chasing me home
to wash myself. Last week's daughter,

twelve years old, heart still for sale.

DANEZ SMITH

dinosaurs in the hood

let's make a movie called *Dinosaurs in the Hood*.
Jurassic Park meets *Friday* meets *The Pursuit of Happyness*.
there should be a scene where a little black boy is playing
with a toy dinosaur on the bus, then looks out the window
& sees the *T. rex*, because there has to be a *T. rex*.

don't let Tarantino direct this. in his version, the boy plays
with a gun, the metaphor: black boys toy with their own lives
the foreshadow to his end, the spitting image of his father.
nah, the kid has a plastic brontosaurus or triceratops
& this is his proof of magic or God or Santa. i want a scene

where a cop car gets pooped on by a pterodactyl, a scene
where the corner store turns into a battleground. don't let
the Wayans brothers in this movie. i don't want any racist shit
about Asian people or overused Latino stereotypes.
this movie is about a neighborhood of royal folks—

children of slaves & immigrants & addicts & exile—saving
        their town
from real ass dinosaurs. i don't want some cheesy, yet
        progressive
Hmong sexy hot dude hero with a funny, yet strong,
        commanding
Black girl buddy-cop film. this is not a vehicle for Will Smith
& Sofia Vergara. i want grandmas on the front porch taking
        out raptors

with guns they hid in walls & under mattresses. i want those
        little spitty
screamy dinosaurs. i want Cecily Tyson to make a speech,
        maybe two.
i want Viola Davis to save the city in the last scene with a
        black fist afro pick

964

through the last dinosaur's long, cold-blood neck. But this
      can't be
a black movie. this can't be a black movie. this movie can't be
      dismissed

because of its cast or its audience. this movie can't be
      metaphor
for black people & extinction. This movie can't be about
      race.
this movie can't be about black pain or cause black pain.
this movie can't be about a long history of having a long
      history with hurt.
this movie can't be about race. nobody can say nigga in this
      movie

who can't say it to my face in public. no chicken jokes in this
      movie.
no bullet holes in the heroes. & no one kills the black boy. &
      no one kills
the black boy. & no one kills the black boy. besides, the only
      reason
i want to make this is for the first scene anyway: little black
      boy
on the bus with his toy dinosaur, his eyes wide & endless

                    his dreams possible, pulsing, & right there.

CLINT SMITH

Your National Anthem

Today, a black man who was once a black boy
like you got down on one of his knees & laid
his helmet on the grass as this country sang

its ode to the promise it never kept
& the woman in the grocery store line in front
of us is on the phone & she is telling someone

on the other line that this black man who was
once a black boy like you should be grateful
we live in a country where people aren't killed

for things like this you know she says, in some places
they would hang you for such a blatant act of disrespect
maybe he should go live there instead of here so he can

appreciate what he has & then she turns around
& sees you sitting in the grocery cart surrounded
by lettuce & yogurt & frozen chicken thighs

& you smile at her with your toothless gum smile
& she says that you are the cutest baby she has
ever seen & tells me how I must feel so lucky

to have such a beautiful baby boy & I thank her
for her kind words even though I should not
thank her because I know that you will not always

be a black boy but one day you may be a black man
& you may decide your country hasn't kept
its promise to you either & this woman or another

like her will forget you were ever this boy & they
will make you into something else & tell you
to be grateful for what you've been given

PHILLIP B. WILLIAMS

Prayer

Help me distinguish between approaching blizzard
and his breath against my ear, causing my skin
to whistle like a blade of grass. Please, help me keep
my mind at ease when he trembles beneath me, cold-
hot and wet, wet all over. The sheets have been
soaked and wrung and bleached. The carpet
vacuumed, the kitchen floor swept. God, help me keep
a clean home, keep the roaches' running prayers
from competing with my own, keep the rats
from gnawing on the bread with filth and squeak.
Plastic won't keep ice crystals from making
a second pane over the window, won't keep
the don't-give-a-damn cold from coming in
and lingering beneath our feet. Give me feet
that can sing, that can sing all over this floor
like a drum battalion, stomp out the pests
and their late night coitus, stomp out winter
crawling from beneath the floorboard, stomp out
the fever pouring from his never-dry back.
I want to heal like You do. God, let me walk on water.

JAMILA WOODS

Ode to Herb Kent

Your voice crawls across the dashboard of Grandma's Dodge Dynasty on the way home from Lilydale First Baptist. You sing a cocktail of static and bass. Sound like you dressed to the nines: cowboy hat, fur coat & alligator boots. Sound like you lotion every tooth. You a walking discography, South Side griot, keeper of crackle & dust in the grooves. You fell in love with a handmade box of wires at 16 and been behind the booth ever since. From WBEZ to V103, you be the Coolest Gent, King of the Dusties. Your voice wafts down from the ceiling at the Hair Lab. You supply the beat for Kym to tap her comb to. Her brown fingers paint my scalp with white grease to the tunes of Al & Barry & Luther. Your voice: an inside-out yawn, the sizzle of hot iron on fresh perm, the song inside the blackest seashell washed up on a sidewalk in Bronzeville. You soundtrack the church picnic, trunk party, Cynthia's 50th birthday bash, the car ride to school, choir, Checkers. Your voice stretch across our eardrums like Daddy asleep on the couch. Sound like Grandma's sweet potato pie, sound like the cigarettes she hide in her purse for rough days. You showed us what our mommas' mommas must've moved to. When the West Side rioted the day MLK died, you were audio salve to the burning city, people. Your voice a soft sermon soothing the masses, speaking coolly to flames, spinning black records across the airwaves, spreading the gospel of soul in a time of fire. Joycetta says she bruised her thumbs snappin' to Marvin's "Got to Give It Up" and I believe her.

BIOGRAPHICAL NOTES

Chris Abani (b. 1966) b. Afikpo, Nigeria. Fled Nigeria during Biafran War, has lived in the U.S. since 2001. Also a novelist. Awarded Hurston/Wright Legacy Award (2005), PEN Hemingway Book Prize (2005), and Guggenheim Fellowship (2009). Currently professor of English at Northwestern University.

Hanif Abdurraqib (b. 1983) b. Columbus, OH. Has also published as Hanif Willis-Abdurraqib. Poetry collections include *The Crown Ain't Worth Much* (2016), *Vintage Sadness* (2017), and *They Don't Dance No Mo'* (2020). Also an essayist and music critic. With Eve Ewing, is one-half of the writing duo Echo Hotel.

Elizabeth Acevedo (b. 1988) b. New York, NY. Published chapbook *Beastgirl & Other Origin Myths* (2016). Also the award-winning author of young adult novels, including *Poet X* (2018).

Ai (1947–2010) b. Florence Haynes in Albany, TX, spent most of her life in Arizona. Poems are often dramatic monologues, including those of historical figures. *Vice: New and Selected Poems* (1999), containing the work of three decades, won the National Book Award.

Elizabeth Alexander (b. 1962) b. New York, NY, raised in Washington, DC. Debut poetry *The Venus Hottentot* was published in 1990. Read her poem "Praise Song for the Day" for President Barack Obama's 2009 inauguration. Chaired African American Studies department at Yale University and is currently president of the Andrew W. Mellon Foundation. In addition to her poetry volumes, she is the author of a memoir about her relationship with her late husband, *The Light of the World* (2015).

Lewis Grandison Alexander (1900–1945) b. Washington, DC. Worked as editor, playwright, and actor; his poems were published in *Fire!!*, *Opportunity*, and *The Crisis* magazines and the anthologies *The New Negro* (1925), *Caroling Dusk* (1927), and *Ebony and Topaz* (1927).

Will Alexander (b. 1948) b. Los Angeles, CA. Published first poetry collection in 1987; notable volumes include *Asia & Haiti* (1995) and *Singing in Magnetic Hoofbeat: Essays, Prose, Texts, Interviews, and a Lecture* (2013), which won the American Book Award. Has written plays and fiction. Other awards include a Whiting Fellowship for Poetry and a Jackson Poetry Prize.

Samuel Allen (1917–2015) b. Columbus, OH. Served in World War II and studied in Europe on the GI Bill. Worked as lawyer from mid-1940s to 1968. First book, the bilingual volume *Elfenbeinzähne* (Ivory Tusks), was published in West Germany in 1956. In later life he taught at the Tuskegee Institute, Wesleyan University, and Boston University. Honors include the Furious Flower Lifetime Achievement Award (1994). Also wrote under pseudonym Paul Vesey.

Maya Angelou (1928–2014) b. Marguerite Annie Johnson in St. Louis, MO. Was also a singer, actor, dancer, film director, and activist. Along with poetry and essay collections, books for children, and cookbooks, she published seven memoirs, beginning with *I Know Why the Caged Bird Sings* (1970). Wrote plays. Read her poem "On the Pulse of Morning" at first inauguration of President Bill Clinton. Awarded Presidential Medal of Freedom by President Barack Obama in 2011.

Russell Atkins (b. 1926) b. Cleveland, OH. Also a composer. Studied music at Cleveland School of the Arts and Cleveland Institute of Music. With Adelaide Simon, co-founded the Black avant-garde journal *Free Lance*, 1952–80. Published mostly in chapbooks. *World'd Too Much: The Selected Poetry of Russell Atkins*, edited by Kevin Prufer and Robert E. McDonough, was published in 2019.

Cameron Awkward-Rich (b. 1989) b. Ann Arbor, MI. Earned BA from Wesleyan University and PhD from Stanford University. Has published poetry collections *Sympathetic Little Monster* (2016) and *Dispatch* (2019). Currently assistant professor of Women, Gender, Sexuality Studies at the University of Massachusetts, Amherst.

Benjamin Banneker (1731–1806) b. Baltimore County, MD. Raised by free African American parents (father had been enslaved) on tobacco farm he would inherit. Around age twenty, invented a wooden clock that kept precise time. Was an astronomer, surveyor, and farmer as well as an essayist and pamphleteer who voiced ideas about abolitionism and civil rights. Published annual almanacs in the 1790s that included astronomical tables, along with short poems, dream narratives, essays, and proverbs.

Amiri Baraka (1934–2014) b. Everett Leroy Jones in Newark, NJ. Served in U.S. Air Force; worked at base library in Puerto Rico and was dishonorably discharged for suspicion of being a Communist. Moved to New York City, studying literature at Columbia and befriending Beat poets. Co-founded Totem Press, the journals *Yugen* and *The Floating Bear*, and the experimental American Theater for Poets. As LeRoi Jones, published *Preface to a Twenty-Volume Suicide Note* (1961), first of many poetry collections. Explored sociohistorical context of Black music in *Blues People* (1963). One-act play *Dutchman*

(1964) won Obie Award. Became a central figure at Black Arts Repertory/Theater School in Harlem; in 1966, moved back to Newark, converted to Islam, and became Imamu Ameer Baraka, which he abbreviated Amiri. Named poet laureate of New Jersey in 2002 and refused calls to step down during furor over poem "Somebody Blew Up America"; post was abolished by state legislature. Taught at Rutgers, Columbia, and Yale Universities and SUNY Stony Brook.

George Barlow (b. 1948) b. Berkeley, CA. Earned BA from California State University, Hayward, and MA and MFA from the University of Iowa. Author of poetry volumes *Gabriel* (1974) and *Gumbo* (1981) and co-editor of *About Time III: A Third Anthology of California Prison Writing* (1987). Teaches African American literature and poetry at Grinnell College.

Gerald Barrax (1933–2019) b. Attalla, AL, moved to Pittsburgh in 1944. Served in U.S. Air Force. Earned BA from Duquesne University and MA from University of Pittsburgh. Taught at North Carolina State University. Served as editor of *Obsidian: Literature and Arts in the African Diaspora*. Among his poetry collections, *Leaning Against the Sun* (1992) was nominated for the Pulitzer Prize and National Book Award.

Quan Barry (b. 1973) b. Saigon, South Vietnam (now Ho Chi Minh City, Vietnam), to a Vietnamese mother and an African American father. Raised on Boston's North Shore. Earned BA from University of Virginia and MFA from University of Michigan. Publications include the poetry collections *Asylum* (2001), *Controvertibles* (2004), *Water Puppets* (2011), and *Loose Strife* (2015), and the novel *She Weeps Each Time You're Born* (2015). Teaches at University of Wisconsin–Madison.

Paul Beatty (b. 1962) b. Los Angeles, CA. Earned BA from Boston University and MFA from Brooklyn College. Winner of Nuyorican Poets Café's Grand Slam in 1990. Published poetry collections *Big Bank Take Little Bank* (1991) and *Joker, Joker, Deuce* (1994). Subsequent career has been mostly devoted to fiction; his novel *The Sellout* (2015) was awarded the National Book Critics' Circle Award and the Man Booker Prize. Teaches writing at Columbia University.

James Madison Bell (1826–1902) b. Gallipolis, OH. Moved at seventeen to Cincinnati and in 1854 to Chatham, Ontario, to pursue abolitionist interests. Befriended John Brown and raised funds for Brown's 1859 raid on the federal arsenal at Harpers Ferry, Virginia; allowed his home to be Brown's planning headquarters. Spent several years in San Francisco, where he began career as poet and orator, joined civil rights conventions, and was active in the A.M.E. Church. Settled with family in Toledo in the mid-1860s. Served as delegate for state and national Republican conventions.

Gwendolyn B. Bennett (1902–1981) b. Giddings, TX, and spent most of childhood in Washington, DC, Pennsylvania, and New York City. Studied art at Teachers College, Columbia University; the Pratt Institute; and later with Aaron Douglas at the Alfred C. Barnes Foundation. Taught art at Howard University, 1924–27; took a yearlong leave to study art in Paris on a scholarship. Designed and edited a weekly literary news column for *Opportunity* and was contributor and co-editor for the short-lived *Fire!!* magazine. After four years in Florida, settled in Hempstead, NY, in 1932. Worked for Works Progress Administration's Art Project; directed the Harlem Arts Guild in 1936. Suspended from post at the Harlem Art Center due to scrutiny from the House Un-American Activities Committee; remained under surveillance into the 1950s. Much of her artwork was destroyed in two fires, the first in 1926 and the second in the early 1980s.

Joshua Bennett (b. 1988) Raised in South Yonkers, NY. Earned BA from University of Pennsylvania, MA in Theater and Performance Studies from University of Warwick, and PhD from Princeton University with a dissertation that is the basis of *Being Property Once Myself: Blackness and the End of Man* (2020). Poetry collections are *The Sobbing School* (2016), *Algorithm and Blues* (2014), and *Owed* (2020). A member of the Harvard Society of Fellows, he is Mellon Assistant Professor of English at Dartmouth College, where he teaches English and African American Studies.

Reginald Dwayne Betts (b. 1980) Raised in Suitland, MD. Earned BA from University of Maryland, MFA from Warren Wilson College, and JD from Yale Law School. Served time in prison after conviction for his involvement in a 1996 carjacking and armed robbery. After release in 2005 he wrote the memoir *A Question of Freedom: A Memoir of Learning, Survival, and Coming of Age in Prison* (2009). Poetry collections are *Shahid Reads His Own Palm* (2010), *Bastards of the Reagan Era* (2015), and *Felon* (2019). Currently enrolled in Yale Law School's PhD program.

Arna Bontemps (1902–1973) b. Alexandria, LA, and moved to Los Angeles at age three. Earned BA from Pacific Union College. Accepted teaching position in Harlem, won prizes from *The Crisis* and *Opportunity* magazines, and befriended other Harlem Renaissance figures. Taught at a junior college in Alabama, 1931–34, and was fired for his political views; was editorial supervisor to the Federal Writers' Project in Illinois and, after earning MA in library science from the University of Chicago, was librarian at Fisk University. In addition to poems, wrote historical novels and children's books and edited influential anthologies with Langston Hughes, including *The Poetry of the Negro 1746–1949* (1949, exp. ed. 1970).

William Stanley Braithwaite (1878–1962) b. Boston, MA. Raised in a prosperous home until his father died; was self-educated after age twelve. Published first poetry collection *Lyrics of Life and Love* (1904) and in 1906 began writing regular column as a critic in the *Boston Evening Transcript.* Founded short-lived *Poetry Journal* in 1912, followed by the more enduring and influential annual *Anthology of Magazine Verse.* In 1935 accepted teaching position at Atlanta University, where he spent ten years teaching creative writing. Moved in 1945 to Harlem, where he lived until his death.

Kamau Brathwaite (1930–2020) b. Lawson Edward Brathwaite in Bridgetown, Barbados. Earned BA in history in 1953 and a diploma in education in 1954 from Pembroke College, Cambridge University, and PhD from University of Sussex in 1968. Lived in Ghana in the period before and after its independence and, with first wife, founded a children's theater there. Poetry volumes *Rights of Passage* (1967), *Masks* (1968), and *Islands* (1969)—collected in 1973 as *The Arrivants: A New World Trilogy*—gained him international renown. Wrote essays and books in cultural and historical studies. His awards include the Griffin International Poetry Prize (for *Slow Horses*, 2005), the Neustadt International Award for Literature, the Casa de Las Americas Prize for Literary Criticism, and the PEN/Voelcker Award for Poetry. Beginning in 1992 he taught as a member of the faculty of the Comparative Literature department at NYU.

Gwendolyn Brooks (1917–2000) b. Topeka, KS, grew up and lived in Chicago her entire life. Published poems as teenager and at sixteen became a regular contributor to the *Chicago Defender*'s poetry column. First of many poetry collections, *A Street in Bronzeville*, was published in 1945; in 1950, for *Annie Allen*, became first Black poet to win Pulitzer Prize. Post-1967 poetry was influenced by the work and aims of Black Arts poets; later volumes were brought out not by mainstream trade houses but by Black publishers, including Broadside Press and Brooks's own small presses. The first African American to join the National Institute of Arts and Letters (in 1976), she received the National Medal of the Arts as well as Lifetime Achievement Awards from the National Endowment for the Arts and the National Book Foundation.

Jericho Brown (b. 1976) b. Nelson Demery III in Shreveport, LA. Earned BA from Dillard University, MFA from University of New Orleans, and PhD in literature and creative writing from University of Houston. Poetry volumes are *Please* (2008), recipient of the American Book Award; *The New Testament* (2014); and *The Tradition* (2019), which was awarded the Pulitzer Prize. Currently professor of English and creative writing at Emory University and director of its creative writing program.

Sterling A. Brown (1901–1989) b. Washington, DC. Earned BA from Williams College and MA from Harvard University. For forty years was professor of American literature in 1929 at Howard University. His debut poetry collection *Southern Road* (1932) was influenced by his travels throughout the South. Served as editor on Negro Affairs in the Federal Writers' Project. As critic his books include *Outline for the Study of Poetry of American Negroes* (1931), *The Negro in American Fiction* (1937), and *Negro Poetry and Drama* (1937); edited poetry anthology *The Negro Caravan* (1941). His *Collected Poems* was published in 1980.

Mahogany L. Browne (b. 1976) b. Oakland, CA. Graduated from MFA writing and activism program at Pratt Institute, Brooklyn, where she later served as instructor and Black Lives Matter program coordinator. A performance poet, she has released recordings of her poetry and published several chapbooks and poetry volumes, including *Redbone* (2015) and *Black Girl Magic* (2018). Co-edited *The BreakBeat Poets Volume 2: Black Girl Magic* (2018). Director of Friday Night Slams at Nuyorican Poets Café and Urban Word NYC; coordinates MFA program at St. Francis College.

Julia de Burgos (1914–1953) b. Julia Constanza Burgos García in Carolina, Puerto Rico. Earned degree in teaching at the University of Puerto Rico and became an elementary school teacher. A political activist, she became an official in the Nationalist Party advocating for Puerto Rican independence. First poetry collection, *Poema en veinte surcos* (Poem in Twenty Furrows), was published in 1938. Moved to New York City in 1940, where apart from two years in Cuba she lived for the rest of her life. Wrote column in the Spanish-language New York periodical *Pueblos Hispanos*. Suffered from alcoholism, cirrhosis of the liver, and respiratory problems. Collapsed on the street and died at Harlem Hospital at age thirty-nine.

Darrell Burton (1971–2002) Raised in Arkansas. Earned BA from the University of Arkansas, Little Rock, and MFA posthumously from Indiana University. Was a scholarship basketball player in college.

Served in the U.S. Navy and later worked as a chef and fashion model. At the time of his death in a fire in his Bloomington, IN, apartment, he had recently completed the manuscript for his first poetry collection.

Olivia Ward Bush (1869–1944) b. Sag Harbor, NY. Raised mostly by an aunt in Providence. Moved to Boston with her two daughters after first marriage ended and took job as assistant dramatic director at the Robert Gould Shaw Community House. Published poetry collections *Original Poems* (1899) and *Driftwood* (1914); after marriage to Anthony Banks, moved to Chicago and opened the Bush-Banks School of Expression, a drama school. Wrote about her parents' indigenous heritage and worked to preserve Montauk language and folklore; composed plays. Worked on theatrical projects for the WPA and wrote an arts column for the *Westchester Courier* in the 1930s.

Cyrus Cassells (b. 1957) b. Dover, DE. Raised in the Greater Los Angeles area in the Mojave Desert. Earned BA from Stanford University. Debut collection was *The Mud Actor* (1982); other books include *Soul Make a Path Through Shouting* (1994), *Beautiful Signor* (1997), *More Than Peace and Cypresses* (2004), and *The Crossed-Out Swastika* (2012). Awards include the Lannan Literary Award and two Pushcart Prizes. Currently teaches at Texas State University at San Marcos.

Barbara Chase-Riboud (b. 1939) b. Philadelphia, PA. Earned BFA from Tyler School of Art, Temple University, and was first Black woman to earn an MFA from Yale University. Based in Paris, she traveled the world extensively; began her writing career in the 1970s and published her first poetry volume, *From Memphis to Peking*, in 1974. *Sally Hemings* (1979) won the Janet Heidinger Kafka Prize for year's best novel and ignited controversy for her unearthing of information about Thomas Jefferson fathering children with Sally Hemings. In addition to her novels, her poetry collections include *Portrait of a Nude Woman as Cleopatra* (1987) and *Everytime a Knot is Undone, a God is Released* (2014). She has received the Hurston/Wright Legacy Award and the Alain Locke International Award, among other prizes; her artwork has been widely exhibited and collected.

Dominique Christina (b. 1974) Raised in Denver, CO. Has won five national poetry slam titles. Poetry volumes include *The Bones, The Breaking, The Balm: A Colored Girl's Hymnal* (2014) and *Anarcha Speaks: A History in Poems* (2018). Has acted in the HBO television series *High Maintenance*, for which she is also a contributing writer.

Benjamin Clark (1825–1875) b. Maryland. Parents had been enslaved. A self-educated man who worked as a dyer, Clark wrote *The Past, Present, and Future: In Prose and Poetry*, a work about slavery published in

Toronto in 1867. (Often confused with the Boston shipping magnate Benjamin Cutler Clark who wrote *A Plea for Hayti*, published in 1853.)

Tiana Clark (b. 1983 or 1984) b. Los Angeles, CA, raised in Southern California and Nashville. Earned BA in Africana and Women's Studies from Tennessee State University and MFA from Vanderbilt University. Poetry collections are *Equilibrium* (2016) and *I Can't Talk About the Trees Without the Blood* (2018). Awards include the Furious Flower's Gwendolyn Brooks Centennial Poetry Prize. Currently teaches creative writing at Southern Illinois University, Edwardsville.

Carrie Williams Clifford (1862–1934) b. Chillicothe, OH. Married attorney William H. Clifford, one of Ohio's first African American legislators. Moved to Cleveland and helped found the Ohio State Federation of Colored Women in 1900; was an editor of the *Cleveland Journal*, an African American newspaper. Wrote articles, stories, and poems published in *Opportunity* and *The Crisis* magazines and was the author of the books *Race Rhymes* (1911) and *The Widening Light* (1922).

Lucille Clifton (1936–2010) b. Depew, NY, and raised in nearby Buffalo. Attended Howard University, where she studied drama. Settled in Maryland in the 1960s, serving as poet-in-residence at Coppin State College and as the state's poet laureate. *Good Times* (1969), her first poetry book, was followed by numerous collections including *Blessing the Boats: New and Selected Poems, 1988–2000* (2000), which won the National Book Award. In 2007, Clifton was the first Black woman to be awarded the Ruth Lilly Poetry Prize.

Anita Scott Coleman (1890–1960) b. Guaymas, Mexico, and moved as a child to a ranch near Silver City, NM. Spent most of her life in the Southwest. Earned teaching certificate from New Mexico Normal School and worked as a teacher. First of some thirty stories published during her lifetime appeared in 1919. Published essays, stories, and poems in *The Crisis* and *Opportunity* magazines, as well as volumes such as the poetry collection *Small Wisdom* (under the pseudonym Elizabeth Stapleton Stokes).

Wanda Coleman (1946–2013) b. Los Angeles, CA. Began writing career as journalist with the *Los Angeles Free Press*. Wrote for the soap opera *Days of Our Lives*; won an Emmy in 1976. Published first of many poetry collections, *Art in the Court of the Blue Fag*, in 1977. Wrote the novel *Mambo Hips and Make Believe* (1999) and short stories collected in *A War of Eyes and Other Stories* (1988) and *Jazz and*

Twelve O'Clock Tales (2008). *Native in a Strange Land* (1996) is a selection of her essays and articles.

Sam Cornish (1935–2018), b. Baltimore, MD. Worked for Enoch Pratt Public Library in Baltimore. Moved to Boston in 1970, where he developed educational projects and served as literature director of the Massachusetts Arts Council. Taught writing at Emerson College. Appointed Boston's first poet laureate. Published six books of poetry, two books for children, and a memoir. Also a photographer.

James D. Corrothers (1869–1917) b. Chain Lake Settlement, Cass County, MI. Moved to Chicago at eighteen and published poetry in the *Chicago Tribune*, at whose offices he worked as a custodian. Studied at Northwestern University and at Bennett College in North Carolina. An African Methodist Episcopal minister, Corrothers contributed to newspapers in Chicago and other cities as well as to magazines; his sketches were collected in *The Black Cat Club: Negro Humor and Folklore* (1902).

Jayne Cortez (1934–2012) b. Fort Huachuca, AZ, and moved to Watts in Los Angeles at seven. Was married to the jazz saxophonist Ornette Coleman, 1959–64. Worked with the Student Nonviolent Coordinating Committee (SNCC) and registered Black people to vote in Mississippi. Founded the Watts Repertory Theater Company in 1964. A key Black Arts Movement figure, she published numerous poetry collections, including *Scarifications* (1973), *Firespitter* (1977), and *Jazz Fan Looks Back* (2002); recorded her poems set to music on albums such as *Everywhere Drums* (1990) and *Taking the Blues Back Home* (1996). Toured with her band the Firespitters, which included her son, the jazz drummer Denardo Coleman. Lived in Manhattan and in Dakar, Senegal; founded the Organization of Women Writers of Africa in 1991.

Joseph Seamon Cotter, Jr. (1895–1919) b. Louisville, KY. Enrolled at Fisk University; returned home during his sophomore year due to the onset of tuberculosis, which would eventually kill him. Worked as an editor and writer for the Louisville *Leader*. Published *The Band of Gideon and Other Lyrics* (1918). Other poems, including the sonnet series *Out of the Shadows*, and his play *On the Fields of France* were published posthumously in 1920.

Joseph Seamon Cotter, Sr. (1861–1949) b. Bardstown, KY. Worked as a ragpicker, a field worker on tobacco and cotton plantations, and a brick maker; was briefly a prizefighter. Completed ten-month night school course at age twenty-two; earned certification as school instructor and principal. Served as principal at Louisville's Samuel Coleridge-Taylor School. Inspired to write poetry after hearing Paul Laurence Dunbar read his poems while visiting Cotter's home. Wrote fiction as well as poetry; books include *A Rhyming* (1895), *Links of Friendship* (1898), and the story collection *Negro Tales* (1912). *Collected Poems of Joseph S. Cotter, Sr.* was published in 1938.

Mae V. Cowdery (1909–1953) b. Philadelphia, PA. Moved to New York City after graduating high school and attended Pratt Institute. Won first prize in a *Crisis* magazine poetry contest and was awarded Krigwa Poetry Prize. Befriended Harlem Renaissance figures. Published a single poetry volume, *We Lift Our Voices and Other Poems* (1936); work fell into obscurity shortly thereafter. Committed suicide.

Countee Cullen (1903–1946) b. Countee LeRoy Porter, exact birthplace unknown. Informally adopted as teenager in New York by Rev. Frederick A. Cullen, an activist minister, and Carolyn Belle (née Mitchell). Earned BA from New York University and MA in English and French from Harvard University. The first of his several poetry collections, *Color* (1925), was published before he graduated from college. His poems earned him numerous awards and enjoyed enormous popularity in the 1920s. His short-lived marriage to Yolande Du Bois, daughter of W.E.B. Du Bois, is best known for their lavish 1928 wedding. Studied in Paris. His African American poetry anthology *Caroling Dusk* (1927) was highly influential. Published a novel, *One Way to Heaven* (1932), translated *The Medea*, and wrote books for children. Became a full-time French instructor at Frederick Douglass Junior High in 1934; students included James Baldwin.

Waring Cuney (1906–1976) b. Washington, DC. Educated at Howard University, Lincoln University (where he was a classmate of Langston Hughes), and the New England Conservatory of Music; later studied music in Rome and at Columbia University. His "No Images" won first prize in *Opportunity* magazine's 1926 poetry contest. Wrote art and music criticism for *The Crisis*. Served as technical sergeant in the South Pacific during World War II. Published first collection of poetry, *Puzzles* (1960), in Holland, and the second, *Storefront Church* (1973), in London.

Pierre Dalcour (1813–?) b. New Orleans, LA. Son of free Creoles of color. Raised and educated in Paris. Contributed twelve poems to *Les Cenelles*, published in New Orleans, the first anthology of poetry by Black Americans. Returned to Paris and spent the rest of his life there.

DéLana R. A. Dameron (b. 1984 or 1985) b. Columbia, SC. Earned BA from University of North Carolina at Chapel Hill and MFA from

New York University. Has published the collections *How God Ends Us* (2009), which won the South Carolina Poetry Book Prize, and *Weary Kingdom* (2017).

Margaret Danner (1915–1984) b. Pryorsburg, KY, spent later youth in Chicago. Attended Loyola, Roosevelt, and Northwestern Universities. In 1951, published "Far from Africa: Four Poems" in *Poetry* magazine and became, in 1956, the magazine's first African American assistant editor. After her appointment as poet-in-residence at Wayne State University, she co-founded Boone House for the Arts in Detroit in 1962. Became active in the Baha'i faith; traveled to Africa in 1966. Publications include *To Flower* (1962), *Poem Counterpoem* (with Dudley Randall, 1966), *Impressions of African Art Forms in the Poetry of Margaret Danner* (1968), and *The Dawn of a Thistle: Selected Poems, Prose Poems and Songs* (1976).

Kyle Dargan (b. 1980) b. Newark, NJ. Earned BA from the University of Virginia and MFA from Indiana University. Poetry collections are *The Listening* (2004), *Bouquet of Hungers* (2007), *Logorrhea Dementia* (2010), *Honest Engine* (2015), and *Anagnorisis* (2018). Worked as managing editor of *Callaloo* and founded the journal *Post No Ills.* Currently associate professor of literature and assistant director of the creative writing program at American University.

Frank Marshall Davis (1905–1987) b. Arkansas City, KS. Nearly killed at age five by older white children. Enrolled in Kansas State Agricultural College's journalism program in 1924. Moved to Chicago in 1927; wrote for various Black newspapers and published the poetry collections *Black Man's Verse* (1935), *I Am the American Negro* (1937), and *Through Sepia Eyes* (1938). Served as executive editor of Associated Negro Press in Chicago. Moved to Honolulu with family and ran wholesale paper business; wrote weekly column for the *Honolulu Record.* Met ten-year-old Barack Obama through his friendship with Stanley Dunham, Obama's grandfather. Davis's *Livin' the Blues: Memoirs of a Black Journalist and Poet* (1992) appeared posthumously.

Kwame Dawes (b. 1962) b. Accra, Ghana, and moved to Kingston, Jamaica, in 1971. Earned BA from the University of the West Indies at Mona in 1983 and a PhD in English literature from the University of New Brunswick in 1992. Poetry volumes include *Progeny of Air* (1994), *Wheels* (2010), and *Duppy Conqueror: New and Selected Poems* (2013); also a novelist, essayist, memoirist, playwright, and anthologist, as well as an actor and reggae singer. Elected chancellor of the Academy of American Poets. Currently Chancellor's Professor of English at the University of Nebraska at Lincoln, Dawes is also the editor of the literary magazine *Prairie Schooner.*

Clarissa Scott Delany (1901–1927) b. Tuskegee, AL. Father was secretary to Booker T. Washington and advisor to President Woodrow Wilson. Earned BA from Wellesley College. Traveled to France and Germany. Lived in Washington, DC, and New York City, where she became a social worker and director of the Joint Committee on the Negro Child Study, which published findings on delinquency and child neglect. Died at twenty-six of kidney disease.

Toi Derricotte (b. 1941) b. Hamtramck, MI, raised in Detroit. Earned BA from Wayne State University in Special Education and MA in English and creative writing from New York University. Worked as a teacher in Detroit before moving to New York City. Has published six poetry collections and a memoir. Founded Cave Canem Foundation with Cornelius Eady in 1996. Elected chancellor of the Academy of American Poets. Awards include the Poetry Society of America's Frost Medal for distinguished lifetime achievement in poetry.

Joel Dias-Porter (b. 1962) b. Pittsburgh, PA. Served in U.S. Air Force, then moved to Washington, DC, after his service, where he became a disc jockey under the name DJ Renegade. Represented Washington, DC, in the National Poetry Slam for six consecutive years. Edited the anthology *The Black Rooster Social Collective: this is the place* (1997). Two-time Heads Up Haiku Slam champion. Released a CD featuring jazz and poetry, *LibationSong* (2002). Awarded James Madison University's Furious Flower Emerging Poet Award in 1995.

Ralph Dickey (1945–1972) b. Detroit, MI. Earned BA at Wayne State University's Montieth College and enrolled in the MFA program at the University of Iowa. Was also an accomplished musician and composer. Committed suicide.

LaTasha N. Nevada Diggs (b. 1970) b. New York, NY. Earned MA from New York University and MFA from California College of the Arts. Also a sound artist. Album *Television* was released in 2003. Co-founded with Greg Tate *Coon Bidness*, journal renamed *YoYo/SO4*. Author of the poetry collection *TwERK* (2014).

Melvin Dixon (1950–1992) b. Stamford, CT. Earned BA from Wesleyan University and MA and PhD from Brown University. Moved to Paris; returned to the U.S. and became an English professor at Queens College in 1980. First book, *Change of Territory* (1983), was a volume of poems; lived in Senegal as a Fulbright lecturer. Published two novels and a book of literary criticism and translated Léopold Sédar Senghor's poetry from French. Died of AIDS; poetry collection *Love's Instruments* was published in 1995.

Owen Dodson (1914–1983) b. New York, NY. Earned BA from Bates College and MFA in playwriting at Yale School of Drama. First of his many plays, *Divine Comedy* (1938), was completed at Yale. Published three poetry collections and two novels. Taught theater and literature at several universities, including Howard, where he taught for twenty years; Amiri Baraka and the choreographer Debbie Allen were among his students.

Rita Dove (b. 1952) b. Akron, OH. As a Presidential Scholar in 1970 she was named one of the nation's 100 most outstanding high school students. Earned BA from Miami University; studied at University of Tubingen in Germany on a Fulbright scholarship; awarded MFA from the Iowa Writers' Workshop. Of her many poetry collections, *Thomas and Beulah* (1986) won the Pulitzer Prize. First African American to serve as U.S. Poet Laureate, 1993–95. Elected chancellor of the Academy of American Poets, which also awarded her its Wallace Stevens Award. Member of the American Academy of Arts and Letters. Currently Commonwealth Professor of English at the University of Virginia.

David Drake (c. 1800–c. 1870s) b. South Carolina, lived in the vicinity of Edgefield, SC, known for stoneware production. Parents may have been trained as potters in Africa. Was first owned by Harvey Drake; was sold by Drake's widow after her husband's death in 1832. Around 1840, began signing the shoulders and sides of some of his glazed pots, some of which contained his inscriptions, usually rhyming couplets. Produced more than 100 signed and dated pots and may have made tens of thousands of enormous stoneware pots left unsigned and uninscribed. Last known pot dates from 1864. Took surname Drake after Emancipation.

W.E.B. Du Bois (1868–1963) b. Great Barrington, MA. Earned BA from Fisk and a second BA, an MA, and a PhD from Harvard University with a dissertation on the African slave trade in the U.S.; also did graduate work at University of Berlin. Taught at Wilberforce University, the University of Pennsylvania, and Atlanta University. Published highly influential book *The Souls of Black Folk* in 1903. Founded the Niagara Movement in 1905, a group of African American intellectuals opposed to Booker T. Washington's accommodationist ideas; began twenty-four-year stint as editor of *The Crisis* in 1910. Literary works include several novels. Became more vocally Communist in the 1950s; U.S. government seized his passport. With restoration of passport, emigrated to Ghana in 1959 at the invitation of President Kwame Nkrumah and renounced his U.S. citizenship. Died in Accra.

Henry Dumas (1934–1968) b. Sweet Home, AK, moved to Harlem at ten. Enrolled at City College of New York; left to join U.S. Air Force and served in Texas and the Middle East; studied at Rutgers University. Active in civil rights advocacy; transported food and clothing to field workers and protestors in Mississippi and Tennessee. Served as editor for little magazines. Shot and killed on a platform of the 125th Street subway station by a New York City Transit officer under circumstances that remain unclear. Poems and fiction collections published posthumously.

Paul Laurence Dunbar (1872–1906) b. Dayton, OH. Parents had been enslaved; father fought with the Massachusetts 55th Infantry Regiment in the Civil War. Only Black student at Dayton Central High School, where he was class poet; Orville Wright was a classmate and friend. Published first volume of poetry, *Oak and Ivy*, in 1893. *Majors and Minors* (1895), a mixture of traditional and dialect verse, received favorable notice from William Dean Howells and made Dunbar the most visible and popular African American poet of his time; read poems during a tour of England. Married to Alice Ruth Moore, who would publish poetry as Alice Dunbar-Nelson, from 1898 until their separation in 1902. In addition to several poetry collections, Dunbar wrote fiction as well as lyrics for the pioneering Black musical comedy *In Dahomey* (1903). Died of tuberculosis at age thirty-three.

Alice Dunbar-Nelson (1875–1935) b. New Orleans, LA. Earned teaching degree from Straight University (now Dillard University) and worked as teacher. Married to Paul Laurence Dunbar from 1898 to 1902; suffered domestic violence at his hands. Also a journalist and activist, she was executive secretary of the American Friends Inter-Racial Peace Committee. Advocate for women's suffrage, civil rights, and the passage of the Dyer Anti-Lynching Bill in 1922; helped establish the Industrial School for Colored Girls in Delaware. Published poems, short stories, and speeches.

Camille Dungy (b. 1972) b. Denver, CO. Earned BA from Stanford University and MFA from the University of North Carolina, Greensboro. Poetry collections are *What to Eat, What to Drink, What to Leave for Poison* (2006), *Smith Blue* (2011), *Suck on the Marrow* (2010), and *Trophic Cascade* (2017). Edited *Black Nature: Four Centuries of African American Nature Poetry* (2009). Currently a professor of English at Colorado State University.

Cornelius Eady (b. 1954) b. Rochester, NY. Earned BA from Empire State College. His eight volumes of poetry include *You Don't Miss*

Your Water (1995) and *Brutal Imagination* (2001), which he adapted for the stage with music by cellist Diedre Murray, who had collaborated with him on his theater piece *Running Man* (1999). Founded Cave Canem in 1996 with Toi Derricotte. Currently holds the Miller Chair in poetry at the University of Missouri at Columbia.

Thomas Sayers Ellis (b. 1963) b. Washington, DC. Earned AB from Harvard University and MFA from Brown University. Founded, with Sharan Strange, the Dark Room Collective in 1988. *The Maverick Room* (2005) won the John C. Zacharias First Book Award. *Skin, Inc.: Identity Repair Poems* was published in 2010.

Mari Evans (1923–2017) b. Toledo, OH. Studied fashion design at the University of Toledo. Spent most of life in Indianapolis. Published first poetry volume in 1968, followed by *I Am a Black Woman* (1970) and subsequent collections. Taught at several universities. Edited *Black Women Writers 1950–1980: A Critical Evaluation* (1983). Worked as director of the Indianapolis-based television program *The Black Experience* and consulted for the National Endowment for the Arts and the Indiana Arts Commission; involved in prison reform activism, community organizing, theater, and efforts to end capital punishment. Published children's books and wrote plays, including *Eyes* (1979), a musical adaptation of Zora Neale Hurston's novel *Their Eyes Were Watching God* for which she also wrote the music.

Eve L. Ewing (b. 1986) b. Chicago, IL. Earned BA from the University of Chicago and education-related degrees from Dominican and Harvard Universities. Has taught in Chicago's public schools and at Wellesley College and Harvard University. In addition to *Ghosts in the Schoolyard: Racism and School Closings on Chicago's South Side* (2018), she has published poetry collections *Electric Arches* (2017) and *1919* (2019). With Hanif Abdurraqib, is one-half of the writing duo Echo Hotel. Currently assistant professor of sociology at University of Chicago's School of Social Service Administration.

Sarah Webster Fabio (1928–1979) b. Nashville, TN. Enrolled at Spelman College at fifteen; transferred to Fisk University and earned BA in 1946. Received MA in language arts and creative writing from San Francisco State College in 1965. Taught at Merritt College in Oakland, as well as at California College of Arts and Crafts and University of California, Berkeley, where she founded the Black Studies department. Severely injured in a car accident on New Year's Day, 1971. Published poetry volumes include the seven-volume *Rainbow Signs* (1973). Pursued further graduate work; taught at Oberlin College and the University of Wisconsin. Recorded four LPs of her poetry set to music in the 1970s; backing musicians included her children. Died of colon cancer.

Jessie Redmon Fauset (1882–1961) b. Camden County, NJ. Earned BA in classical languages from Cornell University, after being denied admission to Bryn Mawr College on account of her race. Earned MA in French from University of Pennsylvania. Was editor at a children's magazine aimed at young Black readers, *The Brownies' Book*, which she co-founded with W.E.B. Du Bois, and at *The Crisis*, 1919–26; published four novels from 1924 to 1933. Studied at the Sorbonne in 1925–26. Taught French from 1927 to 1944 at De Witt Clinton High School in the Bronx.

Julia Fields (b. 1938) b. Perry County, AL. Published her first poem in *Scholastic Magazine* at sixteen. Earned BA from Knoxville University. Traveled in the UK; met Langston Hughes in London. Studied at the University of Edinburgh in 1963. Earned MA from Middlebury College in 1972. Taught high school and at historically Black universities; was poet-in-residence at Hampton Institute. Has published four poetry volumes as well as fiction, including the story "Not Your Singing Dancing Spade" (1967). Has lived in Washington, DC, since the late 1970s.

Nikky Finney (b. 1957) b. Conway, SC. Earned BA from Talladega College. Worked for the Black Women's Health Project (now the Black Women's Health Initiative) in Atlanta as a writer and photographer in the 1980s. Befriended Toni Cade Bambara; joined the Southern Collective of African American Writers, which met at Bambara's home. Taught at University of Kentucky; founded Affrilachian Poets with young local writers and worked to emphasize the cultural contributions of African Americans in Appalachia and other parts of the South. Among her several poetry collections, *Head Off & Split* (2011) won the National Book Award. Currently professor of English and creative writing at the University of South Carolina.

Calvin Forbes (b. 1945) b. Newark, NJ. Earned BA from the New School for Social Research and MFA from Brown University. Traveled widely throughout Europe, the United States, and the Caribbean. Poetry volumes include *Blue Monday* (1974), *From the Book of Shine* (1979), and *The Shine Poems* (2001). Has taught at Emerson College, Tufts University, Howard University, the University of the West Indies in Kingston, Jamaica, and the School of the Art Institute of Chicago.

Sarah Louisa Forten (1812–1884) b. Philadelphia, PA. Born free; privately educated in art, music, and French. Belonged to the Female

Literary Association, a literary group for Black women. Began publishing abolitionist poetry and prose in the 1830s. Worked under the pen names Ada (biblical daughter of Lamech) and Magawisca (a Pequot character in Catharine Sedgwick's 1827 novel *Hope Leslie*). Was the aunt of Charlotte Forten Grimké. Also known as Sarah Forten Purvis, her married name.

Vievee Francis (b. 1963) b. West Texas. Earned BA from Fisk University and MFA from the University of Michigan. Three collections of poetry are *Blue-Tail Fly* (2006), *Horse in the Dark* (2012), and *Forest Primeval* (2016). Awards include the Hurston/Wright Legacy Award. Serves as an associate editor at *Callaloo*. Currently teaches English and creative writing at Dartmouth College.

Ross Gay (b. 1974) b. Youngstown, OH. Earned BA in English and Art from Lafayette College, MFA in Poetry from Sarah Lawrence College, and PhD in English from Temple University. Has published poetry volumes *Against Which* (2006), *Bringing the Shovel Down* (2011), and *Catalog of Unabashed Gratitude* (2015), as well as the essay collection *The Book of Delights* (2019). Prizes include the National Book Critics' Circle Award and the Hurston/Wright Legacy Award. Founding editor of the online sports magazine *Some Call It Ballin'*. Currently teaches at Indiana University and at Drew University's low-residency MFA program in poetry and poetry-in-translation.

Christopher Gilbert (1949–2007) b. Birmingham, AL, raised in Lansing, MI. Earned BA from the University of Michigan, and MA and PhD in Psychology from Clark University. Was a practicing psychologist. Published *Across the Mutual Landscape* (1984), which won the Walt Whitman Award from the Academy of American Poets. Died after long bout with kidney disease. Previously unpublished poems were included in posthumous *Turning into Dwelling* (2015).

Nikki Giovanni (b. 1943) b. Knoxville, TN, raised in Cincinnati suburbs. Earned BA in history from Fisk University; did graduate study in social work at the University of Pennsylvania and in the MFA program at Columbia University. Published poems with Black Arts and militant themes in the collections *Black Feeling Black Talk* (1968), *Black Judgement* (1969), and subsequent volumes. Has written poetry for children, including *Rosa* (2005), winner of the Caldecott Medal. Currently Distinguished Professor of English at Virginia Tech, where she has taught since 1987.

Aracelis Girmay (b. 1977) b. Santa Ana, CA. Earned BA from Connecticut College and MFA from New York University. Her poetry collections are *Teeth* (2007), *Kingdom Animalia* (2011), and *The Black Maria* (2016). Teaches at Hampshire College.

C. S. Giscombe (b. 1950) b. Dayton, OH. Earned BA from State University of New York and MFA from Cornell University. In addition to poetry volumes such as *Here* (1994) and *Prairie Style* (2008), has published an essay collection and a travel memoir. Prizes include the American Book Award. Latest of several university teaching appointments is at the University of California, Berkeley.

Lorna Goodison (b. 1947) b. Kingston, Jamaica. Attended the Jamaica School of Art and the School of the Art Students League in New York. Worked as a painter. Poetry volumes include *I Am Becoming My Mother* (1986), winner of the Commonwealth Poetry Prize for the Americas, and *Goldengrove: New and Selected Poems* (2006). Is also a fiction writer, essayist, and memoirist. Became the first female Poet Laureate of Jamaica in 2017. Is Professor Emerita at the University of Michigan.

Rachel Eliza Griffiths (b. 1978). b. Washington, DC. Earned BA from University of Delaware and MFA from Sarah Lawrence College. Poetry volumes include *Mule & Pear* (2011). Also a photographer. Developed interview series *P.O.P. (Poets on Poetry)*. Teaches creative writing at Sarah Lawrence College.

Angelina Weld Grimké (1880–1958) b. Boston, MA. Named after her great-aunt, the abolitionist and suffragist Angelina Grimké Weld. Attended Cushing Academy and the Carleton School. First published poems appeared in periodicals after the turn of the twentieth century. Anti-lynching play *Rachel* was staged in Washington, DC, in 1916 and published in 1920.

Charlotte Forten Grimké (1837–1914) b. Philadelphia, PA. Graduated from Salem Normal School (now Salem State University) in 1856. Took teaching post at all-white Eppes Grammar School in Salem. Published poems in *The Liberator*. During the Civil War, taught formerly enslaved individuals on St. Helena Island, South Carolina, under the auspices of the Port Royal Experiment; met Harriet Tubman; as a nurse, befriended soldiers in all-Black Massachusetts 54th Infantry Regiment. In Boston, served as secretary of the Teachers Committee for the New England branch of the Freedmen's Union Commission. Her translation from French of Emile Erckmann and Alexandre Chatrain's novel *Madame Thérèse* was published in 1869. Moved to Washington, DC, where she worked as a teacher and as a clerk in the U.S. Treasury Department. A founding member of the National Association of Colored Women, she continued to write essays and poems in her later years.

Nicolás Guillén (1902–1989) b. Camagüey, Cuba. Wrote for newspapers, founded the literary magazine *Lis*, and published debut poetry collection *Motivos de son* (Motifs of Sound) in 1930 to great acclaim; met Langston Hughes when the latter came to Cuba. Fought with Republicans in the Spanish Civil War and published poetry collection *España* (1937). Returning to Cuba, was active in the Popular Socialist Party (later the Cuban Communist Party) and was arrested and exiled during Fulgencio Batista's regime; awarded Lenin Peace Prize from the Soviet Union in 1954. After the Cuban Revolution he served as director of Cuba's Union of Writers and Artists and on the Communist Party's Central Committee. English translation *Man-making Words: Selected Poems of Nicolás Guillén* was published in 1975.

Forrest Hamer (b. 1956) b. Goldsboro, NC. Earned BA from Yale University and a PhD in psychology from the University of California, Berkeley. Poetry volumes are *Call and Response* (1995), *Middle Ear* (2000), and *Rift* (2007). Is a psychologist as well as lecturer at the University of California, Berkeley.

Jupiter Hammon (1711–c. 1806) b. Lloyd Harbor, NY. The first published African American poet, Hammon was born into slavery on the estate of Henry Lloyd, whom he later assisted with business ventures, working as a bookkeeper and negotiator. Converted to Christianity; first broadside printed in 1761. Became a leader among African Americans; attended meetings of abolitionist and Revolutionary War societies. Published poems and sermons. Buried in an unmarked grave on the Lloyd estate.

Frances Ellen Watkins Harper (1825–1911) b. Baltimore, MD. Born free, she was orphaned in early childhood and raised by aunt and uncle, whose Academy for Negro Youth she attended. Moved to Columbus, OH, in 1851; became first female professor of domestic science at the African Methodist Episcopal Church's Union Seminary (later Wilberforce University). Involved herself in abolitionism in Philadelphia; lived at an Underground Railroad "station." Contributed to *The Liberator*, *Frederick Douglass's Monthly*, and the *Anglo-African Magazine*. Continued her activism throughout Reconstruction and for the rest of her life, addressing racial issues, temperance, and support for women's suffrage. Published widely; in addition to her poems and nonfiction, wrote novels.

Michael S. Harper (1938–2016) b. New York, NY, moved to Los Angeles in 1951. Earned BA and MA from Los Angeles State College of Applied Arts and Sciences (now California State University, Los

Angeles); earned MFA from the Iowa Writers' Workshop. Taught in colleges in California and, from 1970 to 2013, at Brown University. First of several poetry volumes, *Dear John, Dear Coltrane*, published in 1970. Edited anthologies of African American poetry, including the post-1945 collection *Every Shut Eye Ain't Asleep* and *The Vintage Book of African American Poetry* (with Anthony Walton, 2000).

Duriel E. Harris (b. 1969) b. Chicago, IL. Earned BA from Yale University, MA from New York University, and PhD from the University of Illinois at Chicago's program for writers. Has published three poetry collections and works frequently as a performance artist. Co-founded the poetry and performance trio Black Took Collective and the performance group Call & Response; is poetry editor of *Obsidian: Literature & Arts in the African Diaspora*. Currently associate professor of English in Illinois State University's graduate creative writing program.

Walter Everette Hawkins (1883–after 1940) b. Warrenton, NC. Parents had been enslaved. Educated at Kittrell College in North Carolina. Moved to Washington, DC, and worked as a postal clerk. Published first poetry volume, *Chords and Discords*, in 1909; revised edition published in 1920. Other books include *Petals from the Poppies* (1936).

Robert Hayden (1913–1980) b. Asa Bundy Sheffey in Detroit, MI; Hayden was name of adoptive parents. Earned BA from Detroit City College (now Wayne State University), then worked for Federal Writers' Project; earned MA from University of Michigan two years after publication of his first volume. Converted to Baha'i faith. Taught for twenty-three years in Fisk University's English department, followed by appointment at University of Michigan. Awarded Grand Prize at the First World Festival of Negro Arts in Dakar, Senegal, in 1966. Poetry collections include *A Ballad of Remembrance* (1962) and *Night-Blooming Cereus* (1972).

Terrance Hayes (b. 1971) b. Columbia, SC. Earned BA from Coker College and MFA from the University of Pittsburgh, where he later became a professor and co-founder of the Center for African American Poetry and Poetics. Spent time teaching in Japan; Columbus, OH; and New Orleans. Poetry collections include *Lighthead* (2010), winner of the National Book Award in Poetry, *How to Be Drawn* (2015), and *American Sonnets for My Past and Future Assassin* (2018). Awarded MacArthur Fellowship. Currently teaches in the English department at New York University.

Josephine D. Heard (1861–1921) b. Salisbury, NC. Parents were enslaved. Raised in Charlotte. Attended Scotia Seminary in Concord, NC (now the historically Black college Barber-Scotia College); graduated with honors from Bethany Institute in New York. Worked as a schoolteacher in North Carolina, South Carolina, and Tennessee. Only poetry collection is *Morning Glories* (1890, exp. ed. 1891). Traveled extensively through the United States, Europe, and Africa; lived in Liberia for several years, accompanying her husband on diplomatic and ecclesiastical appointments.

Essex Hemphill (1957–1995) b. Chicago, IL, raised in Washington, DC. Anthologized in pioneering collection *In the Life: A Black Gay Anthology*; edited *Brother to Brother: New Writings by Black Gay Men* (1991), which won Lambda Literary Award. *Ceremonies: Prose and Poetry* (1992) won the National Library Association Award. Died of AIDS-related complications.

David Henderson (b. 1942) b. New York, NY. At nineteen, was the youngest of the six founding members of the Umbra Poets Workshop. Poetry collections include *De Mayor of Harlem* (1970) and *Neo-California* (1998). Is the author of *Ghetto Follies*, a musical performed in San Francisco in 1978. Recorded with jazz musicians, including Ornette Coleman and Sun Ra; published a biography of Jimi Hendrix and created an award-winning radio documentary on the poet Bob Kaufman.

Safiya Henderson-Holmes (1950–2001) b. New York, NY. Earned BA at New York University and MFA in creative writing at City College of New York. Studied at Columbia University's Teachers College. Published the poetry collections *Madness and a Bit of Hope* (1990) and *Daily Bread* (1994). Died of breast cancer.

Calvin Hernton (1932–2001) b. Chattanooga, TN. Earned BA from Talladega College and an MA from Fisk University, both in sociology. Co-founded *Umbra*, magazine born out of the Umbra Poets Workshop on New York City's Lower East Side. Was writer-in-residence at Oberlin from 1970 to 1972; joined faculty in Black Studies and creative writing in 1973. Books include *Sex and Racism in America* (1964), the novel *Scarecrow* (1974), and the poetry collections *Medicine Man* (1976) and, with Carla Blank, *The Red Crab Gang and Black River Poems* (1999).

Sean Hill b. Milledgeville, GA. Earned BA from University of Georgia and MFA from the University of Houston. Has published the poetry collections *Blood Ties & Brown Liquor* (2008) and *Dangerous*

Goods (2014). Serves as director of the Minnesota Northwoods Writers Conference at Bemidji State University.

Harmony Holiday (b. 1982) b. Waterloo, IA. Earned BA in Rhetoric from the University of California, Berkeley, and MFA from Columbia University. Also works as a choreographer; taught dance at the Alvin Ailey American Dance Theatre. Founded and curates the Astro/Afrosonics archive, a collection of jazz poetics and audio culture. Published *Negro League Baseball* (2011) and several subsequent poetry collections. Awards include a Ruth Lilly Fellowship. Teaches at Otis College.

Frank Horne (1899–1974) b. New York, NY. Earned BS from City College of New York and optometry degree from the Northern Illinois College of Ophthalmology. Practiced optometry in Harlem, 1922–26. Version of poem "Letters Found Near a Suicide" (1925) was included in Alain Locke's anthology *The New Negro* (1925). Served as dean and acting president of Fort Valley Normal and Industrial School (now Fort Valley State College), 1926–35; niece Lena Horne, who would become a renowned singer, actor, and activist, lived with him for a time. Served in numerous positions in federal Negro Affairs and housing agencies; later worked in municipal posts in New York City. Sole poetry collection *Haverstraw* was published in London.

George Moses Horton (c. 1798–c. 1883) b. Northampton County, NC, enslaved on William Horton's tobacco plantation. Began composing verse in his head in 1815; started reciting poems for a fee to crowds; sold mostly to students, who gave him books on poetry, geography, history, and oratory. Published *The Hope of Liberty, Containing a Number of Poetical Pieces* (1829) and *The Poetical Works* (1845). Walked to Raleigh in April 1865 to join the 9th Michigan Cavalry Volunteer Infantry, which took him under their protection. Published his final volume, *Naked Genius*, in 1865; moved to Philadelphia.

Langston Hughes (1901–1967) b. Joplin, MO. Raised by grandmother in Lawrence, KS, then by mother in Lincoln, IL, and Cleveland. After graduating high school, joined father for a year in central Mexico. Moved to Harlem in September 1921. Became a seaman in the summer of 1923; traveled throughout West Africa and Europe. Lived in Paris and Washington, DC, working as a busboy. Published first of many collections, *The Weary Blues*, in 1926. Earned a BA from Lincoln University in 1929; moved to the Soviet Union for a year in 1932 and worked as a newspaper correspondent during the Spanish Civil War. Wrote plays, essays, the novel *Not Without Laughter*

(1930), an autobiography, and children's books; as anthologist, edited *The Poetry of the Negro, 1746–1949* (1949; exp. ed. 1970) with Arna Bontemps.

Erica Hunt (b. 1955) b. New York, NY. Earned BA from San Francisco State University and MFA from Bennington College. Has published poetry collections *Arcade* (1996), *Local History* (1993, 2003), and *Piece Logic* (2002) and co-edited the anthology *Letters from the Future: Black Women/Radical Writing* (2018).

Ishion Hutchinson (b. 1983) b. Port Antonio, Jamaica. Earned BA from the University of the West Indies, MFA from New York University, and PhD from the University of Utah. Poetry collections are *Far District* (2010) and *House of Lords and Commons* (2016). Awards include a National Book Critics' Circle Award and the Windham-Campbell Prize. Teaches in the graduate writing program at Cornell University.

Gary Jackson b. Topeka, KS. Earned BA in English from Washburn University in 2004 and MFA in creative writing from the University of New Mexico at Albuquerque. Author of *Missing You, Metropolis* (2010), which was adapted for the stage; is associate professor of creative writing at the College of Charleston.

Major Jackson (b. 1968) b. Philadelphia, PA. Received BA from Temple University and MFA from the University of Oregon. Joined the Dark Room Collective in 1994. Poetry collections include *Leaving Saturn* (2002) and *Roll Deep* (2015). Currently poetry editor at the *Harvard Review* and Distinguished Professor at the University of Vermont.

Honorée Fannone Jeffers (b. 1967) b. Kokomo, IN, raised in Durham, NC, and Atlanta. Earned BA from Talladega College and MFA from the University of Alabama. Has published four collections of poetry, including *The Gospel of Barbecue* (2000). Was elected to the American Antiquarian Society due to her research on Phillis Wheatley. Currently professor of English at the University of Oklahoma.

Tyehimba Jess (b. 1965) b. Jesse S. Goodwin in Detroit, MI. Earned BA from University of Chicago and MFA from New York University. Competed in two National Poetry Slams with the Chicago Green Mill Poetry Slam team. Adopted first name from the Tiv people of Nigeria that means "we stand as a nation" and legally changed name. His collection *Olio* (2016) won the Pulitzer Prize. Is poetry and fiction editor of the *African American Review.* Currently associate professor of English at the College of Staten Island.

Eva A. Jessye (1895–1992) b. Coffeyville, KS. Parents had been enslaved. Attended the Quindaro Freedman's School (later Western University) at thirteen and graduated in 1914; enrolled at Langston University in Oklahoma. Served as director of music at Morgan College (now Morgan State University) in Baltimore. Moved to New York in 1926; worked as a singer and organized the Original Dixie Jubilee Choir (later the Eva Jessye Choir). Directed chorus for the operas *Four Saints in Three Acts* by Virgil Thomson and *Porgy and Bess* by George Gershwin. The Eva Jessye Choir was selected by Dr. Martin Luther King, Jr., as the official choir for the 1963 March on Washington; performed "We Shall Overcome."

Ted Joans (1928–2003) b. Cairo, IL. Earned BFA from Indiana University. Moved to New York City in 1951 and befriended Beat poets. Graffitied "Bird Lives" throughout the city in 1955 after jazz saxophonist Charlie Parker's death. Also a visual artist and musician. Traveled widely, including abroad. Wrote more than thirty books of poetry, prose, and collage.

Fenton Johnson (1888–1958) b. Chicago, IL. Earned MA from the University of Chicago and a degree from Columbia University's School of Journalism. Published three poetry collections; sequence "African Nights" was included in Alfred Kreymborg's 1919 *Others* anthology. Was a drama critic for the *New York News.* Published story collection *Tales of Darkest America* (1920) and essay collection *For the Highest Good* (1920). Wrote plays that have not survived.

Georgia Douglas Johnson (1880–1967) b. Atlanta, GA. Earned degree from Atlanta University Normal School and studied music at the Oberlin Conservatory of Music. Lived most of her life in Washington, DC; hosted long-running salon for Black writers and artists. Published four volumes of poetry; wrote the weekly syndicated column "Homely Philosophy" in the 1920s and 1930s. Wrote songs, stories, and several plays.

Helene Johnson (1906–1995) b. Boston, MA. Moved to New York City in the mid-1920s, living in the same building as Zora Neale Hurston, whom she befriended. Published about two dozen poems in periodicals. First cousin of the writer Dorothy West.

James Weldon Johnson (1871–1938) b. Jacksonville, FL. Earned BA from Atlanta University. First African American admitted to Florida Bar Association since Reconstruction; practiced law in Jacksonville. After he was nearly lynched, left the South permanently. Moved to New York City in the early 1900s and wrote around 200 songs for Broadway musicals. Published novel *The Autobiography of an*

Ex-Coloured Man in 1912. Served as U.S. consul in Nicaragua and Venezuela; became an NAACP field secretary and later was appointed executive secretary. Books include the poetry collections *Fifty Years and Other Poems* (1917) and *Saint Peter Relates an Incident: Selected Poems* (1935); edited influential anthology *The Book of American Negro Poetry* (1922).

Gayl Jones (b. 1949) b. Lexington, KY. Earned MA from Connecticut College and MA and DA in creative writing from Brown University. Published plays *Chile Woman* (1974) and *The Ancestor: A Street Play* (1975) in graduate school. Her first two published novels, *The Healing* (1998), nominated for a National Book Award, and *Mosquito* (1999), were edited by Toni Morrison. Taught as assistant professor of English, Afro-American Studies, and African Studies at the University of Michigan; left position in 1983 and spent time living in Europe. Along with her fiction, has published three poetry collections.

Patricia Spears Jones (b. 1951) b. Forrest City, AK. Earned BA from Rhodes College and MFA from Vermont College of Fine Arts. Poetry collections include *A Lucent Fire: New and Selected Poems* (2015). Co-edited *Ordinary Women: Poetry by New York City Women* (1978). Currently teaches at City University of New York.

Saeed Jones (b. 1985) b. Memphis, TN. Raised in Lewisville, TX. Earned BA from Western Kentucky University and MFA from Rutgers University–Newark in 2010. Named executive editor of culture at *Buzzfeed* in 2016. First book, the poetry collection *Prelude to Bruise*, was published in 2014.

A. Van Jordan (b. 1965) b. Akron, OH. Earned BA from Wittenberg University, MA from Howard University, and MFA from Warren Wilson College. Has published four books of poetry, including *M-A-C-N-O-L-I-A* (2005). Currently a professor of English and poetry at the University of Michigan and director of the Helen Zell Writers' Program.

June Jordan (1936–2002) b. New York, NY. Involved with the Black Arts Movement, she published some twenty-eight books as author or editor, including poetry collections, beginning with *Some Changes* (1971); wrote children's books, plays, the memoir *Soldier: A Poet's Childhood* (2000), and essays. Also a prominent activist. Was professor of African American Studies at the University of California, Berkeley. Complete poems, *Directed by Desire*, was published posthumously.

Allison Joseph (b. 1967) b. London, England. Earned BA from Kenyon College and MFA from Indiana University. Edits the *Crab*

Orchard Review and serves as publisher for No Chair Press, a chapbook press for women poets. Currently Judge Williams Holmes Cook Endowed Professor of English at Southern Illinois University in Carbondale; directs the MFA program in creative writing.

Bob Kaufman (1925–1986) b. New Orleans, LA. Joined U.S. Merchant Marine as a teenager. Lived in New York City and San Francisco and was at the center of the circle of Beat writers in both cities. Co-founded literary journal *Beatitude*. Began ten-year period of self-imposed silence in 1963. Became a Buddhist. Poetry collections include *Golden Sardine* (1967) and *The Ancient Rain: Poems 1956–1978* (1981).

Douglas Kearney (b. 1974) Raised in Altadena, CA. Earned BA from Howard University and MA from California Institute of the Arts. Has published chapbooks and four full-length poetry volumes; collected three opera librettos in *Someone Took They Tongues* (2016). Teaches English and creative writing at the University of Minnesota, Twin Cities.

John Keene (b. 1965) b. St. Louis, MO. Earned AB from Harvard University and MFA from New York University. A member of the Dark Room Collective, he has been the recipient of the Windham-Campbell Prize and a MacArthur Fellowship, among other awards. Publications include *Annotations* (1995) and *Counternarratives* (2015). Currently teaches at Rutgers University–Newark in the Department of African American and African Studies, the Department of English, and the MFA in creative writing program.

Sybil Kein (b. 1939) b. Consuela Marie Moore in New Orleans, LA, into a family of Creole and Cajun descent; grew up speaking Creole. Earned BS in music from Xavier University, MA in Theater Arts and Communications from Louisiana State University, and PhD in a comparative study of American ethnic literatures at the University of Michigan. A scholar of Creole culture, she is the author of plays, the study *Creole: The History and Legacy of Louisiana's Free People of Color* (2000), and poetry collections such as *Delta Dancer* (1984), among other books.

Donika Kelly (b. 1983) b. Los Angeles, CA, moved to Arkansas in the late 1990s. Earned BA at Southern Arkansas University, MFA from the Michener Center for Writers at the University of Texas at Austin, and PhD from Vanderbilt University. Author of poetry collection *Bestiary* (2016) and the chapbook *Aviarium* (2017). Currently assistant professor of creative writing and English at Baruch College.

Dolores Kendrick (1927–2017) b. Washington, DC. Earned a teacher's certificate from Miner's College (now part of the University of the District of Columbia) and MA in teaching from Georgetown University. Taught in Washington, DC, public schools and at Phillips Exeter Academy. Published four poetry collections, most notably *The Women of Plums: Poems in the Voices of Slave Women* (1989), which were given theatrical and musical adaptations. Appointed poet laureate of Washington, DC, in 2000.

Keorapetse Kgositsile (1938–2018), b. Johannesburg, South Africa. Popularly known as Bra Willie. Left South Africa in 1961 for Tanzania and then the United States, settling in New York City, where he was at the center of the Black Arts Movement. Published poetry collections *Spirits Unchained* (1969), *For Melba* (1969), and *My Name Is Afrika* (1971), among others. Earned MFA from Columbia University; founded Black Art Theater and African Literature Association. Returned to Tanzania and taught at the University of Dar es Salaam. After the end of apartheid, returned to South Africa; appointed its poet laureate.

Etheridge Knight (1931–1991) b. Corinth, MS, raised in Paducah, KY. Served in U.S. Army in the Korean War and was wounded. Imprisoned for eight years on robbery charges; began writing poetry. Published *Poems from Prison* (1968) a year before his release. Active in Black Arts Movement. Married for two years to poet Sonia Sanchez. Taught at the University of Pittsburgh, the University of Hartford, and Lincoln University. Led Free People's Poetry Workshops, open to anyone. Earned BA from Martin Center University in Indianapolis in 1990.

Yusef Komunyakaa (b. 1947) b. James Willie Brown in Bogalusa, LA. Served in U.S. Army during the Vietnam War, including as a correspondent and managing editor of the U.S. army publication *Southern Cross*; awarded Bronze Star. Earned BA from University of Colorado, MA from Colorado State University, and MFA from University of California at Irvine. Legally changed name to surname that according to family lore had belonged to grandfather who had arrived in the U.S. from the Caribbean, likely Trinidad. Among his several poetry collections, *Neon Vernacular: New & Selected Poems 1977–1989* (1993) won the Pulitzer Prize. Elected Chancellor of the Academy of American Poets in 1999. Currently Distinguished Senior Poet in New York University's graduate creative writing program.

Pinkie Gordon Lane (1923–2008) b. Philadelphia, PA. Earned BA from Spelman College, MA from Atlanta University, and was the first Black woman to earn a PhD in English from Louisiana State University in 1967. Published first of several poetry volumes, *Wind Thoughts*, in 1972; became chair of the English department at Southern University in 1974. Was the first Black woman poet laureate of Louisiana.

Armand Lanusse (1812–1868) b. New Orleans, LA. Born free; educated in either New Orleans or Paris. Helped organize the New Orleans Catholic School for Indigent Orphans of Color in 1848; was a teacher and mentor for Black orphans; served as principal from 1852 until his death. Fought for the Confederate Army during the Civil War; initially opposed the Union Army's occupation of New Orleans but later encouraged Black people to leave the state due to racism. Worked on literary journals and Afro-Creole newspapers.

Rickey Laurentiis (b. 1989) b. New Orleans, LA. Earned BA from Sarah Lawrence College and MFA from Washington University. Collections include *Prime* (2014) and *Boy with Thorn* (2015), recipient of a Lambda Literary Award, among other prizes. Currently the Inaugural Fellow in Creative Writing at the Center for African American Poetry and Poetics at the University of Pittsburgh.

Danielle Legros Georges (b. 1964) b. Gonaïves, Haiti, moved to Boston from Zaire at age six. Earned BS in Communications from Emerson College in 1986 and MFA in English and creative writing from New York University. Member of the Dark Room Collective. Has published three books of poetry and was appointed poet laureate of Boston. Currently director of the MFA program in creative writing at Lesley University.

Robin Coste Lewis (b. 1964) b. Compton, CA. Earned BA from Hampshire College, MTS in Sanskrit and Comparative Religious Literature from Harvard University's Divinity School, MFA in Poetry from New York University, and PhD in creative writing and literature from the University of Southern California. Poetry collection *Voyage of the Sable Venus* (2015) won the National Book Award. Appointed poet laureate of Los Angeles. Currently writer-in-residence at the University of Southern California.

Audre Lorde (1934–1992) b. Audrey Lorde in New York, NY. Earned BA from Hunter College; studied for a year at the National Autonomous University of Mexico in Mexico City in 1954; earned MA in Library Science from Columbia University. Worked as librarian in New York City, among other jobs. The first of her poetry collections, *The First Cities*, was published in 1968; prose works include *The Cancer Journals* (1980). A prominent activist, she founded Kitchen

Table: Women of Color Press with Barbara Smith. Taught English at John Jay College of Criminal Justice and at Hunter College; was poet laureate of New York State. Took the name Gamba Adisa (She Who Makes Her Meaning Clear) during an African naming ceremony shortly before her death.

Nathaniel Mackey (b. 1947) b. Miami, FL, raised in California. Earned AB from Princeton University and PhD from Stanford University. Taught as professor at the University of Southern California and directed its Black Studies program. Long served as editor of the journal *Hambone*; edited anthology *Moment's Notice: Jazz in Poetry and Prose* (1993). Of his many poetry collections, *Splay Anthem* (2006) won the National Book Award. Other awards include Bollingen Prize from Yale University. Elected chancellor of the Academy of American Poets. Currently Reynolds Price Professor of Creative Writing at Duke University.

Haki Madhubuti (b. 1942) b. Donald Luther Lee in Little Rock, AK, moved to Detroit in 1943. Served in U.S. Army; worked at Ebony Museum of Negro History and Art (later the DuSable Museum of African American History). First of many poetry collections, *Think Black*, was published in 1967. Active in Black Arts Movement circles; co-founded Chicago-based Third World Press, the quarterly *Black Books Bulletin*, and community educational institutions. Visited Africa and took name derived from Swahili in 1974 (*Haki* means "justice," *Madhubuti* "precise and reliable"). Prizes include the American Book Award.

Clarence Major (b. 1936) b. Atlanta, GA, moved to Chicago at age ten. Earned BS from SUNY Albany and PhD from the Union Institute and University. Poetry collections include *Swallow the Lake* (1970) and *My Studio* (2018). Also a fiction writer, scholar of African American slang, and anthologist; his *The Garden Thrives: Twentieth-Century African-American Poetry* was published in 1996. Recipient of a 2016 PEN Oakland/Reginald Lockett Lifetime Achievement Award, among other prizes. Taught at several universities, including University of California, Davis.

George R. Margetson (1877–1952) b. St. Kitts, British West Indies. Immigrated to the U.S. in 1897; settled in Boston area. Author of four poetry collections.

Mariposa (b. 1971) b. Mariposa María Teresa Fernández in the Bronx, New York, NY, a third-generation Puerto Rican. Earned both BA in Women's Studies with a concentration in English Literature and an

MA in Education from New York University. Poetry collection *Born Broxeña: Poems on Identity, Love, and Survival* was published in 2001.

Dawn Lundy Martin (b. 1968) Raised in Hartford, CT. Earned BA from the University of Connecticut, MA from San Francisco State University, and PhD in English from the University of Massachusetts, Amherst. Collections include *Life in a Box Is a Pretty Life* (2014), recipient of a Lambda Literary Award. Also a video artist whose work was exhibited at the Whitney Museum's 2014 Biennial. Co-founded and directs the Center for African American Poetry and Poetics at the University of Pittsburgh.

Adrian Matejka (b. 1971) b. Nuremberg, West Germany, raised in California and Indiana. Earned BA from Indiana University and MFA from Southern Illinois University, Carbondale. Most recent of four poetry collections is *Map to the Stars* (2017). Appointed poet laureate of Indiana in 2018. Currently an associate professor of English and creative writing at Indiana University.

Agnes Maxwell-Hall (1894–1984) b. Montego Bay, Jamaica. Educated in London, Boston, and New York; attended Columbia University to study short-story writing. Published stories and poetry in American and British literary journals.

Shara McCallum (b. 1972) b. Jamaica, immigrated to the U.S. at age nine. Earned BA from the University of Miami, MFA from the University of Maryland, and PhD from Binghamton University in Poetry and African American and Caribbean Literatures. Poetry volumes include *The Face of Water: New and Selected Poems* (2011) and *Madwoman* (2017). Currently teaches creative writing and English at Penn State University.

Shane McCrae (b. 1975) b. Portland, OR, raised in Texas and California. Earned BA from Linfield College, MFA from the Iowa Writers' Workshop, and JD from Harvard Law School. Has published six poetry collections, including *In the Language of My Captor* (2017) and *The Gilded Auction Block* (2019). Currently teaches at Columbia University.

Colleen J. McElroy (b. 1935) b. St. Louis, MO. Moved frequently due to stepfather's U.S. army assignments, including in Wyoming, Munich, and Kansas City. Earned BS and MS from Kansas State University and PhD from University of Washington. Her many poetry collections include *What Madness Brought Me Here: New and Selected Poems, 1968–1988* (1990); she is also the author of books of short stories and travel writing. Is a playwright, photographer, and visual artist.

Prizes include American Book Award. Taught English at University of Washington and became first Black female full professor in 1983. Was editor of *The Seattle Review*.

Claude McKay (1889–1948) b. Sunny Ville, Jamaica. Published first poetry collection, *Songs of Jamaica*, in 1912, the year he arrived in the U.S. Along with poetry volumes such as *Harlem Shadows* (1922), published novels and memoirs, including *Home to Harlem* (1928) and the autobiography *A Long Way from Home* (1937). Spent much of the 1920s and 1930s in Europe and North Africa.

Tony Medina (b. 1966) b. New York, NY. Earned BA from Baruch College and MA and PhD from SUNY Binghamton. In addition to his poetry books, he is the author of children's books, a memoir, and the graphic novel *I Am Alfonso Jones* (2017); edited the anthology *Bum Rush the Page: A Def Poetry Jam* (2001). Currently professor of creative writing at Howard University.

Anis Mojgani (b. 1977) Raised in New Orleans, LA. Earned BFA from Savannah College of Art and Design. Poetry books include *Over the Anvil We Stretch* (2008) and *In the Pockets of Small Gods* (2018). A spoken-word performer, he has been featured on HBO's *Def Poetry Jam*.

Aja Monet (b. 1987) b. New York, NY. Earned BA from Sarah Lawrence College and MFA in creative writing from the School of the Art Institute in Chicago. Was, at age nineteen, the youngest winner of Nuyorican Poets Café's Grand Slam. First full-length poetry collection, *My Mother Was a Freedom Fighter*, was published in 2018. Co-founded the Miami arts collective Smoke Signals Studio. Manages the poetry workshop Voices: Poetry for the People.

Myra Estelle Morris (1906–1972) b. Tennessee, moved to Los Angeles around age thirteen. Earned BA in Education from UCLA. Published first and only anthologized poems in *Negro Voices: An Anthology of Contemporary Verse* (1938), edited by Beatrice M. Murphy. Was a public schoolteacher in Los Angeles for thirty-three years.

Tracie Morris (b. 1964) b. New York, NY. Earned MFA from Hunter College and PhD in Performance Studies from New York University. Studied acting at Royal Academy of Dramatic Art in London and Michael Howard Studios in Manhattan. Performed regularly at the Nuyorican Poets Café and was a Grand Slam champion. Also works as a sound artist; pieces have been featured in several Whitney Biennials and at the Museum of Modern Art. Poetry collections include

Intermissions (1998) and *handholding: 5 kinds* (2016). Currently professor of Humanities and Media Studies at the Pratt Institute.

Thylias Moss (b. 1954) b. Cleveland, OH. Earned BA from Oberlin College and MA from the University of New Hampshire. Poetry collections include *Wannabe Hoochie Mama Gallery of Realities' Red Dress Code: New & Selected Poems* (2016). Author of children's books and a memoir. Professor Emerita at the University of Michigan's School of Art & Design.

Fred Moten (b. 1962) b. Las Vegas, NV, raised in Las Vegas, Pennsylvania, and Arkansas. Among his many books are the poetry volumes *B Jenkins* (2010) and *The Feel Trio* (2014) and the monograph *In the Break: The Aesthetics of the Black Radical Tradition* (2003). Taught Performance Studies at New York University and is currently professor of English at University of California, Riverside.

Harryette Mullen (b. 1953) b. Florence, AL, raised in Fort Worth. Earned BA from University of Texas and MA and PhD from University of California, Santa Cruz (2000). Active in the Black Arts Movement during the 1970s. Poetry collections include *Muse & Drudge* (1995) and *Sleeping with the Dictionary* (2002). Currently professor of African American literature and creative writing at University of California, Los Angeles.

John Murillo (b. 1971) b. Upland, CA. Earned BA from Howard University and MFA from New York University. Published the two collections *Up Jump the Boogie* (2010) and *Kontemporary Amerikan Poetry* (2020). Co-founded poets' collective The Symphony. Currently assistant professor of English at Wesleyan University.

Pauli Murray (1910–1985) b. Baltimore, MD, raised in Durham, NC. Earned BA in English from Hunter College, JD from Howard University's Law School, LLM from University of Berkeley's Boalt School of Law, and PhD in juridical science from Yale Law School. Arrested in 1940 for refusing to move to the back of a segregated bus; organized sit-ins at Washington, DC, restaurants while attending Howard. Co-founded National Organization for Women. Spent several years teaching in Ghana. Published poetry collection *Dark Testament and Other Poems* in 1970, as well as other books, including the family memoir *Proud Shoes* (1956). Earned MA in Divinity from the Episcopal Church's General Theological Seminary; was the first Black woman to be ordained as an Episcopal priest. Was named, in 2012, a saint of the Episcopal Church.

Larry Neal (1937–1981) b. Atlanta, GA, raised in Philadelphia. Earned BA from Lincoln University and MA from University of Pennsylvania. Served as arts editor for Black nationalist publication *The Liberator*; co-founded Black Arts Repertory Theatre and *Cricket*, a music magazine. Co-edited *Black Fire: An Anthology of Afro-American Writing* (1968). Published the poetry volumes *Black Boogaloo* (1969) and *Hoodoo Hollerin' Bebop Ghosts* (1974); wrote plays and essays. Taught at Howard, Yale, and other universities; was executive director of Washington, DC, Commission on the Arts and Humanities. Died of heart attack at age forty-three.

Marilyn Nelson (b. 1946) b. Cleveland, OH. Also published as Marilyn Nelson Waniek. Grew up on military bases; father was one of the last Tuskegee Airmen. BA from University of California, Davis, MA from University of Pennsylvania, PhD from University of Minnesota. Poetry collections include *The Fields of Praise: New and Selected Poems* (1997); has also published children's books and translations. Elected chancellor of the Academy of American Poets. Served as Connecticut's poet laureate. Professor Emerita at the University of Connecticut.

Richard Bruce Nugent (1906–1987) b. Washington, DC. Writer and visual artist who also published as Richard Bruce and Bruce Nugent. In Harlem in the 1920s, he was involved with short-lived *Fire!!* magazine, to which he contributed "Smoke, Lilies, and Jade," a story about homosexuality with a protagonist who resembles Nugent. Prose poem "Sahdji," published in Alain Locke's anthology *The New Negro* (1925), was later adapted into a ballet with music composed by William Grant Still. Was in the cast of DuBose Heyward's play *Porgy* (1927). Helped found the Harlem Cultural Council with artist Romare Bearden in the 1960s.

Gloria C. Oden (1923–2012) Raised in Yonkers, NY. Earned BA and JD from Howard University. Worked for the federal government. Moved to New York City, where she enrolled in graduate courses at New York University and became a part of the Greenwich Village poetry scene. Edited several academic journals and math and science textbooks in 1960s and 1970s. Taught English for more than twenty-five years at the University of Maryland, Baltimore County. Poetry collections include *Resurrections* (1978) and *Appearances* (2003).

Myron O'Higgins (1913–1978) b. Myron Higgins in Chicago, IL. Was a student of Sterling A. Brown at Howard University. Served in U.S. Army. Won fellowships that enabled travel to Mexico and Cuba. Published, with Robert Hayden, *The Lion and the Archer: Poems*

(1948). Went to Paris in 1949 with photographer Marvin Smith and painter Romare Bearden to study with French painter Fernand Léger. Wrote plays. Worked as archivist at the Museum of Primitive Art in New York and registrar at the Hirshhorn Museum in Washington, DC.

Brenda Marie Osbey (b. 1957) b. New Orleans, LA. Earned BA from Dillard University; also studied at Université Paul Valéry in Montpellier, France. Earned MA from University of Kentucky. Has written in French as well as English. Served term as poet laureate of Louisiana. Has taught at Loyola University in New Orleans, Dillard University, and UCLA. Her collected poems, *All Souls*, was published in 2015. Currently Distinguished Visiting Professor of Africana Studies at Brown University.

Gregory Pardlo (b. 1968) b. Philadelphia, PA, raised in South Jersey. Earned BA from Rutgers University; studies were bookended by service in U.S. Marine Corps. Lived in Copenhagen with his first wife, a Dane. Helped his grandfather run a jazz and blues club in Camden, NJ. Earned MFA in poetry from New York University and MFA in nonfiction writing from Columbia University. Among his poetry collections, *Digest* (2015) won the Pulitzer Prize. Translated a book of Niels Lynsø's poetry from Danish and is the author of *Air Traffic: A Memoir of Ambition and Manhood in America* (2018). Was associate editor of *Callaloo*. Currently teaches at Rutgers University's MFA program in creative writing and is poetry editor at *Virginia Quarterly Review*.

Morgan Parker (b. 1987) b. Highland, CA. Earned BA from Columbia University and MFA from New York University. Poetry collections are *Other People's Comfort Keeps Me Up at Night* (2015), *There Are More Beautiful Things Than Beyoncé* (2017), and *Magical Negro* (2019). Published young adult novel *Who Put This Song On?* (2019). One-half, with Angel Nafis, of the poetry duo The Other Black Girl Collective. Co-founded and co-curates Poets With Attitude (PWA) with indigenous poet Tommy Pico.

Raymond R. Patterson (1929–2001) b. New York, NY. Earned BA from Lincoln University and MA from New York University. Long a professor at City University of New York, he published the poetry collections *26 Ways of Looking at a Black Man and Other Poems* (1969) and *Elemental Blues* (1983) and wrote the libretti for two operas by the African American composer Hale Smith.

Willie Perdomo (b. 1967) b. New York, NY. Has published four poetry volumes, including *The Essential Hits of Shorty Bon Bon* (2014), as well as children's books. Teaches at Phillips Exeter Academy.

Carl Phillips (b. 1959) b. Everett, WA. Moved frequently during childhood because father served in U.S. Air Force. Earned AB from Harvard University, MAT from the University of Massachusetts, and MA in creative writing from Boston University. Has published more than a dozen books of poetry, including *Speak Low* (2009), along with essay collections and his translation of Sophocles's *Philoctetes.* Elected chancellor of the Academy of American Poets. Many prizes include two Lambda Literary Awards. Serves as judge for the Yale Series of Younger Poets. Currently professor of English, African and African American studies, and creative writing at Washington University in St. Louis.

Rowan Ricardo Phillips (b. 1974) b. New York, NY. Received BA from Swarthmore College and PhD from Brown University. Has published the poetry volumes *The Ground* (2012), *Heaven* (2015), and *Living Weapon* (2020). Also the author of *When Blackness Rhymes with Blackness* (2010) and *The Circuit* (2020), about tennis. Currently Ford Schumann Distinguished Visiting Professor at Williams College.

Pedro Pietri (1943–2004) b. Ponce, Puerto Rico. Moved to Spanish Harlem in early childhood. Served in the U.S. army in the Vietnam War. Joined the Young Lords, a Puerto Rican civil rights organization; co-founded the Nuyorican Poets Café in the early 1970s. Became known for eccentric performances; nicknamed himself Reverend and carried leaflets of his poems in a suitcase labeled "Coffin for Rent." Recorded two LPs in 1979, *One Is a Crowd* and *Loose Joints: Poetry by Pedro Pietri.* Books include the poetry collection *Puerto Rican Obituary* (1973). Wrote plays and was an AIDS activist. Died of stomach cancer.

Oliver Pitcher (b. 1923) b. Massachusetts. Attended Bard College. Studied theater at the Dramatic Workshop of The New School and the American Negro Theater. Composed numerous plays, including *Spring Beginning* and *The One.* Published small poetry volume, *Dust of Silence*, in 1958. Taught African American theater at Vassar College. Was poet-in-residence at Atlanta University Center; taught poetry and creative writing. Was also an instructor at Emory University.

Lucia Mae Pitts (1904–1973) b. Chattanooga, TN, raised in Chicago. Lived in Chicago, Harlem, and Washington, DC, among other places, and was active in literary and cultural circles in these cities. Wrote for the *Chicago Defender* and in a column for *The Pittsburgh Courier* entitled "Back Streets of Business," chronicling the professional lives of stenographers. Served in the Women's Army Corps during World War II. Contributed to *Triad* (1945), joint collection of poems by Pitts, Helen C. Harris, and Tomi Carolyn Tinsley. Moved to Los Angeles; started a personnel service. Employed in later years by the U.S. Department of Public Housing.

Ann Plato (c. 1824–1870) May have been born in North Fork, Suffolk County, in eastern Long Island, NY. Was likely of African and indigenous ancestry. Lived in Hartford, CT, where she was a member of the First Hartford Colored Congregational Church. Published *Essays: Including Biographies and Miscellaneous Pieces, in Prose and Poetry* (1841).

Sterling D. Plumpp (b. 1940) b. Clinton, MS. Served in U.S. Army. Earned BA in Psychology from Roosevelt University. Released first chapbook, *Portable Soul* (1969), with Third World Press, for which he became an editor. Took post in the Black Studies Department at the University of Illinois, Chicago, in 1971; was promoted to full professor in 1994. Published essay collection about childhood on tenant farm, *Black Rituals* (1972). Edited anthology of South African poetry. Wrote libretto "My Feeling Tone" for the Swiss composer George Gruntz's *Chicago Cantata* (1991).

Esther Popel (1896–1958) b. Harrisburg, PA. Also known as Ester Popel Shaw. Published first book of poetry while in high school. Earned BA from Dickinson College, the first Black woman to enroll there; was barred from residing on campus due to racial restrictions. Taught in Baltimore and Washington, DC, schools from the late 1920s until 1952. Poetry collection *A Forest Pool* was published in 1934. Wrote plays. Began painting after retirement and lectured at women's clubs in New York and Washington, DC.

N. H. Pritchard (1939–1996) b. Norman Henry Pritchard in New York, NY. Earned BA in Art History from New York University. Was a member of the Umbra Poets Workshop. Published the poetry collections *The Matrix: Poems 1960–1970* (1970) and *Eecchhooeess* (1971).

Khadijah Queen (b. 1974) b. Wayne County, MI, raised in Los Angeles. Books include *Conduit* (2008), *I'm So Fine: A List of Famous Men & What I Had On* (2017) and *ANODYNE* (2020). Taught poetry and playwrighting for the low-residency Mile-High MFA in creative writing at Regis University. Currently Visiting Professor in creative writing at the University of Colorado.

Dudley Randall (1914–2000) b. Washington, DC, moved to Detroit in 1920. Graduated high school at sixteen. Served in U.S. Army in World War II as a supply sergeant in the South Pacific. Earned BA from Wayne University (now Wayne State University) and master's degree in library science from the University of Michigan. Worked as a librarian at historically Black universities. Founded Broadside Press, dedicated to publishing Black writers, in 1965. Visited the Soviet Union in 1966. First of his poetry collections, *Poem Counterpoem*, was published by Broadside in 1966; he also edited anthologies, including *For Malcolm: Poems on the Life and Death of Malcolm X* (1967) and *The Black Poets* (1971). Named Detroit's first poet laureate in 1981.

Camille Rankine (b. 1983) b. Portland, OR. Earned BA from Harvard University and MFA from Columbia University. Published chapbook *Slow Dance with Trip Wire* (2011) and collection *Incorrect Merciful Impulses* (2016). Currently teaches at Hampshire College and at The New School.

Claudia Rankine (b. 1963) b. Kingston, Jamaica, moved to New York City at age seven. Earned BA from Williams College and MFA from Columbia University. Has published five volumes of poetry, notably the best-selling *Citizen: An American Lyric* (2014). Has also written several plays. Was awarded MacArthur Fellowship in 2016; used funds to open The Racial Imaginary Institute, an interdisciplinary initiative exploring the impact of racial ideas on daily life and culture. Elected chancellor of the Academy of American Poets in 2013. Produces the video series *Situations* with her husband, the filmmaker and photographer John Lucas. Currently Frederick Iseman Professor of Poetry at Yale University.

Henrietta Cordelia Ray (1850–1916) b. New York, NY. Graduated from University of City of New York (now City University of New York) in 1891 with degree in pedagogy. Became proficient in Greek, Latin, German, and French. Taught at Colored Grammar School No. 1 in New York for thirty years. Poetry collections are *Sonnets* (1893) and *Poems* (1910).

Andy Razaf (1895–1973) b. Andriamanantena Paul Razafinkarefo in Washington, DC, raised in Harlem. Direct descendant of Madagascar royalty. Worked as successful lyricist in New York musical theater and wrote the words for many songs that are now standards, collaborating with Fats Waller, among others.

Charles L. Reason (1818–1893) b. New York, NY; parents immigrated to U.S. during the Haitian Revolution. Was a math prodigy. Studied at New York's African Free School and became an instructor at the school at fourteen. Graduated from McGrawville College, also known as New-York Central College. Worked as educator and teacher; was an abolitionist and activist. Published essays and poetry in periodicals.

Ishmael Reed (b. 1938) b. Chattanooga, TN, raised in Buffalo, NY. Moved in 1962 to New York City, where he co-founded the underground newspaper *East Village Other* in 1965; has spent most of his career in the Bay Area. Also a prolific playwright, essayist, anthologist, and novelist. Poetry collections include *Conjure: Selected Poems 1963–1970* (1972) and *New and Collected Poems 1963–2006* (2006). Has founded and co-founded various small presses, literary journals, and nonprofit organizations. Prizes include a MacArthur Fellowship. Taught creative writing at University of California, Berkeley.

Justin Phillip Reed (b. 1979) b. South Carolina. Earned BA from Tusculum University and MFA from Washington University. His collection *Indecency* (2018) won the 2018 National Book Award in Poetry. Is the 2019–21 Fellow in creative writing at University of Pittsburgh's Center for African American Poetry and Poetics.

Roger Reeves (b. 1980) b. Willingboro, NJ. Earned BA from Morehouse College, MA from Texas A&M University, and MFA from the Michener Center for Writers at the University of Texas at Austin. Published first collection, *King Me*, in 2013. Currently associate professor of English at University of Texas at Austin.

Victor-Ernest Rillieux (1845–1898) b. New Orleans, LA. Was of mixed-race Creole heritage and descended from a distinguished family; was first cousin to the mother of the French artist Edgar Degas. Composed, in French, odes, satirical songs, and romantic verse and made translations from Spanish; most of his work has not survived.

Ed Roberson (b. 1939) b. Pittsburgh, PA. Earned BA from the University of Pittsburgh; was an undergraduate research assistant in limnology. Went on research expeditions in Bermuda, Canada, and throughout Alaska, including the Kodiak and Afognak Islands. Worked in a steel mill and as aquarium diver at the Pittsburgh Aquazoo before becoming a poet. Befriended Black Arts Movement figures. Has published seven poetry collections, including *When Thy King Is a Boy* (1970) and *Atmosphere Conditions* (1999). Currently teaches in the MFA program at Northwestern University.

Carolyn Rodgers (1940–2010) b. Chicago, IL. Earned BA from Roosevelt University and MA from University of Chicago. Participated in writing workshops sponsored by Gwendolyn Brooks and the

Organization of Black American Culture. Active in the Black Arts Movement, she helped found Third World Press, which published *Paper Soul* (1968) and *Songs of a Blackbird* (1969), the first two of her several books. Was a book critic for the *Chicago Daily News* and a columnist for the *Milwaukee Courier*. Founded Eden Press.

Alison C. Rollins (b. 1987). b. St. Louis, MO. Earned BS in Psychology from Howard University and Master of Library and Information Science from the University of Illinois, Urbana-Champaign. Published debut collection *Library of Small Catastrophes* in 2019. Currently Lead Teaching and Learning Librarian at Colorado College.

Kate Rushin (b. 1951) Raised in Camden and Lawnside, NJ. Received BA from Oberlin College and MFA from Brown University. Poetry collection *The Black Back-Ups* was published in 1993. Was writer-in-residence and director of the Center for African American Studies at Wesleyan University and has taught at MIT and Connecticut College; is recipient of the Rose Low Rome Memorial Poetry Prize and the Grolier Poetry Prize.

Sonia Sanchez (b. 1934) b. Wilsonia Benita Driver in Birmingham, AL. Moved to Harlem with father in 1943; mother had died in 1935. Earned BA from Hunter College. Organized writers' workshop in Greenwich Village attended by Amiri Baraka (then LeRoi Jones), Larry Neal, and Haki Madhubuti (then Don L. Lee). Formed Broadside Quartet of poets with future second husband Etheridge Knight, Nikki Giovanni, and Madhubuti. Moved to the Bay Area; taught and helped create the first Black Studies program at San Francisco State College (now University). Was a member of the Nation of Islam, 1971–76. Poetry collections include *We a BaddDDD People* (1970) and *Shake Loose My Skin: New and Selected Poems* (1999). Wrote plays. Among her several academic appointments the longest was at Temple University, where she taught for more than two decades. Named poet laureate of Philadelphia.

Gil Scott-Heron (1949–2011) b. Chicago, IL. Lived with grandmother in Lincoln, TN; faced abuse and harassment when he was one of three Black children to integrate Tigrett Junior High School. Won scholarship to the Fieldston School in the Bronx. Published murder mystery *The Vulture* in 1970. Released spoken-word albums *Small Talk at 125th & Lenox* (1970) and *Pieces of a Man* (1971), the first of several; published novel, *The Nigger Factory* (1972). Most recent recording is *I'm New Here* (2010).

Nicole Sealey (b. 1980) b. St. Thomas, Virgin Islands. Moved to Apopka, FL, at age eight. Earned MLA from the University of South

Florida and MFA from New York University. Published chapbook *The Animal After Whom Other Animals Are Named* (2016) and poetry collection *Ordinary Beast* (2017). Served as executive director of Cave Canem.

Tim Seibles (b. 1955) b. Philadelphia, PA. Earned BA from Southern Methodist University and MFA from Vermont College of Fine Arts in 1990. Has published six poetry collections, including *Hurdy-Gurdy* (1992). Was poet laureate of Virginia; taught at Old Dominion University for over twenty years.

Charif Shanahan (b. 1983) b. New York, NY. Earned AB from Princeton University, MA from Dartmouth College, and MFA from New York University. Author of the poetry collection *Into Each Room We Enter Without Knowing* (2017). Has lived abroad in several countries. Served as programs director for the Poetry Society of America. Currently Jones Lecturer in Poetry in Stanford University's creative writing program.

Ntozake Shange (1948–2018) b. Paulette Williams in Trenton, NJ. Earned BA from Barnard College and MA in American Studies from the University of Southern California. Active in antiwar and feminist movements. Adopted name from Xhosa: *Ntozake* (she who comes into her own things) and *Shange* (she who walks like a lion). Also a playwright, novelist, essayist, and author of children's books. Play *for colored girls who have considered suicide/when the rainbow is enuf* (1975) was broadcast on PBS and adapted into a film. Prizes include an Obie Award.

Reginald Shepherd (1963–2008) b. New York, NY. Earned BA from Bennington College and MFAs from Brown University and the University of Iowa. Published five poetry collections, including *Some Are Drowning* (1994) and *Fata Morgana* (2007), and two books of prose. Taught at Northern Illinois and Cornell Universities and the University of West Florida. Died of colon cancer.

Evie Shockley (b. 1965) b. Nashville, TN. Earned BA from Northwestern University, JD from the University of Michigan, and PhD from Duke University. Has published five poetry collections, including *semiautomatic* (2017), as well as *Renegade Poetics: Black Aesthetics and Formal Innovation in African American Poetry* (2011). Co-edited the University of Massachusetts's literary journal, *jubilat*. Prizes include Hurston/Wright Legacy Award. Currently teaches English at Rutgers University.

Safiya Sinclair (b. 1984) b. Montego Bay, Jamaica. Raised in a Rastafarian household. Educated at Bennington College, the University of Virginia, and the University of Southern California. Has published the chapbook *Catacombs* (2011) and the collection *Cannibal* (2016). Awards include a Ruth Lilly Prize.

Clint Smith (b. 1988) b. New Orleans, LA. Earned BA from Davidson College. Taught high school English in Maryland in the Prince George's County public school system; received teacher of the year award from the Maryland Humanities Council. Author of the poetry collection *Counting Descent* (2016). Contributed a poem to *The New York Times Magazine*'s 1619 Project. Co-hosts two podcasts: *Pod Save the People* and *Justice in America*.

Danez Smith (b. 1989) b. St. Paul, MN. Earned BA from the University of Wisconsin–Madison and MFA from the University of Michigan. Published chapbook *hands on ya knees* (2013) and four poetry collections, most recently *Homie* (2020). Founding member of the Dark Noise Collective. Awards include Britain's Forward Prize for Poetry.

Lucy E. Smith (1916–2004) b. North Carolina, moved to Philadelphia during childhood. Worked as a furrier. Published poetry chapbook *No Middle Ground* in 1952. Co-authored the poetry collection *Give Me a Child* (1955) with Sarah Elizabeth Wright.

Patricia Smith (b. 1955) b. Chicago, IL. Worked as journalist in Chicago and Boston. Her seven books of poetry include *Blood Dazzler* (2008). Co-wrote *Africans in America: America's Journey Through Slavery* (1998), a companion book to the PBS documentary series, with Charles S. Johnson. Also writes fiction and edited the anthology *Staten Island Noir* (2012). Co-edited *The Golden Shovel Anthology: New Poems Honoring Gwendolyn Brooks* (2017, 2019). Has written and acted in two one-woman plays. Currently teaches at the College of Staten Island (CUNY) and in Sierra Nevada College's MFA program.

Tracy K. Smith (b. 1972) b. Falmouth, MA. Raised in Fairfield, CA. Earned AB from Harvard University and MFA from Columbia University. Has published four poetry collections, a memoir, and two libretti; *Life on Mars* (2011) won the Pulitzer Prize for poetry. Appointed U.S. Poet Laureate in 2017. Hosts the podcast *The Slowdown*. Currently professor of the humanities and of creative writing at Princeton University, where she also chairs the Lewis Center for the Arts.

A. B. Spellman (b. 1935) b. Alfred Bennett Spellman in Elizabeth City, NC. Earned BA from Howard University. In New York City, hosted a radio show and was a jazz critic. Published the first of his two poetry collections, *The Beautiful Days*, in 1964. *Black Music: Four Lives* (1966) is a study of the jazz musicians Cecil Taylor, Ornette Coleman, Herbie Nichols, and Jackie McLean. Academic posts include teaching positions at Emory University and Morehouse College. Became the National Endowment for the Arts' first director of the Arts in Education Study Project.

Anne Spencer (1882–1975) b. Henry County, VA. Parents had been enslaved. Graduated at seventeen as valedictorian of her class at Virginia Theological Seminary and College (now Virginia University of Lynchburg); remained in Lynchburg for most of her life. Opened and managed the library at Dunbar High School. Published in magazines and anthologies.

Primus St. John (b. 1939) b. New York, NY. Studied at the University of Maryland and Lewis and Clark College. Has published four poetry collections, including *Communion: Poems 1976–1998* (1999). Edited the anthologies *Zero Makes Me Hungry* (1976) and *From Here We Speak* (1993). Launched the Poets in the Schools program, sponsored by the National Endowment for the Arts, with five other poets. Taught English, creative writing, and African American Studies at Portland State University for thirty years.

Sharan Strange (b. 1959) Raised in Orangeburg, SC. Earned AB from Harvard University and MFA from Sarah Lawrence College. A founding member of the Dark Room Collective. Published the poetry collection *Ash* in 2001. Has exhibited poetry at the Whitney Museum, the Institute of Contemporary Art in Boston, and other art museums and galleries. Currently teaches in the English department at Spelman College.

Sekou Sundiata (1948–2007) b. Robert Franklin Feaster in New York, NY. Became involved in the Black Arts Movement and changed his name in the late 1960s. Received BA in English from City College of New York (CCNY) in 1972; helped form the Black and Puerto Rican Student Community of City College; started its first Black student newspaper. Earned MFA in creative writing from City University of New York in 1979. Released several spoken-word albums, starting with *Are & Be* (1980). Was the school's first writer-in-residence. Staged the oratorio *Udu* and was the creator of the one-man shows *The Circle Unbroken* and *Blessing the Boats*.

Lucy Terry (1730–1821) b. West Africa. Also known as Lucy Abijah, Luce Terry, Abijah's "Luce," and Lucy Terry Prince. First known African American woman poet. Was kidnapped in infancy, possibly along with her mother. Purchased by Ensign Ebenezer Wells of Deerfield, MA, at age four. Left the Wells household after marrying Abijah Prince, a prosperous free Black man who purchased her freedom. Only surviving poem is "Bars Fight" (1746), transmitted orally until first publication in 1855. Moved to Sunderland, VT, where she died.

Camille Thierry (1814–1875) b. New Orleans, LA. Contributed poem "Les Idées" to *L'Album Littéraire*, a magazine published in 1843, and several poems to the anthology *Les Cenelles*. Spent most of his life in France, first in Paris and then in Bordeaux. Lived in near poverty due to having invested in New Orleans firms that went bankrupt.

Lorenzo Thomas (1944–2005) b. Panama City, Panama, moved to New York City in 1948. Grew up speaking Spanish. Earned BA from Queens College in 1967. Active in Black Arts Movement and the Umbra Poets Workshop. Enlisted in the U.S. Navy; served in Vietnam in 1971. Moved to Texas and was writer-in-residence at Texas Southern University. His six poetry collections include *A Visible Island* (1967), *Dracula* (1973), and *The Bathers* (1981).

Eloise Bibb Thompson (1878–1928) b. New Orleans, LA. Published first book, *Poems* (1895), at seventeen. Graduated from the University of New Orleans and taught in the city's public schools. Moved to Los Angeles and worked as feature writer for the *Los Angeles Tribune*. Joined literary group The Ink Slingers, founded by the sociologist and educator Charles S. Johnson. Also wrote plays, including *Africannus* (1922), based on the life of Marcus Garvey, and *A Reply to the Clansman* (1915), a response to D. W. Griffith's film *Birth of a Nation*.

Priscilla Jane Thompson (1871–1942) b. Rossmoyne, OH, where she spent her entire life. Published two volumes, *Ethiope Lays* (1900) and *Gleanings of the Quiet Hours* (1907).

Samantha Thornhill (b. 1980) b. Trinidad and Tobago, moved to U.S. at age eight. Earned BA from Florida State University and MFA from the University of Virginia. Coached the Virginia Poetry Slam Team. Released spoken-word CDs *Merror, Mirror: The Art of Self Reflection* (2003) and *Odelicious Poems* (2010). Has taught poetry writing and performance at the Julliard School since 2005.

Melvin B. Tolson (1898–1966) b. Moberly, MO. Earned BA from Lincoln University and MA from Columbia University. Taught at Wiley College, where he helped found the black intercollegiate

Southern Association of Dramatic and Speech Arts; created the Wiley Forensic Society, a successful debating club that broke the color line by competing against all-white teams. Published first poetry collection, *Rendezvous with America*, in 1944. Wrote weekly column for the *Washington Tribune*. Appointed Poet Laureate of Liberia in 1947; published *Libretto for the Republic of Liberia* (1953). *Harlem Gallery: Book I, The Curator* (1965) is the first and only completed part of an intended five-volume epic. Wrote unpublished novels and plays. Was mayor of Langston, OK.

Jean Toomer (1894–1967) b. Nathan Pinchback Toomer in Washington, DC. Moved to Greenwich Village in New York City in 1920; assumed the name "Jean" after reading French novelist Romain Rolland's *Jean Christophe*. Wrote two plays in 1922: *Balo, A Sketch of Negro Life* and *Natalie Mann*. *Cane*, a mixture of poetry and prose, was published in 1923. Embraced the philosophy of the Armenian mystic George I. Gurdjieff and studied with him in France; *Essentials* (1931), a collection of aphorisms, and the twenty-page poem "The Blue Meridian" (1936) reflect Gurdjieff's influence. Joined the Society of Friends in 1940.

Natasha Trethewey (b. 1966) b. Gulfport, MS. Earned BA from University of Georgia, MA from Hollins College (now University), and the University of Massachusetts. Author of five poetry collections, including *Domestic Work* (2000) and *Native Guard* (2006), which won the Pulitzer Prize, as well as *Beyond Katrina: A Meditation on the Mississippi Gulf Coast* (2012). Member of the Dark Room Collective; served as poet laureate of Mississippi and U.S. poet laureate in 2012. Elected chancellor of the Academy of American Poets and member of the American Academy of Arts and Sciences. Currently Board of Trustees Professor of English at Northwestern University.

Quincy Troupe (b. 1939) b. St. Louis, MO. Poetry collections include *Transcircularities: New and Selected Poems* (2002). Founded and edited the magazines *American Rag*, *Confrontations: A Journal of Third World Literature*, and *Code*; co-edited the anthologies *Watts Poets: A Book of New Poetry and Essays* (1968), *Giant Talk: An Anthology of Third World Writings* (1975), and *James Baldwin: The Legacy* (1987). Co-wrote *The Inside Story of TV's "Roots"* (1978), *Miles: The Autobiography* (1989), and *The Pursuit of Happyness* (2006), adapted into a film. Prizes include a Peabody Award for co-producing and writing *The Miles Davis Radio Project* and the American Book Awards' Lifetime Achievement Award. Edits the journal *Black Renaissance Noire*.

Lyrae Van Clief-Stefanon (b. 1971) b. Daytona Beach, FL. Earned BA from Washington and Lee University. Poetry volumes are *Black Swan* (2002), *Open Interval* (2009), and, with Elizabeth Alexander, *Poems in Conversation and a Conversation* (2008). Currently teaches English literature and creative writing at Cornell University and poetry at the Auburn Correctional Facility in Auburn, NY.

George B. Vashon (1824–1878) b. Carlisle, PA. Born free to abolitionist parents. Was first African American to graduate from Oberlin College. Attended law school in Pittsburgh but bar examination was denied him because he was Black. Moved to Haiti; became professor of Greek, Latin, and English at Collège Faustin in Port-au-Prince. Earned MA from Oberlin while in Haiti. Moved to New York; became, in 1848, the first African American admitted to state bar. Practiced law in Syracuse. Published poems and essays in Frederick Douglass's newspaper *The North Star.* Was teacher and principal in Pittsburgh public schools; moved to Washington, DC, and worked for Treasury Department and for the Freedmen's Bureau. Was a professor at Alcorn University (now Alcorn State University).

Derek Walcott (1930–2017) b. Castries, Saint Lucia. Earned BA from University College of the West Indies. *Sea Grapes* (1976) and *Omeros* (1990) are among his many poetry collections. Also a playwright, whose plays include the Obie Award–winning *Dream on Monkey Mountain* (1967). Awarded the Nobel Prize in Literature. Other prizes include a MacArthur Fellowship. Taught at several American universities, most notably Boston University.

Alice Walker (b. 1944) b. Eatonton, GA. Earned BA from Sarah Lawrence College in 1963. Spent the summer of 1965 in Africa; was a civil rights activist in Mississippi. Contributed to and served as editor for *Ms.* magazine. In 1984, co-founded Wild Trees Press, which prioritized Black women writers. Her many books include fiction, essay collections, children's books, and poetry volumes. Her novel *The Color Purple* (1982) won the Pulitzer Prize and the National Book Award; was adapted into successful films and plays. Has taught at Wellesley College, Yale University, the University of California, Berkeley, and other schools.

Frank X. Walker (b. 1961) b. Danville, KY. Earned MA from the University of Kentucky and MFA from Spalding University. *Affrilachia* (2000) and *Buffalo Dance: The Journey of York* (2004) number among his several poetry volumes. Co-founded and coined name of the poetry collection the Affrilachian Poets. Edits *Pluck! The Journal* *of Affrilachian Arts and Culture.* Currently associate professor in the department of English at the University of Kentucky.

Margaret Walker (1915–1998) b. Birmingham, AL. Earned BA from Northwestern University. Worked with the Federal Writers' Project in Chicago and joined the South Side Writers Group, founded by Richard Wright. *For My People* (1942) was her MFA thesis at the University of Iowa, which later awarded her a PhD; book won her a Yale Younger Poets Prize, the first given to an African American. At Jackson State College (now Jackson State University), she taught and founded its Institute for the Study of History, Life and Culture of Black People; center was renamed in her honor. Later poetry includes *October Journey* (1973).

Anthony Walton (b. 1960) b. Aurora, IL. Earned BA from University of Notre Dame and MFA from Brown University. Widely read essay "Willie Horton and Me" was published in *The New York Times Magazine* in 1989. Author of the poetry volume *Cricket Weather* (1995) and two works of nonfiction. Short story "Slow Burn" inspired screenplay for 2005 film of the same name. Co-edited *Every Shut Eye Ain't Sleep: An Anthology of Poetry by African Americans Since 1945* (1994) and *The Vintage Book of African American Poetry* (2012), both with Michael S. Harper. Currently senior writer-in-residence at Bowdoin College.

Lucian B. Watkins (1879–1921) b. Chesterfield, VA. Attended Virginia Normal and Industrial Institute. Became a teacher. Published first volume of poems, *Voices of Solitude*, in 1903, followed by *The Old Log Cabin* (1910). Published poems in *Negro World*. Served in U.S. Army during World War I; died in Fort McHenry Hospital in Baltimore.

Tom Weatherly (1942–2014) b. Scottsboro, AL. Educated at Morehouse College and Alabama A&M College. Became a minister in the A.M.E. Church; was assistant pastor of the A.M.E. church in Scottsboro during the mid-1960s. Moved to New York City to pursue a career as a poet. Participated in community arts programs, including St. Mark's Church Poetry Project; led poetry workshops in Harlem, Brooklyn, and for women in prison. Converted to Judaism. Published four volumes of poetry, including *Maumau American Cantos* (1970). Co-edited *Natural Process: An Anthology of New Black Poetry* (1970) with Ted Wilentz.

Afaa Michael Weaver (b. 1951) b. Michael S. Weaver in Baltimore, MD. Joined the U.S. Army Reserves at nineteen. Earned BA at

Regents College (now Excelsior College) in Albany and MA in Theater and Playwriting from Brown University. Has written plays, short fiction, and numerous volumes of poetry, including *Water Song* (1985). Was named Afaa (Ibo: Oracle) by the Nigerian playwright Osonye Tess Onwueme in 1997. Was one of the first faculty members at the Cave Canem retreat; named the organization's first Elder in 1998. Appointed Alumnae Endowed Professor of English by Simmons College.

Phillis Wheatley (c. 1753–1784) Brought to the American colonies from the Senegambia region (present-day Gambia or Senegal) at age seven or eight. Sold on an auction block in Boston to tailor John Wheatley and became the servant of his wife, Susanna. Became literate; published "On the Death of Rev. Mr. George Whitefield, 1770" and achieved recognition in England and the American colonies. A book of Wheatley's poems was commissioned by Susanna Wheatley to be published in England; Wheatley was tested by eighteen men to ensure she could have written the poems in this volume, *Poems on Various Subjects, Religious and Moral* (1773). Visited London for six weeks in 1773 with owners' son. Was freed after return to Boston; remained with the Wheatleys until Susanna's death in 1774. Married John Peters in 1778. Suffered from physical ailments worsened by poverty. Completed another poetry volume but could not find a publisher in Boston; most of the volume's contents remain lost. Was abandoned by Peters after the birth of their third child (two previous children had died in infancy). Died shortly after giving birth to fourth child, who died soon after Wheatley and was buried with her in an unmarked grave.

Simone White (b. 1972) b. Middletown, CT, raised in Philadelphia. Earned BA from Wesleyan University, JD from Harvard Law School, MFA from The New School, and PhD from the CUNY Graduate Center. Poetry volumes include *House Envy of All the World* (2010), *Of Being Dispersed* (2016), and *Dear Envy of Death* (2018). Currently teaches at The New School

James Monroe Whitfield (1822–1871) b. Exeter, NH. Enslaved father had escaped to Newburyport, MA. Whitfield worked as a barber in Buffalo, NY, Portland, OR, and Idaho before settling in San Francisco. Published one volume of poetry, *America and Other Poems* (1853). Edited the American Colonization movement's monthly journal, *The African Repository and Colonial Journal*. May have traveled to Central America from 1859 to 1862 to scout land for an African American colony. Died of heart disease at forty-nine.

Albery Allson Whitman (1851–1901) b. Hart County, KY. Born enslaved. After Emancipation, taught school and attended Wilberforce University; served as an unordained pastor of an A.M.E. church in Springfield, OH. Wrote sonnets, dialect poems, and epic poetic narratives. Died of pneumonia in Anniston, AL.

Phillip B. Williams (b. 1986) b. Chicago, IL. Earned MFA from Washington University. Poetry collection *Thief in the Interior* was published in 2016. Won a Ruth Lilly Fellowship; is poetry editor for the literary webzine *Vinyl*. Teaches at Bennington College.

Saul Williams (b. 1972) b. Newburgh, NY. Earned BA from Morehouse College and MFA from New York University. Was Grand Slam Champion at the Nuyorican Poets Café in 1996. Won acclaim for his leading role in film *Slam* (1997). Has published five poetry collections, including *The Dead Emcee Scrolls: The Lost Teachings of Hip-Hop* (2006). Released *Amethyst Rockstar* in 2001, followed by other albums, including *The Inevitable Rise and Liberation of Niggy Tardust* (2008). Played the lead in the Broadway musical *Holler If Ya Hear Me* (2014). Created *MartyrLoserKing* (2016), a multimedia project.

Sherley Anne Williams (1944–1999) b. Bakersfield, CA. Educated at California State University at Fresno and Brown and Howard Universities. Published the two poetry collections *The Peacock Poems* (1975) and *Some One Sweet Chile* (1982); televised adaptation of the latter won an Emmy Award. Novel *Dessa Rose* was published in 1986. *Working Cotton* (1992), one of her two children's books, was based on her childhood experience as a farmhand. Performed *Letters from a New England Negro* as a one-woman show at the National Black Theater Festival in 1991. Taught at the University of California, San Diego. Died of cancer at fifty-four.

Jamila Woods (b. 1989) b. Chicago, IL. Earned BA from Brown University. Published chapbook *The Truth About Dolls* (2012). Also a singer and songwriter. She is associate artistic director of the nonprofit youth organization Young Chicago Authors and helps organize the poetry festival Louder Than a Bomb. Designs curricula for Chicago Public Schools; teaches poetry to children throughout the city.

Richard Wright (1908–1960) b. Natchez, MS, moved throughout the South during his early youth. Moved to Chicago in December 1927. Joined the Communist Party and worked for the Federal Writers' Project. Published the novel *Native Son* (1940), which brought him literary renown, and the memoir *Black Boy* (1945), among other works. Expatriated to Paris in 1946. Helped launch the pan-Africanist literary magazine *Présence Africaine*. Took up the writing of haiku. Died of a heart attack at age fifty-two.

Al Young (b. 1939) b. Ocean Springs, MS, moved to Detroit during childhood. Earned BA from the University of California, Berkeley. Co-founded, with Ishmael Reed, the literary journals *Yardbird* and *Quilt*. His several books of poetry include *Geography of a Near Past* (1976). Worked on the screenplay for film *Bustin' Loose* (1981). Published books about music, among them *Bodies and Soul* (1966), *Kinds of Blue* (1984), and *Drowning in the Sea of Love* (1995), as well as novels and, with Janet Coleman, *Mingus/Mingus: Two Memoirs* (1989). Appointed poet laureate of California.

Kevin Young (b. 1970) b. Lincoln, NE. Earned AB from Harvard University and MFA from Brown University. Was a member of the Dark Room Collective. Has published ten books of poetry and has edited several anthologies; nonfiction includes *The Grey Album: On the Blackness of Blackness* (2012) and *Bunk: The Rise of Hoaxes, Humbug, Plagiarists, Phonies, Post-Facts, and Fake News* (2017). Was Charles Howard Candler Professor of English and Creative Writing and later Atticus Haygood Professor of Creative Writing and English at Emory University. Also served as curator of Literary Collections at the university's Raymond Danowski Poetry Library. Elected chancellor of the Academy of American Poets. Is currently poetry editor at *The New Yorker* and director of the Schomburg Center for Research in Black Culture.

NOTE ON THE TEXTS &
ACKNOWLEDGMENTS

This volume contains poems by 246 Black poets published from the 1770s through the present (2020, at the time of this writing). The earliest work included here, the poem by Lucy Terry known as "Bars Fight," was likely composed around the time of the event it describes in 1746 but was not published until the nineteenth century. In general, the texts for the poems have been taken from their first publications in books by their authors, and sometimes from later collected editions or in posthumous editions often prepared by scholars. Several poets, and in particular certain figures writing in the first half of the twentieth century, never published a book, and in these cases the texts have been drawn from periodical or anthology publications. In certain instances of more recent poems, texts of works that have not yet been collected in a book by their authors have been printed from periodical, anthology, or online sources.

With regard to copyright, great care has been taken to locate and acknowledge all owners of copyrighted material included in this book. If any such owner has inadvertently been omitted, acknowledgment will gladly be made in future printings.

The list that follows indicates the respective texts for all the poems printed in this volume, along with copyright information where relevant.

Chris Abani, Blue: *Dog Woman* (Los Angeles: Red Hen Press, 2004). Copyright © 2004 Chris Abani. Reprinted with the permission of The Permissions Company, LLC on behalf of Red Hen Press, redhen.org. The New Religion: *Hands Washing Water* (Port Townsend, WA: Copper Canyon Press, 2012). Copyright © 2006 Chris Abani. Reprinted with the permission of The Permissions Company, LLC on behalf of Copper Canyon Press, coppercanyonpress.org.

Hanif Abdurraqib, How Can Black People Write about Flowers at a Time Like This: *A Fortune for Your Disaster* (New York: Tin House Books, 2019). Copyright © 2019 Hanif Abdurraqib. Reprinted by permission of Tin House Books.

Elizabeth Acevedo, La Negra Takes Medusa to the Hair Salon: *The Rumpus*, March 2016, https://therumpus.net/2016/03/the-conversation-angel-nafissafia-elhillo-and-elizabeth-acevedo/. Copyright © 2016 Elizabeth Acevedo. Reprinted with permission of the author, who has made a few revisions for publication here.

Ai, Twenty-Year Marriage; I Can't Get Started; Two Brothers; The Good Shepherd: Atlanta, 1981: *Vice: New and Selected Poems* (New York: W. W.

Norton, 1999). Copyright © 1973, 1979, 1986; these poems are also included in *The Collected Poems of Ai* and used by permission of W. W. Norton & Company, Inc.

Elizabeth Alexander, The Venus Hottentot; Nineteen: *The Venus Hottentot* (Charlottesville: University of Virginia Press, 1990). Race: *Antebellum Dream Book* (Minneapolis: Graywolf, 2001). Ars Poetica #28: African Leave-Taking Disorder; Ars Poetica #100: I Believe: *American Sublime* (Minneapolis: Graywolf, 2005). Praise Song for the Day: *Praise Song for the Day: A Poem for Barack Obama's Presidential Inauguration* (Minneapolis: Graywolf, 2009). Regarding copyright, "Ars Poetica #28: African Leave-Taking Disorder" is copyright © 2005 Elizabeth Alexander; other poems are included in *Crave Radiance: New and Selected Poems 1990–2010* and are copyright © 1990 the Rectors and Visitors of the University of Virginia, copyright © 2001, 2005, 2009 Elizabeth Alexander. All reprinted with the permission of The Permissions Company, LLC on behalf of Graywolf Press, graywolfpress.org.

Lewis Grandison Alexander, Japanese Hokku: *Opportunity*, September 1925. Negro Woman: *Opportunity*, April 1926. Copyright © National Urban League. Effigy: *Ebony and Topaz: A Collectanea*, ed. Charles S. Johnson (New York: National Urban League, 1927). Copyright © National Urban League. Latter two poems reprinted by permission. All rights reserved.

Will Alexander, from *Haiti: Asia & Haiti* (Los Angeles: Sun & Moon, 1995). Copyright © 1995 Will Alexander. Reprinted with the permission of The Permissions Company, LLC on behalf of Green Integer, greeninteger.com.

Samuel Allen, To Satch (American Gothic): *Ivory Tusks* (New York: Poets Press, 1968). Nat Turner *or* Let Him Come; If the Stars Should Fall: *Every Round and Other Poems* (Detroit: Lotus Press, 1987). All poems copyright © 1987 Samuel Allen and reprinted by permission of the Samuel W. Allen Trust.

Maya Angelou, Still I Rise; Phenomenal Woman: *The Complete Poetry* (New York: Random House, 2015). Also included in *And Still I Rise: A Book of Poems*, copyright © 1978 Maya Angelou. Used by permission of Random House, an imprint and division of Penguin Random House, LLC and Little Brown Book Group Ltd. All rights reserved.

Russell Atkins, Narrative; Night and a Distant Church; It's Here in The; Spyrytual: *World'd Too Much: The Selected Poetry of Russell Atkins*, ed. Kevin Prufer and Robert E. McDonough (Cleveland: Cleveland State University Poetry Center, 2019). Copyright © 2019 Russell Atkins. Reprinted with the permission of The Permissions Company, LLC on behalf of the Cleveland State University Poetry Center, csupoetrycenter.com.

Cameron Awkward-Rich, Cento Between the Ending and the End: Poets. org, website of the Academy of American Poets. https://poets.org/poem/cento-between-ending-and-end. First published in 2018. Also included in

Dispatch, copyright © 2019 Cameron Awkward-Rich. Used by permission of Persea Books, Inc. (New York), www.perseabooks.com. All rights reserved.

Benjamin Banneker, A Mathematical Problem in Verse: George Washington Williams, *History of the Negro Race in America from 1619 to 1880*, vol. 1 (New York: G. P. Putnam's Sons, 1883).

Amiri Baraka, Preface to a Twenty Volume Suicide Note; Look for You Yesterday, Here You Come Today; Notes for a Speech; The Liar; Short Speech to My Friends; Three Modes of History and Culture; SOS; Black Art: *S.O.S.: Poems 1961–2013* (New York: Grove Atlantic, 2014). Copyright © 2014 The Estate of Amiri Baraka. Used by permission of Grove/Atlantic, Inc. Any third-party use of this material, outside of this publication, is prohibited. Why's 12: *Wise, Why's, Y's* (Chicago: Third World Press, 1995). Copyright © 1995 Amiri Baraka. Reprinted by permission of Chris Calhoun Agency.

George Barlow, Titta: *Gumbo* (New York: Doubleday, 1981). Copyright © 1974, 1975, 1976, 1977, 1978, 1980, 1981 George Barlow. Used by permission of Doubleday, an imprint of Knopf Doubleday Publishing Group, a division of Penguin Random House, LLC. All rights reserved.

Gerald Barrax, King: April 4, 1968: *From a Person Sitting in Darkness: New and Selected Poems* (Baton Rouge: Louisiana State University Press, 1998). Copyright © 1998 Gerald Barrax.

Quan Barry, loose strife: *Loose Strife* (Pittsburgh: University of Pittsburgh Press, 2015). Doug Flutie's 1984 Orange Bowl Hail Mary as Water into Fire: *Controvertibles* (Pittsburgh: University of Pittsburgh Press, 2004). Poems copyright © 2015 and © 2004, respectively, and reprinted by permission of the University of Pittsburgh Press.

Paul Beatty, Verbal Mugging: *Joker, Joker, Deuce* (New York: Penguin, 1994). Copyright © 1994 Paul Beatty. Used by permission of The Wylie Agency, LLC and Viking Books, an imprint of Penguin Publishing Group, a division of Penguin Random House, LLC. All rights reserved.

James Madison Bell, Song for the First of August: *The Poetical Works of James Madison Bell* (Lansing, MI: Wynkoop, Hallenbeck, Crawford Co., 1901), under the title "The First of August."

Gwendolyn B. Bennett, Heritage; Lines Written at the Grave of Alexander Dumas; Fantasy; To a Dark Girl; Dirge for a Free Spirit; I Build America; Epitaph: *Heroine of the Harlem Renaissance and Beyond*, ed. Belinda Wheeler and Louis J. Parascandola (University Park: Penn State University Press, 2018). Republished with permission of Pennsylvania State University Press: A Division of the Pennsylvania State University Libraries and Scholarly Communications; permission conveyed through Copyright Clearance Center, Inc.

Joshua Bennett, America Will Be: *The Nation*, February 26, 2018. Copyright © 2018 Joshua Bennett. Reprinted by permission of the author.

Reginald Dwayne Betts, A Postmodern Two-Step: *Poetry*, November 2012. Note: poem was revised as "To the Edge of Panic," part of a sequence in Betts's 2015 collection *Bastards of the Reagan Era*, copyright © 2015 Reginald Dwayne Betts. Reprinted with the permission of The Permissions Company, LLC on behalf of Four Way Books, www.fourwaybooks.com.

Arna Bontemps, The Return, A Black Man Talks of Reaping, Southern Mansion, The Day-breakers: *Personals* (London: Paul Breman, 1963), Copyright © 1973 the Arna Bontemps Estate. Reprinted by permission of Harold Ober Associates.

William Stanley Braithwaite, The House of Falling Leaves: *The House of Falling Leaves, with Other Poems* (Boston: John W. Luce and Company, 1908).

Kamau Brathwaite, Blues: *Other Exiles* (Oxford: Oxford University Press, 1975). Copyright © 1975 Edward Brathwaite. All God's Chillun; The White River: *The Arrivants: A New World Trilogy* (Oxford: Oxford University Press, 1973). Copyright © 1967, 1968, 1968, 1973 Edward Brathwaite. Republished with the permission of Oxford University Press; permission conveyed through Copyright Clearance Center, Inc. Sam Lord: *Mother Poem* (Oxford: Oxford University Press, 1977). Copyright © 1977 Edward Brathwaite.

Gwendolyn Brooks, from *A Street in Bronzeville: A Street in Bronzeville* (New York: Harper & Bros., 1945). Beverly Hills, Chicago: *Annie Allen* (New York: Harper & Bros., 1949); The Bean Eaters; We Real Cool; A Bronzeville Mother Loiters in Mississippi. Meanwhile, a Mississippi Mother Burns Bacon; The Last Quatrain of the Ballad of Emmett Till; The Chicago *Defender* Sends a Man to Little Rock; The Lovers of the Poor: *The Bean Eaters* (New York: Harper & Bros., 1960). Malcolm X; The Second Sermon on the Warpland: *In the Mecca* (New York: Harper & Row, 1968). Paul Robeson; The Life of Lincoln West: *Family Pictures* (Detroit: Broadside Press, 1970). The Boy Died in My Alley: *Beckonings* (Detroit: Broadside Press, 1975). Infirm: *The Near-Johannesburg Boy, and Other Poems* (Chicago: The David Company, 1986). I Am a Black: *Children Coming Home* (Chicago: The David Company, 1991). An Old Black Woman, Homeless, and Indistinct: *In Montgomery and Other Poems* (Chicago: Third World Press, 2003). Copyright © 1945, 1949, 1960, 1968, 1970, 1975, 1986, 1991, 2003 the Estate of Gwendolyn Brooks. For permissions, write to Brooks Permissions, P.O. Box 19355, Chicago, IL 60619.

Jericho Brown, Prayer of the Backhanded: *Please* (Kalamazoo: Western Michigan University/New Issues Press, 2008). Copyright © 2008 Jericho Brown. Reprinted with permission of New Issues Press. 'N'em; Another Elegy: *The New Testament* (Port Townsend, WA: Copper Canyon Press, 2014). Copyright © 2014 Jericho Brown. Bullet Points; The Tradition: *The Tradition* (Port Townsend, WA: Copper Canyon Press, 2019). Copyright © 2019 Jericho Brown. Latter four poems reprinted with the permission of The Permissions Company, LLC on behalf of Copper Canyon Press, coppercanyonpress.org and Pan Macmillan through PLSClear.

Sterling A. Brown, Ma Rainey; Old Lem; Slim Greer; Strange Legacies; Southern Cop; To a Certain Lady, in Her Garden; Let Us Suppose: *The Collected Poems of Sterling A. Brown*, ed. Michael S. Harper (Evanston, IL: TriQuarterly Books, 1989). Copyright © 1980 Sterling A. Brown. Reprinted by permission of Jacqueline M. Combs.

Mahogany L. Browne, upon viewing the death of basquiat: *The BreakBeat Poets: New American Poetry in the Age of Hip-Hop*, ed. Kevin Coval, Quraysh Ali Lansana, and Nate Marshall (Chicago: Haymarket Books, 2015). Copyright © 2015. Reprinted by permission of Haymarket Books.

Julia de Burgos, To Julia de Burgos; Ay, Ay, Ay of the Kinky-Haired Negress; Poem of the Unborn Child; Farewell in Welfare Island; The Sun in Welfare Island: *Song of the Simple Truth: The Complete Poems of Julia de Burgos*, Spanish poems trans. Jack Agüeros (Willimantic, CT: Curbstone Press, 1997). Copyright © 1996 Jack Agüeros. Reprinted by permission of the publisher. All rights reserved.

Darrell Burton, A Balance of Blues and Angels: *Ploughshares* 29, no. 4 (Winter 2003–4). Copyright © 2003.

Olivia Ward Bush, Driftwood: *Driftwood* (Providence, RI: Atlantic Printing Co., 1914).

Cyrus Cassells, Soul Make a Path through Shouting: *Soul Make a Path Through Shouting* (Port Townsend, WA: Copper Canyon Press, 1994). Copyright © 1994 Cyrus Cassells. Reprinted with permission of The Permissions Company, LLC on behalf of Copper Canyon Press, coppercanyonpress.org. Sally Hemings to Thomas Jefferson: *Callaloo* 18 (Spring–Summer 1983). Copyright © 1983 Cyrus Cassells. Reprinted with permission.

Barbara Chase-Riboud, from *Portrait of a Nude Woman as Cleopatra: Portrait of a Nude Woman as Cleopatra* (New York: William Morrow, 1987). Copyright © 1987 Barbara Chase-Riboud. Reprinted by permission of the author.

Dominique Christina, Massa's House: *Anarcha Speaks* (Boston: Beacon, 2018). Copyright © 2018 Dominique Christina. Republished with the permission of Beacon Press; permission conveyed through Copyright Clearance Center, Inc.

Benjamin Clark, The Emigrant: *The Past, Present, and Future* (Toronto: Adam, Stevenson, & Co., 1867).

Tiana Clark, Nashville: *I Can't Talk About the Trees Without the Blood* (Pittsburgh: University of Pittsburgh Press, 2018). Copyright © 2018 Tiana Clark. Reprinted by permission of the University of Pittsburgh Press.

Carrie Williams Clifford, America; Character or Color—Which?: *Race Rhymes* (Washington, DC: R. L. Pendleton, 1911). Little Mother: *The Widening Light* (Boston: Walter Reid, 1922).

Lucille Clifton, "in the inner city"; miss rosie; good times; admonitions; "being property once myself"; the lost baby poem; from "some jesus"; cutting greens; homage to my hips; "the light that came to lucille clifton"; jasper texas 1998; why some people be mad at me sometimes; "i am accused of tending to the past"; study the masters; to my last period; wishes for sons; "surely i am able to write poems"; "won't you celebrate with me": *The Collected Poems of Lucille Clifton 1965–2010* (Rochester, NY: BOA Editions, 2012). Jump Rope Rhymes (transcribed): manuscript in Lucille Clifton papers, Stuart A. Rose Manuscript, Archives, and Rare Book Library, Emory University. Regarding copyright, "homage to my hips," "the light that came to lucille clifton," copyright © 1980 Lucille Clifton and reprinted by permission of Curtis Brown, Ltd.; "won't you celebrate with me" from *The Book of Light*, copyright © 1993 Lucille Clifton and reprinted with the permission of The Permissions Company, LLC on behalf of Copper Canyon Press, coppercanyonpress .org; all other poems by Clifton in this selection, copyright © 1969, 1972, 1987, 1991, 2000 by Lucille Clifton. Reprinted with the permission of The Permissions Company, LLC on behalf of BOA Editions, Ltd., boaeditions .org.

Anita Scott Coleman, Portraiture: *Contemporary American Poets*, ed. Horace C. Baker (Boston: Stafford, 1928). Reprinted by permission of Crisis Publishing Co., Inc., the publisher of the magazine of the National Association for the Advancement of Colored People, for the use of the material first published in *The Crisis*. Black Baby: *Opportunity,* February 1929. Copyright © 1929 National Urban League. Reprinted by permission. Impressions from a Family Album: *The Crisis*, February 1930. Reprinted by permission of Crisis Publishing Co., Inc., the publisher of the magazine of the National Association for the Advancement of Colored People, for the use of the material first published in *The Crisis*. Coveted Epitaph; Denial: Elizabeth Stapleton Stokes [pseud. of Coleman], *Small Wisdom* (New York: Harrison, 1937). Reprinted by permission of the family of Anita Scott Coleman. Idle Wonder: *Opportunity*, May 1938. Copyright © 1938 National Urban League. Reprinted by permission.

Wanda Coleman, What It Means to Be Dark; Mastectomy: *Hand Dance* (Santa Rosa, CA: Black Sparrow, 1993). From *American Sonnets*: 4, 5, 15, 24: *American Sonnets* (Milwaukee, WI: Co-published by Light and Dusk Books and Woodland Pattern Book Center, 1994). from *American Sonnets*: 35: *Bathwater Wine* (Santa Rosa, CA: Black Sparrow, 1998). From *American Sonnets*: 91: *Mercurochrome: New Poems* (Santa Rosa, CA: Black Sparrow, 2001). Copyright © 1990, 1993, 1998, 2001 Wanda Coleman. All reprinted by permission of David R. Godine Publisher, Inc.

Sam Cornish, Harriet in the Promised Land: *Songs of Jubilee* (Greensboro, NC: Unicorn Press, 1986). Copyright © 1986 Sam Cornish. Reprinted by permission.

James D. Corrothers, Paul Laurence Dunbar: *Century Magazine*, November 1912.

Jayne Cortez, How Long Has Trane Been Gone; Jazz Fan Looks Back: *Jazz Fan Looks Back* (New York: Hanging Loose Press, 2002). Copyright © 2002 Jayne Cortez. Orisha; Rape: *On the Imperial Highway: New and Selected Poems* (New York: Hanging Loose Press, 2009). Copyright © 2009 Jayne Cortez. All poems reprinted by permission of Hanging Loose Press.

James Seamon Cotter, Jr., A Prayer; And What Shall You Say?; Supplication; A Woman at Her Husband's Grave: *Complete Poems*, ed. James Robert Payne (Athens: University of Georgia Press, 1990).

Joseph Seamon Cotter, Sr., Dr. Booker T. Washington to the National Negro Business League: *A White Song and a Black One* (Louisville, KY: Bradley and Gilbert Co., 1909).

Mae V. Cowdery, Longings; Goal; Farewell; Having Had You; Four Poems— After the Japanese; For a New Mother; I Look at Death: *We Lift Our Voices* (Philadelphia: Alpress, 1936). "Longings," "Farewell," and "Having Had You" are reprinted by permission of Crisis Publishing Co., Inc., the publisher of the magazine of the National Association for the Advancement of Colored People, for the use of the material first published in *The Crisis.*

Countee Cullen, Yet Do I Marvel; Incident; Tableau; Saturday's Child; Heritage; from "Epitaphs": *Color* (New York: Harper & Bros., 1925). From the Dark Tower: *Copper Sun.* Uncle Jim: *Copper Sun* (New York: Harper & Bros., 1927). Scottsboro, Too, Is Worth Its Song: *The Medea and Some Poems* (New York: Harper & Bros., 1935). Copyright owned by Amistad Research Center, New Orleans, LA. Licensing administered by Thompson and Thompson.

Waring Cuney, No Images; Nineteen-twenty-nine; Down-Home Boy; Carry Me Back: *Storefront Church* (London: Paul Breman, 1973). My Lord, What a Morning: *Beyond the Blues*, ed. Rosey E. Pool (Aldington, UK: Hand and Flower Press, 1962).

Délana R. A. Dameron, Dear ——,: *Weary Kingdom* (Columbia: University of South Carolina Press, 2017). Copyright © 2017 University of South Carolina Press. Reprinted with permission of USC Press.

Margaret Danner, The Small Bells of Benin; Etta Moten's Attic: *Impressions of African Art Forms in the Poetry of Margaret Danner* (Detroit: Broadside Press, 1968). Copyright © 1968 Margaret Danner.

Kyle Dargan, nap-i-ness: *The Listening* (Athens: University of Georgia Press, 2004). Copyright © 2004 Kyle Dargan. Reprinted by permission of The University of Georgia Press.

Frank Marshall Davis, from "Ebony Under Granite"; Mojo Mike's Beer Garden; Four Glimpses of Night: *Black Moods: Collected Poems*, ed. John Edgar Tidwell (Urbana: University of Illinois Press, 2002). Copyright © 2002 the Board of Trustees of the University of Illinois. Used with permission of the University of Illinois Press.

Kwame Dawes, Natural; Black Funk: *Duppy Conqueror: New and Selected Poems*, ed. Matthew Shenoda (Port Townsend, WA: Copper Canyon Press, 2013). "Natural," also in *Shook Foil*, copyright © 1997 Kwame Dawes. Reprinted by permission of Peepal Tree Press. "Black Funk," also in *Wisteria*, copyright © 2006 Kwame Dawes. Reprinted with the permission of The Permissions Company, LLC on behalf of Red Hen Press, redhen.org.

Clarissa Scott Delany, The Mask; Solace: *Caroling Dusk: An Anthology of Verse by Negro Poets*, ed. Countee Cullen (New York: Harper & Bros., 1927).

Toi Derricotte, Blackbottom; The Weakness; On the Turning Up of Unidentified Black Female Corpses: *Captivity* (Pittsburgh: University of Pittsburgh Press, 1989). Copyright © 1989. Black Boys Play the Classics: *Tender* (Pittsburgh: University of Pittsburgh Press, 1997). Copyright © 1997. All poems reprinted by permission of the University of Pittsburgh Press.

Joel Dias-Porter, Wednesday Poem: *The BreakBeat Poets: New American Poetry in the Age of Hip-Hop*, ed. Kevin Coval et al. (Chicago: Haymarket Books, 2015). Copyright © 2015. Reprinted by permission of Haymarket Books.

Ralph Dickey, Leaving Eden; from "The Arcanum Poems": *Leaving Eden* (Providence: Bonewhistle Press, 1974). Copyright © 1974. Father: *Iowa Review* 2.2 (1971). Copyright © 1971. All reprinted by permission of The Estate of Michael S. Harper.

LaTasha N. Nevada Diggs, My First Black Nature Poem™: *TwERK* (New York: Belladonna, 2013). Copyright © 2013. Reprinted by permission of Belladonna* Series, Inc.

Melvin Dixon, Tour Guide: *La Maison des Esclaves: Change of Territory* (Lexington: University Press of Kentucky, 1983). Copyright © 1983 Melvin Dixon. Turning Forty in the '90s; Wednesday Mourning; Heartbeats: *Love's Instruments* (Chicago: Tia Chucha Press, 1995). Copyright © 1995. Reprinted by permission of Tia Chucha Press.

Owen Dodson, Sorrow Is the Only Faithful One: *Powerful Long Ladder* (New York: Farrar, Straus & Company, 1946). The Morning Duke Ellington Praised the Lord and Six Little Black Davids Tapped Dance Unto: *The Forerunners*, ed. Woodie King, Jr. (Washington, DC: Howard University Press, 1975).

Rita Dove, The House Slave; David Walker (1785–1830); Adolescence—II; Banneker; from *Thomas and Beulah*; Canary; The Return of Lieutenant James Reese Europe; Hattie McDaniel Arrives at the Cocoanut Grove: *Collected Poems, 1974–2004* (New York: W. W. Norton, 2016). Copyright © 1980, 1983, 1989, 2004 Rita Dove. From *Sonata Mulattica*: *Sonata Mulattica* (New York: W. W. Norton, 2009). Copyright © 2009 Rita Dove. All poems used by permission of W. W. Norton & Company, Inc.

David Drake, Concatenations: Transcribed from Drake's pots.

W.E.B. Du Bois, A Litany of Atlanta: *Darkwater* (New York: Harcourt Brace, 1921).

Henry Dumas, Son of Msippi; Black Star Line; Outer Space Blues: *Play Ebony Play Ivory*, ed. Eugene Redmond (New York: Random House, 1974). Copyright © 1968, 2020 Executor Eugene B. Redmond and Loretta Dumas. Used by permission of the Dumas Estate.

Paul Laurence Dunbar, We Wear the Mask: *Majors and Minors* (Toledo, OH: Hadley & Hadley, 1895). A Negro Love Song; When Malindy Sings; When the Co'n Pone's Hot; An Ante-Bellum Sermon: *Lyrics of Lowly Life* (New York: Dodd, Mead & Co., 1897). Sympathy; A Death Song: *Lyrics of the Hearthside* (New York: Dodd, Mead & Co., 1899). Compensation: *Lyrics of Sunshine and Shadow* (New York: Dodd, Mead & Co., 1905).

Alice Dunbar-Nelson, Violets; I Sit and Sew; The Proletariat Speaks: *The Works of Alice Dunbar-Nelson*, vol. 2, ed. Gloria Hull (New York: Oxford University Press, 1988). "The Proletariat Speaks" reprinted by permission of the Crisis Publishing Co., Inc., the publisher of the magazine of the National Association for the Advancement of Colored People, for the use of the material first published in *The Crisis*.

Camille Dungy, Frequently Asked Questions: #10: *Trophic Cascade* (Middletown, CT: Wesleyan University Press, 2017). Copyright © 2017 Camille Dungy. Published by Wesleyan University Press and reprinted with permission.

Cornelius Eady, The Dance: *Victims of the Latest Dance Craze* (Chicago: Ommation Press, 1986). Also in *Hardheaded Weather: New and Selected Poems*, copyright © 2008 Cornelius Eady. Used by permission of G. P. Putnam's Sons, an imprint of Penguin Publishing Group, a division of Penguin Random House, LLC. All rights reserved. The Supremes: *The Gathering of My Name* (Pittsburgh: Carnegie Mellon University Press, 1991). Copyright © 1991 Cornelius Eady. Reprinted with the permission of The Permissions Company, LLC on behalf of Carnegie Mellon University Press. From *Brutal Imagination*: *Brutal Imagination* (New York: Putnam, 2001). Copyright © 2001 Cornelius Eady. Used by permission of G. P. Putnam's Sons, a division of Penguin Random House, LLC. All rights reserved.

Thomas Sayers Ellis, View of the Library of Congress from Paul Laurence Dunbar High School: *The Maverick Room* (Minneapolis: Graywolf, 2005). Copyright © 2005 Thomas Sayers Ellis. Reprinted with the permission of The Permissions Company, LLC on behalf of Graywolf Press, Minneapolis, Minnesota, graywolfpress.org.

Mari Evans, I Am a Black Woman: *I Am a Black Woman* (New York: William Morrow, 1970). Copyright © 1970.

Eve L. Ewing, I saw Emmett Till this week at the grocery store: *1919* (Chicago: Haymarket Books, 2019). Copyright © 2019. Reprinted by permission of Haymarket Books.

Sarah Webster Fabio, I Would Be for You Rain: *My Own Thing* (Oberlin, OH, 1973). Copyright © 1973. Reprinted by permission of the Estate of Sarah Webster Fabio.

Jessie Redmon Fauset, Dead Fires; La Vie C'est La Vie; Oblivion (trans. from French): *The Book of American Negro Poetry*, ed. James Weldon Johnson (New York: Harcourt, Brace and Company, 1922).

Julia Fields, High on the Hog: *East of Moonlight* (Charlotte, NC: Red Clay Books, 1973). Copyright © 1973.

Nikky Finney, Brown Girl Levitation, 1962–1989; *Concerto No. 7*: Condoleeza {working out} at the Watergate: *Head Off & Split* (Evanston, IL: TriQuarterly Books, 2011). Copyright © 2011 Nikky Finney. Published by TriQuarterly Books/Northwestern University Press and used with permission. All rights reserved.

Calvin Forbes, Some Pieces; Hand Me Down Blues; Dark Mirror: *Blue Monday* (Middletown, CT: Wesleyan University Press, 1974). Copyright © 1974 Calvin Forbes. Published by Wesleyan University Press and reprinted with permission.

Sarah Louisa Forten, An Appeal to Women: *The Liberator*, February 1, 1834. The Grave of the Slave: *The Philanthropist*, March 11, 1836.

Vievee Francis, Sugar and Brine: Ella's Understanding: *Horses in the Dark* (Evanston, IL: Northwestern University Press, 2012). Copyright © 2012 Vievee Francis. Salt: *Forest Primeval* (Evanston, IL: Northwestern University Press, 2016). Copyright © 2016 Vievee Francis. Both poems published by TriQuarterly Books/Northwestern University Press and used with permission. All rights reserved.

Ross Gay, burial: *Catalog of Unabashed Gratitude* (Pittsburgh: University of Pittsburgh Press, 2015). Copyright © 2015 Ross Gay. Reprinted by permission of the University of Pittsburgh Press. A Small Needful Fact: Website of Split This Rock: www.splitthisrock.org/poetry-database/poem/a-small-needful-fact. Copyright © 2015 Ross Gay. Reprinted with permission of the author.

Christopher Gilbert, This Bridge Across; Time with Stevie Wonder in It; Chris Gilbert: An Improvisation: *Turning into Dwelling* (Minneapolis: Graywolf Press, 2015). Copyright © 2015 the Estate of Christopher Gilbert. Reprinted with the permission of The Permissions Company, LLC on behalf of Graywolf Press, Minneapolis, Minnesota, graywolfpress.org.

Nikki Giovanni, Black Power; Nikki-Rosa; For Saundra; Ego Tripping; A Poem for Carol; Legacies: *The Collected Poetry of Nikki Giovanni 1968–1998*

(New York: William Morrow, 2003). Copyright compilation © 2003 Nikki Giovanni. Used by permission of HarperCollins Publishers.

Aracelis Girmay, Santa Ana of Grocery Carts; Teeth: *Teeth* (Evanston, IL: Curbstone Press/Northwestern University Press, 2007). Copyright © 2007 Aracelis Girmay. Reprinted by permission of Northwestern University Press. All rights reserved. Ode to the Little "r": *Kingdom Animalia* (Rochester, NY: BOA Editions, 2011). Copyright © 2011 Aracelis Girmay. Reprinted with the permission of The Permissions Company, LLC on behalf of BOA Editions, Ltd., boaeditions.org.

C. S. Giscombe, Vernacular Examples; Palaver; Sotto Voce: *Prairie Style* (Champaign, IL: Dalkey Archive, 2008). Copyright © 2008 C. S. Giscombe. Reprinted by permission of the author.

Lorna Goodison, For My Mother (May I Inherit Half Her Strength): *I Am Becoming My Mother* (London: New Beacon Books, 1986). For Claude McKay: *Collected Poems* (London: Carcanet, 2nd ed., 2017). Copyright © 2017 Lorna Goodison. Reprinted by permission of the author and Carcanet Press, Ltd.

Rachel Eliza Griffiths, Seeing the Body: *Virginia Quarterly Review* 94, no. 3 (Fall 2018). Published in *Seeing the Body* (New York: W. W. Norton, 2020) after this book entered production. Copyright © 2020. Used by permission of W. W. Norton & Company, Inc., and The Wylie Agency, LLC.

Angelina Weld Grimké, The Black Finger; A Mona Lisa; El Beso; Rosabel; The Eyes of My Regret; Trees; Tenebris; Grass Fingers; To Keep the Memory of Charlotte Forten Grimké: *Selected Works of Angelina Weld Grimke*, ed. Carolivia Herron (New York: Oxford University Press, 1991). You: in Maureen Honey, *Aphrodite's Daughters: Three Modernist Poets of the Harlem Renaissance* (New Brunswick, NJ: Rutgers University Press, 2018). Poems in this selection reprinted by permission of the Moorland-Spingarn Research Center, Manuscript Division, Howard University, Washington, DC.

Charlotte Forten Grimké, A June Song: *The Dunbar Speaker and Entertainer*, ed. Alice Dunbar-Nelson (Naperville, IL: J.L. Nichols & Co., 1920). A Parting Hymn: William Wells Brown, *The Black Man, His Antecedents, His Genius, and His Achievements* (New York: Hamilton, 1863). "In the earnest path of duty": *The Liberator*, August 24, 1855.

Nicolás Guillén, My Last Name: *Man-Making Words: Selected Poems of Nicolás Guillén*, 2nd ed., ed. and trans. Roberto Márquez and David Arthur McMurray (Amherst: University of Massachusetts Press, 2003). Copyright © 1972 Robert Márquez and David Arthur McMurray. Reprinted by permission of University of Massachusetts Press.

Forrest Hamer, Goldsboro Narrative #4: My father's Viet Nam tour near over; Goldsboro Narrative #28; Goldsboro Narrative #33; Goldsboro Narrative #7; Annual Visit of the Quiet, Unmarried Son: *Middle Ear* (Berkeley,

CA: Roundhouse Press, 2000). Copyright © 2000 Forrest Hamer. Reprinted with permission of the author.

Jupiter Hammon, An Address to Miss Phillis Wheatly, Ethiopian Poetess, in Boston: *An Address to Miss Phillis Wheatly* (Hartford, CT: Watson and Goodwin, 1778).

Frances Ellen Watkins Harper, The Slave Mother; Bury Me in a Free Land; Learning to Read; A Double Standard; Songs for the People: *Complete Poems of Frances E. W. Harper*, ed. Maryemma Graham (New York: Oxford University Press, 1988).

Michael S. Harper, American History; Dear John, Dear Coltrane; Nightmare Begins Responsibility; Reuben, Reuben; Tongue-Tied in Black and White; Last Affair: Bessie's Blues Song; The Love Letters of Helen Pitts Douglass: *Songlines in Michaeltree: New and Collected Poems* (Urbana: University of Illinois Press, 2000). Copyright © 1970, 2000 Michael S. Harper. All poems used with permission of the University of Illinois Press.

Duriel Harris, Black Mary Integrates the School House: *No Dictionary of a Living Tongue* (Brooklyn, NY: Nightboat Books, 2017). Copyright © 2014 Duriel E. Harris. Reprinted with the permission of The Permissions Company, LLC on behalf of Nightboat Books, nightboat.org.

Walter Everette Hawkins, Wooing; A Spade Is Just a Spade; Here and Hereafter: *Chords and Discords* (Boston: Richard G. Badger, 1920).

Robert Hayden, Those Winter Sundays; Frederick Douglass; Middle Passage; Runagate Runagate; Ice Storm; A Letter from Phillis Wheatley; Paul Laurence Dunbar; [American Journal]: *Collected Poems*, ed. Frederick Glaysher (New York: Liveright), 1996. Copyright © 1962, 1966, 1978, 1982. Used by permission of Liveright Publishing Corporation.

Terrance Hayes, Touch: *Hip Logic* (New York: Penguin, 2002). Copyright © 2002 Terrance Hayes. Satchmo Returns to New Orleans; The Golden Shovel; Carp Poem: *Lighthead* (New York: Penguin, 2010). Copyright © 2010 Terrance Hayes. All poems used by permission of Penguin Books, an imprint of Penguin Publishing Group, a division of Penguin Random House, LLC. All rights reserved.

Josephine D. Heard, Retrospect: *Morning Glories* (Philadelphia: Published by the author, 1890).

Essex Hemphill, Heavy Corners; Civil Servant; For My Own Protection: *Ceremonies: Poems and Prose* (New York: Plume, 1992). Copyright © 1992 Essex Hemphill. Reprinted by permission of The Frances Goldin Literary Agency.

David Henderson, Do Nothing till You Hear from Me; A Coltrane Memorial: *De mayor of Harlem* (New York: E. P. Dutton, 1970). Copyright © 1970. Reprinted by permission of Georges Borchardt, Inc., on behalf of the author. All rights reserved.

Safiya Henderson-Holmes, "C" ing in Colors: Blue: *Spirit and Flame: An Anthology of Contemporary African American Poetry*, ed. Keith Gilyard (Syracuse, NY: Syracuse University Press, 1997). Copyright © 1997.

Calvin Hernton, Medicine Man: *Medicine Man: Collected Poems* (New York: Reed, Cannon and Johnson, 1976). Copyright © 1976.

Sean Hill, Aunt Flo and Uncle Phineas: *Blood Ties and Brown Liquor* (Athens: University of Georgia Press, 2008). Copyright © 2008 Sean Hill. Reprinted by permission of The University of Georgia Press.

Harmony Holiday, (Afterward) One Corner More/Notes on a Letter to the Singer Abbey Lincoln from Her Lover, Abraham Lincoln: *Boston Review*, April 8, 2011, http://bostonreview.net/poetry/NPM-2011-Harmony-Holiday-Letter-Abraham-Lincoln. Copyright © 2011 Harmony Holiday. Reprinted by permission of the author.

Frank Horne, Notes Found Near a Suicide: *Haverstraw* (London: Paul Breman, 1963).

George Moses Horton, To Eliza; The Slave's Complaint; On hearing of the intention of a gentleman to purchase the poet's freedom: *The Hope of Liberty: Containing a Number of Poetical Pieces* (Raleigh, NC: J. Gales & Son, 1829). Division of an Estate: *Poetical Works of George Moses Horton* (1845). The Art of a Poet; George Moses Horton, Myself: *Naked Genius* (Raleigh, NC: Wm. B. Smith & Co., Southern Field and Fireside Book Pub. House, 1865).

Langston Hughes, The Negro Speaks of Rivers; The Weary Blues; Mother to Son; Jazz Band in a Parisian Cabaret; Beale Street Love; Cross; Personal; Midwinter Blues; Bound No'th Blues; Dream Variations; I, Too; Song for a Dark Girl; Let America Be America Again; Madam and the Rent Man; from *Ask Your Mama*: *The Collected Poems of Langston Hughes*, ed. Arnold Rampersad with David Roessel, Associate Editor (New York: Random House, 1994). From *Montage of a Dream Deferred*: *Montage of a Dream Deferred* (New York: Henry Holt and Co., 1951). All poems in this selection copyright © 1994 the Estate of Langston Hughes. Used by permission of Harold Ober and Alfred A. Knopf, an imprint of the Knopf Doubleday Publishing Group, a division of Penguin Random House, LLC. All rights reserved.

Erica Hunt, Surplus Future Imperfect; Woman, with wings: *Local History* (New York: Roof Books, 1993). Copyright © 1993, 2003 Erica Hunt. Reprinted by permission of Roof Books, an imprint of Segue Foundation, Inc. Should you find me: *Time Slips Right Before Your Eyes* (New York: Belladonna, 2015). Copyright © 2015. Reprinted by permission of Belladonna* Series, Inc.

Ishion Hutchinson, After the Hurricane: *House of Lords and Commons* (New York: Farrar, Straus & Giroux, 2016). Copyright © 2016 Ishion Hutchinson. Reprinted by permission of Farrar, Straus and Giroux and Faber & Faber Ltd.

Gary Jackson, Kansas: Poets.org, website of the Academy of American Poets. https://poets.org/poem/kansas. Copyright © 2016 Gary Jackson. Reprinted with permission of the author.

Major Jackson, How to Listen; Euphoria: *Leaving Saturn* (Athens: University of Georgia Press, 2002). Copyright © 2002 Major Jackson. Ferguson: *Boston Review*, March 2, 2016, www.bostonreview.net/poetry/major-jackson-ferguson. Copyright © 2016. All reprinted by permission of the author.

Honorée Fannone Jeffers, The Gospel of Barbecue: *The Gospel of Barbecue* (Kent, OH: Kent State University Press, 2000). Copyright © 2000 by Kent State University Press. Reprinted by permission of Kent State University Press.

Tyehimba Jess, Charity on Blind Tom; General Bethune on Blind Tom; Blind Boone's Vision; Minnehaha: *Olio* (Seattle: Wave Books, 2016). Copyright © 2016 by Tyehimba Jess. Reprinted with the permission of The Permissions Company, LLC on behalf of Wave Books, wavepoetry.com.

Eva A. Jessye, The Singer: *My Spirituals* (New York: Robbins-Engel, 1927). Copyright © 1927, renewed 1954 Eva A. Jessye. Reprinted courtesy of Bentley Historical Library, University of Michigan. The Maestro: *Opportunity*, August 1933.

Ted Joans, The Truth; Jazz Is My Religion; The Nice Colored Man: *Teducation: Selected Poems 1949–1999* (Minneapolis: Coffee House Press, 1999). Copyright © 1999 Ted Joans. Reprinted with the permission of The Permissions Company, LLC on behalf of Coffee House Press, coffeehousepress.org.

Fenton Johnson, When I Die: *A Little Dreaming* (Chicago: Peterson Linotyping Company, 1913). The Lonely Mother: *Songs of the Soil* (New York: self-published, 1916). Who Is that A-Walking in the Corn?: *Poetry*, June 1918. From African Nights: *Others for 1919: An Anthology of the New Verse*, ed. Alfred Kreymborg (New York: Nicholas L. Brown, 1920); the "Rulers" section of the sequence was published in *The Poetry of the Negro 1746–1949*, ed. Langston Hughes and Arna Bontemps (Garden City, NY: Doubleday and Company, 1949).

Georgia Douglas Johnson, The Heart of a Woman: *The Heart of a Woman, and Other Poems* (Boston: The Cornhill Company, 1918). Cosmopolite; Black Woman: *Bronze: A Book of Verse* (Boston: B. J. Brimmer, 1922). Old Black Men: *Caroling Dusk: An Anthology of Verse by Negro Poets,* ed. Countee Cullen (New York: Harper & Bros., 1927). Common Dust: *The Selected Works of Georgia Douglas Johnson*, ed. Claudia Tate (New York: G. K. Hall, 1997). I Want to Die While You Love Me: *An Autumn Love Cycle* (New York: Harold Vinal, 1928). Interracial: *The Crisis,* January 1944. "Interracial," Reprinted by permission of the Crisis Publishing Co., Inc., the publisher of the magazine of the National Association for the Advancement of Colored People, for the use of the material first published in *The Crisis.*

Helene Johnson, Sonnet to a Negro in Harlem; Poem; Invocation: *This Waiting for Love: Helene Johnson, Poet of the Harlem Renaissance*, ed. Verner D. Mitchell (Amherst: University of Massachusetts Press, 2000). Copyright © 2000 by University of Massachusetts Press. Reprinted by permission of the publisher.

James Weldon Johnson, Lift Every Voice and Sing; My City: *Saint Peter Relates an Incident* (New York: Viking, 1935). Sence You Went Away; O Black and Unknown Bards: *Fifty Years and Other Poems* (Boston: The Cornhill Co., 1917). Go Down Death: *God's Trombones: Seven Negro Sermons in Verse* (New York: Viking, 1927). Regarding copyright, "My City" is copyright © 1935 James Weldon Johnson, renewed © 1963 Grace Nail Johnson. "Go Down Death" is copyright © 1927 James Weldon Johnson, renewed © 1955 by Grace Nail Johnson. Both used by permission of Viking Books, an imprint of Penguin Publishing Group, a division of Penguin Random House, LLC. All rights reserved.

Gayl Jones, Deep Song: *Iowa Review* 6, no. 2 (1975). Copyright © 1975 Gayl Jones. Reprinted by permission of the author.

Patricia Spears Jones, i done got so thirsty that my mouth waters at the thought of rain: *Ordinary Women: An Anthology of Poetry by New York City Women*, ed. Sara Miles (New York: Ordinary Women Books, 1978). Copyright © 1978. Reprinted with permission of the author.

Saeed Jones, Kudzu: *Prelude to Bruise* (Minneapolis: Coffee House Press, 2014). Copyright © 2014 Saeed Jones. Reprinted with the permission of The Permissions Company, LLC on behalf of Coffee House Press, coffeehouse-press.org.

A. Van Jordan, Jesse Owens, 1963; Rope: *M-A-C-N-O-L-I-A* (New York: W. W. Norton, 2005). Copyright © 2004 A. Van Jordan. Used by permission of W. W. Norton & Company, Inc.

June Jordan, What Would I Do White?; These Poems; I Must Become a Menace to My Enemies; Poem about My Rights; Poem for Haruko: *Directed by Desire: The Collected Poems of June Jordan* (Port Townsend, WA: Copper Canyon Press, 2007). Copyright © 2005, 2020 June M. Jordan Literary Estate Trust. Used by permission.

Allison Joseph, My Father's Kites: *My Father's Kites* (Chicago: Steel Toe Books, 2010). Copyright © 2010. Thirty Lines about the Fro: *Little Epiphanies* (Pittsburgh: Imaginary Friend Press, 2015). Copyright © 2015. Both reprinted with permission of the author.

Bob Kaufman, Hawk Lawler: Chorus; I, Too, Know What I Am Not; Would You Wear My Eyes?; War Memoir; Walking Parker Home; Crootey Songo; Heavy Water Blues; Blues for Hal Waters; Oregon: *Collected Poems of Bob Kaufman*, ed. Neeli Cherkovski, Raymond Foye, and Tate Swindell (San

Francisco: City Lights, 2019). Regarding copyright, "Heavy Water Blues," "Crootey Songo," "Hawk Lawler: Chorus," from *Cranial Guitar: Selected Poems*, copyright © 1996 Eileen Kaufman. Reprinted with the permission of The Permissions Company, LLC on behalf of Coffee House Press, coffeehousepress.org. "I, Too, Know What I Am Not," "Walking Parker Home," "War Memoir: Jazz Don't Listen To It At Your Own Risk," "Would You Wear My Eyes," from *Solitudes Crowded with Loneliness*, copyright © 1965 Bob Kaufman. Reprinted by permission of New Directions Publishing Corp. "Blues for Hal Waters," "Oregon," from *The Ancient Rain*, copyright © 1981 Bob Kaufman. Reprinted by permission of New Directions Publishing Corp.

Douglas Kearney, Drop It Like It's Hottentot Venus: *The BreakBeat Poets: New American Poetry in the Age of Hip-Hop*, ed. Kevin Coval, Quraysh Ali Lansana, and Nate Marshall (Chicago: Haymarket Books, 2015). Copyright © 2015. Reprinted by permission of Haymarket Books.

John Keene, Language, Knowledge, a Teeming River of Implications; Texts, Contexts, a Fear of Contamination: *Annotations* (New York: New Directions Books, 1995). Copyright © 1995 Bob Kaufman. Reprinted by permission of New Directions Publishing Corp.

Sybil Kein, Fragments from the Diary of Amelie Patiné, Quadroon Mistress of Monsieur Jacques R------.: *Delta Dancer: New and Selected Poems* (Detroit: Lotus Press, 1984). Copyright © 1984.

Donika Kelly, The moon rose over the bay. I had a lot of feelings: Poets. org, website of the Academy of American Poets. https://poets.org/poem /moon-rose-over-bay-i-had-lot-feelings. Copyright © 2017 by Donika Kelly. Reprinted with permission of the author.

Dolores Kendrick, from *The Women of Plums: Poems in the Voices of Slave Women* (Andover, NH: Phillips Exeter Academy Press, 1989). Copyright © 1989.

Keorapetse Kgositsile, Blues for Some Literary Friends & Myself; For Art Blakey and the Jazz Messengers: *The Present Is a Dangerous Place to Live* (Chicago: Third World Press, 1974). Copyright © 1974 Keorapetse Kgositsile. Reprinted by permission of Third World Press, Chicago, IL.

Etheridge Knight, A Poem for Myself; The Idea of Ancestry; The Bones of My Father; Haiku; For Freckle-Faced Gerald; The Violent Space; Hard Rock Returns to Prison from the Hospital for the Criminal Insane; For Eric Dolphy; Feeling Fucked Up: *Born of a Woman: New and Selected Poems* (Boston: Houghton Mifflin, 1980). Regarding copyright, "For Eric Dolphy," copyright © 1980 Etheridge Knight, is reprinted by permission of The Estate of Etheridge Knight; all other poems, included in *The Essential Etheridge Knight*, are copyright © 1986 Etheridge Knight and reprinted by permission of the University of Pittsburgh Press.

Yusef Komunyakaa, Annabelle; More Girl Than Boy; Letter to Bob Kaufman; Blue Light Lounge Sutra for the Performance Poets at Harold Park Hotel; February in Sydney; from *Dien Cai Dau*; Venus's-flytraps; My Father's Love Letters; Anodyne: *Pleasure Dome: New and Collected Poems* (Middletown, CT: Wesleyan University Press, 2001). Copyright © 2001 Yusef Komunyakaa. Published by Wesleyan University Press and reprinted with permission. Ode to the Maggot: *Talking Dirty to the Gods* (New York: Farrar, Straus and Giroux, 2000). Copyright © 2000 Yusef Komunyakaa. Reprinted by permission of Farrar, Straus and Giroux.

Pinkie Gordon Lane, On Being Head of the English Department: *Elegy for Etheridge: Poems* (Baton Rouge: Louisiana State University Press, 2000). Copyright © 1970, 1972, 1977, 1978, 1981, 1985, 1991 Pinkie Gordon Lane. Reprinted by permission of Louisiana State University Press.

Rickey Laurentiis, One Country: *Boy with Thorn* (Pittsburgh: University of Pittsburgh Press, 2015). Copyright © 2015 Rickey Laurentiis. Reprinted by permission of the University of Pittsburgh Press.

Danielle Legros Georges, Hostage: *Maroon* (Willimantic, CT: Curbstone Books, 2001). Copyright © 2001 Danielle Legros Georges. Reprinted by permission of Northwestern University Press. All rights reserved.

Les Cenelles: Armand Lanusse, Epigram; Pierre Dalcour, Verse Written in the Album of Mademoiselle: *The Poetry of the Negro, 1746–1970: An Anthology*, ed. Langston Hughes and Arna Bontemps (Garden City, NY: Doubleday, 1970). Translation of "Epigram," copyright © Langston Hughes. Reprinted by permission of Harold Ober. Camille Thierry, Ideas: *Les Cenelles: A Collection of Poems of Creole Writers of the Early Nineteenth Century*, ed. Régine Latortue and Gleason R. W. Adams (Boston: G. K. Hall & Co., 1979). Translation copyright © 1979. Reprinted by permission of Régine Latortue. Victor-Ernest Rillieux, Love and Devotion: *Creole Echoes: The Francophone Poetry of Nineteenth-Century Louisiana*, ed. and trans. Norman R. Shapiro (Urbana: University of Illinois Press, 2004).

Robin Coste Lewis, Plantation; from *Voyage of the Sable Venus*: *Voyage of the Sable Venus and Other Poems* (New York: Knopf, 2015). Compilation copyright © 2015 Robin Coste Lewis. Used by permission of Alfred A. Knopf, an imprint of the Knopf Doubleday Publishing Group, a division of Penguin Random House, LLC and The Wylie Agency, LLC. All rights reserved. "Lucy Terry Prince Prepares for Her Marriage": in *The Meeting House: Build Therefore Your Own World* (London: Black Dog, 2017), exhibition catalogue of works by the artist Sam Durant. Copyright © 2015, 2017 Robin Coste Lewis. Used by Permission of The Wylie Agency, LLC.

Audre Lorde, Coal; Revolution Is One Form of Social Change; A Litany for Survival; Power; Lunar Eclipse; Inheritance—His: *The Collected Poems of Audre Lorde* (New York: W. W. Norton, 1997). Copyright © 1968, 1970,

1973, 1974, 1978, 1993 Audre Lorde. Used by permission of W. W. Norton & Company, Inc.

Nathaniel Mackey, Falso Brilhante: *Eroding Witness* (Urbana: University of Illinois Press, 1985). Copyright © 1985. Reprinted by permission of selva oscura press. Song of the Andoumboulou: 31: *Whatsaid Serif* (San Francisco: City Lights, 1998). Copyright © 1998 Nathaniel Mackey. Reprinted with the permission of The Permissions Company, LLC on behalf of City Lights Books, citylights.com.

Haki Madhubuti, But He Was Cool; Don't Cry, Scream: *GroundWork: New and Selected Poems of Don L. Lee/Haki Madhubuti from 1966–1996* (Chicago: Third World Press, 1996). Copyright © 1996 Haki Madhubuti. Reprinted with permission of Third World Press, Chicago, IL.

Clarence Major, Swallow the Lake: *Configurations: New and Selected Poems, 1958–1998* (Port Townsend, WA: Copper Canyon Press, 1998). Copyright © 1972 Clarence Major. Reprinted with the permission of The Permissions Company, LLC on behalf of Copper Canyon Press, coppercanyonpress.org. Hair: *The New Yorker*, May 7, 2018. Copyright © 2018. Reprinted by permission of the author.

George R. Margetson, from *The Fledgling Bard and the Poetry Society: The Fledgling Bard and the Poetry Society* (Boston: Richard G. Badger, 1916).

Mariposa, Ode to the Diasporican: Author's website, archived at https://web.archive.org/web/20140320042942/http://www.universeofmariposa.com/ode-to-the-diasporican.html. Copyright © María Teresa Mariposa Fernández. Reprinted by permission of the author.

Dawn Lundy Martin, from *Good Stock Strange Blood*: *Good Stock Strange Blood* (Minneapolis: Coffee House Press, 2017). Copyright © 2017 Dawn Lundy Martin. Reprinted with the permission of The Permissions Company, LLC on behalf of Coffee House Press, coffeehousepress.org.

Adrian Matejka, from *The Big Smoke: The Big Smoke* (New York: Penguin, 2013). Copyright © 2013 Adrian Matejka. Used by permission of Penguin Books, an imprint of Penguin Publishing Group, a division of Penguin Random House, LLC. All rights reserved. Robot Music: *The BreakBeat Poets: New American Poetry in the Age of Hip-Hop*, ed. Kevin Coval et al. (Chicago: Haymarket Books, 2015). Copyright © 2015. Reprinted by permission of Haymarket Books.

Agnes Maxwell-Hall, Jamaica Market: *The Poetry of the Negro 1746–1949*, ed. Langston Hughes and Arna Bontemps (Garden City, NY: Doubleday, 1949).

Shara McCallum, What the Oracle Said: *The Water Between Us* (Pittsburgh: University of Pittsburgh Press, 1999). Copyright © 1999 Shara McCallum. Reprinted by permission of the University of Pittsburgh Press.

Shane McCrae, Still When I Picture It the Face of God Is a White Man's Face: *In the Language of My Captor* (Middletown, CT: Wesleyan University Press, 2017). Copyright © 2017 Shane McCrae. Published by Wesleyan University Press and reprinted with permission.

Colleen J. McElroy, Gra'ma; Try to Understand Papa: *Music from Home: Selected Poems* (Carbondale: Southern Illinois University Press, 1976). Copyright © 1976. Reprinted by permission of the author. Throwing Stones at the All White Pool; Fade to Black: *Blood Memory* (Pittsburgh: University of Pittsburgh Press, 2016). Copyright © 2016 Colleen J. McElroy. Reprinted by permission of the University of Pittsburgh Press.

Claude McKay, Christmas in de Air; "The white man is a tiger at my throat": *Complete Poems*, ed. William Maxwell (Urbana: University of Illinois Press, 2004). The Harlem Dancer; Harlem Shadows; If We Must Die; On Broadway; The Tropics in New York; The Lynching; America; My Mother: *Harlem Shadows* (New York: Harcourt, Brace and Company, 1922).

Tony Medina, The Keepin' It Real Awards: *An Onion of Wars* (Chicago: Third World Press, 2012). Copyright © 2012 Tony Medina. Reprinted with permission of the author.

Anis Mojgani, Closer: *Songs from Under the River* (Austin, TX: Write Bloody Publishing, 2013). Copyright © 2013 Anis Mojgani. Reprinted with permission of Write Bloody Publishing.

Aja Monet, #sayhername: *My Mother Was a Freedom Fighter* (Chicago: Haymarket Books, 2017). Copyright © 2017 Aja Monet. Reprinted with permission of Haymarket Books.

Myra Estelle Morris, Man and Maid: *Negro Voices*, ed. Beatrice M. Murphy (New York: Harrison, 1938).

Tracie Morris, Blackout 1977: Website of Cave Canem: https://cavecanempoets.org/tracie-morris-poet-of-the-week/. Copyright © Tracie Morris. Reprinted with permission of the author.

Thylias Moss, Life in a Sterile Environment: A Case Study; The Day before Kindergarten: Taluca, Alabama, 1959: *Hosiery Seams on a Bowlegged Woman* (Cleveland: Cleveland State Poetry Center, 1983). First poem copyright © 1983 Thylias Moss. Reprinted by permission of the author. Second poem copyright © 1983 Thylias Moss. Reprinted with the permission of Persea Books, Inc. (New York), www.perseabooks.com. All rights reserved. A Reconsideration of the Blackbird: *Pyramid of Bone* (Charlottesville: University of Virginia Press, 1989). Copyright © 1989 Rector and Visitors of the University of Virginia. Reprinted by permission of the University of Virginia Press. An Anointing; Poem for My Mothers and Other Makers of Asafetida; The Lynching: *Rainbow Remnants in Rock Bottom Ghetto Sky* (New York: Persea, 1991). Copyright

© 2003 Thylias Moss. Reprinted with the permission of Persea Books, Inc. (New York), www.perseabooks.com. All rights reserved.

Fred Moten, gayl jones; cecil taylor; johnny cash: *B Jenkins* (Durham, NC: Duke University Press, 2010). Copyright © 2010. Reprinted with permission. "I ran from it but was still in it," from *The Feel Trio* (Tucson, AZ: Letter Machine Editions, 2014). Copyright © 2014. Reprinted with permission.

Harryette Mullen, from *Muse & Drudge: Recyclopedia* (Minneapolis: Graywolf Press, 2006). Copyright © 1992, 2006 Harryette Mullen. Reprinted with the permission of The Permissions Company, LLC on behalf of Graywolf Press, graywolfpress.org. From *Sleeping with the Dictionary: Sleeping with the Dictionary* (Berkeley and Los Angeles: University of California Press, 2002). Copyright © 2002, reprinted with permission of the University of California Press.

John Murillo, On Confessionalism: *The Common* 16 (October 29, 2018), https://www.thecommononline.org/on-confessionalism/. Published in *Kontemporary American Poetry* (Chicago: Four Way Books, 2020) after the present volume entered production. Copyright © 2018, 2020 John Murillo. Reprinted with the permission of the author and The Permissions Company, LLC on behalf of Four Way Books, fourwaybooks.com.

Pauli Murray, from "Dark Testament," copyright © the Pauli Murray Foundation; Prophecy, copyright © 1970 Pauli Murray: *Dark Testament and Other Poems* (Norwalk, CT: Silvermine, 1970). Used by permission of Liveright Publishing Corporation.

Larry Neal, Malcolm X—An Autobiography; Don't Say Goodbye to the Porkpie Hat: *Hoodoo Hollerin' Bebop Ghosts* (Washington, DC: Howard University Press, 1974). Copyright © 1974.

Marilyn Nelson, A Strange Beautiful Woman; Sleepless Nights: *Mama's Promises* (Baton Rouge: Louisiana State University Press, 1985). Lonely Eagles; Star-Fix: *The Homeplace* (Baton Rouge: Louisiana State University Press, 1990). Copyright © 1985, 1989, 1990 Marilyn Nelson Waniek. All poems reprinted by permission of LSU Press.

Richard Bruce Nugent, Shadow: *Caroling Dusk: An Anthology of Verse by Negro Poets*, ed. Countee Cullen (New York: Harper & Bros., 1927).

Gloria C. Oden, A Private Letter to Brazil; Review from Staten Island: *New Negro Poets, USA* (Bloomington: Indiana University Press, 1964). Man White, Brown Girl and All That Jazz: *The Poetry of Black America: Anthology of the 20th Century*, ed. Arnold Adoff (New York: Harper & Row, 1974). Copyright © 1964, 1974.

Myron O'Higgins, Young Poet: *The Poetry of the Negro 1746–1949* (Garden City, NY: Doubleday, 1949).

Salute: *The Crisis*, August 1934. Esther Popel, "Flag Salute," reprinted by permission of Crisis Publishing Co., Inc., the publisher of the magazine of the National Association for the Advancement of Colored People, for the use of the material first published in *The Crisis*.

N. H. Pritchard, From Where the Blues?: *Umbra* 2 (December 1963). "WE NEED": *Echoes* (New York: New York University Press, 1971). Copyright © 1971. Reprinted by permission of NYU Press. ''; Metagnomy: *The Matrix: Poems, 1960–1970* (Garden City, NY: Doubleday & Company, 1970).

Khadijah Queen, I want to not have to write another word about who the cops keep killing: *LitHub*, August 11, 2015, https://lithub.com/i-want-to-not-have-to-write-another-word-about-who-the-cops-keep-killing/. Copyright © 2015. Reprinted by permission of the author.

Dudley Randall, Booker T. and W.E.B.; An Answer to Lerone Bennett's Questionnaire on a Name for Black Americans; A Poet Is Not a Jukebox: *Roses and Revolutions: The Selected Writings of Dudley Randall*, ed. Melba Joyce Boyd (Detroit: Wayne State University Press, 2009). Copyright © 2009. Reprinted with permission of the Dudley Randall Literary Estate.

Camille Rankine, History: *Incorrect Merciful Impulses* (Port Townsend, WA: Copper Canyon Press, 2016). Copyright © 2016 Camille Rankine. Reprinted with the permission of The Permissions Company, LLC on behalf of Copper Canyon Press, coppercanyonpress.org.

Claudia Rankine, from *Citizen: An American Lyric*: *Citizen: An American Lyric* (Minneapolis: Graywolf Press, 2014). Copyright © 2014 Claudia Rankine. Reprinted with the permission of The Permissions Company, LLC on behalf of Graywolf Press, graywolfpress.org and Penguin Random House UK.

Henrietta Cordelia Ray: Toussaint L'Ouverture; Self-Mastery: *Poems* (New York: Grafton Press, 1910).

Andy Razaf, What Did I Do (To Be So Black & Blue)?: *Reading Lyrics*, ed. Robert Gottlieb and Robert Kimball (New York: Pantheon, 2000). Music by Thomas "Fats" Waller and Harry Brooks, Words by Andy Razaf, copyright © 1929 (renewed) EMI Mills Music, Inc., Chappell & Co., Inc., and Razaf Music Co. All rights for Razaf Music administered by BMG Rights Management (US) LLC. All rights reserved. Used by permission of Alfred Music and Hal Leonard LLC. The Tree of Hope: *Amsterdam News*, June 8, 1932.

Charles L. Reason, Hope and Confidence: *Autographs for Freedom, 1853–54*, ed. Julia Griffiths (Auburn, NY: Alden, Beardsley, 1854).

Ishmael Reed, Beware: Do Not Read This Poem; Paul Laurence Dunbar in the Tenderloin; The Reactionary Poet: *New and Collected Poems, 1964–2006* (New York: Carroll & Graf, 2006). Copyright © 1988, 2000, 2006 Ishmael Reed. Reprinted by permission of Lowenstein Associates.

Justin Phillip Reed, Black Can Sleep: *Indecency* (Minneapolis: Coffee House Press, 2018). Copyright © 2018 Justin Philip Reed. Reprinted with the permission of The Permissions Company, LLC on behalf of Coffee House Press, coffeehousepress.org.

Roger Reeves, Children Listen: Poets.org, website of the Academy of American Poets, https://poets.org/poem/children-listen. Copyright © 2018 Roger Reeves. Reprinted by permission of the author.

Ed Roberson, sonnet; poll; the poor houses; othello jones dresses for dinner: *When Thy King Is a Boy* (Pittsburgh: University of Pittsburgh Press, 1970). Copyright © 1970. Reprinted by permission of the University of Pittsburgh Press. American Jazz Quartet: *To See the Earth Before the End of the World* (Middlebury, CT: Wesleyan University Press, 2010). Copyright © 2010 Ed Roberson. Published by Wesleyan University Press and reprinted with permission.

Carolyn Rodgers, how i got ovah: *How I Got Ovah: New and Selected Poems* (New York: Anchor/Doubleday, 1975). Copyright © 1975. Reprinted by permission.

Alison C. Rollins, Why Is We Americans: *Library of Small Catastrophes* (Port Townsend, WA: Copper Canyon Press, 2019). Copyright © 2019 Alison C. Rollins. Reprinted with the permission of The Permissions Company, LLC on behalf of Copper Canyon Press, coppercanyonpress.org.

Kate Rushin, The Black Back-Ups: *The Black Back-Ups* (Ithaca, NY: Firebrand Books, 1993). Copyright © 1993 Kate Rushin. Reprinted by permission of the author.

Primus St. John, All the Way Home: *Skins on the Earth* (Port Townsend, WA: Copper Canyon Press, 1976). From *Dreamer* (Pittsburgh: Carnegie Mellon University Press, 1990). Poems also included in *Communion: New and Selected Poems*, copyright © 1976, 1990 Primus St. John. Reprinted with the permission of The Permissions Company, LLC on behalf of Copper Canyon Press, coppercanyonpress.org.

Sonia Sanchez, for our lady: *We a BaddDDD People* (Detroit: Broadside Press, 1970). A Poem for My Father: *Shake Loose My Skin: New and Selected Poems* (Boston: Beacon Press, 1999). A poem for my brother; from "Philadelphia: Spring 1985"; haiku (for Osage ave and Doorknop); haiku (for mungu and morani and the children of soweto); two haiku (for Clarence H. Watson and The Count); tanka (for papa Joe Jones who used to toss me up to the sky); haiku (for domestic workers in the african diaspora); haiku ("man. you write me so"); tanka ("like dark old men the"); haiku ("like ermine when i"); haiku ("i want to make you") blues; Song No. 2: *Under a Soprano Sky* (Trenton, NJ: Africa World Press, 1987). Copyright © Sonia Sanchez. Reprinted by permission of the author.

Gil Scott-Heron, Whitey on the Moon; The Revolution Will Not Be Televised: *Now and Then: The Poems of Gil Scott-Heron* (Edinburgh, Scotland:

Payback Press/Brouhaha Books, 2000). Home Is Where the Hatred Is: transcribed from LP recording *Pieces of a Man* (Flying Dutchman Records, 1971). Copyright © The Estate of Gil Scott-Heron. Reprinted with permission.

Nicole Sealey, Object Permanence: *Ordinary Beast* (New York: Ecco, 2017). Copyright © 2017 Nicole Sealey. Used by permission of HarperCollins Publishers.

Tim Seibles, Trying for Fire: *Hurdy-Gurdy* (Cleveland: Cleveland State University Poetry Center, 1992). Copyright © 1992 Tim Seibles. Reprinted with permission of the author.

Charif Shanahan, Gnawa Boy, Marrakesh, 1968: *Into Each Room We Enter Without Knowing* (Carbondale: Southern Illinois University Press, 2017). Copyright © 2017 Charif Shanahan. Reprinted with permission of the author.

Ntozake Shange, from "for colored girls who have considered suicide when the rainbow is enuf": *For Colored Girls Who Have Considered Suicide When the Rainbow Is Enuf* (New York: Scribner, 2010). Copyright © 1975, 1976, 1977, renewed 1997, 2010 Ntozake Shange. Reprinted with the permission of Russell & Volkening as agents for Ntozake Shange and Scribner, a division of Simon & Schuster, Inc. All rights reserved.

Reginald Shepherd, The Difficult Music; The Lucky One: *Some Are Drowning* (Pittsburgh: University of Pittsburgh Press, 1995). Copyright © 1994. Reprinted by permission of the University of Pittsburgh Press. Hesitation Theory: *Fata Morgana* (Pittsburgh: University of Pittsburgh Press, 2007). Copyright © 2007. Reprinted by permission of the University of Pittsburgh Press. My Mother Was No White Dove: *Red Clay Weather* (Pittsburgh: University of Pittsburgh Press, 2011). Copyright © 2011. Reprinted by permission of the University of Pittsburgh Press.

Evie Shockley, from *The Lost Letters of Frederick Douglass*: *The New Black* (Middletown, CT: Wesleyan University Press, 2011). statistical haiku (or, how do they discount us? let me count the ways); ode to my blackness: *The New Black* (Middletown, CT: Wesleyan University Press, 2011). Copyright © 2011 Evie Shockley. Published by Wesleyan University Press and reprinted with permission.

Safiya Sinclair, Safiya Sinclair, Fisherman's Daughter: *Cannibal* (Lincoln: University of Nebraska Press, 2016). Copyright © 2016 Board of Regents of the University of Nebraska. Reprinted by permission of the University of Nebraska Press.

Clint Smith, Your National Anthem: *Harvard Kennedy School Journal of African American Public Policy* (2017–18). Reprinted by permission of HJAAP. Copyright © 2018 the President and Fellows of Harvard College.

Danez Smith, dinosaurs in the hood: *Don't Call Us Dead* (Minneapolis: Graywolf Press, 2017). Copyright © 2017 Danez Smith. Reprinted with the permission of The Permissions Company, LLC on behalf of Graywolf Press, Minneapolis, Minnesota, graywolfpress.org.

Lucy E. Smith, Ballad of American Mores: *No Middle Ground* (Philadelphia: The Philadelphia Council of Arts, Sciences, and Professions, 2nd printing, 1952). Face of Poverty: *New Negro Poets, USA* (Bloomington: Indiana University Press, 1964).

Patricia Smith, Building Nicole's Mama: *Teahouse of the Almighty* (Minneapolis: Coffee House Press, 2006). Copyright © 2006 Patricia Smith. Don't Drink the Water: *Blood Dazzler* (Minneapolis: Coffee House Press, 2008). Copyright © 2008 Patricia Smith. Both poems reprinted with the permission of The Permissions Company, LLC on behalf of Coffee House Press, coffeehousepress.org.

Tracy K. Smith, Sci-Fi; Don't You Wonder, Sometimes?; The Universe Is a House Party: *Life on Mars* (Minneapolis: Graywolf Press, 2011). Copyright © 2011 Tracy K. Smith. Declaration: *Wade in the Water* (Minneapolis: Graywolf Press, 2018). Originally from *The New Yorker*, November 6, 2017, copyright © 2017, 2018 Tracy K. Smith. Reprinted with the permission of The Permissions Company, LLC on behalf of Graywolf Press, Minneapolis, Minnesota, graywolfpress.org.

A. B. Spellman, After Vallejo: *Things I Must Have Known* (Minneapolis: Coffee House Press, 2008). Originally appeared in *African American Review*, copyright © 2008 A. B. Spellman. Reprinted with the permission of The Permissions Company, LLC on behalf of Coffee House Press, coffeehousepress.org.

Anne Spencer, At the Carnival: *The Book of American Negro Poetry*, ed. James Weldon Johnson (New York: Harcourt, Brace and Company, 1922). White Things: *The Crisis*, March 1923. Sybil Warns Her Sister: *Ebony and Topaz: A Collectanea*, ed. Charles S. Johnson (New York: National Urban League, 1927). Copyright © National Urban League. Reprinted by permission. All rights reserved.

Sharan Strange, Offering; Snow: *Ash* (Boston: Beacon Press, 2001). Copyright © 2001 Sharan Strange. Republished with permission of Beacon Press; permission conveyed through Copyright Clearance Center, Inc.

Sekou Sundiata, from Free!: *Free!* (New York: Shamal Books, 1977). Copyright © 1977. Reprinted with permission of the Estate of Robert Feaster.

Lucy Terry, [Bars Fight]: *The History of Western Massachusetts*, Josiah Gilbert Holland, ed. (Springfield, MA: Samuel Bowles & Co., 1855).

Lorenzo Thomas, Inauguration: *Chances Are Few* (Berkeley, CA: Blew Wind Press, 1979); Song: *The Bathers* (New York: I. Reed Press, 1979). Poems also included in *The Collected Poems of Lorenzo Thomas*, copyright © 2019 Estate of Lorenzo Thomas. Published by Wesleyan University Press and reprinted with permission.

Eloise Bibb Thompson, Ode to the Sun: *Poems* (Boston: Monthly Review Press, 1895), as Eloise Bibb.

Priscilla Jane Thompson, To a Little Colored Boy: *Ethiope Lays* (Rossmoyne, OH: Self-published, 1900).

Samantha Thornhill, Ode to Gentrification: *Brooklyn Rail,* April 2015. Copyright © 2015 Samantha Thornhill. Reprinted by permission of the author.

Melvin B. Tolson, Dark Symphony; from *Harlem Gallery, Book I: The Curator: "Harlem Gallery," and Other Poems of Melvin B. Tolson*, ed. Raymond T. Nelson (Charlottesville: University of Virginia Press, 1999). Copyright © 1999 Rector and Visitors of the University of Virginia. Reprinted by permission of the University of Virginia Press.

Jean Toomer, Five Vignettes; Her Lips Are Copper Wire; Be with Me: *The Collected Poems of Jean Toomer*, ed. Robert B. Jones and Margery Toomer Latimer (Chapel Hill: University of North Carolina Press, 1988). Copyright © Yale University. Reprinted by permission of the Beinecke Rare Book & Manuscript Library, Yale University. From *Cane* (New York: Boni and Liveright, 1923). From *Essentials: Essentials*, ed. Rudolph P. Byrd (Athens: University of Georgia Press, 1991). Copyright © Yale University. Reprinted by permission of the Beinecke Rare Book & Manuscript Library, Yale University.

Natasha Trethewey, Flounder; Drapery Factory, Gulfport, Mississippi, 1956; Graveyard Blues; Pilgrimage; Miscegenation; Incident: *Monument: New and Selected Poems* (Boston: Houghton Mifflin, 2018). All but two poems copyright © 2006 Natasha Trethewey and reprinted by permission of Houghton Mifflin Harcourt Publishing Company. All rights reserved. "Flounder" and "Drapery Factory, Gulfport, Mississippi, 1956" (Minneapolis: Graywolf, 2000), first published in *Domestic Work*, copyright © 1994, 2000 by Natasha Trethewey. Reprinted with the permission of The Permissions Company, LLC on behalf of Graywolf Press, Minneapolis, Minnesota, graywolfpress.org.

Quincy Troupe, One for Charlie Mingus; Poem for My Father; After Hearing a Radio Announcement: A Comment on Some Conditions: *Transcircularities: New and Selected Poems* (Minneapolis: Coffee House Press, 2002). Copyright © 2002 Quincy Troupe. Reprinted with the permission of The Permissions Company, LLC on behalf of Coffee House Press, coffeehousepress.org.

Lyrae Van Clief-Stefanon, Strip: *Black Swan* (Pittsburgh: University of Pittsburgh Press, 2002). Copyright © 2002. RR Lyrae: Matter: *Open Interval* (Pittsburgh: University of Pittsburgh Press, 2009). Copyright © 2009. Both poems reprinted by permission of the University of Pittsburgh Press.

George B. Vashon, A Life-Day: *Early Negro American Writers*, ed. Benjamin Brawley (Chapel Hill: University of North Carolina Press, 1935).

Derek Walcott, A Far Cry from Africa; Codicil; Blues; from The Schooner *Flight*; Sea Canes; Volcano; Easter: *Collected Poems, 1948–1984* (New York: Farrar, Straus & Giroux, 1986). Also included in *The Poetry of Derek Walcott 1948–2013*, selected by Glyn Maxwell, copyright © 2014 Derek Walcott. From *Omeros*: Chapter VIII: *Omeros* (New York: Farrar, Straus & Giroux, 1990).

Albery A. Whitman, from *The Rape of Florida*; A Question: *Twasinta's Seminoles; or, Rape of Florida* (St. Louis, MO: Nixon & Jones Printing Co., 1890).

Phillip B. Williams, Prayer: *Thief in the Interior* (Farmington, ME: Alice James Books, 2016). Copyright © 2016 Phillip B. Williams. Reprinted with the permission of The Permissions Company, LLC, on behalf of Alice James Books, www.alicejamesbooks.org.

Saul Williams, Amethyst Rocks: *The Dead Emcee Scrolls: The Lost Teachings of Hip-Hop* (New York: Simon & Schuster, 2006). Copyright © 2006 Saul Williams. Reprinted with the permission of the author c/o Charlotte Gusay Literary Agency and Pocket Books, a division of Simon & Schuster, Inc. All rights reserved.

Sherley Anne Williams, from "Letters from a New England Negro": *Some One Sweet Angel Chile* (New York: William Morrow, 1982). Copyright © 1982 Sherley Anne Williams. Reprinted by permission of the Sandra Dijkstra Literary Agency.

Jamila Woods, Ode to Herb Kent: *Poetry* (December 2015). Copyright © 2015 Jamila Woods. Reprinted by permission of the author.

Richard Wright, Between the World and Me: *Partisan Review*, July 1935. Copyright © 1935 Richard Wright. Reprinted by permission of John Hawkins and Associates, Inc. Selected Haiku: *Haiku*, ed. Yoshinobu Hakutani and Robert L. Tener (New York: Arcade Publishing, 1998). Copyright © 1998, 2012 Ellen Wright. Reprinted by permission of Skyhorse Publishing.

Al Young, How Stars Start; Dance of the Infidels: *Heaven: Collected Poems 1956–1990* (Berkeley, CA: Creative Arts Book Company, 1992). Boogie with O. O. Gabugah; The Old O. O. Blues; A Poem for Players: *Geography of the Near Past* (New York: Holt, Rinehart and Winston, 1976). Copyright © 1976.

Kevin Young, Money Road: *Brown* (New York: Knopf, 2018). Copyright © 2018 Kevin Young. Reprinted by permission of Alfred A. Knopf, an imprint of the Knopf Doubleday Publishing Group, a division of Penguin Random House, LLC. All rights reserved.

This volume presents the texts of the original printings chosen for inclusion here, but it does not attempt to reproduce nontextual features of their typographic design. The texts are presented without change, except for the correction of typographical errors. Spelling, punctuation, and capitalization are often expressive features and are not altered, even when inconsistent or irregular. The following is a list of typographical errors corrected, cited by page and line number: 28.17, thusb egan.; 120.5, high-minded, man;; 141.12, whem; 158.15, futiley; 218.8, The; 218.16, rythmic; 222.7, comon; 222.20, lets; 297.19, Gaugin; 347.15, soverign; 349.22, form; 397.33, cooly; 441.13, apertifs; 463.23, caressess; 472.2, *Literay*; 477.8, fix).; 516.13, easled; 521.18, The; 539.32, The will; 548.22, sachel; 589.32, souless; 598.5, laping; 627.14, Coconut; 670.23, its; 674.1, pass; 717.7, others'; 938.3, Abby; 947.27, returning I home.

NOTES

In the notes below, the reference numbers denote page and line of this volume (the line count includes chapter headings). No note is made for material that is sufficiently explained in context, nor are there notes for material included in standard desk-reference works such as Webster's Eleventh Collegiate, Biographical, and Geographical dictionaries or comparable internet resources such as Merriam-Webster's online dictionary. Foreign words and phrases are translated only if not translated in the text or if words are not evident English cognates. Biblical quotations are keyed to the King James Version. Quotations from Shakespeare are keyed to *The Riverside Shakespeare*, ed. G. Blakemore Evans (Boston: Houghton Mifflin, 1974).

3.7   *Helicon's*] In Greek antiquity, mountain in Boeotia with a spring that, according to legend, gave inspiration to those who drank from it.

3.31   *Sylvanus*] Roman god of forests and woodlands.

4.13   From *Tithon's* bed now might *Aurora* rise] In Greek mythology Tithonus, son of the Trojan king Laomedon, was the husband of the goddess of the dawn, Eos, who was called Aurora by the Romans.

4.25   Mneme . . . sacred nine] In Greek mythology the goddess of memory Mnemosene (Mneme), daughter of the titans Uranus and Gaia, was mother to the nine muses.

5.15   *Maro's*] The Roman poet Virgil.

6.8   *George Whitefield*] The English evangelist George Whitefield (1714–1770), who traveled throughout the American colonies as an itinerant preacher. Whitefield may have visited or stayed in the Wheatley home during his trips to Boston, and it is possible that Wheatley heard him preach. As mentioned in the poem, Whitefield served as chaplain to Selina, Countess of Huntingdon (1707–1791), a Methodist religious leader to whom Wheatley's poem was dedicated.

7.23   *S. M., a young African painter*] The artist Scipio Moorhead (fl. 1773), none of whose paintings are known to be extant. It is possible that the portrait engraving of Wheatley included as the frontispiece to her book *Poems on Various Subjects* (1773) was based on a painting by Moorhead.

8.11–12   twice six gates . . . Celestial *Salem*] In the vision of the heavenly New Jerusalem in Revelation 21.12–13, the city wall has twelve gates, each inscribed with one of the names of the twelve tribes of Israel.

8.23   *Damon's* tender sighs] Damon, in classical legend, offered himself as a hostage in place of his friend Pythias, who had been condemned to death, so that Pythias could return home to settle his affairs. Both were freed in recognition of their loyalty.

9.22 Eolus] Or Aeolus, Greek god who was keeper of the winds.

10.2 Gallic powers Columbia's fury found] A reference to the French and Indian War.

13.28–30 Samaria's flood . . . redeeming blood] See John 4:13–14, when Jesus, traveling through Samaria, stops to speak with a woman at a well and contrasts its water with the water that he can give, the water of eternal life.

15.2 *Bars Fight*] The attack described in the ballad took place in Deerfield, Massachusetts; "Bars" is an archaic term for a meadow.

34.12 Ida B. Wells] Anti-lynching activist, writer, lecturer, and newspaper owner (1862–1931).

35.1 Judith, who Holofernes slew] In the apocryphal Book of Judith (13:1–10), the Assyrian general Holofernes is beheaded by the Jewish woman Judith in his tent after a drunken banquet.

40.7 Cinque] Sengbe Pieh (1814–c. 1879), later known as Joseph Cinqué, was an enslaved African who led the rebellion on the Spanish slave ship *Amistad* off Cuba in 1839. After seizing the ship the rebels sailed north and eventually reached eastern Long Island, where they were arrested and charged with murder and mutiny. In March 1841 the U.S. Supreme Court ordered the mutineers freed, and in November 1841 the surviving rebels sailed for Sierra Leone.

40.15 beard the robber in his den.] Cf. the phrase "beard the lion in his den," which means to contradict or defy a powerful person on their home ground.

48.2 *Song for the First of August*] Bell wrote this poem to be sung to the tune "America" ("My Country 'Tis of Thee"). People of African descent in the Caribbean, Canada, and the United States commemorated the abolition of slavery in the British West Indies and elsewhere in the British Empire on August 1, 1834, with anniversary celebrations and often used these occasions to mobilize against American slavery.

54.13–14 in chains . . . mighty conqueror] After the French colony of Saint-Domingue (corresponding to present-day Haiti) established its administrative independence from France through a revolt led by Toussaint L'Ouverture (c. 1743–1803), Napoleon dispatched troops to the island and forced L'Ouverture to surrender on May 5, 1802. He was incarcerated in France until his death from tuberculosis and malnutrition on April 6, 1803.

56.23 the Great Wahoo.] Swampland in present-day Sumter County, Florida, the site of fighting in the Second Seminole War, November–December 1836.

The area was home to escaped slaves, many of whom fought with the Seminoles during the conflict.

74.10 *the lynching of Mary Turner*] At least thirteen African Americans were murdered by white mobs in Brooks and Lowndes Counties in southern Georgia during a spree of violence in mid-May 1918. Hayes Turner, accused of involvement in the murder of a white farmer, was lynched on May 18. The following day, after his eight-months-pregnant wife, Mary Turner (c. 1885–1918), said she would report the murderers to the police, a mob seized her from her home, brought her to the Folsom Bridge over the Little River, and strung her upside down from a tree before dousing her with gasoline and setting her on fire. Her unborn child was cut out of her body and trampled to death, and Turner's body was riddled with bullets.

76.7 Helicon] See note 3.7.

85.26 "Come to Jesus,"] Hymn written by the Methodist preacher and hymn writer John Hart Stockton (1813–1877), usually sung in a version with words slightly altered by the gospel musician and preacher Ira Sankey (1840–1908).

85.29 "Rock of Ages,"] Hymn whose words, written in 1776 by Anglican cleric Augustus Montague Toplady (1740–1778), were adapted and set to music in the nineteenth century.

86.19 "Swing Low, Sweet Chariot,"] A spiritual.

88.9 de man said, 'Hyeah am I.'"] See Exodus 3:4.

89.2 Gab'el's ho'n] In African American spirituals, the angel Gabriel is said to sound his trumpet on Judgment Day.

89.27–28 de Bible says] Cf. Luke 10:7: "the laborer is worthy of his hire."

94.9 *El Beso*] Spanish: The Kiss.

103.2 *Lift Every Voice and Sing*] Written in February 1900 for a school commemoration of Lincoln's birthday held in Jacksonville, Florida, the poem was set to music by Johnson's brother J. Rosamond Johnson; it has sometimes been referred to as the "Negro National Anthem."

105.18–20 great German master . . . the creation] Most likely Franz Joseph Haydn (1732–1809), composer of the oratorio *The Creation* (1798).

110.18 Joshua, the son of Nun?] The biblical Joshua, an Ephraimite man who was an aide to Moses and later the leader of the Israelites.

129.21 *Alexander Dumas*] The French writer Alexandre Dumas *père* (1802–1870). His paternal grandmother, Marie-Cessette Dumas, was an enslaved woman of African descent who lived in what is now Haiti.

144.4–10 Jack Johnson . . . Jim Jeffries] The boxer Jack Johnson (1878–1946) was the first African American heavyweight champion, 1908–15. On

July 4, 1910, he defeated Jim Jeffries (1875–1953), a former champion touted before the match as the "great white hope," by a technical knockout in the fifteenth round.

144.14   John Henry] Figure of African American folklore (perhaps based on a real person) and the hero of a ballad: a steel-driver who, while working on the Big Bend railroad tunnel near Talcott, West Virginia, in the early 1870s, won a test of strength against a steam drill but died from his exertions.

168.5   Scottsboro] On March 25, 1931, nine Black youths, aged 13 to 20, were accused of having raped two young white women on a freight train in northern Alabama. They were tried in Scottsboro, Alabama, beginning on April 6, 1931, and on April 9 eight of the defendants were sentenced to death (the case of the 13-year-old resulted in a mistrial when a jury deadlocked over whether to impose the death penalty). In 1932 the U.S. Supreme Court overturned the verdicts on the grounds that the inadequate counsel provided to the accused at their trial violated their right to due process under the Fourteenth Amendment. Two defendants were retried and again sentenced to death in 1933, despite the recantation by one of the alleged victims of her previous testimony (the trials of the remaining defendants were postponed pending the appeal of the new conviction). The U.S. Supreme Court overturned one of the new convictions in 1935, ruling that the systematic exclusion of Blacks from grand and trial jury duty violated the right to equal protection of the law under the Fourteenth Amendment. All the defendants were then reindicted by Alabama authorities. Four of the defendants were retried and convicted between January 1936 and July 1937; one was sentenced to death (commuted in 1938 to life imprisonment), one to 99 years in prison, and two to 75-year terms. A fifth defendant received 20 years for assaulting a deputy while in custody, and charges against the remaining four were dropped in July 1937.

168.20   Sacco & Vanzetti] In 1921 Nicola Sacco (1891–1927) and Bartolomeo Vanzetti (1888–1927) were convicted of murdering two men during a payroll robbery in South Braintree, Massachusetts, the previous year. Their case became an international cause célèbre, with their defenders arguing that the two men had been unfairly convicted because of their Italian immigrant backgrounds and anarchist beliefs.

170.1   *Lord, What a Morning*] Cf. the spiritual "My Lord, What a Morning."

170.6–7   Johnson . . . Jeffries] See note 144.4–10.

175.6   *Massillon Coicou*] Haitian poet, playwright, diplomat, and politician (1867–1908).

182.13–14   Iscariot to your Pythias] Bywords for, respectively, a betrayer (from the biblical Judas Iscariot) and a loyal friend or companion (see note 8.23).

212.27   LEONTYNE'S] The soprano Leontyne Price (b. 1927), who in 1961 became the first African American singer to join the Metropolitan Opera Company.

213.9–11 SAMMY HARRY . . . PEARLIE MAE] Prominent African American performing artists: Sammy Davis, Jr. (1925–1990), singer and actor; Harry Belafonte (b. 1927), singer, actor, and activist; Lena Horne (1917–2010), singer, actor, and activist; Marian Anderson (1897–1993), classical singer of opera, lieder, and spirituals; most likely Louis Armstrong (1901–1971), trumpeter and composer; Pearl Mae Bailey (1918–1990), actor and singer.

213.12 GEORGE S. SCHUYLER] Novelist and journalist (1895–1977), a columnist for the *Pittsburgh Courier*, 1924–64, and author of the satirical novel *Black No More* (1931).

213.18–19 "*Hesitation Blues*"] Blues song with roots in the tradition of spirituals, first recorded in several varying versions during the 1910s.

213.23 MOUNT VERNON] George Washington's estate in Virginia.

213.24 VESPUCIUS] From the Latinized form of the name of the Italian navigator Amerigo Vespucci (1454–1512), basis for the name America.

213.26 ARNA BONTEMPS] See biographical notes.

213.28 SHALOM ALEICHEM] Pen name (meaning "peace be unto you," a Hebrew greeting) of Yiddish writer and humorist Sholem Rabinovitch 1859–1916), from Ukraine.

214.4 ORNETTE] Jazz saxophonist and avant-garde innovator Ornette Coleman (1930–2015), a pioneer of free jazz.

214.14 NKRUMAH] Kwame Nkrumah (1909–1972), first president of the Republic of Ghana, 1960–66.

214.16 NASSER] Gamal Abdel Nasser (1918–1970), president of Egypt, 1956–70, a vocal proponent of pan-Arab unity.

214.18 ZIK AZIKIWIS] Nigerian nationalist and political leader Nnamdi Azikiwe (1904–1996), governor-general of Nigeria, 1960–63, and, after independence, the country's first president, 1963–66.

214.19 TOURÉ] Ahmed Sékou Touré (1922–1984), president of Guinea, 1958–84).

214.21 KENYATTA] Jomo Kenyatta (c. 1897–1978), leader in Kenyan struggle against British colonial rule; prime minister of Kenya, 1963–64, and the nation's first president, 1964–78.

215.7 DIXIECRATS] Common name for the States' Rights Democratic Party, a breakaway faction from the Democratic Party that in 1948 held their own convention and nominated segregationist South Carolina governor Strom Thurmond (1902–2003) for president.

215.12 DR. RUFUS CLEMENT] Educator and author (1900–1967), president of Atlanta University, 1937–57 and 1966–67; when elected to serve on the

Atlanta Board of Education in 1953, he became the first African American to hold elective office in Georgia since Reconstruction.

215.13 ZELMA WATSON GEORGE] Opera singer, diplomat, and philanthropist (1903–1994).

215.23–25 FAUBUS . . . PATTERSON] Segregationist politicians. Orval Faubus (1910–1994), Arkansas governor (1910–1994) who opposed school integration in the wake of the Supreme Court ruling in *Brown v. Board of Education* (1954). James O. Eastland (1904–1986), who often called Blacks "an inferior race," was Democratic senator from Mississippi, 1943–78, serving as chairman of the Senate Judiciary Committee, 1956–78, and president pro tempore, 1972–78. John Malcolm Patterson (b. 1927) served one term as governor of Alabama, 1959–63.

216.11 DREYFUS TO CRY, "*J'ACCUSE!*"] On January 13, 1898, the French novelist Emile Zola (1840–1902) published "I Accuse," an outraged open letter to the president of the French Republic following the acquittal of Charles-Ferdinand Esterhazy (1847–1923), the army officer and spy for Germany who had falsely accused fellow officer Alfred Dreyfus of treason.

216.12 DEAD BLIND LEMON] Blues singer Blind Lemon Jefferson (1893–1929).

216.13 CA IRA] "Ah, ça ira" (It will be fine), popular song during the French Revolution.

216.15 LUMUMBA TO CRY, "FREEDOM NOW!"] Patrice Lumumba (1925–1961), a leader of the Congolese independence movement, was the first prime minister of the Congo, June 23–September 5, 1960. He was arrested on December 1 by troops loyal to Colonel Joseph Mobutu and shot on January 17, 1961, by Katanga secessionists led by Moise Tshombe, with possible CIA involvement in the assassination. "Freedom Now" was a slogan used by the American civil rights movement.

216.17 DENMARK VESEY] Denmark Vesey (1767?–1822) was a personal servant to slave trader Joseph Vesey before winning a lottery in 1800 that allowed him to buy his freedom. In 1821–22 he planned a slave uprising in South Carolina set for July 14, 1822. Charleston authorities learned of the plot, and Vesey was executed along with thirty-four other Black men.

216.18 CINQUE] See note 40.7.

216.19 OLD JOHN BROWN] Abolitionist John Brown (1800–1859) and a group of his followers seized the U.S. armory at Harpers Ferry, Virginia (now West Virginia), on October 16, 1859, with the purpose of arming slaves and starting an insurrection. Fifteen people were killed during the raid. Brown was captured, convicted of treason, and hanged on December 2, 1859.

216.27–28 GARRISON, BEECHER, LOWELL] William Lloyd Garrison (1805–1879), editor of the antislavery periodical *The Liberator* and an uncompromising abolitionist; Henry Ward Beecher (1813–1887), prominent pastor of Plymouth Congregational Church in Brooklyn, New York; of the Lowell family in Boston, likely the poet and abolitionist James Russell Lowell (1819–1891).

216.30 MARCUS GARVEY] Jamaican-born Black nationalist and entrepreneur Marcus Garvey (1887–1940), founder of the Universal Negro Improvement Association and the Black Star Shipping Line. He advocated economic self-sufficiency for Blacks and led a movement to establish a nation-state in Africa governed and populated by Black immigrants from the United States and elsewhere.

216.30 SUFI] Labor and religious leader Sufi Abdul Hamid (1903–1938), based in Harlem, an African American convert to Islam.

216.30–31 FATHER DIVINE] African American preacher, born George Baker (c. 1879–1965), who founded the Peace Mission Movement during the 1930s. He made his headquarters in Harlem from 1933 until 1942, when he moved to Philadelphia.

216.32 STOKELY] Trinidad-born American activist Stokely Carmichael (1941–1991), chairperson of the Student Nonviolent Coordinating Committee (SNCC) and the man responsible for the popularization of the phrase "Black Power."

216.34 ADAM POWELL ON A NON-SUBPOENA DAY.] Adam Clayton Powell (1908–1972), civil rights leader and a Democratic congressman from New York, 1945–67 and 1969–71, who was plagued by accusations of financial misconduct during the 1950s and 1960s.

238.24–25 Princess Anne lynching of October 18, 1933] In October 1933 George Armwood (1911–1933) was accused of assaulting an elderly white woman near the town of Princess Anne on Maryland's Eastern Shore. When arrested by police he was severely beaten en route to the Salisbury prison, ten miles from Princess Anne. Reports of a lynch mob gathering in Salisbury led to Armwood being moved to Baltimore for his protection, but on October 17 he was sent back to Princess Anne to await trial. On the night of October 18, 1933, a large white mob broke into the Princess Anne prison with battering rams and dragged Armwood out of his cell, beat and mutilated him, dragged him through the town, and hung his body from a tree on the property next to that of local judge Robert F. Duer. Armwood's corpse was then strung up on a telephone pole and burned.

239.6 feeble-minded black boy!] Contemporary press accounts of the case (including in African American newspapers) characterized Armwood as being mentally handicapped, though it is not clear how accurate these descriptions are.

239.35 The teeth] Members of the lynch mob had taken out Armwood's gold teeth.

241.23–24 mark of Ham . . . curse] See Genesis 9:25, where Noah curses his grandson Canaan, the son of Ham: "a servant of servants shall he be to his brethren." Ham had seen the drunken and naked Noah asleep in his tent. African peoples were listed among the biblical Ham's descendants in Genesis 10:6–20; the "curse of Ham" had often been used to justify enslaving Black people.

242.1 *The Tree of Hope*] Elm tree near the Lafayette Theatre in Harlem, reputed to give good luck to performers.

246.17–18 Juggernaut . . . over each of us] An annual festival held in Puri in eastern India is devoted to the Hindu god Jagannath (Juggernaut in its Anglicized form), an avatar of Krishna. Nineteenth-century Protestant missionaries published widely read accounts of processions in which chariots bearing wooden carvings of Jagannath and other deities crushed people under their wheels as they were pulled through the streets of the city.

257.2 *Satch*] Hall of Fame baseball player Leroy Robert (Satchel) Paige (1906–1982), who played during the height of his career in the Negro Leagues and later played for Major League Baseball.

257.11 *Nat Turner*] Leader (1800–1831) of a slave insurrection in Southhampton County, Virginia, August 22–24, 1831, during which more than fifty white men, women, and children were killed. More than 100 African Americans were killed without trial during the suppression of the revolt, and Turner and twenty others were executed.

261.3–5 John Brown . . . Harper's] See note 216.19.

269.5 "Knock me a kiss."] From the popular song "Knock Me a Kiss" (1942), words by Andy Razaf (see biographical notes), music by Mike Jackson (1888–1945).

270.19–20 a blackish child of fourteen] Emmett Till (1941–1955), visiting relatives near Money, Mississippi, from Chicago, was beaten and shot to death on August 28, 1955, after he allegedly whistled at a white woman. His murder and the acquittal on September 23 of Roy Bryant and J. W. Milan, the two white men charged with the crime (both of whom later admitted to a journalist that they had killed Till), attracted widespread public attention.

274.15 *Little Rock*] After a federal district court ordered nine African American students to be admitted to Little Rock's Central High School, Arkansas governor Orval Faubus used the National Guard to prevent them from entering the school on September 3, 1957. The Guard was withdrawn after the district court ordered Faubus to end his interference on September 20. After a large mob attacked the nine students three days later, President Eisenhower placed the Arkansas National Guard under federal control and sent more than 1,000 paratroopers of the 101st Airborne Division to enforce the desegregation order. The troops remained until November 27.

281.16–17   Paul Robeson] Prominent singer, actor, and political activist (1898–1976). Brooks's poem refers to his well-known rendition of "Ol' Man River," song written for the musical *Show Boat* (1927), with music by Jerome Kern (1885–1945) and lyrics by Oscar Hammerstein II (1895–1960).

291.24   Rocinante] In Cervantes's *Don Quixote* (1605–15), Rocinante, a worn-out workhorse, is the hero's steed.

301.29   Stockyards Fire] Massive fire at the Union Stock Yard on the South Side of Chicago, May 19, 1934, resulting in one human fatality and the deaths of hundreds of livestock, as well as numerous injuries, mostly to firefighters.

306.11   amid the alien corn] See John Keats, "Ode to a Nightingale" (1819), stanza 7: "Perhaps the self-same song that found a path / Through the sad heart of Ruth, when, sick for home, / She stood in tears amid the alien corn." The eponymous heroine of the biblical book of Ruth, a Moabite woman, is widowed and follows her late husband's mother, Naomi, to live in Jerusalem.

306.17   Corinthians: . . . as a man."] Cf. 1 Corinthians 13:11: "When I was a child, I spake as a child, I understood as a child, I thought as a child: but when I became a man, I put away childish things."

308.5   *Jesús . . . Mercy*] Names of slave ships, as are the names at line 308.18.

308.21–23   *Deep in the festering hold . . . were his eyes.*] Cf. "Ariel's Song" in Shakespeare's *The Tempest*, I.ii.397–99.

316.16   Obour] Wheatley's friend and confidante Obour Tanner (d. 1835), the recipient of eight extant letters from Wheatley (no other correspondence to or from Wheatley with another person of African descent has survived).

318.6   dear Nathaniel] Nathaniel Wheatley, the son of John and Susanna Wheatley, who had purchased Phyllis Wheatley in 1761.

318.23   "in a broken tongue"] Dunbar's own characterization of his use of dialect in his poetry from his poem "The Poet": "He sang of life when earth was young, / And Love, itself, was in his lays. / But ah, the world, it turned to praise / A jingle in a broken tongue."

324.11–14   Dizzy Gillespie . . . Cecil Taylor] Renowned and influential jazz musicians and composers: the trumpeter Dizzy Gillespie (1917–1993); saxophonist Charlie Parker (1920–1955), known as "Bird" or "Yardbird"; the bandleader, composer, and pianist Count Basie (1904–1984); the trumpeter and singer Louis Armstrong, known as Satchmo; the pianist Thelonious Monk (1917–1982); the trumpeter Miles Davis (1926–1991); the saxophonist Sonny Rollins (b. 1930); the bandleader and composer Duke Ellington (1899–1974); the pianist Horace Silver (1928–2014); the saxophonist John Coltrane (1926–1967); the pianist Cecil Taylor (1929–2018).

324.17   the days of Buddy Bolden] Buddy Bolden (1877–1931), a New Orleans–style cornet player, is considered to be one of the first jazz musicians.

324.18–19   Ornette Coleman's extension of Bebop] See note 214.4.

329.7   Gabriel exchanged his trumpet] See note 89.2.

330.33   Leadbelly of blues] Huddie William Ledbetter (1888–1949), the blues singer, songwriter, and guitar virtuoso known as Leadbelly or Lead Belly.

333.1   *Parker*] Charlie Parker.

333.7   Hawkins] Jazz musician Coleman Hawkins (1904–1969), often regarded as the first important tenor saxophone stylist.

333.7   Lester] Saxophonist Lester Young (1909–1959), nicknamed Prez or Pres, whose career as a jazz musician began with the Count Basie Orchestra.

334.13   *Heavy Water Blues*] Reference to "Mississippi Heavy Water Blues," recorded by Atlanta blues guitarist Barbecue Bob (Robert Hicks, 1902–1931) in 1927.

335.1   John Mitchell's] John Mitchell (1913–1988), attorney general in the Nixon administration, 1969–72.

337.15   Terry and the Pirates] Comic strip, 1934–73, created by cartoonist Milton Caniff (1907–1988).

338.25–26   Crispus Attucks] In the Boston Massacre, March 5, 1770, British soldiers under Captain Thomas Preston (c. 1722–c. 1798) opened fire on an angry, taunting crowd, killing five Boston residents, the first among them the Black sailor Crispus Attucks (1723?–1770), a leader of the protest.

338.29–32   Hart Crane . . . Gulf of Mexico, the bridge] The poet Hart Crane (1899–1932), author of *The Bridge* (1930), took his own life when he leapt from the deck of the steamship *Orizaba* into the waters of the Gulf of Mexico on April 27, 1932.

341.21   *poll-taxers*] A poll tax was a fixed tax levied on every person within a jurisdiction. In the South after Reconstruction, the payment of a poll tax was often made a requirement for voting as a means of disfranchising African Americans and, in some cases, poor whites. The ratification of the Twenty-fourth Amendment in 1964 made it unconstitutional to impose poll taxes in federal elections; the levying of poll taxes in state and local elections was deemed a violation of the Fourteenth Amendment's Equal Protection Clause by the U.S. Supreme Court in *Harper v. Virginia Board of Elections* (1966).

341.25   *Nat Turner*] See note 257.11.

343.23–24   Hero . . . Leander] In Greek legend, Leander would swim across the Hellespont every night to visit Hero, a priestess of Aphrodite, who lived in a tower and lit a lamp to guide him. One stormy night her lamp was extinguished and Leander drowned on his return home; in grief, Hero leapt from her tower to her death.

347.23 Minos] Tyrannical Cretan king who demanded the sacrifice of Athenian youths every nine years to the Minotaur, a monster with a bull's head and a man's body who was kept in a labyrinth.

352.8 *Lerone Bennett's*] The historian, journalist, and longtime *Ebony* magazine editor Lerone Bennett, Jr. (1928–2018), author of *Before the Mayflower* (1962) and *The Shaping of Black America* (1975).

353.13 riot in Miami?] Riots broke out in Miami, May 18–20, 1980, after an all-white jury acquitted four Dade County police officers of manslaughter and evidence tampering charges in their arrest of Arthur McDuffie (1946–1979) on December 17, 1979, which caused injuries that led to his death in the hospital four days later. Eighteen people died and hundreds were injured in the unrest.

354.16–17 as I wrote about Birmingham] Randall wrote "Ballad of Birmingham" (1965) in response to the bombing by Ku Klux Klansmen of the Sixteenth Street Baptist Church in Birmingham, Alabama, on September 15, 1963, which killed Denise McNair, eleven, Cynthia Wesley, fourteen, Carole Robertson, fourteen, and Addie Mae Collins, fourteen.

362.5 seven-league boots] Magic items in folklore allowing the wearer to take strides of seven leagues (approximately twenty-one miles) at a time.

362.13–14 Okies for *The Grapes of Wrath* . . . Native Son.] References to the influential and best-selling social novels *The Grapes of Wrath* by John Steinbeck and *Native Son* by Richard Wright.

363.22 Tyche's] Greek goddess of fortune and luck.

364.2 Blakean tigers and lambs on the wall] Reference to two poems by the English poet and artist William Blake (1757–1827), which he also illustrated: "The Lamb," from *Songs of Innocence* (1789), and "The Tyger," in the "Experience" poems of *Songs of Innocence and Experience: Shewing the Two Contrary States of the Human Soul* (1794).

364.4 Max Donachie's] A fictional painter.

364.9 scorn of an Ozymandias] In the sonnet "Ozymandias" (1817) by the English poet Percy Bysshe Shelley (1792–1822), an inscription on the pedestal of a monumental sculpture in ruins reads: "My name is Ozymandias, King of Kings; / Look on my Works, ye Mighty, and despair!"

364.16 Satchmo] Louis Armstrong.

364.23 a Doctor Faustus] In German legend, the scholar Faustus, unsatisfied with mortal beauty, summons Helen from the underworld. The Faust story was the basis for Christopher Marlowe's *The Tragical History of Doctor Faustus* (1589–92) and Goethe's *Faust* (1808–32).

364.24 *King Oliver of New Orleans*] The cornet player and bandleader King Oliver (Joseph Nathan Oliver, 1885–1938).

364.28   *Storyville*] Red-light district of New Orleans.

365.1   *Bessie Smith*] Singer (1894–1937) known as "Empress of the Blues."

365.3   *Mister Jelly Roll*] The pianist and composer Jelly Roll Morton (1890–1941).

365.5   *Papa Handy*] Musician and composer (1873–1958), sometimes referred to as "father of the blues."

365.7   *Leadbelly*] See note 330.33.

365.14   *hypodermic needles in Rome*] In June 1959, shortly after arriving in Spoleto, Italy, to play at a music festival there, Louis Armstrong had a heart attack and was hospitalized.

365.14   *Wyatt Earp's legend, John Henry's too*] Wyatt Earp (1848–1929), American frontier law officer and gambler; John Henry, see note 144.14.

366.8   the Laughing Philosopher] Epithet for the ancient Greek philosopher Democritus (c. 460–c. 370 B.C.E.).

366.17   ghost dance.] Originating among the Northern Paiutes of Nevada, a late-nineteenth-century pan-Indian religious movement that promised the renewal of the world and a reunification of the living and the dead. Its most important ritual was a ceremonial round dance repeated on successive nights. There were two distinct strands of the movement; at the center of the second was the messianic figure Wovoka (c. 1856–1932), also known as Jack Wilson.

366.25   "Much learning doth make thee mad."] Statement by Festus, Roman procurator of Judea, to Paul in Acts 26:24.

367.6   Xanthippean spouse] Xanthippe was the wife of Socrates.

367.23   M.-K.-T.] The Missouri-Kansas-Texas railroad.

367.25   Cotton Market Capital] Dallas, Texas.

367.30–31   Diogenes naked in the market place] The Greek Cynic philosopher Diogenes (412?–323 B.C.E.), known for his unconventional behavior such as living in a tub.

368.18   *Old Man River*] See note 281.16–17.

368.28   *ignoti nulla cupido*] Ovid, *Ars Amatoria* 3.397: for what is unknown there is no desire.

369.22   *Dies Irae*] Latin: Day of Wrath: a thirteenth-century hymn describing the day of the Last Judgment, used as part of the liturgy for the Roman Catholic funeral mass.

369.24   Boas] The influential German-born anthropologist Franz Boas (1858–1942), who spent most of his academic career at Columbia University and founded the first anthropology department in the United States; his books include *The Mind of Primitive Man* (1911) and *Race, Language, and Culture* (1940).

369.25   Blumenbach and Koelreuter] The German zoologist and anthropologist Friedrich Blumenbach (1752–1840), who developed categories of racial classification; the German botanist Josef Gottlieb Koelreuter (1733–1806).

369.27–28   Bilbo . . . mouth] Theodore G. Bilbo (1877–1947), U.S. senator from Mississippi, 1935–47, an advocate for white supremacy and segregation; he died of oral cancer.

369.31   rams' horns from Jericho] See Joshua 6:20, when during the Israelite siege of Jericho the priests blow their rams' horns and after the ensuing shouting by the besiegers the city's walls collapse.

370.4   sounding brass] See 1 Corinthians 13:1: "Though I speak with the tongues of men and of angels, and have not charity, I am become as sounding brass, or a tinkling cymbal."

387.22   *Look for You Yesterday, Here You Come Today*] Cf. "Sent For You Yesterday (and Here You Come Today)" (1938), composition by Count Basie and Eddie Durham (1906–1987), with lyrics by Jimmy Rushing (1901–1972).

388.4   "The Poet in New York."] Posthumously published book (1940) by the Spanish poet Federico García Lorca (1898–1936).

388.20–22   James Karolis . . . bathroom?] In the play *The Toilet* (1964), first staged while Baraka was calling himself LeRoi Jones and based on an autobiographical incident: a group of African American high-schoolers confront and fight James Karolis, a white youth, after he has sent a love note to Foots, their leader. Ora Matthews is among the group that roughs up Karolis.

388.26   Kline] American abstract artist Franz Kline (1910–1962).

388.27–28   Frank . . . Jack's] The poets Frank O'Hara and Jack Kerouac. The lines allude to a poetry reading at New York's Living Theatre, March 2, 1959, at which a drunken Kerouac repeatedly heckled O'Hara, who quit reading in exasperation.

389.16   Flowers of Evil] English translation of *Les Fleurs du Mal* (1857), book of poems by the French poet Charles Baudelaire (1821–1867).

389.30   Tom Mix dead in a Boston nightclub] American movie actor Tom Mix (1880–1940), who starred in Westerns mostly during the silent era, died not in a nightclub but as the result of a car accident in Arizona.

390.1   Dickie Dare] Comic strip (1933–57) created by Milton Caniff but drawn by other artists after late 1934.

390.8   Captain Midnight] Serialized radio program (1938–49) that was the basis for films and television programs as well as a comic strip.

391.1   F. Scott Charon] Fusion of the names of American novelist F. Scott Fitzgerald (1896–1940) and Charon, the boatman of Greek mythology who ferried the newly dead to the underworld across the River Styx.

396.12   Willkie or Wallace or Dewey] Wendell Willkie (1892–1944), politician, lawyer, and business executive who was the Republican candidate for president in 1940; Henry A. Wallace (1888–1965), American vice president, 1941–45, and Progressive candidate for president in 1948; Thomas E. Dewey (1902–1971), governor of New York, 1943–54, and the Republican candidate for president in 1944 and 1948.

398.29   Sardi's] Restaurant in New York City's Theater District.

402.19   KLOOK] Bebop jazz drummer Kenny Clarke (1914–1985).

411.6   Akuapim] Area in eastern Ghana; the poem's other geographical references are also to Ghana.

411.10   *nkyekyere*] Guinea grass.

412.22   Sam Lord] The Barbadian pirate Samuel Lord Hall (1778–1844), who became wealthy enough from his piracy to erect a castle on Barbados.

412.23   The Lord is my shepherd] The beginning of Psalm 23; other passages from the psalm are quoted and sometimes altered throughout the rest of the poem.

420.21   *j byrd*] James Byrd, Jr. (1949–1998), a resident of Jasper, Texas, was murdered on May 2, 1998, after three white men, luring Byrd into a pickup truck with an offer of a ride, beat him, spray-painted his face, chained him to the back of the truck, and dragged him for three miles. Byrd's decapitated, dismembered body was discovered outside an African American cemetery on the outskirts of Jasper. All three assailants were convicted of capital murder: Lawrence Russell Brewer and John William King were sentenced to death and executed in 2011 and 2019, respectively, and Shawn Ellen Berry was sentenced to life imprisonment.

428.16   Johnny Ace] R&B singer born John Marshall Alexander (1929–1954)

429.25   Ornette] Ornette Coleman (see note 214.4), who was married to Cortez from 1954 to 1964.

432.4   *Jazz Fan*] The jazz musicians named by a single name or nickname are as follows: Thelonious Monk; the pianist Bud Powell (1924–1966); bebop saxophonist Sonny Stitt (1924–1982); Sarah Vaughan (1924–1990), who sang "Don't Blame Me" (1933), lyrics by Dorothy Fields, music by Jimmy McHugh, including at a concert at New York's Town Hall on November 8, 1947; Billie

Holiday; the singer Dinah Washington (born Ruth Lee Jones, 1924–1963); the singer Ella Fitzgerald (1917–1996), whose performance at the Shrine Auditorium in Los Angeles on January 21, 1956, was part of the long-running Jazz at the Philharmonic series organized by Verve Records founder Norman Granz (1918–2001); Charlie Parker; Lester Young; Coleman Hawkins; the drummer Art Blakey (1919–1990), leader of the band Art Blakey and the Jazz Messengers; the bassist Ray Brown (1926–2002); the drummer Max Roach (1924–2007); Dizzy Gillespie; the bassist and cellist Oscar Pettiford (1922–1960); the vibraphonist Lionel Hampton (1908–2002); the saxophonist Dexter Gordon (1923–1990), who recorded his composition "Dexter's Deck" in 1945; the pianist Oscar Peterson (1925–2007); the trumpeter Fats Navarro (1923–1950). Through performances and recordings, Fitzgerald became associated with the songs "How High the Moon" (1940), music by Morgan Lewis (1906–1968), words by Nancy Hamilton (1908–1985), and "Lady Be Good" (1924), music by George Gershwin (1898–1937), words by Ira Gershwin (1896–1983). "52nd Street Theme": composition by Thelonious Monk.

434.26 *Black Star Line*] See note 216.30.

435.18 Songhay, Kongo, Kaaba] Songhai, fifteenth- and sixteenth-century West African empire with Gao as its capital, a successor to the Mali Empire; Kongo, large sovereign kingdom, 1390–1857, in west and central Africa stretching from the Atlantic coast in what is now Angola and Gabon to the present-day Democratic Republic of Congo; Kaabu, Mandinka kingdom in present-day Guinea-Bissau and Senegal, 1250–1867.

435.19 Mahdi] Sudanese military and religious leader Muhammad Ahmad (1844–1885), who led a successful Islamic insurgency against British and Egyptian forces and took Khartoum in 1885.

435.20 Malik] Born in Ethiopia, Malik Ambar (1548–1626) was captured or sold into slavery as a youth and transported first to the Middle East, then ultimately to India, where, eventually freed, he became a powerful military and political leader in the Deccan sultanate of Ahmednagar as well as an arts patron.

436.2 *Sun Ra myth*] The jazz keyboardist, composer, and bandleader Sun Ra (born Herman Poole Blount, 1914–1993) developed a visionary intergalactic cosmology and declared himself to have been born on Saturn.

437.15 Nat's] Nat Turner (see note 257.11).

437.16 Anzio] During World War II, Anglo-American and German forces fought each other on the beachhead between the towns of Anzio and Nettuno, thirty miles southwest of Rome, January 22–May 23, 1944.

437.18 Da Nang and Pork Chop Hill] Respectively, a major American airbase during the Vietnam War and a hill that, though lacking strategic utility, was the site of fighting between American and Chinese forces in April and July 1953 during the Korean War.

441.17   40 Acres and a Mule] Phrase associated with post–Civil War promises to African Americans, possibly derived from the aftermath of Major General William T. Sherman's Special Field Orders No. 15 (January 16, 1865), reserving a coastal strip of abandoned and confiscated lands thirty miles wide from Charleston, South Carolina, to the St. John's River in Florida for the settlement of emancipated people. By the summer of 1865 about 40,000 formerly enslaved individuals were living on the 400,000 acres of land set apart by the order. Some of the settlers worked their forty-acre plots with surplus mules provided by the Union Army.

442.11   Mau Mau] A Kikuyu secret society that sought independence for Kenya through attacks on European settlers and Africans considered loyal to the colonial regime. The Mau Mau were suppressed by the British in a counterinsurgency campaign, 1952–56, during which approximately 100 Europeans and 13,000 Africans were killed.

442.22   monyihanned] Reference to American politician and public official Daniel Patrick Moynihan (1927–2003), who as assistant secretary of labor issued what became known as the Moynihan Report (*The Negro Family: The Case for National Action*), released in January 1965 by the Labor Department's Office of Planning and Policy. The report made claims that were critical about the state of the African American family. In a 1970 memo to President Nixon, Moynihan also made the widely circulated remark that "the time may have come when the issue of race could benefit from a period of 'benign neglect.'"

444.12   Hollydale] A development of single-family homes outside Cincinnati planned by the Cedargrove Homestead Association, a private group of African American shareholders including the attorney, politician, and civil rights leader Theodore Berry (1904–2004). The association was founded in 1947 and by the following year had raised sufficient funds to purchase land for the development. but it encountered fierce resistance over several years from white residents in the area as well as obstruction from the Federal Housing Association. About 200 houses were eventually built in the mid-1950s.

449.3   black girls blown up] See note 257.11.

449.13   a love supreme] Album (1965) by Coltrane.

450.28   *Naima*] Composition (1959) by Coltrane, named for his wife.

451.3   *Nightmare Begins Responsibility*] Cf. "in dreams begin responsibility," the epigraph for the Irish poet William Butler Yeats's collection *Responsibilities* (1914), attributed to an "old play." Slightly adapted ("responsibilities"), the phrase is also the title of a story (1935) by the American writer Delmore Schwartz (1913–1966).

451.6 him] Harper's son Reuben Masai Harper, who died in the hospital on the second day after his birth.

451.29 two sons gone] Harper and his wife had previously lost a son in infancy.

452.17 "I had a most marvelous piece of luck. I died."] The closing line of "Dream Song 26" (1964) by the poet John Berryman (1914–1972). An earlier title for this poem was "Remembering John Berryman."

452.27 Henry's/Mr. Bones] Personae used by Berryman in *The Dream Songs*, the latter based on a stock character in nineteenth-century minstrel shows.

453.3 Crane's] Hart Crane (see also note 338.29–32).

453.4 Roethke] American poet Theodore Roethke (1908–1963).

453.24–25 Bread Loaf] the Bread Loaf Writers' Conference in Vermont, an annual summer program sponsored by Middlebury College; Berryman taught there in summer 1962.

454.2 The bridge you dived over] Berryman committed suicide by leaping from the Washington Avenue Bridge in Minneapolis on January 7, 1972.

454.4 *asiento*] Spanish: contract, with which the Spanish Crown granted rights to transport African slaves to the New World.

454.4 border ruffians] Term for proslavery Missouri militia who fought with Free Soil settlers in Kansas Territory during the 1850s.

455.3–4 afloat at forty-three on a Mississippi road] Bessie Smith died as the result of injuries suffered when the car she was in collided with a truck on Highway 61 north of Clarksdale, Mississippi, on the morning of September 26, 1937, while she was on tour.

456.1 *Helen Pitts Douglass*] American activist and feminist (1838–1903), the second wife of Frederick Douglass, 1884–91.

456.30 hate of his daughter Rosetta] Rosetta Douglass-Sprague (1839–1906) opposed the interracial marriage of her father and Helen Pitts.

458.4 sapphires . . . Kingfish's] George "the Kingfish" Stevens was a hustler and con man in the radio comedy *Amos 'n' Andy* (1928–55), later also a television series. His outspoken wife, Sapphire, was invariably fed up with his schemes and antics.

458.26–27 carver's grave] The scientist and inventor George Washington Carver (c. 1864–1943) is buried on the campus of the Tuskegee Institute in Alabama, where he long conducted research and was director of its agricultural department. His grave is beside that of educator, author, and civic leader Booker T. Washington (1856–1915), the founder and head of Tuskegee.

458.28 Laly] Probably Laly Charleton Washington (b. 1945).

458.32–33 where the southern cross the yellow dog] From "Yellow Dog Rag" (1914), composed by W. C. Handy (1873–1958), later titled "Yellow Dog Blues" and recorded by Bessie Smith in 1925.

459.9 my favorite things] Title of Coltrane's 1961 album; its title track was an instrumental reimagining of "My Favorite Things," a song from the musical *The Sound of Music* (1959), music by Richard Rodgers (1902–1979).

460.4 Shango] Yoruba god.

469.11 according to the *Times* this week] "C.I.A. Said To Have Aided Plotters Who Overthrew Nkrumah in Ghana," May 9, 1978, by the journalist Seymour Hersh (b. 1937). Nkrumah was deposed in a military coup in 1966.

469.14 Patrice Lumumba] See note 216.15.

472.11 Amilcar Cabral] Agronomist, political theorist, and anticolonialist leader in Guinea-Bissau and Cape Verde (1924–1973), assassinated in 1973 by a political rival. Later that year Cabral's party, the Partido Africano da Independência da Guiné e Cabo Verde (PAIGC), declared independence from Portugal, which recognized Guinea-Bissau as a nation the following year. (Cape Verde became its own independent nation in 1975.)

473.4 *Art Blakey and the Jazz Messengers*] Drummer and bandleader Art Blakey led several ensembles with variants of this group name.

473.16 Blue Note] Jazz record label that issued several LPs featuring Blakey's ensembles.

478.18–19 dry bones in this valley] The sermon known as "Dry Bones in the Valley," based on the vision of the bones in Ezekiel 37, was delivered in individualized variations by African American preachers.

482.2 *Mary don't you weep don't you moan*] From the spiritual "Mary, Don't You Weep."

483.23 *Eric Dolphy*] Bebop and free jazz musician and composer (1928–1964) who played saxophone and other wind instruments.

484.24 fanon] Frantz Fanon (1925–1961), Martinique-born philosopher, psychologist, anticolonial political theorist, and Marxist thinker whose books include *Black Skin, White Masks* (1952) and *The Wretched of the Earth* (1961).

489.22 A policeman who shot down a ten year old in Queens] On April 28, 1973, Thomas Shea, a plainclothes New York Police Department patrolman, shot ten-year-old Clifford Glover in the back while the boy was running away from him. He had approached Glover and his stepfather for questioning about a taxi driver's robbery. Shea was charged with murder and acquitted; in his defense he said he believed Clifford had a gun, a doubtful claim that was never substantiated, and asserted that he did not know that the boy was a child, though Clifford was five feet tall and weighed less than 100 pounds.

489.24   a voice said] Walter Scott, Shea's partner.

491.22–25   dwell in a house . . . no evil.] Cf. Psalm 23.

495.31   after detroit, newark, chicago] Riots in Newark, New Jersey, July 12–17, 1967, led to the deaths of 23 people; rioting in Detroit later that month, July 23–27, resulted in 43 deaths. Rioting in Chicago, April 5–7, 1968, in the aftermath of the assassination of Martin Luther King caused 11 deaths.

498.38–499.1   lightnin' slim] Blues singer and guitarist (born Otis Hicks, 1913–1974).

499.15   *my favorite things*] See note 459.9.

504.4   Small's Paradise] Nightclub on Seventh Avenue in Harlem.

504.14   no Good Man] Song by Dan Fisher (1920–2001), Irene Higginbotham (1918–1988), and Sammy Gallop (1915–1971), recorded by Billie Holiday in 1946. Prez: Lester Young (see note 333.7).

504.17–18   Signifying Monkey] A trickster figure in folklores of the African diaspora.

504.27   Bird] Charlie Parker.

505.12   *Don't Say Goodbye to the Porkpie Hat*] In honor of the recently deceased Lester Young (who had liked to wear porkpie hats), the jazz double bassist and pianist Charles Mingus (1922–1979) composed and recorded the instrumental "Goodbye Pork Pie Hat" with his ensemble in 1959.

505.17   Minton's] Jazz club on 118th Street in Harlem.

505.17   jelly roll] The pianist and composer Jelly Roll Morton (1890–1941); likely a reference as well to the Mingus composition "Jelly Roll," which, like "Goodbye Pork Pie Hat," was recorded for the LP *Mingus Ah Um* (1959).

506.1   Scottsboro] See note 168.5.

506.15   Stop-time Buddy and Creole Sydney] New Orleans jazz musicians: Buddy Bolden (see note 324.17) and the saxophonist and clarinetist Sidney Bechet (1897–1959).

506.35   Waller and Willie The Lion Smith] The jazz stride pianists and composers Thomas "Fats" Waller (1904–1943) and Willie "The Lion" Smith (1893–1973).

508.22   Lester . . . leaps] Young's composition "Lester Leaps In" (1939) dates from the period of his career when he played with the Count Basie Orchestra. References to other jazz musicians in this stanza include Billie Holiday (Lady); Eric Dolphy; the composer and arranger Tadd Dameron (1917–1965), whose compositions include "Our Delight" (1947); Dinah Washington; the pianist Richie Powell (1931–1956); his brother Bud Powell; and Ornette Coleman.

510.2   *26 Ways of Looking at a Black Man*] Cf. "Thirteen Ways of Looking at a Blackbird" (1917), poem by American poet Wallace Stevens (1879–1955).

514.2   *Howlin Wolf*] Blues singer and guitarist (born Chester Burnett, 1910–1976).

515.5   *Big Maybelle*] The blues singer Mabel Smith (1924–1972).

516.17   Kubla Khan] Poem (1797) by the English poet Samuel Taylor Coleridge (1772–1834).

521.18   *Tenderloin*] Name (no longer in use) of the area in Manhattan where the theater district is located.

521.22   *The History of Cakewalk*] *Clorindy, or The Origin of the Cakewalk* (1898), musical with book and lyrics by Dunbar and music by the African American composer Will Marion Cook (1869–1944), a success on Broadway and elsewhere.

521.27–28   wel/don johnson] James Weldon Johnson (see biographical notes).

522.3–4   hayden's *Kaleidoscope*] *Kaleidoscope: Poems by American Negro Poets* (1967), anthology edited by Robert Hayden (see biographical notes) whose headnote to Dunbar's poems contains Hayden's commentary.

522.24   Krazy Kat] Newspaper comic strip, 1913–44, created and drawn by American cartoonist George Herriman (1880–1944).

522.27   Fletcher Henderson] Jazz pianist, arranger, and composer (1897–1952).

522.30   Black Eagle] U.S. Air Force general Daniel "Chappie" James, Jr. (1920–1978).

530.4   billie] Billie Holiday.

533.16   *the MOVE ruins*] On May 13, 1985, the Philadelphia Police Department dropped explosive from a helicopter on a house on Osage Avenue in West Philadelphia that was home to the radical back-to-nature and Black liberationist group MOVE (not an acronym). In the ensuing fire, which was allowed to burn out of control and destroyed sixty-one homes in the area, six adults and five children in the MOVE house were killed; the only survivors from the house were Ramona Africa (b. c. 1955) and thirteen-year-old Michael Moses Ward (1972–2013), then known as Birdie Africa (MOVE members took Africa as a surname).

534.8   *mungu and morani*] Two of Sanchez's children.

535.2   *papa Joe Jones*] Jazz drummer (1911–1985).

539.11–12   John Mitchell, General Abramson] Mitchell, see note 335.1; U.S. Air Force general James A. Abrahamson (b. 1933).

539.17   Bullwinkle and Julia] Bullwinkle, cartoon moose in the animated series *The Rocky and Bullwinkle Show*, title in syndication of series originally broadcast on ABC, then NBC, 1959–1964; Julia, eponymous main character of NBC situation comedy, 1968–1971, starring Diahann Carroll (1935–2019).

539.32–34   Roy Wilkins . . . liberation jumpsuit] Roy Wilkins (1901–1981), executive director of the NAACP, 1965–77, was publicly critical of Black militancy and of the civil rights organizations CORE and SNCC.

540.12   Jim Webb] Songwriter (b. 1946) whose hits include "By the Time I Get to Phoenix" (1966) and "Up, Up, and Away" (1967).

540.15   Rare Earth] All-white soul band that recorded on the Motown label in the late 1960s and 1970s.

543.2   *After Vallejo*] Referencing the poem "Black Stone on a White Stone" by the Peruvian poet César Vallejo (1892–1938).

543.8–9   *congueros . . . bongoseros . . . timbaleros*] Percussionists: conga, bongo, and timbale players, respectively.

543.28   tumbao] In Cuban music, rhythmic patter established and sustained by the clave.

543.29   montuno] Groove or vamp section in a performance of Cuban music.

543.29   guaguanco] One of the three forms of rumba.

544.2–4   *Inauguration . . . Was the Land*] Cf. "The land was ours before we were the land's," from Robert Frost's 1941 poem "The Gift Outright," read at the presidential inauguration of John F. Kennedy.

546.2   *Charlie Mingus*] See note 514.12.

547.5   in the dugout] Trouppe (1912–1993) played catcher for several Negro Leagues baseball teams from 1930 to 1948.

548.5   yardbird] Charlie Parker.

548.12   josh gibson] Negro Leagues star (1911–1947), a catcher.

548.22   satchel paige] See note 257.2.

548.26   "brown bomber's"] Nickname for boxer Joe Louis (1914–1981), heavyweight champion, 1937–49.

548.27   sugar ray robinson] Champion boxer (1921–1989), in both welterweight and middleweight divisions.

548.29   chono pozo] Afro-Cuban conga player and composer (Luciano Pozo González, 1915–1948) who collaborated with Dizzy Gillespie on compositions and played in Gillespie's band.

548.31   "cool papa" bell] Negro Leagues star (1903–1991), an outfielder.

551.23   Peer Gynt's] Hero of the play of the same name (1867) by the Norwegian playwright Henrik Ibsen (1828–1906).

554.5   Laventille] A district in Trinidad.

558.11   *The Twelve*] Long narrative poem (1918) about the Russian Revolution by the Russian poet Aleksandr Blok (1880–1921).

558.27–28   spaghetti West- / ern . . . Van Cleef.] Clint Eastwood (b. 1930) and Lee Van Cleef (1925–1989) were cast together in the spaghetti Westerns *For a Few Dollars More* (1965) and *The Good, the Bad, and the Ugly* (1966), both directed by Sergio Leone (1929–1989).

561.3   *Victory*] Novel (1915) by Polish-born English writer Joseph Conrad (1857–1924).

564.13   Battle of the Saints] Battle of the Saintes, naval battle in the Caribbean off Dominica, April 12, 1782, a decisive victory for the British, under the command of Sir George Rodney (1718–1792), over the French, commanded by François-Joseph-Paul de Grasse (1722–1788).

569.17   *Maumau*] See note 442.11.

571.8   Mal Waldron] Jazz pianist and composer (1925–2008).

572.27–28   the record you made in Paris . . . Morgan] *Paris Jam Session* (1959), with Blakey on drums and Lee Morgan (1938–1972) on trumpet.

572.30   Buttercup's] Altevia Edwards, Powell's companion and manager while he was living in Paris.

573.1   Wayne Shorter] Jazz saxophonist (b. 1933).

574.22   Wes Montgomery] Jazz guitarist (1923–1968).

575.4   Fats for Faust] The pianist and composer Thomas "Fats" Waller (1904–1943); *Faust* (1808–32), play in two parts by Johann Wolfgang von Goethe (1749–1832).

575.17–20   Bird . . . moment's notice] Charlie Parker, Dinah Washington, Billie Holiday, Louis Armstrong, the gospel and soul singer Sam Cooke (1931–1964), the soul singer Otis Redding (1941–1967), Clifford Brown, Eric Dolphy, John Coltrane. "Moment's Notice" is a Coltrane composition recorded in 1958.

576.7   Ionesco, Bullins, Baraka, or Genet] Playwrights: the Romanian-born French playwright Eugène Ionesco (1909–1994), author of absurdist plays such as *The Bald Soprano* (1950) and *Rhinoceros* (1959); Ed Bullins (b. 1935), playwright prominent in the Black Arts Movement whose plays include *Goin' a Buffalo* (1966) and *The Electronic Nigger* (1967); Amiri Baraka (see biographical notes); Jean Genet (1910–1986), French playwright and novelist who was the author of the long-running off-Broadway play *The Blacks: A Clown Show* (1958).

576.12   Ojays] The R&B group The O'Jays, whose hits include "Love Train" (1972) and "For the Love of Money" (1974).

576.16   Diz] Dizzy Gillespie.

576.18   *The Wiz*] The musical *The Wiz: The Super Soul Musical "Wonderful Wizard of Oz"* (1974), later adapted as a film (1978).

576.24   *Ulysses*] Novel (1922) by the Irish writer James Joyce (1882–1941).

576.30   *Amsterdam News*] New York African American newspaper.

585.34   the clown in Piaf's song] "Bravo pour le clown" (1953), written by Henri Contet (1904–1998) and Louiguy (Louis Guglielmi, 1916–1991) and often performed by the French singer Edith Piaf (1915–1963).

586.11   *Atlanta, 1981*] From 1979 to 1981, twenty-four children in Atlanta ranging in age from 7 to 17, mostly African American boys, along with four adults, were abducted and killed in a series of murders whose patterns suggested they were connected. (A ten-year-old boy who went missing in 1980 has also been linked to the murders.) Wayne Williams (b. 1958) was convicted in 1982 of two of the adult murders, after which the cases of 22 of the murdered children were closed, though neither Williams nor anyone else has ever been charged in these cases.

592.3   *Elizabeth Eckford*] One of the nine African American students who integrated Central High School in Little Rock, Arkansas (see note 274.15).

593.11   Sally Hemings] An enslaved woman owned by Thomas Jefferson, Hemings (c. 1773–1835) is recorded as having given birth to at least six children, four of whom survived to adulthood. The preponderant evidence—genetic, circumstantial, and oral historical—suggests that Thomas Jefferson was their father, though his paternity had long been denied by historians, members of the Jefferson family, and others.

595.15   As all the country crowned me] The rumor of Jefferson's relationship with Hemings first received widespread attention in 1802, when the journalist James T. Callender (1758–1803), a former agent of Jefferson's who turned against the president when Jefferson refused to offer him a government sinecure, wrote in a Richmond newspaper, "It is well known that the man, whom it delighteth the people to honor, keeps, and for many years has kept, as his concubine, one of his slaves. Her name is SALLY."

595.34   *enceinte*] French: pregnant.

601.9   to Chicago. baby you want to go?] Cf. repeated line in "Sweet Home Chicago," song recorded by and associated with the Delta blues singer and guitarist Robert Johnson (1911–1931).

603.24   usta be young usta be gifted—still black] Cf. the title of the play
"To Be Young, Gifted and Black" (1968), drawn from the writings of the
playwright Lorraine Hansberry (1930–1965) by her ex-husband Robert Nemi-
roff (1930–1991). Its title was also used for a song recorded by Nina Simone
(1933–2003) in 1969, with music by Simone and words by Weldon Irvine
(1943–2002).

605.2–3   *Harriet in the Promised Land . . . Lawrence*] *Harriet and the Prom-
ised Land* (1968), children's book about Harriet Tubman illustrated with
works by the artist Jacob Lawrence (1917–2000).

614.2   *Tour Guide*] Boubacar Joseph Ndiaye (1922–2009), founder and head
curator of La Maison des Esclaves (the House of Slaves) on the Ile de Gorée
off the coast of Senegal, the site of a hub for transport of enslaved Africans
to the New World.

619.18   *David Walker (1785–1830)*] Freeborn antislavery activist, author of
Appeal, in Four Articles . . . to the Coloured Citizens of the World (1829), a
radical tract that circulated throughout the South despite efforts to suppress
it and to punish Walker, including a bounty by the State of Georgia for his
capture or assassination.

622.14   *Lieutenant James Reese Europe*] Composer, arranger, and bandleader
(1881–1919), a lieutenant of the U.S. Army's 369th Infantry Regiment, known
as the Harlem Hellfighters. He led the sixty-five-member Hellfighters Band,
which helped introduce ragtime to France, from 1913 until his death in 1919.

623.9   *Croix de Guerre*] French military medal (War Cross) instituted in 1915,
which could also be awarded to members of allied armed forces.

627.14   *Hattie McDaniel at the Cocoanut Grove*] Actor Hattie McDaniel
(1895–1952) won an Academy Award, the first for an African American, for her
role as Mammy in *Gone with the Wind* (1939). The awards ceremony was held
at the Cocoanut Grove, a nightclub in the Ambassador Hotel in Los Angeles.

627.21   Wonderful Smith] Comic actor (1911–2008) with roles in Duke
Ellington's satirical revue *Jump for Joy* (1941) and on radio and in films; he
was McDaniel's friend and part-time chauffeur.

628.2–3   "little lady" from *Showboat* whose name Bing forgot] In January
1937, the singer and actor Bing Crosby (1903–1977) wrote to the producer and
film executive David O. Selznick (1902–1965) and recommended McDaniel
for the role of Mammy in *Gone with the Wind*: "The little lady I have in mind
played opposite Robeson in *Showboat*, and to my mind would be a cinch. I
don't know her name, but your hirelings in the casting office could dig it up."
McDaniel had recently played Queenie in the first film version (1936) of the
musical *Show Boat.*

628.3–4   *Beulah . . . Fidelia*] McDaniel's roles in the following films: *45
Fathers* (1937), *Mickey* (1948), *Alice Adams* (1935), *Maryland* (1940), *The Great
Lie* (1941), *Affectionately Yours* (1941), *Since You Went Away* (1944).

628.5 one half of the dark Barrymores] McDaniel's brother Sam McDaniel (1886–1962), also an actor, referred to himself and his sister together as the "dark Barrymores," referring to the renowned family of stage and film actors.

633.2–3 *the young black man Susan Smith claimed kidnapped her children*] On October 25, 1994, Susan Smith (b. 1971) of Union, South Carolina, drowned her three-year-old son Michael and fourteen-month-old son Alex by strapping them into her car and letting it roll down a ramp into a lake. She told police and the media that while stopped at a traffic light she had been the victim of a carjacking by an African American man who then drove away with the children and committed the murders. Nine days later, Smith confessed that she had killed her children and had invented the assailant. She was sentenced to life imprisonment for the murders.

639.13 *Condoleezza*] Condoleezza Rice (b. 1954), national security advisor, 2001–5, and secretary of state, 2005–9.

640.2 *her friend Denise*] As a child Rice was friends with Denise McNair, who was murdered in the bombing of the Sixteenth Street Baptist Church in Birmingham in 1963 (see note 354.16–17).

640.10–12 relocated . . . Steinway] Rice moved with her family to Denver in 1967; as a teenager, having studied music from an early age, she aspired to be a classical pianist.

645.10 Charles Brown, Ruth Brown, Muddy and Wolf] The blues and country singer and pianist Ray Charles (1930–2004), the blues and R&B singer Charles Brown (1922–1999), the R&B singer and actor Ruth Brown (1928–2006), the blues singer and guitarist Muddy Waters (McKinley Morganfield, 1913–1983); Howlin' Wolf, see note 514.2.

645.35–36 "Fingertips?" Little Stevie Wonder] Composition (1962) by Clarence Paul (1928–1995) and Henry Cosby (1928–2002), written for "Little" Stevie Wonder to play as a twelve-year-old piano prodigy. The live recording released in 1962 was Wonder's first hit.

646.22–24 Lt. Col. William Higgins . . . noose on the TV news] On August 1, 1989, NBC, CBS, and CNN broadcast a short videotape showing the hanging of U.S. Marine Corps Lt. Col. William R. Higgins (1945–1989) by his captors in Lebanon, who had taken him hostage in February 1988.

648.23–24 Originally the lyrics . . . Johnny B. Goode] Chuck Berry (1926–2017) told *Rolling Stone* magazine in 1972 that in his smash hit "Johnny B. Goode" (1958) he had changed "colored boy" to "country boy" because the original lyric would ensure "it wouldn't get on the radio."

650.34–35 cho-cho] Chayote.

652.11 *hunted and penned in an inglorious spot*] From Claude McKay, "If We Must Die" (see p. 228 in this volume).

659.2 *Nurse Eunice Rivers*] Eunice Rivers Laurie (1899–1986), a nurse who was the only full-time staff member of the Tuskegee Study of Untreated Syphilis in the Negro Male, an observational medical study conducted by the U.S Public Health Service beginning in 1932. Three hundred ninety-nine poor African American men were told they were being treated for "bad blood" at the Tuskegee Institute when in fact they had contracted syphilis but were unaware of the nature of their condition. None of the men were treated for the disease even after penicillin was developed in the 1940s and discovered to be an effective cure. The program was ended in 1972 after it was brought to public attention. The federal government made payments to survivors and family members under the terms of the settlement of a class-action lawsuit; President Clinton apologized to the study's subjects on behalf of the federal government in 1997.

659.13 Dr. Dibble] Eugene Dibble (1893–1968), African American physician who served as medical director of the Tuskegee Institute's John H. Andrew Memorial Hospital, 1925–36, 1946–65.

674.5 *pendijito*] Diminutive form of Spanish *pendejo*, idiot, stupid man.

678.2 *Jenny*] The imagined speaker of this poem and the next are enslaved women.

680.26 *GOLDEN SARDINE*] Kaufman's 1967 poetry collection (for more on Kaufman, see biographical notes).

682.16–18 Dexter Gordon's] Gordon (see note 432.4) starred as a fictional bebop saxophonist in the film *Round Midnight* (1986), directed by the French director Bernard Tavernier (b. 1941). "April in Paris": song (1932), music by Vernon Duke (1903–1969), lyrics by E. Y. Harburg (1896–1981).

682.25 Bud, Prez, Webster, & The Hawk] Bud Powell (1924–1966), Lester Young (1909–1959), saxophonist Ben Webster (1909–1977), Coleman Hawkins (1904–1969).

683.10 *Dien Cai Dau*] Vietnamese: Crazy in the Head, phrase used to describe American soldiers during the Vietnam War.

687.14–15 Mary Lou Williams'] Jazz pianist (1910–1981).

687.15 "Polka Dots & Moonbeams"] Jazz standard (1940), music by Jimmy Van Heusen (1913–1990), lyrics by Johnny Burke (1908–1964).

691.2–3 *Falso Brilhante . . . Elis Regina*] Album (False Diamond) by the Brazilian singer Elis Regina (1945–1982), who died of an overdose of cocaine at the age of 36.

692.1 Iansã, Ogum] Candomblé deities.

693.1 *Andamboulou*] Mackey has been working on the long serial poem "Song of the Andamboulou" for decades. In a spring 2020 interview with *The Paris Review*, he explained the origin of the work: "In the early seventies, when I was working at a radio station in Northern California, KTAO in Los Gatos, I found an album of Dogon music in the station's library, *Les Dogon*, which had funeral songs on one side, and one of them was [the funeral dirge] 'Song of the Andoumboulou.'" He added that he later read *The Pale Fox* (1945), a book about the Dogon by the anthropologists Marcel Griaule and Germaine Dieterlen, "which talks about the Andoumboulou as an earlier form of human being, kind of a trial form that didn't work out. That's when I got through to the sense of the Andoumboulou as a kind of metaphor for us and our present, you know, failed condition, the Andoumboulou as a failed form, a rough draft of humanity."

693.2   Bukka White] Blues singer and guitarist (1906–1977).

693.4   Ogo's] Dogon god of chaos.

697.18   40 acres and a mule] See note 441.17.

699.9   *after Gwendolyn Brooks*] Inspired by Brooks's poem "A Lovely Love." Terrance Hayes invented the "Golden Shovel" form (see p. 803), in which words from a poem, most frequently by Brooks, are selected to be end words in a new poem.

699.29   Oscar Micheaux] Pioneering African American director and producer (1884–1951), whose films include *The Homesteader* (1919) and *The Conjure Woman* (1926). He was also a novelist.

700.2   Hopalong Cassidy] Cowboy hero of fiction and movies created by Clarence Mulford (1883–1956).

700.3   Ralph Cooper] Actor and dancer (1909–1992) perhaps best known for founding and emceeing the Amateur Night competitions at the Apollo Theater in Harlem.

700.3   Mantan Moreland] Vaudeville and film comedian (1902–1973).

701.8   Boston Blackie] Detective played by Chester Morris (1901–1970) in numerous films in the 1940s.

705.5   *Guess who's coming to dinner?*] Film (1967) starring Sidney Poitier (b. 1927), Spencer Tracy (1900–1967), and Katharine Hepburn (1907–2003) about a liberal white couple meeting their daughter's African American fiancé.

705.9   *from here to eternity?*] Film (1953) based on the novel (1951) by James Jones (1921–1977).

705.11   *Who never sang for my father?*] Reference to *I Never Sang for My Father* (1970), film starring Gene Hackman (b. 1930) and Melvyn Douglas (1901–1981).

709.21   the prophet Jolson proclaiming *Mammy*] Singer and actor Al Jolson (1886–1950) was widely known for his performances in blackface and his "mammy" songs, such as "Mammy" in the film *The Jazz Singer* (1927).

712.7   dry bones in the valley] See note 478.18–19.

712.17   Oshun] Yoruba deity, a river goddess.

712.23   get off your rusty dusty] From "Rusty Dusty Blues" (1943), also known as "Mama Mama Blues," by Louis Jordan, perhaps best known in the 1943 version sung by Jimmy Rushing with the Count Basie Orchestra.

714.1   mannish boy] Blues song (1955) by Muddy Waters.

715.11   Noiseless patient spiders] Cf. Walt Whitman's poem "A Noiseless Patient Spider" (1868).

727.30   en mi casa toman bustelo] "In my house we drink Bustelo," marketing slogan for Bustelo Coffee.

728.9–16   *I said Hey Babe . . . ooooo*] From "Walk on the Wild Side" (1972), song by Lou Reed (1942–2013).

728.25   the Main Line] Upper-class Philadelphia suburbs west of the city.

729.30   the Country Squire] Station wagon manufactured by Ford from the 1950s through the early 1990s.

730.7   Hattie McDaniel] See the four notes about McDaniel beginning at note 627.14.

730.7   Butterfly McQueen] Actor (1911–1985) whose roles included Prissy, Scarlet O'Hara's maid in *Gone with the Wind*.

730.8   Ethel Waters] Singer and actor of stage and screen (1896–1977) whose films include *Pinky* (1949) and *The Member of the Wedding* (1953).

730.9   Sapphire] See note 458.4.

730.10   Saphronia] See "Four Women" (1966), song written and recorded by Nina Simone: "My skin is yellow / My hair is long / Between two worlds / I do belong / My father was rich and white / He forced my mother late one night / What do they call me / My name is Saffronia."

732.11   Ruby Begonia] Name of a woman cited in a gag by Black comedians.

730.31–33   *Mam-mie . . . smiles*] Lines from "Mammy" sung by Al Jolson (see note 709.21).

743.27   *How Stella Got Her Groove Back.*] Best-selling novel (1996) by Terry McMillan (b. 1951).

748.4–5   Earl Weaver . . . Frank Robinson] Earl Weaver (1930–2013), colorful manager of the Baltimore Orioles baseball team, 1968–82, 1985–86; Frank Robinson (1935–2019), outfielder for the Orioles, 1966–71, and later a manager.

749.18   *John Henry*] See note 144.14.

757.2   *The Venus Hottentot*] Name under which Sarah Baartman (1789–1815), a Khoikhoi woman born in present-day South Africa, was exhibited as a curiosity in England and in Paris because of her protruding buttocks. Variant forms of her first name include Sara, Saartije, and Saartje.

757.4   CUVIER] After Baartman died, the French naturalist Georges Cuvier (1769–1832) made a plaster cast of her body and dissected her corpse, preserving her skeleton and pickling her genitals and brain in jars that were displayed in the Musée de l'Homme in Paris until the 1970s. The French government, responding to a request by South African president Nelson Mandela, sent her remains in 2002 to South Africa, where they were interred.

758.3   Broca's brain] The French physician Paul Broca (1824–1880) studied the brain and advocated the preservation of human specimens, including his own (displayed at the Musée de l'Homme), in formaldehyde-filled jars.

759.15   "The Ball of Duchess DuBarry"] Anonymous engraving published in 1829, fourteen years after Baartman's death.

760.2   *sadza.*] Thick porridge made from cornmeal.

767.18   Tuol Sleng prison] Notorious Cambodian facility where prisoners of the Khmer Rouge were tortured and executed, 1975–79, now the site of a museum.

767.24–25   *Doug Flutie's 1984 Orange Bowl Hail Mary*] In a nationally televised game held at Miami's Orange Bowl on November 23, 1984, Boston College quarterback Doug Flutie (b. 1962) threw an improbable touchdown pass on the game's final play, securing his team's victory against the Miami Hurricanes.

771.12   big daddy kane and miss jane pittman] The rapper Big Daddy Kane (Antonio Hardy, b. 1968); protagonist of novel *The Autobiography of Miss Jane Pittman* (1971) by Ernest J. Gaines (1933–2019), adapted as a movie for television in 1974.

775.28   *John Crawford.*] John Crawford III (1992–2014) was fatally shot by the police officer Sean Williams in a Walmart in Beaverbrook, Ohio, on August 5, 2014. He was holding a toy pellet gun when Williams fired on him. A grand jury decided not to indict Williams or his partner, David Darkow, on criminal charges related to the killing.

775.28   *Eric Garner.*] While arresting Eric Garner (1970–2014) for selling loose cigarettes in Staten Island, New York, on the afternoon of July 17, 2014, NYPD officer Daniel Pantaleo placed Garner in a chokehold, then pushed his face to the sidewalk. While surrounded by Pantaleo and other police officers, Garner, who was asthmatic, repeatedly said "I can't breathe" before losing consciousness. He was taken to Richmond University Medical Center, where he was pronounced dead an hour later. His death was ruled a homicide. A Staten Island grand jury later declined to indict Pantaleo on criminal charges.

775.28 *Mike Brown.*] Michael Brown (1996–2014) was killed by the police officer Darren Wilson (b. 1986) in Ferguson, Missouri, on August 9, 2014. Wilson had driven his SUV in front of Brown and 22-year-old Dorian Johnson to question them about a reported theft of cigarillos from a nearby convenience store. According to the report of a Department of Justice investigation into Brown's death, Wilson fired his gun twice during a scuffle between Wilson and Brown while Wilson was still inside the vehicle, wounding Brown's right hand. Brown then fled, pursued by Wilson on foot. When Brown turned around and faced Wilson, the police officer fired several times, including a fatal gunshot to the head. A crowd soon formed at the scene of the shooting; Brown's corpse lay exposed on the ground on Canfield Road for at least four hours. Brown's death, which according to some accounts had occurred while he was surrendering to Wilson, led to days of vigils, protest, and civil unrest, which in turn were met with a curfew and a highly militarized response by the Ferguson Police Department, the Missouri State Highway Patrol, and the National Guard. The events in Ferguson were the focus of national and international attention. Further protests and unrest took place in November after a grand jury declined to indict Wilson for the killing.

776.13 *Y'all too young to know*] From "Too Young to Know," blues song recorded by Muddy Waters in 1951.

776.21 Bernard Allison's] Blues guitarist and singer (b. 1965).

776.31 a statuesque Jesus] The monumental *Christ of the Ozarks* statue on Magnetic Mountain overlooking Eureka Springs, Arkansas, the site of an outdoor dramatization of Jesus's final days.

778.11 Ka'bbah] Cube-shaped building in the Grand Mosque of Mecca.

779.19–20 confession you made on the Cane River . . . desolate places] See Bob Marley and the Wailers, "Trench Town" (released 1983): "Up a cane river to wash my dread. / Upon a rock I rest my head. / There I vision through the seas of oppression [. . .] in desolate places we'll find our bread."

784.11 Quiscalus quiscula] The common grackle.

786.10 Robert Hayden] See biographical notes.

792.20 Eric Garner] Garner (see note 775.28) had worked as a horticulturist for New York City's parks department but had to quit because of the severity of his asthma.

794.7 *Massawa*] Port city in Eritrea, whose capture was a key victory for Eritrea in its war of independence from Ethiopia; Girmay's father was born and largely raised in Gondar, Ethiopia.

803.7 Gwendolyn Brooks] See "We Real Cool," p. 269, and note 699.9.

807.20 the Quiet Storm] Program of R&B ballads on Philadelphia's Power 99 FM radio station.

807.24–25 Luther Vandross . . . "Creepin'."] Song (1985) written by Stevie
Wonder and recorded by the R&B singer Luther Vandross (1951–2005).

808.22 *Ferguson*] See note 775.28.

809.22 Lazarus moment] Lazarus was raised from the dead by Jesus in
John 11:1–44.

813.2 *Blind Tom*] Thomas Bethune (1849–1908), a blind pianist and com-
poser born in slavery in Columbus, Georgia. Bethune was a child prodigy and
amazed audiences with his musical and verbal recall as well as his ability to
mimic natural and instrumental sounds.

813.2 *Blind Boone's*] John William Boone (1864–1927), ragtime pianist and
composer whose eyes were removed in a surgical procedure at six months old.

816.1 *Minnehaha*] Marble bust (1868) by the sculptor Edmonia Lewis
(1844–1907), of African American and Anishinaabe/Ojibwe descent, based
on a character in *The Song of Hiawatha* (1855), long narrative poem by Henry
Wadsworth Longfellow (1807–1882).

821.2 *Drop It Like It's Hottentot Venus*] The title of the hit hip-hop single
"Drop It Like It's Hot" (2004) by the rapper Snoop Dogg (Calvin Broadus,
Jr., b. 1971) featuring the singer Pharrell Williams (b. 1973), fused with a
reference to the Hottentot Venus (see note 757.2).

822.20 Montgomery, My Lai] Montgomery, Alabama, key locale of civil
rights activism by Rev. Martin Luther King, Jr. (1929–1968), and others, most
notably the African American boycott of segregated city buses, 1955–56; My
Lai, central Vietnamese village where American soldiers massacred between
200 and 500 unarmed civilians in March 1968.

822.34–35 Nice work . . . lie] Cf. lines from the chorus of the jazz standard
"Nice Work If You Can Get It" (1937), music by George Gershwin, lyrics by
Ira Gershwin: "Nice work if you can get it / And you can get it if you try."

823.9 Kali] The Hindu warrior goddess of death, time, and fertility.

823.10 Chain of Rocks.] Bridge crossing the Mississippi River from the
northern edge of St. Louis to Illinois.

823.13 Treemonisha.] Name of opera, first published in a vocal and piano
score in 1911, by the ragtime composer Scott Joplin (c. 1867–1917). Set in 1884,
it is named for its central character, a young woman who had been discovered
as a baby under a tree and raised on a former plantation in Arkansas.

823.19 Eugene Field House.] Museum in St. Louis, once the home of the
attorney Roswell Field (1807–1869), who argued unsuccessfully on behalf of
Dred Scott (c. 1799–1858) in *Dred Scott v. Sandford* (1857), in which the U.S.
Supreme Court ruled that Congress could not prohibit slavery in federal ter-
ritories and that free Blacks were not citizens of the United States. Field's son

Eugene (1850–1894) was a humorist and newspaper columnist perhaps best known for children's poems such as "Wynken, Blinken, and Nod."

824.17   Cardinal Ritter] Joseph Ritter (1892–1967), archbishop of St. Louis, 1946–67, after whom Cardinal Ritter Prep High School (founded 1979) is named.

825.7   "Caped Crusader."] Nickname of the comic-book hero Batman.

825.7   Ivanhoe, Pip, and Peter Pan] Protagonists, respectively, of works by English writers: *Ivanhoe* (1820), novel by Sir Walter Scott (1771–1832); *Great Expectations* (1861), novel by Charles Dickens (1812–1870); *Peter Pan* (1904), play by J. M. Barrie (1860–1937). "John": Peter Pan's friend John Darling.

825.28–29   Baldwins . . . Michener's opera] Referring to unspecified novels by the writers James Baldwin (1924–1987), Erica Jong (b. 1942), James Gould Cozzens (1903–1978), Toni Morrison (1931–2019), and James Michener (1907–1997).

825.40   Homer G. Phillips] Prominent attorney in St. Louis (1880–1931) who while attending Howard University had lived with Paul Laurence Dunbar. He was murdered en route to his office after being approached by two assailants on the morning of July 18, 1931; no one was ever charged for the crime. A St. Louis hospital, in operation from 1937 to 1979, was named in his honor.

827.13   *Kenèps*] Fruit common in the Caribbean, sometimes referred to as Spanish lime.

833.10–13   Here . . . corridor] From "Mural" (1998) by the Palestinian poet Mahmoud Darwish, translated by Rema Hammani and John Berger.

837.3   a Bes and an Isia] Egyptian deities, the former a dwarf god.

840.17   Meroë] Capital city in the ancient kingdom of Kush.

842.9   *Lucy Terry Prince*] See biographical note for Lucy Terry.

844.3   *pa' mi gente*] Spanish: for my people.

844.4–8   Mira . . . Boricua] Spanish: Look at my Puerto Rican face / and my nappy hair / and my brown-skinned hands / Look at my heart that is filled with pride / and tell me I'm not Boricua.

846.6–7   ¡No nací . . . mi!] Spanish: I wasn't born in Puerto Rico / Puerto Rico was born in me!

850.11   cast down a bucket] See Booker T. Washington's speech at the Atlanta Exposition in 1895: "To those of my race who depend upon bettering their condition in a foreign land, or who underestimate the importance of cultivating friendly relations with the Southern white man who is their next-door neighbor, I would say: 'Cast down your bucket where you are'—cast it down in making friends, in every manly way, of the people of all races by whom we are surrounded."

850.12–13   the Great Storm] The Great Galveston hurricane, September 8, 1900.

850.13–14   "black ghouls"] See "Ghouls Shot on Sight," *The New York Times*, September 13, 1900, an article about the looting of corpses in Galveston, Texas, in the storm's aftermath in which many of the looters were themselves shot dead by government troops sent to the area: "The ghouls were holding an orgie [*sic*] over the dead. The majority of these men were Negroes."

851.2   Hattie] Hattie McClay, pseudonym of Anna Peterson, a white woman working as a prostitute when Jack Johnson (see note 144.4–10) met her in 1907 in Manhattan. Their relationship, off and on, lasted until 1911.

852.13–14   *"Carefree as a Plantation Darky in Watermelon Time"*] The title and some of the imagery in the latter part of the poem are drawn from newspaper accounts before the Johnson–Jeffries fight, as recorded in Geoffrey Ward's biography of Jack Johnson, *Unforgivable Blackness*: "'To all appearances,' said the Baltimore *American*, 'the black man is as happy and carefree as a plantation darky in Watermelon time.' 'The man is a puzzle,' said the Chicago *Tribune*. 'Physically the greatest athlete the colored race has produced and mentally keen as a razor in a sort of undeveloped way, he fiddles away on his bull fiddle, swaps jokes with ready wit, shoots craps, plays baseball, listens dreamily to classical love songs on the phonograph and is going to fight Jim Jeffries for the world's championship one week from tomorrow.'"

853.8   *Robot*] Dance performed in mimicry of a robot.

853.11   Sergio Valente] Designer jeans first popular in the 1980s.

853.11–12   dance floor . . . no parking] Reference to disco hit "No Parking (on the Dance Floor)" (1983) by Midnight Star.

853.19–20   Soul Train line] On the syndicated television dance program *Soul Train*, 1971–2006, a series of dancers would show off their moves in a procession surrounded by other dancers lined up on either side.

857.1   Cee-lo] A gambling game using three dice.

858.2   *gayl jones*] See biographical note.

858.9–10   nancy wilson] Jazz singer (1937–2018).

858.19   clarence carter] Soul singer (b. 1936).

858.20–21   creflo dollar] Televangelist and entrepreneur (b. Michael Smith in 1962), founder of the nondenominational World Changers Church International.

859.5   *Cecil Taylor*] Classically trained pianist and avant-garde jazz composer (1929–2018); Moten's collection *The Feel Trio* (2014) is named for the ensemble Taylor led in the late 1980s and early 1990s.

860.8–9   just before moses cut new york] Robert Moses (1888–1981) was the public official and city planner who presided over ambitious public works projects in New York City and Long Island in the mid-twentieth century.

860.15   almeida ragland] Maiden name of Taylor's mother, who, though she died when he was fourteen, was an enormous influence on his musical studies.

862.6   j tizol] Puerto Rican trombone player and composer Juan Tizol (1900–1984), who played with Duke Ellington's band.

863.6   free as dred] Dred Scott (see note 823.19).

866.18   ain't I a woman and a brother] Cf. the abolitionist slogan "Am I not a man and a brother?" and the question "Ain't I a woman?" asked repeatedly by the abolitionist and activist Sojourner Truth (1797–1883) in a speech delivered on May 29, 1851.

866.27–28   Broadway production of *A Raisin in the Sun* . . . Diddy, played the starring role.] A 2004 Broadway revival of Lorraine Hansberry's play *A Raisin in the Sun* (1959) featured the stage debut of Sean Combs (b. 1969), hip-hop artist, producer, and mogul whose stage names have included Puff Daddy and P. Diddy, in the role of Walter Lee.

867.13–14   "Get rich or die trying," 50 Cent] *Get Rich or Die Tryin'* is a 2003 album by the rapper 50 Cent (b. Curtis Jackson III, 1975).

867.15   like Ricky Skaggs, "Don't get above your raisin'"] The country singer Ricky Skaggs (b. 1954) recorded "Don't Get Above Your Raisin'," a 1951 song written by Earl Scruggs (1924–2012), in 1981.

867.19–20   conga marching raisins that sang Marvin's hit song.] In 1968 the R&B singer Marvin Gaye (1939–1984) recorded a hit version of "I Heard It Through the Grapevine," written by Norman Whitfield (1940–2008) and Barrett Strong (b. 1941); the song was used in a popular 1986 television campaign for raisins featuring a musical claymation band called The California Raisins.

867.24–25   dreams deferred] See Langston Hughes, "Montage of a Dream Deferred," pp. 200–212, esp. 210.

867.25–26   Marvin Gaye . . . Marvin Sr.] Gaye's father fatally shot him after an argument and physical altercation not long after midnight on April 1, 1984.

868.2   *Bembé*] Cuban drums.

871.17–18   *The Miraculous Translation of the Body of Saint Catherine of Alexandria to Sinai*] Painting (1860) by the Austrian artist Karl von Blaas (1815–1894).

874.9–10   June Jordan's "Poem About My Rights"] On pp. 468–70 in this volume.

874.21 Michael Brown] See note 775.28.

875.3 *Trayvon Martin*] While walking home on the evening of February 26, 2012, Trayvon Martin (b. 1995) was followed by George Zimmerman (b. 1983), a Neighborhood Watch volunteer for a gated community in Sanford, Florida. Perceiving Martin as a threat, Zimmerman called the police and was told to remain in his vehicle; he nonetheless got out and in a scuffle with Martin he fatally shot the unarmed teenager in the chest. Zimmerman was later acquitted of second-degree murder and manslaughter charges in the killing in a verdict that elicited widespread outrage and protests.

881.32 *Take it from me*] From "Someday We'll All Be Free" (1973), song written by the soul singer, songwriter, and keyboardist Donny Hathaway (1945–1979) with lyrics by his friend Edward Howard, and recorded for Hathaway's album *Extensions of a Man.*

885.17 Thomas Auld] Auld (1795–1880) owned Douglass while he was enslaved.

885.27 Anna Murray] Anna Murray-Douglass (1813–1882), Douglass's first wife, 1838–82.

886.9–10 Helen became the new Mrs. Douglass] See note 456.1.

888.1 the tunnel john henry] See note 144.14.

901.26 *Prissy's*] African American maid in Margaret Mitchell's novel *Gone with the Wind* (1936) and its film version (1939).

902.13 Faulkner's Joe Christmas] Black protagonist of William Faulkner's novel *Light in August* (1932).

904.29–30 the song I picked . . . *love me.*] From "I Touch Myself" (1990), hit single for the Australian band The Divinyls.

906.3–4 Ocian in view! . . . Clark] Journal entry, November 7, 1805, of William Clark (1770–1838) during the Lewis and Clark Expedition.

909.22–23 Robert Taylor . . . Cabrini Green] High-rise housing projects in Chicago.

912.5–6 Resurrected like Lazarus] See note 809.22.

914.4–5 Money, Mississippi] See note 270.19–20.

914.8–9 Robert Johnson's muddy maybe grave . . . Little Zion] One of three grave markers for the blues guitarist and singer Robert Johnson in Mississippi is on Money Road, in the cemetery of the Little Zion Missionary Baptist Church in Greenwood.

921.19 el Cibao] Northern region of the Dominican Republic.

923.2 *Cento*] "'Cento Between the Ending and the End' is composed of language scavenged from the works of Justin Phillip Reed, Hieu Minh Nguyen, Fatimah Asghar, Kaveh Akbar, sam sax, Ari Banias, C. Bain, Oliver Bendorf, Hanif Abdurraqib, Safia Elhillo, Danez Smith, Ocean Vuong, Franny Choi, Lucille Clifton, and Nate Marshall. All of whom have made for me a world and for whom I wish the world" (Awkward-Rich's note).

924.3 *after Langston Hughes*] Cf. Hughes's poem "Let America Be America Again," pp. 197–99.

924.15 Bull Connor] Eugene "Bull" Connor (1897–1973), commissioner of Public Safety in Birmingham, Alabama, 1937–63, notorious for the measures he approved in the suppression of civil rights protesters, including the use of cattle prods, fire hoses, and attack dogs.

925.21–22 Sam Cooke . . . river] "I was born by the river in a little tent," the opening of "A Change Is Gonna Come" (1964) by the soul and gospel singer Sam Cooke (1931–1964).

928.2 *basquiat*] The artist Jean-Michel Basquiat (1960–1988).

932.21–22 breath of Apollo . . . Daphne's wild hair] In Greek mythology, the nymph Daphne was transformed into a tree to escape the pursuit of the god Apollo.

934.10 Gorée] See note 614.2.

935.2 *Emmett Till*] See note 270.19–20.

935.3–4 *There is no time to be lost . . . problem.*] From an editorial in the Chicago *Evening American* in response to the racial violence of July 27–August 13, 1919, in which white mobs attacked African Americans throughout Chicago; 23 African Americans and 15 whites died in the rioting.

950.9–29 *Rekia Boyd . . . Sandra Bland*] African Americans who were either killed by police officers or died in the immediate aftermath of an encounter with law enforcement or while in police custody. Rekia Boyd, 22, was shot dead by an off-duty Chicago policeman on March 21, 2012. Tanisha Anderson, 37, who had been diagnosed with bipolar disorder, died after being restrained by police officers outsider her home in Cleveland on November 12, 2014. Yvette Smith, 47, called 911 while trying to mediate a dispute between two men and was fatally shot when she opened the door at a policeman's orders not long after midnight on February 16, 2014, in Bastrop County, Texas. Aiyana Jones, 7, was shot to death by a Detroit police officer during a SWAT team raid on her home shortly after midnight on May 16, 2010. Kayla Moore, 41, a paranoid schizophrenic transgender woman, died at the hospital on February 12, 2013, after being restrained at home by police officers in Berkeley, California. Shelly Frey, 27, was fatally shot by an off-duty sheriff's deputy in Houston who had suspected her of shoplifting in a Walmart. Miriam Carey, 34, was killed after being shot five times from behind in her car by a Washington,

D.C. policeman and a Secret Service agent during a car chase near the White House; apparently confused, Carey had driven her vehicle into a White House checkpoint (her one-year-old child, in the car with her, survived the incident physically unharmed). Kendra James, 21, was fatally shot on May 5, 2003, by a Portland, Oregon, policeman during an arrest of the driver of the car she was in. Alberta Spruill, 57, suffered a fatal heart attack on May 16, 2003, after New York police mounted a mistaken raid in Harlem, throwing a concussion grenade into her apartment. Tarika Wilson, 26, was killed and her 14-month-old son was wounded by gunfire on January 4, 2008, when a SWAT team in search of her companion raided her home in Lima, Ohio. Shereese Francis, 29, a schizophrenic, was fatally suffocated by four New York City police officers on March 5, 2012, after family members called police to her home in Queens because she had not been taking her medications and had been behaving erratically. Shantel Davis, 23, was shot to death in her crashed car by a plainclothes NYPD officer in Brooklyn on June 14, 2012. Shantel Davis, 23, and Timothy Russell were fatally shot during a barrage of police gunfire in East Cleveland, Ohio, on November 29, 2012, at the end of a high-speed car chase. Darnisha Harris, 17, was shot to death by a police officer in Beaux Bridge, Louisiana, after her car collided with a police car and two other cars. Michelle Cusseaux, 50, was fatally shot outside her apartment on August 14, 2014, by a Phoenix Police Department officer while he and three other officers were serving her with a mental health petition. Pearlie Golden, 93, was shot and killed on the porch of her home in Hearne, Texas, by a local police officer on May 6, 2014. Kathryn Johnston, 92, was fatally shot by Atlanta police while she was alone in her home during a raid intended to arrest a man on drug charges. Eleanor Bumpurs, 66, was shot dead by an NYPD officer in her Bronx apartment on October 29, 1984, when police were summoned by New York's Housing Authority after she had refused to accept an eviction notice from city officials; she had a history of mental illness. Natasha McKenna, 37, was a mentally ill inmate at the Adult Detention Center in Fairfax County, Virginia, who died after she was tasered four times while naked by officers of the sheriff's department who were involved with her transport to a different facility. Sheneque Proctor, 18, died in the city jail of Bessamer, Alabama, on November 2, 2015, after her arrest the day before on disorderly conduct charges. Sandra Bland, 28, was found hanged on July 13, 2019, in a prison cell in Walker County, Texas, where she had been held after her arrest during a traffic stop; her death was ruled a suicide.

953.7   Spoke Baraka] In "Somebody Blew Up America" (2002; see also biographical note for Amiri Baraka).

954.26   MMXVI.] "Either the Roman numerals or the year may be recited" (Phillips's note).

958.2   *Why Is We Americans*] Cf. "Why Is We Americans?" a poem by Amiri Baraka featured in the 2002 season of the HBO television series *Def Poetry Jam*.

958.13   Birdland] Manhattan jazz club at 1678 Broadway, at 52nd Street.

958.13   *body electric*] From Walt Whitman, "I Sing the Body Electric," in *Leaves of Grass* (1855–92).

958.25–26   Mississippi goddamned] Cf. Nina Simone, "Mississippi Goddam" (1964), first recorded on Simone's album *Nina Simone in Concert.*

958.28   washed out . . . blood of the lamb.] Cf. the hymn "Are You Washed in the Blood?" (1878), hymn by the Presbyterian clergyman Elisha Hoffman (1839–1929) that repeats the line "Are you washed in the blood of the lamb?"

959.1–2   Radio Raheem and Zoot Suit Malcolm] Character in *Do the Right Thing* (1989), film written and directed by Spike Lee (b. 1957); Malcolm X, who as he recounts in his autobiography, liked to wear zoot suits in the 1940s.

959.20–21   swingin' in the sweet summer breeze] "Black bodies swinging in the summer breeze" is a line from the anti-lynching song "Strange Fruit" (1937), words and music by Lewis Allan (pseud. Abel Meeropol, 1903–1986), widely known through its 1939 recording by Billie Holiday.

966.3   a black man] The NFL quarterback Colin Kaepernick (b. 1987), who initiated a sustained protest among many fellow players and other athletes that involved kneeling during the playing of the National Anthem at sporting events. Kaepernick first clarified the gesture after a preseason game, August 26, 2016: "I am not going to stand up to show pride in a flag for a country that oppresses black people and people of color. To me, this is bigger than football and it would be selfish on my part to look the other way. There are bodies in the street and people getting paid leave and getting away with murder."

968.2   Herb Kent] Radio disc jockey (1928–2016) in Chicago.

968.14   Al & Barry & Luther] Soul and R&B singers Al Green (b. 1946), Barry White (1944–2003), and Luther Vandross (1951–2005).

968.27   Marvin's "Got to Give It Up."] Hit song (1977) for Marvin Gaye.

INDEX OF POETS, TITLES,
AND FIRST LINES

This book is set in 10 point ITC Galliard Pro, a face designed for digital composition by Matthew Carter and based on the sixteenth-century face Granjon. The paper is acid-free lightweight opaque that will not turn yellow or brittle with age. The binding is sewn, which allows the book to open easily and lie flat. The binding board is covered in Brillianta, a woven rayon cloth made by Van Heek–Scholco Textielfabrieken, Holland. Composition by Publishers' Design and Production Services, Inc. Printing and binding by LSC Communications. Designed by Bruce Campbell.

THE LIBRARY OF AMERICA SERIES

Library of America fosters appreciation of America's literary heritage by publishing, and keeping permanently in print, authoritative editions of America's best and most significant writing. An independent nonprofit organization, it was founded in 1979 with seed funding from the National Endowment for the Humanities and the Ford Foundation.

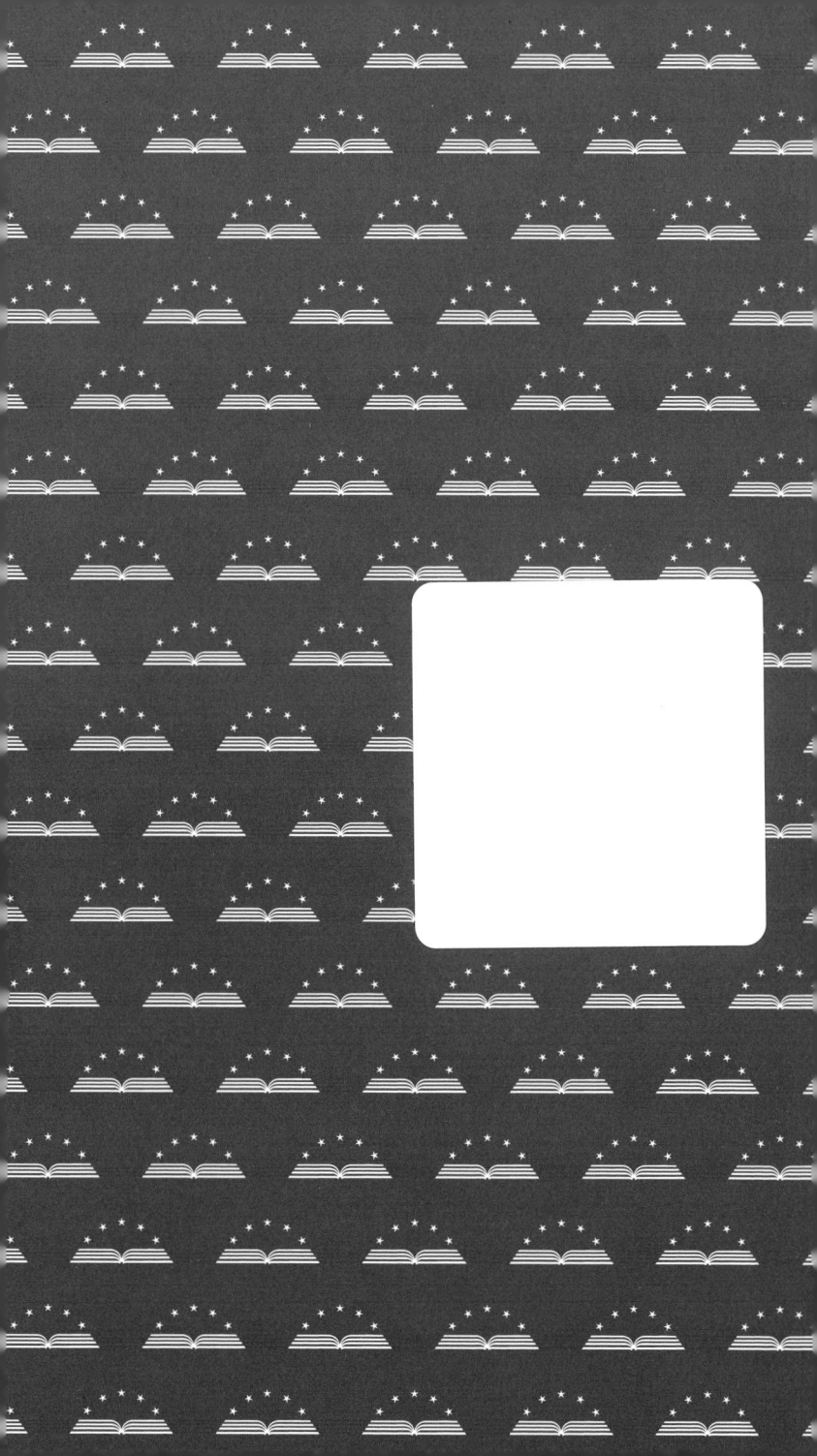